THE
MIGHT
OF THE
WEST

Lawrence R. Brown

Joseph J. Binns—publisher
Washington-New York

TABLE OF CONTENTS

Chapter 4   The Physics of Magic

Chapter 5   The Envy of Less Happier Lands

Chapter 6   The Dragon's Teeth

THE
MIGHT
OF THE
WEST

Prologue:

Of Politics and History

To THE EUROPEAN AND NORTH AMERICAN in the summer of 1913 all the ages of man seemed to have reached a pinnacle of security, prosperity and peace. Ahead stretched indefinite progress. Behind lay unarguable success. The year was the hundredth anniversary of the downfall of Napoleon at the battle of Leipzig. As the centuries run, it had been the age of the great peace, the greatest within the historical experience of Western men.

Not only did peace brood over this world, but the political forms of its states seemed cast in a permanent and hopeful mold. In every Western state the political parties of liberalism were either in power or year by year becoming more powerful. The Liberal Asquith was Prime Minister of Great Britain. Woodrow Wilson had emerged victorious from the three-cornered election of 1912 dedicated to a course of social reform which he called the New Freedom. The vast and alien dominions of the Russian czar were ruled by a creaking, inefficient but Europeanized bureaucracy, and to the other powers Russia was one of themselves, peculiar perhaps, but part of Europe. And even in Russia, the parties demanding democratic reforms seemed to be growing constantly stronger. The melange of languages and what were called, and are still called, nations stretching from Bohemia to the Balkans were united in a non-national state where a pleasant way of life was almost the end and purpose of state policy. To be sure, liberal political theory objected to this state, more perhaps than it did to the slowly disintegrating monarchy of the Russian czars. Its mere existence hindered the national hopes of spokesmen for linguistic groups within and without its borders. The objection was not that Austria was tyrannical or oppressive, but that it existed. Russian despotism could be modified towards democracy, but Austria's existence was a denial of what theory taught on the nature of nations in the modern world. But in Germany and Italy, the theory of liberal nationalism had already been triumphantly actualized. Italy had never before existed, so its creation around the liberal, anti-clerical House of Savoy was unarguable evidence that the declared intentions of democratic politics and romantic nationalism were indeed the motive power of history. Germany, unified after centuries of division, was so far in the vanguard of progress and liberalism that it enjoyed a Socialist Party of immense power and a set of institutions of public welfare that would be modern even today. For France, the Low Countries, Scandinavia and England there were in those years neither doubts nor worries. The empires of England, France and Holland stood firm and peaceful. All these states were both old in existence and modern in their way of life. All enjoyed democratic institutions of government and were as extensively industrialized as their situations warranted.

In the Far East the beneficent march of democracy and liberalism had not yet accomplished as much as in Europe and North America. Japan had jumped, it seemed, in one generation from feudalism to a surprisingly good copy of a Western state—yet was still far from democratic. In China, it was felt, progress was at last about to begin because China had just been made a republic, and the young men who seemed to be in control could use Western democratic slogans as well as anyone in the world. They were able, one or another of them, to make more satisfactory adjustments to the desires of both the missionaries and the Western commercial interests than the reactionary old Empress Tsu Hsi, who had at last been gathered to her ancestors after having so long slowed the progressive efforts of both the men of God and the men of money.

From the point of view of an American, whether he was a liberal or inclined to favor the trusts, the society of Europe and North America was in all important things both satisfactory and enduring. Everyone had minor objections against one or another aspect of this interrelated civilization, but its essential structure was what all approved of and believed in; it was the acme of the long progress of mankind down the ages and the stepping stone to even greater progress.

It was indeed a remarkable society. Its technology, the heir of centuries of theoretical and practical work, was so far above the technology of any other group of men that comparisons cannot even be made. Based on that technology, it had spread its dominion over all the seacoasts of the world and over vast inland areas. With this political power available to force importation of cheap raw materials, with the application of its technology in manufacturing and public health at home, it increased its population in a century at a rate never before attained or imagined by any other society.

In western Europe, it was a process of transforming an ancient peasant countryside with an ancient balance of food supply, birth and mortality. In America, it was a process of easy conquest from savages and the clearing, settling and building of empty country. When the two processes were finished, the results were strikingly the same.

Forty years afterwards in the wreckage of the Western world, it was hard to find anything that remained of that safe and secure society. The lands of the Hapsburg Empire, after a fitful existence as national theory-states, had succumbed first to the German and then to the Russian conquerors. The only parts of Germany not blown up by British and American air raids had likewise fallen to the Russians. Russia itself had changed hands internally. Instead of the Europeanized bureaucracy, the rulers of Russia made no secret of their intention to destroy the West. The Dutch and French Empires had collapsed and most of the British. France itself was barely a power at all, a nation restored by alien arms and kept alive by alien assistance. In the Western world only the United States appeared as a stronger power than in 1913, but in relation to the menaces that threatened us, even we were immensely weaker. Who would have taken the prospect of a life or death war as a serious matter in 1913?

The point about this profound decay in the strength and welfare of Western society is not so much that it occurred, nor even that it occurred so rapidly, but that no one wanted it, no one planned it and no one even expected it. Even the Marxists of 1913 only chattered revolutionary slogans and dreamed of an immense international bureaucracy of men like themselves to replace "capitalist imperialism." They never expected to see their slogans in the export literature of a Russian Empire more powerful, more ambitious and far more ruthless than that of the Romanoff czars. It is hard for Western men of our times, who believe so completely and so passionately in the will, to face this grim contradiction between fact and human intention and realize what it may mean, not alone in light upon the past but in expectation of the future.

To us modern men of the West, steeped, even when we deny it, in the philosophy of scientific materialism, it is an article of both political and deep personal faith that our lives are governed by will and conscious intention. We, as individuals and through our machinery of government, we, as a people, plan what is to be done and take steps to see that it is done. All about us we see tangible proofs—so we feel sure—of this process. Over these same years of imperial decay we have seen the development of the modern automobile and road system, of widespread electric power, of aircraft, of nuclear physics, even of the first pioneering exploration of space. We have seen legislation profoundly altering our social structure, the graduated income tax, the rise of powerful mass unions, federal bank control, agricultural subsidies. All these we see as willed activity, intended, planned and excuted by men conscious of what they were doing and of what they intended to accomplish, and this is as willingly admitted by the opponents of such developments as by their adherents. Yet in the field of world politics, no such pattern can be found. No one intended the world developments of the past generation, not even the lords of the Russian Empire who alone have benefited from them. At most, the Soviet Government hoped for some disaster to the West and assisted toward such disaster where it could. But even the Soviet Government prior to about 1944 never seriously supposed that the day would come when it held such a preponderance of military power that to conquer and annihilate the West would become a program within the compass of real politics.

If we had been twice defeated in two great wars, we would have the enemy as a convenient explanation of our disasters. But we have been twice overwhelmingly victorious. Our intentions were supreme in a world at our mercy, yet nothing—not one significant thing—has occurred in accord with these intentions. Words and programs have triumphed, but facts have escaped us.

True, the day-to-day publicity amid which we unavoidably live does not constantly remind us of our lost political security. No powerful political force of our time is served by any public knowledge of this aspect of our immediate past. Security, therefore, is not pictured to us as something lost but as something to be gained in the future, for this, we are told, is the ceaseless objective of all our politics. But each of us knows better, provided we need not say so publicly, knows that we once did have it even though the authorities of our public life never tell us how it was lost.

This is the central problem to which this book is addressed.

The illusion of a fixed present permits our minds to make a comforting separation of the future and the past. It permits us the illusion that they cover human activities of a different sort. The past is fixed and done for, but the future is malleable, a free field for our will. This is emotion not logic, because all the past was once a future, and all the future will become a past. In fact, there is no difference or boundary between them, and the structure and nature of one are the structure and nature of the other. In the modern fashion, however, this fact is uncomfortable. If the future is free to be molded to our wishes, so too the past must once have been free. Who then willed that it should have become what it did become? The other horn is no more comfortable. If the past was not free, if the events that did occur were somehow determined despite the will of the participants, what freedom can there be in the future? But here we refuse to be logical. We are sure that the events of the past could not have been free;

they must have been determined even if by some mechanism we do not understand. Our belief in causality is too profound for us to feel otherwise. Everything that has happened must have a cause, and everything that has a cause could have happened in no other way than it did. Yet we cannot apply the same rule to the future. Our belief in the will is at least as strong as our belief in causality, and a causally determined future would make nonsense of the conception of the will. In truth, the past enshrouds too many miseries and disappointments, and the future veils too many dear hopes and expectations for us to see that they are one and the same, distinguished only by the momentary position from which we observe them. But to anyone who can bring himself to admit the identity of past and future, the two mesh together in one unbroken series of interlocked lives of living beings. The division between the past and future is an ephemeral personal experience different to each man. The smooth, unbroken flow of the past was so broken into past and future for the men who lived in that past, though to us no chink or crack appears in the endless flow of events.

The two cardinal errors of history and politics are to picture the past as timelessly rigid and the future as indefinitely plastic, to feel that because nothing has yet happened, anything can happen, and because things did happen, they *must have* happened. To realize that these are errors is a difficult intellectual process for a modern man. Our fundamental intellectual premise of the coexistence of both will and causality here brings face to face the concealed and inherent contradiction. It is more comforting to keep past and future far apart; to assert a separation between them that permits the assignment of causality as the governing power of history, and intention as the master of politics.

The recognition that past and future do not exist as separate entities and only appear so to an observer, and appear differently to each observer at each instant of observation, carries with it the recognition that history and politics are equally identical. This is simply another way of saying that politics is the practice of the art of prophecy and that history is the record of prophecies fulfilled or confounded. The problem with which we are then concerned is the same whether it is cast forward over the future or back over the past. All that needs to be changed is the tense: "How did it come about that certain prophecies were fulfilled and certain others confounded?" becomes "How will it come about that certain prophecies will be fulfilled and certain others will be confounded?"

It is the thesis of this book that from an understanding of history there flows an understanding of the future. Such understanding cannot confer foreknowledge of what events will certainly happen, but it can confer insight into the probability and improbability of many things dreaded or hoped for. It can go further. It can foresee great alternatives that face a society and though it cannot reveal which alternative may eventuate, it can foresee many of the consequences that will follow from the choice of one rather than of the other .

But an understanding of history, a sense of the living flow of our society and of other societies, living and dead, which have flourished in the course of five thousand years, is a far different thing from a knowledge, however immense, of a maze of unrelated historical events. Unfortunately it is the latter, in organization if not in volume of material, that our liberal education and our popular reading implant among literate Americans, indeed among almost all literate Westerners. It is not usually the historical facts thus taught and accepted that are wrong. It is the connection between the facts, the asserted causal linkages which in the minds of many have come to replace the facts themselves as the frame of historical reality. The problem with which this book is concerned is therefore far less the accepted facts of history than the accepted philosophy of history. It is from the fallacious interpretation of the facts that have flowed those images of the contemporary world, political and economic alike, that have justified at every step forty years of uninterrupted disaster. The units of political reality, the character and ambition of states and civilizations, the value of arms and international compacts, these are not things whose inner nature is disclosed by their contemporary action. All operate on a time scale so long that even the personal experience of a lifetime cannot give a man a valid understanding of their possibilities and their perils. It is from the past, from our image of history, that we derive those convictions about the nature of political societies to which, for good or ill, for life or death, we commit the destiny of our nation and of the civilization which in a thousand years has made us the sort of men we are.

The nature of this civilization itself is a puzzle to us. We know that something to which we give the name "The West" exists. We even talk about Western civilization. But what this West is we pass over as a matter of no importance. Is it a group of human beings or a set of ethical principals? Is it a geographical or a historical entity? Has it a personality as a nation has or is it a loose coalition of the moment designed for practical advantage? Is it something which we join by choice like a philosophical association or into which we are born like a family? Has it a past or is it a contemporary accident? Is it a race? Is it a political alliance? Is it in some way involved with Christianity or democracy or machine technology? Are the Jews part of the West? The Moslems of North Africa? The Russians? To none of these questions does the liberal philosophy of our day seek an answer or ponder whether the correct answers have any bearing upon the survival of our country and the endurance of the millennial society of which it is the last self-standing state.

Around us we cannot help but see this great, endangered civilization which we have come to call the West. But what is it? Who composes it? What are its boundaries in space and in time? How can we set about preserving something whose essential nature we have never thought it important to comprehend?

To review the life of the West as a self-contained existence is not history as that subject is commonly thought of among us, because it requires identifying and tracing the life of a cultural unit whose existence as a historical entity is usually denied. Furthermore, the intellectual fashion of our times is so strongly liberal that it is of necessity antihistorical. A living past to which we are organically connected is perhaps the greatest of all fetters of which liberalism wishes to be rid. To see the West as a relatively closed group of people century after century sharing a common civilization, and to a large extent a common fate, contravenes liberal theories of the nature of men and of mankind. In fact, modern liberalism not only dislikes the past but seeks to get along with no real knowledge of it. A few anecdotes, a semi-biographical treatment of certain favorite moments of the past, the times of Jefferson, Jackson, and Lincoln, the French Revolution, these serve liberalism with all the data it needs for its antihistorical philosophy of history. For the rest, the basic theory of Marxist history, almost voided of historical fact, does duty as the frame of interpretation, officially of the past, but actually only of the present. As a result, there is really no liberal interpretation of history, and accordingly the notion that serious history can contribute to political understanding and action seems almost an odd idea today. Nevertheless its very oddity may not be without some interest.

Conventional school history, with the purpose of showing the progress of mankind, teaches some selected facts arranged in a cause-and-effect relationship. This can scarcely be called an interpretation of history because much, perhaps most, of the history of men has to be left out or the scheme would be wrecked. Between a century and half a century ago, while the Marxists still thought it desirable to have a complete world philosophy to offer, there was current a Marxist interpretation of history in terms of economic determinism, historical materialism and the theory of the class struggle. It too, however, was more frame than fact. Intellectual conviction being a slow road to power, and the matter not being very convincing even to the minds emotionally drawn to Marxism for other reasons, the whole field has today been abandoned, and we are spared a current Marxist history. All that remains of it is a practice of biographical diatribe to praise or vilify this or that historical personage depending on what is deemed good politics at the moment. That a particular and very special history receives considerable attention in Russia and in the Soviet dominions is without bearing here. In Russia, it is Russian history of a sort, solely for Russians, and it is promulgated by men who are leftists only beyond the picket lines of the Soviet armies and are the lords temporal and spiritual within them.

We Americans are antihistorical for another reason besides the current fashion of liberalism. The insistence on having a specifically American history requires of itself a perversion of Western history and gives to an intelligent mind in childhood a life-long distaste for what appears to be such a senseless, even idiotic, discipline as history. Ripped from its place as part of the history of the West and established as though it were the record of a self-contained entity, American history presents a caricature of what happened to the Europeans who crossed the seas. Further it denies, always by inference and sometimes explicitly, the unity of civilization between these Europeans and those who stayed in Europe. In many textbooks of American history there is little to indicate that had the New World been settled by Orthodox Slavs and Moslems, it might have developed otherwise than it did. All the great influences that are pictured as having made us what we are—the frontier, the natural town-meeting democracy of a land without nobility or men of great wealth, the vast untapped resources—all these should have operated as fully on others as they did on our ancestors. The fact is that during most of the four centuries in which Europeans have lived in the Americas almost everything of importance that happened to Americans happened to them not as residents of the Americas but as people of European stock, happened as the reflection in the Americas of the cultural and political life of Europe. Deeper than this, the whole West, for all its immense historical work, tends to an antihistorical bias, limited but important, in one vital field of history. It is required out of veneration for Western Christendom to assert that Western Christianity is the same as that of Jesus. This passionate belief, so certain that no one ever thought it required any evidence, has not only bedeviled Western politics for centuries but in the field of pure historical thought has made it impossible for most historians to make the necessary classifications of their subject matter; in cruder words, to know what they were talking about.

The problem in gaining a sense of history is, therefore, in reality threefold: the facts of history; the connections, if any, between these facts; and the units of historical action. On the first, there can be almost no quarrel with contemporary historical scholarship. The facts of more than five millennia have been gathered and sifted with a zeal and skill that has made this field of endeavor one of the great monuments of Western scholarship. No other society ever attempted such a task or ever thought it worth the effort. The difficulty enters in the philosophical calculations concerning what the facts show.

The history of the world as it is taught in general American education, and as it is presupposed in such current literature as touches upon history at all, is the picture of history that most people hold. This, not the esoteric history of the specialist, is the image of the past of our life that affects political action. It is a picture of progress, moral and mechanical. It shows man as a species appearing from the other animals by evolution. It shows him advancing through knowledge of tools and husbandry across prehistoric times. It shows him, still mankind, advancing through the ancient societies of Egypt and Babylonia to attain the foundation of real progress in art and philosophy with the Greeks, in law and politics with the Romans, in religion with the Hebrews. Then after an unfortunate setback mankind emerges into true progress again with Western society—or more usually—specifically in the rise of the modern Western states and churches in the fifteenth and sixteenth centuries.

This is the skeletal frame of history to which each attaches whatever detail of knowledge he desires. The past of non-Western peoples like the Moors and Byzantines, whose contacts were close with the West during the past of the West, are treated as branches off the main stem of progress. The past of peoples whose contacts with the West are almost entirely modern, like the Chinese and the Hindus, simply is not considered high history at all. Theirs is the history of annals and, in reality, not a part of history but a division of comparative sociology or anthropology.

The difficulty that forces this exclusion of all peoples who have not involved themselves in our past, and the later affairs of peoples with whom we were once intimate, is that if these peoples be included in history the line of progress picture falls apart, and the record of mankind appears as only a jumble of ups and downs, crimes and victories going nowhere. We have so construed and arranged our own story of human societies that we have created a plot for it, but if we include these aberrant societies, the plot is destroyed, and the book becomes a meaningless jumble of unconnected yarns. Liberalism asserts the equality and unity of all men, but it refuses to consider seriously the history of many men because their histories do not lead to the modern West. Thucydides asserts in the opening of his history of the Peloponnesian War that before his time nothing of importance had happened in the world. We are free from this conviction of the Classical world that there is no real past, but like Thucydides we exclude whatever has no meaning to us, and that part of the past that does not appear to lead to us, that is, all history that falls outside the Egypt-Greece-Rome-West scheme, has no meaning as *history*. The great novelist who contrived the story of mankind has here, we feel, indulged his taste for the bizarre in long and perhaps interesting descriptive passages, or even in subplots involving his minor characters. But all of these passages could be cut out with no harm to the real story—perhaps even with considerable improvement in the coherence of the tale and the tightness and march of the plot.

Of those who do not see the image of history as this line-of-progress, almost all see history simply as bunk, a body of information difficult to acquire and useless to know. These will concede, if pressed, that the present has been unfortunately molded by the past, but they refuse to see the future as simply the present of some other day equally, in its turn, molded by its past. To them the molding process of the past, which they reluctantly admit, is a confusion of luck and misfortune without sense or pattern.

The line-of-progress scheme, while it is a caricature of the history of mankind, is something more than an arbitrary rigging of fact to produce the plot for our own story. There is a reality to the scheme, though not the one assigned to it, and there is good reason why it should have so long remained the accepted image of history in Western society. Historical, in contrast to causal, consideration of this scheme reveals what it in fact is. It is simply the history of the *lands* of the Roman Empire up to what we call the fall of Rome and thereafter the history of Western society itself. Even though we think of ourselves as Christians, this has never altered our attachment to the scheme. Our consideration of the history of Christianity is confined also to the Roman lands. The great spread of early Christianity east of the Roman frontier is left to a handful of historical scholars, not considered part of world history. These Christians had split from Orthodoxy before the schism between the Latin and Greek churches and so were not in the line of descent to us. Similarly after the development of the Latin church in the West, the further history of Orthodoxy becomes of no importance to us.

It is rather amusing that this scheme which defines the structure of the world for both the progress-materialism of the nineteenth century and the economic determinism of the twentieth is a product of medieval astrology. In a popular twelfth century poem explaining how all things are foretold in the stars, Bernard Silvester tells us:[1]

> *Astra notat Persis, Aegyptus parturit artes,*
> *Graecia docta legit, praelia Roma gerit.*
> *Exemplar specimenque Dei virguncula Christum*
> *Parturit, et verum saecula numen habent.*

> *The Babylonians learned astronomy. The Egyptians*
>   *began the mechanical arts.*
> *Greece discovered learning, Rome waged wars.*
> *A virgin bore Christ, the example and type of God,*
> *And the world received its true Lord.*

The earliest historians of the West, likewise men of the twelfth century, necessarily found bulking immense across their past the name of the Roman

[1] Quoted by Lynn Thorndike, *History of Magic and Experimental Science*, New York. 1947. Vol II, p. 105.

Empire, so that the history of Rome became the essential first back step into history. In its turn, the history of Rome raised to importance the preceding history of the lands over which the Roman Empire eventually spread. But these earlier historians were not attempting to write a history of mankind. They sought only a history of their own people, a people whose learned language was Latin and whose religion was Christian, so that the exclusion from their scheme of all history that did not lead to them seemed entirely reasonable. It was an early groping attempt to deal with the perplexing mystery of the growth and change of human societies and would probably long since have been abandoned except for the veneration in which Westerners still hold Rome and Christianity, a veneration that places the past of the Mediterranean lands in a special position above all others, a veneration that requires us to seek our own cultural origin in those lands.

One other aspect of human society gives great difficulty to historical analysis. Although societies differ radically among themselves, both historically and geographically, yet individual men seem much alike. Hunger, love, fear of death operate almost identically on all men, civilized or savage. The life of individual men in all the great societies is molded by a group of institutions and customs which touch the individual in much the same way: religion, state, wealth and poverty, rank and subordination. It has been and can truthfully be argued that the lives of individual men, particularly men living in any one of the great societies, have far more in common than they have points of difference. From this fact a passionate sentimentality has gone on to conclude that since men resemble each other, so societies ought to resemble each other, and for a society to differ, particularly to differ from the historical mean as drastically as ours does, is unnatural and indeed wicked. If society were nothing but the arithmetical aggregate of the individuals composing it, this point of view would be sound. There would be no reason why all men could not and perhaps should not lead almost identical lives in a nearly identical environment. Such is, in fact, the official Marxist doctrine and very nearly the approved position of modern liberalism.

Historically, it is not the intimate resemblance of men but the subtle distinctions among them that are important. Men resemble each other as animals. They differ from each other as the creatures and creators of civilizations. For what distinguishes men in societies from the imaginary man-as-man, which means man-as-animal, is that all men of historical actuality are also molded by some culture. And what distinguishes men of the great historical societies from neolithic men or from the savage peoples of later times is that the men of the great societies are not alone possessed of the static and technical cultures that characterize the simpler societies but are molded by the cultures of growth, decay and intellectualization which are the unique attributes of all the great societies.

Societies are more than the simple aggregate of the individuals or nations composing them. They are historical creations in which the acts of the dead have more power than the intentions of the living. Every society is a tissue out of the past, a web of laws, customs, boundaries, word meanings, property and institutions of all sorts which make of every man within that society something more than merely a man. He is also a creature molded by all these things. There is no natural man. There are only men of certain tribes or certain civilized societies, and we deduce the image of man-as-such from the points of resemblance among the real men who live or have lived as members of the various societies of men. Whether such a creature could exist we do not know. We do know that from paleolithic times to our own day he never has.

Even the conscious intention to change a society, which is so accepted a feature of our own time, is not an assertion of the power of man-as-such against the fetters of historical society. Even the partisans of change are men of a society, either of that which they seek to change or of another. Their conscious goal does not remove from their whole being the centuries of the society to which they belong. They remain like other men loaded with the ideas, prejudices, unconscious ways of understanding, unconscious meaning of words, unconscious pictures of right and wrong, that they derive from the society of their origin. The influence of environment has been a favorite theme of modern sociology, but the greatest environment of all is the historical society to which a man belongs. More than slum or suburb it molds him, but since it molds his observer, too, there is no relative sign of the influence.

The philosophical justification for contempt of history flows from the liberal thought of the eighteenth century. The antihistorical bias of eighteenth century liberalism took the form of denying all logic to history, in asserting that history was not justified by "reason" and seeing it as a mass of meaningless anarchic events, most of which never should have occurred and few of which would have occurred if "reason," that is if the liberals themselves, had been guiding events. From this point of view all the historical institutions of their time, dynasty, nobility, church and province, became "unreasonable," and society was intellectually disintegrated into disparate beings struggling in a web of economic interests and irrational, inherited tyrannies. The higher unity, and the only higher unity, to which a man could belong was, therefore, "mankind." All other unities, state, church, even race, were historical creations and therefore unreasonable and unworthy of being maintained. If the tangible, operating and powerful realities of everyday life, the state and the church, could hardly withstand intellectual distintegration under this acid, how much less such an obscure concept as that of civilization which has no tangible body corporate in the forefront of events but must be discovered as a concept from the slow unrolling of long history?

As a living fact, the church and state survived eighteenth century liberalism, but they were thereafter intellectually justified, as they still are, on rational, not historical grounds. They "do good," or should, and moreover they do good for their current tenants. They are instruments of present advantage not of historical necessity.

So, too, everything that is felt to have come into being over the past but to lack rational justification, that is, to fail to promote egalitarianism, is regarded as something contrary to "liberty," or as we would say today contrary to "democracy." Hence such things should be consciously removed from society. From this point of view, the least rationally justified concept, which is therefore the prime enemy of world egalitarianism, is the concept of Western civilization as a historic entity. The fact that the states of western Europe and the states of European foundation beyond the seas differed both in their history and in their contemporary way of life from all other societies could not be denied. What could be denied, however, was that this fact represented anything more than the coincidence of natural circumstances. From this denial it could be asserted that there was nothing specifically personal about Western civilization, nothing biologically or historically unique, and that its "social progress" and mechanical benefits could and should be equally available to all the world.

The difficulty of grasping and defining the concept of Western civilization long preceded the eighteenth century liberals, but in the earlier times it was not philosophically so important to deny it or explain it away. In the early ages this identity of the Western peoples was comprehended under the inapplicable name of Christendom, and the fact that these communities were Christian was felt to be both the fact and the cause of the difference. Later with the use of the word "Europe" and the growing intellectual importance of the problem, other factors than Christianity were added, again both to identify and explain the difference. These have come well down into our own day and are all causal. Their number is fairly impressive: the Classical literary and artistic inheritance, the innate genius of the Germanic barbarians, the peculiar stimulus of the climate of western Europe, the peculiar soil of western Europe, the extensive coast line and necessity for use of the sea, the innate democracy of Christianity (or of the Germanic tribes) flowering in democratic institutions, the great intellectual borrowings from the Jews and Saracens, the genius of individual kings, the genius of individual rebels. All these have been offered, some constitute a whole library of argumentation, to explain the stubborn and, to the idealist, distasteful fact, that Western society differs drastically from all others both contemporary and extinct.

To a great extent throughout the eighteenth and nineteenth centuries, these explanations more and more tended to obscure the fact that Western civilization existed at all. The explanations came to obscure the thing explained, a natural but erroneous application of the methods then current in the mechanical sciences—a matter discussed in some detail in Chapter 1. Studying thus the postulated mechanics of society, it came to be supposed, as if the data were those of the sciences, that the same mechanics could in theory be applied to different sorts of men; and if that were done, these men would become essentially the same as the Westerners. This belief still endures, though now it is rarely set out in detail, and is the intellectual foundation—the moral foundation is another matter—of modern liberal internationalism. Naturally in this process the existence of the West as a historical personality was lost sight of. By the outbreak of the Second World War probably the bulk of the educated opinion throughout all the Western states would have denied the historical reality of Western civilization and have accepted as an accurate analysis of the world the system of classes, ideals and economic interests that had been alleged as the motive power of history. An embarrassed reservation on the supposed unimportance of races might have been admitted privately, but in all other factors the liberal opinion was unchallenged.

But more than a philosophical objection to history as the grim reminder of the fallibility of human intention and human reason lies in our modern rejection of historical knowledge as a thing of value in the politics of the world. We do not understand the mechanics of history. What has made things happen? What are the causes of history? We assert, of course, that history is a chain of cause and effect; but though we may believe this as an ideal, its practice on the events of history produces no useful body of knowledge. Unlike the mechanical sciences, history yields no guide to the possibilities of the future when analyzed by cause and effect. We deny this in principle, but we accept it as an unfortunate fact.

It is this that makes history so unwelcome. Rigged for us as though it were a causal science, it proves a useless tool in practice. If causality could interpret the past, it could foresee the future. But the accepted history of our day does not really interpret the past. Once the illusion of causal explanation vanishes under detailed scrutiny, all that is left is an inexplicable jumble of meaningless events, which even in the wisdom of hindsight seem completely unpredictable. We can, therefore, scarcely be surprised to find a half century of liberal and democratic prophecies based on such profound misunderstanding, decade by decade flatly contradicted by events.

With the life of more than five thousand years of human society behind us, is there thus no wisdom that can be gathered from that long record?

Among the few books dealing with the philosophy of history that attained any general circulation in the last thirty years only three have attempted to deal with world history from a strictly historical approach: Wells' *Outline of History,* Spengler's *Decline of the West* and Toynbee's *A Study of History.* Such a choice will probably shock a professional historian, but the selection is based on the objective of the author and the reasonably wide audience each obtained—not on the basis of the scholarly excellence of the work. Each of these writers sought to give a purely historical picture of the history of all men—to treat of world history as history—not as random examples of comparative anthropology, jurisprudence or sociology. In three quite different ways each realized that what was essential to the understanding of the lives of men was shown not by the contemporary frame of space but by the eternal arrow of time.

Wells, who was, of course, an earnest liberal, was the earliest and the least successful of these popularizers of world history. Few liberals have attempted as he did to ponder history seriously. They prefer to use it as a convenient grab bag for the extraction of tendencious anecdotes, and rarely notice the contradiction of having to show the progress of mankind by successively disregarding the fate of each particular group of men in order to take up the tale of progress, for awhile, with another. But Wells was one of these few, and he was struck by the essentially illiberal character of the line-of-progress scheme. He struggled emotionally against it but never built any alternate pattern. He was fascinated by the concept of progress and sought to find it anywhere he could, hoping somehow to tie all the separate progresses that he believed he found into one final unity. In the end, the only unity lay in the future, in a renewed vitality for a League of Nations. In essence, the book was dull. History is a drama and so it must have a plot. But the plot of Egypt-Greece-Rome offended Wells' liberal principles so he threw it out. But then he could find no other.

Spengler, in contrast, is all plot. Guizot's [2] concept that there existed

---

[2] The *sense* of the identity of Western civilization had existed since Carolingian times, but its intellectual expression in later centuries seemed in contradiction to both Christian tradition and the progress theories of the Enlightenment. There was a further difficulty with the word "European." Geographically it is arbitrarily applied to certain lands which have no particular geographic identity, no common history, and have never been the seat of a common culture. Culturally, however, it means, when it means anything at all in this sense, simply Western civilization, even though that civilization never covered all Europe—Russia and the Balkans have never been culturally "European,"—and that civilization now occupies parts of the world far removed from Europe. Of course, all Europeans— in the cultural sense of the word—in the back of their minds have always known

a European civilization, essentially self-contained, and despite its national forms, essentially identical throughout Western Europe, provided Spengler with his key historical unit. States and peoples belonged to a higher organization which Spengler called a culture in its early phases and a civilization in its later. All the great societies of the earth, past and present, belonged to one of these cultures which successively have flowered and withered. But—and here was the catch to the popular acceptance of Spengler's scheme—these cultures had an organic quality about them. They had youth, maturity and senility, and the possibilities open to a mature or senile society were quite different from those open to that same society in its youth. Even this might not be too hard to accept—we would not consider it reasonable to expect a revival of the ages of Gothic faith and cathedral building or a new Crusade—but Spengler included in his aging process philosophy, politics and the arts and was not averse to expressing a low opinion of contemporary art and thought. Since artists and intellectuals are so largely the promoters of current fashion in opinion, the opinion regarding Spengler has been shaded accordingly. Besides he was anti-leftist, a German, and, despite his sharp criticism of the blood-and-thunder romanticism of Nietzsche, not beyond using a good deal of it himself. In the end, perhaps, his popular standing as a man of intellectual importance disappeared when his views were confused with Nazi actions and Nazi effusions of the Rosenberg type. Actually this confusion was an injustice to Spengler, both as a man and a historian, but was quite natural. Even today the epithet of "fascist" is thrown at everyone who does not parrot leftist clichés about the nature or future of democratic politics, and Spengler was a strong German nationalist not overly tender with the professional optimism of democratic liberalism.

Considered, however, from the view of scholarly history, Spengler has been the most important historian of modern times. Since the publication of *The Decline of the West,* all historical writing has been forced to take account of Spengler's presentation of the history of men as the history of great societies, each having an inward cohesion and personality of its own. Even those who bitterly oppose Spengler's political objectives have more and more come to accept this much of his interpretation of history. Among serious objections to Spengler's theory of history—his leanings towards Nietzsche are irrelevant to that point—perhaps the only vital one is his

---

that they differed sharply from other men. Even Gibbon in his chapter on the barbarians (Chapter 37 II of the *Decline*) could write: "The perpetual correspondence of the Latin clergy, the frequent pilgrimages to Rome and Jerusalem, and the growing authority of the popes, cemented the union of the Christian republic, and gradually produced the similar manners and common jurisprudence, which have distinguished from the rest of mankind the independent, and even hostile, nations of modern Europe."

inattention to the relations among the different historical societies. This has been a relation which itself has undergone change with the passage of time—in other words a historical fact outside the self-contained life of the individual societies—an item, perhaps the one real item since neolithic times, in which "mankind" has been the historical unit. The ancient societies, arising in the midst of history-less, neolithic man, necessarily differed from the later societies arising on an earth already covered with the monuments, memories and political remains of the earlier. It has not destroyed the inner cohesion of the life of the later societies, but it has made them immensely different from the earlier. It is the difference, in a Spengler-like analogy, between the virgin forests which long ago arose out of the post-glacial prairies of the north, and the tangled second growth forests of today.

Toynbee is a mechanized, liberal Spengler. He believes not only that causality rules human events, but that these events can be explained and proved causally. He is even willing to give examples that, he asserts, consitute such proofs. But he accepts the concept of a culture embracing the various nations within it, and he admits some sort of time pattern within those cultures. It would not be correct to call this time pattern growth and decay—though for long stretches they seem such in Toynbee's pages—because Toynbee denies with anger anything approaching an organic structure in his cultures. Age is an organic necessity in an organism. Even though we cannot explain the process causally, we know that it must occur and can predict a good deal about its effects. But Toynbee will have none of this. He admits the decay of many cultures but insists that this decay flows from causal and mechanistic reasons, usually of a moral kind, the "creative minority" becoming the "dominant minority." These are phrases more useful for conveying moral opprobrium than precise facts and so Toynbee doubtless intended them.

His classification of cultures follows in many important respects that of Spengler. Both see society developing into a "time of troubles" and a universal empire, but Toynbee denies the rigorous life span of a culture that Spengler asserts. Hence what Spengler calls the *fellahin* societies—the long drawn out and often rigid societies of aged cultures, late Egypt, Assyria and Byzantium, modern China, India and the Arab world—frequently are represented by Toynbee as new, successor cultures. A comparison of their respective classification of civilizations, the table on page 18, shows this difference sharply for the ancient civilizations.

It is apparent at once from this table that Toynbee merely divides Spengler's main classifications into subcivilizations which even in his own account are essentially similar. He does not shatter Spengler's underlying structure and in only one case would most historians cavil at grouping

TOYNBEE

Approximate dates (B.C. unless indicated as A.D.) [3]

Civilization	Origin	End
Egyptiac	4000	1660
Minoan	3000	1400
Sumeric	3500	1900
Hittite	1400	?
Babylonic	1500	550
Sinic	1500	175 A.D.
Far Eastern (Main Body)	500 A.D.	extant
Japanese offshoot		extant
Indic	1500	475 A.D.
Hindu	800 A.D.	extant
Syriac	1100	1000 A.D.
Islamic (derived from Syriac)	1300 A.D.	extant
Orthodox Christian (Main Body)	700 A.D.	extant?
Orthodox Christian (Russian offshoot)	950 A.D.	extant
Hellenic	1100	400 A.D.
Western	700 A.D.	extant

SPENGLER

Approximate dates (B.C. unless indicated as A.D.)

Civilization	Origin	Youth	Maturity	Senescence
Egyptian	3400-3000	2900-2400	2150-1800	1800-660(?)
Babylonian				
Chinese	1700-1300	1300-800	800-500	480-modern times
Hindu	1500-1200			
Magian	500 B.C.-0	A.D. 0-500	A.D. 500-800	A.D. 800-modern times
Russian	(no dates indicated)			
Classical	1600-1100	1100-650	650-300	A.D. 200-300
Western	A.D. 500-900	A.D. 900-1500	A.D. 1500-1800	A.D. 1800

Toynbee's division into the major societies as set out by Spengler. That case would be what Spengler called the Magian, or at times the Arabic civilization, which in this book is called the Levantine civilization. To modern Westerners steeped in a Christian tradition, it is initially difficult to recognize as a single civilization nations professing what seem to us such disparate religions as Mazdaism, Judaism, Orthodox Christianity and Mohammedanism. Nevertheless, there are sound historical reasons for doing so though at this point it is only possible to refer to the discussion of this question in chapters III and IV.

Both historians likewise tabulate the ancient civilizations of the Americas. These are not considered in this work primarily because its focus of interest

---

3 This schedule of Toynbee's civilizations is based on the list in *A Study of History*, vol. I, p. 131-3 and upon Table V of his abridgement of volumes I-VI (1947). In volume VII (1954) Toynbee added two new civilizations to his list, the Shang—preceding the Sinic, and the Indus—preceding the Indic. In volume XII (*Reconsiderations*, 1961) he further revised his classification to remove from the list of independent civilizations the Babylonic, the Far Eastern (Main Body), and the Hindu, attaching these eras to their geographic predecessors; thus conforming, in regard to these, to Spengler's grouping. Toynbee further reorganized the whole original list of civilizations by dividing it into "Full Blown Civilizations" and "Satellite Civilizations." The first group (again eliminating ancient America) is divided as follows: (definitions within square brackets are Toynbee's own)

Unaffiliated to Others

Sumero-Akkadian	(corresponds to the Sumeric and Babylonic of the original list)
Egyptiac Aegean Indus	(largely the Minoan of the original list)
Sinic	(includes not only the Sinic and the Far Eastern (Main Body) of the original list but also the Shang civilization of volume VII)

Affiliated to Others [First Batch]
Syriac [to Sumero-Akkadian, Egyptiac, Aegean and Hittite]
Helenic [to Aegean]

Indic [to Indus]	(combines the Indic and Hindu of the original list)

Affiliated to Others [Second Batch]

Orthodox Christian Western Islamic	[to both Syriac and Helenic]

Finally Toynbee defines a new class of civilizations, Satellite civilizations, in which he places the Hittite—satellite of the Sumero-Akkadean, Japanese—satellite of the Sinic, and Russian—originally a satellite of the Orthodox Christian but now a satellite of the Western. He repeats (p. 470) his inclusion of the Jews as members of the Syriac civilization, in fact, as its only living members.

The list of Spengler's civilizations is based upon Tables I, II and III in vol. I of the English translation of *The Decline of the West*. New York. Knopf, 1926.

is the life of the West with which the American civilizations had almost nothing to do, and secondarily because the preliminary work of assembling the factual basis for a study of these civilizations—if there were actually more than one—has not yet been done and, indeed, in the poverty of records may never be done.

The essential difference between Toynbee and Spengler lies in Spengler's theory of the organic nature of a culture and Toynbee's emphatic rejection of all considerations but those of mechanistic causality. The issue requires some analysis and a clearer notion of the idea of organic behavior than we today commonly entertain. The word "organic" as applied to history has been used largely by German writers and has earned a good deal of warranted contempt as a fuzzy product of German pedantic romanticism. Nevertheless, it is not the word but what is sought to be described by the word that is important.

The word "organic" appears at first thought to have a precise meaning. Clearly, all the higher plants and animals are organisms and all the unicellular forms of life equally clearly are not.[4] Here the word has an unambiguous meaning: a functionally interdependent group of living cells. But in areas of life more complex than unicellular creatures, and less so than true organism, the problem becomes much more difficult. In general we mean by an organism a group of living cells differentially specialized so that some cells perform one special function—digestion, nerve transmission, reproduction—and the organism as a whole is enabled to live by the interdependent functioning of the various specialized cells. The word "organism," therefore, is not strictly speaking the name of a thing, but the description of a process, of the manner of interdependent behavior of living cells, a behavior that we find characteristic of all the higher plants and animals. In fact, that is what we mean by "higher" in this case, "partaking of an organic structure." In popular, unthought image there then follows an assumed connection between life and the organism that lives. There is felt to be some "thing" in a man which is alive, that is, as it were, the seat of death when he dies. An organism is felt to have a life of its own distinct from the life of the cells that compose it. Biology and medicine, on the other hand, encounter no such phenomenon. All the life that can be found in a man is in the individual living cells that compose him. When he dies, the complex functioning of the cells ceases though the individual cells are still alive. Inevitably, of course, with the breakdown of the interdependent functioning, the individual cells themselves begin to die for lack of oxygen and food and from the poisoning of

---

4 From a chemical point of view, to be sure, a single cell is a complex of enormous specialization of its different molecular components, in that sense an organism itself, but no self-sustaining living components seem to lie below it.

the now irremovable end-products of their own and their neighbors' metabolism.

Among the higher animals, the life span of no individual differs much from the average of his species and extremes of longevity are unknown. Among the plants, however, the cellular relationships are less dangerously specialized and the life span of many trees and hardy perennials seems capable of immense extension in a favorable, and therefore usually artificial, environment. Between the unicellular creatures and the obvious organisms lies a borderland of creatures, such as the corals, that are known as colonies because while there is sufficient interdependence among the cells to require them to live together for their general welfare, they are not organically specialized and each could, under favorable circumstances, live by itself. So, of course, can the tissue of the true organism if somebody will feed and air it artificially.

The next difficulty in grasping the essential nature of an organism is the supposition that in order to be an organism, a creature must be physically attached together in one obvious, visible piece. This is a natural illusion from the fact that what we usually call organisms are always so assembled. But this fact is irrelevant. The word "organism" is the description of a type of cell behavior and any group of cells that behave like an organism must be considered to be one. The myriad living cells of our own blood, sperm and saliva are not physically connected with their fellows but are not for that reason excluded from the organism of which they are a part. In some of the sponges and hydroids, for instance, appear creatures with all the attributes of an organism, specialization of separate cells for digestion and reproduction. Yet if these creatures are ground up, the separate cells will reassemble themselves again as an organism. Our own practice of surgical tissue grafting is a similar phenomenon and shows again that the question of physical assemblage of the cells is a matter, in these cases, of cell nourishment and is irrelevant to the question of specialization of function which alone defines what we mean by an organism.

In the insect world, we find the other extreme. Individual ants and bees are normally classified as individual organisms in their own right. In addition, however, these creatures belong to a more complex institution, the hill or hive, which has all the attributes of organic behavior and might from some points of view be considered as the prime unit organism of these creatures. Although there is no doubt that the ant in relation to its own cells is a true organism, yet in relation to the hill it has the aspect of an individual cell. Like cells the individual ants are biologically specialized to their tasks. Similarly the queens and drones are the sole reproductive "cells" and the life of the individuals composing the hill comes to an end shortly after the death of the hill which can be brought about by the destruction of its queen.

The development of all the forms of life, animal and plant, shows a constant tendency toward aggregation of individual living cells into functionally dependent units. Whether the cells are physically attached to each other is immaterial. The point is whether the cells function as a unit or as an aggregate of individuals. With a tendency so universal as this among living creatures, it should not be surprising to find behavior tending in the same direction by the higher forms where the unit is no longer the individual cell, but an individual organism itself assuming toward the higher and more complex function, part of the role that its own cells assume toward it. Interestingly, although we do not normally discern the presence of an organic structure in any of the natural associations of individual organisms, what corresponds to the intermediate step between the unicellular creature and the true organism, the colony, is taken for granted. It is found very widely among the higher animals, for example, in the inevitable herd of the ungulates and in the flocks of many of the wild birds. Perhaps the beavers, and certainly the social insects, go further and show an unmistakable tendency to create the specialization of an organism out of their joint life.

The point is not whether the great societies of men are organisms. Let us be done with it and say that they are or are not as anyone pleases, but the point is whether it should be surprising to find in these societies behavior that partakes of a tendency so widespread among all living things. Youth, age and specialization of function are all essential elements of organic life. Unicellular creatures lack all three. All three are strikingly present in all the great societies of men.

They have a crude, passionate beginning, a full powerful maturity, and a rigid senility where growth or even change is no longer possible, and like ancient trees they exist until some outside force destroys them. Colonies, on the other hand, do not have youth and age, and specialization is very slight among these creatures. The same situation exists in the primitive societies of men, the Eskimos, Bushmen, etc., whose individuals live and die as do the corals, but whose society is changeless for millennia. And precisely as we do not know the cause of youth and age in an animal organism—we only know that it occurs and must occur in every member of a species in accordance with the life pattern of that species—so we do not know the causes of youth and age in human societies. But there is no question of our ability to see the fact.

Homeric Greece in contrast to Augustan Rome, the age of the pyramids and the age of Rameses, the Gothic cathedrals and modern architecture, the passion of the Apostles and the wrangles of the church councils of the

Isaurian Emperors, all show a contrast with which we are familiar. From all our personal experience with living things, we become accustomed to this contrast of the young and the old: the hopeful, the unsure, the energetic against the doubtful, the long-practiced and the weary.

These great societies have another attribute that we associate with a higher organism: personality. Inevitably, the strict personality of the West is not so immediately evident to us because we live within it and see rather the multiple minor differences among the various Western nations than the overlying similarity. So, too, members of a family think they all look different, even when strangers can scarcely tell them apart. But the personalities of other societies are instantly apparent and in no aspect of their lives is this personality so clearly displayed as in their arts. The artistic boundaries between the different nations of the same society are vague and often entirely arbitrary, but the artistic boundaries between different civilizations are so real and vivid that no aesthetic text book is required to argue their existence. They instantly strike the eye and ear of every observer. The rankest amateur can tell an Egyptian work of art and never confuse it with the art of any other culture, whether it was produced in 3000 B.C. or in the reign of Alexander. Everything produced in China for three thousand years, pictures, bronzes, buildings, is unmistakably Chinese to our eyes and the derivative origin of the cultures of Japan and Korea is equally apparent. No one ever confuses a Classical building, Greek or Roman, with any other even though we have made a few partial copies ourselves and are said to have copied this architecture since the Renaissance and been powerfully influenced by it before that. We talk of "Oriental" art, but no one confuses Hindu work with Chinese or confuses either with Byzantine or Arabic. Byzantine churches, which, of course, also exist in Italy, can never be mistaken for Western churches, though they can be mistaken for mosques and synagogues and the Mazdaist fire temples of Persia.

So striking is the artistic integrity of each society that had Western historical writing originated in an aesthetic rather than a political and religious focus, the structure of history as the history of separate civilizations would long since have been accepted as an obvious fact of human life. But the history of the arts was undertaken long after the progress frame of political history and had become rigid convention so that instead of being the history of great self-contained aesthetic enterprises, it is a patchwork of asserted "influence," all, of course, progressively leading to each author's favored manifestation in the artistic life of the West. Quite naturally in such a process the marginal areas, both in time and space, between different civilizations, since they and they alone show conscious "borrowing" of alien aesthetic factors, receive an attention out of all proportion to their importance. Thus the inadequate crudities of Carolingian art are mulled over in an earnest endeavor to find in this confusion of Byzantine motifs, Classical structural members and unrealized, unconscious Western ambitions some causal explanation of the immense and sudden artistic development that appeared nearly two centuries later in Western Romanesque. With the same objective what is called "Early Christian" art in the Roman Empire is dissected in the hope of establishing it as a bridge of influence from Classical art to the far later Western, though it is embarrassingly evident on the most superficial examination of this art that if it is a bridge from the Classical world, it is a bridge to Byzantium and the Moslems, not to the West.

It is unfortunate that the historians of art have allowed themselves so generally to fall into the trap of the line-of-progress political historians. Had they not done so they would have seen and been able to show that the arts have been so powerful an expression of human life that they could stamp the style of a society on all its members and sweep along hostile and indifferent nations in one great, unorganized but living enterprise.

All the arts of each of the great societies show this power of a historical personality, not only in how each art was handled but in the types of creative effort that grew to the stature of great arts in each society. The Classical world which is declared in all the textbooks to have been the mother of our arts—in fact to have had arts identical with ours—had an entirely different catalogue of arts and those that superficially agree with our classification were used quite differently. The great arts of the Classical society were architecture, sculpture, vase painting, poetic literature (which seems to have been clearly related to oratory, i.e. for recitation not reading) and the dance. Music and painting were minor, comparable, perhaps, to what pottery (i.e., the equivalent of vase painting) is to us. But even where the arts appear to coincide, the differences are enormous. Classical architecture, with a profound knowledge of the mathematics involved and by brilliant design, removed from every building the possibility of seeing it with any perspective. Every rank of columns is broken against the horizon, every architrave bowed, every column set slightly out of line and out of plumb and built with an entasis that prevents vertical perspective between them. It used to be a silly notion in some textbooks that the Classical men did not understand perspective. They understood it completely and devised skillful technical means to prevent it showing.

Somewhat the same confusion exists about the asserted lack of perspective in Egyptian reliefs. In these, distance is indicated by reducing the size of a distant figure and raising it above the figures that, in our terms, are in the foreground. This is, of course, perspective of a sort, but it seems to us highly artificial and even childish and is made somewhat confusing because the Egyptians also used difference in size to show difference in dramatic importance of their figures. But their perspective as such was not childish. We get this illusion from supposing that our own perspective is "natural," a true image of the way things really look. What we do not realize is that our perspective is exactly as artificial as the Egyptian's or Greek's, and is designed, as was theirs, to show things, not as they look, but as we desire to see them.

Our perspective is said to be the projection according to the rule of the inverse square of the distance, but it is not strictly so. What it actually is, is the integration of an infinite series of such projections. It is this complicated act of integration that converts horizontals into straight converging lines instead of having them appear as converging shallow arcs as they actually appear to our eye. Here, if anywhere, is an interesting example of the power of a culture. Our idea of perspective is so powerful that it is capable of altering our own impressions from our own senses and not one person in a million is aware that he does not see horizontals as he thinks he sees them, as all the pictures he sees show them. Elaborate mathematics is not necessary to demonstrate this. Consider the projection of a brick wall with the mortar joints showing conspicuously. To an observer facing the wall, the courses to the right slant away downward toward the earth, the vertical joints all standing upright and making increasingly acute angles with the courses as the distance increases. To the left the same phenomenon is repeated only now the angles are reversed. What the observer really sees in the horizontal courses is a series of converging arcs, tangent to the plane of the horizon directly in front of him where they are farthest apart and falling away downward on both sides. What perspective must picture, however, is not these converging arcs but converging straight lines and this is done by integrating all images formed as the eye sweeps right or left. But it is impossible to integrate both sweeps in the same picture since the right and left horizontals would then meet at an angle in front of the observer. For this reason no background of long horizontals extending on both sides of a perpendicular from the observer is possible in Western art.

A similar situation exists in the handling of vertical parallels, as the sides of a straight tower or two tall chimneys. These should converge as they rise above the line of sight to the plane of the horizon, as they do to the eye and to a photograph, but in integrating the separate pictures of the sweep all verticals are at all times at right angles to the horizon so in Western prespective they do not converge.

Now Egyptian perspective is equally false but different. Where our perspective holds the eye in a fixed spot and sweeps the field of view with a vector, Egyptian perspective holds the eye at a fixed height above the ground, with a fixed line of sight perpendicular to the plane of view, and moves the eye parallel to that plane. In perfect keeping with these different mathematical conventions of perspective is the different treatment of the eye in the portraiture of the two civilizations. In Western portraiture, the eye is never fixed on the observer because that is not the way we see. The image from a fixed point of projection is not our view of the world. For us to see, the eye must sweep through a vector. In Egyptian portraiture the eye is always fixed on the observer even when it requires an anatomical monstrosity as in profiles.

Consider literature. Classical literature does not have the novel. Its tragedy is confined to myths and only in its late comedies does it even pretend to deal with people, and then predominantly standard literary types. History as we understand it is lacking; current events, the actual lived experience of the author-politician, exists instead. Biography is rare and late, autobiography unknown. The Classical dancer, motion being confined largely to the arms and torso, would probably appear to us as some sort of refined contortionist.

Most striking of all the arts in revealing the difference of personality in these two societies is sculpture, all the more because we never cease praising the beauty of Classical sculpture and suppose that we have continued this art. This is a case of simple dishonesty on the part of several generations of art critics and teachers which historians should long since have exposed and ended. When the aesthetic cult of Classical art was just beginning in the West, say from Petrarch to da Vinci, Classical art was known only by worn and broken fragments, the marbles shattered and their pigments long washed away, the bronzes covered with the patina of a thousand years. These early humanists can be forgiven for not realizing how this sculpture looked to the men who made it. But we today have no such excuse. We know that every Classical marble was painted, flesh color for the body, purple for the eyes, the lips reddened, the hair gilded. We know that the bronzes were kept brilliantly shined. So when we praise Classical sculpture, it is not the ancient fragments in our museums that we should be praising—that is not Classical sculpture and bears no resemblance to it. If we were honest and wished to praise Classical art, we should praise it as Classical man made it and loved it, polychromed and gilded, though to us it would be more nearly a waxwork horror.

Of the great Classical art of vase painting, all we can do is keep it piously in our museums, carefully inking out what we consider its obscenities.

Of Classical music, we know very little for there was never much to know, except that it was a matter of simple monophonic melodies and, to our ears, intolerably sing-song. Apparently it was never more than accompaniment to words.

The arts of the Byzantine-Arab society, what is here called the Levantine society, were again different. Their architecture bore no resemblance either to ours or the Classical. The basic artistic element of their buildings was the inside, the outside being merely structural walls to create an inside, a fact that makes exterior pictures of this architecture both so unattractive and meaningless. They had no sculpture whatever. There was some use of painting and an immense use of mosaic, pictorial but rigidly conventionalized among the Byzantines, largely geometrical among the Mohammendans, Mazdaists and Jews. Literature of all kinds except the drama, music, but again monophonic music quite unlike ours, and the dance complete the list.

The classification of our own great arts differs radically from that of both the Classical and the Levantine societies. Architecture, of course, we have, but except for the vain effort of Michelangelo we have no real sculpture save as an architectural component of Gothic. People other than Michelangelo have created works of sculpture, but they have never created a great art comparable with our literature, music and painting. And significantly, the two latter, far and away two of our greatest arts in the West, were almost lacking, and were certainly lacking as great arts, in the Classical society.

We have another great though esoteric art in the West that has escaped classification as such because we feel we must copy Classical models and to the Classical—and apparently to all the other societies—such a medium was impossible for artistic expression: naval architecture. Other societies have built ships for practical purposes, as we use porcelain without making a great art of it, but only to the West did shipbuilding approach—even though it never reached—the status of architecture. Unfortunately, since this art, like acting and the dance, deals with a perishable medium, knowledge of it outside of its own time can be derived only from records, never from the actual creation itself.

The art of naval architecture necessarily dealt with the mechanics of buoyancy and sailing, as the art of architecture dealt with the mechanics of load and stress. Art entered in the means of solution. The problems of the ship were solved by making her lines and riggings more powerful and graceful, her motions in the sea more sure and delicate. And the ship, the mistress of the endless oceans, became a true artistic symbol to all the maritime people of the West—and most of them are maritime —a symbol of all that is far and lonely.

Other men have mastered the rivers and the inland seas, have skirted

the sheltered coasts of some of the continent, have even made landfall
across some of the great gulfs like the Bay of Bengal. Other men in
wonderfully contrived canoes, reading the azimuth of the sun from notches
on coconut shells, have hedgehopped the islands of the Pacific, but we
Westerners alone of all men ever created an instrument that mastered
the oceans.

We know very little about the early ships or their builders as we know
little about the early architects of the West, but by 1400, the fundamental form of the ocean-going ship had been designed and that form
remained the type of the ship for as long as the art lasted, that is, until
it became purely practical engineering in the days of iron and steam.
This type was the three-masted, square-rigged ship, still showing the marks
of the galley and the Mediterranean in her latteen-rigged mizzen and the
ancient Roman rostrum, the galley's beak, at her bows. From then on
aesthetic refinements took place, many with only incidental practical
significance. There was a maze of inter-related problems in proportion:
the spacing and rake of the masts, the proportion of the lower masts
to the beam and length of the vessel, the proportion of the upper masts
to the lower, the proportion of the three masts, one to another, the angle
and length of the bowsprit, the length and vertical spacing of the spars.
In these problems, within wide ranges, aesthetic not practical considerations determined the final design as Sir Henry Manwayring pointed out
in 1644. "There is no absolute proportion in these, and the like things,
for if a man will have his mast short, he may the bolder make his top-
mast long." The ultimate proportions arrived at were those that created
a moving object of great beauty and symbolic content. Viewed abstractly
a ship is simply a building designed to move over the water rather than
to stand firm on the land. To a society that feels at home on the sea, it is
as natural a means of artistic expression as land buildings have always
been to all societies.

The art reached its final development in the first half of the nineteenth
century and was one of the few arts flowering late enough in Western
life to include Americans among its great practitioners. The two greatest
of the American naval architects were Joshua Humphrys of Philadelphia
who designed John Adam's frigates and Donald McKay of Boston who
established the type of the American clipper. Then the art died, as architecture as a great creative art had died a generation before. The two
techniques are today almost completely parallel: deliberate archaism as in
sailing yachts and ecclesiastical and academic buildings, eclecticism or
modernism spread thin over minimum mechanical workability as in pas-

senger vessels, power yachts, hotels and domestic construction, and unadulterated, undisguised engineering in war ships and freighters, bridges, highways and industrial plants.

Aesthetic textbooks do not condescend to classify naval architecture as an art—probably their authors never thought of the existence of the technique—but that need disturb nobody. These works are universally written under the spell of progress history which has no room for such a striking distinction in historical personality as a difference in basic great arts among the several societies. The "art" of the aesthete like the "mankind" of the political historian must be a universal.

The arts are a wonderful and unconscious expression of the style and personality of a people, but the expression of these historical personalities does not stop there. All Classical politics was city-state politics. There were no dynasties except as myths. There were no territorial states. Each city was a state and hence there was no capital city, the name of the city was the name of the state and later of the empire. Every Western state is a territorial state. Not one is known by the name of its capital city. Each has had a long dynastic history, that of the United States going back, as our law shows, to our English origin. Chinese and Egyptian politics were likewise dynastic, even maintaining the dynastic form through the "Contending States" and the Hyksos Kings, the eras of their periods of democracy and revolution. This we ourselves have not wholly done, though the British and several other dynasties still stand in legal form if not in actual state power. Islamic, Jewish and Byzantine politics were wholly religious, dynastic but with a profoundly different type of dynasty from that of the West and not essentially territorial. Each new sect became at once a nation. Regardless of whether it ruled any territory, it exercised legal jurisdiction over the internal relation of its own numbers. It employed its own script regardless of the language used—as the Orthodox Jews to this day use the Hebrew script.

The identity of other societies is obvious to us. The self-contained life of our own society is more difficult to grasp. Whether we picture an alien civilization erroneously as merely a preliminary stage in the progress of mankind, as we picture Egypt and the Classical world; or whether we contemptuously dismiss it as a branch off the main stem of progress, as we dismiss Byzantium and Islam; or whether, with some embarrassment, we merely footnote it as a completely detached and almost aberrant phenomenon like China and India, in all these cases we recognize an integrated though alien personality, a personality that always has a beginning and sometimes an end. But in regard to ourselves we are troubled by an apparently irresolvable difference between a contemporary and a historical definition of Western society.

Viewing our society as it is currently extended in space, defining it as it exists today in terms of the states and peoples comprising it, is simple. We readily see it as the states of western Europe and the states of European settlement overseas. These states taken collectively are the political organization of Western society and the civilization of that society is the civilization of Western men. Just as there are Chinese and Hindus, just as there were Classical men, so there are Western men, individuals born or molded to the society of which they are a part.

But when the question of identifying the West shifts from what it is today to what it was in the past, serious emotional difficulties arise. We are fairly comfortable in defining who among living men are Westerners. But among these modern Westerners there are peoples with widely divergent pasts. The United States alone contains men of utterly distinct, even hostile cultural ancestry: not only descendants of Pre-Reformation Catholics, but also Jews, Orthodox Slavs, Negroes, men of Chinese and Japanese origin, and even that supposedly most American of all Americans, the Indian. Are all these, then, Westerners? If they are, we must either deny that our society has had a historical existence or else admit that some Americans are Westerners by long ancestry while others are such by recent adoption. On the other hand, if we assert that not all contemporary Americans are members of Western society, we are driven to classify our fellow citizens as those who are members of the civilization of which their country is a part, and those who, despite their legal citizenship, belong to some alien society. Either alternative is impossible in liberal philosophy or in democratic publicity. Thus arises part of the passionate necessity to picture the history of Western society not as the history of particular men but as the history of ideas, ideals and disembodied political institutions.

But instead of attempting to define Western society in terms of those who today participate in its civilization, the definition can as well be sought at some point in the recent past. In that case the problem is no longer complicated, as in the definition of the modern West, by the divergent cultural ancestry of the Westerners of that time. Set thus in a historical focus, to the question, "What was Western society and who were the Westerners in 1500?" the answer is quite simple. At that time, Western society was composed of the Catholic Christians of western Europe. The Reformation had not yet split the Westerners into Protestants and Roman Catholics and the breach with the Orthodox church was already centuries old. These men were a homogeneous cultural group. All of them were Westerners and they constituted all the Westerners there then were.[5]

Western civilization as it stands today in every field of thought, law, and action is the unbroken, lineal continuum of the civilization of these Catholics of 1500. The overwhelming bulk of modern Western men are their descendants. Western civilization is not in any respect the continuum of the civilizations as they stood in 1500 of the Orthodox or eastern schismatic Christians, of the Moslems or of the Jews. The history of Western society is, therefore, the history of these Catholics. Western civilization as a political entity is composed of the states of their descendants in Europe and beyond the seas. We admit that there are Western states and Western institutions. There is also a Western people. It is not that Western society began in 1500 nor that other men from other civilizations and indeed from savage tribes have not by choice or force thrown in their lot with this society and become ineradicably part of it. The essential point is that Western civilization like every other has been the creation of a particular group of men. The creators of Western civilization were the ancestors and the descendants of the Catholics of 1500. It is they who have been and still are the core of Western society.

Now there is one troublesome fact in this definition of the West. By pointing up what is historically evident, that our civilization like others has been the creation of a human strain, the troublesome spectre of "race" is introduced into a political problem. Do the peoples who have constituted Western society also constitute a race? And what, under this definition of the West, is the position of two great groups living within the West and participating in its civilization but by no stretch of the imagination descended from the Catholics of 1500; the Western Jews and the Negroes of the Americas?

The word "race" has become the prisoner of scientific ethnology to such an extent that it has been left almost no meaning applicable to human beings. If applied to other animals, it would mean only spaniels as a race among dogs, angus as a race among cattle. No such strains exist, or for millennia have existed, among civilized men.

The ethnologist in seeking to apply the word "race" to any group of men insists on confining it to a group of men of unmixed ancestry. Untold millennia of wars and human wanderings, of the changeless destiny

---

[5] To avoid ambiguity of nomenclature, the word "Catholic" throughout this book will be applied only to the Latin Church between the Reformation and the semi-official but real break with the Greek church in the eighth century. The church in obedience to Rome after the Reformation will be called the Roman Catholic Church.

of women to accept the seed of the conqueror, forbid there being such groups. The ethnologist, therefore, postulates such groups as once having existed and in studying the origin of actual groups of men seeks to find dominant traces of one postulated stock in one area and less of it in some other. Thus in Europe the physical types of Brittany and western Ireland can be shown to be distinct from those of Tuscany or Bavaria, and this fact is considered a racial distinction. Perhaps so but it is not the historically important point. What is of historical importance is that for more than a thousand years the European Catholics from any area were willing, and to some extent did, marry with people from any other. Almost every descendant of the Catholics of 1500 is more closely related by blood to all other such descendants than he is to any Greek, Turk or Russian.

The Romans, who lacked our squeamishness about human propagation, dealt with this fact of human society even in their law. Roman citizenship and connubium, the right of legal intermarriage, were identical. In the early days, this was limited to corresponding social classes. But after social distinctions disappeared, a Roman could marry only another Roman. No Western state has ever adopted this as a principle of law and citizenship, but Western society as a whole has generally acted on it. Western Europeans, when they did not marry fellow nationals, have generally married other western Europeans and their descendants have carried on the same custom both in Europe and beyond the seas. The connubium of the West is never stated as a principle but widely practiced as a fact and nowhere more obviously than in this transplantation of western Europe which is the present day United States. The descendants of the Catholics of 1500 are all more closely related to each other than they are to anyone else and apparently prefer one another's society, at least for marriage, and so tend to continue and increase that relationship.

A connection between biology and civilization is distinctly unpalatable today. Nevertheless, it is an obvious historic fact. Each of the great civilizations of the world has been conducted by groups of people whose marriage borders were roughly the borders of their civilizations. None of those about which we know enough to say was a race in the ethnologist's sense, but each was the society of a definite group of people and their descendants.

The truth of the matter is that in his wrath at the layman's use of the word "race," the ethnologist has so defined it that it has no real meaning. No human strain of any consequence in the world has an unmixed ancestry and the popular meaning of the word "race" never required such an origin. But the ethnologist has not disproved the layman's notions of race. He has instead given the word a different meaning from the layman's and then discovered that nothing corresponding to *his* meaning exists. But what corresponds to the layman's meaning of race does indeed exist. It is a creation not of nature, which is perhaps why the scientific ethnologist cannot see it, but of history. It is not the product of a strain, like cattle, but of a connubium that out of various strains breeds a historical stock which so long as its society exists breeds true to itself. In this sense, the Jews are a race as are the Westerners and the Chinese, bodies of people formed by centuries of marriages within a relatively closed group.

An understanding of the reality of race is complicated by an inexplicable fact of human life, the different, massive geographical distribution of certain obvious physical characteristics which are hereditary and confuse the evidence of connubium. All men originally found south of the Sahara were black, though not all were related to one another. All the inhabitants of the eastern end of Eurasia are yellow, though again many are not related to others. The Americas were inhabited by red men, ranging from pygmies to the giants of Patagonia, but all red. The distribution of what we call white men, which is a far vaster body than Westerners, is similar. What accounts for these facts we do not know, but these groupings are not races in either the historical or ethnological sense. Races in the ethnologist's sense do not exist. Races in the historical sense are the creations of historical connubia.

Western society as early as 1000 was in the ethnologist's sense a racial hodgepodge and since that time it has incorporated into its civilization and its connubium the western Slavs, the Byzantines of southern Italy and Sicily and the converted Moors and Jews of Spain. Nevertheless it is a race. Today that civilization legally includes the Western Jews and the American Negroes, but to include these groups within its connubium is more than present day Western society is willing to concede or, for their part, the Jews wholly to accept. We then have two great groups which have become part of Western society by adoption, but for two quite different reasons have not yet been fused into its race.

The Western Jews and the American Negroes have, of course, nothing in common except their incomplete status as members of Western society. The barrier between modern Jews and other Westerners is not that they come from different stocks of men but that they come from two distinct civilizations. The Jews are a nation, but a nation of the Levantine society where nations are groups like the Jews, not the combination of a land and its inhabitants like France or Ireland that Westerners think of as nations. But there is no biological bar. Let a Jew give up his nationality, and he disappears without mark into the society of the West. Time and again this happened when Jews were converted to Christianity. This practice went on well into the seventeenth century and it ceased as an effective means of absorption not because individual Jews ceased to be willing to be converted but because the power of Christian faith weakened among the Christians.

Since their own faith had come to have a weaker hold on them, they could scarcely believe in its power to transform a Jew. For the first time there began suspicion on the part of Christians about the sincerity of a conversion, and doubt that it was powerful enough to transform a convert and his children into Westerners. With the eighteenth century conversion became barren of any but social significance, pointedly evident in the fact that no one has the remotest notion of the Jewish ancestry of converts prior to the eighteenth century and almost a meticulous record of families of later conversion like those of Disraeli, Marx and Mendelssohn. Today a man is held to be a Jew whether he attends *shul* or not or even whether he attends the Episcopal Church. These things are no longer held to be the outward and visible symbol of an inward and spiritual change. And unhappily, there is no substitute. There is no symbol, and this is a profound tragedy for the individual Western Jew who, with all justified pride in the greatness of his own past, nonetheless has come to feel himself as a Western man and desires to throw in his lot and that of his descendants with the people of the West. Western society receives him with words and even with laws, but cannot make him feel at home.

No definition of Western civilization as a process in history can avoid pointing up a difference between Jews and non-Jews. If we make the assumption that the Western Jews are today as integrally a part of Western civilization as the descendants of the Catholics of 1500, then it becomes necessary to postulate a conversion of some kind by these Jews, for present day Western society is not by even the most fanciful distortion the lineal descendant of the society of the Jews of 1500. Equally it creates a division in Jewry which can be substantiated by evidence, but is denied by theory, namely between the Russian-Galician Jews and those of western Europe. The division between the Sephardic and Ashkenazim Jews is recognized as a fact by the Jews themselves though not always for its significance, namely the one-time division of the Jewish nation between those who lived intimately with the high civilization of the Arabic society of the eighth to the fourteenth centuries (the *Sephardim*) and those who lived among the less civilized Westerners and the barbarians of Russia and lacked the skill and polish of the great world, (the *Ashkenazim*). A similar division could perhaps wisely be applied today between those Jews whose families have lived long among the Westerners and become Westernized and those who have not. The distinction might be of dubious acceptance among the Jews, but it would at least keep nomenclature better in line with historical fact.

The history of the Jews is something about which the Jews themselves know almost as little as the *goyim*. The general picture of Jewish history as Western Jews see it jumps from the largely mythical Diaspora of the sixth century B.C. to the nineteenth century A.D. when the West became more liberal and permitted the Jews to enter intimately into Western life. This picture is drastically simplified, but it is the outline of the views most Jews, who are not specifically historical scholars, hold of their own history and their historical relations with Western society. It is a version of Jewish history that is further distorted by the supposition, accepted by Jew and non-Jew alike, that the situation of the Jews as a group within Western society has been a phenomenon unique in human history. It has not. It was the exact situation of the Jews themselves and of the eastern Christians under the Sassanids and later under the Mohammedan territorial sovereigns, of the Parsees among the Hindus, of the Nestorians in medieval China. It was, from the Jewish side, the normal situation in every Levantine nation living under a territorial sovereign of different nationality. The distinction between secular and spiritual matters which is so sharp in the West is unknown and impossible in the Levant. In that society not only are church and state one, but so are priest and judge, prophet and army commander, citizen and true believer. The boundaries of a Levantine nation and a Levantine faith are identical.

It was impossible for the Mohammedan conquerors of Syria and Mesopotamia to govern the Jews and eastern Christians who had fallen within the dominions of the caliph. For the conqueror no less than for the subject, those who were not within the fold of Islam had to govern their own internal affairs, live in quarters by themselves and enforce their own law on their own members. The presence of an enclave, or more accurately a dispersion, of an alien nation governing its own internal affairs was unavoidable in the politics of the Levant. In that society it was the natural political relationship and from the point of view of the Jews it was still natural when the territorial sovereign was no longer another Levantine nation, but a Western state.

In the early years of the West this cultural and legal extraterritorial status of the Jews was accepted without too much difficulty by both sides. But as Western society grew in power and self-confidence, it became increasingly a source of grave friction. To the Western Jews, the centuries wore on without the least change in their political image of themselves or of the society about them. But to the Westerners this alien group, neither part of Holy Church nor in essential matters under the sovereignty of the king, came to seem more and more unnatural and, therefore, hostile and dangerous. The growing Western idea of nationality, of a man's "country," differed more and more deeply from the Levantine. Territorial sovereignty to the Jews had no bearing whatever on nationality. A man's faith, not the place of his birth, determined his country. But place of birth came to have an increasing importance for the Westerners until today it is almost the only basis of Western nationality. It was this irreconcilable difference in political concepts, a difference stemming from the different civilizations of the two groups, that lay unspoken beneath so much Jewish-Christian friction from the late eleventh century until the French Revolution, and survives to this day in backward corners of anti-Semitism and in the extremes of Zionism alike. But for a while the Jewish enclaves, what was in effect the Jewish right of extraterritorial status within the West, continued undisturbed.

Two main waves of immigration brought Jews into central and western Europe. The first, and the earlier, came from the western Islamic lands by Jews who had moved along with the Mohammedan conquests.[6] These were the Jews who appeared very early in France and England and by 900 had considerable settlements in the Rhineland. Here they gradually abandoned Arabic as their common speech and acquired the contemporary Middle High German of the Imperial Court, the ancestor of modern Yiddish. The other, and much later movement, came from the Jews living north of the Black Sea. This group stemmed from the wreckage of the Kingdom of the Khazars, a brief barbarian dominion—the Khazars were akin to the Turks of the Asiatic steppes—that held a flickering sway in the triangle between the Caucasus, the Volga and the Don from the third to the tenth centuries A.D. Commanding, as it did, the important Black Sea and Caspian trade it had extensive commercial, cultural and political contacts with the entire Levant, Orthodox Christian, Mazdaist, Jewish and, eventually, Moslem, alike. Originally a pagan people, it was vigorously proselytized by the three surviving Levantine faiths and though all three made many converts, the ruling dynasty and probably the greater part of the population embraced Judaism during the eighth century. It was one of the very few Jewish territorial states that history records. It suffered

---

[6] This is certainly the general view of most historians of the Jews, but there are certain considerations that suggest another origin. Chief among the latter is the fact that there were Latin-speaking Jewish communities in Spain at the time of the Arabic conquest, whose descendants, in all probability, were the Castilian-speaking Jews forcibly converted or expelled in the 15th and 16th centuries. There could easily have been similar groups in Italy, Gaul and even in Romanized Germany. As a simple historical fact, prior to the 6th century, wherever in the Roman Empire there were Greek- or Latin-speaking Christian communities there is no *a priori* reason why there could not have been Greek- or Latin-speaking Jewish communities. The myth of the Palestinian origin of all Jews here confuses even serious historians. The Greek version of the Christian Old Testament was made for the Jewish communities within the Roman Empire two hundred years before Jesus was born. It does not seem ever to have been examined whether the Old Latin text of the Old Testament, superceded in the Vulgate by Jerome's 5th century translation, may not equally have been a Jewish translation, made for Latin-using synogogues of Africa, Spain and Gaul. These matters are considered in Chapter 3.

severely under Hunnish and Tartar invasion and was eventually overthrown by the Russians of Kiev late in the tenth century.

For some centuries the Jews within the West, like the Jews among the Moslems, governed their own internal affairs for themselves and their primary relations, both cultural and mercantile, were not with the less civilized Christians around them, but with the Jewish and Arabic communities to the south and east. Their relations with the Christian authorities were stiff, but they were not treated with systematic cruelty. They were the occasional victims of personal crime—as who is not—but the pogrom was a later and a more eastern, indeed almost a Russian, development. The ghetto was the Jews' own choice just as few Americans in an Asiatic city would willingly live anywhere but in the European quarters. They were constantly pressed for money, of course, as is everyone who has any and lacks the political power to prevent it being taxed away. But they were free to come or go as they pleased or could afford and the whole world of Islam from Cordova to further India was open to them and many traveled widely. Intermarriage with the Christians was out of the question on either side, but the close resemblance of physical type of present day Western Jews to the physical type of the area where their forefathers lived suggest that while personal relations with the Christians were never official, they may well at times have been intimate.

We are told that they were persecuted. Legally they were restricted. In time many of them were expelled from most of the Western states. Sporadically, they were victims of mass outrages particularly during the religious fervor of the Crusades when their supposed guilt in the crucifixion of Jesus made them a natural target and their obvious cultural kinship to the Saracens identified them with the hated enemy. They were again the victims of the mass hysteria accompanying the Black Death. But though they occasionally suffered from personal and even community violence, they were under the generally effective protection of royal and ecclesiastical power. They were free to leave and yet until they were expelled they chose to stay. The whole civilized world of the Dar al Islam was open to them yet they preferred the West. The type of persecution under which they suffered needs more careful examination.

Seen under the public morals and public sentimentality of a liberal and democratic age, the relations of Jew and Catholic in these now distant centuries of the youth of our society appear to us as highly objectionable. Probably most modern Westerners, whether of Jewish or Catholic ancestry, would agree that the Jews of medieval Europe were a persecuted minority. Actually they were not and the reason we so generally suppose that they were is an example of what was said earlier about the difference between historical facts and the relations among those facts.

The Jews of medieval Europe were not treated as the Catholics were treated, that is a correct fact. But this did not make them a persecuted minority because they were not a minority of any Western state, either in their own view or in that of the Catholics around them. They were alien sojourners who had no part and wanted no part in the political or cultural life of the Western nations in which they chanced to reside. They were not excluded. You cannot exclude men from something they have no desire to enter.

In order to appraise this situation with historical realism, we cannot, as we usually do, evaluate the status of medieval Jews as though it were such a status occupied by a so-called minority group in a modern state. Instead we have to compare it with the status of legal aliens in our modern states. These, as we know, are forbidden to take part in domestic politics. Frequently the type of work they may accept or the type of property they may own is restricted. They must always carry papers and can always be expelled, often for actions which would not be a crime for a citizen. Sometimes it is legally possible for them to become citizens. Sometimes it is not. But always their entire status, their entry, their residence, their admission to citizenship, are privileges granted or withheld, not rights to which they are entitled. Even those privileges established by statute are still privileges enjoyed not as a permanent right but at the pleasure of the citizens. Of course, they are not outlaws. They are entitled to protection, which they do not always receive, in all things that they may legally do or own. So too were the medieval Jews.

Because the Jews today are not legal aliens in any Western country in which they are born, we forget that in the past nationality was not established as it so largely is today by place of birth. In medieval Europe, sovereignty was a matter of feudal allegiance for Catholics no less than for Jews. What was, therefore, determinant of nationality in those centuries was not where a woman bore a child but to whom she bore it. Both are important facts in the question and our own exclusive interest with the one does not invalidate the reasonableness of our predecessors in considering the importance of the other.

In medieval Europe, Jews, wherever they were born, were thus as definitely legal aliens as men born beyond a nation's borders are aliens today. And just as modern aliens can become naturalized, so could medieval Jews. What then corresponded to our naturalization was conversion. Today we believe that matters of conscience are of no political relevance and can see no proper way in which conversion could be an act of naturalization. Indeed we hold this view so strongly that we feel entitled to apply moral censure to our medieval ancestors for believing the exact opposite, even though both Jew and Catholic shared in this error. Basically, what we fail to grasp is the change that the centuries have worked in our definition of nationality. The essential difference between our own attitude toward aliens and that of our medieval forefathers lies only in the different elements used in defining nationality. Our definition is almost entirely territorial. Theirs was partly territorial, partly feudal, and—to this extent like that of the Jews themselves—partly confessional.

The situation was thus not one of a persecuted minority on the one hand and a group of tyrannical bigots on the other. The Jews were not a minority within any nation of the West. They were legal and cultural aliens granted leave to reside as a juridical unit within the West, a permission of high value and one given to no other foreign nationality—ever.

In the early thirteenth century, England, and in the early fourteenth, France, both expelled the Jews. France did not then exercise effective rule over Languedoc, but with the establishment of French sovereignty, expulsion of the Jews followed in the fifteenth and sixteenth centuries. As Christian power moved south against the Moors in Spain, the choice of conversion or expulsion was offered both conquered Moslems and the Jews, long resident among them. As a result, by 1550 the only considerable colonies of Jews in Western society were within the territories of the Empire, which by then was a name, not a government, and of Poland which was an anarchy calling itself an elective kingdom. In later times Jews from these areas returned to England and France but never in massive settlements. A trickle of Jews expelled from Spain settled in the Netherlands and England. A few came to the American colonies. Such was the physical distribution of the Jews among the Western nations at the moment when their age-long status as legal aliens came to an end.

With the seventeenth century and above all with the eighteenth, the whole position of Western Jewry changed. At first the ghetto was turned by law into a Jewish prison and then legally abolished. Conversion became politically meaningless at the same time that legal citizenship began to be opened to the Jews. The now mature civilization of the West established its own merchantile and financial arrangements and the Jew instead of being useful—even though alien—became a competitor. Finally, with the French Revolution all legal distinction between Jew and non-Jew was wiped out and Jews were classed de jure as citizens or subjects of the place of their birth. At the same time the Jews gave up the remnants of their unofficial but real extraterritorial status—observe the recommendation, extraordinary to us today, of the Jewish conference called by Napoleon at Paris in 1807 that the Jews forego their own marriage and divorce laws which they had immemorially followed in their own communities and submit themselves in these matters to the civil laws of the Western countries in which they resided. In essence these changes were the legal and social assertion of the theory that the Jews were not a nation but only a group of people who practiced Judaism as a religion. It was a natural theory in an unhistorical age which could not possibly have distinguished the Levantine nationality of the Jews. It was also the practical recognition of the fact that the Jews, too, had changed in the course of centuries of life within the West and had come in part to think of themselves less as Jewish nationals of Western residence than as Western nationals of Jewish faith. Yet the change was not complete, and even in our day, the remnants of more than a thousand years of different cultural histories still vex the inner harmony of the modern West.

The final transformation of the Jewish nation is apparent in our own day in the shift in the consciousness of the Jews themselves of the whole basis of Jewish nationality: the rise of Zionism. Throughout the Middle Ages, Zion to the Jews was not a tangible, earthly hope, but a mystical symbol of the divine deliverance of the Jewish nation. To these Jews, Zion was a heavenly city, but, unlike the Western Christian notion of the Heavenly Kingdom, it did not yet exist; it was to be planted on earth by the Messiah on the Day of Judgment when historical time was to come to an end. In modern times, this notion has been transformed into a wholly irreligious picture of a terrestrial state of the Jews as an actual historical institution in the practical world. Not only does political Zionism thus replace the ancient Jewish image of themselves as a Levantine nation, a community of the faithful, but it also tends to replace the newer image of Judaism as a religion practiced by certain nationals of the Western states. In brief, it *reasserts* the nationhood of the Jews, but it sees this nation no longer as a Levantine consensus but as a Western territorial sovereign.

It is interesting to observe that this transformation has gone much further among the Russian and Polish Jews than among their Western coreligionists. Not only was Zionism developed as a program of political action by eastern Jews, but control of the present state of Israel is very largely held by Jews least influenced by the West and least absorbed into its civilization. The occurrence is one repeated often in recent centuries among non-Western societies exposed to the power, intellectual and political, of the West. It is identical with the establishment of Western constitutional forms in India and Pakistan, with Sun Yat-sen's ideas in the overthrow of the Manchu dynasty and the establishment of the same Western trappings in China. There is an obvious element of the tendency in Meiji's vast changes in Japan and even, in quite different circumstances, in Russia from Peter the Great onwards. In the case of the Jews, this desire to transform themselves from a nation existing as the community of the faithful into a modern territorial state found a perfect Jewish formula in secularizing the ancient religious idea of Zion.

The case of the Amercan Negro is quite different and historically much less complex. Here is a group whose ancestors had never been members of one of the civilized societies. Their basic culture differed little from that of neolithic men and even this was shattered by transportation and slavery. Although probably the majority of the Negroes brought to the Americas came from a restricted group of similar tribes stretching some hundreds of miles inland along the Guinea coast, it was not as tribes nor as parts of tribes but as individuals that they had to live in the New World. Time itself worked against any serious survival of their tribal cultures in the New World. In the two centuries of the intense slave trade, the major source of slaves shifted steadily east and south along the African coast, beginning in Senegal and Sierra Leone in the seventeenth century, traversing the lower valleys of the Niger and Congo and ending in Angola and even around the cape in Mozambique and Madagascar in the nineteenth. Thus decade by decade the Negroes put ashore in the Americas were thrown into a slave population of earlier and different provenance, itself without any tribal coherence and already forced to use the speech of their several white masters. For awhile a few of the African languages lasted, but since increasingly these became languages unknown to the new arrivals, these too died and the only tongues common to the Negroes themselves were those of the whites.

Modern anthropology, which more often deals with "the Negro" than with real Negroes, observes a group of dark pigmented individuals reaching from North America through the West Indies, along the coast of South America, and into Brazil. This group now has little in common except the continental African origin of the majority of its ancestors. It is thus of little significance that in Surinam and in the hills of Haiti are Negroes whose life shows distinct traces of African tribal customs. For the bulk of the Negroes of the Western world, Africa is almost as remote in culture as are the steppes of Asia for men descended from the white barbarians of Roman times. A few traces of African religious practices probably worked their way under Christian disguise into the slaves' new religion. Perhaps a few traits of the African family, that most persistent of all human institutions, survived the promiscuity and animal-like breeding widely encouraged and even enforced by the whites. The break with an African past was even more thorough with the Negroes brought to what is today the United States. In addition to all the other factors separating the slaves from their ancient tribal background was the fact that many of the early slaves of North America were not brought directly from Africa but were Negroes born, sometimes for several generations, in the West Indies. The "salt water" Negro, the man directly from Africa, was often the object of amused disdain to the other slaves.

Thus what was put ashore in the Americas was something unique in human history, for the history of men when it has not been the history of the great societies, has been the history of tribes, of groups of men organized under some cultural pattern. But the American Negroes were ripped almost completely from their culture pattern and thrown ashore as millions of separate individuals, as a black breeding stock almost as though they had been animals. Since then these individuals have been remolded into a special "racial" group whose cultural pattern is that of the West and a considerable amount of white blood has been added. Yet what would otherwise have been a normal, unnoticed physical absorption of this stock into the body of the population has been prevented by the simple fact that Negroes and most peoples with appreciable Negro blood are dark-skinned. This prevents intermarriage, which would otherwise proceed rapidly between poor Negroes and poor whites and well-to-do Negroes and not quite so well-to-do whites. As a result two official "ethnic" groups are frozen and physical mixture proceeds almost entirely in one direction, the addition of white blood to the Negro group through Negro women. With this, of course, comes a bitter and natural rancor. The problem can be dressed up for polite democratic consumption as one of civil rights, or employment opportunities, education or any other superficial aspect that anyone chooses, but the problem is completely simple though not, therefore, soluble. It is, at heart, a problem of sex: the Negro's women are good enough for the white man, but the white man's women are too good for the Negro.

With this brief consideration of the status of the two great Western groups that are not wholly integrated into Western society nor freely included within its connubium, the definition of Western society either in historical or contemporary focus becomes much less troublesome. As this society stands today, it is in historical lineage the society of the descendants of the Catholics of 1500. In contemporary fact it is no longer exclusively theirs. Other men have joined it bringing into the community of the West biological lines from alien civilizations. But these alien civilizations themselves have not been fused with that of the West. The newcomers in accepting Western civilization have either abandoned their own or kept only remnants of it in their personal lives. The civilization of the West has remained the civilization of the Catholics of 1500. These are the peoples whose ancestors and descendants developed the intellectual and political forms of this society and made it almost the master society of the earth. It has been a society capable of incorporating other human stocks into its biological stream and, when it rose to be a mighty group of imperial powers, of becoming the model whose political forms and intellectual disciplines were copied by all the peoples of the globe. But its own history remains something of a mystery even to its own peoples, primarily because of the historical entity involved. The society itself has no outward, simple political form that is capable of popular expression and easy understanding. It is not a question of what learned historians think or write but of what passes current among the people as their image of their own past. In this living history—this view of the past that influences the politics of the present—the concept of Western society is most lacking. Even the existence of the West as an entity in face of the rest of the world is only dimly seen, grudgingly admitted and felt rather as an unfortunate and temporary evil than as a historical necessity and source of immense pride.

True, the history of the West from the sixteenth century to the outbreak of the first World War is a familiar matter to most modern men. But this is pictured as the history of separate nations with little thought of their common origin and common civilization. To Americans even this history is perhaps less clear than it is to other Westerners because we over-emphasize colonial events and colonial conditions. Thus the long contest between the European states for world power, the successive rise of the empires of Portugal, Spain, Holland, France and England is thought of almost as though it had been primarily a struggle for the Americas. The great purpose of that struggle—to become the dominating power among the Western states—is insufficiently noticed. Certainly the consequences of the outcome in North America, that it was British rather than Dutch, French or Spanish, proved in the end to be of greater influence in Western life than the consequences of the struggle in any other colonial area or even than many of the decisions in Europe itself. But the modern United States was not in the mind of any of the participants of the wars of the sixteenth and seventeenth centuries. Transoceanic power was sought primarily for its value in Europe.

A minor consequence of a specifically American view of this period is a misunderstanding of Western technology and an over-valuation of the role of America in this field. There is an unconscious tendency to picture the technology of the West in the seventeenth century as identical with the contemporary technology of the American settlements. From this erroneous base the technological changes of the past three hundred years seem much more accelerated than they were, and much more the result of specific American enterprise. But the American settlements were unavoidably backward technologically. A pioneer settlement could not possibly be otherwise. Scores of handicrafts had to be substituted for the already industrialized production of Europe. Homespun had almost disappeared in Europe when it was about all there was to wear in British and French America. Coal mining was an old shoe in Wales and Flanders by 1400. It was industrial pioneering in Pennsylvania in 1800. By about 1700, the machine shops of England and France were making steam engines—primarily for mine pumps—when the village blacksmith was the highest level of metal-working in North America.

With the social changes of these centuries we are almost too familiar. Barring the error of supposing that the aristocratic society of the sixteenth century was like the feudal society of the twelfth, our general picture is tolerably correct: the new monied men, almost successively merchant, in-dustrialist, banker, were pressing democratic forms on the dynastic states until by the nineteenth century these oligarchies were the governing power in all the great states of the West. Even the subsequent replacement of these oligarchies of money by the oligarchies of mass organization which now rule in the West is familiar to us though we use other names for the process. But this knowledge, pulled from its setting in the millennial history of a continuing, unbroken society, is dangerously inadequate. It is not in these recent four hundred years but in the earlier formative centuries that there lies concealed the key to understanding the historical personality of the West, the type of thought that has governed its intellectual life, the moral perplexities that have so long confused its politics, the fact, even, that it exists as a society. Ours is the society of the Catholics of 1500 But who were they?

It was not always a matter of political importance whether the Western peoples were aware that they constituted above and beyond their individual states a great historical society of their own. The rough and ever-ready hostility of all the European states toward the Mohammedan powers was for centuries quite enough. It was not necessary for the kingdoms of Europe to remind themselves that no Saracenic state was a member of their group and that whatever animosities they had toward each other, these were trifling in comparison with their common hostility toward all the Saracens—Moor or Turk. It was true then as now that money made its own politics and the Christian maritime states of the Mediterranean—Venice and Genoa particularly—found trade in military supplies to the Saracens too profitable to forego. It is true that in later years the kings of France found it ad-vantageous to encourage the sultan to annoy the Imperial Government at Vienna. But until the relief of Vienna and the Battle of Lepanto (1571) removed forever the threat of Mohammedan conquest, the states of Islam were not generally invited into the quarrels of Europe. Fortunately, the bitter division of Europe between Protestantism and Catholicism did not become a political factor until the Saracens had almost ceased to be a powerful menace. Europe was still morally united in the days when that danger existed.

Thereafter, the whole non-Western world sank into such relative weakness, or lay at such remote distances that the consciousness of the existence of a world of states that did not belong to Western society disappeared from the practical consideration of all the Western governments. The world held alien peoples, some savages, some strangely civilized in their own odd way, but it held no states that as political entities counted at all in the politics of the West. The French and the British in their struggle for India involved themselves in Indian politics and sought to use the native states against each other. But as the name itself shows, this was a purely local matter and these states counted for nothing in the politics of the West. And when Russia first appeared as a power on the eastern borders, it was well into the late eighteenth century before her power was considered a serious European political factor and by then she wore the European disguise fashioned for her by the early Romanoff czars. For even as late as 1700 the Russian frontier ran from Leningrad south by east to Smolensk with only a slight bulge west of Novgorod to the east shore of Lake Peipus. From Smolensk, the frontier ran south by west to Kiev, followed the east bank of the Dnieper to the bend and then straggled away southeastward into the Caucasus, at no place reaching the Black Sea. And Russia at that time had never held lands west of that line. Only the Mongols of the Golden Horde had ever pushed farther west during the fourteenth and fifteenth centuries.

The nineteenth century exaggerated the illusion of the seventeenth and eighteenth. Outside the closed ring of the Western states, now half-heartedly expanded to include the United States as a weak member—the non-Western world lay in a complete political vacuum. Wars with the non-Western world were struggles between artillery and spears which is why we Westerners, but not the rest of the world, remember it as the age of the great peace. Only late in the century did Japan emerge as a political power and even then until the Russo-Japanese War no one took her power seriously.

In these centuries of isolation from political realities, centuries of almost complete monopoly of all political power by the states of the West, it is not surprising that all concept of the West as a political entity should disappear. The philosophers taught that all men were equal and that we lived in a world inhabited by "mankind." For their purposes the practical governments found sufficient confirmation of this theory in the universal equality of non-Western "mankind" in possessing neither fleets nor armies. World politics became Western politics and the only problems of war or policy developed in struggles with other Western states. Not one or two, but at least eight or nine generations of political authority—kings, ministers, presidents, party leaders, reformers, journalists, bishops, agitators—rose, ruled, worked, wrote and died in this seemingly eternal sunlight of Western power. All living memory of an "outside" as a political fact disappeared, and with the disappearance of that living memory so too there disappeared any need for understanding the difference between the "inside" and the "outside," the "us" and the "others." And so even the concept almost disappeared.

Suddenly the whole world situation changed. Out of the First World War the power of the Western world emerged badly shaken. How badly was not obvious in the flush of victory over Germany. But out of the Second, it emerged so gravely shattered that we cannot yet tell how much there is left to rally. And therewith in less than a single lifetime the whole relative political balance of the earth is changed. In one sudden shift of power the non-Western world is no longer a mass of natives, colonies, amusing half-Europeanized kingdoms, backward oriental principalities. All at once these people are armed, ambitious, hostile—determined to stay armed and improve their arms. Some are obviously mere tools used by the Russians. Some seem to hope, or pretend to hope, that they can strike out on their own. Some aim to eat the heart of the West. Others will be content for a time to gnaw the finger bones.

And at the same time there emerges within the West itself, intimately entwined in its economy and politics, a powerful, ambitious, relentless group who are the avowed enemies of the West and all its ways, the partisans and hirelings of the Great Khan.

We are not intellectually or morally prepared to deal with all this at once. With the loss of the unity of Western Christendom, and even the loss of the Christian faith as the mark of a Western man, this rallying point that served our ancestors so well is lost to us. We have as yet no great symbol that we can substitute for it. We do not think of ourselves as all members of a great and proud society because we do not clearly see that the world is composed of these great societies and that we are one of them with definite history, culture, intermarriage and boundaries of our own .We talk of a "democratic" world or a "free" world; we declare that we seek "peace" and "collective security" and so do the Russians, and with equal right, for these are words without intrinsic meaning. They are only signs of the emotion possessing the speaker. Sunk in the morass of these almost meaningless words, in this quagmire of liberal clichés that does duty for political thought, we ignore the endangered life of the West in our passion for mere slogans. For these words are indeed only slogans. They correspond to no precise reality either existing or potential. They have in fact only an ethical content and like ethical adjectives, they are applicable to anything and everything in accord with the scale of values of the user. Each sees under them whatever concrete image he desires. Under none of them lies necessarily the historical reality of the West.

In this bog of confusion, we have become men without good conscience, uncertain of right and wrong, uncertain of fact and dream. We are not even aware any longer who are "we" and who are "they." We are the man who has lost his sense of identity and is no longer sure whether his house is his or another's, whether even the tongue with which he speaks is his own.

Let us, therefore, see if we can discover our lost identity.

Chapter 1:

The Dignity of Causality

IN EVEN CURSORY INSPECTIONS of the nations that comprise the West, there is one other thing as strikingly obvious as the medieval Catholic ancestry of their populations: their participation in the development and use of the mechanistic sciences. Although our popular history credits the Greeks with a share in the distant origin of scientific thinking and although in modern times machines, processes and even scientific education have been exported to non-Western peoples, nonetheless even the most liberal history does not deny that the great development of the mechanistic sciences and of the pure scientific thought underlying them was the work exclusively of the Western nations. No one, however devoted to the ideal of the equality of mankind, ascribes the development of these sciences from 1200 to 1850, the years in which their fundamental hypotheses were evolved and their fundamental discoveries made, to the Chinese, Hindus, Arabs, Byzantines, Jews or Russians. The modern liberal feels that this great body of knowledge should now be considered as belonging to "mankind," not because "mankind" developed it, nor because its postulates and methods of analysis are in harmony with the intellectual life of non-Western peoples, but because it is useful. It is capable of conferring power and advantage. But from the historical point of view, what is important is that this body of thought was developed exclusively by Westerners long before its advantages were fully obvious even in the West. It was an attribute of our historical personality before it became the flower of our utilitarian desires.

Mechanistic science is both so powerful and so exclusively Western in origin that any consideration of the West, however insistently it seeks to deal with the world of political reality, cannot entirely exclude this phenomenon if it desires to arrive at any clear conception of the life of the West. There is a further necessity for considering not so much the sciences as scientific thought. This body of apparently esoteric doctrine has not only produced the great machines of modern times, it has profoundly influenced Western thought. It has thus been a part of political history even though it has been highly esoteric and most men have been almost unaware that its philosophy affected their scale of values and influenced their decisions.

The mechanical accomplishments flowing from the sciences have been the subject of an enormous literature, but discussion of the philosophy of Western mechanistic science has been much more restricted. This philosophy has been considered from a religious point of view in the fear that its doctrines combined with the success of its mechanical accomplishments were undermining belief in religion. From a contrary side there has been a considerable liberal literature which, while not penetrating very deeply into the actual nature of scientific thought, still sought to cast an aura of beneficent scientific determinism about the particular egalitarian theory being promoted. Marx was the most famous of these but there have been scores of others equally aware of the value of good publicity who asserted a relationship between their political schemes and mechanistic science. In all this, however, there has been almost no popular discussion of what scientific doctrine really is, its essential premises and the type of conclusions it has proved from these premises. We all know it has been capable of designing the most incredible array of machines, processes and devices, but the core of its thought is rarely considered.

Science is the discipline of causality. Everything that can be called genuinely scientific deals with cause and effect even in those manifestations of causality that have to be handled by methods of probability. There are situations—dice or the kinetic laws of gases are simple cases—in which the immense complexity of the causal factors precludes analysis of the forces operating on each molecule or on each throw of the dice. In these cases the resultant statistical probability, which approaches certainty if there are enough molecules or throws of the dice, is the averaging of the operation of causal necessity, not a substitute for it.[1]

Scientific causality always requires a necessity. An effect is a necessary, unavoidable, predetermined, inescapable result of a cause. This cannot be too strongly emphasized in regard to scientific causality. If a consequence may or might or could follow a preceding event—if necessity

---

[1] In recent years probability has been introduced into the field of subatomic physics, but here too the same situation still holds. The probability averages the unidentified causal necessities. This is discussed further below.

is absent—then causality is absent or incomplete. Some of the operating causes may be known but others essential to knowledge of the result must be unknown since from known causes only known results can follow. If the results are not fully known in advance, neither are the causes. Causality thus means to us necessity, and it has meant necessity throughout Western philosophy and science from the medieval schoolmen to the modern physicists. It is true that necessity is not something that can be observed as such. All that can be observed is temporal sequence. If there are enough identical sequences, the idea of some common origin for all these identical events occurs to the mind of the observer. He calculates a cause, a necessity. He does not see or measure that. If there were no idea of necessity, no observation would ever disclose it. The search has never been to find causality and prove that such a necessitous relationship existed among material forces and objects but simply to discover how it worked, not its existence, but the laws of its operation. And in essence this has been a belief unique to the West. No other society ever entertained such an idea. Inevitably no other society ever developed the great sciences of causal necessity that we have created. They had sciences, but standing on different concepts of causality they were not the sciences that we know. That men could conceive, indeed have conceived, of different types of causality may seem strange to us today. Yet so profound are the inner differences of human societies that even this has occurred.

Since the only method we have for determining the certain presence of causal necessity is to find identical conditions followed by identical changes, what of situations in which identical conditions can never be re-established? We assume, of course, that these, too, are cause-governed because we believe all things to be cause-governed, but since we cannot reproduce the conditions, we cannot establish invariable temporal sequence which alone constitutes our evidence of necessity. Although in these things we assume there is a cause, and often assume what that cause may be, we do not, scientifically at least, know what it is. It is then apparent that there must be at least two great classes of facts about which we seek knowledge, those facts in which causal necessity can be evidenced by invariable temporal succession of identical changes from identical conditions, and those in which no such thing is possible. It is equally apparent that the type of knowledge that we can obtain about one of these classes is not quite the same as the type we can obtain about the other. The first embraces matters of scientific knowledge and with these we apply causal reasoning and obtain scientific laws. It is immaterial whether the identical change from identical conditions is artificially arranged in a laboratory or directly observed in the motion of the planets. In both cases we become able to discover all the variables that determine the consequence of any condition. The second class is much more difficult. With facts of this sort whenever we try to apply causal reasoning, we have to guess at the cause or assume it, or even disregard it since it is impossible to prove what it is. Yet even here we are far from destitute of information. What we lack is the certain knowledge of the causality involved so that all our predictions about such events must be based on other types of reasoning. Only in the first class can we use causal reasoning. With the second, we must employ analogic.

In causal reasoning, what is sought is knowledge of the mechanism by which a change takes place. Superficially it seeks to answer the question "why?" but at bottom it deals only with the "how" of events. Each scientific law is a satisfactory causal explanation of the phenomena below it but not of the type of energy of mass whose effects the law describes. The law of gravity is a causal explanation of the motion of masses acting under attraction of one another, but it is not a causal explanation of gravity itself. Layer by layer up into the innermost structure of matter and energy, scientific laws resolve action into a causal explanation of the behavior of another concept whose behavior is known and measured or partly measured, but whose nature, that is, whose causal relation, is not yet understood. Scientific causality never answers the question "why?" except by putting in a more subtle concept for which the question "why?" again cannot be answered.

Our causality, therefore, extends as it were between the two great boundaries of knowledge. Along one border begins the area of analogy, the whole class of phenomena that cannot be repeated or whose variables cannot be certainly identified. Along the other lies the real frontier of mechanistic science, where the phenomena are no longer explained but identified by concepts that have not yet been decomposed by causal analysis. At these ultimate reaches of scientific thought we encounter what might wisely be called grammatical causality, that is, the employment of a name to cover all the still unanalyzed causal relations that must lie beyond the present state of knowledge. Grammatical causality is expressed in such words as "gravity," "energy," "electron" and so forth. Once "atom" was such a word, but it has yielded to causal analysis and the border of grammatical causality has been pushed deeper into the unknown. Between those two boundaries lies the field of operable causality, the area in which we know enough not only to make foreseeable results follow from identified causes, but enough to explain the mechanics of the changes involved. Beyond the border of grammatical causality we know nothing. Beyond the border of analogy we know many things, but we do not know them by causal reasoning or scientific proof.

Today the grammatical border of causality is the domain of quantum mechanics where causality is formally ignored. The underlying, individual actions of the ultimate particles of matter and quanta of energy are pictured as phenomena of probability. Causal necessity is the impression on the observer of the average behavior of huge numbers of particles and quanta. Newtonian mechanics, for instance, postulates a necessity for a planet to be at a certain place at a certain time, a necessity arising from its mass, prior motion and the masses and motions of surrounding matter in space. Why mass and motion must produce these invariable consequences is, of course, inexplicable. So far as Newtonian mechanics is concerned, we have here crossed the border into grammatical causality. In contrast, quantum mechanics does not postulate a necessity for an electron to be at a certain place at a certain time. It calculates the probability of an electron being at any particular place at a particular time. It finds that there are certain places, in relation for instance to the nucleus of an atom, in which there is a very high probability of finding an electron and other places where the probability becomes almost infinitesimal. The average probabilities of an immense number of electrons then become the "laws" of chemical change as they are observed in the reaction of vast numbers of atoms.

This concept that all macroscopic effects are statistical summations of discrete particle and quantum actions of a quite different sort has been immensely rewarding in the study of all phenomena where the actual behavior of individual particles becomes of consequence. It has supplied an intelligible theoretical base for the operable causality of chemistry, thermodynamics and radiation. It is said to have destroyed the grammatical causality of Newtonian mechanics without in any way affecting the latter's operable causality. It has not itself, however, supplied a satisfactory grammatical causality at its own base and in regard to the problems of pure mass and motion it has added nothing to our understanding of gravity.

Most of the major quantum physicists of today believe they have gone much further. They believe they have destroyed causality as a philosophical principle and substituted statistical probability. But here they have made the tacit assumption that causality, if it exists, must be a phenomenon of nature and that their analysis of nature should, therefore, be capable of discovering it. But causality is not a phenomenon of nature. It is a concept of the human mind, and in the form in which we know it, of the Western mind. It is something we read into nature. When the quantum physicists say they can find only statistical probability not causality in the ultimate reactions of nature, they mean only that they have not assumed causality. It is true that electrons do not obey the causal laws of Newtonian mechanics, but this does not mean that electron behavior cannot be interpreted under causal laws if one wishes to draw such laws. The phenomenon of statistical probability can be imagined as merely a descriptive method and the actual behavior of particles and quanta assumed to be causally determined by laws we do not yet understand. Stated another way, the statistical probabilities of electron behavior can be exactly compared to the statistical probability of the behavior of dice. The latter is not determined by the probability that is shown by the successive fall of dice but by mechanical factors, "causes" which for each throw are pure, rigid necessity, but in throw after throw operate without bias for any one face of a die and so produce a derived probability curve. Under this interpretation, probability differs from operable causality only in describing phenomena where the causal factors are too complex for enumeration—as with dice—or unknown as with electrons.

No one has ever suggested that the electrons, any more than the dice, determine their own positions and motions. To conceive of an electron having choice is as ridiculous as to conceive of a die having it. Whatever happens to it *must* happen to it, even though the number of things that *might have* happened to it are very large and the probability of any one of them almost no greater than the probability of the others.

Consider a box with a small hole containing a large number of marbles. Agitate the box. Now and then one marble will come through the hole. No calculation, only prolonged observation, will enable the probability of the number of marbles per hour to be determined for any particular type of shaking. Pure chance and probability? On the contrary, rigid cause and effect. The marbles are subjected to no other forces than those known to the laws of physics. The position and velocity of each marble are rigidly determined at each instant by the condition of the original assembly and the forces acting on the whole. Deterministic causality seems to disappear only because its detailed operation becomes incalculable. Not that it does not exist but that it cannot be measured. In this case all the laws of motion governing the behavior of the marbles are known, but their actual behavior can only be described in the form of statistical probability. In the situation of which this is a poor simile, the behavior of subatomic particles, the laws are by no means so surely known, but even if they were, they might still fall under the same difficulty as the laws of motion governing the marbles. Their interaction may be too complex for anything but statistical expression. But in neither case does it mean that rigid necessity does not govern the actual behavior.

Nor does the phenomenon of indeterminacy—Heisenberg's famous principle—destroy causality. A certain amount of popularizing mumbo jumbo has been written about this in an almost leftist vein—that it proves the very structure of the universe to be so slovenly as to forbid clarity and determination on our part. Heisenberg's principle has no such implication. It asserts that we cannot precisely know both the velocity and the position of an electron. It does not assert that the phenomena which we embrace under the word "electrons" do not have precise velocities and positions at any moment, but only that we cannot know both with precision. If either is ascertained with great exactness, the other becomes accordingly vague. This is not proof of a fuzziness in the structure of the universe but does involve a profound difficulty and one which has been increasingly troublesome to the theoretical foundation of modern physics—and with good reason. In the ultimate phenomena of nature it is impossible to observe an experiment without influencing it. The minimum observing instrument is a photon of light, involving at least Planck's constant of energy in its contact with an atom, and when the object of study is the atom itself, the energy of the photon, which is an appreciable fraction of the total energy, becomes hopelessly involved with that of the atom. We must always, of course, observe an actual event, but in macrosopic experiments we can eliminate as inconsequential or calculable every thing that particularizes the event under study. We can thus generalize the results and arrive at a Western type scientific law. In ultimate phenomena this cannot be done. What particularizes the event is too large to ignore, too involved to calculate, and cannot be removed or the experiment could not be observed. Thus in these phenomena the only causation we can study is the causation of the actual event itself which, though we rarely realize it, is something outside the intellectual limits of Western scientific causality. It is not surprising that in this, the only scientific situation in which the causation of a particular event is ever sought in the West, modern quantum mechanics asserts that it can never be exactly found.

There is a vital distinction between the cause of an actual event and scientific causality as the Western mechanistic sciences employ that concept. In all practical scientific operations this distinction, whether it is always consciously understood, is always acted upon. Unfortunately it is neither understood nor acted upon in studying the problems of politics and history. In modern popular thought the distinction is not even known to exist. Since confusion on this matter is the very core of modern materialism, there is a certain unwillingness to recognize the distinction—and above all to grasp its importance. Since it is correctly realized that by pursuing the method of causal analysis the mechanistic sciences have developed a vast field of knowledge, it is difficult at first to understand that this type of analysis cannot be applied to discover or explain the cause of any actual event.

Consider a trifling example, for even the most trivial is adequate to show the nature of the difficulty. Consider a schoolboy generating hydrogen with zinc and aqueous hydrochloric acid in a high school chemistry class. What is the cause of the evolution of hydrogen? Is it the replacement of the hydrogen by the zinc according to the laws of chemistry, or is it the act of the boy in pouring in the acid? Both are the "cause" within the accepted meanings of that word, but the two meanings belong to different worlds. In the scientific sense, the cause can be further analyzed back through molecular and atomic structure and remain scientifically meaningful. But nowhere in that long and learned chain is there anything that tells us why the chemical reaction itself was set going, why the boy poured in the acid. Yet if we seek to pursue the alternative meaning of cause, to inquire causally into the reason for the boy's act, we not only gain no answer but acquire no wisdom on the way. In the human sense no chain but nonsense can be woven. What was the cause of his conducting the experiment, the cause of his taking the course, the cause of his going to this school, the cause of schools having chemistry courses? Pursuit of cause in the world of hydrogen ions leads to science. Pursuit of cause in the world of the boy leads in ever widening circles to imbecility.

Reflection reveals that these two almost contradictory approaches can be made to every terrestrial event whatsoever. In each case, regardless of how profound our knowledge of the mechanics of nature that are involved, this knowledge never gives us the slightest information on why the specific event actually occurred. There is only one apparent inconsistency. Causal science, astronomy to be specific, is capable of foreseeing the motions of the planets and in this case the knowledge of the mechanics involved not only explains how eclipses must occur if they are going to occur, but foresees the occurrence of each specific eclipse. But here causality deals with a situation never encountered on the face of the earth, an arrangement of matter and force where *all* the variables, *all* the determining conditions, are known.

Scientific causality operates within those limits and beyond them the pursuit of cause is no longer scientific. Every scientific law describes the certain consequences of known causes, but in order to do so *all* the causes must be known. The very method of acquiring scientific knowledge in the first place permits no other result. A scientific cause can only be determined by exhaustion of the negative. All conditions must be known, all variables under control and then by successively altering the variables the cause can be identified. Manifestly no such method is applicable to actual events for those can never be repeated. Equally the task of isolating and identifying all the relevant causal conditions of an actual event—the boy with the acid—is simply beyond the possibility of human accomplishment.

The difficulty in applying in the fields of history and politics what passes today as scientific thinking, is not that there need be any doubt that the universe is indeed the vast, interrelated system of cause and effect that we believe it to be. The difficulty lies solely in the type of problem that is considered capable of causal solution. Whatever may be popularly believed to the contrary, Western scientific causality never deals with why things actually are as they are or happen as they do. It deals only with the mechanism of how they must happen if they do happen. But the wonders of modern science create the general impression that scientific causality undertakes to explain "reality," and since nothing is more real than an actual event, it is an irresistible temptation to believe that this, too, is within the compass of causality.

Yet the flaw in this popular belief is immediately apparent. If there were causal explanations of past events—as we so generally believe there are —it would mean that all the relevant variables determining the consequences of any condition had been identified. If these could be identified out of our always incomplete knowledge of the past, certainly it would be simpler to identify them out of our more complete knowledge of the present. We could then readily calculate precise future events that must occur. But to this necessary conclusion no one is willing to go. Yet if actual past events could be explained by scientific causality, then scientific causality could predict future occurrence. But it does not.

This we realize in regard to specific prevision. Yet we accept what we are offered as causal predictions of the future provided it is a generalized future, though any future can be only a tissue of specific events not one of which, we admit, could be scientifically predicted. Nevertheless we have whole fields of intellectual study like economics and sociology which call themselves sciences and assert a claim to scientific prevision. Their practitioners believe that they can use and are using the methods of scientific causality in their respective fields. But these fields deal with actual events and their predictions concern what actually will happen, not what will certainly happen *if* precise conditions are present.

We have also an immense popular literature setting forth what is said to be a causal description of the worlds of nature and history. It purports to give a causal explanation of events, but even a brief examination reveals that its concern is not with causality but plausibility. It is incapable, of course, of proving the causes it asserts as operating in political events and always relies on finding this belief already implanted in the reader. Unhappily this reliance is usually justified. Thus to people who believe, for example, that popular injustice is the cause of social revolution, events of the French Revolution or the Soviet conquest of China can be selected and arranged in such a way that the reader's existing conviction leads him to the conclusion desired by the author. The same events arranged against a different pattern of belief lead, naturally, to entirely different conclusions. Even the best of this type of historical analysis shows its real lack of causal structure as soon as it is applied to the problem of the future. Immediately, the method employed becomes apparent as a way of *accounting* for events but not of *foreseeing* them. Yet this very school of scientific thought, the positivism of J. S. Mill and Comte, which is the philosophical atmosphere of our times, asserts that the true nature and possibly even the definition of science is the ability to predict the consequences of known causes. It should long ago have seemed suspicious that this school of historical and political philosophy has always been willing to assert its sure knowledge of causes by working backward from effects but has been consistently unable to calculate forward from such causes and predict effects that have not yet occurred.

We admit that causal analysis cannot foresee the specific future, but we still insist that it can explain the past. The process is not logical, but the motive is sound politically. The illusion of having accounted for the past by a causal analysis permits the extension of plausibility to a desired future. While shying away from foresight concerning specific events, predictions are made in regard to generalities of a democratic and leftist tone. The reader, who is usually not well versed in scientific philosophy, is aware that in practical life even the most rigid scientific prevision, as in engineering, contains some sort of uncertainty. Accordingly he is not too shocked by the imprecise predictions and is willing to accept them as having the scientific base asserted by the author. What is lost track of is the awareness that scientific foresight is never vague but only conditioned, while mechanistic political foresight is never conditioned but always vague. Scientific foresight predicts from definable causes, mass, energy and so forth, exactly what specific events will occur, and when they will occur, so long as definite conditions—about which it predicts nothing—are maintained. Mechanistic political foresight postulates no conditions but predicts general consequences from vague "causes," democracy, class consciousness and so forth, which it asserts to be currently operating in society. The one identifies its causes with measurable reality and predicts exactly their result if they are set operating in a specified circumstance. The other describes as a cause a word which has no precise meaning and asserts that the indefinable maze of fact and opinion represented by this word will bring about a necessary result—a result which in turn is an indefinable maze—under every condition that may develop.

Now in regard to the actual event, our language has a group of words that are indeed distasteful—fate, fortune, destiny, doom—which deal with the unpredictable, unmanageable web of the unending series of actual events. They are unscientific words, and we do not like to use them for they disclose the pit that lies always beneath our feet. Nevertheless, in the very imprecision of their meaning, in the atmosphere of the hidden and the dark that clings to them is disclosed how little we really feel ourselves the masters of the actual. Just as our passion for the concept of security is a desperate flight from the image of death, so our passion to assert a causal explanation of the actual is a flight from the image of fate whose real meaning to us we disclose in our use of its adjective.

The difficulty seems to be this: we assume that all material things that happen occur in accordance with a system of cause and effect. Some schools of thought are inclined to make reservation of the psychological operations of men, ascribing these to something other than cause and effect. The more mechanistic schools include these, too, within mechanical causality, but in any event both schools ascribe all mechanical action, that is, all physical and chemical events, to a system of strict causality. Experiments are then conducted under controlled conditions and these show unmistakably that where all conditions are known, the results are invariable and therefore always predictable. This confirms our belief that all things are governed by mechanistic causality so that we feel entitled to extend the certainty we have attained under controlled conditions to the universe at large where conditions can neither be controlled nor even identified. Now since we never find any physical or chemical situation in which the laws of causality do not appear to apply, we are undoubtedly justified in asserting that such causality governs all events. But in so doing, we forget the controlled conditions which alone make predictions possible. We can say, therefore, that we have good evidence for believing all events to be cause-governed, but we have equally good evidence that without control of condition, or exact knowledge about them, these events are completely unpredictable by causal means. The experimental method which confirms us in our belief that the universe is rigidly cause-governed proves in the same experiments that the method of causality is incapable of predicting actual events since the conditions of the latter are an infinity of unknown and uncontrolled variables.

The hard fact of the matter is that the Western mechanical sciences, despite the popular and even professional belief to the contrary, are not concerned with predicting the future and are really incapable of doing so. Even the apparent predictability of engineering is an illusion. All these complex machines and processes whose future operations seem to be so accurately foreseen are not in fact the object of true prevision. No designer of a dynamo can foresee whether it is going to be destroyed in a fire or shut down by a strike, or even adequately maintained. All his prevision is clouded with the eternal "if." All he can foresee is that if his dynamo is run correctly it will generate a calculable amount of current at a known voltage. Whether it ever does so and how long it does so will depend upon events entirely beyond the scope of technological or scientific calculation.

Scientific prevision is thus negative only. In its estimates of the future, it can in theory divide the mechanically possible rigidly from the mechanically impossible. But in fact, since its knowledge of nature at any given moment is never complete, its analysis always containing some degree of error, the exact division between the possible and impossible is blurred by a class of events where it can only postulate a greater or lesser degree of mechanical probability. For most purposes, however, its prevision of the mechanically possible and impossible is accurate enough for almost all practical operations. In this way it is an invaluable tool both in foreseeing the future and in analyzing the past. It reduces sharply the range of possible events. But this is immensely short of knowing the cause of a past event or predicting what events will in fact occur in the future.

All we can say is that everything that happens or ever has happened must be within a net of mechanistic causation, and must be mechanically possible, but this net is so infinitely complex that in both practice and strict theory we know *nothing* about the causation of events. What we think of in rough practical thought is not causation at all but only the mechanism of the immediate action under the conditions present, conditions for which we can never account. This is a distinction that is popularly overlooked, most grievously by technical men when they are talking beyond their field. Since we know the universe is cause-governed, and we know we can predict results under controlled conditions; it is an irresistible temptation to forget the limiting conditions and assume the ability to predict all cause-governed phenomena, which in modern materialism means everything. And from an assertion of ability to predict follows necessarily the assertion of ability to control. From this illogical extension flows the political fetish of modern materialism and the apologia of modern leftism.

Humility in regard to causation is difficult in the modern world, for in our time the role of natural science tends to be that of religion in the later Middle Ages. It is believed to have all the answers, not only in its field, but in practical life. The open, acknowledged fear of death gave theology its immense political power in the affairs of Medieval Europe. The secret, unadmitted fear of death, which is the hidden shame of all modern men, flowers with us in our preoccupation with "security" and to this the tremendous physical power of the natural sciences makes an unarguable appeal. The psychological replacement goes even further and "science" in our time wears even the image of God and possesses His attributes. It is, in principle at any rate, believed to be omniscient and in practice omnipotent. To the heretic and infidel, that is to the society that will not learn its principles and walk in its ways, it is believed to assure the hell of war, revolution and death by atomic blast. To the believer, it promises the paradise of security, ease and equality.

So immense is this fetish of modern science and so twisted and covered up in our own minds are the terrors for which it offers comfort, that it is as difficult for us to be skeptical towards even its unfounded claims as it was for the intellectually timorous of the Middle Ages to question the adequacy of the truths of religion. But science, for all the mastery of mechanics that has grown from it, can no more be applied to the affairs of politics and history than theology. Like theology, it does not apply to this world, though the believer in each so believes, but to another, theology to the kingdom of the dead, science to the kingdom of the pure. The sciences deal in systems. All their laws and expressions concern systems—imaginary combinations of mass and energy isolated from all else—something which obviously never occurs and never could occur, something which even in a laboratory cannot be constructed and must be created by calculations alone, by making allowances in the data or in the degree of accuracy desired, for the unavoidable influence in the surroundings. But in the world of the impure, the world of life and politics, there are no systems and no ways to create them. Events occur, situations must be anticipated, decisions made, all without a causal base or the possibility of getting one. It is here that the fetish of science is politically most dangerous, its derogation of other methods of knowledge. Under the fetish of science, causality becomes so important that where it is absent, as in all political questions, there is a temptation to invent it and thereby ascribe to a guess or a wish the dangerous certainty of a law, or if this cannot be done, to deny the possibility of any knowledge whatever about the matter in question. Both attitudes are almost universal in the political and economic writing of our time. Both attitudes are the justification of the ruin of our world which we have fought two great wars to achieve.

The study of history and the forecasting of politics are not, therefore, subjects that can be intelligently undertaken through the application of causality, and the more a study of either is dressed in the appearance of causality, the more specious it is and the more the intelligence or the honor of the writer is open to suspicion. The objective of scientific work is not to establish plausibility but at the best certainty and at the worst probability. What is made plausible is not thereby made one bit more probable, and the only purpose of going to great effort to create plausibility is to delude either the writer himself or the reader.

On the other hand, while causality in life is undiscoverable, events do have consequences. The whole fabric of our lives, personal and political, is woven of events and consequences. If we cannot employ the principles of causality, how can we deal with this obvious fact? We cannot foreclose to ourselves all knowledge of the flow of events.

Since we cannot analyze the past nor foresee the future by the use of scientific causality, we must approach the problem frankly by the method of analogy. This is not the weak method that the fetish of modern science might suggest. Actually it is not only the concealed foundation upon which causal laws are raised, it is also the method by which we habitually gain almost all the prevision that we have. It is analogic not causal reasoning which tells us that if we plant a garden in the spring we may have vegetables in the summer, that when our daughter reaches her early twenties, she is likely to marry and have children, that since grandfather is now ninety, his death cannot be far off. The problem in analogic reasoning and prevision is only the problem of classification. If in the tangle of real events, we can discover an identity, we can study its ways and learn to predict them. We do this constantly. We know that one seed, one daughter, one grandfather is each an altogether different individual from any other seed, daughter or grandfather. Yet familiarity has taught us that there is a classification of these things which permits us to predict with greater or less accuracy the likely and unlikely—even the possible and impossible—events that can happen to them. Thus we can predict the quite different life expectancies of a pine tree and an oak tree, not by causal analysis of each tree but by identifying each with the species to which it belongs. Our information is gained by simple observation of enough trees of each species to ascertain the life expectancy of each. We have no knowledge whatever of what causes oaks so vastly to outlive pines. In fact, all our basic knowledge of living things is gained in this way. Causal science in this field has profoundly improved our knowledge of the mechanics of life but tells us nothing about its fate. A living thing is not "caused" by the biochemistry of its metabolism.

To obtain analogic knowledge of individual things is fairly simple. The individuals constituting the class are obvious. But sometimes the classification is one of function, not corporate similarity, and in these cases the similarities that reveal the classification may require intricate search. Such unavoidably are the classifications with which history must deal. Even in the mechanical sciences the problem of identification of the units of action is perhaps the most difficult single problem involved even in these intricate fields. Molecules, atoms, electrons, etc., are not ascertained to exist by being discovered. The possibility of such entities was first conceived in the mind and then nature searched to see whether its behavior was better explained if something somewhat corresponding to these concepts was assumed to exist. Similarly, in the biological sciences we have to ascertain the units that compose living things, the cells, the organs, the species, the genera, the phyla, none of which is a net fact in itself. Each is an intellectual unit, a concept, abstracted by the mind from the data and placed by analogy, not by exploration of its cause, in its proper relation with the others. Even what appears to be so obvious an external reality as an individual animal is not truly a net fact. It, too, is at bottom a concept, for we recognize the existence of the same individual from birth to death, though the continuity is one neither of form nor matter nor of any tangible thing but of the abstraction, "function," alone. So, too, by the same mechanism of observation and thought we must perceive the living units of history.

Fortunately, historical research in the past century and a half has assembled the data in which the real similarities are evident once the mind admits that there is no possibility of finding any scientifically valid causality to explain these events. We can see with distinctness today that the history of men has been a history of great self-contained societies or civilizations, some of which have affected others as two trees growing close together affect one another without either thereby becoming anything but a self-contained tree. What has not been studied in too great detail is the consequence of this on the life of the West. The line-of-progress history which seeks to find causal explanation of these developments in Western life that it chooses to call progress can turn out little but propaganda or nonsense. The scholars who have tried to re-establish world history as the history of these great societies have had necessarily far wider interests than the West itself. The task, therefore, of trying to set forth essential aspects of the life of the West as a self-contained society, yet nevertheless a society in physical contact with living alien societies and in cultural contact with others long before extinct, has yet to be done. Such part of this task as is germane to the political problems of the modern West seems therefore an essential requirement of this study. The very identification of the West requires it.

Before entering upon this task, however, there is still a scientific problem that obstructs an understanding of history. Not only has the misused causality of Western science confused historical analysis; mechanistic philosophy has denied the existence of motive in the world. At best, we are allowed to attribute motives of a narrow, personal sort to an individual man, even these, however, conditioned by his food, friends and infancy. The great flow of events is felt to respond to no purpose but those of an occasional wicked conqueror, himself perhaps a causal victim of underprivilege. That anything remotely resembling purpose operates throughout history as a whole is dismissed as mystical rubbish. The line-of-progress philosophy is one of motiveless causation—we were mechanically lucky in happening to live on coal and iron mines in a temperate climate—and now that progress seems to have turned downward into wars and disasters, we have become mechanically unlucky and perhaps the Soviet Empire has the luck. A mechanistic philosophy does not exclude luck. This is only the human name for a favorable turn of mechanistic probability.

Mechanistic philosophy flows from this same misreading of the nature of scientific causality. It is the grandiose expression of the error of supposing that Western science deals with the cause of events. Taken at its face value, it would require that on some spring morning, say in 20,000 B.C., the state of the men then living and the physical state of the earth and the solar system necessarily caused all subsequent events. Imagine even the most skilled group of investigators armed with the most modern scientific, geographic and geologic information, skilled in the latest techniques of psychoanalysis, attempting to forecast a causal picture from the men—and there were so very few then—and the world of 20,000 B.C. It is obviously, palpably absurd. These ancient men had no notion consciously or subconsciously of what their distant descendants were going to do and no clue in them or in the physical earth around them could have given a hint to our scientific researchers. These might have concluded only one thing, that man differed markedly from other animals and some extraordinary future might lie before him. What it would be, they could not possibly have discovered.

Despite an apparent resemblance between the problem mentioned earlier of predicting the choice of the marbles and the problem of an imaginary research team trying to forecast history from 20,000 B.C., the two cases are quite different. To be sure, in both cases the operation of causal laws are unpredictable by strict causality but in the case of the marbles these causal laws are known while in the case of the men they are not. For practical purposes all the laws governing the behavior of marbles are known. We can study them with any degree of refinement that we choose and we never find controlled behavior of a marble ever anything but what the causal laws allow us to predict. We have, therefore, a warrant for assuming that the marbles are still entirely governed by the laws that we know even when we can no longer trace the operation of these laws. In regard to historical causality, the situation is obviously different. Instead of dealing with known laws whose operations are too complex to follow, we have no knowledge of any laws at all. Certainly we find the mathematical phenomenon of probability in life as we do with dice and marbles, but in neither case does the probability pattern tell us anything of the causality presumed to be operating. We cannot deduce the laws of motion, nor even deduce that such laws exist, from the probability pattern of dice.

Now it is not at all scientific to assert the existence of a cause whose operation is incapable of being shown. Since our research team in 20,000 BC. could not have found the necessary data to make a causal forecast of the future, we have no warrant for the belief that such future was in fact to be causally determined. To believe so is simply an act of faith taken against the evidence. The truth of the matter is that we do not know what makes human history. We know that all events that occur must occur within the frame of mechanical possibility—they must not violate the mechanistic laws of nature—but that does not mean the mechanistic laws of nature are responsible for their occurrence. What then is the nature of this still mysterious universe of physical reality which is at once the stuff and the stage of human history?

Nineteenth century materialism, driven to find a causal explanation of the universe in which it found itself, erected a curiously contradictory philosophy. Faced with the phenomena of life, the development of species and the flow of history alike, it designed a mechanistic progress-optimism. Evolution was interpreted as a purposeless, causal series, but nonetheless a manifestation of progress culminating in man. History was seen as equally purposeless and equally progressing to the democratic states of Western Europe and America. Although the two processes operated on such vastly different time scales that one could have had no mechanical connection with the other, yet an emotional fusion was effected to forecast a similarly progressive future. The whole development was entirely purposeless, but by a happy accident, this resultant of blind, mechanistic causality had produced beneficent progress and would produce still more.

But with the inorganic, which was always pictured as the base out of which the living had arisen and into which the living must some day return, utter pessimism replaced mechanical optimism. The physical universe was seen as a giant clock slowly running down. Its ultimate end was inescapable: dead matter, its energy forever bound in irrecoverable form, extended inert in the frozen night of space. This was the deep, and indeed the great, philosophy of the nineteenth century. The shallow progress-optimism in affairs of politics and history was a mocking trap. It was of immediate advantage in liberal politics and it soothed the outraged emotions of the worldly religiousness of the time, which in slow retreat from its hopes of Heaven the more insistently demanded belief in progress upon earth. In reality it was dishonest and petty, dishonest to the bleak pessimism of the deep thought of the age and suffocatingly petty in what it was optimistic about. The utilitarian—and strictly respectable—future it held out as the goal of progress could make no man's heart beat the faster.

It was probably the only practical philosophy the age could have tolerated. The old belief in the transcendental purpose of life, that history and nature were only the background for the journey of the soul to God, had become more a sacred form of words than a deep conviction. Its power to give an ethical direction to the actions of a lifetime had largely disappeared from the upper intellectual and political circles. At the same time, the worldly ethics of rank and responsibility which had come down from a long-vanished political nobility were becoming increasingly ridiculous in a society of egalitarian theory and arriviste millionaires. The ultimate pessimism of mechanistic science was probably necessary to remove from the study of phenomena the teleology of a transcendental purpose once and for all revealed—the curse of the earlier rationalists. But as a philosophical base for the affairs of a human world, mechanistic pessimism denied any deep stream of purpose, anything greater than himself by which a man could be moved, and left life to ethical evaluation by the crass and ephemeral standards of progress-optimism. It is not surprising that on this philosophy nothing but political ruin was erected, the ruin that today lies about us.

But upon the deep pessimism of universal death the nineteenth century completed the great structure of the Western causal sciences—and utterly destroyed the foundation of its own pessimism. The scientific expression of this pessimistic cosmology is set forth in the laws of thermodynamics which assert the principle of the conservation of energy but also require that this energy must continuously flow toward an ultimate equilibrium in which available energy no longer exists. Now there is no doubt that these laws are invariably true of all the phenomena of life or of the inorganic as we can expect to encounter them on this planet. Modern nuclear phenomena have required redefinitions of mass and energy but have not altered the correctness of the laws so far as they apply to the narrow space and brief time of the earth's surface. But the nineteenth century mechanistic philosophers did not stop with the application of these laws to the earth. They took a practical operating rule of the earth and extended it as the philosophical principle of all creation. It is this extension that modern cosmology, itself the development of nineteenth century mechanistic casuality, finds unwarranted.

Since we do not consider purpose as part of our system of causality, we never reckon it in natural phenomena and therefore calculate as though it did not exist. As a result no trace of purpose appears in our accepted scientific picture of the material universe. Now this may be because nature is indeed without purpose. It may likewise be that we find no evidence of purpose because our structure of causality excludes it from the beginning. We find everywhere evidence of the existence of the necessity which we always assumed to exist. It is not surprising that we find nowhere traces of a purpose whose existence we have refused to assume. In the biological sciences, a narrow purpose has to be admitted, the attempt of the organism to stay alive for a time and reproduce itself, but nature as a whole in modern scientific analysis is postulated to be purposeless. But purpose does exist, and it exists as part of the natural order of phenomena covered by the laws of mechanistic causality. For nineteenth century physics to strip phenomena of any assumed transcendental purpose was essential if those phenomena were to be seen as they actually occurred, not as some theory concerning God's purpose in creation would have required that they occur. But there is an immense difference between assuming a purpose and discovering the evidence of a purpose. Modern causal science out of unalloyed atheism—certainly in its teleology—has reached that point.

Purpose is the carrying out of a pre-existing design. In mechanistic language, it is the manipulation of mass and energy to bring about a result in accordance with some pattern that in some fashion is in existence before the result occurs. When a man undertakes to carry out a purpose, the design of what he intends to accomplish is in his mind before he acts. When a seed starts to grow a plant, it is our fashion to deny purpose to the seed. Our prejudice makes us assume unnecessarily that purpose must exist as a conscious image in an intellect. What proceeds without that conscious image we like to call "nature" or "instinct." But "instinct" and "nature" in this sense are only meaningless words to cover a vast and embarrassing ignorance.[2] Such usage is as unscientific as the four elements of Aristotle or the term "chemical affinity," which was used to describe observed, but inexplicable, chemical phenomena in the days before our knowledge of subatomic structure brought some causal order into this field. "Instinct" has no intrinsic meaning, nor does "nature" when used in this sense. Both describe purposeful behavior of living things when we are unwilling to admit the existence of purpose.

The alternative to purpose is not cause and effect, as it seems to some observers. All purpose is *also* cause and effect. The alternative to purpose is chance, which, too, is cause and effect. We cannot even know phenomena, as we see the world, that do not show cause and effect, so that there is no valid physical distinction between chance and predictable causality. It does not look so because we consider the laws of astronomy rigid and the celestial motions wholly predictable while the motions of dice seem free. But the motions of the dice do not vary in

---

[2] This difficulty is no monopoly of the West. In Levantine thought the divine guidance by which, for instance, Mohammed was able to receive the Koran is described by the same Arabic word that is used to explain what we call "instinctive" knowledge, as for example, among bees.

essence from the motions of the planets; it is simply that the motions of the dice are affected by too many unknown and unascertainable variables to permit a calculated prediction of the result of a single throw. In popular usage, to be sure, the word "chance" is confined to such causal operations as those of dice where the variables effecting the result are unknown. But this is only the personal view of a limited observer and does not change the underlying identity between chance and the predictable. Each is the manifestation of the identical causality that we see as the operating mechanics of all things that are. The difference between purpose and chance is, therefore, not the difference between the unreal and the real. Both are real. The difference is whether the mass-energy relations are handled within a system or simply operate freely with the environment.

Technical literature defines a system in the following terms: "a system is taken to mean that real or ideal space confined by known boundaries through which pass, in or out, the various forms of energy that are involved in the process in which the given system is participating. When any system takes part in any process whatsoever, the amount of energy resident in the system changes only by the net amount of energy (of any form) which may be absorbed or given off by the system during the process." [3]

The prime definition of a system, therefore, requires the establishment of its boundaries. A gasoline engine as a system can be defined with boundaries through which the heat of combustion of the fuel passes inward and the waste heat and mechanical energy pass outward. A system can be, in fact, any process or combination of processes whatever for which the mind desires to establish boundaries and is able to count or estimate the flow of energy inward and outward through those boundaries. Every living thing, in this sense, can be considered as a system. There is only this difference: When an engineer establishes the boundaries of a system that he wishes to study, he places them with a view to the requirements of his calculations and these boundaries are boundaries in his mind and have no actual existence. The systems of science are imaginary. They are isolated by image and calculation from their surroundings and have no actual existence as either "things" or functions, though their energy relationships are none the less real. When the mental concept of the boundary of the system is dropped, the existence of the system itself ends, and the matter and energy that composed it become once more part of the vast undifferentiated system that is the face of the planet in its energy exchanges through space. If, on the other

[3] *Chemical Engineers Handbook*, McGraw-Hill, 1941, page 628.

hand, we wish to consider a living thing as a system, the boundaries of the system, placed as they are by mental image, nevertheless coincide with an actual boundary that was there before and will remain when the image is withdrawn, the actual boundary of the living thing itself.

The difference between life and non-life is thus neither a matter of arbitrary distinction nor the result of a mystic feeling. It is a physical difference in the handling of energy. All forms of living things are at base organizations of molecules that are capable of absorbing energy and using it to maintain and increase the mechanism by which they absorb energy. If we consider each one as a scientific system, they are engines that can run uphill by means of their ability to absorb energy from their surroundings. They do not violate the laws of thermodynamics. They cannot absorb energy from a lower potential and discharge it against a higher. Like all real engines, they absorb from a higher potential and discharge to a lower, but they are able to use the difference for the advancement of their own interests. The energy cycles of all the engines of art are the same, but they cannot use that energy to maintain or better themselves.

Now it is because living things can constitute themselves as systems, can abstract energy from their surroundings and use it to manipulate the physical realities within and abutting their systems that they are capable of purpose and are not wholly subject to chance. If they could not do this, their physical and chemical reactions would proceed indistinguishably with those of their environment. They would be neither systems nor living things.

We mask concrete purposeful activity in animal life under the term "instinct." For the more subtle examples of purpose in plants we have devised no such comfortable word. We can say that an animal knows what is good and bad for it by "instinct," but we are forced to say that an acorn produces an oak by "nature." Now, if by the word "nature" we mean mechanical cause-and-effect—which is what we often mean by nature—the expression is incomplete. Is it cause-and-effect operating on and within a system, or is it cause-and-effect operating on the unorganized but assembled molecules of a thing which is not a system? We should specify that an acorn produces an oak by cause-and-effect by chance or else by cause-and-effect by purpose, because the word "nature" includes both notions of cause-and-effect. We are forced to choose one meaning or the other because all the causal operations that we know are either those operating in an undifferentiated field—that is, there is no distinction of function between the object of study and the surroundings, there is nothing, in effect, but surroundings—or those operating within a system and between a system and its surroundings. The first we call chance and the second we have no choice but to call purpose. In the case of the acorn, the distinction is simply whether the acorn is dead or living. In the first case, its structure as a thermodynamic system has been destroyed and its cause-and-effect relations with its surroundings are those we call chance. The acorn is now simply one with its surroundings and what happens to its molecules is entirely the result of the chemical and biological condition in which it is. On the other hand, if the acorn is alive, it is a system and while its purposeful operations are conditioned by the state of its surroundings—it may be eaten by a pig—these by themselves, no matter how favorable, cannot make it into an oak.

Even in purely mechanical operations, this distinction holds. An operating engine operates by cause-and-effect but not by chance. It is a system and handles its input and outgo of energy in accordance with purpose, not its own but still purpose, and is built to maintain a rigidly controlled energy relationship with its surroundings such that while the total available energy of the system and its surroundings declines, the available energy of the system alone, or of parts of the system, are for a time increased. On the other hand, an abandoned engine continues to operate by cause-and-effect, but it is no longer a system. Its energy relations with its surroundings are no longer under any kind of control. It is now thermodynamically indistinguishable from its surroundings, and its operations are those of cause-and-effect by chance, the rust and corrosion of undifferentiated surroundings where not only the total energy must decline, but the energy of every part.

It cannot be helped that the mechanist fashions of two hundred years are opposed to the concrete expressions of this issue. The issue is nevertheless there not as mystical yearnings but as an inevitable conclusion from the laws of thermodynamics. Nor can it be helped that there is no discrete individual whom we can endow with this purpose. Even though the operation of an acorn in producing an oak can be seen by consideration of its thermodynamic operations to be a matter of purpose, we still feel that this purpose in no way resides in the acorn. The operations of the acorn display purpose but only as a thermodynamic system, not as an individual. Here the acorn only obeys mechanistically the causal laws of its own structure and chemistry. The purpose, if it can be lodged anywhere, is the species oak which employs this mechanism to endure as an endless succession of thermodynamic systems; for each oak tree in producing acorns in turn only mechanistically follows the same causal laws of its structure and chemistry as does the acorn in producing an oak. We have, therefore, a series of purposeful acts for which we can find no purposeful agent. But that for the sake of which all this is done is evidently the species oak tree, and it would appear that we must assign purpose to the species even though we cannot envisage a purposeful mechanism in something operating through disparate individuals across time and therefore, according to our way of thinking, only a concept, not a reality. Perhaps the wisest step would be to revise our way of thinking about the latter. Species are something more than concepts. We understand them as concepts by abstraction from the many real and concrete individuals composing them, as indeed we abstract such concepts as mass and energy from bodies and the changes they undergo. Species are actual existences but more clearly evident in time than in space. They do not exist solely in our minds. They also act in the world by purposefully continuing to exist.

The death of species, which for no good reason we call extinction, does not seem comparable to the death of conscious organisms. We cannot imagine any element of choice or rigid necessity in their death. They seem either to have perished under new adverse interference from the environment, or their own development, their life in a sense, reduced their ability to withstand outside pressures they had formerly mastered. The development of each species shows a youth, maturity and senescence, that is, a period of rapid organic development in which the basic character of the species is set, a period of increase in members and geographical extension and a final period of changeless endurance and often slow geographical retreat. But their ends seem fortuitous, not organically determined. Nothing, not even species, lives for ever, but the definite life spans of individual animals do not exist among species.

It would be simpler to grasp the nature of living unities like species if we could rid our minds of the illusion that an individual must be something all of which must be contained within a definite spacial boundary at some specific moment of time. Although we know that countless cells of our own bodies are not physically attached to us, and that countless more constantly die and are replaced by newly-born cells, still we find it difficult to extend the concept of a soma beyond the boundaries of some visible skin and the continuity of some observable nervous structure. But the evidence is against our prejudices in this matter, and it is better to accept the evidence than stick by the prejudice. Species *act* like an individuality of some kind and it is, therefore, better to recognize them to be what they obviously are than avoid consideration of the evidence in the hope of protecting the prejudice.

But there is evidence of an additional purpose operating among living things. Just as we mask under the names "instinct" and "nature" the purposeful behavior of individuals, so we mask the purposeful behavior of species under the name "evolution." The same consideration applies here. Evolution describes a cause-and-effect process, so we must specify whether it is cause-and-effect by chance or cause-and-effect by purpose.

The history of the development of species over geologic time is a history of the increase of specialization and complexity. From early unicellular life and from creatures that are little more than cellular aggregates there have developed in two unrelated but functionally similar lines the great groups of the higher vertebrates and the higher arthropoda. It is perhaps unappealing to our vanity to recognize the higher mammals— by which we mean primarily ourselves—and the hymenoptera as the two pinnacles of evolution, but by any objective standards the social insects are at least as far from primitive life, both in specialization and in intellectual mastery of environment, as are the social mammals. This is not always easy for us to realize. The psychic life of mammals and even of birds is so akin to ours that it is possible to understand the idea of thought by these creatures. In contrast, the psychic life of insects is so distant that we cannot conceive of these creatures as capable of thought. But here again we are forced to cover our essential ignorance of the mechanics of purposeful activity by use of the word "instinct," for insects do pursue purpose and do so with specific reactions to specific occasions. Since that is part at least of what thinking is, they, therefore, think even though we do not understand how they do it.

Placed against the scale of time, therefore, it is evident that in living things there is a purpose to become more specialized and complex, that is, to become both more conscious of the environment and more surely the master of it, not in the interest of the individual cell nor of the individual animal, who remains fated to die, but in the interest of the species or of those special groups like ant hills and historical societies that form an organic type of structure—whether we call them organisms or not is immaterial—within the species.

The same type of problem faces us in the immense aesthetic development of design and color in flowers, insects, birds, fish, and even reptiles and mammals. To what end? To be beautiful? Who cares? For whom to see and enjoy? The mechanistic nineteenth century and the liberal-leftist twentieth century assurance that this was all purposeless cause-and-effect —each individual bird developing the feather pattern of the species in its own interest or by chance in the interest of the species—is logically absurd and mathematically impossible. No conceivable statistical odds could account for a purposeless, by chance, appearance of the same aesthetic standards of design and color in such disparate forms of life as flowers, fish, birds, snakes and insects.

There is another and curious fact that is apparent from the evolution of living things. Despite the clear evidence of relationship among species there is no case where we can feel sure that one species is the direct offspring of another, living or extinct. It is as though our knowledge of our personal ancestry were confined to uncles and great-aunts with never a sure knowledge of the direct maternal and paternal line. Whether this is significant of anything but our ignorance of the mechanics of change of species, it would be impossible to say. But despite our ignorance of its significance, it remains a fact of nature.

But though we men stem from the same source, the life of the individual animal and the human person are separated by a psychic gulf which no identity of organic mechanism can ever bridge. The psychic life of man has separated him from his fellow mammals as completely as the mechanized psychic reaction of the hymenoptera has separated them from their fellow arthropods and from all vertebrates. The thought processes of the hymenoptera—we have no notion of the mechanism— produce specialized individuals designed to take care of the problem that stimulated the thought. The thought processes of the higher mammals enable each individual to deal intelligently with a series of unrelated specific events. The thought processes of man, which alone we think we understand, also produce ideas, that is the abstraction of the similarities found, or at times invented but felt to be found, in disparate things. Even this, however, is not unique to man for beavers obviously have ideas of water level when they plan a dam and ants certainly have the idea of the equivalents of agriculture and animal husbandry. The primary difference lies in the human ability, indeed the human necessity, of abstracting such ideas concerning the entire environment. The power of creating ideas is the property of the human person while in other creatures it appears, to us at least, to be the property of the species and limited to those fields of activity in which members of the species have been engaged for innumerable generations.

For man the ideas become more meaningful than the tangible realities from which they are abstracted. We act as though that inward picture were in fact the outer reality. A structure of ideas replaces the mere sum of tangible sense impressions as the "real" world in which we live. The nature of these ideas differs between primitive men and men of the historical societies, and differs among the men of the different societies, but for all men, external reality is seen in the form of a human abstraction from the sense impressions, seen as images and ideas. Needless to say, to the men who hold them these images and ideas appear not as human abstractions but as the external, actual realities themselves. And this is equally true of such ideas as God or the Kingdom of Heaven and gravity, mass or energy. The sense data, the assemblage and interpretation of which lie beneath the various ideas, differ enormously. Different men at different times find one image convincing and another absurd, but all these ideas are identical in being mental images put together by the human mind from such sense data as the mind is willing to accept as germane to the image. It is, of course, almost impossible for a man who is convinced that he holds no ideas, but relies solely on objective data or true revelation, to understand that the world as he sees it is not the world that exists but only an image in his own mind, projected like the images of a magic lantern on the dark screen of unknowable reality. But such is the fact, and from this fact men and animals, inhabiting the same globe together, have come to live in two separate environments which coincide only in limited areas, which seem completely identical or completely distinct only to those whose ideas already contain these specific images.

The history of animals is, therefore, the history of creatures operating in a world of sense impressions. The history of men is the history of creatures operating in a world only partially one of sense impressions and primarily one of ideas that interpret, and therefore largely replace, these sense impressions. The difference is the immense distinction that we see about us. To outward appearances our paleolithic ancestors differed little from their animal contemporaries, but in fact, and perhaps without even being aware of it, they lived in a different environment. That environment despite all these ages is still the essential environment of man: his own ideas and images.

We have come then to this, that living things in their operations as species display a type of behavior that must be called purposeful if we are to apply that word to operations that accord with its meaning. This is a demonstrable fact of the physical universe. It is not, to be sure, a purpose according with the conscious purposes of men or the purposes that the religions which have prevailed among men have ever asserted. It includes not alone the purpose of the species to survive but quite evidently the purpose of the individual to die. Not only is this an evident fact of the behavior of living things—it is a logical necessity. Immortal individuals and an immortal species are mutually exclusive. A species is a chain of interrelated individuals across time, and without mortal individuals no species could exist. A group of immortal individuals who continued to propagate would run out of food and either have to cease propagating or cease to be immortal. A group of individuals which does not propagate is no longer a species.

This knowledge of the necessity of death is almost universally accepted as a prime factor in the psychic life of man. But it is probably more than a knowledge of the necessity only. There is probably a dim awareness that not only is his death necessary but that it is intended as part of the order of things. There cannot help but be a conflict between the intellect of man and the world of nature. However hidden the thread of this hostility, it weaves through all the intellectual works of man, his arts, his religions, his sciences and his philosophies. Behind the joyous forefront of nature lies always the implacable purpose to kill him.

These considerations on the nature of nature and the world of living organisms are not prompted by a belief that the secret of human history lies buried in the record of organic development on the earth. It is simply that it is essential to bear in mind in all consideration of human history that whatever else man or historical societies may be, both are part of the organic scum on the face of this planet, like all other living things stemming from the same origins, subject to the same forces, imprisoned alike within the vacuum walls of this globe. What is characteristic of life is necessarily characteristic of history and there is nothing in history that has not its analogue somewhere in the vast drama of living things. Both are great enterprises whose purpose and direction are not revealed solely by the causal mechanisms they employ.

But is there evidence of the existence of purpose in history? Does human history as part of a vast organic process display any of the same purposeful traits that are so evident and so fiercely denied in the development and fate of species? It would be absurd if it did not, for it is merely a part of the same whole. Even the acceleration of change is consistent with the pattern of life: five or six thousand years of the societies of historical man, perhaps a hundred thousand years of neolithic man, perhaps half a million years since the biologic origin of man. These compare reasonably with the great acceleration of organic development: the slow changes during the incredible ages of the Paleozoic, the considerable changes during the long peace of the Mesozoic, the tremendous mammalian changes during the few million years of Tertiary times, the biologic revolution that followed the appearance of man during the trifle of geologic time that constitutes the Quaternary.

The operation of purpose in history, therefore, resembles the operation of purpose in organic evolution. Again we find that the changes are not in the interest of the changers. In biological development we have changes that are solely in the interests of the species, or at times against them, and a spectacular development of species as such. We find a growth of awareness and complexity, physical and psychic whose pattern is obvious but whose point escapes us for we cannot establish by rational or sensory means the existence of anything or anybody in whose interest it is so to develop living forms. It is certainly not in the interest of any individual creature. Had he not been born, he would have no way of discovering this fact and had he been born a different sort of creature, he would have no way of knowing or evaluating what he was missing. It is the awareness that life is not in the interest of those who live that lies beneath both extremes of religious thought, the ultimate pessimism of transcendentalism and atheism.

To recognize purpose requires only a knowledge of the sense of the change, not of its ultimate extent, of the steps and the direction they bear, not of the goal, nor of whose goal. It does not, therefore, need to bear any relation to what we as conscious men could conceive as a possible, much less a desirable, goal any more than our far-off ancestors in Mesozoic times could have conceived of us as worthy offspring, had they possessed any organ capable of entertaining such a concept. It is dangerous to suppose, as we do, that man as a species expresses the purpose of evolution precisely, as it is dangerous to suppose that Western society expresses the purpose of history. Not man nor the West but what they represent expresses the purpose of evolution—the interdependent complexity of human life, the power of the developed human mind. These are examples of the type of thing that the purposeful cause-and-effect of evolution have brought into being. But we even as a species are not the indispensable instrument of this purpose. It is too evident in all that surrounds us for us to suppose that some mutant strain from our own bodies, some hybrid, some mutant of another species, from another phylum for that, might replace us should we ever fall back from the historical plane of life on which human societies have lived for perhaps six or eight thousand years. As historical societies, man creates his environment, not wholly of course, but enough to protect himself against the two great destroyers of organic life, stagnation and overpowering enemies. It is herein that the historical society shows itself as an evidence of the purpose that pervades life. It provides man, as a species—of course, not every man—with the means of power and the necessity of growth. The primitive, unhistorical societies of men are powerful relative to the other creatures of the earth, but they have no organic structure; they are analogous to colonies, not organisms, and can neither grow nor die, though, like animal colonies they can be warped or destroyed. The historical society as a type is an evolutionary development within man as a species entirely comparable with the development of organisms out of colonies of cells. Their life expectancy, if we may judge by the relatively few that have existed, is of the type of the life expectancy of species. Their periods of youth, maturity and senescence have been generally comparable in time span, one to another, but their ability to continue living has varied widely from one to another. Some have died and some almost as ancient are still living. Historical societies have no skins, and thus reproduce their component members by sexual reproduction from the individual members and enforce a functional but not an organic specialization. So far as we know there is nothing comparable to a specialized function for reproducing new societies—though it must be admitted that the intellectual and organic relations between old societies and the preformed period of new ones are extraordinarily intricate. Animal organisms, in contrast, have skins, reproduce their component cells by partition, carry out specialized functions by organic not functional specialization and do have specialized organs for reproduction of new organisms. Amidst all the welter of different mechanical means used by living creatures for accomplishing identical objectives, these differences are in accord with natural practice.

The artist of evolution has been the dramatist of history. There is the same pattern of the flower in the seed, the same operation through individuals for distant ends that bear no relation to their own tangible interests. There is the same rankling fact that progress in history, like evolutionary progress, is largely an abstraction from the separate fates of individuals or societies that have only the most remote biological connection one with another. In all evolution we cannot find the missing links, and the successive flowerings of animal forms are of creatures that are never descended from one another but always from some common, but unknown, ancestor. In history the great societies which have succeeded one another for over five thousand years are not lineal offshoots one of another. The biological group that has constituted each society stems from some common but unknown human ancestry and the contemporary biological connections among different societies apparently have been fortuitous and always minor. For it is a society that forms a people. No doubt this people is affected in turn by the qualities of the ancestral stocks from which it was formed, but the act of creation is that of the society, not the component stocks.

But the peoples thus formed by historical societies have not lived in a world of naked sense impressions. They have lived in a world of ideas and images, each a complete, but different, unity for each society, yet each succeeding unity touched by the earlier. But these ideas and images, being human abstractions from sense impressions, are themselves part of nature, so that though different men have lived in environments different from each other, these have been natural environments in which cause-and-effect by chance and cause-and-effect by purpose both operated. Furthermore, though human history has been a history of men in a world of ideas, this is not the same thing as a history of ideas and it is very far from a history of philosophical or religious concepts, of words, or of those verbal sounds of equivocal meaning or of no meaning that in modern terminology we call ideals. Ideas, in the sense in which these are the environment of man, are illusions, but they are illusions that appear to the mind not as something *in* the mind but as something actually existing outside it. They are in the mind the way sense impressions are in the mind as the terminal of the nerve impulses, but like the latter they appear to be part of the surrounding wall of reality. "Cause" is such an idea and so are "time," "space" and "God." To each man who holds these ideas these words are unequivocal. Each stands for an actual reality that does not appear to be reasoned or thought out but to be seen as it is in the tangible reality round about. It is true that the idea of cause or of God—which are simply the mechanical and emotional words for the same basic idea: that which accounts for the unaccountable, explains the inexplicable—or of any of these words is different in one man from what it is in another, but to each man his own idea is reality itself. Philosophical conceptions such as "righteousness," "duty," "truth," "conservation of energy," "inertia," are mental conclusions knowingly drawn in the mind and asserted as existing in external reality. They are calculated, not seen. Ideals, as we today use the word, are simply equivocal names for conscious programs, "progress," "democracy," "peace," which are neither entities nor abstractions but agglomerates of infinitely complex sets of real events which the speaker supposes can and should be polarized, as it were, in a direction he deems socially desirable. The very difficulty of giving them a precise meaning indicates their use.

A society itself is an idea in the sense discussed above. It is an observed fact of the environment as the members of that society see the world about them. The early men of the great societies see about them the world of nature, the sky and the earth with its men and its animals, and in the middle of this vast mysterious universe it finds *"us."* "We" differ from all other men. Not only do we live differently, but we care deeply about different things than the "nations," the "barbarians," the "gentiles," the "heathen," even the "natives" round about us. Nothing is more evident than the sudden awareness of this unbridgeable gulf in the early days of a society. Hellenes versus barbarians, Jews versus gentiles from Ezra's time onward. The Egyptians simply called themselves "the men" (cf. the original meaning of Dutch and Deutsch). Our own medieval forefathers called themselves Christians in the heart of the western lands but Franks, or Latins, or Catholics in the Mediterranean and along the religious frontier, and a man was all three whether he came from Scotland or Castile.

To observe an "us" surrounded by alien peoples is not a monopoly of the great societies. Every primitive tribe sees itself as a separate group.

but the nature of the idea in the two cases is profoundly different. The primitive idea is humble. Each tribe sees itself perhaps as better than others but not essentially different in structure from the others. The world is seen as composed of a large number of similar tribes differing from one another in fortune and bravery but all members of the same species of human organization. The concept of self in the great societies is, in contrast, of the most appalling egotism. Each sees itself as unique. All other tribes of men constitute a species, but "we" are a species by ourselves. We are the chosen, the favorite of our God. We, and we alone, understand the secret cause of all things. The life of others is the life of blindness, perversion and folly.

Coupled with this different idea of the "we," the great societies form an image of a definite pattern of change. They see themselves from their earliest times possessed of the secret of why the universe is as it is, and the universe itself thereby becomes the object of deliberate change. Primitive tribes seek power, greater wealth, more women, sheer adventure, perhaps, and so indeed do the men of the historical societies. But the historical societies alone seek to transfer an intellectual image of the universe, in the early days in emotional form, into objective reality. This, of course, is what the word "creative" means, and all the great societies have been properly called creative.

Of all the creative acts of the great societies, the deepest and perhaps the most revealing of the character of each was the image each created concerning death. If there is any one thing that is most characteristic of the beginnings of all of them, it is the belief in another world. They solved death not by ameliorating it but by abolishing it. The great civilizations and their religions are assertions of individual mastery over the universe, of survival of the self against the implacable death purpose of nature. Without such a belief, conscious man must see himself in the role of a mere instrument to be used, worn out and destroyed for the unknown purposes of a species whose very being is on a time scale beyond meaning to him. Few can attain such abnegation of self.

Inevitably, therefore, the fate of the civilization remains intertwined with the rise, development and decay of the great religion that accompanied its birth.

The realization that historical societies are living entities, as characteristic of life as species, requires us to expect in their histories and in their futures the kind of conduct that our knowledge of life leads us to expect but that our political ethics urges us to deplore. We know that living entities act in ways that are causally inexplicable, and from the special view of any particular observer, often irrational. We know that the passion to survive and dominate is deeply implanted in all living things. It is not, to be sure, always present. Individuals, species and historical societies alike, become at some point in their lives exhausted and indifferent. But it is a passion we can always expect to encounter in living things.

Nowhere is awareness of this reality of world politics more needed than in the present age of exhaustion of Western society. We no longer feel ourselves driven by the passions of our ancestors. Most of us do not wish our society to die, but almost all of us want it to be left alone without considering too deeply whether the organic nature of others can really permit them to leave us alone. Our fond hope is that by some accord of conscious purpose among the states of the world the passion to expand and master can be eliminated from the politics of men.

But when we grasp the living quality of human societies, we realize that this is a vain and, indeed, a perilous hope. Because they are living entities, not conscious associations, these historical societies unavoidably struggle with one another. We know from the nature of living things that they are certain to do so. We can anticipate the type of situation that must always develop between two societies, as it must develop between two competing species. The details of such historical struggles, being among the societies of men, will not resemble the struggles of species of wild animals but the essential patterns will be the same. Each society will seek to live its life regardless of the welfare of others or, if such be advantageous, at the expense even of the life of others. We know historically that some societies have destroyed others, as some species have destroyed other species. We know also of societies that have existed together. But we know equally that no society has ever long existed through the forebearance and charity of another. Each that has survived has survived by its own material power.

In one other aspect of our life, perhaps the deepest and most vital of all, the knowledge of the living reality of these great societies can be of value to us: the ethical. To survive is the duty of the living. That is what ethics is at bottom and it takes the form of accepting the risk of death when the more complex unit to which a living being belongs is threatened and must be defended. Thus even animals defend their mates and their young—ethically in behalf of their species, and men defend their tribes, their states and at the last their civilizations. It is this same ethic of survival that becomes the religious ethic to men who feel that true reality is not the organic and political life of which they are a part but their image of God. What must then survive is this new higher reality, this greater "life" which has come to embrace the lesser. To be sure, we know that in time all things die, men, states, civilizations, concepts of God and even species alike. But to each while it lives, its ethical duty is to survive. The attempt to maintain each individual life is the essential mechanism of the unknown purpose that pervades all things that are, since all life, the only life, resides in these transient things.

The great ethical problem of our lifetime is to keep our society alive. In the forefront it is a practical problem of understanding our dangers and devising workable means of countering them. In the background it is an intellectual problem of identifying the existence and the nature of what is endangered. Living as we do surrounded by the clamor of liberal and leftist publicity, it is a hard thing to think our way through this mechanism of demagogic ambition and alien intrigue, to reach an understanding of what lines of action are truly ethical and not specious frauds promoted for the welfare of our deadly enemies. To have even a chance of doing so with the internal and external dangers that have now risen to destroy us, we need not only a sense of the living nature of human history but an informed, conscious awareness of what sort of men we are, of the character and personality of our society, of the historical and biological unit which has given us life as civilized men and to which we owe a deep allegiance. We must see the courses open to us that will be consistent with our honor and that will call forth our courage.

But to understand our own society—for what we do not recognize as existing we can scarcely see as endangered—requires more than the assertion that it is today a society in the contemporary world. It requires disentangling the personalities of alien societies that time and custom have long fused with the image of our own.

Chapter 2:

The Grave Of Alaric

EDWARD GIBBON WAS AS LOGICAL A MAN as could be found in the late eighteenth century to crystallize the fashionable historical opinion of his time concerning the past of Western society. His flair for historical insight was sufficient for him to assess the American Revolution as the inconsequential act of a group of rebel colonists who should be brought to heel. His liberal principles led him to aid and applaud all the revolutionary theories of the French Encyclopedists, never anticipating that he would recoil in horror from the practical consequences of these principles in the Revolution. His complete inability to understand the political realities of human societies, his theoretical liberalism, his deism and his smug prejudices all fitted him to compose the masterpiece of eighteenth century misunderstanding of history, *The Decline and Fall of the Roman Empire*. To Gibbon the years from Augustus to the Antonines represented a society as close to the ideals of the eighteenth century philosophers as ever existed. It appeared free of political and religious emotions, comfortable, urban, but fond of pleasant country places not far from town. It gave a dignified position to sages and authors. It appeared to have eliminated war forever. It maintained good order over large areas of land and sea so that travel and commerce were both secure. Almost everything seemed prepared for it to become the ancestor of the eighteenth century then and there. But, alas, so it was not to be. The empire degenerated into military feebleness and was overrun by barbarians. Its religious indifference was replaced by cruel zeal and mysticism, its worldliness by a passion for the transcendent. More than thirteen hundred years had to roll by before the damage was undone and Europe again became sufficiently civilized to appreciate the serene and crowning virtues of deistic liberalism as exemplified in Gibbon and his friends. He tells us himself that he describes the triumph of Christianity and barbarism, which meant the defeat of religious indifference and civilization, two concepts always firmly linked in eighteenth century liberalism. So he saw the relation of Western society to Rome; so he framed it with exhaustive detail and in Ciceronian prose in his *Decline*, and so the English-speaking world to this day largely accepts it.

Only on one feature of his picture of Rome have later historians taken severe issue with Gibbon. His account of the fall of the empire in the west and his implicit causal theory to explain it fit admirably into the line-of-progress scheme. But his inclusion of the history of the Byzantine Empire as an integral part of the history of Rome is a shocking contradiction of this scheme. Rome to us is progress, and we see ourselves as the heirs of its virtues. But to connect Rome to the Orthodox Christians, the Moslems and modern Greeks—and at that with a closer political tie than to us—that is not progress but embarrassing perversion. Gibbon was accepted and is still accepted as a great historian. His general picture of the fall of Rome and rise of the Christian West is still the generally prevailing, popular image, but his treatment of Byzantium as a *part*, not even an heir, of Rome is universally ignored. No one argues it. It is just not mentioned or it is dismissed by citing the relative disproportion between the few pages devoted to the thousand years of Byzantium and the many devoted to four centuries of decline in the west.

We know, when we stop to think of it, that the historical facts of the six centuries between the "fall" of the Roman Empire in the west and the rise of the states of modern Europe do not fit very intelligibly into the theory that "mankind" progressed through a dark age from the fall of Rome to the modern West. Only by anchoring our attention in Gaul and Britain can we create even momentarily the illusion that such a chain of events took place. Naturally we are interested in ourselves. The lands where our society was later to flower properly receive our attention when we concern ourselves with our own fate. But Britain and Gaul are not "mankind" and however important they may loom in later times, in the fifth and sixth centuries they were an insignificant part of mankind. We are aware that the legal existence of the Roman Empire continued for a thousand years after what we are pleased to call its fall, but in these later centuries we prefer to call it the Byzantine Empire, partly because it was an essentially different society from the Classical empire and partly because another name conveniently removes it from the imaginary chain leading to us. We know that the most important territories of the empire, containing the overwhelming bulk of its population, the territories where Classical civilization had begun and always flourished, were not overrun by the German barbarians. We know that as Gaul, Spain and Britain sank into cultural and economic ruin under their barbarian conquerors, a high civilization flourished in the unconquered Roman Empire and in Sassanid Persia. We know that this high civilization continued undisturbed through the religious Reformation—using the word as we apply it to the cognate event in our own society—which we call the Mohammedan conquest. But though we know these things as isolated historical facts, we still insist that the continuity of "mankind" occurred in the western provinces of the Roman Empire and hence must go from a fifth century "fall" of Rome to eleventh century Europe. Hence when Gibbon insists on treating this thousand year continuation of Rome as an essential element of the history of Rome, we cannot follow him. This "Rome" leads not to the modern West but to the Orthodox Greeks and Moslems of today.

But Gibbon had to handle a difficult matter. He was a pioneer to the extent that he sought to popularize Classical history for the mercantile well-to-do of England and he lacked the foundation of the prevailing intellectual fashion that today permits an avoidance of the problem. Our modern liberal historians are more fortunate. For well over a century accepted history has dwelt upon the Roman Empire in the west, accentuating a purely administrative division as though it represented a political or even cultural division and playing up the linguistic differences of the parts. It became necessary for emotional and philosophical reasons to prove that Rome fell in the fifth century and to accomplish this the surest way was to define whatever it was that fell in the fifth century as the Roman Empire. The most convenient way, as it turned out probably the only way, was to magnify the administrative machinery of the east-west division, to focus the reader's attention on the western administrative areas and then, when the continuity of this particular line of administration came to an end in military disaster, to proclaim as the fall of Rome the fall of what the reader had now forgotten was not originally the Roman Empire at all.

The full development of this piece of historical sleight of hand was later and Gibbon lacked an audience already trained for the proper response. He was faced with a practical problem. He knew that the east-west division was wholly administrative and that the language difference had existed without influence for centuries. If Constantine was a Roman emperor— and everyone, himself and his contemporaries included, said he was—then so were the later Christian emperors like Theodosios, Valentinian, Honorius, Justinian. And if Justinian, so were the obviously Byzantine rulers like Irene and Leo, Basil and all the strange Greek and Armenian dynasties to the very end. There was no place where the name or the formal legal continuity of the Roman Empire came to an end until 1453. And so Gibbon felt bound to include these eastern provinces with their unbroken political continuity, not as an heir but as a part of the Roman Empire.

The modern version that Byzantium belonged to a different civilization from that of Rome is correct factually, but is left only as an assertion of fact without explaining the difficulty that bothered Gibbon: where did the Roman Empire stop and the Byzantine begin?

There is a further and very serious difficulty here. Modern historians have come far from the war-and-politics conscious historians of the past. They deal quite comfortably with cultural and social forces and see in them, usually, deeper significance than the transient forms of the political surface. From the modern point of view, and quite soundly, the Roman Empire represented far more than the military victories of the Roman armies. It had a Roman political form but as a civilized historical entity it was a product of the whole Classical civilization, Hellenic as well as Roman. In all the aspects of culture it was as much an Athenian empire as it was a Roman, in some respects perhaps more so. No one, then or since, has ever pictured the Roman annexation of the political remnants of the Hellenic city states as an alien conquest like those attempted by Darius and Xerxes. The Roman Empire represented the political consolidation of the whole Classical world, as the Athenian might have if the Peloponnesian War had been successful. The Romans were considered boors from the far west with no manners and little culture, as Europeans consider Americans, but not alien barbarians, "outsiders." They did not destroy Hellas. They continued it.

This then being what Rome was, the official "fall" of the Roman Empire in the fifth century seems rather an invention to solve an intellectual difficulty than a historical fact discovered in the flow of events. What precisely did "fall" in the fifth century? First, the imperial administrative machinery in the west. Then certain recently acquired territories of the empire were overrun and settled by the barbarians. Finally Italy was conquered by Alaric's Goths, but the *Hellenic* world was not overrun. Almost none of it passed even briefly under barbarian control. And even many of the barbarian inroads in the west were pushed back. Africa was reconquered from the Vandals, southern Spain and Italy and the head of the Adriatic from the Goths. The city of Rome itself was retaken and, along with the major cities of Italy, held for nearly two hundred years. What was not reconquered were the lands where Western society was to rise half a millennium afterwards, but that fact has no conceivable bearing on the history of *Rome*.

Long after our official fall of Rome all the lands where the Classical civilization had lived and grown stood intact under the unbroken political continuum of the empire. Even after the city of Rome itself was lost, this loss was a matter of no ascertainable significance. The name had long since become the name of the empire and the city itself had long ceased to be the capital and had indeed been of no importance culturally or politically for at least two centuries. Athens, Syracuse, Corinth, Ephesus, Alexandria, all these famous Classical cities still stood and still flourished under the continuing empire.

So far as the Classical world is concerned, all that our world-shaking "fall of Rome" would seem to amount to is the loss of some recent conquests of non-Hellenic and non-Roman lands and the loss, but not even that in the fifth century, of the city of Rome, after that city had become of no importance. And because it was no longer of any importance, the empire made no serious efforts to hold it. Should we take the position that the loss of one ancient, historic, but useless, city either marked or caused the end of a millennial society still, to all appearances, flourishing on the lands where it had always lived? It really is not too hard to brush aside our natural preoccupation with ourselves and see what the events that we call the "fall of Rome" really were.

The disappearance of Classical society from the face of the earth is not a simple matter, but the events that we call the fall of Rome were not the occasion of that disappearance and are simple. These events in substance add up to this: the far northern and western provinces of the Roman Empire, Spain, northern Italy, Gaul, Britain, and the bit of Germany, lands where the Classical civilization had never grown but had been brought by Roman arms, and in most areas only a few centuries before, were overrun and never reconquered. That is what happened and that is all that happened. It appears as a cataclysm to us because these were the lands where Western society was to arise, but in the history of Classical civilization it is barely a stir.

We can speculate either way we please, whether it was a world disaster or a world deliverance for the Roman Empire to be driven out of these lands, but either speculation is immaterial to the fate of Classical culture itself. It may be all-important to us Westerners whether Classical society held or lost its recent conquests in the north and west. Down in the ancient heart of that society in Hellas and Magna Graecia, what difference did it make that these distant annexations were retained or abandoned? They were Roman plantations of day before yesterday. They were not the cities of Aristotle, Praxiteles, Phidias, Plato, Thucydides and Archimedes.

We have the historical record of another great and aged society, China, which was wracked by barbarian inroads, even conquered by them, which was the object of extreme conversion by alien religions but still maintained the unbroken continuity of its style and culture. The Buddhists made immense conversion in China in the third and fourth centuries A.D. The Nestorian Christians, the Mazdaists and the Mohammedans converted extensively, but less widely, from the eighth to the fourteenth. Western Christianity after a brief attempt in the fourteenth resumed its efforts late in the seventeenth. The whole land was overrun by the Mongols in the thirteenth century and by the Manchus in the seventeenth. And yet through all these alien pressures and military disasters, the same essential society continued through all the eighteen centuries that separate the dynasties of Han and Ch'ing.

In the Roman world everything was the reverse. With an unbroken legal continuity of emperors, unlike China, the empire ruled by the Julian-Claudian house bore no resemblance to that ruled by the Comnenian dynasty. In this extraordinary process of converting the Classical empire into the Byzantine Empire, our fascination with ourselves and our notion of our own origins has fixed our attention on the crude military operations in the west and led us to magnify the loss of a few unimportant and sparsely inhabited provinces into the *coup de grâce* of a great society.

The story is more complicated and much more difficult to follow. Military operations are easily identified and their consequences show in the immediate flow of events. The complex changes in the whole culture and way of life of a people are slower and seemingly less spectacular. Furthermore, there is no other example known to us in the history of the world of such a process as the conversion of the Classical Roman Empire into the Orthodox Byzantine. India was invaded but not absorbed by either the Mohammedans or the West. Egypt, it is true, was superficially Hellenized by the Classical society and later completely absorbed by the Mohammedan conquerors, but Egypt had long been the prey of alien conquerors and had sunk to a mere province of other peoples' empires. At the end of the second century, the Roman Empire appeared to be the lord of the western world.

If Augustus, Tiberius and Claudius were Roman emperors, and they obviously were, and Andronicus, Isaac II and Alexius III were not Roman emperors, as they obviously were not, somewhere in this unbroken legal chain of emperors there should be a point where the last emperor of Rome was succeeded by the first emperor of Byzantium. There is no such point but there is an area. The mere numbers of the emperors show it. In the 207 years from the accession of Augustus to the death of Marcus Aurelius there were sixteen presumably legal emperors of Rome. In the 104 years from the death of Marcus to the accession of Diocletian there were twenty-eight. In the succeeding 190 years from the accession of Diocletian to the death of Leo II, the years in which the western provinces were lost and Christianity became the state religion, there were eighteen, counting only the emperors of the whole empire and of the eastern division. In contrast, during the 110 years in which there were separate emperors of the west, there were fifteen such emperors while there were but eight during the same period in the east. (Theodosius I is counted in both lists.)

The average life expectancy of any class of persons is a statistical entry that may be of considerable significance and these crude figures alone suggest that there were two periods where something extremely serious was occurring in the Roman Empire: 180 to 284 throughout the whole empire and 364 to 475 in the western division. Actually, however, the last figure is of itself meaningless. After the death of Theodosius I and the division of the empire between his sons, Arcadius and Honorius in 395, the power of the western emperors was only nominal. Arcadius gave up an inheritance that Honorius was unable to defend. In his reign the Goths were the real masters of most of Italy, Gaul and Spain. Under his successor, Valentinian III, the Vandals took western Africa. During the twenty years following the death of Valentinian III, nine puppets held the title at the pleasure of Odoacer, the Gothic chieftain, until the latter tired of the farce and suppressed it, announcing instead, his dutiful but meaningless allegiance to Zeno, new sole Roman emperor at Constantinople. This allegiance for some reason is never counted as continuing the Roman Empire in the west, but it was no more empty and just as legal as the fiction of all the emperors in the west since Honorius.

The earlier period of multiplicity of emperors is quite different. This century and four years does not mark the loss of a single important province, nor a break in the legal continuity of the institutions of the empire, nor the adoption of the Christian religion. It marks instead the extinction of Classical society. Marcus Aurelius died a Roman emperor. Diocletian came to the throne a Byzantine.

Consider first a matter of obvious importance to us today, money. Roman and Greek money was exclusively coinage. Nothing resembling the bill system of Egypt or our own credit mechanism existed. Coinage was at once money and the medium of exchange, that is, it performed the functions of our debt structure, our bank check system, and our circulating currency. Under Caesar the *aureus* contained 8.18 grams of gold. Nero reduced it to 7.4. By the reign of Septimius Severus (193-211) it contained less than 3 grams. Under his son Caracalla (211-217), the *aureus* disappeared as worthless to be succeeded by the *antoninianus*, containing at first a trace of silver but by the reign of Claudius II (268), degenerating to copper and usually lead with a touch of silver wash. Prices acted accordingly, despite innumerable imperial edicts ordering them to remain fixed.

With Diocletian, the process came to an end, not with the re-establishment of sound money but with the disappearance of money as a medium of exchange. It is true that Diocletian established a new coinage, largely silver, with a firm standard of metallic value, but it no longer circulated as in a sophisticated, urban economy. It counted as a measure of value but it passed from one owner to another only on rare and exceptional occasions, as metallic money passed in the early Middle Ages. It was money in the sense that prices were quoted in terms of its units, but it was no longer tendered in exchange for goods. Goods and services were exchanged directly. From Diocletian on, tax laws and payrolls, army and administrative, tell the story. No longer are these in terms of money, but of lands and goods. The tax laws of these emperors call for payment in bread, wine, oil, lard, forage for animals, clothes, mules. By Valentinian I (364), it was even forbidden for landlords to attempt to collect rent in anything but goods and services. Cash was not wanted.

Necessarily, imperial payments had also to be made in goods. Great and minor officers of state had to be paid in sustenance and, for more enduring rewards, in land. The salaried soldier became the sustenance soldier rewarded on retirement with land which his son could inherit if he in turn was willing to serve.

To us who live inextricably enmeshed in a money economy, the significance of so drastic a change in economic life should be apparent with only the briefest reflection. In the days of the Julian-Claudian emperors, Roman society was as completely dominated by money as our own. Hardly two hundred years afterwards money had disappeared. It was not simply that it was inflated to valuelessness. That too had happened, but in Diocletian's Rome no new money took the place of the worthless old as in Western states that have debased their money. Instead, the use of money came to an end and feudal barter replaced it. Nor was this solely the result of the terrible destruction of life and property during the anarchy and barbarian invasions of the third century. These had an enormous, crushing effect on commerce, but with the restoration of order and firm government in the beginning of the fourth century, production of goods and services revived, though not the old money and slave economy. If we consider the consequence that would result in our own times from such a change in our entire way of life, we can estimate how deep must have been the revolution in Roman life during the third century.

The changes in the army were equally profound. The ancient legion was broken into six independent detachments scattered at strong points, not only along the frontier, but throughout the interior of the empire. Cavalry made its appearance, no longer an occasional auxiliary as in Caesar's day but the center of tactical operations. Heavy individual armor and great reliance on archers altered the whole method of Roman warfare. The title of "duke" (*dux*) appeared for the high army commander, that of "count" (*comes*) for the personal agent of the emperor who took over more and more the management of imperial affairs.

The territorial organization of the empire was completely altered. Instead of the ancient *civitates* and *provinciae*, the Roman Empire became based upon the *iugum*, an economic concept—so many acres of productive land, an area containing so many bearing olive trees—whatever division, differing necessarily province by province and crop by crop, that would produce a livelihood for one peasant family. These *iuga*, which became the basis for assessment in kind on their proprietors, were assembled into *civitates*—an old name but an entirely different institution—and these in turn into provinces, now increased to more than a hundred and incorporated into a new administrative area whose name has survived, the diocese, ruled by the emperor's vicar.

And in these ninety years appeared also that powerful political figure unknown to the Classical world and to us, but a commonplace to the Byzantines and Mohammedans, the court eunuch.

The decadence of Classical art in this period is taught in every school book. Constantine could do no better than rip reliefs from the arches of Trajan and Marcus Aurelius to decorate his own. In such bas-relief and sculpture as was still made, the Classical taste for the human body gave place to drapery for pictorial effect. Stone was no longer worked with a chisel but with drill, a tool never used by Classical sculptors but a favorite of the Egyptians. The old Classical sense of the importance of all the surface was replaced by alternation of intricately designed areas and unimportant, bare space between.

The only exceptions to the general decline noted by the school books are the mosaics, the Christian basilicas and a few "pagan" temples in the east. But while decline is a fair evaluation against Classical art, since the new had no purpose of symbolizing what the old had done, it is a meaningless consideration if it is slanted towards Western art eight hundred years later. It was not Western art that was imprisoned within a dying Classical surface. Here the end of the road is clear at its commencement: Byzantium and Islam, where there were no plastic arts, where the graven image was an affront to God, where abstract design became the principal means of plastic expression. The early mosaics were still pictorial, but they are far better designs than they are pictures. Like the dome of the Pantheon, this anti-representational tendency appearing in Imperial Rome in the third century is not just an oddity marking the end of Classical art, though it does that; it is equally the earliest expression in Italy of a style that was destined to be the master style over the eastern Mediterranean for more than a thousand years.

The early Christian basilica of Italy appears to be somewhat more of an oddity because it was a type of building that never equalled the domed basilica in the east. Nevertheless even it, built as it was from the wrecked pieces of Classical buildings, carried in it one of these same seeds that was to come to great flower among the Byzantines and the Moslems: the arch on column.

So commonplace is this feature to us today, and so frequently is it found in Renaissance construction, that it is popularly considered a normal feature of Classical art. On the contrary, its first appearance in any public building is in the basilica of Constantine. What seems to us such an ordinary idea had never been used until the first Christian emperor, until the very last and open act that symbolized that Classical society existed no more. And again, like the dome and non-representational art, it was not a local fluke but an artistic arrangement that survived throughout the life of Byzantium and Islam.

It was not barbarism as Gibbon thought that was rising within the disintegrating forms of the Classical empire. It was Levantine feudalism, Levantine art, thought and taste, above all Levantine religiousness, and these were in control of the structure of the state and the style of society many years before Constantine changed the name under which he worshiped God from Sol Invictus to Jesus Christ.

The religious identity of these Levantine churches is obscured by the fact that the only contemporary detailed statements about them have survived in the works of their most bitter Christian opponents. "Cutting the throats of wretched boys and sacrificing children of hapless parents and opening up the entrails of new born babes," are among the crimes charged against some third century "magians," presumably Mithraists,[1] undoubtedly with as much truth as the charge that the Christians universally practiced incest and cannibalism.

The only identifiable rival Levantine church in the early third century was Mithraism, the only form in which Mazdaism seems to have been widespread as an organized church within the empire. There is, indeed, a strong and significant parallelism here. Both Judaism and Mazdaism, when they operated within the imperial frontier, did so successfully only in the form of their Hellenized offspring. Later a heretical offshoot of Mazdaism, Manicheanism, spread as an outlaw religion, and one powerful heretical Christian church, that organized by Marcion, existed for a time. There were many sects and splinter movements to which it is customary to apply the name "Gnosticism" and there were even attempts to organize a Levantine church using the names of the Classical gods. There was also Neo-

---

[1] Eusebius, *The Ecclesiastical History,* VII, x, 4. The translation here and in the balance of this chapter is that of Oulton and Lawlor in the Loeb Classical Library. However, the word here translated "magians" they translate "magicians." The Greek word is the same as that used at Matthew ii, 1 and Acts xiii, 6, indicating adherents of a rival religion, rather than what is meant today by the word magician.

platonism and in the early years Stoicism, both posing in the Classical manner as schools of philosophy, but both becoming bodies of Levantine religious feeling.

The core of the thought of all these churches, sects and philosophies was the discovery and promulgation of the secret of salvation. It was not quite the concept of salvation that has been the common doctrine in the West, that is, forgiveness of sin so that the soul in the hereafter may enjoy Heaven and escape the agonies of hell. This is the sense we usually read into the Levantine texts, but this was not exactly what was involved from a Levantine understanding of the world. To all the Levantines, salvation consisted in being saved from the power of the Prince of Darkness who ruled the present physical world, so it was not only escape from a future but from a present hell, which was still a hell even though the Prince of Darkness, as part of his plot, often made it delightful for his elect and even not always too unpleasant for the godly. Each sect and church had knowledge of the secret that gained this salvation, so to that extent it would be proper to call them all gnostic. All were dualistic, some frankly, some implicitly, but all saw the physical world of time and history as both ungodly and ephemeral, very far from God or actually the dominion of his enemy.

Mithras is not the sun, despite the fact that the Romans called him Sol Invictus, but the "light," the messenger, the *logos* of God. He is born of a rock, not a Virgin, but only the lowly shepherds understand the miracle and adore the infant. He then clothes himself with the leaves from a fig tree and proceeds forth to conquer the world from the god of darkness and evil. In the process he encounters the sacred bull created by God and is ordered to kill it so that from the blood of this sacrifice of God's own creation, the life of the world might flow. Then follows a universal flood from which one man and some cattle are rescued by a marvelous boat, a great fire, and finally Mithras is translated to Heaven where he awaits, ever helping the loyal, the upright and the chaste until at the last day he shall descend to open the tombs and judge the dead, when the wicked shall be consigned to hell and the blessed drawn up to Heaven.

The ritual that accompanied this was close to that of the Christian: baptism, communion in bread, wine and water, holy water and candles, observance of Sundays and December 25. Nor is there any evidence that either myth or ritual was borrowed from the Christians. All were complete in Mithraism when it appeared on Roman soil in the middle of the first century. This was the faith of Constantine's family and of his boyhood.

The intellectual side of this wave of anti-Classicism, of essentially Levantine thought, permeating the Roman world from the second century onward goes under the name of Neoplatonism. But even it was intellectual only in relation to the mythological content of the new religion. It too was concerned with personal salvation after death, but it sought for its holy writings among the Classical philosophers rather than among the historical and mystical writings of the Jews and the Persians. The first great systematic writer of Neoplatonism was Plotinus, a man of Roman family born in Egypt and brought up in the east where he spent his early manhood. In his *Enneads*, he sets out a system of mystical philosophy that bears no relation to the rational philosophy that had been the objective of all the different schools of Classical philosophy. To him the corporeal world, the sole concern of all the Classical philosophers, no longer has any real existence. Although Plotinus is not a dualist to the extent of postulating two antagonistic forces, good and evil, light and darkness, struggling for the mastery of the visible world, nevertheless against the world soul which emanates from God and generates the universe there stands opposed the dark formlessness of matter which is without energy, to be sure, but is in principle evil. Only the logos emanating from God can mold this formless principle of darkness into the corporeal facts of the visible world. Man's sad lot is that through lust and sensuality, he has to some extent dissociated himself from the world soul and seeks, falsely, to make himself even more independent. His salvation lies the other way, by shedding the false values of all things earthly and seeking his way back to communion with the world soul from which he has departed. For this, of course, the ascetic life is required. From this it likewise follows that knowledge can not be obtained by studying the illusory, material surface of the universe, but by closer access to God through nearer return to the world soul, which again, by requiring a shedding of corporeality, can only be attained in the ecstasy of a trance.

Plotinus' great pupil and the popularizer of his doctrines was Porphyry, a Syrian who taught at Rome and died probably in the early years of Constantine's reign. More clearly than Plotinus, Porphyry taught that the prime function of what he called philosophy was the salvation of the individual soul. To him evil was more the evil desires of the human heart than the dark principle of matter. Hence what was important was an ascetic life. So far as the myths of the various religions were concerned, these did not matter. Therefore he attacked bitterly the current religious practices of his time and yet defended the myths of the pagan gods. His attacks on the Christians, for example, were not against Jesus or the teachings of the gospels but against the practices of the Christians, so that had he not defended the non-Christian cults he could perhaps be classed as a heretical Christian himself. He said of Origen [2] that his outer life "was that of a Christian and contrary to law; but as far as his views of things and of God are concerned, he thought like the Greeks, whose conceptions he overlaid

[2] Eusebius, *The Ecclesiastical History*, vi, 19.

with foreign myths." This compliment was universally returned by the Christians who declared that the Neoplatonists obtained all their central doctrines from the Christian books.

The political triumph of Orthodox Christianity affected the philosophical aspects of the Neoplatonist movement very little. The attempt of Porphyry and his pupil Iamblichus to insert the new religious philosophy under the names of the old pagan cults came to an end, but the work of interpreting the Classical philosophers into harmony with the new religion continued. It reached its conclusion late in the fifth century with the work of Proclus who established a canon of text and interpretation of Plato and Aristotle as they should appear from the world view of Plotinus. It was this canon that became "Greek" philosophy in the Byzantine and Mohammedan worlds, and in due course, for many centuries in the West. Even today our text of Aristotle is a tissue of this Levantine editing and interpolation.

All these movements, despite their different names for God's messenger, constituted in their inward feeling "of things and of God" one great religious expression. These religions from Mithraism to Neoplatonism all had in common with all the early Christian sects one identical religious view of the world. In all of them good and evil struggled for mastery of the ephemeral world of visible things, which itself was little more than an illusory forefront of the real and invisible world that lay veiled behind visible things. All saw the emanation of God, the *logos*, the light, as the immediate, effective cause of all things. All saw the great blessing of religion to be the freeing of man from his mortal dross and his reunion with God, who was at once his creator and his saviour. All preached and sternly attempted to practice the ascetic life. All knew that knowledge was not gained by study of the forefront of the world but by the knowledge of God, which was gained only in the ecstasy of revelation. So for all, there was immediately a set of sacred books, where the knowledge of God acquired by the founders in their ecstasy was recorded for those who did not receive this blessing. Both Porphyry and St. Paul describe this process of revelation with complete candor.

These sects and religions differed among themselves in the source of the myths in which they encased the sacred story. The Jewish, Persian and Greek textual sources are obvious enough. But all made their different text tell the same holy story of creation and redemption.

The view that Orthodox Christianity fought its way to power against the ancient pagan religion of Classical antiquity has long been dropped by the historians of religion, but it persists in the popular image. But Christianity did not overthrow the gods of Greece and Rome. The irreligion of the late republic and early empire had done that. Religion in Virgil is a pious form out of respect for public convention. In Juvenal there is not even that. In Seneca, Epictetus and Marcus Aurelius at least a faint tone of respect reappears, but it is a religiousness of utter weariness, of resignation to the harsh and meaningless fate of this world where death is neither a punishment nor a salvation, but simply a release from the intolerable *tedium vitae* of a finished and dying society.

The establishment of Christianity as the church of the new political structure that emerged from the anarchy of the third century followed by only a few years the organization of that structure by Diocletian. It had become in fact the Byzantine Empire, though it did not call itself by that name, then or ever. Byzantium has been our name for it, never its own. The political organization still calling itself the Roman Empire had become a semi-feudal Levantine state, but what was its nationality? The Levantine concept of nationality differed as profoundly from the Classical concept as it does from our Western. To the Classical world nationality meant citizenship in a *polis* and this concept lasted through the reigns of the Antonines. To us it means allegiance to a territorial sovereign, personal or corporate. To the Levantine world it meant, and to a great extent it still means, membership in the same religious sect. The Classical Roman Empire could embrace an infinity of local gods, which to us would seem to mean a multiplicity of religions. It did not. Innumerable gods, each entitled to his own cult, were one religion in Classical society. But when the empire became a Levatine feudal state it could no longer, like the Classical empire, have a multiplicity of cults. It had to have one true god and only believers in this god could constitute the nation of which the empire was the political apparatus. Hence the great political struggle of the century from Septimius Severus to Constantine was to establish the nationality—in the Levantine sense—of the emerging Byzantine Empire. Of which church was the empire to be the political state? Christianity engaged in no struggle with Classical paganism; that was long dead. Its struggles were with the Levantine churches like itself, some denying Christ, some venerating Him. Some used the same myths. Some used quite different symbols. But all expressed the same beliefs in the nature of God, of this world and of the world to come. The new religion was founded in the Roman Empire well before 300. The battle was to determine which church, and therefore which nation, would prevail.

The details of the political history of this battle are lost forever because the historical myth of the victor did not picture the struggle as one between rival nationalities, embryonic to be sure, but still national in a Levantine sense. As a result there is almost no formal historical survival that relates the military anarchy of the third century with the political struggles of rival Levantine sect-nations. Received history does not even recognize the existence of such a struggle because it does not admit the existence of such entities as Levantine sect-nations, and to it the rise of a religion, even a Levantine religion, is fundamentally an operation of propaganda and belief, not a political struggle involving war, revolution and dynastic power. Thus in received history Christianity does not acquire a true political history until Constantine, in other words, not until the essential political struggle is victoriously concluded. Hence the anarchy of the third century must be represented as merely the pointless personal struggle of candidates for the imperial throne, simply as an example—actually quite inexplicable—of "militarism." Thus the military anarchy and what has come down to us as the "persecutions" of the Christians appear to be unrelated, and the exact coincidence of their occurrence is coincidence and no more.

Ecclesiastical historians, both ancient and modern, tell a single, connected story of persecution of the Christians from Nero to Constantine, but the story always breaks into two quite different parts and the division point is the reign of Septimius Severus. Prior to his reign there were no systematic persecutions and, to the extent that individual Christians were martyred, little sure information about it was known even to third century Christian writers. It seems tolerably clear that most Christians who suffered martyrdom under the Classical empire either deliberately sought martyrdom or were the victims of personal animosity. The correspondence of Pliny and Trajan, even if it be forged—or perhaps just touched up a little—accurately reflects the condition under the Classical empire. Christians were not bothered unless as individuals they aroused enmity, official or private, for some other reasons. When that happened their Christianity made it easy to injure them *as* Christians, but not *because* they were Christians. The notion that the blood of the martyrs is the seed of the Church is true only so long as there are not too many martyrs. Very possibly the traditional slaughter under Nero has a basis of fact, but Nero's conduct was that of an individual madman, not a reflection of imperial policy. Origen, writing about 249, says that the number of martyrs up to that time had not been very great, and his figures include victims of the Severan persecution.

From Septimius Severus on, however, the story is quite different. It is no longer a case of sporadic individual victims about whom we really know almost nothing, but a systematic legislative and administrative action against the Christians as a political body. So far as the number of individuals actually put to death in the later persecution is concerned, we are again without reliable information, but the fact of action against the church is indisputable.

A series of persecutions is recorded by the ecclesiastical historians, principally by Eusebius, under Septimius Severus, under Decius, under Valerian, under Aurelean and under Diocletian. The persecution under Severus was directed only against the attempt to make new converts. The persecution of the other emperors was against all Christians. As Eusebius tells it, of course, these persecutions were inspired by motiveless evil; for Eusebius tells us nothing of Christian history that is not wholly edifying, but even in his text there is an occasional hint of explanation of the curious see-saw of persecution and favor that marks this century of anarchy.

"When Alexander (Severus) had brought his principate to an end after thirteen years he was succeeded by Maximin Caesar. He, through ill will towards the house of Alexander, since it consisted for the most part of believers, raised a persecution, ordering the leaders of the Church alone to be put to death. . . ."[3] What Eusebius does not tell us is that Alexander had gained power by military revolt against his predecessor, and that Maximin, in turn, led a successful revolt against Alexander.

"When after six whole years, Gordian brought his government of the Romans to an end, Philip . . . succeeded to the principate. It is recorded that he being a Christian. . . ."[4] Philip had been Praetorian Prefect under Gordian, an able soldier who had defeated both the Persians and the Germans, and gained the imperial throne by murdering Gordian.

"When Philip had reigned for seven years he was succeeded by Decius. He, on account of his enmity toward Philip, raised a persecution against the churches . . ."[5] Philip and Decius engaged in civil war during which Philip was killed.

"When Decius had reigned for an entire period of less than two years, he was forthwith murdered along with his sons, and Gallus succeeded him." Eusebius then quotes Dionysius, bishop of Alexandria at the time: "But not even did Gallus recognize the fault of Decius, nor yet did he look to what had caused his fall, but he stumbled against the same stone that was before his eyes. For when his reign was prospering, and matters were going according to his mind, he drove away the holy man who were supplicating God for his peace and health. Therefore along with them he banished also their prayers on his behalf."[6]

"Gallus and his associates held the principate for less than two entire years, and then were removed out of the way; and Valerian along with his son Gallienus succeeded to the government." Eusebius then quotes again at length from Dionysius in regard to Valerian: ". . . note especially the nature of his previous conduct, how mild and friendly he was to the men of God. For not a single one of the emperors before him were so kindly and favorably disposed towards them, not even those who were said to

[3] Eusebius, *op. cit.* VI, xxviii, 1.
[4] Eusebius, *op. cit.* VI, xxxiv, 1.
[5] Eusebius, *op. cit.* VI, xxxix, 1.
[6] Eusebius, *op. cit.* VII, i, 1.

have been openly Christians, as he manifestly was, at the beginning. Indeed all his house had been filled with godly persons and was a church of God. But (Macrianus, apparently supported by the Mithraists in Egypt) persuaded him to get rid of them as being rivals and hinderers. Now this man (Macrianus) in his mad desire for the imperial rule of which he was not worthy put forward his two sons."[7]

"But not long afterwards (Valerian's) son (Gallienus) succeeding to the sole power conducted the government with more prudence, and immediately by means of edicts put an end to the persecution against us." Macrianus and his two sons were captured and killed.[8]

Finally with the persecution under Diocletian, Eusebius points out that it began against Christians in the army. "Then one could see great numbers of those in the army most gladly embracing civil life, so that they might not prove renegades in their piety towards the creator. (They had) a choice whether they would obey and enjoy the rank they held, or else be deprived of it if they continued to disobey. A great many soldiers of Christ's kingdom preferred to confess Him than retain the seeming glory and prosperity that they possessed. And already in rare cases one or two of these were receiving not only loss of honor but even death in exchange for their godly steadfastness, for as yet the instigator of the plot was working with a certain moderation and daring to proceed into blood only in a few instances; fearing presumably the multitude of believers and hesitating to plunge into the war against us all at once. But when he had prepared himself still further for the battle, it is quite impossible to recount the number or the splendour of God's martyrs."[9] Some splendid martyrdoms are then described in detail, followed by this passage: "Such were the things that were done in Nicomedia at the beginning of the persecution. But not long afterward, when some in the district known as Melitene (in Armenia) and again others in Syria had attempted to take possession of the empire, an imperial command went forth that the presidents of the churches everywhere should be thrown into prison and bonds."[10]

This is the first place where Eusebius' pious mask slips and we catch a tiny glimpse of political fact: *after* an attempt by Christians in Syria and Armenia to seize the empire, Diocletian moved against the ecclesiastical organization. Indeed everything about the Diocletian "persecution" shows that it was simply one episode in a long civil war, in which cruelties against the Christians are lovingly recorded by the Christian victors but the inevitable counter cruelties consistently ignored. For nineteen years Dio-

---

[7] Eusebius, *op. cit.* VII, x, 1-3.
[8] Eusebius, *op. cit.* VII, xiii, 1.
[9] Eusebius, *op. cit.* VIII, iv, 2-4.
[10] Eusebius, *op. cit.* VIII, vi, 8.

cletian had ruled the empire without injuring the Christians. Early in his reign he had required that Manicheans be burned alive and it seems probable that this act, so satisfactory to both Christians and Mithraists, illustrates his policy of avoiding a forced decision between the two powerful Levantine sects within the empire. However, his projected abdication, which he planned and accomplished at the end of his twentieth year, brought the conflict again into the open.

Diocletian was attempting to establish a mechanism of succession which was neither hereditary nor subject to the immediate whim of the troops. His system was to have two senior emperors with the title of Augustus and two juniors with the title of Caesar. The four men were to govern as a collegiate body, though each had areas assigned to his immediate administration, and the senior Augustus alone could create new emperors of either rank. On Diocletian's retirement in May, 305, his co-Augustus, Maximian, retired with him and the new Augusti were Galerius and Constantius Chlorus, both formerly Caesars. The new Caesars named by Diocletian before he abdicated were Galerius' son-in-law and nephew, Maximinus Daia, and Severus. Constantine, the son of Constantius Chlorus, who had hoped to be Caesar instead of Severus, on the death of his father at York in 306, revolted and named himself Augustus. At the same time Maxentius, son of the restored Emperor Maximian, revolted and gained control of Italy. The struggle immediately came into the open with Constantine in the west supporting the Christians and Maximinus Daia in Syria and Anatolia supporting the Mithraists. There followed some years of intermittent civil war in which Maxentius and Severus were both killed and a new Augustus, Licinius, named by Galerius shortly before his death. Constantine and Licinius then joined against Maximinus Daia, killed him and took over control in the east. Eusebius: "When Maximinus [Daia] was thus removed—he was the only one left of the enemies of godliness and showed himself the worst of all—by the grace of Almighty God the renewal of the churches from the foundation was set on foot, and the word of Christ received a due increase upon its former freedom while the impiety of the enemies of godliness was covered with the most abject shame and dishonor. For Maximinus [Daia] himself was the first to be proclaimed by the new rulers as a common enemy of all and posted in public edicts on tablets as a most impious, most hateful and God-hating tyrant. . . . Next, all the honors of the other enemies of godliness also were taken away, and all who were of the party of Maximinus [Daia] were slain, especially those in high government positions who had been honored by him, and who indulged in violent abuse against our doctrine; when Licinius came to Antioch he made a search for charlatans and plied with tortures the prophets and priests of the new-made idol and inflicted a just punishment upon them all, putting to death after a long series of tortures the partners in charlatany. To all these were added the sons of Maximinus [Daia]. Thus verily when the impious had been purged the kingdom that belonged to them was preserved steadfast and undisputed for Constantine and Licinius alone, who made it their first action to purge the world of enmity against God."[11]

This was not the afterthought of a historian. These opinions are those of a contemporary and, indeed, Eusebius wrote that last sentence too soon and himself apparently cut it out of his later editions when he added the tenth book of his history after Constantine had destroyed Licinius and made himself sole emperor. Again Eusebius has no doubt about the exact religious alliances: "in (Licinius') decision to make war at close quarters against Constantine, he was already hastening to battle also against the God of the universe whom, as he knew, Constantine worshipped; and so he designed an attack, quietly and silently at first, upon his godly subjects, who had never at any time done any harm at all to his rule. And he did this because his innate wickedness had perforce brought upon him terrible blindness. Thus he neither kept before his eyes the memory of those who persecuted the Christians before him, nor of those whom he himself destroyed and punished for the evil deeds they had pursued. . . . First he drove away every Christian from his palace. Then he gave orders that the soldiers in cities were to be singled out and deprived of honorable rank, unless they chose to sacrifice to demons. . . . in the final stage of his madness he proceeded against the bishops, and deeming them opposed to his doing forthwith plotted against them, not openly as yet—for he feared his superior—(Constantine was not his superior), but once more with secrecy and guile. . . . (finally) the Emperor (Constantine) the friend of God, reckoning that Licinius was no longer to be endured, summoned his sound powers of reason, and tempering the stern qualities of justice with humanity, determined to succor those who were being evilly treated under the tyrant's power. . . . the defender of the good went forth with that most humane Emperor, his son Crispus. . . . Then inasmuch as they had God, the universal king and Son of God the Saviour of all, as their guide and ally, the father and son both together easily won the victory. . . . Constantine the mighty Victor, resplendent with every virtue that godliness bestows, together with his son Crispus, an Emperor most dear to God and in all respects like unto his father, recovered the east that belonged to them, and formed the Roman Empire, as in the days of old, into a single united whole, bringing under their peaceful rule all of it from the rising sun around about in two directions, north as well as south, even to the uttermost limits

[11] Eusebius, *op. cit.* IX, xi, 1,3.

of the declining day. Thus when all tyranny had been purged away, the kingdom that belonged to them was preserved steadfast and undisputed under Constantine and his son alone: who, when they made it their very first action to cleanse the world from hatred of God, displayed their love of virtue and of God, their piety and gratitude towards the Deity, by their manifest deeds in the sight of all men."[12]

Constantine defeated Licinius in September, 324. In July, 326 he killed his son Crispus and shortly afterwards had his wife, Fausta, daughter of the old emperor Maximian, murdered. With her fortune, he and his mother Helen financed the excavation at Jersualem that disclosed to the world not only the exact tomb of Christ, but the three crosses of Calvary, that of Christ being identified by the miraculous cure of a sick woman who touched it.

Quite evidently with Eusebius we are not dealing with a Classical historian. Tacitus' portrait of Germanicus is as false as Eusebius' of Constantine, but where the first is made heroic, the second is made pious. It is a trait of all Levantine historians, Greek and Moslem alike, always to see the significance of history displayed not in the struggle of the historian's hero against an enemy hero (which is the structure of all Classical history), but of the historian's saint against the wicked of the enemy. It is part of the profound dualism of the Levant and has been a model long copied in the political pamphleteering of the West.

In regard to the particular use of this technique by Eusebius in his portrait of Constantine, Western historians have long since applied the necessary correction, but Eusebius' equally false picture of the political triumph of Christianity has been left undisturbed. We ignore the Christian emperors who preceded Constantine because the Levantine Christian myth asserts that the great historic role of Constantine was to *tolerate* Christianity. Once tolerated it just naturally grew to be the exclusive sect of the empire. The evident facts are quite different. Christianity had been in fact tolerated since the days of Trajan and edicts of *de jure* toleration went back at least to Alexander Severus. What Constantine did was not to tolerate Christianity but to establish it *de facto* by suppressing its opponents, and their later *de jure* suppression by Theodosius was little but routine.

Classical paganism died of disbelief, of Classical atheism. It was not overthrown by Christianity. Christianity did not emerge victorious from an intellectual and moral struggle with the gods of Homer. It emerged victorious from a bitter civil war against Levantine sect-nations much like itself.

[12] Eusebius, *op. cit.* X, viii, 8,14; ix, 5,6.

There remains one last great field of life and thought where Classical civilization is said to have survived and left a priceless heritage to our own society: the law.

Two questions are involved. From the point of view that is presented here, that all vital elements of Classical society disappeared between Marcus Aurelius and Diocletian, it is necessary to examine what constituted Roman law before and after this period. On the question of the transmission of Roman law to the West, it is necessary to discover what was transmitted. The latter question is the simpler. The transmission was almost wholly the *Corpus Juris Civilis* of Justinian, put together by that emperor at Constantinople in the early years of the sixth century. Other than Justinian's compilation, nothing to which even the name of Roman law could be applied ever reached the West save a few scraps of the Theodosian code incorporated in the early laws of the Gothic and Burgundian conquerors. In substance, "Roman law" in the West has meant only the *Corpus Juris Civilis*.

The structure of Classical Roman law was of two parts. The *jus civile* applying to Roman citizens and the *jus gentium* applying to all other legal persons, and hence not slaves, within the Roman jurisdiction. The first was administered by the Urban Praetor, the second by the Peregrin Praetor. There was no law at all for the slave. He was a piece of property, legally not a human being, even his life being at the private disposal of his master. Each Praetor served for a year and at the beginning of his term announced in the edict for the year the various forms of legal action he would consider and the remedies he proposed to apply. No Praetor's edict was binding on his successors and although a considerable continuity was maintained, the successive Praetors developed a good deal of new law to fit conditions as they arose. Some permanent statute law existed, acts of the Comitia and the Senate, but these largely concerned governmental functions and the bulk of Roman law governing the relations of persons and property was maintained year by year in the Praetors' edicts.

Early imperial times scarcely changed this, for the legislative powers of the emperors were in theory at least limited by Senatorial acceptance and the early emperors made little alteration in the traditional private law of Rome. Almost the only outstanding exception was the legislation initiated by Augustus attempting to improve marital fidelity and encourage the bearing of children by requiring the disherison of childless heirs within certain age limits.

Roman private law of the republic and the early empire was based upon the structure of the Roman family and the paramount importance of form. The Roman family was a social and legal fiction which ignored completely what we consider the ties of blood. The family was the dominion (*potestas*) of the paterfamilias and the only recognized relationships were the agnatic, that is, ascent and descent through persons who were under the same dominion, or would have been except for the death of a common ancestor. Originally marriage transferred a woman from the dominion of her father, or grandfather, to that of her husband or her father-in-law. In later republican and imperial times, this older confarreate marriage became more and more rare, particularly among the wealthy. The new form of marriage, while it left a woman's property intact, kept her as an agnate of her own father and therefore legally related neither to her husband nor her own children.

The paterfamilias cannot be called simply a father, because his authority extended over his wife even when there were no children and over his grandchildren by his sons. All the property of the family, including any property acquired by his sons and unmarried daughters, was legally his, regardless of their age. Correspondingly all their obligations, whether for debt or damages, were equally his. His role went further. As the person legally responsible for his family, he occupied toward them a role that partook of a state office, for he was required to exercise a religious and criminal jurisdiction over them. The power of a paterfamilias to dispose of his property by will, to the complete exclusion of wife and children, if he desired, was unlimited. If he died intestate only his surviving agnates inherited, his wife taking the share of an unmarried daughter if she was under his dominion, but nothing if she had married by the newer forms.

The Classical family was thus primarily an instrument of state and property. Even a word that means what we mean by "family" is lacking in Latin. *Domus* was a home and *familia,* which we translate as family, was a concept that included both family property and the relation to it of heirs who had a right to it. "Household" is perhaps as close to it as English can come. In the standard Roman testament what is bequeathed is described as *"familia pecuniaque mea,"* "my household and my money." The Classical family was not even officially supposed to satisfy the erotic life of men and often not even of women. Not only was an extra-marital erotic life assumed for a man, but it could be quite properly, and often was, homosexual. It is, indeed, an important point in the position of Hadrian as the turning point of the disappearance of Classical civilization that he was the last of the many Roman emperors who were openly homosexual.

The role of the individual as quasi officer of state extended outside the family to legal relations, both criminal and civil, with strangers. The prosecutor of crime was often in fact, and always in theory, whatever private person felt he had been injured by the criminal. In civil action it was the duty of the plaintiff by his own means to bring the defendant into court. A man who received a favorable judgment was obligated himself to enforce it against the loser by seizing his property or even his person if necessary to enforce payment.

Legal procedure was conducted in two steps. The nature and the form of the dispute was first argued out before the Praetor and if the form, and usually an intricate form, was proper and the case fell within one of those classes that the Praetor's edict had announced he would consider, the Praetor himself formulated the factual issue and except in rare cases sent it to a *judex* for decision on the facts sent forward. The *judex* was not an officer of state but a private person satisfactory to both parties. These were the proceedings *in jure* and *in judicio*.

The form of every legal step was of paramount importance. Wills had to have the exact number of seals and signatures. Certain classes of goods could only be validly transferred by touching a pair of scales with a copper coin (*res mancipi*); others passed by simple delivery. In order to bring a legal action at all a plaintiff had to bear a narrowly defined relation to the matter in dispute. For example, a purchase-sale agreement which had been half-completed gave the cheated party a very dubious legal standing. If he had paid the money but not yet received the property due him, he could not plead that he had been robbed because he had never had the property. He could not plead a debt, because the only debt recognized was for money loaned and he had loaned no money. He could not force delivery of what he had bought because if it was a *res mancipi,* the lack of the formal transfer alone withstood any attack, and if it were movable property he held no instrument of pledge covering it. A contract was not a "thing" and as long as Classical Roman jurisprudence lasted, nothing but the most cumbersome and roundabout methods were ever devised to deal with problems of this nature. In substance, it was the personal responsibility of each man to see that he did not get himself into difficulties of such a nature and this, not our modern rendering, is the meaning of *caveat emptor.*

This Roman law of citizens and non-citizens, of the agnate family, of tangible property rights and strict insistence upon form, of what, in effect, amounted to annual reinterpretation by the Praetor, was in fundamentally unchanged substance the law of Rome from the early republic to the reign of Hadrian, a period of some seven hundred years.

With Hadrian began the first slight alterations of substance that mark the beginning of a total and immensely rapid change. Under Hadrian with the Edictum Perpetuum of Salvius Julianus appeared the first attempt to end the law-making function of the Praetors and establish once and for all an eternal body of law, a tendency the importance of which is easier to recognize later when it flowered into the canon of an eternal and *sacred* law, both civil and religious. Under Hadrian also occurred the first breach in the agnate family in the provision that a child could inherit from a non-agnate mother. Antoninus Pius took a similar step by forbidding formal defects in wills to bar an inheritance otherwise presumed to have been desired by the testator. Marcus extended Hadrian's right of inheritance by a child from a non-agnate mother to inheritance by a mother from a non-agnate child.

But it was Septimius Severus and Caracalla, the soldier emperors at the start of the great anarchy, who began the complete transformation of Roman law. It was in the reigns of these emperors that the immense substantive changes of the law began, and it was these reigns that produced the legal writings that became almost the entire body of legal principles of Justinian's Digest.

Form as an important element of legal right rapidly began to disappear. The doctrine of legal fiction, such a vital part of later Mohammedan jurisprudence, made its appearance. A man, for instance who could not have brought an action under the old law because he lacked, say, title to a piece of land and no one could bring such action except the title holder, was fictionally endowed with title for the purpose of the suit. Every impediment of form in the old law was done away with by fictionalizing the existence of whatever was necessary.

Most striking of all, the distinction between *jus civile* and *jus gentium* was abolished; for Caracalla extended citizenship to all the inhabitants of the empire. A little later the remission of cases to a *judex* ceased. Diocletian ordered the Praetors to determine cases themselves if they were not too busy, and Julian, the so-called Apostate, required them to determine all but trivial matters. The judge was no longer a private person satisfactory to the parties but an officer of the state. At the same time, personal enforcement of judgments by the interested parties began to be forbidden, and after Constantine all enforcement and all criminal prosecutions became solely the functions of government officers.

Limits began to be placed on the right of a paterfamilias to disinherit his children, culminating finally with Justinian's Novel 115, which forbade such disherison except for a few specific causes which had to be named in the will. Along with this Justinian in Novels 118 and 127 ended all traces of the agnate family.

What has been received as Roman law and is always called Roman law in the West is, in contrast to the law of the city and Empire of Rome, the *Corpus Juris Civilis* of Justinian. The name itself is recent and unfortunate since it appears to indicate some connection with the old *jus civile* which came to an end 350 years before Justinian. The Corpus itself apparently had no specific name in Justinian's time and a later revision of it by the Emperors Basil and Leo was called the Basilica, which even if anachronistic would be a more pertinent name. The collection itself is in three parts, the Code, a collection of constitutions, that is, in effect, statutes of earlier emperors which were deemed to be still in force, the Digest, also called the Pandects, the collected and edited opinions of the earlier jurisconsults, and the Novels, a collection of Justinian's own legislation.

The Code alone shows the nature of the immense legal change. It contains no constitution earlier than Hadrian, one from his reign, only twenty-three prior to Septimius Severus, one hundred and sixty from his reign, two hundred of Caracalla's and from Diocletian on they became numerous.

But the Digest is the revealing part of Justinian's collection for here are set out the great principles of the new law. The change in statutory requirements might well be explained by changed outer circumstances. The United States Code of today would show few statutes passed prior to 1840, but a change in legal principles and in private law is a change not in the outward organization of a state, but in the inner structure of its institutions and the life and morals of its people.

The Digest, which is represented as the great epitome of centuries of Roman law, is composed almost entirely of the work of four men. Of the three of whom we know enough to identify their existence, not one was a Roman. All three worked together, and all three lived under Septimius Severus and Caracalla: Papinian, Ulpian and Paul. Over half the Digest is the work of these three alone, and of earlier writers other than Gaius and Salvius Julianus, the author of the Edictum Perpetuum under Hadrian, the bulk of the writings are in quotations imbedded in the works of the great three.

There are two different aspects from which the work of these jurists must be considered. The first is obvious, the use made of their writings two hundred and fifty years afterwards by Justinian. The second is more difficult: how far do their writings represent the actual changes in the Roman society of their own time? Were they reflecting what was actually going on about them in their own times or were they attempting to proclaim a new body of legal principles which came to official and social acceptance only many years after their death? Involved in this question is, of course, the basic question, how much of Classical Rome was still in existence by 300 A.D.?

It is true that their canonization as the authors of the legal principles of Byzantium did not begin until Valentinian's law of citations, but the nature of their official position, the subjects with which they concerned themselves and the acts of succeeding emperors indicate that they were not so much prophets as reporters. Prior to their time Roman law was temporary law declared for a year and valid only for that year. Scattered through it were various permanent enactments, special legislation on particular subjects, but there was no general code of law on all subjects that remained always in effect unless repealed by subsequent statute.

Roman law of Classical times has sometimes been compared with English common law because of the large areas in both where there is, or once was, no statutory coverage. Yet it was not a common law as we understand it because it had no binding precedents. The Praetor's annual edict gave the only precedents that were to be followed, and then for only a year. In this respect it followed the style of the older Hellenic cities where law was always a thing of immediate necessity, not of enduring force.

The beginning of a change from this type of law can be seen in Julianus' edict under Hadrian and in that emperor's edict that the unanimous decision of the jurists had the force of law.[13] But with Papinian and Ulpian the change was complete. There was no longer any thought of temporary law to fit changing circumstances, but of a body of eternal, valid legal principles to be binding at all times and upon all men living under the same sovereign. With Gaius there was expressed an entirely new concept of the philosophical basis of law.

Gaius was long afterward said to have lived under the Antonines or Hadrian but there is no contemporary mention of his existence. The only thing that is certain, from the scraps of his writings that have survived, is that he was neither a jurisconsult nor a public official. The earliest record that refers to him is in a law of Theodosius II and Valentinian III in 426, nearly three hundred years after his supposed life, where he is suddenly established as a legal authority equal to Ulpian. Of his writings there survive passages in the Digest, and an independent copy of his *Institutes*.

Gaius in his *Institutes* gives us our chief source of information about Classical Roman law. But as well as being a historian of the dying law of the republic and early empire, Gaius also enunciated some of the deep principles of the new Byzantine law. Legally in his time, if he did in fact live under the Antonines, the *jus gentium* was the law of aliens living under the Roman jurisdiction. It was neither international law supposedly applicable between states nor an ideal law toward which practical legislation should strive. But Gaius invented a new meaning for the term. He applied it to a law established among all men by "natural reason" and kept by all peoples equally. Its foundation he saw as a *jus naturale,* a wholly new legal term, which "nature" taught all

---

[13] *Institutes* i, 7.

living things.[14] To us these views do not seem strange. We have been absorbing them from medieval philosophy and from canon law ever since the West began, though to us they are ideals, not legal principles. But against Classical law they are completely foreign, even as ideals. Though Gaius accounts for but a small part of the Digest, the appearance of the idea of *jus naturale* as the foundation of a universal *jus gentium* makes him a figure of great importance in the shifting of Roman to Byzantine law.

Of the three historically identifiable authors of the Digest, Papinian, Ulpian, and Paul, much more is known. Papinian, probably a Syrian, was the elder, serving as Praetorian Prefect under Septimius Severus while the two younger men, who later succeeded to this office, served under him as assessors. His contribution to the Digest is the least of the three. Ulpian of Tyre, the intimate friend of Alexander Severus who made him Praetorian Prefect, rose to prominence under Caracalla and must have been the legal father of that emperor's extension of Roman citizenship to all inhabitants of the empire in 212, the year of Papinian's murder. Even in the Digest, Ulpian's language on this was still quoted: "Those who are within the Roman dominion are made Roman citizens."[15] Over a third of the Digest is his. Of Paul, little is known except the quotations from him in the Digest, about half the volume of Ulpian's, and some bits of his *Sententiae Receptae* incorporated in the so called Breviary of Alaric.

In the works of these men, every fundamental principle of Classical Roman law was altered. The doctrine of the *jus naturale* was developed in Gaius' sense as the standard or righteousness that ought to be effective among all men for all time. Working from this principle they demolished the old Roman legal doctrine of form as the essential of all legal obligation. They introduced instead the concepts of intention, responsibility and good faith, regardless of the outer form of any particular legal instrument. They went far also in breaking down the legal structure of the agnate family, inserting personal responsibility as among living members, and lines of blood relationship in inheritance.

Justinian may have falsified some of their writings, for where there exist comparative texts of writings quoted in the Digest, the changes are numerous, and he certainly omitted great portions of their works. But in these jurists Justinian found exposition of legal principles sufficiently close to the legal principles of a Christian Byzantine Empire to

[14] *Quod naturalis ratio inter omnes homines constituit, id apud omnes populos peraeque custoditur, vocaturque jus gentium. . . . Jus naturale est quod natura omnia animalia docuit.* (Inst. i, 1; Digest i, i, 1, 3.)

[15] *in orbe Romano qui sunt . . . cives Romani effecti sunt.* (Digest 1, 5 from 17)

use them as the basis of his great canon. For Justinian's work was indeed a canon. No one was allowed to compare the Digest with the writings of the jurists quoted in it. All other legal writings of these authors were destroyed so far as the government could reach them. All commentary on the Digest was forbidden. Tertullian, who was both a Christian and a lawyer under the Severans, used the legal word "digesta" as the proper description of the Christian Gospels. It was in this same sense that Justinian used it, the sacred, authoritative, canonical writings of the founders.

Tertullian has also left us a telling testimony of how revolutionary and how desirable to him as a Christian was the legal revolution of the "pagan" lawyers and emperors of his own time. "All that old and foul forest of laws was cut down by the new axe of royal rescripts and edicts."[16]

It is customary in Western historical writings to regard the *Corpus Juris Civilis* not as the foundation of more than a thousand years of Levantine law but as the barren conclusion of Classical law. It is considered a work that influenced Western law through study of its texts and elaborate commentaries on it, commentaries that usually drowned the texts, from the eleventh to the sixteenth centuries. But because the western provinces had been overrun before the composition of the Corpus Juris, it was naturally not in the direct line of ancestry of any Western law, and therefore, we feel, composed too late. It fell out of the main line of development and so our law is not as much influenced by Roman law as it might have been.

But the significant fact to which we pay little attention is what happened to the Corpus Juris in the east. It remained the law of Byzantium till 1453 and was resumed as the law of modern Greece when that country was established in 1822.

Here again is the same awkward dilemma. If Papinian, Ulpian and Paul living under the Severan emperors were Romans, then the Digest of Justinian was Roman and the legal principles of Byzantium to 1453 were the legal principles of Roman society. In fact so innate were these Roman legal principles that when the Greek-speaking Orthodox Christians set themselves up as a territorial state in modern times, they were so Roman that the principles of Papinain and Ulpian were natural as the base of their law.

The extension of Roman citizenship to the entire empire is alone one

---

[16] *Totam illam veterem et squalentem silvam legum novis principalium rescriptorum et edictorum securibus truncatis et caeditis.* Apologet c. 5 page 50, edit. Havercamp. This involves a double meaning impossible to translate. By extension from the axes in the Roman fasces the word "securis" also meant "state power."

of the most remarkable legal operations of this period. To us, to whom citizenship and place of birth are almost automatic, this seems a normal and long overdue step, and our historians pay to it little attention beyond passing praise as a sign of growing enlightenment. Yet that empire had gone for two hundred and fifty years without it, and the republic far longer than that. Roman citizenship as a legal concept, an attribute of Roman or agnate birth or treaty status, was old and deeply founded in Classical society. Our own concept that citizenship follows the sovereignty of the place of one's birth is no more deeply founded with us. We can better judge, therefore, the magnitude of Caracalla's act if we compare it with, say, the grant of American citizenship to all persons throughout the world who would declare their belief in democratic principles. Caracalla's act appears to approach our type of citizenship and, therefore, it appears normal to us. Against the historic background of Classical Rome, it was as extraordinary as such an extension of American citizenship would be.

It is a commonplace of historical commentary on this subject to point out that Caracalla did it as a means of raising more taxes. No doubt he did, and no doubt the United States today could raise revenue by selling its citizenship even if it restricted the sale to believers in democratic principles. The point is whether the conditions of the times would permit a government to take so drastic a step. In Caracalla's case they did and it is this evidence of the profoundly different sense of nationality in his time from the sense of nationality under Augustus that is revealing.

There is a final extraordinary point about the Severan jurists that is passed over with little emphasis by Western historians. To the political and social historian, the technicalities of law are of little interest and the age of the Severans is pictured as one of violence, anarchy and social breakdown. The work of the jurists is pictured largely as a codification of traditional Roman law and the significance of the revolutionary legal change is ignored. To the legal writer, law is the all-important subject. The breakdown of Roman society is unimportant in comparison with the extraordinary development of law during this period. Although the legal historian is well aware that the law of Papinian and Ulpian is not the law of the republic and the earlier empire, it is still called Roman law, and by ignoring the social and political breakdown that accompanied its creation, it is entered in legal history as one of the great milestones of human progress.

"Under the weakest and most vicious reign, the seat of justice was filled by the wisdom and integrity of Papinian and Ulpian, and the purest materials of the Code and Pandects are inscribed with the names of Caracalla and his ministers," says Gibbon. This simply dismisses the matter as one of the oddities of history.

The fact of glaring significance is that in the middle of the third century a few jurists composed the basic principles of jurisprudence that for well over a thousand years served in spirit and to a large extent in letter as the basic law of Christian Byzantium and have remained for an even longer period the admired and partly declared principles of many of the Christian states of the world. If Papinian and Ulpian had been Christians, the historians would have had no trouble. It would have been clear to all that ennobled by the light of Christian teachings they had utterly recast the ancient pagan law into a proper Christian mode. This is, in substance, what Gibbon says above and what Tertullian said before him, but since these men were not Christians, the phenomenon cannot be fitted into the official doctrine that Rome was changed by Christianity and overthrown by the barbarians.

One other phenomenon of these centuries is significant: The disappearance from public affairs of Romans and even of Italians and Greeks. Syrians, Dalmatians, Africans became the emperors, jurists, and philosophers. Goths, Franks and Vandals commanded the western armies. After Marcus Aurelius, almost every important man in the intellectual and civil life of the empire came from those parts where Byzantium and the califate were later to flower.

The deep change in Classical society after the Antonines has been apparent to all historians. So overpowering is the impression of breakdown that through every account of this age runs the question of how the political existence of the Roman Empire managed to endure through this century of anarchy, weakness and universal violence. But since we are committed by convention to define the loss of the western provinces a hundred and fifty years afterwards as the "fall" of Rome, the death of Classical society remains in our accepted image of history a perplexing mystery—admitted as a fact but unmarked by any monument.

The political and economic organization of the empire, the social structure, money, the style of the arts, the structure and tactics of the army, religious feelings, the family, and the basic law, all these had been changed and all changed in a Byzantine direction before Constantine was born. On a colossal scale, it was precisely an example of the parable of the new wine in the old bottles. For it was in that fashion that it turned out, not in a clean break with the past, but an infiltration, an absorption, new men in old offices, new meanings to old words. At last nothing of Classical society remained but the bottle itself, the name of the Roman Empire and under this name new strains of men in all the leading posts of society lived a new way of life, a new and different civilization. In this process the loss of the barren, far western provinces, which had scarcely been Classical and never became Byzantine and only partly Mohammedan, was a matter of no significance.

Why should an alien civilization rising within and beyond the eastern borders of the Roman Empire have infiltrated that aged society, devoured its tissues to create its own until at last within the meaningless shell of the old name there was a completely different civilization? Regardless of where one cares to place the date of the "fall of Rome," or even the importance one ascribes to the loss of the western provinces, this is the question: "Why did Rome fall?" Like all causality in history, it is unanswerable. There is nothing by which we can explain the origin of the Byzantine-Mohammedan civilization. The "how" but not the "why" can be followed. And in all the multitude of means through which this process worked, one common quality always appears, the nature of the defense, the soul of Classical civilization itself. This civilization of the little, of the statuesque that lived for the day, improvident and irresponsible, could make no spiritual or intellectual stand against a vital alien. The grandiose empire that we picture under Augustus is a childish invention. It was a patched-together collection of broken-down Greek city states and empty border forests and deserts. One and only one military power touched it, Parthia, on its far northeastern frontier. Elsewhere there were oceans or the savage inhabitants of forest and desert. No Classical state ever had an enduring political structure or ever pursued a consistent policy, except the policy, if it can be called a policy, of doing nothing.

The Classical sciences, which we are taught to admire, are ridiculous by our standards. They are an attempt to explain in verbal categories the surface of things, not how they work, but why in the Classical senses of causality they have the *appearance* that they do. On Classical mechanics even the enthusiastic classicists are silent. There were none. The personal idiosyncrasies of Archimedes do not make the mechanics of a great society. It was a civilization whose mechanical answer to the ocean was a rowboat, to war the short sword, to industry the slave. Nor is time any explanation, that these things had not yet been learned by "mankind." They were contemporaries of the Chinese who sailed the Pacific in ocean-going ships, whose techniques in mining, metal working, weaving, paper, cavalry were even then at least the equal of sixteenth century Europe.

Against the spiritual strength, the vital curiosity of the new civilization which lay partly within its borders, Classical society resisted only on the formal surface, which was perhaps all that it understood. It asked for awhile that one go through the form of emperor worship, the form of titles in the Roman army, the form of language of the Greek philosophers, the form of maintaining the distinction of Roman citizenship. And then even these forms were abandoned, though a few of their names and superficial usages survived. But to find the epitaph of Classical society, it is not necessary to seek the lost grave of Alaric in the bed of the Busento. It was written by Ulpian himself, the open acknowledgment that a way of life had died: *in orbe Romano qui sunt . . . cives Romani effecti sunt.*

Chapter 3:

By the Waters of Babylon

AFTER FORTY-SEVEN YEARS OF WARS against the Roman Republic, Mithridates Eupator, King of Pontus, had himself put to death by one of his own mercenaries. His defeated army was in revolt, his conquered kingdom was occupied by Pompey's legions, his attempts to poison himself had failed. Thus in 63 B.C. perished the last unsuccessful opponent of Roman expansion in the Levant.

Ever since the armies of the republic under the two Scipios had crossed the Aegean and won the battle of Magnesia in 190 B.C., Roman arms, Roman intrigue and Roman money had been pushing steadily beyond the easternmost of the Greek city states, beyond the last outpost of Classical civilization to the east. Less and less was there serious resistance from the crumbling remnants of Alexander's empire. Its political unity had long before dissolved and its Hellenized upper crust—never very thick—was growing thinner and less Hellenic in each generation. Egypt had acknowledged Roman overlordship in 168 B.C., and in 164 B.C. the last remaining western fragment of the Seleucid kingdom had accepted a Roman protectorate. But it was not until the defeat of Mithridates that outright Roman dominion was firmly established in these lands. Fresh from his success in Pontus, Pompey entered Syria. There he abolished the last legal thread of the existence of the Seleucid kingdom and going on to Jerusalem annexed the disputed Seleucid dominions in Palestine.

But while Rome was advancing out of the Classical west, the decaying dominions of Alexander were likewise being devoured from the east. The Mazdaist kingdom, which the Romans of Pompey's time called

Parthia, and which under a different dynasty was afterwards called Sassanid Persia, had advanced from the Iranian highlands to the western bow of the Euphrates. Thus when Pompey wiped out the last western remains of Alexander's dominions, Rome, for the first time in more than a century, came face to face with a strong military power in the east. Where the Roman border did not meet the Parthian, only the mountainous buffer state of Armenia or the deserts of Syria and Arabia intervened. Roughly the frontier ran from the eastern end of the Black Sea close under the rampart of the Caucasus, southward to the western tributaries of the Euphrates, thence along that river into Syria and then southward along the vague line where the arid grass lands of Moab and Edom blend into the wastes of the desert. Now and then in the course of succeeding centuries this border was moved briefly a little east or west, but for seven hundred years Pompey's line was substantially the military frontier of the republic and of its legal successors, the Roman Caesars and the Basileis of Constantinople. Long after the border ceased to exist as a military frontier, it remained in the thought and literature of the West as an intellectual barrier. In the popular consciousness of the West it has been almost the boundary between the known and the unknown.

In the image of world history as convention has sketched it for us, what by analogy will be called received history in these pages, Pompey's line is where history stops. East of it lies the field of the scholarly specialties, Sumerian, Semitic and Indo-European philology, Assyrian and Hittite archaeology. History set as the tale of human progress touches upon this area only with reluctance and only to the extent that events occurring within it manifestly impinged on the life of the Classical society or of the West. It forces itself on our attention in much of the Old Testament. We again consider it for a moment in the rise of the Assyrian Empire and for still a third time in the wars of the Greek city states against the Medes and against the Persian Empire of Darius and Xerxes. For a period received history even moves into the area with the empire of Alexander, though it ignores the fate of the eastern ends of this brief dominion. As "Parthia" in Roman times, and as Sassanid "Persia," events of this area for almost the last time enter the penumbra of our historical consciousness. Finally with the rise of the Mohammedan Empire we close our consideration of this vast area which for more than five thousand years has been the site of human civilizations.

The spot where Pompey's victories chanced to place the Roman frontier was not without important consequences in the Levant itself but fewer than we usually suppose. Religion and language, the basic structure of civilization, on each side of this frontier, remained as they had been before it was established and as they remained after it was abolished. The extraordinary influence of this frontier has been an intellectual one and one felt primarily in the West. In our historical picture of the Roman and Christian past, it is we, not the Roman garrisons that held it, who have erected this frontier as a line of cultural importance. We like to think of it as the division between two civilizations, though it is impossible to define any two civilizations meeting at that line. Actually, it is the division between those events we are willing to receive into our accepted picture of world history and those things we do not care to know about. Here lies, perhaps, one of the cardinal errors in our image of the history of ourselves. The intellectual barrier which we ourselves erect along Pompey's military frontier destroys our understanding of historical Christianity, of Byzantium, the late Roman Empire and of the great Arabian Empire that so long molded the West. Under the illusion of this arbitrary cleavage we forget that for three thousand years no such division had existed. We forget how new this line was at the birth of Jesus or even at the Council of Chalcedon. It has not only affected Christian thought; necessarily, it has also reinforced among the Western Jews their historical myth that they and their religion are particular products of Palestine.

Pompey's line shields our image of history from the "Orient." Almost every history of Rome, of the Middle Ages, of Judaism and Christianity, almost every philosophical consideration of the origin of the modern West, here begins speaking of "oriental" influences. Some of these influences are identified as indigenous to Egypt, Palestine and Anatolia but always even these are correctly seen as influences reinforced from beyond the Roman frontier. Yet the common element of all these influences, the word "oriental" itself, is never defined. It is assumed to be self-evident. Yet what precise or even intelligible meaning can inhere in a word that covers more than five millennia of human life over an arc of more than a quarter of the earth's surface? The Japanese, the Chinese, the Hindus, the Mongols, the Babylonians, the Persians, the Mohammedans all are "orientals." What common element can there be among so many peoples so disparate in time, in space and in civilizations? How can we describe China and India as "oriental" and still speak of "oriental" influences appearing in late Roman life, or class Christianity and Judaism as religions of "oriental" origin?

The word has a meaning but a meaning of which most of those who use the word are not clearly conscious. It is a meaning exclusively negative. It means whatever is not of the Classical civilization nor of the West with the single proviso that these alien and utterly different civilizations thus embraced under a common label must lie to the eastward. The word serves merely as a device to avoid seriously considering this apparently complex maze of peoples who have lived between the Euphrates and the China Sea. Obviously the only thing in common between the Mohammedans and the Chinese, between the Nestorian Christians and the Hindus, between the Babylonians and the Japanese is that all these different peoples were members of neither Western nor Classical civilizations.

In journalism and in modern political writing the word "oriental" is, to be sure, usually confined to the Far East, and the Moslems of the Levant and Africa are therefore excluded. But in historical writing, the all-embracing use is retained and even the journalistic use does not change the intrinsic meaning of "non-Western." This use, too, lumps together such different societies as those of the Hindus and the Chinese and for good measure throws in the Japanese and the Moslems of India and the East Indies. Usage in regard to Russia varies. In the historical usage, Russia is not involved since it has too brief a past. In journalism Russia may or may not be described as "oriental" or at times "semi-oriental."

By suspending our serious understanding of history at Pompey's line and by blanketing under this almost meaningless word everything ancient that is not Classical and almost everything modern that is not Western, we have created for ourselves an image of vast and almost senseless confusion covering all events for five thousand years from the Mediterranean to the Pacific. We have left this area to the literature of specialists and in our general picture of human life see it primarily as a lot of strange and often unpleasant people doing odd and apparently meaningless things.

But the confusion is not in the "orient" but in ourselves. This area that was neither Classical nor Western has been the scene of five great historical societies. Once the histories and personalities of these societies are disentangled and each society seen as a self-contained living entity, the confusion disappears and the "orient" becomes as clear and intelligible as the Classical world or the West. The history of the "orient" is the history of these five great societies, their rise, their relations with each other and with barbarous peoples and, for two of them, their death. These five societies are the Egyptian, the Babylonian, the Chinese, the Hindu and the Levantine. The two most ancient are, of course, the Babylonian and the Egyptian. The two others which least concern either the Classical society or the other three, or the West during its youthful centuries, are the Hindu and the Chinese. Their histories until modern times have been almost remote from contact, particularly political contact, with any other society or with each other. It is impossible here to do more than identify the existence of these four.

Of all the civilizations of men the Classical is the most familiar to us Westerners so much so that it needs no more than to be mentioned at this point. Whether in fact it was so close to us as we think, or whether it constituted, as is often said, the first stage of a "European" civilization are matters that must be touched upon later. But for the history of the Classical society itself, in all its aspects, no historical field has been so exhaustively and so competantly covered in Western historical writing. Here all that is required is a brief identification.

The historical origin of the Classical society was unknown to its own later members, or at least it was not known as a series of names and dates as we Westerners must frame our sense of history. The Classical history of its own origins was written in Homer and the Greek dramas and so its own historians of later times clearly understood, but since this is not the kind of history we Westerners understand, we have had to reconstruct from this history-as-myth and from archeology a history of the Classical society that fits our own comprehension of history. Since, however, the late Classical historians understand their own society in their own way, not in ours, and since the authority of these historians has been very great in the intellectual life of the West, it has been a slow process for our received history to grasp the fact that the early stages of the Classical society—corresponding to everything in the West that occupies the eight or nine centuries from the barbarian migrations to the sixteenth century —was recorded by the Classical itself in the form of myth and poetry. Indeed, it was only the stubborn conviction of a few nineteenth century archeologists defying the flat intellectual prohibitions of the received history of their time, that finally exposed the historical reality enshrined in the Greek heroic and mythical poetry. Until this was accomplished received history began Classical history where its intellectual and artistic life comes to our attention, that is with the sixth century B.C. not because it began then but because the oldest records—by our definition of what constitute records—begin then. But by then the Classical society was some six or seven hundred years old, an urban, mercantile, international society which had spread into Sicily, southern Italy and along the shores of the western Mediterranean, embracing the Etruscans, and hence the Romans, and the Carthaginians. During the fifth century occurred its period of artistic and intellectual flowering and the beginning of "enlightenment," a period roughly comparable to the life of the West from 1650 to 1750. The next two hundred years marked an age of increasingly democratic forms of government, of oligarchic power and then of mob power, that is, of the leaders of mobs, increasingly vast and increasingly ruthless wars and a see-saw of empires. First, there was the struggle between Athens and Sparta at the end of the fifth century. This was followed by the rise of border powers, Classical in civilization but not lands in which Classical civilization had begun, Macedonia, Carthage and Rome. All this is thoroughly understood and has been exhaustively discussed in Western historical writings.

The remote historical origin of the Hindu society goes back to a conquest of northern India by a blond people who called themselves Aryans.[2] They spoke a language related to Greek, Latin and ancient Celtic. The lands they conquered were inhabited by a negroid people today called Dravidians. All details of the conquest, even its date, are unknown, 'and the political conditions for many centuries afterwards can only be inferred from later conditions and from oblique references in surviving epic and religious poetry. We can guess that the conquest occurred somewhere around 1500 B.C., but the guess cannot be based on much in the way of evidence. We do know that at a later time there were several independent Aryan kingdoms. We know that the social organization was that of every society during its youthful period, the three great classes of the realm, nobles, priests and commoners. Below these three were the conquered black Dravidians, not originally part of Aryan society at all. Thus has arisen the four basic castes of modern India, but no such rigid system existed until the late mercantile imperialistic times more than a thousand years after the conquest. In earlier days there was simply an impassable social barrier against the Dravidians. These were in theory and probably largely in fact the base of the Sudra, the fourth caste, the "untouchables," today a group of castes. But within the social classes of the ancient Aryans men moved up and down as they did in medieval Europe. However, the present physical types in most parts of India indicate that except in Rajputana and parts of the Punjab a good deal of Dravidian blood must have been taken into the three Aryan classes. Also the priestly class of this Aryan society was a hereditary class, unlike its counterpart in the West—and probably in China—which was always, as it still is, a professional class.

We are not well informed about the religious beliefs of this society prior to its late irreligious days, the times of Siddhartha Gautama, the Buddha, whose title the ages have substituted for his name. We know little more than that these ancient beliefs differed sharply from modern Hinduism, which certainly contains traces of religious customs and beliefs surviving from the Dravidians. By the time of Buddha in the sixth century B.C., belief in the ancient Aryan pantheon—obviously related in nomen-

---

[2] Long before this, probably earlier than 3000 B.C., there had been settlements in the Indus valley that had some contact with Sumer but seem not to have been part of that civilization. When and how they were destroyed are unknown and they seem to have left no trace upon Hindu civilization. See Sir John Marshall's *Mohenjo Daro and the Indus Civilization.*

clature if not in religious significance to the Classical pantheon—had become little more than pious formalism and the surviving texts of Buddha's teachings, buried under an immense volume of wholly fanciful teaching about him, have little bearing on the contemporary significance of Buddha's doctrines.

It has always been difficult for Westerners to comprehend the core of Indian religiousness, ancient or modern. The perishable "I" of modern materialism, the immortal "I" of the Middle Ages, both assume that all consciousness rests upon the relation between a personality—a discrete, utterly separate individuality of some kind—and all the rest of the universe. This is so evident to us that it appears to require neither thought nor specific language capable of differentiating such an understanding of self and reality from any other view. It is hard to comprehend that there could be a different view. The intense personal focus in which Westerners have always lived makes it difficult for us to sense the pluralized personality of the Levant, the "we" of the community of the faithful, and almost impossible to grasp the "anti-I" the "de-selfing"—naturally no words exist in a Western tongue for a thought almost incomprehensible to a Western mind—of our far-off kinsmen of India. That salvation should lie in the riddance of self seems to us absurd since to us nothing would be left to be saved. But such was—and to some extent still is—the basic meaning of Indian religiousness. The separateness of self, the separate existence of anything, is then felt to be the deep cause of change; and all change, soon or late, means decay and death and the end of separateness. Thus the transient arc of separateness returns in itself to form the closed circle of "unseparateness." In nirvanah immortality was at last attained in shedding the last trace of self, the last seed of the cause of death: the self.

The enlightened irreligiousness of Buddha lay in teaching that nirvanah could be attained in this life, precisely as the eighteenth century began the doctrine that the good life, previously foreseen in the Heavenly Kingdom, could be lived in this world. We do not ordinarily recognize early Buddhism as an irreligious movement; partly because we are confused by the later development under the Buddhist name, of a salvation-religion beyond the borders of India; partly because we do not understand ancient Indian religious concepts; partly, perhaps mostly, because we are accustomed to recognize as irreligious only Western irreligiousness, only the denial of personalized causality when the causality itself is Western.

In the time of Buddha, the Indian society embraced a group of sixteen kingdoms and aristocratic republics extending from the valley of the Indus to the bend of the Ganges and from the Himalayas to the

Vindhya hills. The most eastern, the most powerful, and the state least thoroughly inbued with the ancient Vedic tradition, was the kingdom of Magadha. Nothing of the political history of these states has survived. We know only that by the sixth century B.C. the Indian society was already eight or ten centuries old and that the class structure of the past had largely broken down while the caste structure of the future had not yet formed. The politics of the two succeeding centuries is again almost unknown. There was, however, the usual story of an aging society; social and political disorder and the rise of alien enemies. Even in the time of Buddha the empire of Darius had threatened the northwest and succeeded in occupying the Indus valley in 518 B.C. This did not serve to cement the Indian states. Some two hundred years later Alexander of Macedon appeared on the Indus and found many Indian states and Indian individuals anxious to help him sack the entire Indian world. It was not Indian resistance but Greek reluctance that checked the conquest.

One of the adventurers bent on helping Alexander conquer all India was a former Magadha army commander, Chandragupta Maurya. Disappointed in his hope of Greek aid in furthering his political ambitions, he returned to the lower Ganges to try his hand again at strictly domestic politics. In the anarchy of the time he succeeded in organizing a personal army with which, after some years of struggle and intrigue, he gained control of the entire Kingdom of Magadha, a state which had already fallen into the hands of Sudra rulers. With this as his political base he moved against all the independent and largely ruined Indian states, and before his death in 296 B.C. he organized all the ancient Aryan states into a consolidated empire, which from his dynasty carries the name of Maurya. He had also checked Alexander's successor, Seleucus Nicator, and restored for many centuries to come the political independence of India.

Unfortunately, we know nothing about the mass politics that must have been operating in India from Buddha's time to and beyond that of Chandragupta. The Indians kept no history and the Greek chroniclers recorded little but the surface of political personalities. The Chinese chronicles had not yet begun. We can tell, however, from the details known about Chandragupta's empire that the time was distinctly democratic, though naturally in an Indian fashion. No trace of a nobility remained, and it is probable that it had disappeared in Magadha under its Sudra kings before Chandragupta gained control of that state. In any event, in his empire birth counted for little and men rose to power on their ability to acquire wealth or political office. Caste was beginning to form, but except for the Brahmans, who as hereditary priests were sharply set off from all others, it had not yet hardened.

War, public welfare and commerce were the three great concerns of this modern-style empire. The core of the army was entirely professional with popular levies being used as needed. There was a great body of commercial law embracing tariffs, laws against monopolies and restraints of trade, price-control regulations, factory regulations and market controls. There were laws providing for care of the sick and for government irrigation projects.

This empire in Chandragupta's reign differed in no essential way from its condition in the time of his grandson Asoka, the most famous of the Hindu emperors of India. Asoka added to it most of the Dravidian lands south of the Vindhya hills and himself became a Buddhist. In the three hundred years since Buddha, irreligion had grown and then begun to wither. By Asoka's time, traditional piety, and indeed Dravidian religious beliefs, were more and more widespread. In the process, Buddhism had gradually ceased to be a movement of intellectual enlightenment and had become a religion. Buddha himself—who had declared his own convinced atheism—was already being revered as a god. Under Asoka's patronage the Buddhist church prospered in India and Buddhism was preached beyond the borders, where the name still survives. In India, however, it gradually fused with a revived and much altered Hinduism from which Indian Buddhism as a religion did not then or later ever materially differ. What men of other civilizations made of Buddhism had no bearing on the nature of Buddhism in the land of its birth.

The Maurya empire did not long outlast Asoka. India fell apart again into separate states and invasions again came from the northwest. Once more from 32 to 470 A.D. a Hindu dynasty, the Guptas, re-established a consolidated empire but that was the end. Anarchy, petty states, foreign conquests have been the political order in India ever since.

A society that has no sense of history seems likewise to lack a sense of politics, as not only the history of India but the history of the Classical society seems to show. There is indeed much in common between India and the Classical world, the curious lack of a sense of will as the core of a human character, the impersonal focus of the self, the phallicism, the lack of any sense of integrated causality and the corresponding technical and scientific poverty of both societies. Both had mathematics, but no other sciences. Both abutted extensively on the sea, but both shrank from it. Until their late imperial times both preferred to build with wood rather than with stone so that nothing corresponding to Western medieval architecture or the Old Kingdom in Egypt has survived in either society. Both kept few records and had no real chronology. Both refrained from developing an alphabet until late imperial times and then took it from others. Both found in the immobility of sculpture and the changelessness of mythical poetry their prime means of artistic expression. That one survived and the other perished is perhaps an accident of external circumstances, of the mighty barriers of the Himalayas, the Hindu Kush and the deserts of Baluchistan.

In complete contrast to the history of India is the history of China. Instead of a lack of records, there is an immense profusion of them going back for more than two thousand years. Instead of oral recitation of traditional poetry, there is a written literature from an unknown antiquity and a printed literature going back to the tenth century. Instead of political anarchy, there is a long history of kingdoms and enduring dynasties. Instead of a flight from the realities of personal and terrestrial life, there is a passionate embrace of all things of this world. Indeed, so immense are the records of China that no lifetime is long enough to permit the full study of all of them. With the history of the other ancient societies, the problem of a historian is to extend his knowledge from chance and always inadequate survivals. In China his problem is, as it is in the West, to find the significant and the truthful among the detailed and the tendentious.

True, the records of Chinese history for the span of centuries that correspond in that society to the entire history of the West have not survived in their original form. Yet these records once existed and parts of them, and later Chinese interpretation of others, have come down to us.

Chinese history as Chinese tradition has formed it relates the history of China to the history of the creation of human society. It, therefore, opens with a series of mythical rulers, the "five sovereigns" and the "three emperors," who even in orthodox traditions are not seriously considered to have been actual historical figures. To them is ascribed the introduction of patrilineal matrimony into a previously matriarchal society, the discovery of agriculture, textiles and metal working, the invention of writing—in short, prehistory first turned into myth and then rearranged as pseudo-history.

History that at least purports to be real history begins with Yu the Great, founder of the dynasty of Hsia. Unfortunately no events of any kind are recorded and the sole interest of later historians in the dynasty—if it existed—was to use it as a base for moral discourses on virtuous and wicked rulers. The Hsia, like the earlier mythical sovereigns, merely illustrated the perfect etiquette and concord that was asserted to have existed in the distant past.

Of the successor dynasty, that of Yin or Shang, much the same can be said. Again the Chinese historians offer moral lectures on political and family virtue and a complete absence of facts. Perhaps only one thing is notable about the accounts of these two dynasties—the vigorous assertion of royal succession by primogeniture, something quite at variance with the practice of ancient Chinese society, and always a precarious principle in later times.

To the Yin succeeded the dynasty of Chou whose origin is treated in the same vein as are the dynasties of Hsia and Yin, but whose later centuries come into the range of a more sober and detailed historical knowledge. Under the early Chous, China was pictured as a single feudal state, the emperor reigning over everyone, but the barons in their great fiefs holding all the real political power. Later under the last of the Chous, a group of these fiefs had become, in fact, independent states and waged about two centuries of war with each other for the hegemony of the civilized world. One of these, Ch'in, in what is roughly the modern province of Shensi, conquered the others and founded the centralized empire of China, though this first attempt, not being founded in virtue, failed and the real foundation is ascribed to the first or western Han dynasty some twenty years after Ch'in's conquest.

Chinese chronology for the mythical emperors is meaningless. For the dynasties of Hsia, Yin, and the origin of Chou it is possible. It dates the Hsia from 2205 B.C., the Yin from 1766, and the Chou from 1122. (An alternative Chinese system gives the corresponding dates as 1989 B.C., 1557 B.C., and 1049 B.C.) After the eighth century B.C. it is trustworthy and generally precise.

This traditional history is neither a series of fanciful inventions nor a conscientious attempt to discover and set forth a record of events. That a historical period corresponding to the Yin dynasty once existed, the archeology of ancient China amply proves, as it proves the existence in China of a neolithic period whose dim reflection colors the accounts of the mythical emperors. On the other hand there was never an age of virtue in the past, near or distant, and the filial piety ascribed to feudal China is an invention of far later moralizing historians.

China in the uncertain centuries of the Yin dynasty was slowly emerging from a primitive, historyless tribal culture. There is no way of knowing how long this culture had lasted nor what its ethnic composition may have been. Archeology shows, however, that an unbroken continuity existed from these far off days to the full flowering of late civilized life.

Feudal China began under the early Chous. Nowadays the word "feudal" is often used to describe almost any social system in which political power is held by others than state or party officials, but the sense here intended is the sense in which it is applicable to the Western Middle Ages. Land tenure and political power stemmed up through a series of grants and reciprocal obligations almost identical with those of medieval Europe. At the bottom were the serfs who could neither be deprived of their land nor move from it. At the top was the titular sovereign in whose name all power was held but whose actual rule was confined to his own hereditary dominions. Beyond, the great tenants-in-chief were the lords to the extent that they had not so subinfeudated their dominions that they, too, ruled only in their own hereditary lands.

The nobility, as in the West, was a class devoted in the beginning exclusively to war and government. It fought, as in the West, only with noble weapons, the chariot taking the place in China of the mounted knight of Europe and archery instead of swordsmanship being the exclusive skill and prerogative of the nobility. Its wars were conducted like those of feudal Europe. Life, even one's own, was of little consequence. What was vital was honor. Chinese wars of this period are full of heralds courteously announcing an intention to attack, of delays to permit an opposing army to deploy for combat, since to take advantage of a disordered enemy would be ungentle, of senseless slaughter or impolitic mercy depending upon the particular point of chivalry involved, of exquisite courtesy before and after the bloodiest conflicts, and, over and over again, that familiar European device of fierce wars ending in dynastic marriages.

The barons of ancient China like those of medieval Europe slowly hacked arable land out of the great forests, slowly drained the marshes and diked the rivers. Like the Germans of the Saxon emperors faced by the heathen Slavs, they slowly drove back the barbarians and brought into civilized communion the marshmen and hill people left behind and enclosed by the spreading tide of Chinese civilization. Around the earth-walled castles of the barons—ancient China had little stone—grew small villages of artisans and traders. In the pillared south-facing court of every Chinese nobleman, where justice was pronounced and where council was held, there grew up an elaborate ritual of etiquette—in dress, in manners, in word—as perfect a structure of courtesy and symbolism as in the long vanished courts of Europe. As the manners of the West today come from the courts of Hohenstaufen and Capet, those of China come from the courts of Chou.

Feudal China extended from the bend of the Huang-ho in modern Shensi across northern Honan and southern Shansi into western Shantung. Around this ancient and narrow seat of civilization there grew up a ring of border powers, themselves in the beginning wholly Chinese but each reaching out further and further into the barbarian world around about. From barbarian conquests came wealth and military power and these were required in ever increasing quantities to effect desired political settlements back in the ancient middle lands. By the sixth century, with the rise of several powerful, independent kingdoms, feudal China was becoming more accurately dynastic China. The real political power was held by the border states, and the last of the Chous, like the later Holy Roman Emperors, were no more than titular figureheads. In the border states themselves, feudal power was being increasingly replaced by a central administration. The old fortified burgs were disappearing and growing commercial cities were rising everywhere.

At the same time a phenomenon about which we are very poorly informed was going on. The ancient priestly class, which with the nobles had once ruled feudal China, was disappearing or, more accurately, was losing its sacerdotal functions and becoming instead a professional class of clerks (in the old sense), the "sages" of earlier times, the intellectuals of the days of the empire. The nature of Chinese religiousness was such that its sacerdotal functions could be performed by a non-professional priest. Each sovereign and each head of a family—himself a tiny sovereign —tended to acquire these functions.

So ended Chinese feudalism as it ended in Europe with a religious revolution—though quite a different type of religious revolution. Equally, it ended with a group of border powers bent on turning the resources of the world to the struggle for supremacy. In the end, after two hundred years of the varying fortunes of wars and treaties, the victor was Ch'in and from its name has come the name of all China itself. It was Ch'in that first and most effectively broke the political power of her own terri- torial nobility and built as strong a central administration as any state of ancient China ever had. It was Chêng the king of Ch'in who, in ten years of war, conquered the other states. Certain victor at least in Honan, he wiped out the then phantom dynasty of Chou, and in 221 B.C. proclaimed himself Emperor under the title of Shih Huang Ti.

Shih Huang Ti did more than destroy the sovereign independence of the old kingdoms. He created the basic frame of China that was to last for two thousand years. He created a central administration of able men of his own selection and abolished all locally based political power. He unified the widely different methods of writing then prevalent in the different states. He built a great network of imperial roads and canals. He standardized the gauge of vehicles so that no part of the empire was closed to the equipment of any other. Despairing of ever subduing the Huns of the northwestern steppes, he began the construction of the Great Wall. To the south he conquered and colonized Fukien, Kuantung, Kuangsi, and the coast of Annam. He ended the last traces of servile tenure by extending to the whole empire the land laws of Ch'in which long before had provided for full individual ownership of land.

Shih Huang Ti failed to found a dynasty, but few men have left such enduring traces in the political history of human societies. But for this great politician, Chinese tradition has nothing but curses and abuse. He was the enemy of the intellectuals and the oligarchy, and though they could not undo all his work, they have effectively blackened his memory. "He was a man with a prominent nose, large eyes, the chest of a bird of prey, and the voice of a jackal. He lacked benevolence and had the heart of a wolf or a tiger always ready to devour his fellow men." [3] This is all the Han historians have allowed to reach us, the sole description of the founder of the Chinese Empire.

Parallel with the political struggles of the old kingdoms there existed throughout Chinese society two interrelated movements, intellectual and economic: a literature of enlightenment growing constantly more liberal and the rise of an oligarchy becoming constantly more hostile to any traditional or political restraint on the power of the new men. The origin of the first is credited to the times and, indeed, to the persons of Confucius and Lao-tse in the sixth century B.C. but much of it is probably considerably later, being credited for reason of prestige to the older "sages." This Chinese liberalism differs from ours in the technical means by which it avoided history. It objected to history as deeply as Western liberalism does but instead of minimizing history as of little value against the achievements of modern progress, it deliberately falsified history. It asserted that in the golden age of the past, kings reigned but did not rule. They were concerned only with the welfare of their subjects and the latter enjoyed a kind of Chinese democracy by being in celestial harmony with their sovereigns. That is, by grace of this harmony, kings never did anything but what their subjects desired. The intermediaries in bringing to the king's attention the mundane, practical steps toward this harmony and, of course, the natural administrators of all state policy were the "sages," the intellectuals. These alone had sufficient knowledge to enlighten the inherent but uninformed virtue residing in the mystic harmony between king and people. The resemblance of this myth-as-history to the myth-as-sociology of Western liberalism is obvious. To us the mystical harmony of king and people is replaced by the equally mystical harmony of the will of the majority as the virtuous but inherently uninformed base of all political power. But to govern virtuously or democratically—which mean the same thing—government must be guided by the learning of the liberal intellectual who alone knows how to guide the respective fonts of power. This school of thought developed in an ever more extremist direction until, a century before Shih Huang Ti, it flowered in such men as Mencius who taught that the only thing of importance in a state was the mass of the people, and Mo Ti, who preached confiscation of all property and its equitable division.

At the same time mass industry and monetary speculation became the dominant economic operation of the society. The old handicrafts, particularly weaving and metal working, had been family and guild enterprises. The Chinese lacked Western sources of mechanical power but this did not prevent the development of an industrial type of production. (Indeed, in the West industrial production began before mechanical power was thought of.) Syndicates and wealthy proprietors of manufacturing establishments grew up. Inter-provincial and foreign trade developed increasingly in the hands of wealthy merchants. Speculators in land and staples became commonplace. More and more, these men became figures of political importance. In place of the old family alliances, there grew up a network of political associations of men of like purpose or parallel interest.

To all this movement, Shih Huang Ti was a bitter opponent. Although he used able men of common birth in his administration and suppressed almost all titles of nobility, he attempted to curb the oligarchy and to break up the associations. He distrusted the anarchic tendencies of the teachings of the intelligentsia and his destruction of their propaganda is the famous "burning of the books," for which Shih Huang Ti has been remembered as the bigoted foe of learning. "He burned the teachings of the Hundred Schools (i.e., the so-called Confucian movement of the time) in order to keep the people ignorant,"[3] says the Han historian. What he destroyed was not learning but subversive propaganda, as we can tell from scraps of it that survived.

The Han historians have quoted for us the gist, probably accurate, of a discussion before the Emperor of the proposed destruction of this literature. Against the argument that the example of the ancient dynasties proved that the Emperor should distribute political power to irremovable subordinates in order to break down his strongly centralized administration, his chancellor, Li Ssu, is quoted: "The three royal dynasties (Hsia, Yin, and Chou) did not imitate one another. Times had changed. Today Your Majesty has for the first time accomplished a great work and founded a glory that will last for ten thousand generations. It is this that the narrow intellectuals are incapable of comprehending. In antiquity, China was divided and troubled. Since no one could unite it, the local lordlings all grew powerful. The intellectuals falsify the past only for the

[3] Ssuma Ch'ien quoted by M. Granet. *La Civilizasion Chinoise*, Paris, 1929. p. 47.

purpose of deprecating modern times. They involve the masses in their false abuse. If they are not stopped, the imperial power will be shattered and the power of their own associations will grow stronger." [4]

Shih Huang Ti's dynasty outlasted him by only a few years. His death in 210 B.C. left no successor who could think in terms of the political future of his society. The literate population of the empire had written and intrigued against all he had sought to do. No articulate force in China opposed his generals when they began to carve out private dominions for themselves. Even in Ch'in, his dynasty had few friends and was easily overthrown by a man of the people, the first emperor of the new Han dynasty, Kao-tsu (205–195 B.C.). But Kao-tsu became in fact only King of Ch'in though he kept the imperial title. The old kingdoms re-appeared in name, mostly under Shih Huang Ti's old generals, but the old nationalist spirit that had fired centuries of war was no longer present. Nevertheless, neither a commoner as emperor nor the lack of a nationalistic or even patriotic spirit was able to bring peace. There ensued sixty years of civil wars, utterly different from the national wars that had preceded Ch'in's conquest and far more ruinous. It was faction against faction and general against general, never state against state, and ended with the reign of Wu, the third Han emperor, in exhaustion, famine and universal ruin. It ended also in the triumph of the intellectuals and the leaders of the masses. The Hans themselves were not of noble stock and under Wu, only commoners were appointed to office. This did not, however, bring on a socialist millennium. All that happened was the personal advancement of the moneyed men and the leaders of the proletariat who, themselves, soon became rich and before long were being granted revived titles of nobility. But in the world of letters, the triumph of liberalism was complete. The entire political structure was set free for those to operate in who could. The obligations of the past were shed by falsifying the past. To the triumphant liberals and the oligarchy turned office-holders, Shih Huang Ti became the hated exemplar and symbol of state responsibility, of the obligation which a great political past lays upon men to concern themselves with a political future. They blackened his memory, and they expunged his political philosophy from the public life of China. All that remained and all that has carried China to this day was not the strength of the concept of the state, nor even of the concept of China, but the strength of the Chinese family. In the family alone were maintained the standards of honor and responsibility, of thought of the past and care for the future that made possible civilized relations between men as individuals. But the state was left as the mere arena for the family affairs of those who could control it. So it has remained ever since.

[4] Ssuma Ch'ien, *ibid,* p. 44.

The rest of the history of China is chiefly the history of events from the outside affecting a finished and almost changeless society. For almost three hundred years after the Emperor Wu, political emotion—increasingly religious in its formulation—still continued to influence the dynastic destinies of China. The Western Hans fell in 23 A.D. in a combination of palace intrigue and religious excitement. The Eastern Hans fell in 220 A.D. in an even more violent religious disturbance, the revolt of the Yellow Turbans. The one-time philosophical schools of Confucianism and Taoism had at last become mass religions. Thereafter, the history of China is only the history of the family politics of the successsive dynasties, the endless struggle of ministers, concubines and dowager empresses for personal and family power. Sometimes there were several states, sometimes two—from one of which we get our old name of Cathay—sometimes there was one. In the sixth century, many Chinese became Buddhists as in the nineteenth and twentieth many became Christians, without much effect in either case on their way of life. In the thirteenth century, China was conquered and much of it sacked by the Mongols from beyond the Wall. In the seventeenth, it was conquered again from the north by the Manchus. From the eighteenth to the twentieth it was pressed more and more by Western arms and Western intrigue, and by a Westernized Japan.

With these two great civilizations of China and India identified, it is possible to return much closer to Pompey's line in the effort to disentangle the history of the Levant. It is also a step many millennia back into the past, for in the river valleys of the Levant the beginnings of historical societies antidate the origins of even India and China by more than a thousand years.

In the valleys of the Tigris and Euphrates, archeological evidence indicates that, as in the valley of the Nile, the beginnings of a civilization stood without interruption on the preceding neolithic culture, but of the early historical period of these people, whom we call the Sumerians, we know far less than of the earlier historical period of the Egyptians. Chronological conjecture is likewise difficult, but somewhere before 3000 B.C. the inhabitants of the lower courses of the Tigris and Euphrates ceased to be changeless neolithic men and began the earliest historical civilization, a civilization which from its late political form is generally called Babylonian.

We know little of the early political history of this society. If it wrote histories of itself, they have not survived, and its written remains are chiefly a few epics and a vast mass of commercial records from far later times. As a result, our knowledge of Babylonian society while extensive in some fields is often superficial. We have little understanding of its religion and no knowledge of its inward thought. Apparently, in the early centuries there were several states or city states and several cult cities of which the two most important were Eridu, once at or near the head of the Persian Gulf, and Nippur about one hundred miles up the Euphrates. Archeological exploration at Nippur has revealed the development from mud huts to great brick towers and somewhere after 3000 B.C. of written Sumerian. Later this language came to be supplanted by a language of Semitic origin, and it is generally believed that this followed a conquest of the original Sumerians by Semitic-speaking tribes. The insufficiency of our knowledge of the political history of these early times makes any assumption unsure. But in any event there appears to have been no breach in the continuity of the civilization, and Sumerian remained for many centuries the religious language of the entire society, gradually becoming more and more loaded with Semitic words and more and more a priest's jargon.

Most of the site of the ancient home of this civilization is today a wilderness of marsh and desert. During the flowering of this society it was universally fertile, the rivers being kept under control by a system of canals designed both for irrigation and commerce. There was a good deal of shipping in the inland waterways and on the Gulf.

Little more than legend reports that this society was consolidated under a single dynasty, that of Sargon of Agade (or Akkad) who probably lived about 2800 B.C. His dominions were of uncertain extent, but they were evidently those of a civilized people. There is evidence of a system of roads and canals, royal posts, trade in stone and copper with the Red Sea. Whatever Sargon's dominions may have been and whatever the political and social conditions of his time, his reign remained a tradition for two thousand years.

The chronology after Sargon of Agade remains confused. Apparently, a dynasty ruling at Ur in the region later known as Chaldea on the southwest bank of the Euphrates became the dominant political power. Chronology appears to be on surer grounds in dating one of the principal later kings of this dynasty, Ur-Gur, at about 2300 B.C. He styled himself King of Sumer and Akkad and ruled over a dominion extending to the Mediterranean. How far east his power extended is unknown. By his time, Sumerian society was at least seven centuries old and had become a complex, urban, mercantile civilization. Its political history is largely lost, but some of its legal and commercial documents, chiefly on clay tablets, have survived. A significant sign of the age and condition of this society was Ur-Gur's devotion to the forms of the past. He busied himself restoring ancient temples that had fallen into disrepair, particularly those of Ishtar at Erech and Baal at Nippur, but he apparently did not attempt like the later Assyrian kings, to revive dead beliefs or busy himself with empty political forms. Under this dynasty, Sumerian civilization had reached a stage comparable with that of Egypt in the Twelfth Dynasty, a fact that appears to indicate an origin of Sumeria some three centuries earlier than Egypt.

The dynasty of Ur ended in a period of some two centuries of war and revolution. There were civil wars among the provinces, and ambitious individuals struggling for the supreme power. Alien tribes crossed the frontiers and made themselves political masters of all the north. It was during this period that Sumu-La-Ilu, one of the northern kings, made the city of Babylon a fortress—though the city itself may have been far older—and his successors slowly consolidated their power about it. Finally, his great-great-grandson, Hammurabi, brought all the ancient Sumerian dominions under his control. Thus was founded the dynasty of Babylon and the name of the final imperial form of the Sumerian civilization.

Hammurabi established this late Babylonian Empire about 1900 B.C., again some three centuries before Ahmosi I, founder of the Eighteenth Dynasty, established the corresponding New Empire in Egypt. A copy of Hammurabi's codification of Babylonian law has been found at Susa and from it we can derive an accurate picture of that society. It was by that time completely commercial. The only trace of feudal customs remained in purely nominal forms between the king and a few of the great officials—perhaps something like such remnants in the British peerage. Otherwise, the relations between men and property were commercial. Agriculture was intensive, being carried on by means of a complex irrigation system and both it and animal husbandry were universally on a cash basis with no remaining traces of peasant holdings. Apparently, the temples were the principal banks, though there was a good deal of private lending and private risk investment. The immense scope of Babylonian commerce is still not disclosed. We know this trade reached into the Mediterranean and Red Seas. Having the means for maritime traffic, their trade probably went far to the east also, but we have no record of such voyages.

The early Sumerian religion was a complex polytheism in which each natural force and important object had its special god. There was a distinct ranking in this multiplicity of gods, the great triad being Anu, the god of heavens, Ea, the god of the sea and the dead, and Bel, the god of the earth. Beside these more abstract gods, there were three specific personifications, Shamash, god of the sun, Sin, god of the moon, and

Ishtar, goddess of sex. The name Bel was a title, Lord, and in early times En-lil of Nippur was the Bel. Hammurabi, however, transferred this title to the local god of Babylon, Marduk, and during imperial times, Bel Marduk tended to absorb into himself all the functions of all the older gods except Ishtar, whose identity was never lost. We know this surface of names and identification of gods, but we probably do not know the inner meaning of Babylonian religiousness. We realize that religions—even our own—are in some way always involved with sex, but when this involvement takes a phallic rather than an ascetic form, it is difficult for us to follow, or credit, the genuineness of the religious emotion.

Babylonian religion was phallic both in cult and ritual. Accordingly, it had an institution which for lack of a better name we call sacred prostitution. Each temple had a group of women dedicated to its shrine whose duty it was to participate in the necessary religious exercises. This was quite evidently a holy and honorable calling, and girls could be dedicated to a temple by their fathers while still infants, and married women could take refuge in it from the burdens of an unhappy marriage.

Of Babylonian science, only scraps have survived. They had a well-developed algebra and a descriptive astronomy. We have found tables of lunar longitudes and records of the observations of the phases of Venus, the latter certainly indicating the use of a telescope, a not impossible conclusion since a turned lens has actually been found in the ruins of Nimrud near Nineveh. But of their philosophy of science we know nothing and we can guess nothing of their concept of causality.

The political history of Babylonia after Hammurabi is a history of dynastic and imperial politics that never changed the basic frame of Sumerian society. The first Babylonian dynasty remained in power for about two hundred years and then was overthrown by a Kassite dynasty from Elam, one of the eastern provinces of the empire. Western Syria was lost and Assyria became independent. Assyria was originally the Babylonian settlements in the upper reaches of the valleys and was an integral though provincial part of the Babylonian civilization. It differed from southern Babylonia, however, in that, where the latter was by Hammurabi's time a society of priests and merchants, Assyria as a late settlement and frontier province, was a society of soldiers and merchants. After official independence from the kings of Babylonia under Shalmaneser I (c. 1300 B.C.), Assyria rose rapidly as the dominant military power in the now ancient Babylonian world. The western provinces were reconquered by the Assyrian kings and Anatolia occupied. For a while, Babylon was under joint kingship.

Finally under Shalmaneser II (c. 850 B.C.), Babylonia was formally annexed, and the Assyrians were in complete control. Another series of palace revolutions changed the family on the throne, and under the new dynasty founded by Tiglath-pileser III (c. 745 B.C.) war and trade were spread over western Asia on a scale never before attempted. Round about stood the armed, restless barbarians. Inside lay the arena for the clash of personal ambition, more and more ruthless in its means and more anarchic in its purpose. In the entire Babylonian society, the only force with political purpose or political coherence was the Assyrian army. It was the creature of the Assyrian kings and, for more than a century, they used it to maintain the last flicker of life in the dying Babylonian society.

Armenia and Phoenicia were conquered and the northeastern mountains invaded. But always at home, disorder and political decay increased. Tiglath-pileser went through the ancient and empty form of coronation at Babylon which did not prevent his son's being overthrown by an ambitious general, who revived after two thousand years the ancient name of Sargon of Agade, which in turn did not prevent the Babylonians from revolting. The new Sargon's son and successor, Sennacherib, was so profoundly impressed by his father's pious veneration of the past that he massacred the inhabitants and razed the walls and public buildings of Babylon, using the rubble to block the canals.

The dreary, hopeless and bloody record of the Assyrian dynasty, more properly the Assyrian army command, ground on for a few decades. Sennacherib was murdered and his son, Esar—Haddon, who was fortunate enough to be in the field with an army, succeeded in taking Nineveh and keeping the crown. He patched up Babylon sufficiently to go through the ancient rite of being crowned there and then set off to conquer Egypt. This he succeeded in doing in 670 B.C., but could only hold his conquest for ten years. His son, Assurbanipal, continued the war in Egypt and destroyed Susa in an attempt to suppress revolt in the east. But by his death, there was little left of the Assyrian military machine. There was nothing to hold back the barbarians of the northeastern mountains and Nineveh itself was beseiged. In the south, Nobopolassar, nominally the Assyrian viceroy of Babylonia, decided the time was appropriate for a new revolt and allied himself with Cyaxares, one of the barbarian kings of the eastern highlands. Together they captured and destroyed Nineveh in 612 B.C. For only about seventy years, Nabopolassar and his son, Nebuchadrezzar II, enjoyed the fruit of their barbarian alliance. This was the Babylon of what legend calls the Jewish captivity, but it did not long survive the barbarian power it had helped turn loose on Assyria. Another barbarian king, Cyrus the Persian, did away with Cyaxares' dynasty, made himself master of Elam and then, in 538 B.C., took over Babylonia without resistance. Cyrus was duly crowned by the ancient Babylonian rites. With him appeared the first foreign dominion over a society that had governed itself for over three thousand years.

Something under a thousand miles to the westward of Babylon in the valley of the Nile was the nearly contemporaneous civilization of Egypt. Of the political life of ancient Egypt we know considerably more than we do of the politics of the Sumerians. The major Egyptian dynasties and most of the great kings, can be placed not only in proper chronological order, but with some approach to absolute chronology and in fair relation to the major political events of over two thousand years.

Inevitably, however, the early dynasties are not known in detail. There is an almost mythical king of Upper Egypt, known as Menes, whose Egyptian name meant the Fighter. He conquered Lower Egypt and founded Memphis near modern Cairo, roughly on the border between these two districts. There is no doubt that the kings of the First and early part of the Second Dynasty came from Abydos in Upper Egypt and, in later times, this city and its shrines remained the symbol of the dim past. It is with the last king of the Third Dynasty, Snegru, however, that authentic history emerges from tradition.

From the Fourth Dynasty date the three great pyramids set along the escarpment of the valley southwest of Memphis. They were built to be viewed from the valley floor whence they appeared as great shimmering triangles of polished stone, pointing forever to the eternal god of heaven. This was a period of sculpture in the round of a noble simplicity and of beautiful hieroglyphic and figure design in the inscriptions. Politically, it was a period of consolidated feudalism. All Egypt was ruled by great feudal lords. It is the period of Egyptian history known as the Old Kingdom.

Feudal conditions lasted through the Sixth Dynasty and then culminated in an interregnum of about 180 years covered by the Seventh and Eighth Dynasties. The Ninth, Tenth, and Eleventh Dynasties were contemporary in different parts of Egypt. With the Twelfth Dynasty, about 2000 B.C., centralized royal power was restored, and the eight kings of this dynasty ruled over a monarchy in which the ancient feudal lords had been replaced by royal officers holding feudal titles and the feudal courts had given way to royal courts. This period has always been known as the Middle Kingdom.

The occasion for the fall of the Twelfth Dynasty we do not know, but its end marks the beginning of two centuries of civil war and revolution. The orderly records of the dynasties break off. From later records, from monuments, from fragments of papyrus, we can reconstruct accounts of over one hundred and fifty pretenders, upstarts and foreign adventurers who claimed to be kings of Egypt in these years. The northeast was held by a foreign dynasty called the Hyksos, about whom we know nothing except that some of these kings must have held power all over Egypt at certain periods. Of strictly Egyptian rulers all is war and confusion. The lists of the dynasties of Egypt in the tablet that Seti I in the Nineteenth Dynasty erected at Abydos simply ignore all dynasties between Twelfth and Eighteenth. All we know is the record of what is left of those two centuries, the tombs of innumerable upstart leaders, the discontinued records, the shattered monuments, the degenerate art and the end in military dictatorship. The first unified dictatorship was that of a Hyksos, King Khyan, who gave himself new titles and appeared to have established his dominion over a wide area, since objects bearing his name have been found as far away as Crete and modern Baghdad. A counter-revolutionary power, however, established itself in Thebes under the style of the Seventeenth Dynasty and began reducing the area of Hyksos power. The Eighteenth Dynasty completed this task and founded what is known as the New Empire. This was a wholly different political organization from the aristocratic Twelfth or feudal Sixth. This was a centralized, administrative bureaucracy. Both military power and civil administration were placed entirely in the hands of professional government officials. A professional, organized army replaced the local levies of ancient days. Tactics of war were altered. Chariots and specially armed regiments appeared.

Military expansion began with the dynasty itself. Ahmosi I conquered Palestine and part of Syria, where the Babylonian civilization had already been implanted firmly, so firmly that even the official reports of the Egyptian governors of Syria, which have been found at Tel-el-Amarna, are in the Babylonian language and written in cuneiform. A few years later under Tethmosis I (c. 1540 B.C.) Egyptian power was pushed to the Euphrates and into Nubia to the fourth cataract of the Nile.

The New Empire is the most compact example of the combination of archaism, imperialism and degeneration that the history of human civilizations has left us. This may not be because it differed particularly from others at a like state of development, but simply that our detailed knowledge of Egypt is so complete for this period. Our knowledge of ancient Sumeria is too sketchy to allow us to compare Hammurabi's empire with the kingdom of his predecessors. Similarly, concerning China before Han times, we have only fragmentary knowledge of its politics and almost no knowledge of its art. The degeneration of the Classical and

Levantine societies is confused in both by the contemporaneous rise of new civilizations. But in Egypt after 1500 B.C., we can see the whole process undistorted.

The political history of the New Empire is of little significance. After the consolidation of domestic power and the opening of foreign conquests in the Eighteenth Dynasty, the Nineteenth and Twentieth, the ages of the Rameses, continued the same policies with decreasing vigor. The army soon became primarily an army of alien mercenaries. The church of Ammon became the supreme political power in all matters that concerned it. The frontiers in Syria became more and more difficult to defend and domestic order gave way to private violence. During the Twenty-first Dynasty, Syria was lost and the Egyptian kings became mere instruments of the church of Ammon. There followed about four centuries of undistinguished alternations of military and ecclesiastical rule and then conquest by the Assyrians in 670 B.C. For about one hundred and thirty years, Assyrian rule alternated with local rebellion, and then over Egypt, as over Babylonia, appeared the power of Cyrus and his Persians.

By 2000 B.C., it will be recalled, there had developed in the lower valley of the Euphrates and Tigris as there had in the valley of the Nile, a great, complex, urban, sea-going civilization, complete with all the paraphernalia of civilization, property rights, elaborate records, money, courts, armies, police, civil administration, dams, canals, vast irrigation systems, post roads, a priesthood and an organized property-holding church devoted to the ritual of an immemorial religion. After Hammurabi's time, it had that most modern of all the attributes of civilization, a great metropolitan city. Surrounding this already aged society, which had now become primarily a vast commercial enterprise, were a series of primitive and half barbarian peoples. Only in Egypt was there a civilized, urban way of life, and in Egypt there was no city comparable to Babylon. What happened was what we would expect to happen. The names and ideas of Babylon, and to a lesser extent of Egypt, spread to unknown limits among the savage and semi-civilized peoples around them. More, the image and memory of Babylon remained implanted for centuries, perhaps for millennia, in the lands it had dominated.

Far to the north of the civilized middle lands, wholly out of contact with Egypt, lay Bactria between the Oxus and the Ochus, and Parthia between the Ochus and the eastern shore of the Caspian. To the north beyond the mountain range of the Zagros and west of the Caspian was Media. The date at which men speaking an Aryan language appeared in these regions is unknown. By 1600 B.C., they were farther east in the Punjab and a little later men with distinctly Aryan names appear as high military officers in the services of the Assyrian and Egyptian empires. In the periods of anarchy that were interspersed with periods of renewed military consolidation of these empires, many of these men established themselves as local princelings in northern Syria. It was not until Shalmanassar II in 836 B.C. that any serious attempt was made to establish Assyrian power deep in the eastern highlands, but by 715 B.C. the whole western escarpment with its predominantly Aryan-speaking population was incorporated in the empire. It is probable also that it was from these Aryans that the horse was introduced into western Asia and the Mediterranean world. It seems clear that the Aryans had used the horse from remote times, but it first appeared among the Babylonians and Egyptians at about 1700 B.C. The horse, of course, became an important military factor, but it was not possession of this military advantage that gave the Aryan barbarians the power to overthrow these ancient empires. Centuries elapsed between the first contact between the Assyrians and the Aryans, and long before the overthrow of the last Assyrian dynasty the horse had become a familiar weapon in both the Assyrian and Egyptian armies.

To the northwest of Babylonia, in northern Syria and throughout the peninsula of Anatolia, Babylonian civilization seems to have spread its influence, not its conquests. Here was the domain of the Hittites.[5] The origin of these people is unknown, but their language was Aryan. It was originally written in cuneiform but as time went on the Hittites developed a hieroglyphic script of their own which gradually supplanted the cuneiform.[6] The first record of their existence is an attack on Babylon about 1800 B.C. It is apparent that they were then considered barbarians, not fellow members of the Sumerian-Babylonian civilization. Some two hundred years later they possessed a powerful state in Cappadocia, with its capital at Boghaz-Keui, and shortly afterwards conquered Syria and part of northern Mesopotamia. They remained as an important military and increasingly commercial state in intimate contact with both Babylonia and Egypt until about 1200 B.C. when they collapsed under a new Caucasian invasion. Their possessions in Syria were conquered by the Assyrian kings during the ninth century, B.C. Their dominions in Anatolia became the Lydian and Phrygian kingdoms that lasted into Classical times and were well known to the Greeks. Their religion was that of

[5] So the Bible calls them. What they called themselves has so far not been discovered.

[6] It was long believed that two peoples were involved but the recent decipherment of the hieroglyphic has shown otherwise.

Babylonia, essentially the worship of Ishtar. The truth of the matter is that we know very little about the Hittites except that as masters of Anatolia and Syria for several centuries before 1200 B.C., they were superficially at least a civilized people and participated in the commercial phases of the Babylonian civilization. They were not originally a part of it nor did they survive its eventual destruction, either as a people or a state. Perhaps, on a far greater scale, they bore to the Babylonians something of the relation that Macedonia afterwards bore to Hellas, on a smaller scale, perhaps, something of what the Russians bear to the West (except that the future of Russia is as yet unknown). The phenomenon of a semi-barbarian border people acquiring some of the superficial aspects of a great civilization on which it abuts is often observed. Japan has participated in the civilizations of both China and the West, and Carthage participated in those of Babylon and the Classical world.

In contrast to the apparently intrusive character of the Hittites, the coast states, that is Phoenicia, seem to have been of direct Babylonian origin, although all details of the early settlement of this area are unknown. Our knowledge becomes definite with the Egyptian conquest of this area by Ahmose I. For about four hundred years Egyptian power, sometimes real, sometimes shadowy, existed over this coast, but the religion remained that of Babylon and the script, the cuneiform. For a brief period between the withdrawal of the Egyptians and the conquest by the Assyrian kings, the maritime cities of Phoenicia, particularly Tyre, became important Mediterranean powers, established colonies as far west as Carthage and Cadiz and held naval mastery of the eastern Mediterranean practically till the rise of the Athenian Empire in the fifth century, B.C.

On the sea was Crete, whose ancient civilization, the Minoan, had certain features that suggest an old and close contact with early Egypt and Libya. The great flowering of wealth and power in Crete came, however, between the end of the Egyptian Middle Kingdom and the great invasions that destroyed the Hittite Empire, a period during which the Cretans apparently held the naval mastery of the Aegean. They were overthrown about 1400 B.C. by the early ancestors of the Classical Greeks.

When Cyaxares destroyed Nineveh he founded what received history calls the Median Empire. Actually it was only an interim dynasty among the alien overlords of Babylonia. It lasted for fifty-three years and then the Persian Cyrus overthrew Cyaxares' son shortly before his own occupation of Babylon. Actually the Medes and Persians were simply separate tribes or clans of a general Aryan group, all of whom soon came to be known as Persians. Thus was founded the Achaemenean

Empire which was, in fact, not a new empire, but a new and barbarian dynasty as lords of the ancient Babylonian civilization. It was a situation quite comparable to that of the Mongol and Manchu dynasties of China. It was an alien conquest of the seats of power in which the ancient society was not uprooted, but simply taken over. The old language, religion, social institutions and commerce, so far as they did not bother the new masters, were all left undisturbed. The Persians had a language and religion of their own, but no letters or learning, and they depended on Babylonian scribes and wrote Persian in cuneiform script.

The immediate reaction to the overthrow of the Medean dynasty and the re-appearance of a strong military power in Assyria was the organization of a coalition by the fractured pieces of Assurbanipal's empire that still lay beyond the control of the Persian armies. Nabonidus, heir of that Nabopolassar who in league with Cyaxares had cracked the northern frontier and betrayed Assyria to the barbarians, found himself faced with destruction by the more vigorous successors of these same barbarians. Nabonidus allied himself with Egypt, now again independent, and with the Hittite fragment calling itself the Lydian Empire in Anatolia. To strengthen the alliance, they brought in another alien, this time not a barbarian tribe but a civilized state of a new civilization which had risen in the west, Sparta. Although individual Greeks as merchants, pirates, and mercenaries had long participated in the disintegration of the Egyptian and Babylonian societies, this was the first appearance of a Classical state as a political factor in this world of ruin and decay.

Cyrus made short work of this league of contradictory interest. In a few years, he destroyed Lydia and occupied Anatolia, Greek city states and all. In 539 B.C. Babylon fell, and in 525 B.C. his son Cambyses conquered, or in a manner of speaking, reconquered Egypt. The empire of Assurbanipal was restored, but this time under barbarian overlords. Less than ninety years had elapsed since the destruction of Nineveh.

This so-called Achaemenean Empire, this dynasty of Persian overlords of the then ancient Babylonian and Egyptian civilizations, enjoys a position in our received history quite out of scale with its importance. It was the campaigns of the successors of Cyrus, Darius and Xerxes, against the Hellenic states that led to the famous battles of Thermopylae, Marathon, Plataea and Salamis. Viewing these battles not simply as the Greeks saw them but also as we see the role of Hellas in world events, we consider these battles among the most important in history and the Achaemenean kings as the great enemies of the unborn future. But the true military and cultural power of his Persian dynasty is revealed by the ease and speed with which it acquired the empire and the east and speed with which Alexander of Macedon utterly destroyed it two hundred and twenty years afterwards. It was only in name an empire. In fact, it was a group of alien barbarians who had become masters of the wealth of the Babylonians and Egyptians, and it could remain powerful only so long as the ancient economic machinery of Babylonia and Egypt continued to function and so long as there remained enough Persians willing to forego the delights of wealth and ease and accept the dangers and discomforts of the army. This was not long. When Cyrus destroyed the Lydian power at Pteria in 546 B.C., he had a small army of skilled Persian archers and cavalry. When Darius III attempted to check Alexander in the last disastrous action near Arbela in 331 B.C., his army was a huge, immobile mass of conscripts with a few Persian officers and only a handful of Persian troops. In fact, the only serious military opposition that Alexander met was from the Persian cavalry, from fellow Greeks in the Persian service, from the walled cities of Tyre and Gaza and, far to the east, in Bactria where the Persians still lived as a people, not as a handful of alien conquerors.

Except for his possessions in Greece, the civilized part of Alexander's new empire was again simply the empire of Assurbanipal under a new master (Alexander had also conquered all the eastern highlands and even had briefly held the valley of the Indus) but this was the last time it was reconstituted, and Alexander's tenure of its throne was short. Almost immediately on his death, leaving a half-witted brother and a posthumous son, a struggle for power broke out among the provincial governors. After more than forty years of war, the struggle ended in the organization of three fairly enduring states. Egypt became the kingdom of the heirs of Ptolemy. Macedonia fell to a dynasty founded by Antigonus, while most of Anatolia dissolved into independent states, principally Pergamum, Pontus and Cappadocia. The rest of the empire, Palestine, Syria, Babylonia and the eastern highlands, fell to the heirs of Seleucus and his Persian wife. The kingdom of the Ptolemies in Egypt came increasingly under Roman influence after 190 B.C. and its independent existence was ended by Roman annexation in 30 B.C. Macedonia and the states of Anatolia were one by one incorporated into the Roman Empire between 168 and 63 B.C. The fate of the Seleucid dominions was more complicated. The Indus Valley was lost in 302 B.C., and the eastern and northeastern provinces were gradually lost so that by about 160 B.C. the Seleucid dominions were confined to Syria and Mesopotamia. The highlands were once more in Persian hands. In this eastern region some Scythian elements had been added to the Hellenic and Persian, and the chief power had come into the hands of a Parthian dynasty known as the Arsacids.

About 130 B.C. Mithridates I, the Parthian king, conquered Mesopotamia to the Euphrates leaving the Seleucids nothing but Syria and a dispute with a Jewish dynasty for control of Palestine.

Having disintegrated as rapidly as it had, the Seleucid Empire, left to itself, would probably have succumbed in a few years and most of the Achaemenean Empire, except Egypt and western Anatolia, would have reappeared under the Parthian name. But the consolidation of the Classical world in the Roman Empire altered the military balance in the Near East. Instead of the irritating job of tiny Sparta against Cyrus, the desperate Greek alliance against Darius and Xerxes, or the wild exuberance of Alexander, there appeared the persistent, institutionalized military power of Rome. Rome appeared as the decisive power in the eastern Mediterranean at the particular moment when the Seleucids had lost Mesopotamia and before the Parthians were able to take Syria. The momentary Seleucid-Parthian frontier, Pompey's line, became the approximate and permanent eastern frontier of Rome and of Byzantium afterwards.

By the time of the Roman annexation of Syria, the lands of the Babylonian civilization had been under a succession of alien overlords since Cyrus took Babylon in 538 B.C. The mere number of years is not very great, particularly to a society that was nearly three thousand years old even in the time of Cyrus. Four hundred years ago the character of Western society was as evident as it is today: America was being settled, the Reformation had begun, the printing presses of Europe had been turning out books for nearly a century. But these particular four centuries had destroyed the civilization of Babylonia. Today, the cities of Babylonia are vague mounds and rubble heaps in the deserts and marshes of Iraq, few have even been excavated. The complex canal system that once controlled the waters of the two rivers and made the plain of Sumer the Garden of Eden (so the Babylonians called the west bank of the Euphrates) have disappeared in flood lands and desert. In the days of the Parthians, much more of the physical plant of Babylonia was still standing, though these four centuries of alien overlords must have worked prodigious ruin for Nineveh itself and the complex of great cities around it were all uninhabited ruins even when Xenophon passed there on the famous march of the ten thousand in 401 B.C.

Few things have so confused our understanding of history as the existence of the Levantine society. We have no trouble seeing that the Babylonians, the Egyptians, the Chinese, the Hindus, the Classical peoples, each constituted a group politically and culturally self-contained, each an evident historical personality. No one argues this. No one finds it difficult to understand. Even the inward life of these peoples, their youth, maturity and the rigid, uncreative formalism of their old age is evident to us. In them the pattern of growth and senescence of a historical organism is apparent almost at a glance. But with the Levantine society none of this is the case. We do not readily comprehend its unity nor easily detect its origin or its boundaries. Since this lack of comprehension leads us to confuse our own origin and our own historical identity, an understanding of the existence and the personality of the Levantine society is perhaps the most pressing problem to anyone who seeks an understanding of the historical flow of Western life. For the odd thousand years since the origin of our society we have lived in intimate physical and cultural contact with the Levantine and all that we have inherited from the Classical past has reached us through the hands and often through the interpretations of the Levant.

In the modern world we can observe the aged, sterile fragments of the Levantine society. Not only are they entirely distinct from the West, but they are equally as sharply separated from the other living, though more aged, societies of India and China. We see these fragments in the tiny sect of Parsees in India, the Jews of the Near East, in the modern Christian Armenians, Syrians and Greeks. We see without difficulty the Levantine origin of the Western Jews; and the less the influence of the West has altered any group of Jews, the more clearly Levantine is their way of life and the pattern of their civilization. Above all we see the modern remains of the Levantine society in what survives of its final imperial political form, the empire of the Arabs which as Islam still sprawls over the world from the Atlantic coast of Morocco to the East Indies, from Zanzibar to western China. But the origin and inward development of all this great piece of world history, of Jew, Mazdaist, Levantine Christian and Moslem alike, is almost lost to us. The basic political units of this society agree neither with ours, nor with those of China, nor with those of the Classical world and so at first view escape our understanding.

Every society has had its own *style* of political thought, its own units of political life and action: its nations. In the West these units have been those of territorial sovereignty, our "countries," a concept which men of other societies have never had. In the Classical world the political unit, the nation, was the city state, the *polis* or *civitas*, and we endow this Classical concept with enough of our own sense of territorial sovereignty to make ourselves think we understand Classical patriotism, to see in Classical phenomena like the Athenian or Roman states the distant cognates of our own political units. We can do much the same with the ancient states of China before Han times. With the ancient Hindus, the Babylonians and the Egyptians we feel able to ignore political matters altogether, if for no other reason than our almost total ignorance of them. But with the Levant we can do neither. We cannot relate Levantine political life to our own nor, as with Egypt, Babylonia and India, ignore it. The political divisions of the Levantine world are too evident to overlook, yet at first sight they seem hardly to be political divisions at all. They seem to be—indeed they are—religious divisions.

Every society has had a religion. Every society has been, among other things, the expression in time and space of the eternal, immaterial concepts that lay at the base of its own religious thought. In every society religion and politics have been inextricably interrelated. Every Classical city state had its own cult, its own special and corporeal manifestation of a god, Diana of Ephesus, Athena of Athens. Every Chinese sovereign was a sacerdotal official, as every Western monarch had to receive a religious consecration. But in none of these cases did religious boundaries coincide with the boundaries of a political unit. An overriding religion, common to the society as a whole, embraced all the nations belonging to that society. In the West, to be sure, nothing comparable to the Classical cults has ever existed. The West became in time divided into mutually hostile sects, but even these, despite the clear evidence of nationalism in their origin, have never been the definition of a Western nation. Most Frenchmen are Roman Catholics just as most Swedes are Lutherans, but neither Roman Catholicism nor Lutheranism determines any man's nationality.

In the Levantine society, on the other hand, while one great religion of dualism and salvation embraced all the members of the society, each sect of that overriding religion was automatically the basic political unit, the nation. We can see that these national units were sects, that each shared with the others the same religious convictions. But it is harder for us to see that each thought of itself not as a sect, but as a nation possessed of the one true revelation of the common religion. We Westerners, whose overriding religion stems back in sacred text and in ecclesiastical traditions to one of those Levantine sect-nations, indeed to two of them, must understand the difference between surface and reality in our own religious life in order to understand these facts. It is not "Christianity" that has been a unit of secular history for two thousand years. It has been different groups of men who have, at different times and with quite different understandings of first and last things, both successively and contemporaneously, called themselves Christians.

Since the Levantine nation was a sect, not a territorial sovereignty, Levantine history becomes absurd if it is thought of as though it had been Western history. The history of the West must be written in terms of countries. These with us have been the units of political action even though the isolated history of no single nation can give an intelligible picture of Western civilization. But if these great political units were ignored and

Western history were written as though it had been primarily a history of religious sects, not only would the unity of the West be missing from the resulting picture, but the political and intellectual life of the West would disappear also. Precisely the same thing, but in reverse, is true of the Levantine society. If the history of that civilization is written in terms of what were its secondary units, its geographical dominions—Persia, Syria, Palestine, Arabia, Anatolia, Greece—the identity of civilization uniting all the subsidiary groupings of this society passes almost without record.

Even our received history partially adjusts itself to this fact, but reluctantly and with a sense of bafflement. It does not grasp the nature of the difficulty. We write histories of Byzantium but even in the most conventional, Byzantium is not a geographical country like Spain or Bohemia, but a political function, the Orthodox Christian state whose boundaries are always ephemeral and whose political, but not whose cultural existence, is terminated in the Turkish capture of Constantinople in 1453. The history of no Western state could be written this way. Poland has always been Poland whether it was a nation with a state of its own or conquered territory; but not so with Byzantium. Greece, Thessaly, Anatolia, mere geographical areas, remain. Orthodox Christianity as a sub-state under the Moslems remains. But Byzantium comes to an end. A similar thing is true of "Persia," a shifting name first applied to the highlands east of the Tigris, then to the Achaemenian Empire, then to the Parthians and finally, in the exact sense of Byzantium, to the Sassanid dominion, primarily in Mesopotamia. When this last state came to an end under Moslem conquest in the seventh century, this "Persia" likewise came to an end and the name, in our usage, reverts to the old geographical meaning of the northeastern highlands. Among the Levantines themselves, however, the name followed the same fate as the Byzantine name for themselves—namely, "Roman." Just as the latter became in the entire Levant the name of the Orthodox Christians, so "Persian" became the name of the adherents of the Mazdaist faith, the name which still survives as Parsee, that is Persian. So, too, no one can write the history of Mohammedanism or the Moslem Empire as though it were the history of Arabia or the history of the Jews as though it had much to do with the fate of territorial Judea.

The political units of the Levantine society were these sect-nations. They were in that society the cognate of what territorial states have been with us. In them was lived the full political life of that society. Whether any one of the sect-nations also held territorial sovereignty was a fact of importance in the life of the nation, but it did not determine—as it would in the West—the continuing political existence of the sect-nation. This continued as a sub-state, master of the life of its own nationals, submissive to the alien territorial sovereign in its external affairs. The meaningful history of the Levant, therefore, lies in the history of its sect-nations and thus appears to us to be religious history, as it would be if applied to Western life. But in the Levant it is political history.

In first encountering the beginning of Levantine society it is therefore necessary, because of our own traditions of religious history, to consider whether that society was in fact more religious than any other. Certainly it usually seems so to us and the fact that its nations had religious boundaries reinforces this view. Yet it is probably an illusion. Although we are familiar with the old age of all previous societies, the Levantine is the only alien civilization whose early history is known to us in significant detail; and since the early periods of all civilizations are more religious than the later, a disproportionate amount of religious material has survived from the Levant. Furthermore, the official outward form of our own religion stands on a set of Levantine documents and thus makes religiousness and Levantine modes of thought appear an inseparable identity to us. Even in late irreligious Levantine work, the basic thought is so suffused with what we call magic and superstition that it seems to us merely debased religion. In fact, our identification of religion with Levantine thought is so great that we sometimes feel that all religious thought must be based on Levantine concepts or it is not truly religious, that there are no genuinely religious concepts except those of the Levant. Thus, we exaggerate the religiousness of the Levant and lose sight of our own.

If belief in the reality of powers, personal or impersonal, that are not within the observable universe yet interfere in its affairs is what we mean by religion, then the Levantine society was religious throughout all its history, and the West scarcely religious at all. On the other hand, if by religion we mean belief in a causality that is not displayed within the observable universe but operates in a non-physical world of the spirit, then Western society has at times been religious but the Levantine never. But if again we mean by religion a belief that beneath all the complex web of the observable universe there exists a God whom we can only dimly comprehend, but whose purpose, as well as we can estimate it, is carried out by the normal, mechanical operation of that universe (as each society understands what is normal and mechanical) often in utter disregard of our dearest personal hopes and ideas, then both the Levant and the West have at times been religious and at times irreligious.

In considering the history of the Levant it is wise to use the third definition of religion. If the first is accepted, and we are always under a temptation to do so because of the Bible, we are really talking about Levantine physics, not religion, and end by deciding that the whole Levantine world was either more in tune with religious truth than ours has ever been or possessed from beginning to end by the most arrant and nonsensical superstition. It was neither. It just had a different physics.

Finally the Levantine society found in the book a suitable vehicle for its primary religious symbolism and this no other society has ever done. What sacred architecture was to the religious youth of the West, the holy writings were to all the sects of the Levantine religion. These were the concrete expression in symbolic form of the deep and hidden realities of the universe. No one would think of "reading" a Gothic cathedral as he would read a book. The great system of vault, pier and buttress, the intricate design and color of the windows, the vast detail of the sculpture, are not there for their literal reading in engineering and technology, though these are there also, as are the edifying traditions and Bible stories. But the deep meaning, the hauntingly intertwined longing for faith and hope and for immense power over physical reality, which only the buildings as complete wholes are able to display, is only symbolized, never expressed.

So with the book to the Levantine world; what it says is truth, but it is no more than a fraction of the truth that lies concealed, here in detailed allegory, there in the symbolism of the whole. But when we Westerners read such books all we can read is the text. And the literal sense of the text expresses only a tiny fraction of the meaning of the whole. The symbolic meaning of having a holy book at all is largely lost to us. We take it as a record of religious progress or as establishing a moral standard to be approached. We do not see it as the living witness of a compact with holy powers covering the brief but critical period between the magical creation of the world and its magical transformation in the last times, in the near-approaching day of judgment.

There is a further point in connection with the symbolic role of the book in Levantine life: script. To us, script is an attribute of language. We would never write Arabic in our modern so-called Roman script just as we would never write English in Greek script. But to the Levantines, script was a symbol of sectarian nationality and had nothing to do with language. Every Levantine sect-nation immediately adopted its own script, the script in which it wrote its holy books, and this script became its badge of nationality regardless of what language it used in ordinary life. When Arabic became the principal spoken language of the Levant, the Arabs wrote it in Arabic script, the Jews in Hebrew, the heretical Christians in the special scripts of their respective Bibles. When the Mazdaist of Iran became Moslems they promptly wrote their native Persian in Arabic script. The Samaritans wrote their Hebrew Penateuch in their own script, and when the Jews of Europe adopted Medieval German instead of Arabic as their spoken language, they wrote it, as their Orthodox descendants still do, in Hebrew script.

The new Levantine religious feeling that began to show itself in the ancient Babylonian world in the period between Cyrus and the Romans comes to our notice in two religious movements with different myths but the same religious content. Both were soon to become sect-nations. Both were to undergo extensive modifications, suffer extensive schism, and both were to be very largely absorbed into Mohammedanism. They were by no means the only religious movements of their times, but they were the two whose historical continuity was to bring them from the very earliest Levantine days down to our own times. They are Mazdaism and Judaism.

Just as the Bible tells us that God selected Moses to carry the true religious teaching to the Jews, so the Avesta casts Zoroaster in an identical role as the founder of Mazdaism. In both cases, the men as instruments of God are credited with vast religious reform, reform which in fact occurred centuries after their supposed lives. With Zoroaster as with Moses we can be sure neither of his teachings nor his existence. In neither case have we any firm historical evidence upon which to decide whether the lives of actual men underlie the legendary figures of the religious text.

We do know that the Achaemenian kings after Darius worshipped God under the name of Ahura Mazda. We also know that by the time of Herodotus, the Magi, the Mazdaist priesthood, were powers in the empire. Finally from Hermippus, an Athenian writer of comedies at about the time of the Peloponnesian War, we learn for the first time from outside sources that Zoroaster was the founder of the Magi and was the author of a great book, that is, of the Avesta. It is thus clear that somewhere between 500 B.C. and 400 B.C., it was believed throughout the Achaemenian Empire that Zoroaster was the founder of Mazdaism. A similar belief concerning Moses, and at about the same time, arose in Judaism.

The Avesta teaches that from the beginning of time, there were two equal powers, Ahura,[7] that is the Lord, creator of life, truth and goodness, and Ahriman, that is, Satan, the author of all evil, wickedness and death. It is the discovery by each of these mighty powers of the existence of the other that is the cause and occasion of creation. All the universe is rent by a vast spiritual chasm and across this God and Satan, through their angels and various creations, struggle for the mastery of the universe. The life of man and the earth, the history of all the kingdoms of this world, is the history of this titanic struggle.

Man is one of God's creations with a being and a mind fashioned after the mind of God and, therefore, necessarily man has freedom of the will and can, if he chooses, go over to Satan's side. However, since he is God's

---

[7] The Avesta, like the later books of the Bible, gives no name to God. He is called "Lord of Wisdom," in Persian, Ahura Mazdao, hence the modern name of the religion.

creation, it is only just that God should require his voluntary allegiance and punish him if he falters in the struggle. It is, therefore, every man's duty under pain of everlasting punishment to engage all his life in the war against evil. To be certain of the matter, God has established a recording angel, the original role of the Archangel Mithra, who enters every act and thought, good or evil, of every man, and on his death each is faced with this account and judged by it. A man whose good works outweigh the bad enters Paradise immediately upon death. The man of evil goes immediately into Hell. Those whose books balance closely are confined to a limbo of indecision until the last judgment when their fate will be finally decided.

Such, it is said, was the state of the world and the fate of man before Zoroaster. For it became apparent to God that man was a weak creature and blind, troubled in his judgments and all too often unable to distinguish the demons of Satan from the ministers of God. Out of his great love and mercy, therefore, God determined to send into the world a messenger to open the eyes of men and show them the way of salvation. At first, God considered selecting a great and virtuous king for this task, but this king himself pointed out how unfitted are even the best of the kings of this world for the task of teaching men the truths of the world to come. And so God selected instead Zoroaster, the humble man, perhaps a camel driver or a cowherd, to teach his great message.

The history of Mazdaism is of interest primarily as an independent indication of the type of religious feeling that existed in the area where Levantine civilization was beginning to form. It is likewise useful to demolish the opinion that there was anything particularly Semitic about the secular and religious philosophy of this civilization. The ancient Persians were Aryans and indeed not too distantly separated from the Aryan conquerors of India. On the other hand, the history of Judaism is of wider significance to the modern West. Not only are Jews an important element of modern Western society, so that their image of themselves is of political importance, but the Christian myth stands upon the Jewish and even the most irreligious of modern Westerners is molded by the Christian myth of his society. The continuum, which received history and revealed religion alike affirm, is not only the identity of Western and Orthodox Christianity, but equally the lineal progression of the latter from post-exilic Judaism which in turn is asserted to be the same basic religion as that delivered by Moses to the Hebrews. This belief in the long continuity of religious thought furnishes the strongest member in the structure of our line-of-progress image of history. If a continuity, even allowing for development, exists in first and last things then the picture of mankind progressing cannot be wholly false. But the continuum is a myth, and curiously the one place where accepted opinion feels the linkage to be the least firm, namely, between Judaism and Orthodox Christianity, is the one place where a real continuum of religious view did in fact exist.

The Bible as we have it today is not an ancient document. The Jewish books that correspond to the Old Testament of the Protestant churches (and to the corresponding books of the Roman Catholic Bible) all go back to a single Hebrew manuscript of the reign of Hadrian from which was derived the standard Masoretic text, which has been the canonical Hebrew version ever since. No other orthodox Hebrew text exists and the only variants are the Samaritan text of the Pentateuch in Hebrew and the Septuagint, the Greek translation made for the Jews of the Roman Empire. The Jewish-Samaritan rift cannot be earlier than the fourth century B.C. and the translation of the Septuagint began after 300 B.C. so that these two texts do not represent widely different dates.

In addition to the canonical Jewish and Protestant books, there is a group of books considered canonical by the Jews at the time of the translation of the Septuagint and hence included in that translation. Though these books were subsequently expunged from their canon by the Jews, the Christians, whose original Bible was the Septuagint, never the Hebrew Scriptures, had in the meantime accepted them in the Christian canon. Thus has arisen the Protestant Apocrypha, the books of the traditional Christian Old Testament for which no Hebrew texts could be found at the time of the Reformation, these having been destroyed by the Jews after the closing of the Hebrew canon. The principal books in this group are: Esdras, Maccabees, Wisdom and Ecclesiasticus, rarely printed in a Protestant Bible, but (except for III and IV Esdras) still canonical to Roman Catholics.

Seventy-five years of Biblical criticism have successfully disentangled the structure of the Bible and arrived at reasonably conclusive estimates of the several religious and political viewpoints responsible for its different parts and responsible for the form in which the Bible has come down to us. This long, painstaking and scholarly endeavor has established the lateness of the compilation, and the fragmentary and contradictory character of older material incorporated by the several layers of later compilers. This criticism has established that the major image of Jewish and Hebrew history as the Bible displays it, and was compiled to display it, is completely false in every important aspect. Yet oddly enough this criticism has been unable to sketch an intelligible counter-image and, for lack of showing an understandable motive for the falsification, has never been able to make its criticism entirely convincing. Yet the difficulty was simple. It was, however, the type of difficulty that the philosophy of the eighteenth and nineteenth centuries made it natural for Western scholars to ignore. Our scholarship has been a masterly technique for tracking down detailed historical neglect and detailed falsification, but it has been innocent and almost helpless in the face of the really great historical lie, of a falsification not of a historical fact but of a historical image, not of a detail but of a whole. This has been true of our misunderstanding of the history of Rome and Byzantium regardless of how many individual facts have been set straight. It has been true of our confused history of the Christianities. In Biblical criticism, it has led to our inability to comprehend that Yahweh worship of "pre-exilic" times was an utterly different *religion* from "post-exilic" Judaism and that the Jews as a race or nation bear no significant biological or cultural relation to the inhabitants of the Kingdoms of Israel and Judah or the mythical tribes of the Hebrews. In fact, if there were any evidence offered in the Bible for either proposition its dubious character would probably long ago have led to its rejection by modern criticism. But these propositions are not evidence. They are assumed, and, the later the Biblical compiler, the more fully and more rashly he displays these assumptions. Deuteronomy and the early revisions of Kings are very guarded about the nature of the earlier Yahweh worship. Chronicles and Ezra-Nehemiah display no doubt that it was precisely like the worship of their own day—though, of course, subsequently corrupted. Ezra in turn is obviously embarrassed by the question of the Israelite ancestry of the Jews of his time, but by the time of the Apocrypha and the Talmud, as to this day, all Jews are obviously known to be descended from the tribes of Israel and the Hebrews of the days of Moses.

Since the Masoretic text, the Samaritan Pentateuch and the Septuagint do not furnish an extensive base for textual comparisons, the reconstruction of the development of the Bible is primarily a work of examination of internal inconsistencies. The difficulty is further increased by the fact that the ancient Hebrew text was consonantal only and without word spacing, two facts which make even the Masoretic text itself, with its spacing and vowels, only the official Jewish interpretation of the final revision. It is a further important fact that though the composition of the Old Testament is supposed to have covered perhaps five hundred years, and even older fragments are believed to be incorporated in later books, yet through all this time the Hebrew appears to show no real linguistic change. There are slight variations in style but nothing comparable to the changes that always occur in a living language over a comparable stretch of time. It seems necessary, therefore, to suppose one of three alternatives: either that the composition of the books did not stretch over so great a time as is supposed, or that the older parts were later rewritten into a more modern

Hebrew, or—what seems by all odds the most likely—that Hebrew was no longer spoken and had become entirely a closed priests' language before the great bulk of the canon was written.

Back of the late form in which we now have the Bible lay a long series of compilations and drastic revisions. Some of these changes were for such minor purposes as establishing the antiquity of certain priestly customs and advantages, or to discredit Samaria and Israel in favor of Jerusalem and Judah. But beyond all such trifling matters three great purposes dictated the major frame in which the Bible was cast and determined the basic selection, editing and composition of material. Since these purposes were necessarily not those of the early prophets of Judaism, the compilers' task was not alone to manipulate older Hebrew *non-Jewish* material, but also to adapt to newer conditions genuine Jewish material of an earlier age. These three purposes were to show first, that Judaism was the religion revealed by God to Moses, second, that Judaism was the ancient national religion of the Hebrews of Palestine and, third, that these pre-exilic Hebrews were the ancestors of the Jews. Since these three propositions are unqualifiedly without historical basis, the task of composition and editing was exacting and continuous. From the middle of the fourth century, and probably from earlier times, some sort of canonical or semi-canonical text must have been in existence so that major alteration or suppression of texts became increasingly a difficult problem. In earlier times, it must have been easier. The Pentateuch and Joshua, for instance, show distinctly that they were put together from separate narratives by at least two different schools and then interlarded with totally new material by at least two others. In contrast, the later difficulties in reconciling the historical series, Judges, Samuel, Kings, with the newer political and theological standards could no longer be met by again rewriting all these books. Instead, only bits and pieces were changed and the proper emphasis was supplied by writing an entirely new and parallel history, Chronicles.

The historical structure of the Bible is more evident in the order of the books in the Jewish canon than it is in the Christian. The Jewish Bible is divided into three groups of decreasing sacredness. The Torah, that is, the "Law," corresponding exactly with the Christian Pentateuch; the "Prophets," composed of Joshua, Judges, Samuel, Kings, Isaiah, Jeremiah, Ezekiel and the twelve minor prophets counted as one book; and finally, the third section, the "Writings," consisting of all the other books. The arrangement of the Christian Bible follows that of its parent, the Septuagint, which, with the exception of the untouchably sacred Torah, attempted an order somewhat according to subject. The present Jewish order follows the actual historical order of the acceptance of the sacred character of the respective books. Thus, the Pentateuch was held to be sacred before the translation of the Septuagint while the Prophets must have lacked something of this status since the Septuagint broke the group apart. The Writings were clearly somewhat fluid. How long before the translation of the Septuagint the Torah had become sacred is impossible to tell with certainty. It must have been before the Samaritan separation, the date of which is debatable: between 330 B.C., according to Josephus (*Antiquities* xi, 7, 8), and 440 B.C. (twentieth year of Artaxerxes, by the most extreme chronological calculation from the statements in Ezra and Nehemiah). On the other hand, it could not have long preceded the events recorded in these books since these are the earliest that refer to the existence of anything corresponding to the Pentateuch.

The frame of the Bible as we have it today is, therefore, the series, Chronicles, Ezra, Nehemiah. These books are the original creation of the school of thought that dominated the compilation of the earliest canon. Their religious and political point of view is the point of view towards which the older books were altered. To be sure, Chronicles, Ezra, Nehemiah reflect only one of the two powerful trends in Judaism at the time of their composition around 300 B.C., the priestly in contrast to the prophetic. Yet despite the immense influence of the prophetic trend in the development of Judaism as a religion, it was the priestly point of view that controlled the writing or alteration of the holy books and perhaps to some extent their survival, though the technical establishment of the complete canon as it now exists was the work of the much later rabbinical synods, after the priests and the temple at Jerusalem had come to an end.

The historical myth which the Bible seeks to establish is that the Hebrews or Israelites were a nomadic tribe of northwestern Arabia enslaved by the Egyptians. They escaped by the aid of their tribal god, Yahweh, and later conquered and settled Palestine, forming the Kingdom of Israel. This was later divided into the two kingdoms, Israel and Judah. Here the pure religion revealed to Moses was corrupted but never entirely lost. With the overthrow of the two kingdoms, the worshippers of Yahweh were carried away to Babylon but later allowed to return. Yet despite this permission to return, in some unclear way, the Jews have remained in a dispersed "captivity" throughout the world ever since.

Until the mid-nineteenth century, this story was accepted by the great bulk of Western opinion as true and Biblical scholarship worked on minor points within the major frame. Such questions were considered as under what dynasty did the Egyptian captivity occur, what was the probable date of the Israelite entry into Palestine? Today, archaeological and historical investigation has demolished every important feature of this story, but because the name Yahweh was carried from the days of the Hebrew kingdoms into the later religion of the Jews—even though it soon ceased to be used—we still try to re-arrange the story to show the continuance of one people and one identical religion.

Scholars have been at great pains to disentangle the early history of the Israelites from the involved and contradictory stories in the Bible. Chronicles has long since been given up as a source of anything but the view of late "post-exilic" writers, but Judges, Samuel and Kings have been mined to assemble a fairly just picture of the Israelites of Palestine. Unfortunately, it is primarily a cultural picture that emerges and a record of historical events is as lacking as ever. We have no idea when the Israelites may have conquered Palestine and so far as the cultural picture is concerned it is consistent either with no such conquest ever having taken place or of having occurred at such an early date that the references to it in the Bible can be no more than the recording of tales long become purely mythology.

In the confusion there are only two firm anchors of fact: first, the archaeological remains in Palestine; second, for the period about 1400 B.C., the Tell-el-Amarna correspondence of the Egyptian governors and of the Palestinian princes subject to Egypt. The archaeological remains show a sharp change in the population of Palestine somewhere around 2500 B.C. They show also an unbroken continuity of style and cult thereafter. From this continuity, it is evident that the invaders of 2500 B.C. were of the same basic Semitic-speaking stock that was still there in later times when more definite historical evidence becomes available. Prior to the Egyptian XII Dynasty this people showed only the influence of Babylonia. Later certain Egyptian practices began to show. With the XVIIIth Dynasty and its wars and conquests in Palestine and Syria, the Egyptian influence becomes widely evident. Yet the language remained unchanged and Babylonian written in cuneiform remained the official language even of the Egyptian governors in their correspondence with Ahmose III and IV (c. 1400-1350 B.C.).

No one has ever found a satisfactory date for the Israelite conquest of Palestine. It has never been supposed that it could have occurred before the Egyptian conquests of the XVIIIth Dynasty because no Egyptian records give any account of a prominent group of Yahweh worshippers resident in Palestine and on the other side the Bible records no incident that would indicate an Egyptian sovereignty over Palestine. But there remain these difficulties: the Tell-el-Amarna correspondence, though written in Babylonian, shows by its errors and its glosses that the spoken language of Palestine was Hebrew. Furthermore, the archaelogical remains show conclusively that there was no interruption of the continuity of civilization in Palestine from the XVIIIth Dynasty to the fall of Assyria.

It seems necessary to conclude, therefore, that the story of an Israelite conquest of Palestine is considerably exaggerated if not invented. The account in the Bible probably represents a few mythological matters going back to the general Semitic occupation before 2500 B.C. fused with the accounts of some small clans struggling for power in a population composed of people exactly like themselves. Whether these clans were at that time Yahweh worshippers or were the only Yahweh worshippers, are facts that cannot be surely determined. There is no doubt, however, that Yahweh was an important god to some people in Palestine but in no way distinguishable from the other baals of the country. How long he had been one of the gods of Palestine is unknown. Later he became the state god of the Kingdom of Israel and was such when that state appears for the first time in the light of partially verifiable history under David and Solomon (about 900 B.C.).

The Kingdoms of Israel and Judah, with their respective capitals at Samaria and Jerusalem, only briefly united under David and Solomon, continued with Yahweh as their state god. Their history is that of Balkan principalities of the Babylonian civilization rising as minor states in the few centuries that intervened between the collapse of the Egyptian Empire in the XXI Dynasty and the westward advance of Assyria. The two kingdoms lay on the land routes between these two great civilized worlds, and Judah in addition controlled the prosperous portage trade from the head of the Gulf of Akaba to the Mediterranean. They were rich, but they were only as powerful as the weakness of their great neighbors.

It is almost impossible to establish any detailed history of these kingdoms. There is little external evidence on the subject and the Bible, in addition to picturing all events from one or another far later religious and national points of view, was compiled at Jerusalem, not Samaria and adds here a specific distortion to justify and glorify Judah and paint Israel in an unflattering light. If any conjecture at all can be pieced out of the confusion, it is that Judah from the time of Jehu, about 845 B.C., remained a client and ally of Assyria, even assisting Assyria against Israel.

The religious situation in the last days of the Kingdoms of Israel and Judah was complicated by the political and economic. The Empire of Assyria in its last years must have seemed to its contemporaries as essentially unstable. There were constant rebellions against it, in Babylon, in the frontier provinces and in Egypt. True, these were put down, but they never ceased. The worlds of Babylonia and Egypt were manifestly approaching some vast catastrophe. The two Hebrew kingdoms had apparently involved themselves on different sides, Israel generally hostile to Assyria and seeking Egyptian support, Judah generally cooperating with Assyria. But the political situation was constantly growing worse. Egypt was weak and meddlesome, Assyria armed and brutal. With the political ignorance not unknown to religious leaders, Hosea[8] speaks of the problem of Israel with contempt as the politics of "a silly dove without heart. They call to Egypt, they go to Assyria." (vii, 11) But the political situation was not to be cured by a stout or even a pure heart.

There is also the picture of the poor and the rich, (Amos viii, 4):

> *O ye that swallow up the needy, even to make the poor of the land to fail, saying, 'when will the new moon be gone that we may sell corn? and the sabbath, that we may set forth wheat, making the ephah small, and the shekel great and falsifying the balances by deceit? That we may buy the poor for silver, and the needy for a pair of shoes, yea and sell the refuse of the wheat?'*

From Amos v, 7, 10-13:

> *You who make justice a bitter thing, trampling on the law, hating a man who exposes you, loathing him who is honest with you!—for this, for crushing the weak, and forcing them to give you grain, houses of ashlar you may build, but you shall never dwell in them; vineyards you may plant, but you shall drink no wine from them. I know your countless crimes, your manifold misdeeds—browbeating honest men, accepting bribes, defrauding the poor of justice. (It is a time when the prudent make no protest, so evil is the time!)*

In Hosea, a contemporary of Amos, there also appears hostility to the established priesthood of Yahweh (iv, 1-4):

> *No fidelity, no kindness, no knowledge of God in the land, nothing but perjury, lying and murder, stealing, debauchery, burglary— bloodshed on bloodshed! . . . But none protests, no man complains, for my people are no better than their priestlings.*

The northern kingdom, Israel, settled and quaking of its dove's heart and faithful to its political traditions, entered an Egyptian confederation against Assyria. Isaiah, who understood the political realities better than

---

[8] Despite the religious and literary veneration for the King James version of the Bible, quotations hereafter are usually made from the translation of James Moffatt, Harpers, 1935, with the exception that the original "Yahweh" is usually replaced for Moffatt's euphemism "The Eternal." The King James version was based on a defective text and was a revision more than a new translation. Its language was already archaic in 1611 and at certain spots is today almost unintelligible.

a north country shepherd, however religious, opposed the idea in Judah, and Israel fought alone. Egyptian support amounted to little and Samaria and all northern Palestine fell to Sargon in 721 B.C. The memory of this perhaps lies in God's curse on Egypt in Ezekiel (xxiv, 6), "since you have been a poor staff of reeds to Israel, breaking when they seized you, tearing all their hand, breaking when they leant on you." It is not clear whether Judah aided the Assyrians, but from then on the kingdom was little more than an Assyrian province. Under Esar-Haddon and Assurbanipal there were apparently Assyrian garrisons in the country, though local government was not interfered with.

But the Assyrian power was decaying rapidly. The Medes were more aggressive in the north, Nabopolassar, the Assyrian viceroy of Babylonia, established a brief independence and a momentarily reorganized Egypt revolted and moved eastward. In all that decaying empire of revolt and intrigue only Judah seems to have remained with the Assyrians and its great reformer king, Josiah, fell at Megiddo in 609 B.C. fighting the armies of Egypt on behalf of an Assyria that had already come to an end three years before in the ruins of Nineveh.

The battle of Megiddo and the fall of Assyria mark the end of the Israelite kingdoms. All that remained was a twenty-four year epilogue of the neo-Babylonian Kingdom and its brief relations with Judah. This remains large in tradition but changed nothing.

The fall of Assyria was the destruction of a world. It began a period of several centuries of anarchy and conquest in which the Babylonian and Egyptian civilizations came to an end. It is the great funeral dirge of these civilizations that lies in Isaiah and Ezekiel, particularly Isaiah xxiv, 4-20. In chapters twenty-six to thirty-two of Ezekiel the whole downfall of a great mercantile civilization is spread before our eyes.

An Assyrian client state like Judah went with the rest of the wreckage. For a few years, the tottering kingdom shifted its allegiance from vanished Assyria to wavering Egypt even though Egypt had been driven out of Syria by Nabopolassar and it was obvious that the new Babylonian Kingdom was for the moment the strongest power in the shattered political structure of western Asia. The details of these years are hopelessly lost in the contradictions and omissions that the compilers of the Bible employed in an attempt to adjust the facts of this period to the requirement of a later religious and national point of view.

But it is significant to note Isaiah's partiality to Assyria and his deep hostility to Egypt. Equally, in later times, Jeremiah is so manifestly the partisan of the new Babylonian king that he was directly accused of being his agent. There is every indication in the Book of Jeremiah that the events leading up to the destruction of Jerusalem had many of the aspects of a civil war, Jeremiah and the Babylonian party against the king and the pro-Egyptians. All that seems certain is that Jerusalem surrendered undamaged to Nebuchadnezzar in 596 B.C. and then, apparently on the promise of non-existent Egyptian support, revolted, and was again captured in 586. This time its walls were demolished and the temple and palace burned. Some of its inhabitants and some country people were removed to Babylon. There is no way to ascertain the figure and even the later Biblical accounts are contradictory. We do know, however, that it was nowhere near the population of Israel and Judah. Thus began the "Babylonian captivity" which was to become such a decisive phrase in the history of Judaism.

What is presented to us as the "Babylonian captivity" is the end of the Hebrew kingdoms and the beginning of the Jews. Somewhere between the fall of Jerusalem, that is, the destruction of the Assyrian Empire, and the establishment of the Kingdom of the Seleucids, the Jewish religion came into being and formed the Jews. Certainly also certain persons must have had a hand in forming Judaism, but unfortunately it is impossible to ascertain precisely who these were, if indeed they were a cohesive stock at all. That they were not the Judeans and Israelites of Biblical tradition can be reasonably conjectured, though there were undoubtedly Judeans and to lesser extent Israelites among the founders of the new faith. But in this matter historical fact was entirely secondary. Since the great shrines of the god adopted by the new religion had been first at Shiloh and later at Jerusalem, and since the earliest prophets whose teachings became incorporated in the canon of this religion were Judeans and Israelites, nothing was more seemly than that the Jews should see as their physical as well as their spiritual ancestors the inhabitants of the Kingdoms of Israel and Judah.

The early prophets whose work furnished a spiritual Judaic ancestry of Judaism were Amos, Hosea, Isaiah and Jeremiah (the two later books contain a great deal of later material). Later times pictured the teaching of these seventh and eighth century prophets as a call upon Israel to return to the pure Mosaic faith; and the books of each of these prophets contain interpolated accounts of how Israel had turned its face from its true Lord and wandered after foreign gods, though the message of the prophet himself is altogether different. This change of emphasis was in accordance with the required tradition and has even been accepted unquestioned as part of the Christian myth, but there is no shred of either historical or Biblical evidence that the religion of Palestine in the days of Amos and Hosea differed in any significant aspect from the religion of the land when it first came within the sphere of Babylonian civilization more than a thousand years before. Indeed, the only continuity of a religious nature that carries from the time before Amos to post-exilic days is the name of Yahweh.

Everything else amounted to no more than trifling ceremonial customs and generalized myths. Even the name of Yahweh became an embarrassment to the later Jews and they no longer used it. Officially this was because the name was too holy to be uttered. But to the earliest chroniclers who began using "Elohim," God, for "Yahweh," it may have seemed deeply necessary to use a style that could not be applicable to all the personally named gods of dying Babylonia. Perhaps the great and only God could be better designated than by the name of a local demon identified with the Babylonian storm god, given Ishtar as a wife and worshipped as every other baal in Palestine with phallic rites on sacred hilltops and under every tall tree.

It was the natural, genuine Babylonian quality of the people and culture of Israel and Judah that the later compilers of the Bible wished to identify as utterly alien. Babylonian customs were not Jewish, so it must be shown that they were not the customs of Israel and Judah. Thus customs of unknown antiquity in Palestine, like the worship of Ishtar and sacred prostitution, were asserted to have been perversions of the pure faith of Moses brought on by the backsliding of a wicked and stiff-necked people. At certain passages such customs are even described as the specific introduction of some wicked king, the favorite for this role, despite the impossible chronology, being Manasseh, who reigned only a few years before Josiah. This is impossible because by the time of Josiah, in the decaying world of Assyrian power, the religious situation had reached the point of violent revolution. The story is told with great fullness in II Kings, xxii and xxiii. Chapter xxii described how an unknown book of Moses was found in the temple and the king suddenly realized how unlawfully he and his people had been acting. But chapter xxiii speaks for itself:

II Kings xxiii:2-24

> *King Josiah went up to the temple of Yahweh, accompanied by all the men of Judah and all the citizens of Jerusalem, the priest, the prophets, and all the people, young and old. He then read aloud to them all the words of the book of the compact, which had been found in the temple of Yahweh, and, standing on the platform, he made a compact in presence of Yahweh to follow Yahweh, to obey his orders and his warnings and his rules heartily and honestly, maintaining the compact laid down in this book. All the people confirmed the compact.*
>
> *Then the king ordered Hilkiah the high priest and the vice-priest and the warders to bring out of the temple of Yahweh all the vessels made by Baal and Astarte (Ishtar) and the star-worship; these he burned outside Jerusalem in the lime-kiln of Kidron, removing their ashes to Bethel. He put down the pagan priests whom the kings of Judah had appointed to burn incense at the shrines in the townships of Judah and at the shrines round Jerusalem, along with those who*

*burned incense to Baal, to the sun, the moon, the planets, and all
the stars. He took the idol of Astarte out of the temple of Yahweh
to the Kidron-ravine outside Jerusalem, where he burned it grinding
it to powder and flinging the powder on the graves of the common
people. He demolished the houses of the sacred prostitutes who were
in the temple of Yahweh, where the women wove tunics for Astarte.
He took all the priests away from the towns of Judah, desecrating
the shrines where the priests had been burning incense, from Geba
to Beersheba. (However, the priests of these shrines did not serve
the altar of Yahweh at Jerusalem, they ate their unleavened bread
along with their fellow-priests.) He broke down the shrines of the
satyrs that stood at the entrance to the house of Joshua, the governor of the city, on the left as one entered the city. He desecrated
Topheth in the valley of Benhimmon, so that no one might burn his
son or daughter to Molek.*

*He removed the figures of horses set up for the sun by the kings
of Judah, at the entry to the temple of Yahweh, beside the chamber
of Nathanmelek the chamberlain, in the annex; he burnt up the
chariots of the sun, and as for the altars on the roof, made by the
kings of Judah, and the altars made by Manasseh in the two court-
yards of the temple of Yahweh, the king demolished them and bore
them off, flinging their dust into the Kidron-ravine. The king desecrated the shrines east of Jerusalem, on the south side of Destroyer-
hill, which had been erected by Solomon, king of Israel, for Astarte
the detestable idol of the Phoenicians and for Kemosh the detestable
idol of the Moabites and for Milkom the detestable idol of the Ammonites. He smashed the obelisks, cut down the sacred poles, and
filled up their site with dead men's bones.*

*As for the altar at Bethel erected by Jeroboam, who led Israel into
sin, that altar and its shrine he demolished, smashing its stones to
pieces, crushing it to powder, and burning the sacred pole. . . .
The king ordered all the people to hold a passover in honour of
Yahweh their God, as enjoined in this book of the compact. For
no such passover had been kept since the days of the heroes who
had ruled Israel, not even under the kings of Israel or the kings of
Judah. This passover was held in honor of Yahweh at Jerusalem
in the eighteenth year of King Josiah.*

*Moreover, the mediums, the wizards, the household idols, the
fetishes, and any detestable idols that were to be seen throughout
the land of Judah and in Jerusalem, Josiah put away, that he might
carry out the terms of the law written in the book found by Hilkiah
the priest within the tempel of Yahweh.*

It is not surprising that the Book of Kings was an endless problem to the
compilers of the Bible as its truncated ending and the serious variations
between the Masoretic and Septuagint texts clearly show. Here, there is no

argument of an anciently pure religion corrupted by the abominations of the Philistines and the Canaanites. As Jesus, the son of Sirach, perhaps the most thoughtful and honest of the semi-canonical Jewish commentators, said of him long afterwards (Ecclus. lxix: 1, 3), "The remembrance of Josiah is like the composition of . . . perfume . . . He behaved himself uprightly in the conversion of the people and took away the abominations of iniquity. He directed his heart unto the Lord and in the time of the ungodly he established the worship of God."

But in the canonical account the myth must be stressed. Chapters xxxiv and xxxv of II Chronicles recount Josiah's famous passover and the finding of the lost book. But all traces of ancient religious practices and of the evident fierceness of the struggle are swept away and the proper interpretation is placed upon the event: "Josiah removed all the abominable idols from every district belonging to Israel and made everybody within Israel offer worship of Yahweh their God, during all this reign they never gave up their devotion to Yahweh the God of their fathers."

Perfectly in the spirit of Chronicles and in the name of the same myth, though for a derivative purpose, more than two thousand years afterwards the Reverend Dr. Owen Charles Whitehouse, Professor of Hebrew, Biblical Exegesis and Theology and theological tutor, Chestnut College, Cambridge, tells us, "The definite ethical character of the religion of Yahweh established by Moses is exhibited in the strict exclusion of all sexual impurity in His worship. Unlike the Canaanite Baal, Yahweh has no female consort and this remained throughout a distinguishing trait of the original and unadulterated Hebrew religion. Indeed Hebrew, unlike Assyrian or Phoenician, has no distinctive form for 'goddess.' From first to last the true religion of Yahweh was pure of sexual taint; the Kedeshim and Kedeshoth attendants [sacred prostitutes, female and male] in the Baal and Ashtoreth shrines (cf. the Kadishtu of the temples of the Babylonian Ishtar) were foreign Canaanite elements which became imported into Hebrew worship during the period of Hebrew settlement in Canaan."[9]

Furthermore, the evidence of the early prophets themselves is against any idea that the religion of Yahweh in eighth century Israel had been corrupted from a pure, even if primitive, worship practiced by their distant ancestors before they came in contact with the abominations of the Canaanites. That idea occurs only to the writers of the much later books. Amos is concerned only with the crimes and vices of his contemporaries, particularly with the exactions of the rich. Not once does he suggest that a one-time pure religion has been corrupted by alien contact, so clearly so, that later editors apparently thought it wise to inject this note, as in Chapter iii, 4 which is a subsequent interpolation. Hosea is primarily the enemy

[9] *Encyclopedia Britannica*, 11th Ed., vol. 13, p. 179.

of the royal government, the priesthood and the prophets' guilds, and while he objects strenuously to sacred prostitution he does not consider it at all an alien custom. It is true that this book has a few passages asserting that the Israelites have departed from Yahweh to worship baals and idols and that this has brought on them Yahweh's wrath, but the most emphatic passages calling for a return to Yahweh, vii, 10, viii, 6 and ix, 14 are known to be later interpolations. Most significantly, the great Isaiah has not one word of reproach for the religious practices of his time—and he died before King Josiah had desecrated the shrine of Astarte that Solomon had built at Jerusalem. Isaiah's fury is against the human relationship of the inhabitants of Israel and Judah. It is not for worshipping the baals and Astartes on every high hill and under every green tree that God will punish Israel, but for bribery, oppression, robbery, murder, defrauding the poor and the widows (i, 21-23, iii, 14, v, 7, 8 and x, 1-5; the passage at x, 10-13 is a later interpolation). Even Ezekiel writing at Babylon after the fall of Jerusalem with the Jewish myth well into flower did not present the story as one of a pure religion corrupted. To him Israel had *never* been faithful to Yahweh; the Israelites had *always* spurned his laws howsoever often he aided them, howsoever often he once more showed them the way of life and truth. Ezekiel xx is a revealing chapter, for here is the frame of the Jewish myth as the Book of Ezra afterwards gave it completed form, but in the early version of Ezekiel it is not foreign idols and wicked foreign ways that have seduced Israel from the true faith. Israel has been since the day it was chosen, a rebellious, impudent and obstinate race (ii, 3-4).

War and bitter religious revolution, the fall of Assyria and the destruction of Jerusalem, anarchy, scattered peoples and the fierce preaching of the new faith—such was the end of the little provincial outpost of a dying society. By our standards of morals and of the proprieties of history, the destruction of that society might seem a highly desirable accomplishment. It is interesting, however, that we have left to us a faint echo of some of the emotions that moved the people who lived through the opening scenes of that historic drama.

Some years after the fall of Jerusalem and the ruin of the Kingdom of Judah, Jeremiah found himself among some refugees in Egypt. He took the occasion to reproach them bitterly for their failure to accord the proper observance to the new faith. He got this reply from a group of women (xliv, 16-19):

> *We will not listen to this word of yours that you have uttered as from Yahweh. No, we mean to keep without fail this oath of ours to offer sacrifices to the Queen of Heaven, and pour libations in her honour, as we used to do, we and our fathers, our kings and leaders,*

*in the towns of Judah and on the streets of Jerusalem. Then we
had plenty of food, we prospered and came to no harm. But ever
since we gave up sacrificing to the Queen of Heaven and pouring
out libations in her honour, we have been in utter need and at the
mercy of the sword and famine." "Yes," cried the women, "and
had we not the consent of our husbands when we sacrificed to the
Queen of Heaven and poured libations in her honor and made
cakes in the shape of her?"*

Since all Levantine religions see the world as having a definite miraculous creation and as ending in a divine catastrophe, the divine truths that
exist today must always have existed. Hidden books and secret oral truth
that were revealed only as required were commonplace. King Josiah's discovery of a single book of the Mosaic law was trifling, as the account of
Ezra will show. The notion of growth and natural evolution does not exist
in this philosophy. The holy books are revealed. They may be discovered
perhaps seriatim for awhile, but they are not written by men. They are
dictated to men in dreams or even physically given to them in a finished
roll, for they are the work of God and they have existed since the world
began. When revelation stops, alteration becomes impossible and only
commentary, no matter how tortuous the interpretation, is left to adjust
unalterable truth to inexorable time.

Amos, Hosea, Isaiah and Jeremiah (again, the parts of the two
latter that are of the same period) preached a religious awakening during the destruction of the Assyrian world empire. The foundation of the
new faith and its organization as a great religion were the work of Ezekiel,
Ezra and Nehemiah. Or, to be on the safer historical grounds, these were
the work of men whose words and actions are recorded under the names
of Ezekiel, Ezra and Nehemiah, living at or within two hundred years
after the time assigned by the Bible to these men.

Looking back from the vantage point of Seleucid times, the historians
of the established Jewish temple at Jersusalem wrote an account of the
political foundation of their religion. There are two accounts generally
coinciding but inconsistent in some respects. They are the Books of Ezra
and Nehemiah in the King James Bible, I and II Esdras in the Vulgate,
a single Book in the Jewish canon.

In Chronicles, of which these books are the sequel, the historian's
central problem was to cast back over a different past the religious beliefs
of his own time, to identify the Jewish religion of his own day with the
Hebrew religion of Assyrian times. In Ezra-Nehemiah, on the other hand,
the problem is to identify the new Jewish people, that is, the adherents
of the actually new faith, with the ancient people of Palestine in the time

of the Hebrew kingdoms. In the case of Ezra-Nehemiah, we do not have the advantage of a divergent account, but the inner inconsistencies are sufficiently revealing.

The story of the two books is the migration of several parties of Jews from Babylon to Jerusalem, the reconstruction of the city walls and the building of the new temple. By the use of genealogies, or more accurately, catalogues of ancient Israelite families, many of the immigrants are given an Israelite origin though a considerable number are described as unable to prove such ancestry (Nehemiah vii, 64).

The version of the story given in Nehemiah assigns to Nehemiah himself the whole credit for the expedition and the restoration of Jerusalem. He is a cup bearer to Artaxerxes. Unfortunately, we do not know which of the three Achaemenian kings of that name is meant. Nehemiah hears of the ruin of Jerusalem where lie the tombs of his ancestors, his only apparent connection with the city. The king discovers his grief and sends him as governor with orders to rebuild the city. The account in the first six chapters of Ezra is that Cyrus, "King of Persia" (a Greek title made up long afterwards), ordered the restoration of the city and the return of the exiles. Both books agree that the work went forward with considerable opposition from many of the local peoples. In Ezra, the "enemies of Judah" came and offered to help rebuild the temple because, they said, they had worshipped the God of Israel ever since Esar-Haddon, King of Assyria, brought them into Palestine. The offer was refused. Nehemiah records no offer of help but bitter opposition, particularly from Samaria, Samaria of all places, the ancient capital of Israel, where people object to the "feeble Jews" proposing to rebuild the walls of Jerusalem. It is interesting that in both books there is no trace of a single "Jew" resident in Palestine. All the "Jews" (these are the earliest books that consistently use this name) are either "exiles returning" from Babylon or "natives" converted to the faith which the "returning exiles" bring with them. In connection with the opposition from Samaria, it is important to recall that Samaria retained an independent form of Judaism using only the Pentateuch as the entire Holy Scripture. A few of these survive to this day, and at one time there were numerous Samaritan synagogues in the Near East. The difference was apparently quite strong. Probably the accounts of both Ezra and Nehemiah have been edited from the view of later times after the Samaritan rift when it was desirable to show that these heretics had never been of the blood of Israel—hence their identification with the Assyrian colonists of II Kings xiv, 25—as though there had been no Israelites, nor true worshippers of Yahweh in Israel. Otherwise the extraordinary conclusion follows that in all Israel and Judah there was not left one single person of Israelite blood, and, if Nehemiah be followed, no believer in Yahweh. The first is certainly absurd. Even Biblical accounts do not suggest that Nebuchadnezzar removed all the population of Judah. The weight of Biblical evidence and the weight of human historical experience indicate that the bulk of the population of Israel and Judah in 586 B.C. must still have been there when the first exiles were said to have returned in the "second month of the second year" of the reign of Cyrus, "King of Persia" (Ezra xiii, 7), 551 B.C. To be sure, this is a most suspicious date since the reason for it is to confirm a prophecy of Jeremiah's. If Nehemiah's more reasonable chronology is accepted instead, the twentieth year of Artaxerxes, 445 B.C., would indicate a lapse of one hundred and forty years, or two hundred, or two hundred and forty-five years if the Artaxerxes referred to was, as is more probable, one of the two later kings of that name. Time gaps such as these could well account for considerable social and religious changes, but they would put the composition of the Pentateuch well into Seleucid times and require a reconstruction of Jewish history equally at variance with the received tradition. There can be no question, however, that for the authors of Ezra and Nehemiah the Jews, and originally the only Jews, were the "exiles" who "returned" from Babylon. Ezra refers to everyone else as "natives," non-Jews, of course, ("people of the lands" is the rather poor translation of the King James Version following the Vulgate) and Nehemiah (v, 17) refers to the "natives" and the "surrounding foreigners" ("Heathen that are about us," in the King James Version).

But perhaps the most extraordinary thing in these two books is the account of the origin of what must obviously have been intended to mean the Pentateuch itself. In other words, Ezra and Nehemiah are the first books of the Bible, not that other books do not contain older matter, for they do, but these two books record the first presentation of the books that deal with earlier times and were supposedly in existence long before.

In chapter seven of Ezra, it is stated that Ezra who lived in Babylon "was an expert scribe in the law of Moses . . ." and that ". . . he had set his heart upon studying the law of God, upon obeying it, and upon teaching its rules and regulations in Israel." He is also given a genealogy of sixteen ancestors to carry him back a mythical thousand years to Aaron. He lived at Babylon in the reign of Nehemiah's King Artaxerxes, whichever number he was, and equipped with a letter from the king (who here is given his current title "King of Kings"), he came up to Jerusalem "to hold an enquiry," according to the king's letter, "upon Judah and Jerusalem in terms of the law of your God, which is in your possession."

What happened after he arrived from Babylon is told in the eighth chapter of Nehemiah. Ezra, on the first day of the seventh month, opened the book he had brought with him in the sight of the assembled people and for seven days read to them in the open space by the water gate, while the Levites translated as he read so that the people could understand. It is obvious that it was not a brief book, and it is obvious that whatever the date, Hebrew was not a language then understood by these people who now called themselves Jews. At the end of the reading on the first day and on the eighth day there was a great celebration, and then on the twenty-fourth of the month the people assembled again, "separating themselves from all the foreigners," spent a quarter of the day reading from the new book of the law, another quarter conferring, and then assembled for the long prayer in Nehemiah (ix, 5-17), which, so far as history records, was the first full promulgation of the great myth of the Jews. It is worth reading with care, bearing in mind its setting, surrounded by the newly-built walls of Jerusalem, facing the new temple in the midst of "natives" and "foreigners" three weeks after Ezra from Babylon had read and had translated line by line the book of the law of Moses that he had brought with him. This prayer is, in fact, a preparative outline or guide to the composition of the Bible. What agreed with it has been included. What disagreed has been dropped.

Whether this prayer was ever spoken by the priests from Babylon in the presence of Nehemiah, King Artaxerxes' governor of Jerusalem, or was a somewhat later literary composition is of little historical consequence. What is of importance is that the account of the "return from exile" not only contains the earliest account of the promulgation of a collection of sacred law, it also contains the earliest complete and inwardly consistent national credo of the Jews. Something like the events recorded in Ezra and Nehemiah must actually have occurred, probably in the opening decades of the fourth century, and in those events the Jewish religion and the Jewish nation, which shortly came to be thought of as the Jewish race, made their first appearance on the stage of history. Before these events, the Jews did not exist any more than Islam existed before Mohammed or the Mormons before the teachings of Joseph Smith. Earlier events were seen in the light of the new concept of the religious nation of the Jews. Historical and mythical records of earlier times and of peoples having no religious connections and little or inconsequential ancestral connections, were assumed and necessarily somewhat altered to serve as the essential but invented past for the new sect-nation. It was not that some of these events had not in fact occurred; the inventions lay in ascribing them to the Jews, though the basic invention was the basic con-

cept of the religion-as-nation which then and thereafter, and never theretofore, came to be called the Jews.[10]

The biological side of this process is frankly set out in both Ezra and
Nehemiah. As would necessarily be expected with the new concept of a
nation, there appears a new connubium. Far too many of the "exiles" had
married "native" women. Now this would not be surprising in the case of
exiles returning to their own land among their own people. But Ezra, who
was willing to accept "natives" who had forsaken the pagan gods, was
bitterly opposed to the exiles marrying "native" women. Since "natives"
could join the Jews by accepting the doctrines Ezra had brought with
him from Babylon, the only possible meaning of this, particularly as it
took a commission of inquiry three months to study the matter (Ezra x,
16), was that men could not marry women who did not profess the new
faith. Obviously a very troublesome matter, as discussion of it occupies
all chapters nine and ten of Ezra, and it aroused distinguished opposition.
Unfortunately, we are not told the outcome. After giving a long list of
men who had married "foreign" wives, the Book of Ezra comes to an
abrupt close. The variant form of the Book of Ezra, however, I Esdras,
says the wives and children were sent away. Nehemiah gives us only the
oath not to marry non-Jews described as "natives of the land" (Nehemiah
x, 31) and gives us the further absurdity that he encountered children
of those mixed marriages who could not speak "Jewish." Hebrew being
no longer spoken, Aramaic being the general language from Egypt to the
Tarsus mountains and there being neither then nor since a "Jewish"
language, it is difficult to decide what this is intended to mean; perhaps
a slight difference of dialect; or, what would be most significant, that the
"exiles" spoke the Babylonian east Aramaic and not the western Aramaic
of Palestine, which must have been the speech of any exiles who went to
Babylon; or a possible third alternative, not too impossible in view of
modern examples, is that the "exiles" had taught themselves the extinct
priestly Hebrew and were attempting to use it as a household language.

There is one final matter of interest in these books that record the
origin of the Jews. The natives who bother Ezra and Nehemiah so much
are named, and their names are most curious. They are the Canaanites,
the Hittites, the Jebusites, the Amorites, the Perizzites, the Ammonites,
the Girgashites and the Egyptians. It is now, at the very earliest the
twentieth year of Artaxerxes I, 445 B.C., or 384 B.C., if the king was

---

[10] The word is used in Jeremiah in a description of what appears to have been civil
war during the neo-Babylonian invasion. Either the name was just coming into
current use or was employed by a later scribe. It is also used anachronistically in
Isaiah xxxvi, 11-13 (and II Kings xviii, 26) in the passage in which the Assyrian
commander before Jerusalem is told to speak Aramaic, not the "Jews' language,"
so that the inhabitants on the wall cannot understand him.

Artaxerxes II. Who then are these people whose women Ezra, the returning exile, finds too attractive for his coreligionists? Five of them are the peoples whose lands are promised to Abraham, in Genesis xv, 20, by official chronology fifteen hundred years before. Four of them are the tribes whose survivors Israel had "been unable to exterminate" and as slaves were building Solomon's temple (I Kings, ix). One of them, the Ammonites, was supposed to have been nearly destroyed by King Jephthah (Judges, x) and subsequently overthrown anew by Saul (I Samuel, xi). It is as though the Promised Land were being granted anew, as though the days of Joshua and the Judges, of the kingdoms of Israel and Judah had been wiped out without trace. What the scribe who wrote Ezra has obviously done is to dig up ancient, half-mythical names to explain the hostility between the Semitic-speaking inhabitants of Palestine, undoubtedly the same basic stock that lived there at the time of the fall of Jerusalem, and the immigrants from Babylonia. The latter probably were, in part at least, descended from former inhabitants of Judah and worshippers of Yahweh, but they came now as a new nation with a new religion. What they "returned" to was not their country but to the spot they had adopted as their scared shrine. By blood, no doubt, the leaders came from Judah, but even Ezra, the racist nationalist, tells us that not all the returning "exiles" were of Hebrew ancestry. They returned to it as Godfrey of Boulogne and Richard of England "returned" to it, in the name of a different myth, to be sure, but in the name of a myth.

The fact that the Jewish nation and the Jewish religion, which are historically indistinguishable, took their origin in events around 400 B.C., substantially as the Books of Ezra and Nehemiah describe, is not only indicated by the Bible but is testified to by ancient tradition. The unknown prophet who wrote the later Isaiah stated it precisely:

> *Did ever land bring forth its people in a single day?*
> *Was any nation ever born thus all at once?*
> *Yet Sion had no sooner travailed than she brought her son to birth.*

About two centuries later, Josephus, the first historian of the Jews, said the same thing in more prosaic language (*Antiquities* xi, 5-7). Talmudic tradition and the apocryphal II Esdras (xiv) alike assign the "revival" of the Mosaic law to Ezra. Before the closing of the canon this book was considered part of the Holy Scriptures and was so retained for a time by the Greek-speaking Jews of the Roman Empire. The method of revival delineated in Esdras is of interest. (II Esdras xiv, 20-48)

> *"Behold Lord,"* says Ezra, who in this book is called Esdras,
> *"Behold, Lord, I will go, as thou hast commanded me, and reprove the people which are present; but they that shall be born afterward,*

*who shall admonish them? thus the world is set in darkness, and they
that dwell therein are without light.*

*For thy law is burnt, therefore, no man knoweth the things that are
done of thee, or the works that shall begin.*

*But if I have found grace before thee, send the Holy Ghost into me,
and I shall write all that hath been done in the world since the
beginning, which were written in thy law, that men may find thy
path, and that they which will live in the latter days may live." and
he answered me saying . . .*

*"I shall light a candle of understanding in thine heart, which shall
not be put out, till the things be performed which thou shalt begin
to write.*

*And when thou hast done, somethings shalt thou publish, and some
things shalt thou shew secretly to the wise; tomorrow this hour shalt
thou begin to write."*

*Then went I forth, as he commanded, and gathered all the people
together, and said,*

"Hear these words, O Israel.

*Our fathers at the beginning were strangers in Egypt, from whence
they were delivered:*

*And received the law of life which they kept not, which ye also have
transgressed after them.*

*Then was the land, even the land of Sion, parted among you by lot:
but your fathers, and ye yourselves, have done unrighteousness, and
have not kept the ways which the Highest commanded you.*

*And forasmuch as he is a righteous judge, he took from you in time
the thing that he had given you.*

And now are ye here, and your brethren among you.

*Therefore if so be that ye will subdue your own understanding and
reform your hearts, ye shall be kept alive, and after death ye shall
obtain mercy.*

*For after death shall the judgment come, when we shall live again;
and then shall the names of the righteous be manifest, and the works
of the ungodly shall be declared.*

*Let no man therefore come unto me now, nor seek after me these
forty days."*

*So I took the five men, as he commanded me, and we went into the
field, and remained there.*

*And the next day, behold, a voice called me saying, "Esdras, open
thy mouth, and drink that I give thee to drink."*

*Then opened I my mouth, and, behold, he reached me a full cup,
which was full as it were with water, but the colour of it was like fire.*

*And I took it, and drank: and when I had drunk of it, my heart
uttered understanding, and wisdom grew in my breast, for my spirit
strengthened my memory:*

And my mouth was opened, and shut no more.

The Highest gave understanding unto the five men, and they wrote
the wonderful visions of the night that were told, which they knew
not: and they sat forty days, and they wrote in the day, and at night
they ate bread.
As for me, I spake in the day, and I held not my tongue by night.
In forty days they wrote two hundred and four books. And it came
to pass, when forty days were fulfilled, that the Highest spake, saying,
"The first that thou hast written publish openly, that the worthy and
unworthy may read it:
But keep the seventy last, that thou mayest deliver them only to such
as be wise among the people:
For in them is the spring of understanding, the fountain of wisdom,
and the stream of knowledge."
And I did so.

There is no doubt that inhabitants of the Kingdom of Israel were
removed by the Assyrians (this "captivity" is curiously of no interest to
the compliers of the Bible), and members of the royal and princely families,
priests and artisans were removed by the Babylonians. No doubt these
men were worshippers of Yahweh but that many of them were devout
adherents of the new revelation about him is highly doubtful. Nothing
in the tone of Isaiah (i, 1-39) or of Jeremiah suggests it. Yahweh is
represented to us as the territorial god of the Kingdoms of Israel and
Judah, but in the foundering Babylonian world there were a host of terri-
torially-based gods of general jurisdiction. Marduk of Babylon, Ea of
Eridu, had long become generalized and these places were merely their
great shrines. Yahweh of Shiloh, who became Yahweh of Jerusalem after
Solomon built the great temple, probably did not differ, in that respect,
from these other deities. Even Ezra and Nehemiah testify that in southern
Chaldea there were adherents of Yahweh who could not trace their ancestry
to Israel, and these are the prime books of the priestly, racist theory of
Jewish nationalism. It seems altogether likely that there were worshippers
of the Yahweh of the great shrine of Jerusalem scattered throughout the
Babylonian world before the "exile" of 586 B.C. Even in these early days
there was a colony of Yahweh worshipers at far-off Elephantine in
Egypt, and there must have been many similar groups in the Babylonian
world. Some may have been forcibly removed from Palestine by the
Assyrians, some may have left for trade or business, some, perhaps most,
may have adopted the cult without either they or their fathers ever having
been west of the Euphrates.

Whatever may have been the physical stock of the Yahweh worshippers
of Mesopotamia in the last days of Babylonia and the early Achaemenian
kings, the religion evidently prospered there. Perhaps the leaders of the
group were Levites and nobles from Israel and Judah, but for the great

bulk of adherents of the growing faith even then, Jerusalem must have been their spiritual rather than their ancestral home. Only on such an assumption does the Bible, the policy of the Achaemenian kings and subsequent historical facts make any sense. To be sure, it is not necessary to believe the Biblical accounts of Nehemiah's position at the court of Artaxerxes. But if it is a correct picture, it is wholly inconsistent with the notion of a little group of nationalistically-minded captives suspected and maltreated by their captors. It makes sense if Nehemiah was a great Babylonian nobleman of Jewish faith who gained the king's permission to restore the sanctuary of a god whose followers were a significant political factor in the king's dominions. And what Nehemiah did was to restore that sanctuary and surround it with a little, hierarchic, non-political state to serve it. The bulk of the Jews remained in Mesopotamia and their descendants remained there under their own ruler, the Resh-Galutha, the exilarch, and their spiritual head, the Gaon, until after the Mohammedan conquest almost a thousand years later.

Although the Holy Scriptures, that is the Torah, Prophets and Holy Writings, are officially ascribed to a Palestinian origin (which can only be true in part), the Targums are primarily Babylonian. And even the received Jewish tradition admits that the Talmud, the great commentary without which the Jewish meaning of the Scriptures is lost, was the work of the Jews of Babylonia,[11] and that from Babylonia went the missionaries who converted the "Scythians" north of the Black Sea, that is the Khazars, the ancestors of many of the Jews of the present day. The bulk of the Jews living in the lands that came under Mohammedan rule themselves became Mohammedans or Nestorian Christians within a few centuries. The only massive Jewish population outside the dominions of the caliph was this group of converted Scythians and a handful of Negro Jews in northeastern Africa. Within the Mohammedan lands, the Jewish families who remained faithful were long a distinguished, but small, minority— resembling, in some respects, the traditional Catholic families of England. These were the Sephardim. A few entered western Europe in the early Middle Ages, and a few after the fall of Moslem power in Spain. The rest have lived amidst the Moslems, undisturbed by the involvement with the West that overtook the descendants of the Jews of Gaul, Spain and Scythia.

Something of the origin of the Jews becomes evident in considering a question to which we have no positive historical answer, certainly no documented answer, but whose mere existence as an unanswered question conveys an important inference. What became of the Semitic-speaking population of ancient Babylonia after the Persian conquest? These were far more than the inhabitants of the Kingdoms of Israel and Judah. These

---

[11] There exists also an uncompleted Palestinian Talmud.

people must have been sharply reduced in numbers by the havoc of their ruined society, but they were not wiped out without descendants. The worshippers of Ea, Marduk and Ishtar, of all the baals of Babylonia, had descendants. What gods did these descendants worship? By Seleucid times throughout the area that had once been Assurbanipal's empire, the old religion of Babylonia was extinct. There was, as the dominant religion, the Mazdaism of the Persian conquerors of three hundred years before. There were Gnostic sects, though how numerous their followers were, we do not know, who had evolved into a group of ritual and mystical cults of dualistic creation and salvation in which the ancient Babylonian gods clearly appear as demons. The tiny sect of the Mandeans may be the only surviving remnants of this group. Finally there was Judaism, the one surviving religion the name of whose god (though no longer used) was still the name of one of the gods of Babylonia, the one surviving religion, as the Books of Esther and Daniel tell us, which had once been a religion of the conquered subjects of the Achaemenian kings. The descendants of the ancient Babylonians must have become either Mazdaists or Gnostics or Jews, for there were such descendants and at that time there were no other religions generally practiced throughout this whole area. How many embraced Judaism and when they did so we have no way to discover. But Ezra clearly tells us that some had done so before the "return" to Jerusalem, that is, before the Pentateuch itself had ever been published in Palestine. Every surviving piece of evidence shows that whether the bulk of the descendants of the ancient Babylonians became Jews, many must have done so—the numerical density of the Jews in Mesopotamia for many centuries, the continuing Semitic speech of Mesopotamia and of Judaism in contrast to the Persian of the Mazdaists, the numerical insignificance of the later Gnostics, the web of memories of ancient Babylonia that interlaces the Bible, the fact that while Jerusalem was the holy shrine of Judaism, Mesopotamia from the times of Ezra to the rise of Mohammedanism was its intellectual center. To the question then, "Who were the original Jews?" the most probable answer is, "The descendants of a numerous but unknown proportion of the Aramaic-speaking subjects of Cyrus and Cambyses, almost all the offspring of the worshippers of Marduk, Ishtar—and Yahweh—who did not become Mazdaists." Out of the wreckage of one of the cults of their ancestors, they fashioned a religion of utterly different spiritual content expressing the deep values of a new society.

The erroneous popular image of these events flows from the two accepted myths, Jewish and Christian, having other ends in view than the recitation of sober history. The Jewish myth asserts the Palestinian origin of the Jews and works details of that myth into every event and record of Jewish history. The Christian myth accepts the Jewish myth up to the advent of Jesus and then ignores the Jews altogether. Yet from the very beginning of Judaism, its center lay in Mesopotamia, not Palestine. There Ezekiel prophesied, there Ezra became an expert in the law of Moses, and there, despite his famous return to Jerusalem, Jewish tradition has placed his tomb. From the Babylonian destruction of Jerusalem until the Mohammedan conquest, every important event in the development and history of Judaism with the single exception of the career of Jesus occurred in Mesopotamia. But our received picture of history ends at the Roman-Parthian frontier. Hence, the Jews appear in profane history (as it used to be called in contrast to Old Testament mythology, which was known as sacred history) only in two quite untypical events; the Palestinian rising under the Maccabees against Antiochus Epiphanes, the Seleucid king, about 170 B.C. and in the fierce, ruinous revolt against Rome that ended in Titus' destruction of Jerusalem in 70 A.D. Neither of these was the work of the Jewish nation, most of whose citizens lived east of the frontier, and our chief knowledge of them comes from the Classical historians and from books which the Jews themselves have stricken from their canon. We consider these events important elements of Jewish history not because they were important to the Jews nor because the Jews have ever thought so, but because knowledge of them comes to us as part of Classical history, and no other ancient or distant history is quite real to us. The symbol, not the fact itself of the destruction of Jerusalem, was important to the Jews and even this event, as well as the Maccabean revolt, was not in the deep stream of Jewish life. They were the heroic, but wild gambles of a handful of Palestinian Jews who misunderstood the political means at their disposal, and perhaps, even, the very nature of the Jewish nation, and sought to turn Nehemiah's holy shrine into a Classical *civitas* of Jewish nationality. Neither was characteristic of the great body of Jewish life flourishing under Levantine political conditions in Mesopotamia.

But, in fact, there were not two streams of Jewish life, the Palestinian and the Babylonian, but also a third—the great bulk of the Jews within the Roman Empire. These spoke neither dialect of Aramaic and their Holy Scriptures were not in the original Hebrew but in the Greek translation, the Septuagint, dating from about 200 B.C. This was not a paraphrase, a Greek Targum for the benefit of the unlearned like the Aramaic Targums, but a true translation with all the religious standing of the original; for it was used in the western synagogues as the Hebrew text was used in the east. These Jews of the Septuagint were, therefore, a unique phenomenon in over two thousand years of Jewish history. No other group of Orthodox Jews from Ezra's time to our own has ever used anything but the Hebrew in their religious services. Yet curiously this extraordinarily odd group has received little historical notice. Profane history merely mentions that there were such people and then ignores them. The religious tradition of the Jews barely acknoweldges their existence and is quite barren concerning their fate. Christian tradition substantially ignores even their existence. In Christian tradition, and even in conventional Christian history, Christianity stems directly from Hebraic Judaism. Only the history of Christian theology, by being forced back upon Greek texts of the Old Testament, reveals for a moment a group for whose sake these texts came into existence at all.

Even with the best will there is little direct historical evidence that can be brought to bear upon these Greek Jews. Their origin is beclouded by the fable that all Jews are descended from the Hebrews so that these Greek Jews must somehow be emigrants from Palestine. Of course, sober history knows better, knows that Judaism in those centuries was an active proselytizing religion and that the great bulk of these Greek Jews may have been from any and every region within, and perhaps without, the empire except Palestine. They must have been men whose forefathers brought them no tie to the Hebrew scriptures or they would never have needed the Greek. At most, a Greek Targum would have served, as the emigrants' ancestral Aramaic was replaced in popular speech by Greek. Like the Khazars of Scythia, these Greek Jews were converts but while the Khazars were converted some centuries afterwards and had as their native language only the speech of semi-barbarians, the Greek Jews were converted at the height of the great Greek-speaking Roman Empire whose native language contained the greatest contemporary glories of literature and learning. It was not surprising that the Khazars kept the Hebrew scriptures but that the Greeks made a translation of their own. So much we can estimate of their origin. Of their fate we know nothing by external evidence. Two such figures as Philo and Josephus appear in the record of remembered history. The names of a few revisers of the Septuagint appear in the writings of the Christian fathers, and then nothing. But it is possible to make a reasonable conjecture of what happened to them.

The early history of Christianity contains in it a peculiar circumstance upon which neither the church fathers, eastern or western, nor the historians have been prone to ponder. Jesus was an Aramaic-speaking Palestinian Jew, as were all his disciples. He lived and died in Aramaic Palestine. Yet all that we know of him is written in the Greek language and all that early Christianity took from the Jews it took from the Septuagint. Christian tradition asserts the Hebraic origin of its religion, yet almost every scrap of the Old Testament quoted in the New is not from the Hebrew Scriptures but from the Greek. In Matthew alone are a few quotations unique to this gospel that are original translations from the Hebrew Scriptures.

There is a further difficulty, particularly to the Protestants, for they more than the Roman Catholics have been fascinated by the problem of reconstructing the objective, secularized history of early Christianity. In the Protestant Bible there is an unbridgeable gap between the whole spirit and direction of the two Testaments. The New seems not to be the continuance and fulfillment of the Old, as orthodox tradition teaches us, but almost its antithesis. Yet this difficulty is really simple. In attempting, as it thought, to restore "historical" Christianity, Protestanism demanded a Hebrew source for all of the Old Testament it was willing to consider canonical, unaware that the Jews, subsequent to the life of Jesus, had edited their Scriptures to remove every trace of apocalypse, which was almost the whole content of Jewish religious life for more than a century preceding the ministry of Jesus. Thus the Protestant Old Testament is book for book, word for word, the Hebrew Scriptures as these were established more than a century after the death of Jesus. Yet the writers of the gospels and epistles of the New Testament used the Septuagint in which this apocalyptic world feeling was still reflected.

The attempt to reconstruct the history of the origin of Christianity suffers from some of the same difficulties that surround an attempt to do this with the origin of Judaism. In both cases the primary evidence is a collection of documents preserved by the respective believers. The documents taken as a whole, therefore, correspond to the theories of the believers about the origins of their faith. But there were always difficulties of detail in assembling these documents. In the Jewish case there were older documents that might be edited slightly but could not be eliminated. On a much tighter time scale the same thing is true of Christianity. But this fact presents only mechanical difficulties. There are others, far harder to resolve, that obstruct an understanding of Christian history.

Unhappily, in the struggle of the Reformation and Counter Reformation in the sixteenth century, both sides turned to history as the ultimate justification of their religious opinions. Christianity, according to both Protestants and Roman Catholics, was exactly—no more and no less—the teaching of Christ to the Apostles. The only difference dividing Catholic and Protestant was their disagreement about what that teaching had been and how accurately the Western church had transmitted it. No one then and few now seem disposed to feel this interpretation of Christianity to have been historically tragic and intellectually absurd, not only the betrayal of the West but ominously dangerous to the future. For if Christianity is what Jesus taught and nothing else, then religion becomes forever the slave of historical research and historical interpretation, at the hazard, even, of chance discoveries of lost manuscripts and scraps of papyrus. It means that a man must be prepared to change his religious beliefs if the weight of evidence shows that his understanding of Jesus' teaching has been in error, or—what is just as ruinous to the peace of his soul and perhaps even worse for the integrity of his character—deliberately deny what his rational intelligence tells him he should affirm. True, this was not what either Reformation or Counter Reformation meant to do or indeed was conscious of doing when they introduced history as the ultimate authority for Christian beliefs. Each was certain that their own immediate understanding of this special piece of history was true and unalterable, but both were convinced that their understanding was justified or even proved by texts produced, they believed, by direct divine inspiration. Both overlooked the consequence of the essential point—the point itself, of course, they admitted—that this inspiration had occurred during the flow of ordinary terrestrial history. Thus the means and methods by which the documents had been written, edited, copied and finally transmitted to the sixteenth century were necessarily human means and methods, and therefore subject to critical analysis and the application of purely human standards of fact and probability. In the end it was therefore history that provided the content of revelation, and therefore history—not life— that justified faith. There was thus opened a door that it has never since been possible to close. Conceivably the defense of Christianty might have been not on the basis of the origin of its documents (about which in reality nothing was then known and not too much even now) but upon its living magnificence, that it was partly source and partly consequence of the civilization that had risen in Western Europe in the previous seven or eight centuries; that the Christian religion as Western men believed in it was simply whatever had made life noble and death contemptible during these centuries, was what might be thought of by analogy with a similar crisis in legal development, as the religious Common Law of Europe. There was an element of this view in opposition to the Reformation and equally to the militant precision of the Counter Reformation, but it was drowned in the clamor of polemical historicity and ever since all Western Christians have been required to believe (in any sect that required any belief at all) that whatever they believe to be the fundamental tenets of Christianity, they also believe to have been taught by Jesus.

As a result the history of Jesus and of the origin of the Christian Church occupies a unique place in Western historical writing. The difficulty experienced by even the most objective historian in correcting a national bias is trifling compared to the struggle in seeking to correct a confessional. Nor does this bias affect solely historians consciously identified with a a particular Christian sect. To the irreligious historian so much turmoil over something that means nothing to him comes to seem essentially irrational. The historians of Jewish origin cannot help but wonder where the record has been twisted against the honor and intelligence of the Jews.

The first problem arises with the text of the New Testament. Since history has been made the arbiter of revelation, there has been a desperate struggle during the past century and a half to try to establish by secular historical methods that the New Testament is what on its face it claims to be, that the Epistles of St. Paul were written by him, that the Gospels of Matthew and John were written by these apostles, the Gospel of Luke by a companion of Paul, the Gospel of Mark by a companion of Peter—finally that each of the books of the New Testament is an integral unit, the product of a single writer, written from beginning to end at one time, not a composite representing the work of various men with different doctrinal worries, writing at different dates.

It is deeply to be regretted that the moral and intellectual authority of the Western Christian Church should have been maneuvered onto such shaky foundations as these, because these basic assumptions, dear and necessary as they were to both sides in the sixteenth century, are today impossible of acceptance by any general consensus of historical scholarship. Partisan confessional, like partisan anti-confessional positions, exist, both of whose advocates deny that their historical opinion flows from their religious affiliation, though the infallible correspondence indicates that it must.

There were from the very earliest Christian times dissident Christian movements. None survived in Greek and Latin lands, at least not as an organized public church, except the Orthodox Catholic Church of the time of Constantine. In retrospect this Church necessarily saw itself as the Christian Church founded by Jesus. The historical difficulty is that if one of the dissident Christian movements had become the great Church of the Empire, it, too, would have seemed to itself to have been the church founded by Jesus and the documents it prepared and, above all, the documents it preserved, would have been in general harmony with this view. The assertion, therefore, of the third century church that it was the institution founded by Jesus and the superficial harmony of the New Testament with this assertion are historically of no weight.

Nor do the earliest secular historians of the church supply any better evidence. Eusebius, a contemporary of the Emperor Constantine, whose complete history survives, clearly knows almost nothing of the religious history of the first century and a half of Christianity. He knows, or at least he names, the chain of bishops of a few cities; he quotes the worthy Christian sentiments of some of the earlier writers; he knows the fragmentary information Papias recorded two centuries before him on the authorship of the Gospels of Matthew and Mark. But that is really all he knows before his own time. The rest is edifying tales of martyrdom without his always being quite sure whether the martyrs were Orthodox or heretics. Yet Eusebius had available the greatest library of Christian documents of the time and as confidant of the Emperor Constantine, had access to the imperial archives. It is pointless to measure Eusebius against the utter paucity of information from other sources, in which case he is an invaluable mine of information—in fact almost the only source we have. What is important is that even he, as early as he was and as well-placed to obtain information, could not give us what to our way of thinking is the history of the development of the early church. Consider his own view of it:

> *Before I begin my history I must make an indispens-*
> *able observation lest any one think that Jesus Christ our Lord is*
> *only from yesterday because of the time when he appeared in the*
> *flesh. In order that no one should suppose that his doctrine was*
> *recent or unusual, the work of a new man just like other men, it is*
> *necessary to explain this matter briefly. Without question there is no*
> *dispute that our Saviour Jesus recently manifested his presence to all*
> *men. It is equally certain that a people never before seen suddenly*
> *arose, neither little nor weak, nor crowded away in some corner of*
> *the world, but the most numerous and the most religious of all, in-*
> *destructible and invincible because it received without interruption*
> *the constant help of God. This is the people whom all honor with*
> *the name of Christ. This people made its appearance en masse at*
> *the time appointed by the mystery of the Divine Will. A prophet*
> *was struck with astonishment in foreseeing this in the future by the*
> *illumination of the Divine Spirit and he cried (Isaiah lxvi, 8)*

> > *Whoever heard of such a thing,*
> > *Whoever saw he like?*
> > *Did ever land bring forth its people*
> > *in a single day*
> > *Was ever any nation born thus all at once?*[12]

Our received history, the view of the rise of Christianity accepted by most modern Christians, is more elaborate than Eusebius' but not essentially different. We go to great lengths to ferret out "influences" visible in the intellectual and theological development of Christianity: the effects

[12] Eusebius, *The Ecclesiastical History,* I, iv, 1 The translation given here is adapted from the French of Émile Grapin, Paris, 1905.

of Mithraism, Mazdaism, Orphism and the mystery cults, Stoicism, Neo-platonism. We find sources, generally Jewish, for the early ritual and for the pattern of church organization. But for the history of the rise of the Christian Church, that is, of a group of believers in distinction to the history of the rise of Christianity, that is, of a body of beliefs and religious practices, we have barely got beyond Eusebius. In received history the Jews were always a people, a distinct, identifiable people with some of the aspects of nationality (not surprising, since they were in fact a Levantine nation). But Christians are felt not to be and never to have been a people, nor possessed of any of the attributes of nationality. They are and always were simply everybody who embraced Christianity as a religion. Hence we have the history of ideas, not of a people, and the history of this people—as Eusebius saw it to be—remains about where he left it.

It is true that modern Western Christians are not and never have been a people, but we have no right to cast back over the Christians of the Roman Empire definitions that are valid only for Western Christians. The Christians of Rome (and quite evidently of Byzantium) were a Levantine nation, and as such they had a national history before Constantine, today almost completely lost in detail, but still not quite so barren of merely human events as Eusebius might lead us to suppose.

The ancestry of this Christian people of the time of Constantine was, of course, the population of the empire in the days of Augustus. The situation was quite similar to that of the Aramaic Jews of the same years whose ancestry was—in bulk—the population of ruined Babylonia.

The respective myths of the origin of these two peoples differed. With the Jews, the magical acts of choice and compact were set in a mythical past and no attention paid to the mere mechanics of continuity of this people, to the real physical ancestry of the Jews of the moment. With the Christians the magical act was quite recent, as Eusebius describes it, and again little attention was given to the mechanics of the matter, to the actual human operations by which the sudden and massive creation of the Christian people had been brought about. But it is only in modern times with the belief that the Jews have always been the physical descendants of the Israelites and the Hebrew tribes, and the Christians everybody who professed this faith, that the Jews of the time of Augustus seem altogether different from the Christians of the time of Constantine.

If we had no formal account of the rise of the Christian Church except what Eusebius gives us, Western scholarship might have reconstructed the major lines of this development, if by nothing but historical probability. But there is a formal account, The Acts of the Apostles, and since Acts is part of the canon of the New Testament, there are strong confessionalist reasons for accepting its account of events, even though its account is at times directly contradicted by other equally canonical material and is at all times inherently improbable.

If we had a wealth of material on early church history, Acts and its place in the canon might be dismissed as an accident. But we do not. Acts is all that exists, a fact that makes it certain that Acts was written (or perhaps compounded of earlier fragments) and earned a place in the canon because the material it contained served a doctrinal purpose. It is therefore necessary to examine this purpose since this, not impersonal modern historical objectives, governed what Acts contains.

The first twelve chapters of Acts constitute an apparently incoherent collection of random bits put together with no evident causal or chronological relationship. But this is actually not so. The parts, however little they have factually to do one with another, are intimately interwoven by doctrinal connection. Consider the series: The church is commissioned by the risen Jesus, i, 1-14; a mechanism for apostolic succession is established, i, 15-26; the preaching to all nations is approved, ii, 1-41; the healing power of the spirit shown to have been granted to the apostles, iii, 1-10; salvation offered to the Jews, iii, 11-26 and promptly and snidely rejected by them, iv, 1-22; the sacred character of church property is then established, v, 1-11, and the proof that the spread of the church is God's work, not man's, and so useless to oppose, is established by the concession even of its enemies, the Jews, v, 12-42. As a final doctrinal point the seven Hellenic Jews are chosen and duly receive the layings on of hands by the Twelve, thus establishing the chain of Christian authority, vi, 1-6. With doctrine thus well established, doctrinal history is then begun. At great length and in detail it is shown that the true succession of divine favor from Abraham through Moses was always rejected by the Jews but has now been taken up—as proper heirs—by the Greek Jews, vi, 8-vii, 60. (Note how "our fathers" and "we" suddenly become "your fathers" and "you" in vii, 51 and 53.) The Samaritans are then annexed and the future rival Simon Magus humbled, viii, 1-13. Eunuchs who could not become Jews are found eligible to be Christians, viii, 20-40; the conversion of gentiles without circumcision is then approved by Peter, x, 1-48; and the Jewish food regulations suspended for all Christians, whether of Jewish or gentile provenance, xi, 1-18. Finally, it is shown by the failure of Herod to hold Peter that the Jewish hold on divine favor is now finished and Peter (i.e., Aramaic Jewish-Christians), his work now done, is unceremoniously dropped from the scene and Herod eaten alive by worms, xii, 1-25. Chapter nine, 1-30, and chapter ten, 19-30, alone do not fall into this series, being concerned with the subordination of Paul to the Jerusalem apostles, the problem with which Acts deals later (ix, 31-32 seems merely to repeat the point of iii, 1-10).

It is hard to suppose that events themselves so neatly supplied allegories for so many necessary and useful doctrinal points. It has been argued that the story of Stephen[13], of the Twelve Apostles and the seven deacons in chapter six and the scattering of the Hellenistic Judeo-Christian in chapter eight, if not history, at least reflects it. It perhaps does reflect that a Judeo-Christian community—apparently undisturbed by the Jews—existed in Jerusalem at least down to Vespasian's siege. Eusebius gives the names of the heads of this community beginning with James the Just, Jesus' brother, and his successor Simeon, son of Clopas, said to be a cousin or nephew of Jesus (III, xi) and even continues the chain of circumcised bishops down to Hadrian's destruction of the city, though he removes all the Christians from the city by a miraculous vision prior to Vespasian's siege. But it seems that the author of Acts knows as little about this church of the circumcision as Eusebius and cares as little. It has served its purpose for him in passing on to Judeo-Hellenic Christianity the succession from Moses and Abraham. The rest of Acts is concerned with St. Paul.

The author here has two problems, first of showing that Paul's authority to preach was not directly conferred upon him by the vision of Jesus but stemmed, in fact, from the authority of the Twelve; and secondly that Paul's teaching was something altogether different from what his epistles show it to have been. The first task he accomplishes by having Paul learn nothing in his vision but that he will be told what to do, and then having the telling done by obscure or unnamed disciples. Then Paul is returned to Tarsus and only called back to preach by Barnabas who comes to Antioch and Tarsus directly from the Twelve. Finally, in chapter fifteen, Paul sits silently by while Peter and James announce God's approval, which had existed from the first, that is, from long before Paul's vision, of conversion of the gentiles, and the assignment of this duty not to Paul but to Peter.

What actually is the message Paul is given to preach in the Acts? "Remission of your sins is proclaimed to you through him, and that by him everyone who believes is absolved from all that the law of Moses never could absolve you from." (xiii, 39). Elsewhere we are told *where* he preached but not again *what* he preached, so this is the solitary gem of its kind in Acts, the only place where the author risked putting any theological statement in Paul's mouth. Such a travesty could scarcely be the result of incomprehension. Quite evidently Paul's intense eschatology (I Cor. xv, 50) and his basic doctrine of redemption by Christ's death, of the "trap" or

---

[13] The name alone would indicate the symbolic meaning of this passage. It is the Greek for the victor's crown and is so used literally in Matt. xxvii, 29; Mark, xv, 17; John xix, 2; I Cor. ix, 25 and II Tim. ii, 5 though probably with an intended symbolic double meaning. It is also symbolically the crown of blessedness obtained by the saints who die in Christ and is found in the fairly late epistles II Tim. iv, 8; James i, 12; I Peter v, 4.

"stumbling block" of the cross, are not at all to the author's taste. So much is this the case that the author of Acts seems to go out of his way to avoid saying that Christ was crucified. In the seven places in Acts where the method of Christ's death is mentioned (ii, 23; ii, 26; iii, 15; iv, 10; v, 30; x, 39; xiii, 28, 29) only twice does the Greek text use the universal gospel word for crucifixion (ii, 36 and iv, 10), and in both, the word is in material at complete variance with the context, strongly suggesting later doctrinal editing.[14] Elsewhere the author seems to be conscious of the Pauline notion of the cross, a trap or stumbling block to the Jews, folly for the Greeks, the "shame of the Cross" as Hebrews (xii, 2) phrases it, and seeks to keep this method of death out of the text.

With the exception of the brief Petrine passage in chapter fifteen, the rest of Acts is concerned with Paul, or at least with the surface of Paul. It never gives his theology or the teachings that his epistles would lead us to expect. Instead it purports to record his missionary journeys and puts in the mouths of everyone, apostles, proconsuls, hostile Jews, brief little speeches that are perfectly appropriate for the occasion: How a Roman official should treat Christians, how mercenary are the motives of pagan opposition, how deceitful and criminal those of the Jews. Then after the elaborate development of Paul's arrest and voyage to Rome, it stops without telling the results of the trial towards which the entire last eight chapters had been building. Why? A school of historical criticism, which should not be insulted by being called naïve, argues that this is because the author completed his work before the trial and, of course, could not know the result. More plausible hypotheses are based on the assumption that there was something in connection with Paul's trial that the author preferred not to draw to his readers' attention. Some critics think this was merely that Paul was convicted and executed. Others, noting Clement's remark that Paul "Bore a martyr's witness" as a result of strife and jealousy (I Clement v, 5), think this fact the more probable explanation of the silence of the author of Acts.

It is the quiet, skillful opposition to Paul's doctrines—never a word

---

[14] In fact the use of this word in the gospels themselves requires very careful evaluation. It occurs in all the crucifixion accounts but elsewhere it is used in passages that on other grounds may be conjectured to be later interpolations: Mark x, 21, where there is even textual basis for doubt, Mark viii, 34 and Matt. xvi, 24 (parallels, but Luke ix, 22 lacks it) and Matt. x, 38, while the parallel in Luke xvii, 33 lacks it. In the parallel in Thomas 55 the Coptic text uses the Greek word. The word is used in Matt. xx, 19 but the parallel passages in Mark x, 34 and Luke xviii, 31 have no crucifixion, only burial. The parallel passage to Matt. xxvi, 2, Mark xiv, 1 and Luke xxii, 2 again lack mention of crucifixion. The word is used nowhere in John except in the specific account of the crucifixion itself in Chapter xix. The passage at Matt. xxiii, 34 has no parallel.

openly spoken against them—that reveals the purpose of Acts: to annex the name of Paul without his doctrines, to attach the Pauline wing of Christianity to the Septuagint wing, that is, in fact, to Hellenistic Judaism. This is all that concerns the author and everything that he gives us—and fails to give us—fits into this purpose. Of course he knows, as legend quite rightly knows, that Paul was executed; but he knows what legend, thanks to him, has forgotten, that Paul was executed because of the "jealousy and strife" of the Hellenistic Jewish community at Rome, which to the author of Acts is the same community that in his time calls itself Christian.[15]

This concern of the author of Acts with the connection of Christianity to Septuagint Jewry is by no means confined to him. Traces of this situation are present in all early Christian documentation. Almost every quotation from the Old Testament used in the New is from the Septuagint, not from the Hebrew, and the few exceptions are historically revealing. Every document in the New was composed in Greek, not Aramaic.

Most telling, perhaps, was the handling of the Old Testament by the rising church. If we try to imagine events having taken place the way convention pictures them, this becomes absurd. Paul supposedly began the conversion of the gentiles, Peter preached to the Jews (here convention follows Paul, not Acts). Why then a Greek Old Testament? If Paul's work had been organizationally the foundation of the church, it is difficult to see how an Old Testament could have been kept at all. If Christianity had been preached as a complete unit by Jesus and carried almost exclusively to gentiles why should it have brought the Old Testament with it? What would be convincing about a set of documents whose sacred observances were said to be superseded and whose covenant was said to be canceled? A set of documents, furthermore, that constituted the Holy Book of a competing and hostile church? Marcion in rejecting the Old Testament would have been the gentile Christian, but it was not the followers of Marcion who became the Christian Church.

On the other hand, if Peter's work, as the Pauline epistles define it, had been the foundation of the church, if the Aramaic Jews had been converted, the Old Testament would have been derived directly from the Hebrew Scriptures. If ever Greek or Latin texts came to be needed they would have been supplied by new translations directly from the Hebrew following not only the Hebrew text, as the Septuagint often does not, but also following the Hebrew order of books. But precisely the reverse occurred. It was the dwindling number of Greek Jews who rejected Chris-

---

15 If the theory developed here is sound, the original Acts must be older than the general run of secular critics believes. It would have to be later than Paul's epistles but earlier than the present version of Luke. Note also that as well as being evasive about crucifixion, Acts says nothing about any tomb.

tianity who made the new translation. It was the Christians who held the continuity of use and possession of the Septuagint.

The efforts of St. Jerome and the Protestant translators of the sixteenth century have brought the Latin and Western texts of the Old Testament into harmony with the Hebrew, but the order of books in all the Christian Bibles is still that of their parent, the Septuagint.

That Christianity was founded among Hellenistic Jews and developed by them is not only a deduction from such facts of this history as have survived, it is something we are told, almost precisely, in the John Gospel. From the vantage point of the closing years of the first century, the author of that gospel looked back over the rise of Christianity in the empire and pointed out the facts as he saw them. Long since this book has been recognized as a piece of history, but not of the kind we Westerners would write. It is not at all what on the surface it pretends to be, a factual account of the life and teaching of Jesus. That is why its "facts" bear no relation to those in the synoptic gospels, for the latter are in form biographical narratives, not history. John is history. It is one immense allegory woven of interplays and double meanings in which each figure and each act has a symbolic significance in the author's history of the end of Judaism and the rise of Christianity. It has long ago been recognized as absurd to try deriving any biographical items about Jesus from this gospel, but there has been some reluctance to read it as, for instance, Revelation is read— that is, purely as a tissue of Levantine symbolism. Yet both are considered the works of the same school of Christian writers—though almost certainly not of the same author—at the close of the first century.

In regard to the symbolic interest of an author, Westerners are at most willing to read a book like Revelation as so written; that is, they will permit the recognition of a symbolic meaning only when the surface or material meaning is quite impossible. The fact that a Levantine work usually has both meanings is something we ignore because Western authors do not write that way. Above all, though we are familiar with Levantine reading of books in this way, we somehow do not feel that even Levantine authors could have consciously written them this way. We should note therefore the precise, scientific discussion of this matter within the normal frame of Levantine thought made about a thousand years after our gospels by the Mohammedan theologian and Sufi, Al-Ghazzali. "The annulment of the outward and visible sign is the tenet of the Spiritualists, who looked, utterly one-sidedly, at one world, the Unseen, and were grossly ignorant of the balance that exists between it and the Seen. This aspect they wholly failed to understand. Similarly, annulment of the inward and invisible meaning is the opinion of the Materialists. In other words, whoever abstracts and isolates the outward from the whole is a Materialist, and whoever abstracts the inward is a Spiritualist, while he who joins the two together is catholic, perfect."[16]

In the John Gospel the person of Jesus is only the symbol of the Logos, the spirit or messenger of God who is, of course, not born of a virgin or, in fact, born in any other way.[17] He appears and is recognized by John the Baptist on behalf of the vague group of apocalyptic baptists, groups which then existed in every Levantine sect, Jewish and Mazdaist alike. At the wedding at Cana, the Logos-Jesus' mother, the Jewish church, finds she has no more spiritual wine—her spiritual mission is completed—and the Logos-Jesus makes new and much better wine from water, and makes it in inexhaustible quantities (chapter two). The Logos-Jesus then abolishes the old rites by cleansing the temple, yet establishes the true line of revelation through the Jews, not the Samaritans (chapter four) and supersedes both. The Logos-Jesus then shows that through him come all spiritual nourishment (chapter six), all spiritual sight (chapters eight and nine)—the passage concerning the adulterous woman is an interpolation—and the only entrance to salvation (chapter ten). The Logos-Jesus then raises Lazarus (chapter eleven) to show that the Logos has power over death and for this, the basic challenge to Satan, the Prince of This World represented by the Jewish authorities, seeks to destroy him (chapter thirteen). The Prince of This World is condemned for failing to recognize the Logos and the reason for the Logos revealing itself in future through the Church rather than directly to all men is explained (chapter fourteen). The Logos-Jesus then establishes his witnesses to cover the period between the departure of the Logos and the return of the Helper (chapter fifteen). The powers of this world then go through the empty form of putting the Logos-Jesus to death. They, of course, do not know it is empty, but the Logos does (chapters eighteen and nineteen). He establishes the unnamed "beloved disciple," that is, the Christian Church, and makes him the son of the "mother" Jewish Church. After the Prince of This World thinks he

[16] Mishkat Al-Anwar, *The Niche for Lights,* translated W.H.T. Gairdner, p. 77 The Royal Asiatic Society, London, 1924.

[17] The original version of John was not merely evasive about this matter, as is the modern text, but explicit. The text at John i, 13 originally read: "*He* who was not born of the will of the flesh etc." That is, this whole verse referred to the Logos Jesus, not as—very awkwardly—the modern text applies these conditions to the Christian believer. There is no MS evidence for this reading, but there is evidence considerably older than any existing MS. It was the reading known to Justin, Irenaeus, Tertullian and the author of the second century Epistula Apostolorum. It is also the concept of the origin of the Christ similar to that held by the author of Hebrews. The New English Bible, despite the multiplicity of minor variant readings which it gives in its footnotes, does not give this one. The variant readings can be found in A. Merk, S.J. *Novum Testamentum Graece et Latine,* Rome, 1951.

has killed the Logos-Jesus, the Logos appears to his disciples, commissions his witnesses as fishers of men (chapter twenty-one), supplies them with bounteous spiritual nourishment, and then announces that of all the witnesses only one, the "beloved disciple," the Orthodox Church, will live to see his return.

Such is the barest outline of the history of the origin of Christianity as the author of the John Gospel saw it and set it out in allegory webbed with symbolic detail. Needless to say, a Levantine document cannot be read as though it were written within a Western frame of thought. To attempt to do so always produces nonsense and the John Gospel has long produced only nonsense for those Western Christians who sought to make literal Western sense out of it or hoped to find some magic formula to make it agree with the synoptics. It cannot be made to agree because it is written about an altogether different subject.

Among the patterns of symbolic details that fill the pages of John, one bears directly on the geographical development of Christianity. After the Logos-Jesus has made himself known to the Jews and shown their departure from God by their inability to recognize the Logos-Jesus, he announces that he will go where they cannot follow. Where, they wonder, will the Logos go that they cannot follow? "Is he off to the Dispersion among the Greeks, to teach the Greeks?" (vii 35). The fact that the Logos was to go to the Jews of the Dispersion is announced for everyone to understand.

Even long afterwards in the Christian Levant the tradition of its own Greek-Jewish origin must have held. Late in the seventh century Anastasius of Sinai, a Byzantine theologian, could so far confuse outward form with inward reality as to write "so the more ancient interpreters of the church, I mean Philo, the philosopher and contemporary of the apostles. . . ."[18] Philo, the very exemplar of Septuagint Jewry.

By the middle of the second century there was still no Christian canon, no New Testament, though the books that now compose it were in existence. Holy Scripture for the Christians was still only the Jewish Septuagint, and in Africa and the far west, its Old Latin translation. When Christianity was brought to our ancestors in northwestern Europe, it was brought as the gospels. The Old Testament served only as historical and prophetic background. We almost forget that Christianity spread through the Roman Empire before the gospels were even written and long before they were held to be the sacred word of Scripture. In the early centuries they were, in essence, Midrash. In the beginning, the New Testament was the Talmud of Greek Judaism. As in so many other instances the super-

---

[18] *Consideration of the Hexaemeron.* Quoted by E. I. Goodspeed, *The Apostolic Fathers*, p. 268. New York, 1950.

ficial historical perspicacity of Protestantism was correct in elevating the Old Testament to primacy over the New. It was an essential step if one wished to restore Levantine Christianity.

The first man who sought to establish a sacred New Testament was Marcion. In the middle of the second century this Christian bishop asserted that he was in the true tradition of Paul. He denied that anyone could be a true Christian and accept the Old Testament. He went further, and his followers and successors went further still in seeing Yahweh of the Old Testament as a subordinate God, just but not merciful, and therefore essentially a God of evil whose reign was overthrown by the Christ.

The Pauline epistles do not go so far; except for phrases here and there that express a conviction that Satan rules the world of tangible reality, these writings are silent on the identity of the powers of evil. They do not go on to the frank dualism of Marcion and Mani, yet nothing of Marcion's position that all terrestrial creation and the Old Testament are the work of an enemy of the Christ is not logically deducible from parts at least of the Pauline position. Redemption is necessarily dualistic even though the pious of Orthodoxy and Western Christianity both balk at this inescapable consequence. God does not redeem his own from himself. He does not offer a sacrifice to release his own creations from his own power. Jesus as prophet, Jesus as the revealer of truth reviled and ignored by men is not dualistic, but Jesus as God's sacrifice, as the World's Redeemer, requires always an unmentioned power from whom the world is redeemed by this fearful pledge. Marcion drew the logical, verbally expressed consequences of the Pauline position and thereby openly broke with the continuity of Septuagint tradition, and his name and works have vanished from the stage of history. Seen from this view it is easy to understand the efforts of the author of Acts to take over the name and repute of Paul but without this doctrine.

Modern critics lay it as a charge against Marcion that he was dualistic and see in the rejection of his theory by other Christians the assertion of a principle of monotheism. This is absurd. Levantine Christianity of all shades and sects was dualistic. Satan was real to all of them, though there was debate over the extent of his power, whether over all material things or over a more restricted field; debate over his relation to God, whether of equality or permissive existence. It was not Marcion's open dualism that shocked Orthodox Christians as it does academic Western Christians. It was his rejection of the real continuum of Greek Christianity—its Hellenic-Jewish origin confirmed and symbolized in the retention of the sacred Septuagint. But despite the rejection of the Marcion Christians from the fold of Orthodoxy, the Orthodox Church did accept a New Testament as equally sacred with the Septuagint. One final compromise in the direction of Pauline tradition—the abandonment of circumcision and Jewish food restrictions—produced the Greek Christianity that became the Orthodox Church.

The tradition that it was Paul who directed the teachings of the new church to the gentiles rather than to the Jews expresses only part, and not the most significant part, of the earliest Christian preaching. All Christian preaching was to those who spoke the Greek language, Jew and gentile alike, and more important than Paul are the unremembered missionaries who convinced all the Jews of the Septuagint that Jesus was the fulfillment of their existing faith. The historically important factor is that no voice which has come down to us within the canonical or heretical frame of ancient Christianity directed its teachings to the Aramaic-speaking people beyond the frontier. No teacher of Christianity stood directly on an unbroken Aramaic or Hebrew tradition. Aramaic was spoken in Syria and Palestine, but Greek was the overriding official language and the language of the Christian church there as well as further west was always Greek. In the Aramaic east there was only the tiny sect of the Ebonites, the only Christians with a Hebrew name, who derived their Christianity from other than a Greek source. They followed Jewish customs and an apocryphal gospel which they attributed to Matthew. They asserted that they were the real successors of the disciples, as they probably were, rejected the Pauline epistles and soon fell out of communion with the Greek-speaking church. They lasted for a few centuries east of the Jordan.

There were other ancient and curious Christian fragments, but they were without exception Greek, the Montanists and the Paulicians in particular, whose separation from Orthodoxy preceded the foundation of Orthodoxy itself. The Paulicians, if they did not derive their system from Marcion and the Manicheans, certainly adopted many of their views, being openly dualistic and denouncing the Old Testament as the work of Satan. They were probably the spiritual ancestors of the Cathari of southern France, who so long troubled the Catholics and the king during the Middle Ages. The ritual of this curious cult went back to a Christianity so ancient that the distinction between priest and bishop had not yet been established, as it is not, for instance in the earlier Pauline epistles, everyone confirmed in the faith is a saint, everyone has potentially the full power of the Spirit. But they, too, stood on a Greek, not an Aramaic tradition.

But whether we can identify the rift between Orthodoxy and the heretical churches, or whether the division goes back to the dim past before there was a canon or a creed or a fixed ritual, all these dissident fractions of Christianity grew from the Septuagint. Only the brief and tiny Hebraic Ebonites held to the ancient Aramaic line. The Christian movement in the early days grew up in Greek-speaking lands and only some centuries later was carried back into the Aramaic east. To say "carry back" is, of course, a spiritual sense of the term, for physically it was a matter of carrying the faith beyond the Roman frontier. But "back" is really the correct word, for the world of Jesus was not the world of the Roman Empire, but of Aramaic Arabia and Mesopotamia and even of Persian-speaking Iran. Some unknown form of preaching about Jesus apparently spread beyond the Roman frontier before the establishment of the historical churches in the fourth and fifth centuries, but the final churches in these areas all go back to Greek sources. No Aramaic church stands in uninterrupted continuity on Aramaic sources.

All the Christian churches, modern and ancient, are, therefore the off-spring of the Septuagint, of Greek, not Aramaic, Jewry even though their founder was himself from Aramaic Palestine. Jesus lived in a land whose vernacular was Aramaic, and his Aramaic coreligionists extended far to the south and east of the Roman frontier. But the religious movement that grew from his name was the creation of men whose Holy Scripture had been in Greek some centuries before he was born, and who stamped an approximate Greek translation of "Messiah" for all time and for all tongues as the name of those who claim Jesus as the founder of their faith.

The first Christian preaching was to the Greek Jews. Of what did this preaching consist?

Christianity teaches that Jesus was not only God but man, an actual historically real man, as real as his contemporaries Seneca or Pliny or the Emperor Tiberius. With him and him alone divine events entered the world of history, and in the ultimate, whether it is sacred faith or historical fact that must justify the truths of Christianity, no church has ever been willing to deny the reality, as a piece of terrestrial human history—whatever else they may also have been—of the life and teachings of Jesus.

To a modern materialist, the greatest difficulty in any purely historical study of the life of Jesus might seem to be the miracles. Actually, however, this is not a difficulty. The supposition that Western sciences preclude miracles rests on ignorance concerning the nature of Western science and a pointless confusion between the form and the essence of a miracle. It is true that the naïve Levantine reporting of certain events in both the Old and New Testaments appears directly contrary to mechanical possibility, to which the most probable explanation is that the reporting—by our standards—was bad. Of course, to a man who must accept with complete literalness a Levantine report of a Levantine version of a miracle, the conflict with Western scientific thought is inescapable. Consistent Westerners must, of course, reject mechanical impossibility because our faith and our knowledge—which are not Levantine—cannot envisage God doing anything of the sort, any more than our faith and knowledge could allow us to attribute imbecility or evil to God. The mechanical order of the universe, as we see it, is simply one aspect of the mind of God as best we can comprehend it, an aspect concerned not with the purposes but the processes of creation, and we cannot for a moment suppose that God suffers from the human shortcomings of vanity, pique and lack of foresight which alone would require mechanically impossible events as a way out of an unforeseen difficulty in the attainment of purpose. The mechanical order is simply the means chosen by God to actualize his creation. That order does not determine what events shall happen, but merely the mechanism of physical action—if something else, which is not mechanical, determines that an event shall take place.

To deny that any event can occur that is outside the frame of mechanistic possibility is not to deny the possibility of miracles. It only seems so if the structure of Western scientific determinism is not understood. Western scientific thought does not even pretend to predict the future and in essence does not even seek to ascertain the causes of particular events. It only seems that if all events must occur within the frame of the mechanistically *possible*, they must also be mechanistically caused. Our complete ignorance of the cause of particular events forbids any such rash extension.

There is another class of events which both in ancient and modern times leads to confusion on the question of miracles: the so-called miraculous cures of the sick. Whether these cures are miracles in the sense defined above is unknowable, but they certainly are not mechanically impossible events. Levantine thought readily accepted the concept of demonic possession and most of the cures reported in the synoptic gospels involve this. Modern medicine does not accept the existence of demonic possession, not because the idea is empirically unjustified—for it might be simpler to obtain a patient's cooperation against a hypothesized outside demon than against an equally hypothetical internal complex, to which a much less tangible image can be attached—but because it disbelieves in demons. But regardless of the preferred explanation of such illusions, such cures are not in contravention of Western mechanical principles. Equally the cures of serious and evident bodily ailments and injuries often reported, either from shrines or even as acts of individual faith, do not traverse the structure of Western causality. The present level of medical knowledge is so far from that required even to begin organizing a causal science that it is difficult to understand how these cures can be considered an argument for the possibility of mechanically impossible events, or even much of a buttress for the Christian faith, since they are equally common in most of the religions of the world, past and present, civilized and barbarian.

Finally, we must notice that any event that proceeds in accordance with the Divine Will, even though it be entirely within our ideas of mechanistic possibility, must in a final Levantine analysis be of a sort that Westerners can only label miraculous. That is, it must be to the Levantines a consequence of direct divine intervention in the natural order. This is inevitable because to the Levantines, the natural order is not felt to be directly under divine control; often indeed—as it clearly was to St. Paul—it is under direct control of the enemies of God. Hence, all terrestrial events, natural or human, were hostile or at best indifferent towards God, and anything God wished to accomplish in terrestrial affairs could *only* be done by a miracle, *only* by a breach of the natural order.

What, then, is a miracle to the Western mind? Not something that happens "outside" nature, for such events have no existence, but some event produced through the unknowable web of real happenings that asserts what we believe to be the divine purpose. Obviously, we cannot prove divine purpose any more than we can prove causal necessity from temporal sequence. Both are inner connections with which the mind interprets the succession of phenomena. Nor can either be disproved, though each is seen quite differently by men of different societies.

The historical reality of Jesus is, therefore, not disturbed by the fact that our records of his life are necessarily Levantine records, written and for centuries edited by men whose concepts of causality differed profoundly from ours. Inevitably they would report the causation of events as they understood causality—as their irreligious scientists continued to do centuries afterwards. We cannot always figure out the Western version of a reported event, but we can be sure if the event is well authenticated that a Western version of it is just as authentic as a Levantine. Both causalities are equally capable of accounting for the mechanics of anything that can ever happen.

Though we lack the religious emotions of our ancestors and though Christianity today is only the historical and no longer the official religion of our society, the authority of Jesus is still far too precious to risk to the hazard of objective historical criticism. Thus any study of the life of Jesus, if that study goes beyond a pious harmony of the gospels, and all such harmonies are even less intelligible than the bare, unharmonized gospels themselves, is likely to be an unpopular enterprise. The worldly irreligious have a positive distaste for the question because to them the name of Jesus is a reminder of a faith that they have lost. True, they do not consciously regret the loss of this faith, but, unconsciously aware of the absence of any transcendental belief within themselves, they find it more comfortable to know as little as possible of this man whose name is a symbol of all they have rejected from their lives. To the consciously religious, also, an objective study of the life of Jesus can be an embarrassment less subtle, but perhaps much deeper. They too have an image of Jesus to protect. They do not want to know nothing about him, like the irreligious, but they may not want to know too much, and the solution to their psychological problem usually lies in ignoring the historical, human Jesus and focusing their attention on his divinity. This solves the psychological difficulty, but it hopelessly embroils the historical. Objective historical criticism becomes inapplicable to the life of a god. What can be considered possible or impossible, probable or improbable, what test of veracity could apply to the biography of a god? But verifiable history shows that Jesus was a man, and theology teaches that as well as God, he was also man, so that in fact we solve nothing by taking refuge in his divinity as an explanation of the apparent inconsistency of his actions and the impossibility—in human life—of his ethical system. The problem of his human life as the synoptic gospels picture it remains as baffling as ever. Admittedly the conventionally pious do not find his life baffling simply because they rarely seek to understand it. They rarely ask themselves by what warrant they assume some of his teachings to have been intended for practical application and others to be only symbolic of lofty but unattainable goals. They rarely ask themselves whether he foresaw and made provision for the church of the twentieth century or whether the historical development of Christianity was beyond or even utterly contrary to his expectations. They do not realize that these doubts, and scores of others equally disturbing to the tradition of the Christian faith, lie openly in the pages of the New Testament. Too often the conventionally pious have built for themselves out of tradition and isolated scraps of quotations, remembered or partly remembered, a vague, inconsistent image of a Holy Being to whom they give the name of Jesus Christ. To them, quite understandably, the course of intellectual and moral peace is to leave this image undisturbed.

Aside from a mere impersonal interest in objective history, there is however an important—almost political—reason for the modern world to attain a clear understanding of the personality of the human Jesus despite the pain that this understanding may cause. At present the publicly-admitted conception of the life and teachings of Jesus is a lie at the core of our society. In the name of Jesus we proclaim a set of ethical concepts which we do not practice and of social and political goals the practical consequences of which are almost the direct contrary of the declared intentions of their protagonists. At every turn this historical and moral confusion is ruinous to our society. Yet under the protection of this mighty name these goals and concepts are unassailable. What then, if they bear no valid relation to the life and teaching of their supposed author?

Even if these difficulties can be set aside, the life of Jesus is not easily comprehended by modern men. The Levant differs from the West not merely in trifling surface matters but in the deepest concepts of reality, of human destiny and of divine purpose. It was, as its aged remnants still are, firmly and consistently dualistic. In its early centuries it was also apocalyptic. The mundane earth of nature and history was seen as only the ephemeral theater of the struggle between God and Satan, and Satan was not one of God's creations living only by permission of his stronger rival as we of the West feel compelled to picture him when we admit his existence at all. Satan was the Lord of Evil and also the Prince of this World. True, his reign was to be overthrown in the dreadful cataclysm of the near approaching last days when time and history were to come to an end, when the dead were to be raised, the living judged and the natural earth magically transformed into the Heavenly Kingdom with the Messiah at last replacing Satan as its Lord. But in the meantime, this world was the dominion of Satan and all earthly glory, all wealth and power could be obtained only with the aid or at least with the acquiescence of Satan, so that the possession of these things was an infallible sign of the side to which a man had been predestined.

Such a world is intellectually remote from ours, not simply because we are moderns—for our medieval ancestors were equally remote from it— but because we are Westerners and find it difficult to understand honest, consistent dualism, predestination and the notion of the will, not as the responsible arbiter of a man's life, but as a mere servant, predestined for good or ill. To us a man is evil because he wills to do evil. To the Levant a man wills to do evil because, being evil, God predestined him to have an evil will.

Since we do not think too highly of this set of ideas, many would prefer not to find it as the philosophical base of our Christian documents. They would prefer our religious documents to set out with pedestrian literalness the detailed items of what is to be believed as religious truth. They do not take kindly to the fact that these documents, being products of the Levantine society, must necessarily express a concept of truth far different from our own, so different, indeed, as to be absurd if read in a literal Western sense. We can know nothing of any objective value about the life of Jesus until we are able to let the Christian documents say what they do say and not insist on misunderstanding them to make them say something that would make us intellectually more comfortable.

To scholars it has long been evident that the different books of the New Testament and even different parts of the same book are of entirely different historical validity, but there is no consensus concerning the relative authenticity of the different parts of the text. In the end, the final decision on what parts to accept as genuine and ancient and what parts to reject as later, doctrinal or explicative must rest on their consistency with a judgment of what Jesus did and what Jesus taught. To phrase the matter another way, the four gospels and Acts taken complete, word for word and without any deletion, present a picture of Jesus that is inconsistent, contradictory and inherently unintelligible and impossible. No one has ever been able to make any historical sense of the life and teachings of Jesus if he must retain and accept as true everything that is said about him in the four gospels and Acts. Certainly there are many devout persons who would deny this, but the flaw in their denial is that they have not sought to comprehend the life and actions of the human Jesus. Under the unconscious assumption that Jesus lacked a full humanity and was in essence only a divine being, was indeed God and nothing else, the sources present no problem. The incomprehensible, inconsistent, contradictory or impossible are simply divine mysteries which our frail human intelligence cannot entirely grasp. But this does not in any way solve or even aid the problem of the human Jesus.

There is therefore no escape from the necessity of selection if it is knowledge of the life of the human Jesus that is sought. From the canonical texts something must be retained and something else rejected, and unhappily there are few objective criteria for accepting or rejecting any particular part. Even the seemingly easy solution of rejecting everything that to Western mechanical science seems impossible produces no solution. Not only is the residue, stripped of the mechanically impossible, less comprehensible than the original whole, but this criterion rejects much that from a historical standpoint is the most firmly "factual" of all, the transfiguration, the feeding of the multitude, the walking on the water. There is an immense historical difference between miracle mongering—between the invention of pious marvels which a later time bootlegs into a text—and a stubborn fact, however miraculous it seems, that can only be in the story because it happened and the later chroniclers no longer understand it but cannot get rid of it. The test of Western mechanistic possibility can make no distinction between these so that while it is correct in rejecting the first, it is woefully erroneous in rejecting the second.

The problem of the historical validity of the different parts of the Christion documents can be approached, therefore, only by the slow and difficult route of induction and hypothesis. Some consistent pattern and theory of the life and teaching of Jesus must be formed in the mind, must be imagined even, and the authenticity of the text accepted or rejected by the consistency of the text with the theory. There is no other way. All we can ask is that such patterns be honestly set out so that in time by inward evaluation of the different patterns we perhaps someday may agree upon one which best solves this ancient and vexing problem.

In this confusion and disagreement it is only proper, therefore, to state frankly the assumptions upon which the following study is based. They are these:

1. The Gospel of Mark *contains* material going back to the recollection of St. Peter, but the finished canonical book is something altogether different.

2. The Gospel of Matthew *contains* many direct sayings of Jesus not in Mark, but otherwise has no authoritative information about Jesus not derived by its author from Mark.

3. The Gospel of Luke is similar in structure to Matthew, but its last editor had a more clearly defined and probably later theological point of view.

4. The Gospel of John was not written by a disciple of Jesus and was not really written about Jesus at all, the Jesus of its pages being a symbol used by the author for purposes other than a biography.

5. Acts was not written to be a history of the origin of Christianity. In a measure it follows a method somewhat like that of the John Gospel in setting out real or invented matters—neither author seems to care which—that can be employed symbolically for the author's purpose. This in the one is not biographical nor in the other historical, but doctrinal—though slightly different doctrine—in both.

6. The ten so called "undisputed" epistles of St. Paul (Romans, I and II Corinthians, Galatians, Ephesians, Philippians, Colossians, I and II Thessalonians, Philemon) are basically his but have been edited, interpolated and rearranged to the extent that the original meaning must be partly conjectural. This is a position not widely accepted. Few scholars have questioned the Pauline authorship of the ten major epistles, and this acceptance has been extended to accepting each letter as a largely unretouched product of its original author. Some mechanical reshuffling is supposed to have occurred, particularly in Second Corinthians, but the reshuffled pieces are all themselves accepted as Paul's. However, the same person could hardly have told the Galatians that the gospel he preached to them was "not according to men" or received from men, but was a direct revelation from Jesus Christ to the author, and also told the Corinthians that this supposedly identical gospel was what the author had received from the apostles. (Gal. i, 11, 12 *vs.* I Cor. xv, 1-5) The same person could hardly have written across the complete break in sense at Romans i, 18. The great mystical hymn in Romans viii, 18-39, could hardly belong with Romans

ix to xv immediately following it. The intrusion of I Corinthian xiii, 1-12, is flagrantly advertised not only by the continuity of subject before and after but by the clumsy sutures of verses xii, 31 and xiii, 13. There are many other examples of inept textual breaks, of completely different theological views. The whole subject of the age and integrity of the Pauline corpus is in need of exacting restudy. The difficulty seems to be that nineteenth century Protestant scholarship, which accomplished the basic textual analysis of gospels and Old Testament on which all subsequent historical work depends, was naturally reluctant to approach the Pauline corpus with the same unflinching objectivity, since it was these writings traditionally attributed to Paul, rather than the sayings attributed to Jesus, that furnished the declared intellectual basis for the break of Protestantism with medieval Catholicism.

7. The canon of the New Testament did not create the church. On the contrary the church created the canon, which was at first fluid, not merely in regard to the particular books that were or were not considered canonical, but in regard to the contents and structure of each book. That is, two forces were at work between the death of Jesus and the freezing of the canon about 200 A.D.: (1) authentic historical traces of the life and teaching of Jesus, (2) the need to confound Jews and heretics.

8. Where confoundment of Jews or heretics seems to be the purpose of a passage in the gospels, it may also be a correct reflection of a teaching of Jesus but it need not be. On the other hand a statement in a synoptic gospel directly contrary to third century church doctrine is almost certain to reflect correctly an earlier view, and if it is not a view known to have been held by the church in earlier times, it is almost certainly a teaching of Jesus.

9. The historical Jesus was a man and must have acted like a man, necessarily a man of his time and society. His divine nature, to speak theologically, could not have made his life inhuman. This is a necessary historical postulate because if Jesus is to be considered as not human but wholly a god, his life falls outside the natural and historical order and cannot be dealt with historically.

The New Testament as it stands today, as we and our ancestors have read it since the origin of Western society, has a logical, fairly consistent structure. There are inconsistencies and inner disharmonies but the volume as a whole appears to flow rationally. It begins with the birth, life, teachings, death and resurrection of Jesus, then with the doings of the early apostles and closes with various theological and moral papers on the significance of the life, teaching, death and resurrection. The volume thus appears to correspond with the sequence of events. But this is not at all a valid correspondence for the book was written in almost precisely the reverse order. The important theological and moral papers— the "undisputed" Pauline epistles—are older, considerably older, than the biographies. To us the gospels appear to be the foundation of the church, but historically this was not so. Historically, the church existed before the gospels and this of itself creates a serious problem of historical method. If the structure of the New Testament is taken at face value, then the sensible foundation of church history is the life of Jesus as depicted in the gospels, from which the historian then proceeds downward in time to the foundation and spread of the church, noting here and there inevitable human compromises and departures from the pure thought and purpose of the founder.

For a century and a half this has been the method assumed in about all Christian history and in the majority of the lives of Jesus. Leaving aside as not serious historical writing the merely pious lives that made no attempt to consider the various layers of historical validity, even most of the serious work was still imprisoned within the same historical mirage. These authors have attempted to disentangle the historically valid parts of the gospels from what they considered later or erroneous emendation. But while with rare exceptions, they have, so to speak, questioned the letter of the gospels, they have unconsciously accepted as genuine the apparent logical structure of the New Testament. Some have questioned whether Jesus founded the church, but only by questioning the existence of Jesus himself, only by asserting that Christianity is a myth and Jesus an invention of its later believers, by which process they emerged with a worse problem than the one they started with. Almost everyone else has assumed that since the church knew Jesus as the Christ and the gospels— as a whole—picture Jesus as the Christ, that in historical fact, Jesus in his lifetime was accepted by his followers as the Christ—and equally, of course, so rejected by his enemies. Under all the superficial differences among these biographies and histories they have all, therefore, wrestled primarily with the problem of what *kind* of a Christ Jesus must have represented himself to have been—a Davidic earthly Messiah who would restore a mundane Jewish kingdom in Palestine, a heavenly Messiah who would judge the dead, an eschatological Messiah who would bring the world to an end, a spiritual Messiah who would gradually lead mankind by spiritual insight to higher things, a socialist Messiah who would overturn the rich and distribute the good things of this life evenly to the poor, an internationalist Messiah who longed for the complete brotherhood of man. Almost all who have accepted the historical existence of Jesus have accepted the church of the late second century as the institution founded by him; distorted, corrupted, changed, perhaps, or inspired and unchanged; but as a corporate organization, not only using his teachings and carrying out his intentions but having been brought into existence by these teachings and intentions.

The alternative is difficult and has rarely been followed. If the apparent logical structure of the New Testament is too suspect to take at face value we must begin a study of the life of Jesus, not with Jesus but with the church about a century after his death—since that is the earliest set of facts with verifiable rather than conjectural dates—and seek to work backwards. Implicit in this method, however, is the recognition of a historical possibility that tradition makes it hard even to consider. We know by all outward verifiable evidence that the church created the New Testament. What we implicitly assume, however, is that the unwritten substance of the New Testament, the life and teachings of Jesus, first created the church. But suppose this assumption were to be questioned? What evidence is there for it? Suppose that in the brief forty years of contact between the Greek world and the Aramaic Jewish-Christians who had known Jesus, that is, during the years from the crucifixion to the sack of Jerusalem and Judaea by Vespasian and Titus, there passed to the Greek world neither a complete, nor from the Greek view, a satisfactory picture of Jesus? Suppose that, despite the clearly Aramaic details, the assembled picture of Jesus as the New Testament gives it is not the Aramaic, historical picture passed to the Greeks, but a Greek invention incorporating only distorted Aramaic fragments. How would we know?

On the surface there would be no way in which we could know whether such tampering with fact had been done—or know that it had not. We almost always assume, however, that it could not have been done, essentially because we cannot envisage the men or institution that could have done it. The church, we are sure, was founded by Jesus—could only have been founded by Jesus—and, therefore, while it might have misunderstood and misinterpreted, it could not have invented. The Christian Church must originally have been a tiny group of men who had known Jesus and who went out to convert the world to the religion he had taught them. These teachings must have been in existence in order to bring the church into existence, and once in existence why should anyone falsify its history?

Unfortunately this apparently firm chain is an illusion. The existence of the church not only preceded the creation of the New Testament, as we admit; it also preceded the life of Jesus, however paradoxical this may seem. The church adapted itself and its name to the life, and above all to the death, of Jesus, but in everything except outward surface— and even in part to this too—it was in existence before he was born, the church of the Hellenic Jews.[19]

When this is realized, what is otherwise so odd about the New Testament becomes comprehensible. The inverse order in which it was written is seen to have been natural and the fact that all the gospels and Acts are literary compositions—the component items selected and edited from a definite dogmatic point of view—makes sense. Acts is not just some chance annals of Saint Peter and Saint Paul. It is a piece of literary composition organized with a purpose. Mark, which often seems like a mere disorganized, random collection of recollections of Jesus, is in reality also a literary composition, even though it is the oldest and simplest of the gospels. No documentation of the life and teachings of Jesus is the simple, unretouched memoirs of anyone who knew him. No document was ever intended to be his biography. All of them were intended not to tell the life of Jesus but to confess the Christian faith as it stood when the canon was closed in the last half of the second century. All of them, therefore, were assembled, composed and edited during something like a century in which they were not sacred scripture (and therefore untouchable), nor impersonal historical records that it would be intellectually dishonest to falsify; but sermons, cathechisms, articles of belief, exclusively designed to advance and justify the faith—a faith whose unalterable sacred scriptures already existed in the Septuagint, but whose precise Christian form was still fluid so that its strictly Christian documents were necessarily fluid also.

There has long been scholarly debate on the dates of composition of the four gospels. Beyond the complete unanimity in recognizing that they must have been written well after Paul's epistles, the details of the different arguments are of only minor consequence in regard to the historical facts about Jesus contained in them. It is a debate, indeed, that cannot even be accurately focused on a clear issue because there are two inextricably confused questions: When was the first form of a gospel written? When was each gospel as we now have it finally edited or re-edited? For the former question the answer would seem to be: not possibly before 60 A.D. for Mark, 80 A.D. for Matthew and for Luke, and 95 A.D for John. For the latter question, since we have no manuscripts earlier than the fourth century and only fragments of the text

---

[19] To call it a synagogue is to yield to an anachronism in the interest of a tradition of received history. The rough synonym, church and synague (ecclesia and synagoga), did not originally have a Jesus-Christian division of meaning.

from earlier times, the answer is largely guesswork based on each expert's own theory on how much change was desired and how much would have been possible in the ancient Christian communities.

All gospel dates are arrived at, of course, by the labors of learned men. The difficulty is that there are just too few facts on which learning can work, and the number of possible contingent combinations makes the number of possible solutions enormous. Accordingly, any answer becomes a guess which is not made any the less a guess because it is the guess of a learned man. Nor is it any less a guess when the guess is pushed out of the text—for example by proving early dates for the gospels on the basis of early dates for the Ignatian epistles, with no mention of how dubious is the assumed early date for these. The fact that the division of these learned men by adherence to early, middle and late dates is in very close agreement with their confessional allegiance, indicates more convincingly than anything else how few are the facts and how subjective the process of estimating these dates actually is.

On the other hand there is much more scholarly agreement—and such disagreements as exist do not divide so strictly along confessional lines—on the relative dates of different types of religious beliefs, of different religious symbols, of different degrees of ecclesiastical organization. Thus the intense eschatology, the vivid expectation of the Messianic transformation of the world in one's own lifetime, is very early. Attempts to account for the delay in this transformation are necessarily later, and acceptance of an indefinite extension of terrestrial life are obviously later still. Similarly, in the beginning the followers of Jesus were strict Aramaic-speaking Jews, next Hellenistic Jews, next Hellenistic Jews conscious of their break with Aramaic Jews, next Hellenists of Jewish origin who thought of themselves as Christians in religious rivalry with Aramaic Judaism, Hellenic Judaism having meanwhile almost entirely disappeared.

Similarly in the beginning, at least, of Hellenistic Christianity, all baptized with the spirit are saints, each capable of receiving, though not all actually do receive, the spirit, speaking with tongues and having other manifestations of religious ecstasy. Later, organization appears with presbyters and deacons, later still superintendents whom we call bishops. Later still came the idea that the bishops constitute a chain, both in person and in function, back to men who had known Jesus and these, in turn, came to be thought of as a group specially selected by Jesus and commissioned to begin—among other things—this very chain. Similarly, in the beginning, there is no clear distinction between the eucharist and the love feast, the *agape*—and the latter is a real meal. In the very beginning there is the Johannine baptism, then baptism in the name of Jesus, finally in the name of the Trinity.

With these changes as a standard of analysis it is possible to arrive at a rough relative chronology of the New Testament, provided it is admitted that not only Luke-Acts, but Mark and Matthew as well are compositions in which material of earlier dates has been incorporated by a final hand. This, however, is an extremely difficult admission for a modern Christian of traditionalist tendencies, since it makes parts of a gospel more credible than others—whereas the whole is divinely inspired —and perhaps more than that, it appears to make the authors and editors responsible for the present form of our canonical synoptics men entirely without modern literary scruples. No one, we feel, responsible for transmitting a divinely inspired document could deliberately tamper with it— particularly for doctrinal reasons—unless he consciously intended to pervert the faith delivered by Jesus to the saints.

There is much wrong with this view, primarily complete lack of understanding of the mechanics of the creation and transmission of our gospels. They have been scripture so long that today it is hard to feel that they once were not, that there was once a period when men could quite properly take liberties with their texts.

The condition of early transmission must be remembered. A learned and earnest Christian receives from someone a copy of a gospel. He finds in it what he believes to be traces of error. He has no written standard to which he can refer it. He cannot be sure that in the transmission from its supposedly apostolic source someone has not altered it. Why should he not correct it by striking out the error and putting in what he knows to be the truth, a truth perhaps literally but perhaps symbolically expressed? What could we suppose that the Paul of Galatians i, 11, 12, would do with a manuscript, however highly certified by a chain of men, even by Peter (Gal. ii, 11), that failed to harmonize with Paul's views? Granted that we know of only one Paul, the reliance he had on self-certainty as a result of direct revelation was present in other early Christians. True, this could not be continued for many decades because the weight of outstanding numbers of manuscripts would make further changes impossible. When that happened these particular documents could no longer be changed, and if new material needed to be added to the holy story or new interpretations made, a completely new document had to be prepared. Since it, too, had to have, or at least plausibly cite, ancient apostolic authority, this process, too, could not last very long and still remain wholly credible. The apocryphal gospels show that the process did indeed finally outrun its credibility.

Thus the formation of the Christian canon underwent, on a shorter time scale, the process that had earlier operated on the Jewish. When the point was reached that the series Judges-Kings could no longer be edited and interpolated, then Chronicles-Ezra-Nehemiah were written. When these became established in the canon, then III and IV Esdras, Enoch and so forth appeared. In the New Testament canon Mark, the Aramaic Matthew and the undisputed Pauline epistles correspond to Judges-Kings. Luke-Acts correspond to Chronicles-Ezra-Nehemiah. The Apocrypha of the two testaments likewise parallel one another.

It is not an accident that the oldest manuscripts of the gospels are from the fourth century. The older ones were not lost but destroyed because they differed from the approved text of the fourth century—our present text. Something of the changes during the third century and the last half of the second can be estimated from the translations then made into languages other than Greek and from quotations in the early Christian writers, but there is no external witness for changes made prior to about 140 A.D. It therefore does not mean very much for a historian to insist that a gospel ascribed to Mark was in existence in 65 A.D. Since this Mark of 65 A.D. was a form of the gospel that the ancient church itself long ago blotted out of existence, insistence on its mere antiquity without attempting to ascertain the relation of that ancient form to its modern canonical version may comfort the troubled but does not encourage historical comprehension.

Although variant texts were systematically destroyed, the changes in the accepted texts were additions rather than deletions. So long as the necessary doctrines were present it was not too important that contradictions to these doctrines might also be present, since the later could always be explained by an appropriate symbolic interpretation. On human grounds also, it would be evidently easier to add material to a sacred text than to delete it. It must have been easier to convince a congregation that it had received an incomplete text than that it had received—and believed—one containing positive error. Undoubtedly it is from this fact that we have not only interpolated gospels but four of them. There was a good century for this process to work between the time that teachings about Jesus began to spread through the Greek synagogues and the public acceptance of four gospels and ten Pauline epistles approximately like those we now know. Because this was primarily a process of addition, it is possible to try to estimate what parts still record the history of the origin of Christianity and the life of Jesus.

There are four canonical gospels and fragments of others. Nothing in these fragmentary apocryphal gospels offers any information of positive value about the life of Jesus. All are clearly of later composition than the first form of the canonical gospels, and so far as they do more than affirm the state of Christian belief at a particular time and relate material already present—sometimes in another form—in the canonical gospels, they present little but pious and miraculous invention. The recently discovered logia calling itself the Gospel of Thomas is the sole important exception. The wisdom of the early church in rejecting them from the canon is beyond question, but it is important to recall that during the century or so in which they were written, all were accepted by some Christians so that their existence and their contents do have a value in reflecting contemporary beliefs. By being themselves obvious literary fabrications, they also prove that what was offered to the world in the early days of Christianity as a gospel could be a literary fabrication. When it is recalled, further, that the three synoptic gospels were not written to hold equal authority side by side as they do today but that both Matthew and Luke were written to supplant all others and each remain the sole gospel, the importance of the possibility of literary fabrication—even the most honest and pious—cannot be overlooked. If either Matthew or Luke had alone survived, our knowledge of the human Jesus would be entirely different from what it is, and this difference reveals a tendency in the early church to ignore or alter certain historical facts about the human Jesus that it no longer understood.

The existence of the apocryphal gospels does more than warn us of this literary alteration of an older and more mundane record of Jesus. If we arrange a series beginning with parts of the canonical gospels and ending with these aprocryphal gospels, we get an interesting result. Such a series starts with the sections of Matthew and Mark dealing with the Galilean preaching and the journey to Jerusalem, then follows Luke's account of the same incidents, then the resurrection accounts in Mark, then the birth and resurrection accounts in Matthew and Luke, then the entire John Gospel and finally most of the apocryphal fragments. This series shows a development from almost simple, straightforward narrative to conscious doctrinal safeguards, then to doctrinal teachings, pious reflection and finally to exhortation and miracle-mongering. The extremes lie fully developed in the apocryphal fragments, but the beginnings of these same tendencies appear in the canonical gospels also. As a first historical sieve, the apocryphal fragments thus serve a valuable purpose: the more any material in the canonical gospels resembles the aprocryphal, the more dubious is its historical validity, the more surely it is evidence of later tampering with an eariler and simpler form of the gospel.

The only external information we have concerning the origin of the gospels is in the surviving fragments of Papias. This man, who lived in Hierapolis in Anatolia early in the second century, made it his practice to collect what we would perhaps call gossip from all the elderly Christians he met. About 140 A.D. he gathered this together in a work entitled

Interpretations of the Saying of the Lord, of which fragments exist in the surviving writings of the early fathers, particularly Irenaeus and Eusebius. The work was still used in Byzantium through the ninth century and copies existed as late as the fourteenth. Its disappearance is a little commentary on the intellectual decay into which the whole Levantine world, Christian, Jewish and Moslem alike gradually sank.

In a fragment which Eusebius quotes, Papias says that a certain John the Elder who had known some of the apostles told him: "Mark became the interpreter of Peter and wrote down accurately but not in order, as much as he remembered (or possibly, "as related") of the sayings and doings of Christ. For he was not a hearer or a follower of the Lord, but afterwards, as I said, of Peter, who adapted his teachings to the needs of the moment and did not make an ordered exposition of the sayings of the Lord. And so Mark made no mistake when he thus wrote down some things as he remembered them; for he made it his especial care to omit nothing of what he heard and to make no false statements therein." Concerning Matthew, Eusebius quotes Papias: "So then Matthew recorded the oracles (or sayings, logia) in the Aramaic language and everyone translated them as well as he could." [20]

The age of this testimony is impressive but there are difficulties. First it is curious that Papias himself knows nothing about the authorship of the gospels. Apparently it was not common knowledge even in his time, since the sole authority he cites is one old man who, according to Papias, had known some of the apostles. More significant, however, is the fact that we have no way of knowing that what Mark wrote, assuming the complete accuracy of the elder, is our canonical gospel. Even if we assume that it is, we still do not know what changes may have been made in it since the elder acquired his information about it. Certainly some changes are evident. Chapter thirteen is largely interpolated. There is a double account of the feeding of the multitude, one in chapter six, the other in eight. The passages in chapter nine, 2-13, must belong at least ahead of chapter eight, 27, and the material in nine, 14-29, has no fixed place. The end, from sixteen, 9 is new.

With regard to the modern Matthew, the situation is different. Whatever our modern Matthew may be, it is not a translation of Papias' Aramaic Matthew, but Matthew and Luke may both contain extensive quotations from the latter. We can form a probable idea of what this Aramaic Matthew must have been like by the recently discovered Coptic Gospel of Thomas, as it styles itself.[21]

---

[20] Eusebius, *op. cit.* III, xxxix, 15, 16.

[21] *The Gospel according to Thomas,* New York, Harper & Bros., 1959. A preliminary publication of the Coptic text and English translation. This collection of sayings is a fairly complete logia containing a series of disconnected sayings

For the documentation of the life of Jesus we, therefore, have this: Mark as far as sixteen, 9, with, however, interpolations that remain to be identified, going back through one intermediary to an actual companion of Jesus. The language of its original composition was Greek. Matthew and Luke both may be quoting from a Greek translation—made "as well as they could"—of an Aramaic collection of the sayings of Jesus made by another companion. When they agree on something absent from Mark, yet consistent with that Gospel, it is a fair presumption that they are quoting Papias' Aramaic Matthew. Each may have other material from this source which cannot be certainly identified because it is not duplicated in the other.[22]

We have, therefore, one document which contains the recollections of an eyewitness originally written by a man too early and too much in awe of his source to be concerned about the doctrinal consequence of what he wrote. The problem here is to identify the recollections from material that has been added afterwards. We have two other documents, each composed by a deliberate act of literary creation, knowingly drawing on existing written sources, selecting, rejecting and rearranging these sources with an eye to their story and to its doctrinal consequences. Of the two, Matthew was more inclined merely to draw on his sources, Luke to rewrite them. With these, as with Mark, the problem of how far they have suffered later editing remains partly unexplored and completely beyond agreement among scholars.

But the differences between Luke and Matthew are really more startling than their resemblances. Where they agree, they add material to the Marcan account but do not change its essential atmosphere and character. It is

---

attributed to Jesus. It was evidently translated into Coptic from Greek but an Aramaic original clearly lies behind the Greek, probably with a Syriac layer between. Along with many parables and sayings of Jesus identical or similar to those in the canonical synoptics it contains some strange new material. The manuscript of the gospel is placed at the end of the fourth century and the guess of scholars is that the composition goes back to the first half of the second century but what is of particular importance is the problem of the source of its sayings.

The question which will certainly involve long scholarly debate is whether Thomas depends exclusively on the canonical gospels or represents an independent textual tradition. Does it, for instance, despite its Gnostic editing, derive ultimately from Papias' Matthew? Except for the Gnostic editing it answers closely to the descripiton long made of this Aramaic logia. If it is dependent on the canonical gospels its author effected a weaving of Matthew and Luke which is precisely the reverse of what these gospels have supposedly drawn from the Aramaic logia. Tentatively it seems most probable that it is a Gnostically edited version of the ancient logia, probably influenced at certain points by one or another of the canonical gospels, as they have influenced one another.

[22] For example, Luke xii, 16 which is in *Thomas* Log. 63.

where they differ that they paint a picture of Jesus unlike that of Mark and somewhat unlike one another. Mark, of these conclusions no less an authority than Peter, reports nothing of the birth or childhood of Jesus and of the resurrection, only the empty tomb and an unidentified young man in a white garment—tradition and Matthew, but not Mark, make him an angel—who announced to the terrified women that Jesus had risen and that they were to tell the disciples that he would "go before them" into Galilee, a reference perhaps to this promise in Mark xiv, 28. However, the women were too terrified to tell anyone. Here the gospel stops (at xvi, 8), and if it ever had a different ending that end was lost or destroyed very early, for the present ending dates from the second century.

In contrast, both Matthew and Luke record the virgin birth and give details of the resurrection. But the differences are grave. Matthew has Joseph told in a dream that his wife, Mary, is pregnant by the Holy Spirit in order that the prophecy of Isaiah xii, 14 should be fulfilled. We are assured, rather awkwardly, that though married Mary is still a virgin. Then follows the birth at Bethlehem to fulfill another prophecy, the bit of Mazdaist astrology about the star and the three Magi (Mazdaist priests), Herod's slaughter of the innocents, to fulfill another prophecy, and for the same reason the flight into Egypt and return. Then with chapter three, the gospel returns to the Marcan frame with the preaching of the Baptist. Now in Luke, the Virgin is unmarried when the angel announces that she will conceive by the Holy Spirit and, in chapter two, Joseph merely appears to take his family to Bethlehem without any account of how they came to be married. Further, the birth of the Baptist is here assigned to a kins-woman of Mary's and the births are about simultaneous and doctrinally interrelated. Nothing is mentioned of Herod's slaughter or any flight to Egypt. Then follows the shepherds visiting the infant Jesus and the temple preaching of the boy Jesus which reads like the apocryphal infancy gospels. Finally in chapter three, Luke reaches the beginning of the Mar-can frame, the preaching of the Baptist.

It is manifest that these are not two accounts of the same *events*. It is impossible that both could be true since they do not supplement but con-tradict each other and of the only points in which they agree, the date, the virgin birth and the birth at Bethlehem, the two latter are items of doctrinal importance for which each had the same doctrinal reasons but an entirely different version of the actual event. We are thus presented not with an account of facts but with a statement of beliefs where all that is important is the symbol, not the historical reality. It is impossible, therefore, to conclude that we have any historical evidence for either point and what historical events underly the stories of Bethlehem and the virgin birth we have no way to ascertain.

In fact both gospels seem to have had an earlier form which was exclusively concerned with establishing Jesus as the Jewish Messiah, hence the Davidic genealogies and the birth at Bethlehem. Later this became of no interest as Christianity became entirely Greek and the wholly un-Jewish idea of a virgin birth was inserted. Matthew i:18-25 and Luke i:34-35 can be dropped from each gospel without producing any break in the continuity or requiring any other textual adjustment.

In the account of the resurrection, Matthew has Pilate at the request of the high priest appoint a guard over Jesus' tomb so his disciples cannot steal the body and announce his resurrection, a version of events which on its face must be later than the belief in the resurrection. However, an earthquake and an angel who rolls away the boulder from the mouth of the tomb terrify the guards. Then the angel delivers to the women the same message as in Mark, that the disciples will see Jesus in Galilee. Here, however, the women meet Jesus himself who repeats the message about Galilee. The high priest then bribes the guards to keep silence about the events at the tomb, and a meeting of Jesus and the disciples takes place on a hill in Galilee. Here Jesus announces a theologically late message that the disciples are to make converts of all nations, baptize in the name of the Father, Son and Holy Ghost (the idea of baptizing in the name of the Trinity is well post-apostolic) and teach obedience to all the commands he had laid down. Nowhere in Jesus' teaching during his lifetime is there any instruction remotely comparable to this, but the relation to the late ending of Mark is striking.

In Luke, the same women find the empty tomb and are met by two men "in shining garments" who assure them that Jesus has risen from the dead. Instead of a message to meet in Galilee, however, there is a reminder of a statement of Jesus made in Galilee that Jesus had to be betrayed, crucified and rise on the third day. This message conveyed to the disciples leaves them skeptical, but two followers on a journey encounter a stranger who points out all the prophecies that prove the necessary suffering and resurrection of the Christ. Suddenly they recognize the stranger as Jesus, whereupon he vanishes. Jesus then appears to the disciples, eats a piece of broiled fish—to prove he is not a mere spirit—and then gives them a commission to preach repentance and remission of sins, without, however, the same formula as in Matthew. In the supposed continuation of Luke's account in Acts, Jesus stays with the disciples forty days, instructs them to remain in Jerusalem to be his witnesses, tells them they will be baptized with the spirit and is then drawn up into Heaven.

In the account of the resurrection, these two evangelists are in agreement only on what they have in common with Mark—the women finding the messenger at the empty tomb—and a doctrinal point, the duty of preaching to the world. It is curious also that Luke inverts the message about Galilee, Mark has no sequel to it and Matthew uses it to introduce the late baptismal message.

Confused and contradictory as these accounts are, it is clear that the resurrection story originally had some connection with a journey by the disciples to Galilee, something so at variance with even very early church doctrine that Mark's account of it was altered, lost or destroyed, Matthew's was made an anachronism, while Luke bodily suppressed the whole thing, covering himself against the others by making two inverted references to Galilee. But that tradition had a long stubborn life. The apocryphal Acts of Pilate, perhaps as late as the third century, still knows only of Galilean resurrection appearances. Indeed the very difficulty in handling this stubborn traditional memory makes it apparent that unlike the stories of the Davidic ancestry and the virgin birth, an event of a historical sort underlies the story of the resurrection.

One can conclude from St. Paul and from the whole early spread of Christianity that belief in the resurrection of Jesus was the cardinal doctrine of the new faith. Some event must have given rise to this belief, and it must have been an event very close to Jesus' death. The habit of centuries is to identify this occurrence—whatever it may have been—as a physical event, a dead body restored to organic life, and then either accept the synoptic accounts substantially verbatim or else reject the entire story as a physical impossibility and the belief of early Christianity as superstition founded upon fraud. That there is another class of historical events, psychological events, as real to those who experience them as physical events, has rarely been considered by students of the life of Jesus and the spread of Christiantiy, because the gospels on their face seem to give no suggestion of this possibility in regard to the belief that Jesus rose from the dead. In the case of Paul, it is quite clear that his resurrection experience was of the psychological, not the physical sort, but this is not so clearly evident in the resurrection accounts in the synoptic gospels.

But there is even more wrong with the synoptic account of the resurrection than the discrepancies noted above. First of all arises the crass question, "Where did the money come from?" Rock tombs are not cheap. How many victims of Roman crucifixion were buried in rock tombs, were indeed permitted any kind of burial at all? We know very well the disposition of the corpses of those the Romans crucified: a common pit or a ditch, nothing more. Even the Marcan account, therefore, suggests a background of money and powerful friends, in fact does so explicitly in introducing the figure of Joseph of Arimathea, the "councillor." Interestingly the background of money and powerful friends was precisely the condition of the Christians at about the time Mark's gospel received the form it now has, but it was not the condition of Jesus' last days at Jerusalem. Furthermore, there is a radical difference between the account of the crucifixion and the earlier parts of Mark. Earlier there were no witnesses, no sources. No authorities are named. The recollection of Peter is quite authority enough. But with the crucifixion and resurrection, it is different. It is almost as though the author kept worrying over the question, "How are we supposed to know that?" And so Simon the Cyreanic, "the father of Alexander and Rufus," carries the cross, Joseph of Arimathea gets the body. The two Marys and Salome find the empty tomb. The centurion recognizes the "Son of God" (a most un-Jewish phrase, compare the form of Caiaphas' question). Heretofore it had always and only been Jesus and the disciples, now it is outsiders, witnesses, *proofs*. But what is perhaps most significant is that even with the curiously different method of this part of Mark, the original part of the gospel records only the empty tomb and the encounter with the messenger, not with the risen Jesus. There appears then a rather startling conclusion. The Mark gospel contains no account whatever of the resurrection. Furthermore, on the assumption of the basic historicity of Mark, and the later and therefore less firm authority of the other two synoptic gospels on matters where they disagree with Mark, there appears to be no historically valid account of the resurrection in the gospels at all. What is recited in Matthew and Luke is as much a later fabrication as the second century end of Mark.

But the account in the synoptics is not the oldest concerning the crucifixion and resurrection. There is one older one, the earliest Christian account that exists and it is indeed curious that students of the life of Jesus have made so little use of it. This account is in Paul's First Epistle to the Corinthians, chapter fifteen, beginning at verse three. It was written some years before even the earliest version of Mark and probably many years before the Marcan text reached its present form. This is what Paul says: "First and foremost I passed on to you what I had myself received, namely that Christ died for our sins as the scriptures had said, that he was buried, that he rose on the third day as the scriptures had said and that he was seen by Cephas, then by the twelve; after that he was seen by over five hundred brothers all at once, the majority of whom survive to this day, though some have died; after that he was seen by James, then by all the apostles, and finally he was seen by myself, by this so called 'abortion' of an apostle." [23]

---

[23] It is, of course, impossible to reconcile this with the statement at Gal. i:11 that Paul had not acquired his gospel from men but by direct revelation from the risen Christ. Neverthless, though this passage is almost certainly not from Paul's own hand, it represents the state of Christian belief between Paul's death—say 60 A.D., and the formation of the canonical resurrection accounts now found in all three synoptics—say, after 90 A.D. The reasons to question the passage as

This is far indeed from the gospel accounts, no confused or terrified women, no stage setting of heavy boulders and shining garments, nothing but a simple statement that was foretold by scripture: Jesus had been buried and rose on the third day, and that as a matter of oral testimony of various people he had been seen again after his death.

Since this is, by many years, the earliest written account of the resurrection, it is both the most important and the most revealing document on the subject. Every detail is worthy of study and careful meditation. To Paul, and therefore to the Christians of his generation, the fact that there was scriptural prophecy for the burial of Jesus and the three-day interval until he rose from the dead was the only fact of importance about these events. Was it perhaps also the only fact known about them? Considering the importance to Paul of his conviction that Jesus did rise from the dead and the stress he places upon it in this very chapter (verse 19, for instance), if he had more convincing proofs it is hard to suppose that he failed to mention them. But what he mentions is not an empty tomb or a removed boulder, but the testimony of those who saw the risen Jesus, and quite evidently did so on occasions and in circumstances which are not mentioned in the gospels, for nothing in these accounts agrees with Paul's tabulations. Matthew has the eleven disciples meet Jesus on a hill in Galilee. Luke has two unnamed disciples meet the unrecognized Jesus on the road to Emmaus, says that Peter saw him and then has Jesus appear to the eleven and their friends, substantially the account in the addendum to Mark.

So much for the negative value of Paul's evidence. It has likewise a positive aspect of great value. It confirms, to be sure, what the entire early spread of Christianity confirms at every point, that there was from the beginning a firm conviction that Jesus had risen from the dead, but it casts a light on how that conviction arose, something which the gospel accounts do not do. Paul mentions by name three persons who have seen the risen Jesus: Peter, James and himself. His own experience is in no way distinguished from that of the others. He distinguishes himself from the other aspostles most sharply, but he does not distinguish his resurrection experience from theirs, nor is there any hint anywhere in the New Testament that they insisted on any such distinction. The friction between

---

personally from Paul are several. First, it directly contradicts Galatians. Second, it bears no relation to what precedes it and very little to the long and earnest discussion of the resurrection of the dead that follows it. Third, it uses the phrase, 'the twelve," which exists nowhere else in the epistles and seems to have been a concept that did not exist in Paul's time. Further, some early texts have corrected this to "the eleven," obviously because of the Judas story in the gospels—but without attending to the adjustment later made in Acts—indicating a certain fluidity in the text between, say, 90 and 150 A.D. In any event, the passage in I Corinthians, being at clear variance with the gospel accounts, must not only be older but represent an older form of the resurrection tradition.

Paul and the original disciples is amply evidenced, even in the deliberately harmonizing account in Acts, but one charge that is *not* made against Paul is that his vision of the risen Jesus was different from the vision of the others, less real, less true or in any way less valid. This is of importance because, while we do not have a detailed account of the resurrection experience of the others, we do have it from his own hand, from Paul, in Galatians i, 16: "But the God who had set me apart from my very birth called me by his grace and when he chose to reveal his Son to me, that I might preach him to the Gentiles, instead of consulting with any human being, instead of going up to Jerusalem to see those who had been apostles before me, I went off at once to Arabia, and on my return I came back to Damascus."

Whether this is the only basis for the thrice repeated details in Acts (ix, 3-7; xxii, 6-21; xxvi, 13), as it may well be, does not invalidate the conclusion from all of them that not only Paul, but other early Christians accepted such an experience as identical to the resurrection experiences of the other apostles. It is only in the later versions in the canonical gospels that the experiences of these others were made material, indeed at certain points almost offensively material.

Since, therefore, the earliest and the only personal account of a resurrection experience is that of a psychological sort, not in our Western sense, a physical event, and since Paul without evidence of dispute identifies this experience of his own with that of Peter and the others, we can conclude that their resurrection experiences—despite the gospel texts—were in fact equally psychological events. The accounts of empty tombs, terrified women, strangers on the road, were all later attempts to defend orthodoxy and to make convincing to a later generation a conviction that in the beginning rested entirely—and in the beginning wholly convincingly—not on extrinsic objective but on internal subjective evidence; not on "proof" but on experience. If, then, we start with the hypothesis that the conviction of Jesus' resurrection arose among his disciples from a personal psychological experience—from what we would today call a "vision"— we can search the gospels for evidence of such experience. Since the final form of the story was externalized, made to appear miraculous, we could not expect to find the resurrection experience openly set forth as such. But in a disguised form it may still be there. It appears that it is there and in Mark, and in an early form of Mark since it has been taken over intact in Matthew but not in Luke.

It has always been somewhat of a puzzle to New Testament scholars to explain the double account of the feeding of the multitude in Mark. They are obviously symbols of the Messianic banquet expected at the beginning of Messiah's reign, but why should there be two such similar accounts? It cannot be, like minor words in manuscript copying, a mere scribe's mistake. Neither can it be the work of the original author of Mark (presumably Mark himself). The duplication must have been the work of an editor and of an early editor, for if many manuscripts of the gospel giving only one account had been in widespread use among the churches, it is difficult to believe that a version of the gospel with the dual account could have replaced the single version. This editor for some reason that seemed persuasive to him felt that there was enough difference in the two accounts, which to us obviously describe the same event, to require the retention of both. In the present form of the gospel where the two are in close series, no such important difference seems discernible. It is possible to assume, however, that the editor had before him two versions of Mark, each containing a single account of the feeding of the multitude sufficiently different, not in the details of the actual feast, but in the setting, to persuade the editor that the two versions described different events. It is an additional hypothesis that one of these versions contained substantially our Mark, chapter six, verses 30 to 52 (first feeding and water walking) and something much like the modern ending of the gospel, while the second and older version contained Mark, chapter eight, verses 1 to 10 (second feeding) and an end entirely unlike the modern end, an end which gave as an account of the first vision of the risen Jesus substantially what we find today in chapter six, verses 45 to 52—the story of Jesus walking on the water of the Sea of Galilee.

That this miracle depicts a resurrection experience of Peter and some of the disciples is indicated by many considerations. In the first place, the episode is manifestly out of context and very awkwardly fitted into the narrative. Unlike the natural flow of the story in the rest of Mark, where events either follow in orderly sequence or the narrative is sharply broken without transition or apology, here the narrator has to prepare for his miracle artificially by having Jesus leave the disciples to go up a hill by himself while they started across the lake by boat. How, then, when they set off, did they expect him to join them? Worse still, the narrator has his geography confused. The disciples without Jesus set off for Bethsaida on the east shore of the lake, but after Jesus walks out to them they proceed to land on the west shore at Gennesaret.

Still more conclusive is a detail appropriate in a resurrection experience but absurd in the context in which the episode is now placed. According to the present form of Mark, Jesus' purpose in walking out on the lake was to join the disciples and help them with the rough weather they were meeting. But what the text says is that as he approached the boat, "He would have passed them by," and it is they who first called out to him and he turned and entered the boat.

It is not difficult to picture the disciples perplexed and distraught after the death of their beloved master and the apparent failure of his promise to appear as the Messiah, returning heartsick and lonely to their old trade as fishermen on the Sea of Galilee. Probably there had been no promise to meet them in Galilee. It would have been quite inconsistent with Jesus' statement before the Sanhedrin of where he would appear. The promise in Mark xiv, 28 (and Matthew xxvi, 32) has no connection with its context and actually interrupts the thought. It probably was inserted when the Galilean appearance was the only version known to Christians, and the discrepancy of this appearance with Jesus' promise before the Sanhedrin needed explanation. But the disciples had been promised his return, of that there is no question, and they would have been prepared for a resurrection experience such as Mark describes, a phantom of mist or cloud on the dark lake seeming to pass them by and then turning and becoming in their mind's eye the vision of their master. It must also have been evident very early that this resurrection vision had several glaring defects when set out in the narrative as an episode in the course of the ministry of the living Jesus. For one thing, Luke who used the version of chapter six of Mark for his account of the feeding of the multitude, never used the episode of walking on the water at all, presumably because either he had at hand a version of Mark that did not include it in the ministry of the living Jesus, or he questioned its validity in its present context. The editor of Matthew used it, but he made significant alterations in the story. He suppressed the fact that Jesus would have passed the boat had the disciples not called out, and perhaps aware that the original form of the story was not a physical miracle at all, he made certain of driving home the miraculous to his readers by having Peter leave the boat and walk out to Jesus—which he does satisfactorily till his faith begins to fail. Then, as a final touch, the narrator, has the men in the boat declare Jesus to be the Son of God, which is not only missing in Mark but absurd at this point in the gospel when the confession of Peter had not yet occurred.

There survives a small fragment of an early apocryphal work known as the Gospel of Peter. Eusebius (VI, xii) quotes Serapion, bishop of Antioch about 190 A.D., as approving the use of this gospel until after more careful study he decided it had a Docetic tinge. The fragment that survives is an account of the crucifixion dependent on all four of our canonical gospels, though with additional and later embellishments. Nevertheless, the beginning of the resurrection story is substantially that of the synoptics: the heavy stone mysteriously removed, the empty tomb, the women and the young man in shining costume. Here, however, instead of being cut off as Mark is cut off, this gospel has a few more lines before the fragment ends:

Then the women were afrighted and fled. Now it was the last day of unleavened bread, and many were coming forth of the city and returning unto their own homes because the feast was at an end. But we, the twelve disciples of the Lord, were weeping and were in sorrow, and each one being grieved for that which had befallen, departed unto his own home. But I, Simon Peter, and Andrew my brother, took our nets and went unto the sea, and there was with us Levi, the son of Alphaeus, whom the Lord . . .[24]

It is true that this might be dependent on John xxi, 1-3, but the context is quite different. It is more likely that both accounts depend on the same conviction of a Galilean resurrection experience that has been deleted from the synoptics.

These puzzles and contradictions are not in the New Testament by accident or carelessness, nor is it possible that we are dealing with divergent but equally authentic accounts derived by different, but equally authoritative oral traditions. In the nature of the relations between the Hellenistic and Aramaic lands and the sack of Judaea by Vespasian, there were no such oral traditions. Papias was certainly old enough to be in contact with oral traditions and indeed he did have knowledge of some of them though hardly of a sort that buttresses Western credibility. Eusebius says of him: "Papias received other things which he said came to him in oral tradition, such as certain strange parables and teachings of the Saviour and certain other completely fabulous stories." (III, xxix) Remnants of a truthful oral tradition lie in Mark, in Matthew and in Paul, and nowhere else, save as derived from these after they were written. "Oriental memory," sometimes proffered as the source of inconsistent material, is a fiction as applied to the New Testament. What is remembered and transmitted orally in the Levant and formerly in India is not tradition, not general accounts of important matters with possible variation of unimportant detail, but specific, exact texts learned word for word, sense and nonsense equally protected and transmitted with equal rigor. Nothing of this kind of historical transmission exists in regard to any text in the New Testament canon. There does exist in some of the parables and sayings of Jesus a structure and rhythmic balance that convinces most scholars that a Semitic verse-like structure essential for oral recitation lies behind the Greek text. This is persuasive of the authenticity of many sayings of Jesus, but by that very certification raises grave questions about the balance of the gospels. Someone acquired a collection of Jesus' sayings, possibly long transmitted orally in Semitic verse-like structures. He translated them and worked them into a narrative frame.

[24] *The Apocryphal New Testament*, M. R. James, Oxford, 1955 p. 93.

What were his authorities for the different parts of his narrative frame? That the sayings and the narrative need have no connection with one another we know not only from Papias' statement about the Aramaic Matthew, but by the discovery in our own time of the Gospel of Thomas, actually a logia, without any narrative at all.

Oral tradition, therefore, may be called upon as witness for some sayings of Jesus, but it cannot be relied upon to authenticate statements about Jesus. On the contrary the historical core in Mark, Matthew and Paul is pretty closely identifiable and the chain of its transmission reasonably well attested. The rest is invention. It is not, however, fiction, like the later biography and martyrologies. The unhistorical parts of the synoptic gospels are in general explicative of matters affirmed, but not always clearly affirmed, in the historical core. The birth stories are a necessary consequence of a Levantine account of a divine being. Mark is still close enough to the source to need no such crutch. All he needs to invent is the innocent little device of having the demons recognize Jesus as the Son of God, thus asserting the historical fact of this belief at the time Mark wrote, but at the same time allowing the facts of Jesus' human life and preaching to be told with historical verisimilitude, for Jesus did not publicly announce to the crowds of Galilee that he was the Son of God.

Later more elaborate supports had to be developed—but even then they were neither contrary to the historical atmosphere nor developed without a purpose—primarily because different views about Jesus came into existence, and it was desirable to make clear the Orthodox view of what constituted the true faith against the assertions of the non-Orthodox. That is, the canon, as everyone has always known, represents the reaction of the church against heresy. All that is disputed is the extent of that reaction.

The oldest heresy, one so old that it may well be as old or older than Greek Christianity, goes under the name of Docetism. As with all ancient heresies, what we know about Docetism is what disapproving Orthodox writers chose to tell us, but with respect to the synoptic gospels they tell something of use. The Docetae seem to have completely subordinated or even eliminated the humanity of Jesus. To them, he was for all practical purposes wholly God. Hence they believed that he could only have "seemed" to suffer on the cross and the body of the risen Jesus could only have been pure spirit without any materiality at all. But all three of the gospels that mention the risen Jesus are explicit, though quite inconsistently so, about the materiality of the risen body. Luke even goes to the extreme of having the risen Jesus require, or at least eat, a piece of fish for breakfast, though for Luke no less than for the other two, this risen body is capable of appearing and disappearing like a phantom.

The next oldest heresy is that of Marcion which had some affinity with Docetism and actually must have existed as a Christian movement before Marcion organized it and gave it his name. Eusebius is not always quite sure whether some of the martyrs he records were not Marcionites. Marcion is chiefly remembered for rejecting the Old Testament, but his influence in the formation of the New was more significant. He was the first Christian to assemble a group of Christian writings and declare them to be the inspired word of God. In self-defense the Orthodox Church established its canon, not like Marcion as a substitute for the Old Testament, but at least as having equal rank. Marcion's canon was roughly our Luke, but without the first two chapters, and the ten undisputed Pauline epistles. Whether Marcion became thereby responsible for forcing the Orthodox Church to accept these epistles is conjectural, but if so it would explain the willingness of the author of Acts, who clearly knew these epistles, to write in direct contradiction to them. In his time they were not accepted in the circles for which Acts was written and there did not then seem to be any compelling reason to include them in a canonical collection.

Once the later and doctrinal alterations of the synoptic text have been identified and understood, the historical record of the living Jesus remains for study. Between the preaching of John the Baptist and the crucifixion, we have a solid account, the main stem of the narrative in Mark and many additional discourses of Jesus, consistent with those in Mark but not reproduced there, appearing in Matthew and sometimes in Luke.

The story in outline is this. From the Baptist's preaching that the end of the world was at hand and the Heavenly Kingdom in view, Jesus moved on to the conviction, not only that this was so, but that he himself was to be the Messiah of this Heavenly Kingdom. The concept had nothing to do with the ancient and never very real notion of a Davidic Kingdom of the Jews as a political entity in historical time, and even less to do with the modern theological notion that the Kingdom of Heaven is a state of spiritual development within individuals in a mundane world. It was not to be a development, but a cataclysm. It was not to be spiritual, in our sense, but completely physical, though not of the physics of this earth. It was not to exist in Heaven or in the hereafter while the mundane earth of historical time continued to exist, but to replace that earth and its time with an earth and a time that were real but magically different.

It was a Kingdom that was to wrest dominion over the earth from the Prince of Darkness who now held it. It was to bring death—and birth—to an end. And the Messiah was to rule over it forever. This concept is what the theologians call eschatology, and it was the belief not only of Jesus and the Baptist, but the expectation of all the Levant for some centuries before and after the birth of Jesus. It is not a belief of the West. It never has been, although in a more naïve and honest time this image drawn from the Bible touched our art and our theology. But in the modern world it is so distasteful and its logical consequences in ethics and theology are so disastrous for modern liberal religious convention that every effort has been made to argue that it could not possibly have been the basic concept of Jesus, or that at least if he started with that concept he "developed" one more suitable to us moderns.

The accepted view of the Jews of those times in regard to the Kingdom of Heaven was that first Elijah would return with a great outpouring of "the spirit," the powerful presence of God, which would seize men and give them many remarkable powers particularly the powers of curing the sick and of speaking "in tongues," that is, speaking indefinitely in senseless words.[25] Then was to follow the dreadful days which flesh and blood could hardly endure in which the Prince of This World was to be overthrown. This, in turn, was to be followed by the coming of the Messiah on the clouds of Heaven. The living were to be transformed, and the dead raised and history was to come to an end.

What the Baptist preached was not that the Messiah was soon to come, but that the coming of Elijah, a necessary preliminary, was close at hand (Mark i, 7, 8). After his arrest began the preaching of Jesus.

"Repent, for the Kingdom of Heaven is at hand." "Blessed are the poor," the mourners, the humble, the hungry and persecuted. Are these things then good? Not in themselves for they are to be reversed in the Kingdom, but in this world they are signs that those who suffer such hardships are not the favored of the Prince of Darkness who rules in this time. It is, therefore, in an apocalyptic sense that "ye are the salt of the earth" and "the light of the world." (Mathew v, 3-14)

To desire a woman is of itself adultery, and some have, therefore, made themselves eunuchs for the Kingdom of Heaven's sake. If you are struck on one cheek, turn the other. If anyone sues you for your shirt, give him your coat also. Love your enemies. Store up no treasure for yourself on earth. Never trouble about how you will get your food or how you will be clothed. Does not God care for the wild birds and the

---

25 I Cor. xiv. 1-33, but observe that Acts is either ignorant of this older custom or chooses to suppress the true nature of it.

very grass of the fields, and are you not better than they? Never trouble about tomorrow. God will take care of tomorrow.

These are the ethics of Jesus and they are officially the ethics of all the Christianities, but to us men of the West, to us and to our medieval forefathers alike, they have always been no more than an honored ideal. At best we feel they can be partially approached and even then not by everybody, or human society would fall apart and even the generations of men would come to an end. We feel that since they are not literally possible we have a right to pick and choose from them such as we feel practicable of application, if not for ourselves at least for others, or temper each of them to the inescapable requirements of life: lust enough to continue our breed, resist enough to maintain our peoples and our states, trouble enough for the morrow so that we do not starve or freeze to death on a winter night. These compromises, we feel, are not real dents in the ethics of Jesus. It is obvious that he could not have meant literally what he said. No such ethical code as is set forth in Matthew can be practiced in the millennial life of a society or even through a single lifetime by more than a handful of men, kept alive by a community which does not practice these precepts. Obviously, therefore, Jesus could not have meant them literally.

But he did and, as he intended them, they were entirely practicable, all of them and with complete literalness. For they were not the ethics of centuries or even of a lifetime. They were the ethics of a few weeks.

Chapter ten of Matthew records how Jesus sent his disciples, not to the gentiles and not to the Samaritan towns, but to the lost sheep of Israel; not to preach but with a message: "Repent for the Kingdom of Heaven is *at hand*." They are to take neither money nor any ethical teaching. They will have the power of the spirit to cast out demons and cure the sick. The spirit will speak from their mouths as needed, but they must expect to be reviled and even killed. Nothing that has so far been covered shall not now be revealed and what he has told them in darkness they are to speak in the light. They are not to suppose that he has brought peace but a sword. Brother will betray brother to death; father will betray child. It is to be the agonies of the "time of the end." For their fearful message of the end of the world they will be hated, but he who endures to the last shall be saved. And the end will not be long. They will not have traveled through the towns of Israel before the Messiah comes.

It is this powerful discourse and this alone that makes sense of the ethics of Jesus. In it lies no ambiguity, no doubt, no confusion, nor can it possibly be the interpolation of the later church. The time of the end did not arrive. Brother did not betray brother. The Messiah did not come.

Would anybody forging a Christian text so forge it that he proved Jesus so pointedly mistaken? [26]

It is stubborn hypocrisy to read Matthew five and six as a source of truth and rip it from its historical setting against Matthew ten. The eschatology of Jesus is not of the world of Western men, but to accept the ethics of his eschatology and then deny its physics is not to save the character of Jesus for the West. Taken in his time and with his world view he towers over history, which he molded in a way no man ever molded it. But to believe that he preached his ethics on the basis of.our physics is to paint him as a mere incompetent who mouthed empty sentimentalities.

The question that rests on the conscience and judgment of every man who calls himself a Christian is how much of this ethical system can be valid when the validity of the whole is shattered? The Messianic Kingdom did not arrive as Jesus had expected and therewith historical fact demolished the vital doctrinal fact on which stood the moral and intellectual justification for an ethic that abandoned the realities of this world. It was not an ethic of "renunciation," the introduction of a "higher" and "spiritual" valuation to ride along above the mundane ethics of practical worldly life, as our watered-down modern theology attempts to interpret it. It did not accept worldly things and go on to preach that there are better things which should be reached by "spiritual development." Such a notion is alien to the thought of Jesus as the historically evidenced text of the gospels shows. It was not an ethic added to some practical ethic of this world. It was a complete substitute. It was not only that the things of this world were evil as the dominion of the Prince of Darkness—which is implicit in the account—but that the things of this world were *finished*, which is the explicit statement.

And yet when the disciples returned and surprisingly the last time had not arrived, the Messiah had not yet come on the clouds of Heaven, Jesus did not recall these ethical teachings. Did he then justify modern theology by concluding that, after all, they could in some way be justified as the ethics of a continuing terrestrial life? Certainly he did not revise the ethical system, but neither did he revise his eschatology. All he altered was the date of the Messiah's coming, and that by only a few months.

26 It may be derived from the ancient Aramic source. Mark describes the sending out of the twelve (vi, 7) but quotes no instructions at this point. A considerable part of the Matthean instruction, however, appears in the badly interpolated chapter thirteen. Here they are probably quoted from Matthew itself as part of the interpolation. Luke splits the material at ix, 1 and x, 1, perhaps to get instructions for a sending of seventy disciples, which is otherwise unheard of, and furnished in this Gospel with additional instructions drawn from the Mark. Thomas gives Matt. x; 26-28; 34-39. Log. 5, 6, 33, 55, 56.

There was no reason to revise the ethics. They were still the ethics of the end of the world.

The change in the actions and discourses of Jesus that followed the return of the disciples has been a grave difficulty to most of his modern biographers. Suddenly, instead of preaching to crowds, he tries to be alone with his disciples. Suddenly he begins to speak of his approaching death. To account for this change, explanations are invented for which there is not a shred of evidence in the gospels. The fickle people must have turned on him. The hostility of the scribes and Pharisees must have become more intense. On the contrary, the people still pursued him, but it was now he who tried to avoid them. The great event that marks the change, the only event, is the failure of Jesus' expectation that the Messiah would arrive while the disciples were announcing his coming to the towns of Israel. This fact, which is so evident in the text, which reasonably and fully accounts for the change in Jesus, cannot help modern theologians to solve the problem. They are compelled to make tenuous inventions because they are committed by their policy of modernizing Jesus to deny that he then or ever expected the end of the world as a real physical event in time and space. Yet by denying that he so believed they are forced to paint his Galilean preaching as that of an incompetent and his journey to Jerusalem as that of a madman.

One vital question of the early preaching remains: who was to be the Messiah whom Jesus expected? In the earlier days he never said. In the later, he was explicit. It was to be himself. Now it is possible that this conception "developed" within him as we moderns so like to picture psychological operations. It is much more probable, and entirely consistent with the texts though not affirmed by them, that from his baptism onward he so pictured himself. But whether he thought so from the beginning of his preachings, or only came to this conviction later, the identity of the Messiah remained a secret almost to the end. Even when the disciples told him that they believed him to be the Christ, he charged them strictly to tell no one. It is misleading, however, to put this in quite such modern phraseology. Our image of him, as we Westerners understand the nature of God and of man, was that he considered himself the Messiah. To us, the earthly and the heavenly phases of that messiahship are not capable of real division. But in his own image of himself as best we can reproduce it, they were indeed entirely separable. He was now the one who *was to become* the Messiah. They are not the same thing. He already held the sacred *character* of the messiahship, but he did not yet hold its *powers*, for the Messiah as such could not come into power—could not really come into existence—until in the terror of the end of the world the Kingdom of Heaven came into being.

With the peaceful return of the disciples and the failure of the last times to arrive, a serious messianic problem arose. Somewhere in the mysterious mechanism through which God was bringing on the Kingdom there was something that Jesus had not comprehended correctly. Should we be surprised that such a problem would lead him to flee crowds and seek solitude? In the beginning he had supposed the coming of the Kingdom firmly predestined by the rigid causality of God, as its elect were rigidly predestined. But this was apparently not so since the Kingdom had not arrived when it was destined to arrive. Perhaps in Jesus' doubts about the fate of the rich young man we see, in regard to the elect, the same train of thought that he must have followed about the certainty of the coming of the Kingdom. To all outward signs readable by man, the rich young man could not be among the elect, and yet it could possibly be, for to God all things are possible. We do not know the inner mechanism of Jesus' change from acceptance of the predestined inevitable to determination to act, not in history—he had always acted in history—but to act in the world of eschatology itself. We cannot follow the process—nor could the disciples to whom the whole thing was incomprehensible—but we can see its beginning and its end. From acceptance of predestination Jesus turned to violence. Not violence as Western men understand it, not riot and revolution, but ghostly violence. He will do no less than force the hand of God. It is not for nothing that Jesus has been remembered as a man of courage even by those who do not understand wherein that courage lay.

This is more easy to understand if we will ponder the eschatology of the early Fathers. In their image the Prince of This World had been tricked. He thought he had to deal with only a wayward girl, never realizing that it was a virgin with child by the Holy Spirit. He thought he was crucifying only a troublesome man because the Messiah wore the flesh of a man. And it was that fatal error in crucifying the Messiah that was to cost him his dominion over this world.

Violence, Jesus tells us, had already begun. Since the days of the Baptist, men had been forcing the coming of the Kingdom. Beyond that his expression did not go, but from the situation itself we can perhaps estimate the logic of his thought. These acts of violence since the time of the Baptist had been small and they had not yet brought the Kingdom. But suppose God's own elect for the messiahship were to be crucified by the Prince of This World? Surely, in the face of that fearful and insulting violence, God's hand would be forced. Surely, with that he could delay no longer in bringing the world to an end. Indeed it is this view and only this view that makes the parable of the wicked vinedressers intelligible, (Matt xxi, 33; Mark xii, 1; Luke xx, 9; Thom. 65), for Jesus quite evidently pictures himself as the son whose death at the hands of the wicked vinedressers will bring the absent owner back to repossess his vineyard. Furthermore, if so mighty a figure as God's elect were to suffer, would not this more than equal the world suffering that the last times might bring? Would it not both bring on the Kingdom and raise "the many" from the horrors that flesh and blood could scarcely endure?

With this consistent and courageous determination of Jesus—to defy the Devil and manipulate God himself—modern theology flounders even more pitifully than over the ethical question. There is no doubt that Jesus went up to Jerusalem knowing he was to die there. About this no one any longer argues. How did he know? By supernatural revelation or by rational calculation of the forces and intention of his enemies—if he had any real enemies at that time? Was it foreknowledge or was it *intention*? And if it was foreknowledge only, why did he go? What did he seek to accomplish? To teach ethics? He could have taught undisturbed to the crowds of Galilee. He could even have taught delighted and devoted crowds in Jerusalem as long as he wanted to if it had been ethics and abuse of the Pharisees he wanted to teach. We invent a wave of popular antagonism towards him. There was no such wave. Until the evening he was brought before Caiaphas he was the hero of the crowds of Jerusalem as he had been to those of Galilee. He had insulted the priests and treated the Pharisees with withering contempt. He had outraged the hierarchy and all conservative religious feeling, but he was popular and invulnerable. Why then did he have to die? For what was he put to death?

He was not put to death for teaching unpopular ethics, nor for rebellion, nor for having been a thorn to the hierarchy. He was put to death for a simple statutory crime—blasphemy. We do not exact the death penalty for blasphemy, but we still count it a crime.

It has been a desperate struggle for liberal theology to find some plausible connection between the supposed spiritualizing ethics which they ascribe to him, and his public statement at the last that he was the Messiah. But there is no connection. The two have nothing to do with each other. Even the weak-kneed messianism of some moderns does not help, the pious argument that when Jesus said he was the Messiah he meant it in a "spiritual" sense, whatever that is. If he meant something other than his hearers' normal comprehension of the term, he took a strange way to enlighten them. To the question of Caiaphas whether he was the Christ, the Son of God, he answered, "I am: and ye shall see the Son of Man sitting on the right hand of power and coming in the clouds of heaven," using an accepted scriptual image of the last days to be certain that nobody did think he meant anything else.

And if the messiahship was an essential part of the ethical teaching, why had it never been asserted during the preaching in Galilee or even to the crowds in Jerusalem? Why had the disciples been ordered to conceal their knowledge of it? Why bring it forward of all times and at all places to fling it in the teeth of Caiaphas and the Sanhedrin? There was never any doubt, to Jesus or to anyone else, about what that claim meant. It was a claim in effect to be God and to make it was blasphemy, punishable by death. Anyone who made it had better be prepared forthwith to unroll the doom of the last things. That Jesus knew this is apparent from all his statements. That he knew also that he did not yet have the power of the Messiah is equally apparent. This he was to receive when God, compelled by his heroic act, set the machinery of the end in motion.

Jesus intended his crucifixion. He forced it, as he expected it to force God. It was entirely consistent with his ethical system. "Do unto others as ye would that they should do unto you." He would be forced to accept death as God would be forced to accept his Messiahship. He was not going to reform or spiritualize society. He was not going to found a church or set an example to the virtuous. With one single act, he was going to bring the wheels of the universe to a standstill. There is nothing inconsistent, nothing petty and nothing "spiritual" about this defiance of both this world and the next. It does not accord with our image of reality, but within the world view of the Levant it was an unparalleled epic.

With the last days, the betrayal and the trial, the moderns have as hard a time as with the determination to go to Jerusalem to die. He announced that he was to be betrayed by one of his disciples. How did he know? By supernatural foreknowledge or by rational calculation? In either case why permit the betrayal? Hardly to satisfy a late ecclesiastical redeemer-doctrine, no shadow of which ever brushed one of his discourses or parables. The ransomed many of Mark (x, 45 and xiv, 24) are those who are to be spared the terror of the last time. In the first it is even set in a discussion concerning which disciples are to have thrones on the right and left of Jesus in his glory. The question of why it was his purpose to die is here the same as it was earlier, an essential part of the machinery of the end. The new question is why did he have to be betrayed. To die, it would have been sufficient, instead of scorning the scribes and Pharisees, to the delight of the crowds, to have announced to those crowds that he was the Messiah. That would have served, as the scene before Pilate amply shows. But he did not. If he did not want to be betrayed and he knew Judas would betray him, why not exclude Judas from his company? The only possible answer is that he wished to be betrayed. It is silly to suppose that a man of such iron character and decision as Jesus, a man of such inflexible courage, was swept away by a petty plot which he could see through himself. From the return of the disciples till he was fastened to the cross, there was not one event involving him of which he was not the complete master. If he was betrayed, he intended to be betrayed. What dogmatic consideration led him to select that means in preference to others for setting in motion the machinery of the world's doom, we do not know. All we know is that this was the means he chose.

Was Judas really a traitor and what did he betray? Matthew and Mark simply say that it was a betrayal and give no details. By the time that Luke's Gospel was written this problem must have begun to be troublesome, for Luke adds the absurd detail that Judas sought a good opportunity to betray him in the absence of a crowd—as though a man who daily taught in the temple, perhaps the most noted man in Jerusalem, could not have been picked up by the temple personnel, or even by the Roman garrison, any night they pleased to arrest him. No, it was not *where* Jesus was that Judas betrayed, but *who* he was. What else was there to betray about a man who openly day after day said everything else precisely as it pleased him to the very faces of the religious authorities? And even then without the intentional assistance of Jesus the betrayal would have betrayed nothing.

Hauled before the Sanhedrin, various charges were brought against him. Some are stated, others are not. They all collapsed. The evidence of the different witnesses did not agree. At last Caiaphas calls no more witnesses. He has none. Under Jewish law, *one* witness is no use to him. Instead he asks a question: "Art thou the Christ, the Son of the Blessed?" Before him stands the master of verbal fencing, the man who had turned the answer on Caesar's taxes, confounded the questioners on his authority to skimp the sabbath regulations and preach in the temple, silenced the accusers of the adulterous woman, who in all the months of his ministry had never answered a question except in the way he wanted to answer it. But this time, there is no answer like, "Render unto Caesar" or, "The Baptism of John, was it from Heaven?" This time, to the amazement and horror of all, the answer was, "I am."

No wonder Peter denied him. No wonder Jesus foresaw that he would. This blunt and terrible answer was too shocking and unexpected. It was one thing to have an innocent, holy secret in the bosom of the disciples, a secret that was somehow to be magically carried out in the future. It was another thing for the innocent secret to turn suddenly into deadly blasphemy in the cold, mundane court of the Sanhedrin. When Peter was told what had happened in the court his first statement was the bewildered, "I don't understand." The driving purpose of his master was always far beyond his comprehension.

And Judas? No one betrayed Jesus without his leave. Judas did what he was told to do. When he told Caiaphas that Jesus said he was the Messiah, it was because Jesus told him to. And when he hanged himself, if he did, it was not from remorse for a crime he never committed, but from horror that things turned out far otherwise than his master had told him they would.

The hearing before Pilate was only a variant of the trial at the Sanhedrin. It is obvious that Pilate thought it a religious quarrel among the Jews and wanted to keep the Roman power out of it. But it was Jesus himself who would give him no chance to do so. To all the Jewish charges against him—the gospels do not say what they were but blasphemy must have been one of them—he refused to make any plea whatever. But to the drummed-up, nonsensical political charge—for which there was no evidence and could be no evidence—but the one charge that could involve him in the Roman criminal jurisdiction, was he the King of the Jews, to this he answered that he was. Even then Pilate wanted no part of this now confessed rebel against Caesar, since obviously there was no rebellion, but the crowd, now incensed by their former hero for his blasphemy, would not permit Pilate to release him. And so, as always, Jesus had his way.

The figure of the straw-stuffed reformer whom modern respectable "religion" tries to traipse through this ancient Levantine drama is not only one of the most dishonest caricatures of history but one of the most odious. How can anyone respect, let alone worship, a character who is so dull-witted he does not know that people cannot live as the birds and plants live, who cannot protect himself against a stupid traitor about whom he knows already, who cannot find an intelligent answer to a deadly but unprovable charge, who does not realize when the whole ground of the case is shifted in a different jurisdiction? When we try to make Jesus modern, all we do is make him dull-witted. Instead of being willing to realize that his physics were not our physics, that reality to him was not what reality is to us, we want to have him motivated by calculations and principles that would motivate us. And so his motives instead of being different become inane, and a mighty would-be conqueror who had the courage to force both heaven and earth to his will becomes a pusilanimous victim of petty mistakes, petty intrigues, petty men. Perhaps his sense of reality was wrong and ours is right—or at least so it seems today. But within his own world, within the Levantine concept that cannot ever entirely separate this world from the next, he is the epic hero beyond comparison. He alone dared to stop the clock of the world. True, it did not stop, and we Westerners do not believe it is a clock that can be stopped. But we cannot have Jesus both ways. If we insist on judging him under our sense of the real, he becomes familiar but empty. If we judge him within his own, he becomes one of the mightiest men of history and one of the most tragic—but a total stranger.

The story can be read by following this order in the gospels:

> Mark i, 4—ii, 15
> Matthew iv, 25—ix, 38
> Mark iii, 13—vi, 6
> Matthew x, 1—xi, 24
> Mark vi, 14—vi, 44
> Matthew xii, 38—xii, 42
> Mark ix, 2—ix, 13
> Mark vii, 27—vii, 33
> Mark viii, 11—ix, 1
> Mark ix, 30—xii, 44
> Mark xiv, 1—xv, 37
> Mark vi, 47—vi, 51

These passages are by no means free of later adjustments of the text, but these are mostly fairly obvious.

The principal objection to the foregoing interpretation of Jesus' actions is that the texts of the passages in which Jesus announces his own death, as these are read today in our canonical gospels, are without exception the product of later editors. This fact has convinced many critics that the entire idea must also be later, that Jesus could not have expected to die, let alone deliberately have courted death. It is true that the early church did not wish to show Jesus as unaware of the consequence of his journey to Jerusalem—his divine foresight required such awareness—and therefore the church would necessarily have inserted in the gospels statements appropriate to show such foresight if they were required. But this does not prove that similar statements were lacking in the earliest form of the gospels, even though later editorial changes were required to make these statements conform more exactly with the final, canonically accepted version of events. That this must have been the case is indicated by the belief, which existed from the earliest times, in both the messiahship and resurrection of Jesus. If Jesus during his lifetime had not announced to his followers his expectation of both death and resurrection as Messiah, the idea of the importance of his resurrection and its connection with his messiahship would never have occurred to anyone. Despite their long association to us because of their association in the gospels, there is no natural or logical connection between them. Dreams and visions of the dead are not so uncommon, even today, that such an experience alone would lead any man or group to attach messianic importance to the experience, and in those days it was even less so. It was not an unexpected resurrection experience that suddenly convinced the disciples that Jesus was the Messiah. It was that this experience, when it occurred, appeared to confirm what he had previously told them: that he would die and return as Messiah—or, more likely, that the act of putting him to death would precipitate his messiah-ship. Undoubtedly the disciples were anxious to believe this, and un-doubtedly this anxiety made the visions powerful and convincing, but it was the original belief that made the resurrection experiences important, not the experiences that gave rise to the belief. Belief in appearances of the dead was common, far too common to make such an experience the source of a conviction concerning the identity of the Messiah. Samuel was hardly considered Messiah because Saul had persuaded the woman of Endor to summon him from the dead. The author of Revelation seems to have believed that Nero would return from the dead, but not therefore as Messiah.

The pious may feel it pointless and even offensive, to salvage Jesus from the pettiness of modern theology, only to present him, however powerful and heroic, as the victim of such an absurd belief as the possibility of bringing the world to an end. Far better accept the implicit Roman Catholic position that Jesus was *not* a historical figure in the world of actuality but a divine being whose life cannot be ascertained by the usual methods of historical criticism and in whose career on earth neither human consistency nor intelligible motivation is to be expected. But if we seek even a faint image of the actual historical Jesus, we cannot obtain it by stripping him of the essential beliefs of his time and his society. And it is toward these that we need to be a little humble, not denying the validity of our own to us, but merely hesitating to be certain that ours are the only intellectually sound beliefs for the estimation of all times and all societies. For we Westerners who cannot know how absurd our own basic beliefs seem to men of other societies, cannot wisely estimate the stature of other men by their acceptance of the beliefs of our society. Worse, because as well as being Westerners we are now practical "moderns," pragmatists of old age, we fall into the error of misjudging all things heroic. The ethos of heroism, Western no less than Levantine, seem to us "poetic," that is, unreal and ridiculously impractical. As weary cynics, we judge the mundane success or failure of an enterprise, not its grandeur of purpose and iron resolve. But in fact how practical and how successful have been the heroes of any society? Did they ever accomplish what they set out to do? Historical reality has always made something quite unintended from the work of heroes without making them the less heroic.[27]

To grasp the history of early Christianity something of this must be understood. The men of the Greek Levant of Jesus' time did not take our modern view of eschatology. They found no need to interpret the basis out of his ethics, to imagine him as a reformer. They were perfectly willing to accept him as the force that would break the reality of history and bring the world to an end. They, too, believed as Jesus did that the Prince of This World would be soon overthrown and the Messiah would come on the clouds of heaven. All they had to do with the historical reality of Jesus' life was to juggle the dates a little. He had planned to rise as the Messiah from his crucifixion. Well, he had risen but not yet as the Messiah. But that was a minor flaw since he would soon return in glory to establish the Heavenly Kingdom by bringing all earthly things to an end. That was what to be the Christ meant in the early days, precisely what Messiah had meant in Aramaic. Only gradually as eschatology died away from an immediate present possibility to a distant event of an almost mythical future did it come to mean a character in heaven, wholly confined to heaven. And so for the first century or more the vivid greatness of Jesus, his world-conquering character, his unshakable will and courage did not have to be interpreted out of existence. They moved men directly as vast ambition, great wit and iron courage always move men.

As time went on the image of Jesus crystallized, only a little changed from the historical reality. The birth and resurrection doctrines were worked up, but they were not strange to the essential messianic character of the historical Jesus. Only the Redeemer doctrine was carried beyond the history. Jesus' act in seeking to concentrate on himself the world suffering of the time of the end could not stand because the world had not come to an end. But it became instead the Pauline redemption of sin, not a wholly logical development, but one not too distant from its historical source. Only one other subtle change occurred. The messiahship-elect, which apparently was Jesus' actual concept of himself, became the concept of the Messiah as visitor on earth, the God who declines for awhile to exercise his divine powers. It was an attribute of divinity which Jesus had not claimed and it was destined to have great consequences in the history of the Orthodox Church.

[27] A discussion of the importance of eschatology in the life of Jesus can be found in Albert Schweitzer's *Das Messianitats—und Leidensgheimnis.* (*Sketch of the Life of Jesus*), Tubingen, 1901. For a full survey of the problems of the historical biography of Jesus see Schweitzer, *The Quest of the Historical Jesus,* New York, 1950. (*Von Reimarus zu Werde,* 1906). A compact but exhaustive treatment of the problem of the historical Jesus can be found in Ch. Guignebert's *Jésus,* Paris (Albin Michel) 1947.

It would be futile to try to guess why the eschatological expectations attached to belief in Jesus' resurrection spread through the Greek rather than through the Aramaic Jews. Something in the difference in life under a formally Classical empire in contrast to life under a Mazdaist empire, something, perhaps, of already existing dilution of strict Judaic standards among the Greeks, images of this sort come to mind, but here is a problem of historical causality, in its nature unanswerable. We can see what happened, something of how it happened, but not really why it happened.

The image of Jesus, and one by no means free of inconsistencies, that the Jews of the Septuagint accepted during the century in which they became the Christian Church is, of course, the image of Jesus as the New Testament reveals it. But the Septuagint Jews were not the only men to be influenced by the life and teaching of Jesus, and it is these other Christians —for so they too must be called—whose existence confuses the historical picture. Tradition sees all Christians outside the fold of Orthodoxy as secessionists from Orthodoxy, if not physical secessionists like the Marcionites, then at least as movements that went off with part of the Christian doctrine. Increasingly it has become the fashion to label all these as Gnostics, a name necessarily associated with the gross follies and evils attributed by the Orthodox fathers to these rivals who used some of the same sacred writings. This helps maintain the illusion that the Orthodox doctrines were the only true Christian doctrines derived in unbroken apostolic succession from Jesus.

But this does not seem to represent quite the way events happened. The link of either Orthodoxy or Gnosticism to Jesus is not quite so easily perceived. Jesus certainly did not commission either twelve or seventy apostles. The numbers alone show the symbolic Levantine author at work. Twelve messengers go to the twelve tribes of Israel. The Seventy brought the Old Covenant to the Diaspora; another seventy will bring the New. Jesus certainly did not found a church since he did not expect the world to last through the coming autumn. However difficult for tradition, the evidence seems overwhelming that the linkage between Jesus and the Christian Church does not lie in the conscious intention of the human Jesus. When their conviction of his resurrection moved men to spread the good news (which as everyone knows is what gospel means) of the coming Kingdom of God through the Roman Empire, it was not an organized and certainly not a uniform movement. It is clear that for nearly a century there were many different preachings and some different texts. That is one reason we know nothing about the so called "foundation" of the church in every great city of the empire, and why we have four gospels only partially harmonized and some serious differences among the rest of the books. For what we have is fundamentally the assembled texts partially setting forth these several slightly divergent doctrines that were preached successfully to the Jews of the Septuagint and the gentile fringe, the "God fearers" closely associated with these Jews. The Christianity that was preached directly to the gentiles—and this preaching may have been as old and must have been as authentic—disappeared into what appear to us as the splinter movements that we call Gnosticism. Despite the inclusion of the name of Paul within the fold of Orthodoxy, and the inclusion of some anti-Jewish texts under his name in the Orthodox canon, the rejection of the Jewish past was refused; and the attempt to establish Christianity as a new religion of the gentiles, which was in effect the movement we call Gnosticism, was a failure. But so far as Jesus was concerned both sides, Gnostics and Septuagint Jews, had only the same traditions and texts to start with. One and only one narrative about Jesus seems ever to have existed anywhere either in Greek or Aramaic lands—the frame of our Mark. One and only one collection of sayings of Jesus—Papias Aramaic Matthew—seems ever to have reached the Greeks. Both sides therefore, Septuagint Jews and Gnostics, took these texts, expanded them, altered them and in later times fancifully embroidered them to make these texts suitable to their own religious needs. One side in time became the Byzantine Empire which gave it the power to defame its rivals and destroy their texts, Gnostic, neo-pagan and heretical Christian alike. This did not make the texts of Orthodoxy necessarily more accurate.

The basic religious transformation that the Jews of the Septuagint accomplished by asserting in Jesus a divine fulfillment and deliverance, the slow, patient work of the rabbinical schools of Mesopotamia achieved for eastern Aramaic Jewry. The eastern rabbis established Talmudic Jewry. By Midrash, by the slow process of commentary, by reason and charity, the great rabbis introduced those conceptions of God's mercy and personal forgiveness for individuals that are so conspicuously lacking in the Torah and the Prophets.

With the destruction of Jerusalem by Vespasian, territorial Judaism, either as fact or hope, came to an end and temple Judaism ended with it. Two great branches of Judaism remained, Talmudic in the east, Orthodox Christianity in the Roman Empire. The former was the religion of a communion, a type of nation but not a political state, living largely in Sassanid lands. The latter became afterwards the state religion of the late Roman, that is, the Byzantine Empire. Its problems were complicated by considerations of state, by the survival of Classical forms and methods of speech and by the concept of Jesus as the Divine Redeemer, which had flowered from the seeds of this concept in the historical life of Jesus. A God on earth, a

God who dies, entangled Orthodox Christianity in immense theological controversy, complex formulae and constant religious revolt.

The essence of the question was whether the Christ was wholly God, partly God, or Jesus a man, the greatest prophet of God. The Logos, the Holy Ghost, presented no difficulty. Regardless of what opinion was taken about the Christ, all Levantine thought had no difficulty in envisaging the Spirit of God, the Logos, the *pneuma,* the impalpable yet substantial essence or substance of God that perfused all created things and could dwell more or less fully in any man. This was simply ordinary Levantine physics as we can see in certain old-fashioned names that have come down to us from Arabic alchemy where the word "spirit" is used in this precise sense: spirits of niter, spirits of hartshorn, spirits of wine or grain from which we call alcohol simply "spirits."

The real difficulty was not the Trinity as such but the Christological problem that underlay it. If Jesus had been the great prophet in whom dwelt most fully the spirit of God, then one could accept the formulation of two persons (considering one person as the Logos) and one substance (*ousia*). Jesus suffered on the cross, but not God. On the other hand, if Christ were wholly God and not a real man at all, his manhood being merely the outer form that God assumed, the crucifixion would be logically absurd. A being wholly God could only pretend to be crucified.

But into neither of those extremes could the Redeemer concept be fitted except by following Marcion and Mani into acknowledgement that the whole material world was under the rule of Satan. This would have meant discarding the Old Testament and thus the entire historical foundation of the Orthodox church. It was, of course, never even considered. It is true that the Redeemer doctrine had grown out of the rather special problems in the three-cornered relationship among Septuagint Jewry, Palestinian Judaism and Greek gentiles in the first century, but by the fourth century it was ineradicably set in Christian holy writings. It could not be followed to its logical conclusions without splitting the church, but it could not be ignored without ignoring the most ancient and authentic Christian writings the church possessed, the epistles.

It is a natural conviction of Western Christians that they are in the true lineal succession of the one and only religion founded by Jesus. Protestants, of course, more often than not, dismiss medieval Catholicism as a departure from the true faith which Protestantism again re-established, but Protestants and Roman Catholics alike would agree that the true faith was carried by the church that emerged as Greek Orthodoxy from the Councils of Nicaea, Ephesus and Chalcedon. Arians, Nestorians and Monophysites are regarded as deviators from the true way and the implication is left that the church that was finally formed at Chalcedon represented the true consensus of the faith as it had existed since the earliest times. It is the latter proposition that is historically unsound. The doctrines and creed established by the first four oecumenical councils dealt with problems that had never been formulated before Christianity became the state religion of the Roman (i.e. Byzantine) Empire, or phrased more accurately, before the Byzantine Empire became the state apparatus of the Orthodox Christian nation. It was only then that precise and politically effective formulations were sought of the relations of Jesus, God and the Holy Ghost.

The first great controversy was the Arian. It led to the Council of Nicaea and the establishment of the doctrine of the identity of substance of Christ and God. (So we and the creed customarily translate *ousia* though apparently Aquinas would prefer "essence.") The Arian heresy, because of its brief influence on the western barbarians, is treated as an important item in our traditional history. Actually, its specific consequences were nil, but what is significant about it is the light it casts on affairs in the east. It was the theological school of Antioch, probably closer to Aramaic thought than any part of the empire, which pressed for part at least of the Arian position. It was the Antioch school which stood out for a similar view of Jesus in the next great controversy that broke out about a century later and led to the fateful decisions of Ephesus which ended forever the unity of the Christian church. After Ephesus there was the national church of the Greek empire, which we consider "Christianity," and the non-Greek church of the east, which in historical honesty must be considered as much "Christianity" as the branch that eventually and after profound inner changes led to us.

This great Christian church of the east ostensibly was the creation of dissidents from the Orthodox Church. It was a case of Greek development being carried back into Aramaic lands, and probably incorporating into its membership and structure some older non-Septuagint elements, but primarily it was the expression of an Aramaic view of Jesus. It considered itself, and for long called itself, simply the Orthodox Church, but time has finally attached to it inseparably the name of Bishop Nestorius even though he was not its founder and its views would have been anathema to his orthodox soul, had he lived long enough to learn of them.

Nestorius himself was condemned by the Council of Ephesus in 431 for views about the relation between God and Jesus that he certainly did not hold. He apparently was simply a victim of ecclesiastical politics. However, the views condemned accorded with the prevailing view in the Aramaic-speaking parts of the empire, and the rebels were soon identified with the name of the deposed bishop whose cause was not theirs and whose views they would not have accepted.

The primary issue concealed in the theological struggle between Greek

Orthodoxy and the Aramaic-speaking world was whether Jesus was God or man, Redeemer or Prophet. This is always the nub of the long controversy on the relation of Jesus to God. The Arian heresy of the "similar substance" of God and Christ and the Nestorian of the two persons, both God and man united in Christ, tend to make the historical Jesus not God but Prophet.

Arius himself was unimportant, but the Nestorian position denied the essential Pauline thesis of the unique divinity of Jesus. Instead it saw him as God's greatest prophet and the revealer of the new law and the true way of salvation. The step from this to Mohammed, who accepted the virgin birth, the divine creation and the divine prophetic mission of Jesus, but not the Pauline Redeemer's mission, is not great. The same phrase that afterwards rankled the Mohammedans rankled the Nestorians (on this alone perhaps they agreed with Nestorius): *theotekos*, the Mother of God, as an appropriate name for the Virgin. How could God be born of a woman? Are we back in the days of Ishtar and Isis, the Queen of Heaven?

On this rock, the Orthodox Church of the east broke apart, almost precisely along the Greek-Semitic language frontier. Once Orthodoxy was firmly in control with the backing of the Imperial Government at Constantinople (the two were in fact identical), the easterners left by thousands for the welcome sanctuary of Mazdaist Persia, the Sassanid dominions beyond the Euphrates. Those who remained, of necessity the great majority, were an abiding danger to the empire and two centuries later welcomed the Moslem armies as deliverers in the name of the true faith. Behind the Byzantine garrisons, Orthodoxy was official and Nestorianism underground, but after the Council of Ephesus, Christianity from the Mediterranean to China meant the Nestorians.[28] Today almost all this people has

---

[28] The Nestorians never adopted a formal creed, but the following is representative:
"I believe in one God, hidden, eternal, without beginning and without end, Father and Son and Holy Spirit, three equal Persons, inseparable, in whom there is not a first or second, nor a younger and elder, who are in one Nature but in three Persons, the Father Begetter, the Son Begotten, the Spirit Proceeding; that at the end of the time one of the Persons of the Royal Trinity, to wit, the Son, clothed Himself with perfect man, Jesus Christ, of the Holy Virgin Mary, and was united with him personally, and in him redeemed the world; who in His Godhead was eternally of the Father, and in His humanity in time was born of Mary, a unity not be dissolved nor broken forever, a unity without intermixture or confusion or articulation; and this Son is of a unity, perfect God and perfect Man, two Natures and two Persons, one Personality."
This creed was given to the Cardinals at Rome by Rabban Bar Sauma, emissary from the Il Khan of the western Mongols and the Catholicos of the Nestorians, i.e. the Nestorian Patriarch of Ctesiphon (resident at Baghdad since Ctesiphon no longer existed). Bar Sauma and the Catholicos were both Chinese Christians, Bar Sauma from Peking and the Catholicos from Shansi, who had come west and risen high in the Nestorian Church with the Mongol conquest of the Levant. At the time of Bar Sauma's arrival at Rome the papacy was

been destroyed by the Mongols or converted by the Mohammedans, but as late as 1000 al-Biruni, the Mohammedan geographer and mathematician, recorded that Nestorian Christians constituted the bulk of the population of Syria, Iraq and Khurasan.

There was one other important fragment of the Orthodox Church, the Monophysites, who agreed about the full divinity of Christ but in effect denied his humanity. They fused God, Jesus and the Holy Spirit into one. "His divinity was not separated from his manhood for the twinkling of an eye," their creed says of Jesus. When Chalcedon required belief that there were two natures in Jesus, they thought this little better than the Nestorians' two persons and refused to accept the new formulation. They were influential for a while in Egypt, and it is from them that the existing Coptic Church of Abyssinia is derived. Another Monophysite fragment, the Jacobite Church, still survives in northern Syria and Armenia, but it never represented so widespread a religious view nor founded so great a church as the Nestorians.

In the end, all forms of this same religious thought, Jewish, Mazdaist, Orthodox and heretical Christian alike, were largely absorbed into Mohammedanism.

Historical accident has here warped our focus. One relatively small group of Talmudic Jewry remained outside Moslem influence and long afterwards became entangled with the West. The holy books of Orthodoxy, in their far west Latin form, remained in the western lands to become the received revelation of another religion, or, to phrase it more softly, of another and quite different body of religious thought. But within the scope of Levantine life and history, Mohammedanism became the terminal form of this body of religious thought.[29] Talmudic Judaism, Orthodox and Nestorian Christianity, Manicheism and Mazdaism remained as fragments, sometimes composed of ancient aristocrats, sometimes of humble men who, faithful to an older and more complex tradition, refused to be submerged in the easy and popular salvation system that Mohammed distilled from the holy books of these older churches.

The consequences of Mohammed's life on our Western picture of his-

---

vacant, Pope Honorius IV having just died. He went on to France where he conferred with Philip the Fair and afterwards with Edward I of England. The next year at Rome he met the new pope, Nicholas IV, and then returned to Baghdad where he died in 1293. The above creed its quoted in *The History of Yaballaha III*, translated by J. A. Montgomery, New York 1927.

[29] We are not today accustomed to think of Mohammedanism as a variant of Christianity, though the Middle Ages did. A much more convincing proof, however, is that John of Damascus, as a summarist, one of the greatest theologians of the Orthodox Church, so considered it in his study of heresies written about 750. In a sense it was the joint Protestantism of all the Levantine nation-sects.

tory is far greater than its consequence on the spiritual and cultural life of the Levant itself. The religious tendencies of that time would have produced something comparable from one or another church of this religious group. The materialization of religious beliefs is a phenomenon that appears inherent in the history of all religions. Something of this shows in Protestantism and the accompanying Roman Catholic reaction; and the condition of religion in the West in our own day is a complete commentary on how far this tendency can go in four hundred years, a development parallel to that of the Levantine world between Mohammed's "Reformation" in the seventh century and the irreligious times of the tenth and eleventh when, as in our own day, religious concepts were applied to the affairs of this world as moral justification for the ambitions of social revolution.

But Mohammed made a tremendous change in our Western view of the past. His work wiped out Pompey's line, the eastern frontier of the Roman Empire, and re-established an evident political unity over the spiritual and cultural unity of the Levant, a unity that to our eyes had not existed since Alexander destroyed the Achaemenian Empire nine hundred years before. From Arbela to Yarmuk our received history sees the Levant divided at the Euphrates between the Classical world and the "Orient," whatever that word is supposed to mean.

With the Roman eastern frontier taken from the map, Western traditional history accepts the subsequent cultural unity of the Near East with only the demurrer of pious orthodoxy. Since we are Christians we insist that Greek and Syrian Christians ought to resemble us more than they do the Moslems. But in practical life, no one questions that all these groups, Orthodox and eastern Christians, Sephardic Jews of Iraq and the Yemen, Coptic Christians of Egypt and Abyssinia, Parsees, Mandeans, Manicheans and Mohammedans, all constitute a great segment of human society in which all resemble one another more than they resemble any other men.

The question that is implicit in all the history of the Near East, and of the origin of Western society is what we mean by the word religion. It is obvious that it is much broader than the word church, but does it have any real meaning if it is used to embrace all sects and churches which allege a common founder or use a common name for their god or their prophet? Buddhism in Ceylon, Buddhism in Tibet and Buddism in Japan cover religious, ethical and social practices and beliefs that have no common factor but the name of their nominal founder. Mohammedanism, Orthodox and heretical eastern Christianity and Talmudic Judaism, all grew from the same stock of original holy books and legends, all express the same view of the basic causality that each people believes governs the world. All have much the same ethical standards and look to the same last judgment and end of the world. Are they different religions because they have varying authors for part of the true revelation of each? Or are they separate great sects of the same basic religion?

Western Christianity and Orthodox Christianity in contrast, profess the same founder, venerate the same holy books and some of the same saints. The formal difference in creed between the two is almost absurd. Yet the lives and histories of the peoples who have lived under the faiths of these two groups of churches differ in almost every aspect of life, in everything that determines the culture of a people, their arts, their intellectual pursuits, their politics and their deep religious emotion. The two interpretations of the same set of holy books, when removed from theological definition and reduced to the practice of life, express two sets of religious feelings, two views of things and of God. The very pettiness of the official theological separation of the Orthodox from the Western church, the *filioque* clause in the creed, indicates more powerfully than an open and great quarrel could do that it is not over this petty matter, but over deep and inexpressible differences that the name of Christian is divided.

The development of Western Christianity out of Orthodox is almost impossible to trace on the surface of religious history. The Latin-speaking church in Spain, Gaul and Italy did not begin to be pressed by Western religious feelings until long after canon, creed and ritual had been firmly established and until there was an immense body of Orthodox patristic literature in existence. Western religious feeling, therefore, had the choice of accommodating itself to the holy forms or abandoning the name of Christian. In reality the latter choice does not seem to have existed. Except for Orthodox Christianity, there was no formal religion left in the west except suppressed sects like the Cathari and the Manicheans, who had been little better than outlaws since the reign of Constantine. The ancient Celtic religion of the Druids apparently had perished completely. The early barbarian invaders, the Goths, Burgundians and even the Franks arrived while the might of the Christian Empire, the polish of a civilized society and the great monuments of the Classical past, identified of course with the Christian present, were still realities of the tangible and psychological world which the barbarians entered. They became Christians automatically, imitatively and at once. The paganism of the latter Germanic invaders who never knew "Rome" was a collection of formless myths of some ethical power and psychological insight but devoid of any element of the transcendent. Their causality was that of neolithic men, with no central unifying thesis. Against these myths, both mundane and fantastic, the emotional and dramatic power of the gospels was overwhelming. And it was the gospels and almost the gospels only that were translated into

the ancient heathen tongues and carried into the north. More than anything, the living example of men moved by these gospels, the saints, above
all the Irish saints, who carried the gospel into Britain, Gaul and Germany, convinced the heathen invaders that men who lived and preached
and loved their fellow men as these men did, had indeed the secret of
the last things.

And so the future of Western religiousness was set forever within the
holy frame of Orthodoxy, forced to the devices of interpretation and
mental evasion of the meaning of words. It was not a question of mental
reservation, of repeating holy words with conscious disbelief in their meaning, but of repeating these words with a quite unconscious blank as to
their meaning. In early times there was also little or no attempt to force
to verbal precision all the theological implications of Orthodox Christian
dogma. For the formative centuries of Christianity in the West, the
religious life was almost wholly an emotional life. How deeply it moved
the bulk of the people of Europe prior to the tenth century is an unanswerable question. The scanty literary and artistic evidence from
those times suggests that crude formalism and petty superstition were
more prevalent than the faith of the saints. During these early times,
Christianity seems to have had little influence on the lives or manners
of the West. Yet it manifestly rooted itself and manifestly even in that
early day gave men that security they seek above all securities, the
security against death.

Another factor which perhaps influenced the deep allegiance of Western
Europe to a Christian profession of faith was the rise of Mohammedan
power early in the eighth century. However divided they were among
themselves, the men of the primitive West were united against the
hated Saracens, not simply because they were Christians and the Saracens
were Moslems, but because they were simple, emotional, hopeful,
yearning and awkward, while the hated Saracens were polished, skillful,
cynical, rich, organized and powerful. The Christian name served as
the great banner of unity against the Saracens and in unifying Europe
against these powerful, civilized aliens embedded itself even deeper
in the hearts of the West. Christianity became and remained for centuries the West's own image of its own unity. Christianity, Western
society, civilization, these words were practically synonymous and remained so, in public formalities at least, till our own day. The West
even invented the fable, which is still believed, that the Saracens were
the enemies of Christianity and that as defenders of the faith, not as
defenders of the soil of their civilization, Europe stood off the world
conquerors. It is, however, a fable. In those centuries, the Mohammedans never proscribed Christianity, never forced conversions, never

interfered with the full practice of that faith. They accepted willing converts, of course, but in the east, Nestorian and some Orthodox Christians along with the Jews were among the most important intellectual figures of Mohammedan society. They did not, of course, participate in Mohammedan politics. The basic structure of Levantine nations was and is the identity of state, nation and religion. The Jews and the Christians had communion substates of their own and governed their own internal affairs. Even in Spain, where the Mohammedans were lords over a different type of Christian, the ancient Gothic church, the Mozarabic church from the ritual of which much of the liturgy of the Church of England is derived, survived through the whole period of Moslem rule.

The difference between formal adherence to a religious dogma and actual belief in its meaning is evident in the doctrine of the Trinity. The problem of the Trinity was the greatest that troubled the Orthodox Church. It tore the Orthodox Christians into three great and many little pieces. The enforced political decisions ripened the greater part of the Byzantine Empire for the Mohammedan Reformation. In contrast, among the Western Christians this and related problems have never been more than theological curiosities. Few have ever become excited about these issues and none of the great heresies that shook the West ever turned on one of these points. Nor was this dutiful acceptance of the creed of Chalcedon because the problems had been satisfactorily solved once and for all. It was because these problems simply did not exist for Westerners. Aquinas, who was convinced that reason could reach a knowledge of God, frankly asserts that reason could not give us knowledge of the Trinity, such knowledge could come by revelation alone; and his own exhaustive treatment of the matter in the *Summa* [30] scarcely clarifies the revelation. In other words, to put it in blunt and unbecoming terms, to the West it was holy nonsense. But the intelligibility of this doctrine was never important. No side of this issue presented a symbol of what Westerners cared about and so long as men thought of themselves as Christians, they accepted this doctrine without difficulty. It came to bother them, not as they became sectarians over this or that religious issue, but when they began to doubt religion itself.

Western theologians have, of course, written on the subject of the Trinity in the vein of schoolroom duty pieces, but the evidence of art and literature shows that Western men pictured the Trinity in any way they personally chose and were able to do so without having to balk at the specific words of the creed. Only one vital point was ever involved here, the question of Christ as the Redeemer. That was settled at the

[30] Part I, Q. 27-43.

very outset. Even Anselm, as early as he and as good an Augustinian, rejected the idea that Christ redeemed man from sin in the pawnbroker's sense of the word—and that is the sense, and the only sense, in which St. Paul meant it. We still use the venerable word, but we have made it mean what it does not mean and was not intended to mean, the teacher, the one who shows the way. That is rescue, if you like, but it is not redemption.

Except for this, the Trinity in the West meant what anybody wanted it to mean. To most simple people, it has probably been the picture of three independent Gods, a sort of consultative committee of the Godhead with God the Father as Chairman and for many with the Virgin as a fourth and most important member. To others it has seemed only different manifestations of one great God as human frailty reaches knowledge of him in the different relations of man to God, God's power, God's love and mercy, God's wisdom. But to almost no one has his own image of the Trinity seemed something that required quarreling about the image held by his neighbors. The functions of grace and free will, the interpretation of scripture, the nature and meaning of the eucharist, these have involved war and torture for centuries, but not the compromise language of an Orthodox political settlement, which in cold logic, if Christianity be one religion not two, lies at the core of the faith.

How could it be otherwise? We Westerners for a thousand years have recited the Nicene and the Apostles' Creeds believing that we believed every word of them. And indeed most of the West has convinced itself that it believed the words, but it has done so by never thinking of the meanings that underlie these words. Not only we in these irreligious times, but our religious forefathers never believed that "for us men and for our salvation" Christ came down from Heaven and "was crucified also for us," because though we use the word we are incapable of believing in the only intelligible meaning of redemption by death of the Divine Being. We associate it in our minds with the heroic sacrifice of a soldier to save his companions or of a father to save his endangered children, but these are the acts of humans faced with greater powers than their own, they are not the acts of one "by whom all things were made." When Western Christians say they are redeemed by Christ, they mean that Christ has shown men the way, not that God at a great price has bought man free of pledge from a *coequal power of evil*. We use the words, we make prayers and hymns of them, but no balanced mind of the West is capable of believing their meaning. Nor do we believe that Christ "shall come to judge the *quick* and the dead," because we cannot believe, and never have believed, that this world will so pass away. There is no end of the world to us in that sense. That He shall judge the dead, yes, though currently as they die, but not blow Gabriel's trumpet and bring this world all standing into the next.

The last act of these great theological struggles of Orthodox Christianity was the only one played in the Latin language. Its consequences for the future religious and intellectual history of the West were grave. Its principal actors were an obscure and largely forgotten heretic, a great, calm bulk of a man from Ireland, one Pelagius, and the famous ex-astrologer, ex-Manichaean, Augustine, Bishop of Hippo.

Pelagius, whose name in his native Ireland was probably Morgan, came up to Rome somewhere around 400 A.D. He does not seem to have been a monk or priest, but his sole interest apparently was the religion of his time. He objected to it. He thought the doctrine of original sin nonsensical and monstrous. He denied that there could be any redemption since there could be no power counter to God from whom man could be redeemed. Adam had sinned, but he was responsible for his own sins, as each man was responsible for his. Nor could Pelagius accept the doctrine that men were compelled to sin by their nature and could only be saved by God's grace. Only an act of free choice could be a sin. If it was a compulsory act, the doer could not be held responsible and, therefore, there could be no sin. Though God's grace immensely eased the task, he asserted that man could by his own will and intellect conduct his life to keep it free from sin, and thus some of the people of old, and even some of the contemporary heathen who had never heard of Christ, could be saved.

To a man whose faith in predestination had once made him an astrologer and whose conviction of the abiding evil of this world had made him a Manichaean, every article of Pelagius' beliefs was the most intolerable heresy. Augustine immediately entered into fierce controversy and in arguing for his position pushed it to an extreme far beyond anything accepted by the more cautious Greek fathers. Man was wholly base. Only grace could save him and there was nothing, literally nothing, that man could do to attain grace. Only the arbitrary whim of God (these were not Augustine's words but his meaning) determined whom He would save and whom damn. Christ died on the cross to make it possible to save us (we see Ahriman's presence but, of course, he is not mentioned). Augustine stopped just short of holding sexual intercourse inherently sinful even in lawful marriage but did hold that it was in some way always shameful. It is obvious that he thought it was, in fact, sinful in all circumstances but such a position would have been heresy and he stood clear of that.

These were the views that the last father of the Orthodox Church, its only great theologian who used Latin, bequeathed to the unborn church of the West. Interestingly enough his extreme views earned him sharp condemnation among the few Greek theologians who paid attention to a Latin writer. Bishop Theodore of Mopsuestia, afterwards held by the Nestorians to be one of the greatest saints, denounced Augustine's anti-Pelagian views as open dualism and contempt for God's earthly creation, little better than the Manicheism from which he had come.

Pelagius founded no permanent heresy and was certainly never considered a saint by the Western church or any of its sects. It is curious, however, to see so early and from the far and never Roman rim of the world the first expression—tentative and ill-thought out as the formulation was—of the fundamental ethical concepts that have underlain the moral values of Western society. The later Irish saints had a sounder estimate of man's frailty and a deeper sense of God's love, but like Pelagius they knew that the world of God's creation was not a foul thing of evil and that God had not condemned his children out of hand. They knew and were able to convince others that between man's will and God's love there was a way to live in the hauntingly beautiful world of this life and come in due season to the blessedness of the life to come. No church, ancient or modern, could ever admit Pelagius to its hagiography. Yet he was the true predecessor of the great company of the Irish saints who were the founders, to the extent that there were individual founders, of Western Christianity.

Chapter 4:

The Physics of Magic

THE COMPLEX INTERTWINING of the moral and intellectual surface of the lives of three great civilizations, Classical, Levantine, and Western, has produced no field of greater confusion than the history of the sciences. Even the difficulty of separating Western Christianity from Levantine, which lies deep in our misjudgment of history, has not produced such profound intellectual disorder nor furnished the fallacious base for so much political folly as our misunderstanding of the history of the sciences.

To us modern men of the West the physical sciences appear as perhaps the greatest intellectual triumph of mankind. We are taught to regard these disciplines as a slow accretion, as the product of millennia of human thought and effort. We feel that as part of this general accumulation of many ages of technical knowledge, the great masterful sciences of modern times were created as a necessary outcome of all scientific thought that had gone before. We see them as impersonal and their conclusions as unalterably true. Against the impermanence of all human things, they—and to the irreligious, they alone—constitute a body of imperishable truth. Certainly those who thus deify the role of the sciences often know nothing of the logical structure and little of the factual content of these esoteric disciplines, but they nonetheless assert in this body of human experience and human hypotheses something which is both eternal and universal.

By being established thus as universal truth, it is impossible under the modern fetish of science to see that scientific thought and experience, like aesthetic or political, are aspects of a civilization, tinged like all other aspects of human life, by the historical society that developed them. Each civilization has had its own body of scientific thought standing on its own concept of causality. Ours has been operably the most powerful, has delved far deeper than any other into the mechanical secrets of the universe. Ours has lent itself more readily than the science of any other civilization to practical exploitation. But our sciences like the sciences of other societies have been the creation not of mankind but of a historical civilization.

But the unique technical power of the Western sciences makes it difficult for us to compare our body of scientific thought with that of others. The vast difference of consequence between our sciences and those of other societies creates the illusion that only the West has ever developed genuine scientific thought. The little alien scientific thought with which we are acquainted— primarily scraps from Hellenic times—appears to us only as a brilliant but confused forerunner of our own. Yet even though we dismiss the scientific thought of others as trifling or unscientific and deal with Western scientific thought as though it had been almost the only scientific thought of the human species, nevertheless, because we officially deny the historical reality of Western society we are forced to picture our own thought as the thought of all men and our sciences as the sciences of mankind. Thus we come to think of the sciences not as an attribute of each particular society but as a function of time. Our world, we feel, is a scientific world not because it is a Western world but because it is a twentieth-century world. Science seems not so much specifically Western as merely modern.

Thus, despite the philosophical universality which we assert for scientific thought, when we touch upon its detailed history, we ignore the sciences of almost all men and confine ourselves not only to the West, but to only the last four centuries of the West. With little more than a conventional bow to the noble but groping first efforts of the Greeks, we date the beginning of real scientific creation at the sixteenth century with the names of Copernicus, Galileo, da Vinci and Bruno. This work, we are assured, was one of the results of the spirit of enlightenment which the Renaissance was supposed to have engendered. The dark centuries of superstition which succeeded Hellenistic times had at last come to an end, and humanity, but in the person of the West, picked up the work where Aristotle had left off. Some few dissenters file a claim for Arabic science, particularly Arabic mathematics and astronomy, as important contributors, but even these merely desire to insert a few Arabic scientists in the chain from Aristotle and do not seriously question the existence of the chain itself, let alone suggest that Western science began long before the sixteenth century and comes neither from Aristotle nor al-Farabi.

Even so eminent a mathematician as A. N. Whitehead succumbs to the confusion of our traditional picture of history: ". . . apart from remote developments that have not in fact seriously influenced the great structure of mathematics of the European races, it [mathematics] may be said to have had its origin with the Greeks, working on pre-existing fragmentary lines of thought derived from the Egyptians and Phoenicians. The Greeks created the sciences of geometry and of numbers as applied to the measurement of continuous quantities. The great abstract ideas (considered directly and not merely in tacit use) which have dominated the sciences were due to them—namely ratio, irrationality, continuity, the point, the straight line, the plane. This period lasted from the time of Thales, c. 600 B.C., to the capture of Alexandria by the Mohammedans in 641 A.D. The medieval Arabians invented our system of numeration and developed algebra. The next period of advance stretches from the Renaissance to Newton and Leibnitz and the discovery of gravitation."[1]

Here there are almost as many errors as there are statements in that passage, and the necessary condensation of an encyclopedia is not the reason for them. Between the confusion and falsity of our accepted historical image, even an eminent mathematician can lose his way in the origins of his own subject.

This passage, by its text, is not attempting to summarize the history of mathematics, but only the history of European mathematics. Chinese and Hindu mathematics are not involved. Yet in contrast, Classical and Arabic mathematics are neither ignored like Chinese and Hindu, nor treated as self-contained subjects like European but, along with Egyptian, relegated to the status of an introductory phase of European mathematics and considered only insofar as Western mathematics has chosen to pick some element out of them. This would be beyond criticism if it were not for the implication, which inheres in all "line of progress" historical analysis, that *all* of Greek and Arabic mathematics is an introduction to the Western and that Western causally depends upon these predecessors. By giving to the sciences of other societies the status of mere grab bags from which the West has extracted a few valuable items, the relationship of scientific thought to the life of a society is lost and the pattern of growth and decay of the sciences, like the growth and decay of all historical phenomena, is smothered under a rigged scheme of progress.

Whitehead's brief passage contains one other interesting feature, the continuance of Classical civilization down to the time of Mohammed. This is a grouping of civilizations that no analyst from a cultural, aesthetic or political point of view would ever make or accept. It is, of course, here again the old problem of where Byzantium begins. In political and cultural history the problem can be kept from seeming acute because the political

---

[1] In his article "Mathematics" in the XI ed., *E.B.*

and cultural developments of the Levant branch away from the historical development of the West and can be relegated to specialists and footnotes. By the time of Constantine, the eastern end of the Mediterranean has already fallen out of the "line of progress." It no longer leads to us and can be ignored. In mathematics, however, this is impossible. The West came later into contact with the whole body of Levantine mathematics: the early written in Greek and the later written in Arabic alike. Hagia Sophia, mosaics, the iconoclasts, the Holy Orthodox Church, Justinian, Heraclius and Nicephorus Phocas can all be dismissed as a branching away from the main stem of human progress—that is—us. But Diophantus and Pappos cannot so easily be brushed aside in a line-of-progress history of mathematics. And for lack of anything better to do with them in the classifications of received history, they are lumped with the Hellenic mathematicians of half a millennium earlier. Their sole actual bond in common was that they both wrote in Greek. But Newton and Leibnitz wrote in Latin without our finding it necessary to classify them with Balbus and Hyginus as "Roman mathematicians."[2]

There is a curious point also about the great abstract ideas we are said to have obtained from the "Greeks" even after the necessary correction of assigning irrationality and non-geometric continuity to the Byzantines. The question is how much are they worth? Neither Chinese nor Hindu mathematics required someone to tell them about the basic concepts of numbers in order to elaborate their brilliant, though to our minds, limited systems. Mathematical thinking presupposes the ideas upon which its thought is based. We note what we call a development from Classical mathematics to the Levantine "Greeks" of Alexandria because the basic ideas of Levantine mathematics differed profoundly from those of the Classical. We find a similar "development" in the early centuries of Western mathematics, for a cognate reason. In each case, however, the mathematical manipulations of the earlier civilizations were utilized but the basic ideas discarded as absurd or limited.

In contrast, the theory that our mathematics (and equally the rest of our scientific thought) has been "dominated" by these "influences" from the sciences of other societies presupposes that a society capable of producing the immense mathematical thought of the West would never have got started on the subject unless copies of Euclid had happened to survive or copies of al-Khwarizmi happened to get translated. It might even be a delicate question whether any time gained by early access to the great abstract ideas of the Greeks was not more than offset by the centuries of opposition to breaking away from other Greek ideas that to the West were neither

---

[2] There were, in truth, no Roman mathematicians. The Roman Republic rose to power too late in the life of Classical society. Balbus and Hyginus were a pair of expert surveyors.

great nor abstract. Finally, of course, Western mathematics began its great development long before the Renaissance.

In studying the scientific interrelationship of the three civilizations, it is first necessary to define what is meant by a science.

In his *Essay on Human Understanding*,[3] Locke defines science as, "The knowledge of things, as they are in their own proper beings, their constitutions, properties and operations." Since Locke is perhaps the father, certainly the grandfather of modern scientific rationalism, his definition is probably as fair a start as any. This certainly is what most people today would accept as a definition of science. Science may be more than this, nor does Locke give this as an exhaustive definition, but whatever else science is thought to be, it is certainly also the knowledge of things as they are.

Yet if we accept that definition literally, we have a very restricted science. We have only the science of this moment. What was thought to have been science a generation ago is now seen not to have been science because, as we now see, it contained basic errors. Perhaps even the science of today may not be science either if in a generation some profound error is discovered in our present understanding.

In all science there is something more than fact and theory. There is intention. Science includes the intention to know things as they are and therefore means the knowledge of things *as we have reason to think them to be* in *what we have reason to believe to be* their own proper beings, constitutions, properties and operations. After all, despite our vast knowledge of the physical universe we cannot assert that we know things "as they are." We know them at any one time to the best of our knowledge at that time. We cannot do better.

Under this definition, then, we had sciences a generation ago, or in Locke's time. But similarly other peoples have had quite different sciences if they possessed a knowledge of what they thought things really were in their proper being and had their reasons for thinking them to be so. The mark of a science then is not truth against falsehood, but system and rational intention. The differences among the sciences of the different societies is, therefore, a difference in what is considered rational by each society.

Since the sciences are the rational explanation of things as they are in their proper being, in order to understand the nature of the sciences of a civilization, it is necessary to understand what is rational to that civilization and what attributes of being are those that would be considered proper

3 IV, c. 21

to a thing. The structure of causality displays what is rational and the structure of physics displays what is considered proper.

Now there is nothing shocking in there being great differences in what is considered to be rational. For a thing to be rational means that it accords with the appropriate premises, and premises cannot be wholly derived from objective facts. Some element of belief always adheres in them. This is not to say that some beliefs may not accord more nearly with the actuality of the universe than others and so may give to their respective premises more or less value for analyzing the facts of the universe or for building operable mechanisms. For this purpose there are perhaps better and worse beliefs, but it is doubtful whether any society is entitled to intellectual credit for these deep underlying beliefs. Societies seem to have them rather than derive them and these beliefs determine the kind of sciences as well as mold the other activities of a society.

Perhaps the key concept that reveals the nature of these underlying beliefs is the concept of causality. Every society of which we know more than the surface of its politics and the nomenclature of its religion reveals a different concept of causality. To us, of course, our own is true and the concepts of others are false. Thus we tend to judge the worth of the scientific thought of others by how closely their concept of causality parallels our own. We dislike to accept so deep an alien concept as a basic premise beyond proof or disproof and then examine the resulting scientific thought as a self-contained entity consistent with its own premises.

For us, it would be highly irrational to attempt to formulate the causal explanation of any actual event occurring within the atmosphere of the earth. And since it seems to us irrational to attempt such causal formulation, it seems consequentially equally irrational to predict the actual happening of any such actual event. Beyond our atmosphere, the conditions that our causality requires for the prediction of events are present. The number of variables effecting the motions of the sun and the planets are sufficiently few and sufficiently well known. We cannot control these variables, but we know all there are, or at least know all those that effect changes within the scope of our instruments. So we can predict with great accuracy eclipses, transits, the times of moonrise, sunset and all the other phenomena of solar and planetary motion.

Where actual events on the face of the earth are a consequence of planetary motion, we can approach prediction, but it is no longer so accurate. The number of unknowable variables increases. We can predict the increase and decrease of the variation of the compass very closely. After prolonged study of the tides at any particular place, we can predict reasonably well the time and rise of the tide at that place. We can predict the major seasons of the year and the approximate rainfall of various places.

But our foreknowledge is getting increasingly vague. We know there will be winter frosts and snow storms in Pennsylvania, but we cannot predict the temperature and precipitation at Philadelphia next February 21.

In the affairs of life, we deny all ability to make causal predictions about actual events, although oddly enough it is all the fashion to make causal predictions about nations, political movements or mankind as a whole. But so far as anything remotely scientific is concerned terrestrial prediction of actual events does not exist in Western thought. All our causal predictions are contained within established conditions, and no one will undertake to develop a causal analysis of what leads to the establishment of the necessary conditions. We do not consider the cause of *this* ship, *this* statue, *this* chemical experiment, though in ordinary conversation and in slipshod reasoning we often talk as though we did. With the problem of the existence of an actual thing or the occurrence of an actual event, Western scientific causality has nothing to do. It is a mighty science of what must happen in specified circumstances. But it does not and cannot predict the actual occurrence of these circumstances. It describes the mechanism by which all things that will happen must happen, but it leaves to political economists, astrologers and the readers of palms and tea leaves the prediction of what things are to happen. But this is not causality. This is only Western causality.

Despite Aristotle's explicit and detailed exposition of his type of causality, neither historians nor students of philosophy seem willing to consider it seriously. We regard it as an error, a misunderstanding, that further centuries of data-gathering have shown to be wrong. Against the background of the vast scientific accomplishments of the West, it seems almost silly to consider Aristotle's physics as physics, his causality as a full and genuine expression of a rational system of cause-and-effect. And so instead of studying Classical science in terms of what it was about, what function it performed in Classical society, we dismiss it as a noble attempt, the first halting step toward our own great structure. Of Levantine science and how it differed from either Classical or our own, we have little to say.

In every problem of cause-and-effect, there is an implied question: "Cause of what?" of the specific thing or of the underlying phenomenon. Western causality asks, "Why does a match burn?" never, "Why does this match burn?" To us, the first question is in the field of the sciences, the second, in its ultimate ramifications, in the world of politics. Classical causality asked *both* questions. This is Aristotle's efficient cause, and he appears to have considered each an integral part of the scientific explanation of phenomena, although the second was considered unanswerable in many classes of questions and was let go as the operation of chance, which in the Classical view was not, as it is in the West, the result of causal factors where the cause is unknown, but something altogether outside the structure of causality. But in regard to the first question, the position of Classical causality was that of Western causality. These are Aristotle's formal and material causes. We see no reason to split our picture of cause in this way, for we do not make a scientific distinction between form and matter. But to the Classical world, form was as real a concept as energy is to us and it necessarily appeared in the field of causality.

Though Classical and Western causality have this in common, that they both see the explanation of the structure of the universe as a task of causality—in our case, the sole task—they differ profoundly in the type of causal relations that they seek to study. Where we seek an explanation of the mechanics of action always in dynamic terms describing changes of state, and so far as any actual event is concerned, always potential, Classical causality sought to envisage a structure of physical reality that would permit "things" to have the physical existence they appeared to have. Our sciences ask the question, "How does a certain change take place? What differentiates one type of change from another?" Classical causality asked, "How does a certain thing exist? What differentiates one thing from another?"

To be sure, in the last reaches every causality is purely grammatical, ours no less than the Classical. The causal picture, as we Westerners understand it, of the last reaches of energy and sub-atomic physics is a system of verbal concepts in proper grammatical relationship. We do not present a causal explanation of energy or positrons. We define them not in terms of their causes but of their operations and relationships, so that we have at the end only a grammatical causality, the names we have given things arranged in proper sentence structures. As Aristotle would put it, we predicate certain things of these subjects.

But where, at the end of a long chain of analysis, we have to employ grammatical causality, Classical science did so at the very forefront of physical knowledge. We have introduced a vast chain of what we should call operable causality—a series of partial answers that may not be true but are useful. No concept similar to operable causality existed for the Classical thinkers. Their entire structure of cause-and-effect was grammatical while with us only the last inexplicable phenomena are so treated. The idea of an infinite regress of causal analysis capable of explaining the successive "hows," a regress that reached from the surface phenomena back to the ultimate grammatical, and therefore inexplaicable, "why," was an intellectual position that the Classical world could not take. Throughout Aristotle, the idea of an infinite regress is held profoundly irrational. To us it is an everyday comfortable companion of thought.

Only a person who knew nothing of Classical physics could ascribe this vast difference in the sciences of the two societies to ignorance or lack of data on the part of the Classical world. Their thinkers knew precisely what they were doing, why they were doing it and, dimly, something of the consequences of our approach.

Their understanding of the universe was not feeble. The correct apparent motions of the sun and planets, the cause of eclipses, the sphericity and the order of magnitude of the earth, sun and moon were all known. They had a correct understanding of displacement, of the weight of air, an incomplete idea of surface tension and of gravitational attraction toward the center of the earth. On the last point, Aristotle made one of his few errors of observation in reckoning the speed of fall proportional to the weight of different bodies. Here, he must have been confused by air resistance and his inability to admit the existence of a vacuum plus, perhaps, an unavoidable prejudice for so corporeal a ratio as weight to weight equals speed to speed. Since acceleration involves either the mathematics of infinitesimals or non-Euclidean curves, it would have been impossible for the Classical world to make a correct analysis of that.

The Classical society, however, even had thinkers like Leucippus and Democritus, who postulated atomic bodies in perpetual motion in a vacuum producing all substances by their differing combinations. Needless to say their idea of atoms bore no relation, logical or historical, to ours.

Where this science fell so far short of ours was not from ignorance and inexperience but from a fundamentally different picture of what was reasonable.

"The 'impossible' and the 'false'," Aristotle writes, "have not the same significance. One use of 'impossible' and 'possible' and 'false' and 'true' is hypothetical. It is impossible for instance on a certain hypothesis that the triangle should have its angles equal to two right angles, and on another the diagonal is commensurable. Thus it is not the same thing to make a false and to make an impossible hypothesis; and from the impossible hypotheses impossible results follow." [4]

"Mortover, there can always be something between points (for all lines are intermediate between points), whereas it is not necessary that there should be anything between units; for there can be nothing between the numbers one and two.[5]

"Moreover, it is plain that everything continuous is divisible into divisibles that are infinitely divisible, for if it were divisible into indivisibles, we should have an indivisible in contact with an indivisible, since the extremi-

[4] *De Caelo*, 281[b]
[5] *Physica*, 227[a]30

ties of things that are continuous with one another are one and are in contact"[6]

On these bases, there is this objection to Democritus' atomic theory: "For if the various elements [i.e., the atoms] are constrained by one another to move as they do, each must still have a natural movement which the constrained contravenes, and the prime mover must cause motion not by constraint but naturally. If there is no ultimate natural cause of movement and each preceding term in the series is always moved by constraints, we shall have an infinite process."[7]

Democritus' writings have come down to us only in fragments but his doctrines are clear from the writings of his two great followers, Epicurus and Lucretius. The Classical atom bore no resemblance to ours. It was not something that ever could be found or its actions traced. It was a name to explain the immense variety of tangible substances. Atoms were pictured as completely solid but differing in shape, weight and movement. Liquids were said to be composed of spherical atoms that rolled along together, solids, of jagged atoms that interlocked. The motion of atoms was seen as a combination of an eternal fall downward by reason of their weight, motion resulting from collision, and motion from a third and unidentified source which, says Lucretius, "breaks the laws of fate and prevents an infinite succession of causes." (*quod fati foedera rumpat, ex infinito ne causam causa sequatur* II 254.) It is from this last movement that the freedom of intention of animal life is derived.

These are not the considerations of shallow and incompetent minds. Neither are they the result of failure to observe the data of nature nor are they erroneous conclusions from observations. They are the expression of an intellectual viewpoint that precedes the acquisition of data and that necessarily required the interpretation of data in accordance with these same views. The fact that Aristotle denies that any numbers exist between one and two, that is, that to him all numbers are necessarily integers, does not mean that he and his society observed nature improperly but that his primary instrument of analysis differed radically from ours. Number to the Classical world meant only one of the many kinds of numbers that we are able to envisage and therefore employ. Number to the Classical world was an attribute of bodily individuality. It is impossible to have 1.414 cows or 3.1416 sheep, let alone 2.7182 oxen so these first two ratios, $\sqrt{2}$ and π, which are unavoidable in geometry, presented great difficulty to the Classical world and the third (the limit of the sum of an exponential series, the base of natural logarithms) was inconceivable.

The inability to conceive of numbers as merely reference indicies on

[6] *Physica,* 231ᵇ15
[7] *De Caelo,* 300ᵇ12

an infinite continuum, indeed on different continua, that intersect only at zero (i.e. the so called imaginary numbers involving $\sqrt{-1}$ as a factor) or do not intersect at all, may be the mark of a vastly different intellect from ours, but it is not the mark of failure to observe the data of nature. Nor is our ability to conceive of numbers as we do the result of patient improvement on the work of the Classical or Arabian mathematicians. The difference is both too profound and too simple. Any child can grasp the concept of numbers as a continuum if his society is capable of seeing them that way. It is also important to observe that these differing concepts of numbers agree with the differing concepts of causality. Our causality deals with action and action is a process, not a state. Its numerical representation is not a series of integers but of infinitesimals. On the curve of change there are many numbers between one and two.

Similarly, Aristotle cannot quite dissociate magnitude from the material over which a magnitude is measured, and so for him anything continuous must be a continuum. We, on the other hand, find no difficulty in making this separation and compose all things, even light, of finite, irreducible and indivisible minima, once of atoms, today of protons, nuetrons, mesons, electrons, quanta of energy and photons of light. True, we know that these things do not really exist any more than Aristotle's four elements existed but they—and the wave mechanics that accompanies them—reflect reality as it appears under our method of analysis. That is, they are neither reality nor an image of reality but human images drawn from our mathematical analysis of reality. How much our modern educated public is aware of this subjective nature of our physical images is a question, but our physicists are aware of it.

What Aristotle calls the prime substances, the individual existing things, this man, this horse, are the things to which and to which alone Classical number is applicable. To abstractions, to geometrical figures and to magnitude both as a concept and as a physical extension of elemental and, therefore, unformed matter, the Classical world could not apply number. It could not conceive of number of that kind, and therefore, could use nothing but Euclidian geometry as a tool of analysis. Other geometries were, as Aristotle said, hypothetical, but to the Classical world, impossible.

We, on the other hand, consider the prime substances to be those as yet unreduced mental entities on the frontiers of physics. But we do not consider even these as necessarily final minima, but merely the minima that we have reached, the furthest significant decimal place so far evaluated. But we are willing to accept far short of them operating irreducibles like atoms, ions and molecules, that break all the forefront of matter into a maze of discontinuities.

Under the kind of analysis that the Classical concepts of number, magnitude and motion could permit, it was rational for their philosophers to view the world of nature in a way entirely foreign to us. "For the nature of things," Aristotle says, "is the nature which most of them possess for most of the time." And, "Nature means a source of movement within the thing itself, while a force is a source of movement in something other than it. . . ."[8]

"Nature as it exists," writes Lucretius late in the twilight of Classical science, "is composed of two things: bodies and the void in which bodies are set and in which they are diversely moved. . . . Nothing exists which you can say exists separately and apart from bodies and space. . . . Moreover every object which exists in itself, either will itself act, or will suffer itself to be acted upon by other agents, or will be such that in it things can be and be brought about." [9]

Lucretius' acceptance of the idea of a vacuum makes his theory appear superficially an improvement over Aristotle's rejection of it. It seems more in line with our understanding of reality. It is worth noting, however, that Aristotle's rejection of a vacuum shows him to have been a far more powerful thinker than Lucretius. Lucretius was not, of course, a scientific thinker. The purpose of the *De Rerum Natura* was a liberal, not a scientific, purpose: to free the Romans of his time from what he considered their religious superstitions. Within the premises of his society Aristotle reasoned much more acutely and saw with surprising clarity the kind of nature that would appear from contrary premises— our kind of nature.

"How," Aristotle asks,[10] "can there be natural movement if there is no difference throughout the void or the infinite? For insofar as it is infinite, there will be no up or down or middle, and insofar as it is void, up differs no whit from down: for as there is no difference in what is nothing, there is none in the void. . . . Further, in point of fact things that are thrown move though that which gave them their impulse is not touching them, either by reason of mutual replacement, as some maintain, or because the air that has been pushed, pushes them with a movement quicker than the natural locomotion of the projectile wherewith it moves to its proper place. But in a void none of these things can take place, nor can anything be moved save as that which is carried is moved. Further, no one could say why a thing once set in motion should stop anywhere; for why should it stop *here* rather than *here*? So that a thing will either be at rest or must be moved *ad infinitum*, unless something more powerful gets in its way."

[8] *De Caelo*, 301ª8, 301ᵇ18
[9] *De Rerum Natura* I, 420 ff.
[10] *Physica*, 215ª

Here is the root of the inertial dynamics of the West, like non-Euclidian geometry seen in principle and consciously rejected. "Things" and only "things" existed for the Classical society. Motion, which is only the handiest manifestation of energy, is what "things" do—not, as with us, something whose existence is disclosed by the illusory "thing" that moves.

But the proof that Classical science, though utterly different from ours, was of very great intellectual stature lies in the work of three men, Archimedes, Eratosthenes and Aristarchus of Samos. Archimedes, who is remembered even in non-scientific history for his engineering works during the Roman siege of Syracuse, was one of the few Classical scientists who applied mathematical analysis to mechanics. He reduced Aristotle's concept of a center of gravity to geometric precision and thereby solved the problem of the lever that had baffled Aristotle. Through his work in hydrostatics, he approached the concept of specific gravity. By geometrical methods he ascertained that π lay between 3.1411 and 3.1428, though he used an interestingly different method of numerical expression, and discovered the formulae for the surface and volume of spheres. He developed the method of exhaustion, that is, the use of inscribed and circumscribed polygons whose perimeters, as the number of their sides increases, approach the value of their common curve, to an extent that it reached in part, the analytical power of the integral calculus.

His contemporary, Eratosthenes of Cyrene, was not so great a mathematician as Archimedes, but applied mathematics to geography. He calculated the obliquity of the ecliptic to be 23°51'20",[11] or at least so Theon of Alexandria said of him some centuries afterwards, and he certainly calculated the polar circumference of the earth at 252,000 stadia which on the most probable value of his stadia, gives a polar diameter of 7850 statute miles against the actual figure of 7900.

Aristarchus of Samos lived at least a generation earlier than Archimedes and Eratosthenes. His astromical reasoning was brilliant—and quite without results. He proposed to solve the difficulty of explaining the varying motion of the planets by assuming a daily rotation of the earth and an annual revolution about the sun—in short, what at first glance looks like the Copernican system. The fact that no stellar parallax had ever been observed, he explained by assuming the fixed stars to be on a sphere so distant that the semi-annual change of position of the earth, great though it was, was still proportionally so small that it would show no visible shift of the stars. But the inequality of the seasons, resulting from the elliptical orbit of the earth, where Aristarchus was assuming a circular, he was unable to explain.

[11] The actual value in his time was 23°43'47", i.e., 23°27'8.26"-0.4684(t-1900)

It is curious that this daring theory, which seems so much closer to our own, made no stir whatever even among the scientific men of the Classical society. Some commentators recorded that he had prepared such a system and let it go at that. Yet even it was vastly different from the Copernican system and despite its radical shifting of the earth from the center of the universe, it still did not become so un-Classical as to postulate infinity. Aristarchus enclosed the stars in a finite, tangible crystal sphere.[12]

The last great Classical mathematician, whose work closed forever this whole development of mathematical thought, was Apollonius of Perga, a slightly younger contemporary of Archimedes. He completed the study of conics, discovering about all there is to know about the static sections of cones. To him we owe the words: ellipse, parabola and hyperbola. Archimedes died in 212 B.C., Eratosthenes in 192 B.C. and Apollonius a few years afterwards.

The Classical concept of nature was not only completely undynamic, but of an orderly rather than simply an ordered structure as we see it. There was a "natural" arrangement of nature that was almost aesthetic and toward which nature strove, not always successfully. It was a purposeful nature of proportion and fitness, not the dark, demonic field of energy that we live in. It was also a nature of the forefront of things that anybody could understand with a little study, not the maze of esoteric specialties that consumes the whole lifetime of the few Westerners who can understand it at all. Even the profound and brilliant geometry of its last great mathematicians, which is not understandable without deep thought and study, was not felt as an analysis of nature but simply of the intangible form of geometry itself. It was number for number's sake. The type of analysis that accompanied the Classical view of nature—who can say which was the cause of the other?—could distinguish between the concepts of density and mass, but not between mass and specific gravity; between hot and cold but not between heat and temperature; between speed and motion but not between speed and acceleration, nor between motion and energy—nor even conceive of energy as a reality apart from the things energized.

Within that limited frame of Classical mathematics and physics stood all the mechanical accomplishment of Classical society, the mechanics of Archimedes, the engineering of Vitruvius, the Greek architrave and the

---

[12] Aristarchus' theory does not survive in any writing of his own but is referred to by Archimedes in the *Arenarius* as one of his theories. His only surviving writing gives a correct method of calculating the distances and size of the moon and the sun which he himself lacked the instruments to employ with any accuracy.

Roman vault, the Classical rowboat and the Classical slave power. Beyond these, Classical mathematics and physics could not take it.

To the development of Western thought, Classical science and mathematics added nothing. Most of it was unknown during the early period of Western life when the foundation of our scientific thought was laid.

It is even doubtful whether Classical science ever harmed our thought. It is true that for centuries the fashion of opinion recited isolated texts from Aristotle and Euclid—no one, not even the most ignorant, ever accepted their full corpora—and many absurdities were popularized in their names. But it remains doubtful whether men who could convince themselves that they should accept such absurdities would ever have had the intellectual insight and courage to have been of any value in the early development of Western scientific thought. This was always, as it still is, a field of the very few. Whether the others chanted incantations from Aristotle or from the Volsunga Saga could have made little difference. The essence of our interpretation of nature, an interpretation as old as our society—which is discussed in the next two chapters—is too deeply at variance with the universe of reality as Classical men saw it for us to suppose that a sentence or two of Aristotle, or indeed the entire discipline of Euclidian geometry, was a prerequisite for the origin of Western scientific thought. The fashion of many centuries does not change these facts. Our science is no more a continuation of Classical science or even a development stemming from that source than our politics, our morals, our arts or our religion. It has been with the Levant that our life has been entangled.

By a coincidence that has become monotonous, Claudius Ptolemaeus, known to history as Ptolemy of the Almagest, lived and wrote at Alexandria in the reigns of Hadrian and Antoninus Pius around 150 A.D. Most of his work on astronomy and mathematics is a mere compilation of the works of his predecessors. But it contains two things utterly new in the lands ruled by the Roman emperors: a numerical table of chords and a treatise on astrology, the *Quadripartitum*. The growing belief in the Roman world that human fate was governed by the course of the stars had been mentioned before by Pliny and particularly by Marcus Manilius, but a scientific treatise on the subject was new. The second novelty in Ptolemy's work was that here for the first time numerical calculations and numerical expressions replaced the geometrical ratios of Classical mathematicians. This seems hardly startling to us who always use numbers and would never dream of using a geometrical method of calculation, but against the scientific thought of the Classical world it is startling. Aristotle's dictum that the only numbers are integers still rings in the word the early Levantine mathematicians assigned to those ratios, which could neither be integral nor a ratio between integrals, a word we still employ though it now has no meaning: irrational.

In Ptolemy's table of chords appears for the first time the casual use of approximate numbers, since most chords bear an incommensurable ratio to the diameter. Using numbers instead of relations of magnitude (though, of course, these relations lay at the base of the numbers), the art of calculation became possible. Here then begins trigonometry since the chord is twice the sine of half the angle.

Some slight evidence of a departure from Classical mathematics appeared perhaps fifty years before Ptolemy. Nichomachus of Gerasa in Arabia, about whom nothing else is known, wrote the first treatment of arithmetic as a branch of mathematics independent of astronomy. It is interesting that it so appealed to Apuleius as new and noteworthy that he translated it into Latin. Since we consider arithmetic as the childish foundation of all mathematics, it comes as something of a shock to realize that Classical mathematics never had a science of arithmetic at all. Simple operations for practical purposes they knew about as they knew how to dye cloth without thereby having a chemical science. Their mathematical science and their only mathematical science was geometry, which dealt not with quantitative magnitudes but only with ratios that could be expressed by the proportional length of lines, proportional surfaces of areas, proportional volumes of solids, proportional sizes of angles. The diagonal of a square is of a complete simplicity as a figure. As a number, it is irrational.

Ptolemy's table of chords raises for the first time a historical problem that perplexes, indeed confounds, all attempts to deal with the history of thought, religious, scientific and philosophical during several centuries at the beginning of the Christian era. That problem is the misuse of sources, the invention of sources and downright forgery. For example, Ptolemy says that he derived his table of chords from Hipparchus, an astronomer who lived about 150 B.C., thereby, of course, labeling it as a piece of late but genuine Classical science. Ptolemy likewise says that Hipparchus discovered the precession of the equinox. He also reports the observation of various equinoxes by Hipparchus and gives some of his own observations, but the values of the two series cannot be made to reconcile with the times of either Ptolemy or Hipparchus. There is, further, a series of Ptolemy's astronomical calculations for latitude 36° north, that of Rhodes where Hipparchus lived. Finally, Ptolemy gives a table of stars, but all his celestial longitudes are uniformly in error for his own time. These complicated discrepancies have always bothered students of Ptolemy, but they are not inexplicable.

In regard to the discrepancies in the equinoxes, Newcomb[13] estimates that Ptolemy arbitrarily attempted to reconcile his figures with those of Hipparchus and used for his reconciliation a year six minutes too short, a year which he supposedly also derived from Hipparchus. The authorship of the table of stars has been long in dispute. Delambre [14] calculates that if $2°40'$ were subtracted from all the longitudes, the table would fit the times of Hipparchus. Equally, if the longitudes are taken at their face value, they will fit the middle of the first century, A.D., a hundred years before Ptolemy.[15] The most striking difficulty, however, is that not one astronomer before Ptolemy mentions Hipparchus' great discovery of the precession of the equinox, and even after Ptolemy's time it is never mentioned by early writers except by Theon of Alexandria and Proclus, both of whom were commenting on Ptolemy.[16] The only writing of Hipparchus that has come down to us is an unimportant commentary on Aratus and Eudoxus and some fragments on geography. In short, the only reason for believing that Hipparchus did any of the things ascribed to him, is because Ptolemy says so. In dealing with all the works of the Levantine civilization this is not a sufficient reason. The massive forgeries of this civilization are far from being disentangled even yet. It is equally if not more probable that Ptolemy drew on a "Chaldean" astronomer of about a century before his time ($36°$ is the latitude of Nineveh and Mosul as well as of Rhodes) and attributed it to an obscure Greek of a much earlier period. What must be considered otherwise an extraordinary coincidence is that Ptolemy cites as his principal source of new geographic knowledge, which was primarily of Asia and Africa, an otherwise unknown Marinos of Tyre, who too used latitude $36°$ north as the base parallel for his map making.[17]

This process of creating an artificial past can be seen in the organization of Justinian's Digest and the Bible. It was applied equally to Aristotle. The *Liber de Causis*, the *Theology* and the *Secret of Secrets*, circulated for centuries under his name. These can be identified as forgeries because the *Liber de Causis* is an obvious abstract of Proclus' *Theological Institition*; the *Secret of Secrets* was evidently originally composed in Syriac or Arabic, not Greek; the *Theology* is clearly a commentary on the *Enneads* of Plotinus. How much material still circulating under the

13 Neucomb, Simon, *Researchers on the Motion of the Moon*, Washington 1912 Apx. D., page 20.

14 Delambre, J. B. J., *Histoire de l'astronomie ancienne*, Paris 1817 ii, p. 264.

15 Almagest, Books VII and VIII, ed. C. H. F. Peters and E. B. Knobel Carn. Inst., Wash. 1915.

16 Sarton, George, *Introduction to the History of Science*, Washington 1931 Vol. 1, 367n.

17 Sarton, *op. cit.* Vol. I, p. 279.

name of Aristotle may be a forgery whose sources we lack, there is no way to tell. One difficulty is that while the Classical society lasted, Aristotle was not a particularly important thinker. He was not at all the great, dominating intellectual figure that later times pictured him. It was not until Levantine thought seized upon him as its canonical authority in philosophical matters that he became famous and his work widely read. Exactly when these works were first published we do, not know. The oldest list of works ascribed to him is that of Diogenes Laertes, compiled during the third century, A.D.; in other words, seven hundred years after his death. This is not only late but differs radically from the writings we have under his name today. The earliest evidence of the widespread existence of a text of Aristotle, and it was clearly not our text, was with Apellicon in the time of Sulla. After Cicero more than a century passed without further mention of Aristotle's writings in any work that has come down to us. The first quotation resembling the text that we possess today begins with Galen; and the spread of Aristotle's fame began, as we could begin to expect, in the reign of the Severans when Alexander of Aphrodisias wrote the first tentative set of Aristotelian commentaries. Unfortunately, the whole tradition of Western scholarship is to accept as genuine everything ascribed to Aristotle that cannot be proved otherwise. Yet if great parts of the *Metaphysics* had been written by Plotinus or any other great Neoplatonist, they could hardly differ from their present text. This is not to say that great sections of genuine Classical thought have not been retained in the Aristotelian text that we know today, but it is framed in a Levantine setting and interpolated with Levantine concepts.

The early Levantine world lacked our modern idea of a definite personal connection between a particular man and his works. Even the Western Middle Ages was far from entertaining our present scruples in this matter. Above all, the Levantine civilization was a society that required ancient authorities. In every field it repeated this process. A great and canonical authority was found or composed, and thereafter this was for over a thousand years the unchallenged authority in its field. Men could write endless commentaries on these canonical works. They could not discard them as wrong or outdated. Most of them were given a fraudulent antiquity. In philosophy, Aristotle, genuine and false— and how much textually altered we do not know—served the same purpose. In geography, astronomy and astrology, Ptolemy with his ancient, and perhaps predated, reference to Hipparchus became the canon. Among the Byzantines, Justinian's Digest became Roman law. In medicine, the works of Galen served the same purpose. In all these fields, except religion, some older, often far older, writing of the Classical world was interwoven with Levantine principles and established as a millennial canon. Even in the field of religion, this was true of the Neoplatonists and many of the Gnostics, but these sects died out and their canons either were never completed or have disappeared from our notice.

As a result, the line of separation between Classical and Levantine civilization is extraordinarily difficult to draw, more difficult even than the political line between where the Roman Empire ended and the Byzantine began. The two civilizations interpenetrated physically and intellectually, the new tried wherever it could to rely on the great names and texts of the old. Perhaps more important than anything else, great areas of our knowledge of the Classical world have come down to us in texts transmitted—that is, copied and recopied—by Levantine men. There are a few, very few, ancient fragments. There are almost no ancient manuscripts. Almost all the Classical writings we possess have passed through a process of deliberate selection and, to some extent, of conscious editing. How far the latter has gone we probably cannot ever surely know.

The separation is further complicated by the comparative lateness in Western life of our access to knowledge of much of the writings of the mature Levantine civilization. Some, but by no means all, of its great thinkers were known to the Middle Ages, but thereafter all intellectual contact with the Levantine world was abandoned, and it was not until nineteenth century historical scholarship recreated a knowledge of Arabic literature that even a partial understanding of Levantine thought and history became possible. As a consequence any conception of the Levant which stands on Western knowledge prior to the late nineteenth century— as schoolbooks and popular information necessarily do—is unavoidably false.

The problem of understanding the Levantine civilization is, therefore, different from the problem of understanding the Classical world. The latter we feel to have been our progenitor and hence, though we color it to suit our political and sexual prejudices, we do not seek to ignore it. Furthermore, our distant ancestors, who have contributed to the formation of our opinions, were neither at war with Classical society nor possessed of much less of its writings than we ourselves possess today. On the other hand, Levantine society, though its flower and greatness is today as extinct as Hellas and Rome, was once a powerful contemporary of our ancestors. We have, therefore, the necessarily prejudiced opinions of our forefathers handed down to us with the addition of our own prejudices about any opinion they held, particularly if the opinion dates back much beyond 1500. The intense medieval interest in Levantine thought is alone almost enough to make us wish to ignore it.

To return, then, to Ptolemy and the table of chords allegedly of Hipparchus. It is with Ptolemy that we have the first definite sign of a new type of mathematics: trigonometry, geometry conceived as calculable numbers rather than demonstrable linear and spacial relations. We have certainly for the first time the use of irrational numbers. When Aristotle said there were no numbers between one and two, he did not mean that no line was half again as long as another. He was quite aware of the latter relation. He meant this was not a numerical relation. To us these seem synonymous, to Aristotle they were not. In essence, of course, any number is the expression of a ratio, and the essential issue is whether number is suitable to express other ratios than those between discrete entities. Classical mathematics insisted that only line, surface, and volume—not numbers, which are in the mind, but bodily extension in space—were capable of expressing the ratios of incommensurables, that is, in essence of nondiscrete things. Both Aristotle and Archimedes so thought of numbers. Ptolemy did not.

Astrology is mentioned by writers of the Roman Empire before Ptolemy. Some doubt it, some accept it, but all ascribe it to the "Chaldeans." Like Christianity, Manicheanism, Mithraism and the other Levantine religions, it is a way of picturing fate and the physical universe that did not originate with the Classical thinkers of earlier time, but was owed, and was contemporaneously ascribed, to sources east of the Roman frontier. Fate was not a new concept to the Classical world. It was the senseless spinning of the three sisters, and it was read in the flight of birds, the livers of sacrificed animals and the ambiguities of the oracles. It was not, as in astrology, a causally governed process flowing from the motions and natures of the stars and there readable by one skilled in the science.

In his *Quadripartitum,* Ptolemy devotes four books to a complete exposition of astrology, very crude by later standards, but the first in the Roman world.

Ptolemy starts by pointing out the obvious influence of the heavens upon earthly affairs; the seasons and the weather, and the ability of seamen to navigate. In these, knowledge of the heavens permits prediction of events on earth, therefore, a deeper knowledge of the causes involved can lead to deeper and more certain foreknowledge. In Ptolemy, astrology is much wider than the narrow prediction of individual fate that is alone still unofficially practiced in the West. The latter branch of astrology, known technically as genethlialogy, is only a part of what to Ptolemy is a vast science, the science of the causality of all things that actually happen. The distinction that we make between individual fate and a general system of scientific causality is unknown to Ptolemy. There is no distinction, not only none in theory but none as a practical matter, between the cause of tides, rain, eclipses and the individual fortune of a particular man or a particular piece of stone. There is here no trace of Aristotle's formal and material causes, the explanation of how things happen if they happen. Nor is the astrological causation like Aristotle's efficient cause since the latter is often pure chance and the efficient causes of disparate things bear no relation to each other. In Ptolemy's astrological causality there is one great common cause for everything, but it is not the explanation of how they would happen if they did happen, but of why each thing does happen, and of why it happens *when* it happens. In all terrestrial matters, neither Classical nor Western causality ever is concerned with time in this way. Classical causality ignores it because the effective cause, the apparent cause of any particular event, is disconnected from the apparent causes of other events. Western causality ignores it because Western scientific causality never deals with the cause of an event and so never has in it any consideration of absolute time. Time in Western causality is "how long" between two defined states. Just as all our causal laws must be preceded by an "if" clause concerning the establishment of the necessary conditions, so all our scientific statements about time concern duration after the establishment of these conditions. We do not have scientific laws predicting actual occurrences below the moon. Since we cannot predict what things will occur at all, we certainly cannot deal with the time of their occurrence.

In Ptolemy, the Levantine causality of the actual event is explicit as the basis of knowledge. Its basic hypothesis as a scientific proposition in astrological form is that the force and nature of the stars provide the mechanism by which events are brought about. It is a scientific proposition because Ptolemy supposes that the motions and forces of the stars are subject to system and rational analysis. From his time onward, astrology remained one of the great sciences of the Levantine world, and because it was thought of as science its necessary mechanical foundation, what we now call descriptive astronomy, was immensely developed.

This Levantine causality of the actual event was not confined to astrology. It permeated all Levantine thought in every field. "The generation of all things," writes Boethius, "and all the proceedings of mutable natures, and whatsoever is moved in any sort, take their causes, order and forms from the stability of the Divine mind. . . . Fate is a disposition inherent in changeable things by which Providence connecteth all things in their due order. For Providence embraceth all things together, though diverse, though infinite; but Fate puteth every particular thing into motion being distributed by places, forms, and time; so that this unfolding of temporal order being united into the foresight of God's mind is Providence, and the same uniting, being digested and unfolded in time, is called Fate. . . . Wherefore whether Fate be exercised by the subordination of certain Divine spirits to Providence, or this fatal web be woven by a soul or by the services of all nature, or by the heavenly motion of the stars, by angelic virtue or by diabolical industry, or by some or all of these, that certainly is manifest that Providence is an immovable and simple form of those things which are to be done, and Fate a moveable connection and temporal order of those things which the Divine simplicity hath disposed to be done." [18]

Almost a thousand years after Ptolemy in the irreligious days of this society, it was the scientific causality of Averroes: "A knowledge of causes is a knowledge of secret things, because the secret is a knowledge of the existence of a thing before it comes into being. And as the arrangement and order of cause bring a thing into existence or not at a certain time, there must be knowledge of the existence or non-existence of a thing at a certain time. A knowledge of the causes as a whole is a knowledge of what things would be found or not found at a certain moment of time." [19]

That is the causal kernel of every pseudo-science of modern times, economics, sociology and of the politics of those who think of politics as a department of these. But it is not the causality of the great physical sciences of the West.

Besides astrology, there was one other great Levantine science, alchemy, and besides trigonometry and what the Arabs afterwards called "mobile geometry," in contrast to the static geometry of the Classical, one other great branch of mathematics and this, like trigonometry a new development of the Levantine science, completely unknown to the Classical, algebra. The history of the origin of both alchemy and algebra is therefore much less difficult to disentangle from the Classical past.

The earliest development of Levantine algebra—there was, as has been noted, some sort of algebra among the Babylonians—appears in the writing of Diophantus of Alexandria. From one letter of an eleventh century Byzantine mathematician, Psellos, we are told that he lived toward the end of the third century, that is approximately in the times of the Severans. He was the first mathematician to introduce the use of a symbol for the unknown in an equation and to employ a sign for minus. He developed determinate and indeterminate linear and quadratic equations. Before his time the only approach to algebraic handling

---

[18] Sixteenth century trans., Loeb Classical Library, p. 341.
[19] *The Philosophy and Theology of Averroes*, p. 269, Tr. Mohammed Janil-ur-Rehman, Baroda, 1921.

of mathematical problems appears in works attributed to Hero of Alexandria who probably lived somewhere around the reigns of either Hadrian or Diocletian.[20]

The beginning of "mobile geometry" seems to lie with Pappos, an Alexandrian mathematician who probably lived a little later than Hero. The essence of this type of geometry is the curve, surface or volume resulting from the given motion of some given point, straight line, curve or surface. It was, therefore, a geometry of mensuration, which Classical geometry, with the lone exception of part of Archimedes' work, never was. Euclid, for instance, does not even know the theorem for the area of a triangle. It was also the geometry of that interesting conception of these early Levantine mathematicians which has been so difficult for Western mathematicians to define: the porism. Euclid is quoted as using this word, but he meant by it a conclusion from a demonstrated proposition. With Pappos and his successors, the porism is something unknown to Classical mathematics and very difficult for us Westerners to define. It was a process of finding and bringing to view hidden relationships between given data, usually variable data. Hence there was frequently no "solution" in our sense of the word since the conditions proposed might lead to an infinite number of numerical answers, but each expressed one and the same actually existing relationship, the numerical value of which would depend on the instantaneous state of the variables. Ponder Averroes' extraordinary definition of causal knowledge and the meaning of mobile geometry and the porism becomes clear. Where Classical mathematics was interested in the static relations between pure, immobile geometrical forms, the Levantine sought to discover the instantaneous actual relationship between specific variable geometrical constructions or numbers. Hence, they developed admirable methods of mensuration, but at the same time a host of number relationships that seem to us merely childish: magic squares, series with such useless properties as having their digits sum to the same number and a maze of other hidden, but to us pointless, relationships.

In our received history, these early Levantine mathematicians who wrote in the Greek language are a constant embarrassment. It is perfectly obvious to everyone that Classical mathematics came to an end with Aristarchus, Eratosthenes, Apollonius and Archimedes. No one disputes it or argues anything but that the "influence" of Classical mathematics continued. Nearly five hundred years separate the lives of these four great Classical mathematicians from the times of Diophantus and

---

[20] Hero's date has long been disputed. Earlier scholars assigned him to the first century B.C. Modern scholarship places him as above. See Sarton op. cit. I, 208 and Thorndike, Lynn, History of Magic and Experimental Science, I, 188.

Pappos. In all that period there is not one mathematician of even secondary quality. This is such an extraordinary gap in the continuity of any science that even if wholly new mathematical thinking had not begun with Diophantus, the time gap alone would warrant serious pause. "If his work was not written in Greek," says Cajori [21] of Diophantus, "no one would think for a moment that they were the products of a Greek mind . . . Except for him, we should be constrained to say that among the Greeks algebra was always an unknown science." Diophantus presents no such difficulty when it is realized that he belonged to a civilization other than that of Euclid. But convention adoring at a Greek shrine ignores the vast time gap and asserts a continuity that is based on two things alone: the use of the Greek language, and the vague statements of those later mathematicians that they were just doing a little differently what Euclid or Archimedes had done before. The first reason should persuade no one. People still write in Greek and Latin but are not considered thereby part of Classical civilization. In the light of the known habit of the Levantine world to find ancient authorities for itself, the statement by a Levantine writer that such and such was in Euclid (of course, in a book now lost) is worthless as evidence. When Proclus whose business it was to provide himself with an aura of antiquity says that the geometrical curve called a quadratrix was discovered in a now lost work of a friend of Plato's, such a statement is not evidence, any more than Ptolemy's statement about Hipparchus' observation, which it must be noted, will not check out astronomically.

It is curious also to note the fate of the seven books on conics that bear the name of Apollonius of Perga. Books one to four are brilliant but strictly conventional Classical geometry. They exist in Greek and were translated into Arabic by Hilal-al-Himsi and revised or retranslated afterwards by Abu-l-Fath. On the other hand, books five to seven, which are extraordinary, do not exist in Greek nor in the Arabic of either of the above translations, but in an Arabic text bearing the name of Thabit-ibn-Quarra (d.c. 901) who did some translating, to be sure, but was a great mathematician in his own right.

There is no evidence that alchemy appeared in the Roman world before the end of the second century A.D. The alchemical texts themselves, of course, cite a great antiquity—though even then not a Classical antiquity—for their art, but it is not borne out by any surviving evidence. It was always entirely a Levantine art.

With the foundation of astrology, "mobile" geometry, algebra and alchemy, we have the basic scientific corpus of the Levantine world.

[21] Cajori, Florian, *History of Mathematics,* Macmillan, New York 1894 p. 74

None of it stemmed from the great Classical mathematicians and naturalists. All of it continued and flourished under the Byzantines and the Mohammedans. Further, all of these sciences are consistent with the Levantine causality of the actual event. Astrology is obvious enough, but algebra is no less a vehicle of the causality of the actual. Where Classical geometry deals with the properties of some abstract form, hence proof by superposition is possible, algebra is the method of finding the instantaneous quantitative value of some specific unknown. Similarly alchemy was not an attempt to formulate the laws of physics as they apply to what we call chemical change, but to bring about a specific chemical reaction. We have been able to transform alchemy into what we today call chemical engineering (and *not* what we call chemistry) because we have been able to develop what we call chemistry not from Levantine alchemy but from Western theoretical physics.

By the end of the fifth century, Levantine religious thought, which should not be confused with church history, came to an end. Under Shapur II (d. 380) the Avesta of the Mazdaists was substantially completed and its canon closed. After Chalcedon in 451, the religious philosophy of the Christians was settled in a permanent split of the three irreconcilable groups: Orthodox, Monophysite and Nestorian. Between 380 and 427 the active lifetime of Rabbi Ashi, the head of the Jewish Academy at Sura, the Talmud was completed and closed. With this completion of religious thought in each of the five great nations of the Levantine society, the almost exclusively theological problems which had theretofore dominated the keenest minds of this world, began to give place to more mundane and more scientific interests. It appeared in the characteristic form of this civilization, the commentary. Late in the fifth century, Proclus had completed his commentaries on Plato, Euclid, Ptolemy and Aristotle. He was the last great Neoplatonist. Indeed to the extent that Neoplatonism was a church—it was always a religion—Proclus completed the canon with his commentaries infused throughout with the spirit of Neoplatonism. During the sixth century, Philoponos of Alexandria wrote an extensive series of similar commentaries on Aristotle, on Nicomachus' arithmetic and the earliest known treatise on the astrolabe. Alexander of Aphrodisias had made a tentative beginning at scientific writing in the form of commentary back in the reigns of the Severans, but the full development of the form seems to begin with Proclus and Philoponos. It continued thereafter without interruption down to the time of Averroes. The form was, of course, picked up in the early imitative centuries of Western thought.

Beyond the frontier, the Sassanids had the University of Jundishapur near ancient Susa which enjoyed the support of their kings and of the Abbasid Caliphs after them. This was the period of the grand monarchs of the Levantine world, Justinian and Chosroes I, comparable in many respects to the social and political aspects of our own sixteenth century. The Orthodox Christians and the Mazdaists, to superficial appearances the Greeks and the Persians, were the two great territorial nations of this society and in the main dominated the intellectual and political life of the other three, the Jews and the two heretical Christian nations. Their relations with each other were those normal between political states of the same society: war, peace, commerce and a common intellectual tradition. The Sassanids held the greater empire and the intellectual life of the Levantine world probably centered more at Ctesiphon and Jundishapur than at Constantinople. Translations went both ways, but Jundishapur also sought out a good deal of Hindu material. In hindsight the impressive intellectual life of Persia after the Mohammedan Reformation, which far exceeded that of Byzantium, suggests that even in these earlier centuries, the Byzantines were becoming gradually a provincial nation. The revolt of the Nestorians to found a Christian nation of their own had removed some of the strongest intellectual traditions from Orthodoxy which was rapidly becoming exclusively the nation of those who spoke the Greek language. Viewed from the contemporary condition of western Europe, Byzantium of the sixth century seems the center of all learning and civilization. Viewed from Jundishapur, Ctesiphon and the yet-to-be-founded Baghdad, it does not appear so impressive. We have, however, far fewer surviving works from the Persian areas during these earlier periods. After all, one requirement for the survival of Levantine material was its appeal to medieval Western translators. This required that it should be in Greek, Arabic or Hebrew to begin with and that it be physically available in the Mediterranean area. In the end, the destruction of Iran and Mesopotamia by the Mongols in the thirteenth century left us with very little that was not already in Syria or farther west.

The establishment of Mohammedan power in the middle of the seventh century appears to have had little effect on the intellectual life of this society. The same interests were pursued and by about the same peoples. Many Monophysites, Nestorians, Jews and Mazdaists became Moslems in the course of succeeding centuries, and the appearance of men of Arab stock outside of military and political affairs was extremely unusual. The Arabs gave a unified political organization to the bulk of the Levantine world and provided a syncretic and popular answer for many of the theological difficulties of all the Levantine nations. The greatness of their dominion also coincided with the period of mundane interest, urbanization and religious skepticism of the Levantine society, roughly the four centuries from 700 to 1100, approximately comparable in intellectual and social development, allowing for the immense intrinsic differences between the two societies, to the four hundred years in the West, from 1600 to 2000. No exact coincidence is possible, of course, any more than it is between the lives of two men. All men of twenty have much in common, and all men of sixty have rather different things in common, but the specific time patterns of the individual lives in each age group never exactly coincide.

So general is the confused image of the rise of Mohammedanism and of the Empire of the Arabs that a brief clarification of these events seems wise. There are a number of widely accepted key opinions that are quite false and make it difficult to understand the Levantine world and its relation to the West. Near-eastern scholarship during the nineteenth and twentieth centuries has shown the lack of foundation for these opinions, but the correction has not yet spread to the accepted popular image. The greatest confusion perhaps flows from the opinion that Mohammedanism was a new religion. It was a new church, and hence in the Levant a new nation, but it was not a new religion. Also our opinion of what it looks like today in contrast to modern Western Christian sects is meaningless. The point is how did it compare with Orthodox, Nestorian and Monophysite Christianity and with Judaism in the seventh century? On this point the testimony of contemporaries and the opinions of modern scholars are in agreement; it was a *heresy*. Its contrast to Mazdaism, of course, was much sharper because the Koran draws more on Jewish and Christian mythology and sacred traditions than on Persian. It venerates the names of Abraham, Moses, Ezra, John the Baptist and Jesus, but does not mention Zoroaster. Yet the philosophical and ethical content of Mazdaism is so akin to Levantine Christianity and Judaism that even in Persia, Mohammedanism was not in essence a new religion.

The Mohammedans themselves felt this. The Koran states that Judaism and Christianity are, like Mohammedanism, God's creations. Not quite such a specific provision is made for the Mazdaists, but even so, Mazdaism is named a licit religion, one with a revealed book. There was, therefore, no shock of contact with something strange and horrible when the Levantine world suddenly found itself faced with the teachings of the Prophet. In fact, as has been touched on already, part of Mohammed's teaching was in direct accord with the heretical position at each of the great Christian councils. The acceptance of Mohammedanism by most of the Levant was assisted by these facts and also, inevitably, by the immediate political situation in the Byzantine and Sassanid Empires in the middle of the seventh century.

Another misconception is that the Arabs were barbarians. They were not. Like all civilizations, the Levantine had its centers of prolific cultural attainments and its simpler provincial areas. The Arab clans of central and southern Arabia belonged to the latter. Christianity and Judaism were widespread through Arabia and there was constant commercial and intellectual contact with Mazdaist Mesopotamia, and Christian Syria, Egypt and Abyssinia. Like Scotland and Ireland of the Western Middle Ages, the clan structure of Arabic society before Mohammed far outranked the principle of kingship. There were nominal Arabic kingdoms, but the great political principle throughout the whole peninsula was the clan, so that the real rulers of Arabia were the handful of great families that controlled the clans.

In the beginning the great Meccan families were Mohammed's most bitter enemies, but after the force of his arms convinced them of the political expediency of joining him, the whole political structure of his movement changed. He himself became very tender with these former enemies, and within a few years after his death, it was they, not the old companions of the Prophet who had stood by him in the years of hardship and danger, who succeeded to the empire of the civilized world. These great families were not only rich, they were also a hereditary nobility and while they were provincial like a Scots lord, they were nonetheless men of the world.

There are other misconceptions about the rise and decay of the Empire of the Arabs, but these really flow from the two preceding: that the Mohammedans forced conversion, that they butchered populations and destroyed learning, that they poured out of the desert in millions. All these are absurd.

To understand the creation of this great empire and the establishment of Islam, it is necessary always to bear in mind that Levantine nations are constituted on a different principle from Western nations. Both are nations, both are groups which enjoy connubium and constitute in the minds of their members a natural grouping of men. Both usually have or seek a political entity of their own. But where Western nations are always territorial and are never coterminous with a religion, that is, they share a religion with other nations of their society or embrace more than one sect among their own people, or both, a Levantine nation is the group of people belonging to the same church. In a Western nation, church and state are always separate institutions. However intimately they may at times have been involved with each other in common enterprises or in bitter hostility, they are always to Western men two utterly distinct manifestations of human life and action. They could no more be fused in the religious thirteenth century than in the agnostic twentieth. Only the Bible Protestants, the Kirk of Scotland and the Huguenots of the sixteenth century, the congregationalist theocracy of New England in the seventeenth, the Mormons in the nineteenth, only men who had by force of will steeped themselves in Levantine religiousness as best they could understand it, could temporarily forego this essential distinction.

On the other hand, no Levantine nation ever existed with a separate church and state.[22] There was never a spiritual sovereign comparable to the pope in the Orthodox Church. As long as the Byzantine Empire lasted the emperor was the head of the church, and the apparatus of state and church were indistinguishable. And when the empire fell to the Turks, the patriarch of Constantinople became the temporal as well as the spiritual head of the Christians in all their internal affairs; just as the catholicos of Ctesiphon, later of Baghdad, was the ruler of the Nestorian Christians first under the Sassanids and then under the caliphs; just as the resh galutha governed the Jews under the Achaemeneans, the Parthians, the Sassanids and for a time under the caliphs.

When, therefore, a new sect appeared in the world of politics and government in the seventh century, it created anew a situation to which this society had been long accustomed. To the Jews, Nestorians and Monophysites, it meant nothing. They had been nations with substates of their own under the Byzantines and the Sassanids. Their states and nations were not being attacked merely because the Arab armies invaded the territories of Byzantium and Persia. They shifted readily from being substates of the old territorial sovereign to being substates of the new. That was one reason why these vast populated areas put up so little resistance. Most of the inhabitants of great parts were not citizens either in feeling, law or fact of the state being attacked. Sometimes as in Syria and Egypt, the "neutral" nation was legally suppressed, but it was there and welcomed a new territorial sovereign who was willing to give it the autonomous status it desired.

There is also the fact that for more than thirty years before the Arab attacks the Byzantine and Sassanid states had been in almost continuous war. The Byzantine Emperor Maurice invaded Mesopotamia in 591 to restore Chosroes II who had been deposed by factions of the Persian nobility. On Maurice's murder by the usurper Phocas, Chosroes began a war against Phocas that was to prove the ruin of Persia and very nearly

---

[22] The modern states of Moslem population are simply artificial imitations of the West, usually actual colonies of some Western state that has since been driven out. They represent not nations but the area of licensed power of the individuals in control. The situation in Iran and Pakistan is somewhat different, however. Iran is the remnant of the Persian Shi'ites and Pakistan is not Moslem against Moslem but all the Moslems of the area against the Hindus.

the ruin of Byzantium. Three times the Persian armies reached Chalcedon across the Bosphorus from Constantinople. In 611 Antioch was taken, Damascus in 613, Jerusalem in 614 and Egypt in 619. Here, as in the Arab invasion that was to come shortly, the hostility of the Monophysites and Nestorians was a serious weakness of the Byzantines. Very soon, however, the situation was reversed. Heraclius, son of the Bzyantine governor of Africa, succeeded in overthrowing Phocas and set to work to rebuild the shattered Byzantine army. This took him over ten years and then he in turn invaded Mesopotamia. His success was overwhelming. Chosroes was deposed and murdered in 628, and for five years complete anarchy prevailed throughout all the Sassanid dominions. Finally in 632, the Persian aristocracy united in setting up a child, Yazdegerd III. Late in that year the first Arab raiders began probing the Persian frontier.

By the time of his death, Mohammed had gained control of all the Arabian peninsula that was not held by the Sassanids and Byzantines. This gave him a stretch of productive agricultural and trading communities along the three coasts and the pastoral tribes of the interior. His position at Medina permitted him to cut all the caravan routes from Syria and Iraq into southeastern Arabia, and his willingness to use this advantage, despite accepted religious custom, forced the mercantile aristocracy of Mecca to come to terms with him. And terms to Mohammed meant acceptance of Islam. From this base of power the pastoral tribes were easily overcome for they could never stay united. Their paganism, probably the last island of it in Arabia, could make no intellectual stand against the Koran. The Jews, Christians and few Mazdaists of southern Arabia were divided into little semi-feudal principalities and cut off from the Christian and Mazdaist powers in the north. There was no political reason to resist Islam in southern and central Arabia.

Mohammed died at Medina, in June of 632, a few months after the death of his last surviving son, the infant Ibrahim. It was agreed that the community at Medina should name his successor, the caliph, the commander of the faithful, but no agreed-upon mechanism of succession existed. Two conflicts appeared at the outset between the emigrants and the more populous community of Medina as a whole. The emigrants were, to be sure, men from Mecca who had joined Mohammed on his forced flight to Medina, but they had since settled their quarrels with their aristocratic families in the south. Hence the emigrant group at Medina commanded money and power, the power of the great families of the south. Across this social and economic split ran the thread of personal and sexual politics. The struggle was between Ayesha, Mohammed's young and ambitious widow, his last wife, and Fatima, his daughter by his first marriage, the wife of his nephew Ali. In the selection of the first caliph, the contest was smothered by Omar, the head of the emigrant faction, who postponed his own claims and supported the aged Abu Bekr, old friend of the Prophet and Ayesha's father. Although Abu Bekr reigned for only two years and did little more than bring back to subjection the Arab tribes that revolted on Mohammed's death, his brief occupancy of the caliphate had great historical consequences in the internal politics of the Arabian Empire. As a precedent, it destroyed the dynastic principle that the caliphate belonged to the heirs of Mohammed. When Ali's followers later tried to assert this principle, even though Ali himself had become fourth caliph, his failure to have been the first was a fatal flaw in the tradition.

On Abu Bekr's death in 634, Omar gained what he had postponed two years before. It was under him that the great military successes of the Arabian armies began. Damascus fell in 635 and, after the battle of Yarmuk in 636, the Emperor Heraclius abandoned the Syrians to defend themselves, which most of them refused to do. Ctesiphon fell in 637, Mesopotamia in 639, Egypt in 640, Iran and Tripoli in 644. In the Byzantine Empire only the regular imperial troops from Constantinople did any serious fighting. Among the Sassanids, the anarchy that had followed Heraclius' invasion and the deposition of Chosroes II had destroyed the military power of the state and only in Iran proper did the Persian-speaking Mazdaists make a desperate resistance. The attitude of the great mass of Jews, Nestorians and Monophysites was either neutral or of no consequence. The Byzantine Empire was reduced to Anatolia, Greece proper, Sicily, southern Italy, Rome and Ravenna. The dynasty and dominions of the Sassanids were wiped out. The Moslem Arabs became the chief political nation of the Levantine world, but they neither destroyed this world nor resettled it. To begin with they simply took over the machinery of state as they found it. For nearly sixty years Greek remained the official language in the former Byzantine provinces and Persian in the Sassanid. Byzantine and Sassanid coinage was continued in use for many years. The administrative officials of the old regimes very largely went on administering the affairs of the new. Far from any forced conversion, the attitude of the early caliphs was opposed to it for fiscal reasons. The Koran forbade taxing believers for more than the stated alms rate, and theoretically land owned by a Moslem would be tax exempt. Practical considerations, however, had to override the holy text, and for many years new converts were not allowed to avail themselves of this method of tax avoidance. It was not until the impractical and pious Caliph Omar II (d. 720) decided to stand by the text of the Koran that new converts were released from normal taxes.

The resulting conversions wrecked the finances of the empire and ended in a disguised form the exemption from taxation of any Moslem old or new. (The "tribute" of the school histories exacted by the Moslem conquerors from their Christian subjects was an income tax that would seem very old-fashioned today.)

The political affairs of the Arab nation did not proceed so smoothly however. Omar was assassinated and the aged Othman, an emigrant and a member of perhaps the most powerful Meccan family, the Ommiads, became caliph, again at the expense of the "legitimist" claims of Ali. Omar had had Meccan ties but they were not to be compared to those of Othman. Othman, old and weak, scarcely attempted to rule himself. All policy and all high appointments were the monopoly of the Meccan aristocracy, the men who had fought the Prophet and attempted to murder him.

Ali became the symbol of all the assorted discontents of the empire. Othman answered with nothing but promises and did not even attempt to garrison Medina. In 657 a group of pilgrims from Persia and Egypt demanded his abdication in favor of Ali. When he refused they stormed the house of this undefended old man of eighty and put him to death. Ali perhaps had no part in the death of Othman, but he accepted the caliphate from his killers.

The instant consequence of Othman's death was the outbreak of civil war. His cousin Moawiya had been for a number of years governor of Syria; he had administered it skillfully and had gained the support of its fairly homogeneous Aramaic and Islamic Arabic population.

Ali's enthusiastic but temperamentally difficult religious support and the dubious loyalty of the Persian Moslems was not the equal of the secular interest assembled by Moawiya. Partly by military defeat, partly by dissolution of his following, Ali's position became hopeless, and finally Moawiya was spared the problem of how to dispose of the son-in-law of the Prophet when an individual fanatic assassinated him in 661.

The death of Ali ended the first stage of the civil war. But the Arabian south, which was becoming increasingly unimportant in a nation that ruled the great centers of world trade and culture, accepted the new caliph only under a show of force. It was also required to accept the transfer of the capital from Medina to Damascus. Thus Moawiya founded the Ommiad Caliphate of Damascus. But the rifts that divided the Arabian world empire were only suppressed.

On his death in 680, civil war was immediately resumed and for over twenty years consumed the lives and energies of the Arabs. In the course of this war, Hosain, Ali's son, grandson of Mohammed, and Ibn Zobair, grandson of Abu Bekr and the last powerful descendant of the friends and companions of the Prophet were killed by the Syrians. Medina was sacked and Mecca besieged and taken. By the opening years of the eighth century, the Ommiad caliph, Abdal-Malik, had eliminated the political power of the Arabic nobility still resident in Arabia. Although he was the first caliph to introduce Arabic as the official language of the administration and he maintained the social position of the Arabic nobility outside of Arabia proper, he governed the empire primarily through Syrian civil servants regardless of ancestry and to some extent regardless of faith. His successor, Walid I, carried this policy so far that Byzantine provincial governors who had fought the Mohammedans were reappointed to their old provinces on an oath of submission to the caliph. Julian, for instance, the Byzantine governor of Tangiers after a long resistance surrendered and was placed in charge of far west Africa from which, with the assistance of a Christian faction across the straits, he and Tarik began the Moslem annexation of Spain.

In the east, however, the destruction of the House of Ali and of the political power of both the religious fanatics and the nobility of Arabia had been accompanied by bitter hostility and heretical religious movement, the Shi'a, which ended forever the religious unity of Islam and soon contributed to its political break up.

The Shi'ites, who are the present-day Moslems of Iran, are regarded with loathing by all Sunnite (orthodox) Moslems past and present. The Shi'ite surface doctrine is simply that all the caliphs except Ali were usurpers and that only a descendant of the Prophet can lawfully be caliph. Their real difference is perhaps that they are Persians and have attached a good deal of Mazdaism and Nestorianism to Mohammedanism. Their veneration of saints, particularly their own, Ali and Hosain, is extreme, and in some sects their doctrine of the Mahdi and the Hidden Imam amounts to a second coming of a Saviour. The grave of Hosain at Kerbela is probably more holy to Shi'ites than Mecca itself.

For about forty years after Abdal-Malik, the Ommiad caliphs of Damascus ruled in domestic peace. The reigns from Walid I (d. 714) to Hisham (d. 743) mark the high tide of the Empire of the Arabs. It was a period of architecture, poetry and imperial military adventures. Theology as a rational pursuit was finished and mysticism, fanaticism and empirical science had not yet begun. The territorial power of the nobility was ended but the social structure was still aristocratic.

The destruction of the Ommiads was accomplished during four brief reigns that occupied the years following the death of Hisham. A peculiarity of Levantine dynasties was the apparent occasion for this. To us Westerners, dynasty and primogeniture are almost synonomous but this has never been the case in the Levantine society. Not one of their dynasties from Constantine to the last Turkish sultan operated on the principle of primogeniture. Sometimes an eldest son succeeded his father but not because he was the eldest and not even essentially because he was a son. Any member of the family was as lawful a successor as another depending on the designation of some present or past sovereign and, informally but effectively, the choice of the high community around the throne, the Senate at Constantinople, the informal group of great Arabic lords at Damascus. It had, of course, been the same with the Arsacid and Sassanid dynasties in Persia and the view of the Shi'ites only changed the sacred family, not the principle of succession. As a result the question of succession in a Levantine state was always potentially open and in times of weakness, disorder or revolution, a "legitimist" contest could always be started. Such a period followed the death of Hisham. Its primary occasion was the growing dissatisfaction of the Arab nobility with their gradual but constant loss of political power. This time the civil war was not between the caliph and the distant fedual nobility of southern Arabia, nor even, yet, against the Persian Shi'ites, but was war among the Ommiad princes in Syria and Iraq.

During this civil war of the Ommiads, the effective conspiracy that was to overthrow them got under way. The Shi'ite leaders, who were distinctly not of the upper Arab nobility, had long maintained an effective secret organization. A complete knowledge of their machine and method of correspondence came into the possession of one Mohammed-ibn-Ali, no relation to the Shi'ite saint, a descendant of Abdullah-ibn-Abbas who had been an elder uncle of the Prophet. He entered the Shi'ite conspiracy secretly, and after his death in 743 his sons sent as their agent into Khurasan a Persian convert, one Abu Moslim. Abu Moslim provoked the rival Ommiad factions against each other, indicated to the Shi'ite that he was aiming to restore the house of Ali, to the Persians that he was seeking to get rid of the Arabs, to the pious that he detested the religious laxity of the Ommiads, and to the poor of all nations and factions that he sought the seizure of the property of the wealthy. Catalogued, the program was simple. Operated, even in a province of Persian roots, it required the most consumate political skill in duplicity and demagogy.

Finally in 747 with two Ommiad armies fighting each other in Khurasan, Abu Moslim came into the open with his personal army, mostly Shi'ites of Persian descent, and destroyed them both. As master of Khurasan, Abu Moslim began immediately exterminating the local Arabic nobility and organizing an invasion of Iraq. By late 749, he had taken Kufa, the capital of Iraq, and then executed his final political stroke. Depending on the strength of his hand-picked Khurasan army, he turned on the pious Shi'ites who were expecting a caliph of the family of Ali, and proclaimed instead

Abu'l Abbas, son of Mohammed-ibn-Ali. Thus was founded the dynasty of the Abbasids of Baghdad, half Shi'ite and wholly revolutionary.

Wierwan, the last Ommiad caliph, organized a final army in Syria and invaded Iraq only to be hopelessly defeated after a long-drawn-out battle along the banks of the Tigris. He fled to Egypt and was killed a few months later.

With the fall of the Ommiads, even the surface political and religious unity of Islam disappeared. The Shi'a ceased to be a conspiracy and came into the open. Spain broke away at once and Africa and Egypt not long afterwards. Above all, the power of the Arabs was destroyed. The great families that traced their ancestry back to the feudal chieftains who came out of Arabia had become the hereditary aristocracy of the empire they had founded. They had been the creators and became, in effect, the destroyers of the Ommiad dynasty. Many were killed at its final fall, as was every descendant of the house of Omar on whom the new caliph could lay hand. The Arabs had never been more than a thin upper crust outside of Arabia proper. All were not aristocrats, of course, but rank for rank they had enjoyed advantages over the rest of the population. Those that survived the Abbasid revolution no longer constituted either a favored group or an aristocracy. The religion they brought with them remained the principal faith of the Levantine world. The Arabic language supplanted all the Semitic dialects and remained far superior to Greek and Persian as the language of culture and learning. But the Arabs themselves ceased to be of importance.

The early Abbasid caliphate was anti-aristocratic and anti-Arab. It was later to become thoroughly democratic—needless to say in a Levantine form. Incidentally, one of the early acts of its first competent caliph, Abu Iafar (known as al—Mansur, the Victorious), brother and successor of Abu'l Abbas, was to execute Abu Moslim. Even Levantine revolutions eat their children.

The founding of Baghdad was the work of this second Abbasid caliph, al—Mansur. The caliph not only made it a great commercial city. He made it a great center of scholarly learning. Arabic was a new language in civilized lands. It had almost no written literature and nothing whatever of a learned literature. To be sure it was a form of the basic Aramaic that in one dialect or another was spoken from Syria to the eastern highlands, but it was sufficiently different from Syriac and what is sometimes called Chaldee, respectively the principal western and eastern forms, to require translation. Also the replacement of the Mazdaist Sassanids by the Moslem Abbasids as the reigning dynasty and Mazdaism by Mohammedanism as the ranking religion, relegated Persian to a far lower level. Although it was still spoken, as it is now in Iran, it ceased to be used as a learned language.

Syriac and Chaldee were sufficiently close to Arabic to disappear as spoken languages and have survived only in the Nestorian and Monophysite religious works and in parts of the Talmud. Greek also was an important Levantine language, as well as being the language of the philosophical canon of this society, "Plato" and "Aristotle." Far to the east along the ancient frontier since the days of the Parthians the out-posts of the Levantine world in the Indus valley encountered the Hindus with their restricted and specialized learning embalmed in the long-extinct Sanskrit. Al—Mansur brought to Baghdad Syriac, Persian, Greek and Sanskrit translators and organized a systematic translation of the great bulk of important Levantine literature into Arabic. There had been sporadic translations before and they continued sporadically into the tenth century, but by perhaps the middle of the ninth century almost every important work of the past seven or eight centuries within the Levantine orbit was available in Arabic. Actually this was not a matter of making learning available to the Arabs if by Arabs is meant the men who came out of the south under Omar in 638. There were few of these or of their descendants and few of them cared about learning. But Arabic for political and religious reasons had become the master language of the Levantine world and men whose fathers wrote in Syriac, Greek and even to some extent in Persian now needed Arabic translations to read the works of their own ancestors. So in reverse Westerners need vernacular translations of the literature and learning of their medieval forefathers.

In the closing years of the ninth century appeared the early Levantine masters of strict scientific thought: al-Khwarizmi, the mathematician; Abu Ma'shar (Albumasar), the astrologer; al-Fargani (Alfarganus), the astronomer; and above all the great al-Kindi, mathematician, physicist and astrologer. These names are now obscure and generally forgotten but in the intellectual childhood of Western society they were ranked among the great scientists of all time. Al-Khwarizmi's work on arithmetic and algebra set the general form which these branches of mathematics retained among later Moslem mathematicians and in which they were taken over in the early days of the West. It is for this reason— not for any intrinsic preparatory value in the subjects themselves—that our lower schooling still starts mathematical teaching with Euclidean geometry and Moslem arithmetic and algebra. These subjects were the entire discipline of mathematics back in the days when our educational system was founded. As Western society has developed its own mathematics and mathematical methods, these have been added as "intermediate" and "higher" mathematics without any consideration of whether the old subjects were logically the base of what we consider the essence of mathematical analysis or were merely earlier in historical, not logical, order.

Al-Khwarizmi furthermore used Hindu numerals and position throughout his work, probably the first mathematician outside of India to do so. He was familiar with both real roots of quadratic equations for which he gave both analytic and geometric solutions. A table of sines and tangents is ascribed to him but this may be partly a later revision.

Al-Fargani's *Book on Celestial Motions* was a thorough exposition of observed planetary and stellar motions reduced, of course, to a geocentric system. It became one of the standard text books of astronomy in the Western Middle Ages.

Since we Westerners do not consider astrology to be a science, Abu Ma'shar must be reckoned within the Levantine frame of thought. He composed in his *Great Book of Introduction* the first attempt at complete assemblage of astronomical data and astrological deductions. However fallacious they are for us, they were thought in the Levantine world to be scientific and in a system of causality that seeks the cause of events, astrology may be factually a failure but it is not *a priori* irrational. As pointed out earlier, we never seek the scientific causation of an event so we are neither intellectually nor emotionally in touch with any scientific attempt to do so. In fact, we dismiss the type of problem itself as unsuitable for scientific solution. In the early days of the West, however, the present clarity—in practice, not in formal scientific philosophy—in regard to the type of causality at the root of Western thought, did not exist and Moslem astrology, Abu Ma'shar in particular, occupied a position of immense intellectual and even popular importance.

Al-Kindi was in many ways the most interesting of this group. For one thing he was an Arab and not, like the others, from the far northeast, Khurasan and Transoxania. In fact he was the only Arab who is remembered as a person of intellectual consequence. Secondly, his interests were far more encyclopaedic. He was rather a philosopher of science than a strict scientific specialist. He wrote on optics, both geometrical and physiological. He attempted to find a rational mathematical basis for dosage quantities in medication. He wrote on music with a precise understanding of pitch and a method for determining it. He considered positional numerals greatly superior to any other method of mathematical notation and wrote extensively on their use. Above all, al-Kindi was a profound scientific thinker. He realized that alchemy was incapable of scientific base within the frame of Levantine thought, and that what was being practiced under that name was a fraud. He was necessarily a convinced and eminent astrologer and gave the subject perhaps stricter mathematical treatment than any of his predecessors. His *De Aspectibus* (or *De Causis Diversitatum Aspectus*) was one of the most influential astrological works in the West. His most original astrological work, the development of the theory of the different conjunctions—the lesser conjunctions which occur every twenty years, the intermediate, every two hundred and forty years, and the great conjunctions which recur every nine hundred and sixty years— was plagiarized by his pupil, Abu Ma'shar, and known in the medieval West only through the latter's work, the *De Magnis Conjunctionibus*. Al-Kindi's own treatment, contained in an astrological study of the future of the Arabian Empire, postulates that the influences of these different conjunctions are highly progressive and that the great conjunctions open new phases of world history. It is a temptation to wonder whether Spengler picked his thousand-year cycle from al-Kindi rather than from observed data, which seem not to substantiate either quite such a short, and certainly not such a universal, life cycle for the great historical societies.[23]

From the reference of Western thought, it seems absurd to consider a man gifted with profound scientific insight who pursues astrology, however mathematically, and rejects alchemy. Admitting that the alchemical theories were absurd, there was still much useful empirical knowledge to be gained —and much was gained—of the behavior of elements and compounds, even if these were not yet surely identified as such. And more, in the light of modern nuclear techniques, even the idea of transmuting elements is seen not to be absurd, once the principle of the structure and relationship of the elements is understood.

But within Levantine causality, this is not so. If we are charged with ascertaining the scientific cause of an actual event, there can be no chemistry and, therefore, no science into which alchemy can grow. A thoughtful scientific observer, operating within the unconscious limit of Levantine causality, must inevitably come to the sound conclusion that the factors determining chemical and physical change on the face of the earth are of such a nature that predictions about physical and chemical changes that actually must happen, not about what must happen *if* something else happens, are beyond our powers. We cannot gather the necessary data and we could not integrate them if we could gather them. On the other hand, wherever the earth shows the influence of forces originating beyond its atmosphere, tides, days, seasons, part at least of the weather, in these fields accurate prediction of actual events is possible, and here, therefore, must be held to lie the basis of any causality of the actual. In fact, even from a Western scientific approach, exhaustive analysis of the cause of any actual event, hopelessly incomplete though it may be, inevitably reaches back to these same transatmospheric forces that have molded the development of life and history on this globe. These, of course, are a long way from the aspects of the planets, the houses of the zodiac and the mansions of the

---

[23] Al-Kindi's text exists in a Western language only in Loth's *Sendschreiben des al-Kindi über das Reich der Araber und wie lange es dauern wird, Leipzig*, 1875.

moon, but the habit of counting and measuring what you see in fields that you consider causally significant and attempting to correlate these observations with what can be counted and measured in another field, this is the basic research method of all science. The attempts at crude correlation in Levantine astrology differ in this respect not at all from the early attempts at crude correlation in Western physics. The problem always comes back to the question to which you seek an answer. We do not ask how things have the form that they have and so we consider Classical science the work of precocious children. We do not ask how things that happen come to happen, so we consider Levàntine science tinged with demonology and magic—the intellectual world of a nightmare. We ourselves ask how does the mechanism operate by which things happen, and to us this is the only intelligent question about nature that an adult can ask.

One of the most interesting figures of this era, for the light he casts upon Levantine scientific thought, was al-Farabi. He was not a scientific observer but a general philosopher and sociologist. He wrote commentaries, of course, on Plato and Aristotle, but composed works openly his own on music, ideal political conditions and the role of the sciences in human society. In the latter field a little pamphlet ascribed to him survives in a twelfth century Latin translation[24] entitled *De Ortu Scientiarum, The Origin of the Sciences.*

This work is an epitome of Levantine scientific philosophy, and because al-Farabi was not himself a scientific specialist it presents the Levantine scientific philosophy in a matured and generalized form. The work has an additional value. It shows the tenor of Levantine thought as the Western Middle Ages encountered it. The early European thinkers were far more exposed to the type of thought represented in the *De Ortu Scientiarum* than they were to Classical thought. Greece and Rome were names often sifting down only through early Levantine texts, but the perfumes of Arabia and the fleets of the caliphs were vivid facts of early Western society.

Al-Farabi, to follow his logic rather than his order, bases all scientific knowledge upon language. "The first principle of all the sciences," he writes, "is the science of language, of the attachment of names to things, that is, to substance and accident." The concept of substance and accident is one Western physics no longer employs and therefore needs a brief definition. There was little substantial, in the modern meaning of the word, in the Levantine concept for which our forefathers used the Latin word *substantia*. It was this that they used for the Greek word *ousia* so that the creed still declares that Christ is of one "substance" with

[24] In *Beiträge zur Geschicte der Philosophie des Mittelalters,* XIX, 3,31. Münster, 1916, p.19ff.

the Father, not meaning thereby that there was any identity of gross physical matter between them. Substance, in this sense, is by modern standards entirely immaterial. It is not the matter contained in things but, to coin a word for a conception almost impossible for us, the "matterness" of them. The substance of an apple was its "appleness." Its color, its taste, its shape or weight were its accidents. "The five senses," al-Farabi writes, "apprehend the accident by sight and contact without the intervention of anything between the accident and the senses. . . . On the other hand only reason apprehends substance, the accident serving as a contact between the substance and the reason."

Once things are named properly, the second root of the sciences is grammar, "which is the science of ordering the names applied to things and composing expressions which indicate the arrangements of substance and its accidents and consequence. Third is the science of logic, which is the science of ordering declarative propositions according to logical forms in order to draw conclusions, by which we attain knowledge of the unknown and the ability to judge whether the propositions are true or false."

On this quite modern semantic foundation al-Farabi stands the four learned sciences: arithmetic, geometry, astronomy and music. "And these complete the learned sciences, these four, which are also called the masterful sciences—because they master him who searches into them and then return him wise. They show him the right way to learn most correctly that knowledge which comes after them. . . . Because substance at one place glows and at another pales, here is prolonged and there shortened, here increased and there decreased, here generated and there destroyed, here sickened and there cured, from all this it was necessary to have a science which would make known these facts, a science by which we would arrive at a knowledge of the change thus made and of the occurrence and causes of such change, and of how we could avoid dangerous events when we wished to prevent them and how, when we wished, we could bring events about. Thus arose natural science, which is the science of action and of things acted upon.

"Inquiring into its origin we find four elements, fire, air, water and earth—which are the mass of substance extended under the orbit of the moon. It is from the four qualities of these (namely, heat, cold, wetness and dryness) that events occur in substance and things act and are acted upon. From these four roots, together with the four learned sciences, there has arisen science as it exists beneath the orbit of the moon."

The function of the orbit of the moon is, of course, to eliminate theological matters from his discussion of mundane science. Otherwise al-Farabi's logical structure seems not only sound but not at all unscientific until it is realized that the causality with which he is concerned is **the** causality of the actual event. If there is still confusion about the significance of following this type of causality rather than the causality of Western thought, al-Farabi's catalogue of the divisions of natural science should clear it up.

"The divisions of this science according to the most eminent thinkers are eight: the sciences of astrological judgments, of medicine, of divination from natural events (*nigromantia secumdum physicam*), of astrological images, of agriculture, of navigation, of alchemy—which is the science of changing the species of things—and the science of catoptrics (i.e., that part of optics dealing with reflection only). . . . In natural science there is perfected the knowledge of all accidents of changeless substance beneath the orbit of the moon, and the knowledge of all the mass of that substance which undergoes change of form by growth and decay."

From terrestrial substance, al-Farabi argues, inquiry turned to the nature and origin of the stars not as an astronomical question, which as a learned science he considers limited to the study of the positions and proper motions of the stars and planets, but as a metaphysical problem. This higher inquiry, he writes, "was the cause of knowing God and arriving at a knowledge of the Creator of substance and accident. . . . And this science is called metaphysica, that is, divine science. This is the last of the sciences and completes them and beyond this there remains no inquiry; for this is the goal toward which all inquiry aims and in it comes to rest. It is thus clear whence divine science arose. It is now equally clear whence have arisen all the other sciences that are prior to it. For they have been shown to arise from events in the arrangement of substance and its accidents and the concomitants of this, which the senses perceive and the intellect understands."

It is not the general fashion in our picture of history to consider the integrated structure of alien thought. We prefer to pick isolated scraps and indulge thereby in a comforting image of progress. We would, therefore, reject al-Farabi's classification of the natural sciences as absurd and superstitious. The embarrassment, however, is that the logical development of his foundation is unassailable. We, too, realize that precision of nomenclature and adherence to logical structure are the essential base of all knowledge. We accept without question that the foundation of scientific knowledge lies in basic mathematics and mensuration. "A knowledge of the occurrence and causes of changes," sounds exactly like our own off-hand idea of the role of natural science. But what evaluation can we make of a philosopher of science who introduces divination and two departments of astrology as serious practical sciences? Yet careful consideration of al-Farabi's eight divisions of natural science reveals that none is out of place. Of the eight, five are admitted as practical sciences even in the modern West. Catoptrics is not thought of as very important—though motion pictures and television use its principles—and alchemy has been planted on quite different theoretic foundations. Of medicine, navigation and agriculture there would be no question. What al-Farabi was listing, therefore, were the principal fields of the technology of his time—that is, those fields where theoretic knowledge was applied to actual events—and since his causality was wholly the causality of actual events, astrology and divinations were as properly practical sciences as medicine or agriculture. We would be vastly in error to consider this as superstition. It was not. *We* consider these fields the arena of superstition because their practice in Western lands in the atmosphere of Western scientific thought *is* superstitious. It cannot be justified within the only strict causality that our sociey knows, for we do not possess a scientific causality capable of analyzing the actual. But we have not disproved astrology. It is simply a field of mensuration and analysis incapable of ever being a Western science. But to minds to which the cause of the actual event is the only strict and significant causality it remains seriously meaningful. The pitful and degenerate chicanery that passes under the name of astrology in the intellectual gutters of the modern West is beside the point. In a great society whose only picture of cause was the cause of the actual event, where the stars were not strictly the cause of events—the will of God was that cause—but where the stars made manifest to the learned what that will had ordained, astrology was a powerful science. However limited its theoretical foundation and however strange it seems to us, it remains the most thorough effort of man to account by a system of strict causal necessity for all the events and occasions—*sub circulo lunae.* We must take care not to throw away lightly our respect for the inner soundness of an alien mind.

There is another point of profound difference between Levantine and Western scientific thought that appears in al-Farabi's brief treatise: the role of God. Despite pious and false assertions, Western science nowhere leads to God. It is the analysis of a machine, not of a purpose, of how, not why or when, and therefore our science can never come to rest in anything except its own exhaustion. Unlike Levantine science, there is no goal toward which it is aimed. There is no final "why" which it might some day answer. Under the strict and essential axioms of Western causality the universe, endless and purposeless, stretches away forever. It is part of the greatness and tragedy of Western man. "Beyond this there remains no inquiry; for this is the goal towards which all inquiry aims and in it comes to rest." No Westerner could say that.

For about a century following al-Farabi's death at Damascus in 950, Arabic science continued to flourish. It became, however, increasingly commentary on work previously done, the completion of details and the composition of all-embracing cyclopedias. Thus abul-Wafa, who died at Baghdad about 997, was almost the last translator from Greek to Arabic. He commented, as usual, upon Euclid and Diophantus but also on al-Khwarizmi, whose work was already becoming an Arabic classic. His original work was the final touch of Levantine trigonometry: recalculation of the sine and tangent tables, exposition of the relation of the sines of the sum and difference of two angles and a full analysis of the basic relations holding between all six trigonometric functions, with all of which he was familiar. Contemporary with him was al-Kuhi who worked on equations of degrees above the square and made extensive studies of the condition of solvability of these equations. At the same time al-Sijzi completed Arabic mobile geometry with the solution of trisection of the angle using the intersection of a circle and an equilateral hyperbola. Some fifty years later a similar rounding off of Levantine astronomy was accomplished by Ibn Yunus who died at Cairo in 1009. He prepared new and more accurate tables and recalculated the standard astronomical constants: inclination of the ecliptic 23°35′, longitude of sun's apogee 86°10″, solar parallax 2′, precession 51.2″.

The last great Arabic physicist was Ibn al-Haitham, Alhazen of the Western Middle Ages, who died at Cairo about 1039. Understanding what we today call the refractive index, he calculated the angular depression of the sun below the horizon at the beginning and end of twilight and thus sought to calculate the height of the earth's atmosphere. He analyzed the magnifying power of lenses and applied this correctly to the functioning of the lens of the eye. He concluded that vision was something that reaches the eye, not radiates from it as many had long argued.

From the Arabic world of this time, there has survived a document which is probably unique from any society or period, the Fihrist al-Ulum of al-Nadim, who died at Baghdad in 995. It is, to quote his own subtitle "The index of the books of all the peoples of the Arabs and non-Arabs whereof somewhat exists in the language and script of the Arabs, on all branches of knowledge." But of this vast catalogue of books not one in a thousand is still extant—a fact that makes an understanding of Levantine society at its height a problem of historical creativeness, not of statistical flummery.

Levantine science and philosophy came to an end in the middle of the eleventh century, an end marked, as in the Classical world, with two of its greatest figures, and, indeed two of the greatest scientific figures that any society has produced: al-Biruni and ibn-Sina. Al-Biruni was born at Khiva in 973 and died at Ghazna in Afghanistan in 1048. Ibn-Sina,

Avicenna in the West, was born near Bokhara in 980 and died in Hamadhan in 1037. Both men were of Persian descent and al-Biruni was officially a Shi'ite though in fact neither was a religious man. Curiously, al-Biruni was unknown in the Western Middle Ages and his establishment as one of the great thinkers of the Levantine world has been the work of nineteenth and twentieth century Western scholarship. Avicenna, of course, was a familiar name in the intellectual life of the West before Aquinas was born.

What seems most remarkable about the breadth of al-Biruni's mind is that, hardly fifty years before the rise throughout the whole Levantine world of intense provincialism and fierce religious fervor, he could display so vast and catholic an interest in all the affairs of this world, of nature and of human societies alike, and a complete indifference to the woes of the faith or the prejudices of the Moslems.

For some years he lived in India and made a deep study of the Hindu society and its people. He translated two Sanskrit astronomical works (by Varahamihira) into Arabic and on his return to the Moslem world wrote a learned account of India (the *Tarikh al-Hind*) and the best Arabic exposition of the use and value of Hindu positional numerals. His interests were, however, of far wider scope and a few random notes on his observations and conclusions give a crude picture of the range and critical ability of his mind. He composed a comparative study of the different chronological eras and systems used by the different peoples of the world. He analyzed stereographic projection. He redetermined with great accuracy the latitude of many places and improved, not so successfully, the calculation of their longitudes. He considered whether the earth rotates on its axis and refused to make a definite decision one way or the other, which was by far the soundest scientific conclusion with the instruments at his disposal. He understood and explained the hydrostatic principle of springs and fountains. Study of the alluvium of the Indus valley convinced him it was an ancient sea bed filled in by the erosion of the valley—a conclusion that implicitly challenged the Levantine chronology of the creation of the world according to the Book of Genesis, as sacred to Moslems as to Jews and Christians. He understood the difference between weight and specific gravity and made accurate determinations of the specific gravity of eighteen metals and gems. He attempted a comparative study of light and sound and concluded that the propagation of light resembled that of sound but at an incredibly greater velocity.

Al-Biruni's great contemporary and personal friend, ibn-Sina, was primarily a physician—author of the final compendium of Arabic medicine, the *Quanun* (the *Canon*)—and philosopher, though he wrote on a number of mathematical, physical and astronomical questions, some clearly as a result of his correspondence with al-Biruni. Such, for example, seem to have been his observations on light and sound, though in the latter he appears to have been the first to observe that in successive sound vibrations with frequencies according to the series $\frac{n-1}{n}$, when n exceeds 33 the human ear can barely distinguish the difference, and beyond $n=45$ the sounds are completely indistinguishable. A quarter tone on our scale is $n=32$.

In philosophy ibn-Sina, like all the learned Levantines of his time, considered himself a disciple of Aristotle, but his philosophy is, in fact, the final, scholarly—and in a Levantine sense—irreligious summation of the world view of Plotinus and St. Paul. It may at first thought seem absurd to suppose that there could be an irreligious form of the views of the great Neoplatonist mystic and of the author of the Epistle of the Romans, but there is, in fact, a religious and an irreligious way of grasping—it could not be called thinking—the same basic beliefs about "things as they are in their own proper beings." To each, the view of the other is the complete antithesis, but to an outsider who sees in the universe around him different "things" altogether and has different concepts of what constitutes the proper of being, the deep identity of the views is apparent.

In his autobiography, ibn-Sina says that as a boy he was deeply affected by the *Isagoges* of Porphyry and in his early teens read and reread an Arabic version of Aristotle's *Metaphysics* without being able to resolve in his mind the philosophical messages that seemed to be hidden. Finally, he says, from a copy of al-Farabi's commentary, he obtained the key and proceeded to formulate his own systematic exposition of Levantine philosophy.

In ibn-Sina, the logos, the holy spirit, is the active intellect, an impalpable, incorporeal substance, in fact a depersonalized, rational God. The human mind has no creative power of its own. At best it can receive impressions from the active intellect. The universe has an intelligible order and by aid of the light from the active intellect, man can within himself mirror this order and bring himself into harmony with it. Though the radiance of the active intellect falls upon all, yet not all can receive it alike and a man can prepare to receive more of it by removing from his life those habits that impede the reception. In short, it is an intellectual reception of an intellectualized holy spirit by those who, by intellectual asceticism, have prepared themselves for it.

In his own society, ibn-Sina's intellectualization of the Holy Ghost was soon forgotten in the revival of pious, emotional religion, but as a physician his fame has endured. The *Qanun* is still used in Islamic lands. In the West, though he was most noted as a physician, his philosophical fame was considerable for some centuries.[25]

With ibn-Sina the intellectual life of the Levantine society came to a close. After him there continued for a century or more to be minor writers who now and then rehashed old subjects. Omar Khayyam, who was born the year after ibn-Sina died, even carried algebra a little further, but effectively Levantine science, whether it had reached its goal or not, came to rest. There was not a sudden loss of scientific personnel. There were plenty of these. Commentaries continued to be written, astronomical observatories continued to operate, new ones were even established. The whole Levantine scientific corpus was mulled over again and again for several centuries. What came to an end with al-Biruni and ibn-Sina was the development of Levantine science. After them nothing ever changed any more. Nothing was ever again found to be wrong with the world picture as these men and their predecessors left it. As the centuries wore on, the general level of interest and intellectual competence of the upper classes and the learned fell lower and lower into fanaticism and superstition. Among the Jews, whose scientific interests, like those of the Byzantines, had never equalled those of the Moslems, the intellectual decline seems and perhaps was less sharp. Jewish philosophical writings, more and more a mere repetition of what had been said before, continued down through Avecebrun (ibn-Gabirol, d. 1058) to Maimonides (d. 1204) and Levi ben-Gerson (fourteenth century).

In all three faiths, that is, in all three nations, the same change was taking place: the rise of a popular mysticism, increasing unwillingness to consider theoretical questions rationally and increasing deterioration of the social structure including, of course, the political structure. The Jews, having no political state, were spared the latter evil directly, but the Jews in the Moslem world suffered it as the states of their hosts fell into anarchy.

---

[25] Al-Biruni was almost unknown in the West prior to the publication of Wustenfelds' history of Arabic physicians and naturalists in 1840. A few excerpts were published in the learned journals in the following decades, but full texts only became available with the publication of his chronological studies at Leipzig and London in 1878 and 1879 and his account of India at London in 1887. In contrast to the utter neglect of al-Biruni, the dates of publication of some of ibn-Sina's works are of interest. Partial editions of the *Qanun* (Latin translation of Gerhard of Cremona, 12th century): Milan, 1473, Padua 1476, 1497, Venice 1483; complete text Venice 1544, 1582, 1595, Louvain 1658. *Metaphysics*: Venice 1508, 1550. *De Anima*: Pavia 1490. *Compendum de anima*, Venice 1526, 1546. *De Morbis Mentis*, Paris, 1659. All these and other works had circulated for centuries in manuscript.

Even by the death of ibn-Sina, the political structure of the Levantine world was far different from what it had been when al-Mansur executed the founder of his dynasty nearly three hundred years before. The Abbasids still were caliphs of Baghdad but by the middle of the eleventh century the caliph ruled over nothing and was himself the creature of the actual and legally "unofficial" political powers of the Moslem world, the Turks and the Ismailiya.

For some decades individual Turks had been coming over the northeast frontier, embracing Islam, and serving the caliphate in various military and civil positions. As a political power they first began to have weight about the time of the accession of the Caliph al-Mutasim, in 833, when it became apparent that the opinion of the Turkish officers was a powerful factor in the choice of a successor. These early Turks were simply individuals, not tribes or masses of men coming over the frontier. Certain Western historians, considering the decay and ruin of the Arabic Empire, have assigned a causal role to these Turks, as foreigners unwisely permitted to occupy all but the very highest office of state. Yet these Turks were not legally aliens at all. They had complied with every legal and, one might say, "constitutional" requirement for full nationality in the Islamic state. Of course, they were utter foreigners in their culture and long-range political interest, but they had gone through all the outward formalities required by the constitution of the Islamic nation, the Koran. They were thus full nationals and legally entitled to be so treated. The reasons that impelled Mohammed to make adherence to Islam the one fact and symbol of Islamic nationality were valid for the conditions of his enterprise in the early seventh century. That they had no meaning at all in the tenth did not remove them from the Koran.

The Ismailiya was a native movement. To call it Levantine liberalism— it was a Jewish and Christian movement also—is a reasonably accurate tag for it. It was, of course, like all things Levantine, cast in a religious mold and so while it advocated democracy and the rights of the poor, it was mystic and communed with God through ecstatic trances. In this, of course, it resembled its contemporary, Sufism—Mohammedan mysticism which has survived to the present day —but Sufism has stuck to the central doctrine of all the Levantine religions: God's Kingdom is not of this world. The Ismailiya in contrast was an active political movement. Originally a small Shi'a sect during the last quarter of the ninth century, it was soon organized as a secret political society. Its outward propaganda stirred the usual magic rigmarole of the Levantine world, allegories and number symbolism. It claimed a special line to its own lost, true and only perfect imam, Mohammed ibn-Ismail, hence its name. It preached equality and social justice as was manifestly called for in the Koran, but its actual operation was that of a secret political society bent on gaining and holding power for its leaders.

It sympathized with, but stopped just short of joining, Ali Mohammed's Negro slave insurrection that broke out in 869 and held Basra for fourteen years. Later it, too, moved from intrigue and political pressure to open civil war. In 930 the movement was powerful enough around Kufa to become the local government and from there launched a raid that sacked Mecca and seized the holy Black Stone. In the west, the Ismailiya gained the government in the Berber areas and from there in 969 took Egypt, founding the so-called Fatimid califate of Egypt (969—1171). More important, perhaps, than these conspicuous positions of power was the more obscure but real day-to-day power of this group within the Islamic dominion. Everywhere in political life they had connections and scattered throughout the country were actual forts of the Ismailiya into which a wanted man could flee and from which assassins and minor raids could issue. It was one of the posts of this society encountered by the Crusaders that has given us the word "assassin."

The disorders of the end of the ninth and opening years of the tenth centuries were put down, but not by the caliphs. There was a reaction lasting something over a century, from 945 to 1055, during which the Buyids, Persians claiming descent from an ancient Sassanian family, ruled as sultans. The caliphs were maintained almost as prisoners and kept strictly to their religious functions. The political stability of the Persian sultanate covers the period already touched upon of the encyclopedists and philosophers of science, from al-Massudi and al-Farabi to ibn-Sina.

In the far northeast, however, the military situation became increasingly worse. Here the cities and farms of civilized Islam ended and the mountains and high barren plains of central Asia began—the land of hunters and nomad herdsmen. So long as Islam enjoyed a government that could govern and maintain a serious military force this frontier was not difficult to hold against the constant but vacillating attacks of the outer barbarians. As time went on, however, to hold the cities of Transoxiana became the task of each city for itself. So Bokhara fell in 999, and the Turks began coming not as individual officers, but as solid tribes. Toghrul Bey, chief of the Seljuk Turks, took Nishapur in 1038, and at the invitation of the caliph, took Baghdad in 1055, ending the Buyid sultanate. The Turks in their turn began a brief line of sultans, Alp Arslan and Malik Shah. After the latter's death in 1092, the Seljuk power likewise fell apart into petty principalities—the anarchy which our ancestors found so essential to the success of the early Crusades and the establishment of the Latin Kingdom of Jerusalem.

After the fall of Jerusalem in 1099, the major part of the Moslem world was left undisturbed by foreign invasion for more than a century. The Mediterranean islands had already been lost and Moslem Spain was being continuously reduced, but in the center of Moslem life, say roughly Cairo to Bokhara, there was no serious foreign trouble. Yet everywhere there was anarchy. The phantom caliph at Baghdad presided over an empire from Egypt to India, ruled, in fact, at every town or every few hundred miles by some new strong man.

Among the Christian nations of this Levantine society, affairs were little different. The Nestorians and Monophysites, like the Jews, had no political states of their own. However, the Orthodox Christians of Byzantium fared little better than their Mohammedan neighbors. Mysticism and democracy were on the march there also. Back in the ninth century at the time of the rise of the Ismailiya, the monks of Studion began the same clamor in Greek. "If the Emperor," wrote the Abbot Theodore of Leo V (813-820), "is not subject to the law, there are only two hypotheses possible: either the Emperor is God, for God alone is not subject to law, or we are living in anarchy or revolution." The "law" to which the emperor was to be subject, was, of course, the opinion of the monks on any matter they cared to consider a religious question— in this particular case the controversy concerning the use of icons. The principle, however, was general and was the same as that of the pious assassins of the Ismailiya. It is, of course, the echo of every revolutionary movement.

But the struggle of the government and the monks early in the ninth century was only the democratic phase of the revolution. The socialist phase began about a century later under Romanus I (920-944) when the government, at last on the side of the common man, began attempting to legislate the rich out of existence—first by taxes and control of the acquisition of property, eventually by confiscation. Among the Byzantines the emperor, though supreme over religious as well as temporal affairs, was not himself a sacerdotal person. That is, the twin functions united in the caliph were among the Byzantines split between emperor and patriarch. There was not, therefore, the same restriction as there was concerning the caliph that only members of the sacred family could hold the office. Accordingly in the growing decay of government at Constantinople, emperors were not made imprisoned figure heads. They were deposed and the office itself remained the seat of political action. Nothing like the sultanate ever grew up among the Byzantines, but the old constitutional dynasties were nonetheless wiped out, and the throne filled by anybody strong enough in church, army and city mob to get it and keep it.

With occasional interruptions the succession of governments serving God and the common man continued till almost the end of the eleventh century. By this time the anti-property party, lay and ecclesiastical, had been forced to destroy the military establishment because the officer corps and the Anatolian rural area, the principal source of military strength, were incurably conservative and objected, often by force of arms, to the leveling of society to which these emperors, creatures of the monks and the city mob, never felt they had sufficiently attained. This fatal weakness cost the empire Anatolia to the Turks under Alp Arslan at the Battle of Manzikert in 1071. It was never thereafter a military power of serious consequence. It lasted for one hundred and thirty years longer, standing off four serious attacks by the Normans and then going down under the Fourth Crusade in 1204. The date, 1453, that every school child is taught is quite meaningless. It is the date at which the Turks took the city of Constantinople. The empire was destroyed by the Latins, not the Turks, in 1204. The city, after fifty-seven years of Latin rule, was again ruled by Greeks, but it was little thereafter but a city. Trebizond, the Aegean islands, Negroponte and the Morea were never recovered. Epirus was soon lost and by the middle of the fourteenth century the "empire" was little more than the present extent of Turkish territory west of the straits plus an area around Salonika.

It is to be noted that the Levantine world as a whole—regardless of whether it was Moslem or Christian—was under constant attack by the rising West. Again the picture that is drawn for school children of the Christian West attacking the Moslem East is not false but incomplete and misleading. The Christian West was attacking the Moslems, but at the same time and with the same energy the Christian West was attacking the Christian East as well. Naples, Apulia, Calabria, the Morea, Athens, Negroponte, Crete, the Aegean Islands, Rhodes, Cyprus, these are not insignificant parts of Byzantium to have been hacked away and kept by the Latins. (Some afterwards fell to the Turks.) Add to these the fifty-year possession by the Latins of Constantinople and all the Byzantine possessions west of the straits and it is evident that the supposed religious community made little difference.

To the direct and almost childish Westerners of those days—the Franks to Byzantine and Moslem—this whole Levant, regardless of religious faith, was too civilized, too luxuriant, too tricky, to be part of their world— whatever faith any of it professed.

The political conditions of this society were bad though outwardly they did not appear to be so bad as they were. Everywhere the external forms of a Levantine state were preserved, the great cities were intact and agriculture and commerce were everywhere actively pursued. The stagnation of the intellectual life was somewhat similar. In neither case was the true state of affairs admitted. If anything, in the period after 1100 there was perhaps more boasting of the greatness of Islam than during the centuries when there was more to boast about. Yet in the intellectual as in the political world there were signs that a shrewd eye could read—for instance the life and writings of al-Ghazzali, a professor at Baghdad in the sultanate of Malik Shah.

Al-Ghazzali was born in Khurasan in 1058 and died at Baghdad in 1111. He was educated in the accepted scientific general philosophy of his basically irreligious times and rose to distinction, first at Nishapur and then at Baghdad. In middle life, however, doubts began to arise. "Reflecting on my situation," he writes in his autobiography,[26] "I found myself tied down by a multitude of bonds—temptation on every side. Considering my teaching, I found it was impure before God." Later he writes, "feeling my own weakness and having entirely given up my own will, I repaired to God like a man in distress who has no more resources. He answered as he answers the wretch who invokes him. My heart no longer felt any difficulty in renouncing glory, wealth and my children. So I quitted Baghdad, and reserving from my fortune only what was indispensable for my sustenance, I distributed the rest. I went to Syria where I remained about two years with no other occupation than living in retreat and solitude, conquering my desires, combating my passions, training myself to purify my soul to make my character perfect, to prepare my heart for meditating on God—all according to the methods of the Sufis as I had read of them."

In his retreat al-Ghazzali sought, and on brief occasions attained, that ecstasy or transport, that sense of direct communion with God, which St. Paul describes and which the methods of the Sufis sought to make routine for the initiate. "Whoever has no experience of the transport," he writes, "knows of the true nature of prophetism (religion?) nothing but the name. . . . As there are men endowed only with the sensitive faculty who reject what is offered them in the way of objects of the pure understanding, so there are intellectual men who reject and avoid the things perceived by the prophetic (religious?) faculty. . . . Just as the understanding is a stage of human life in which an eye opens to discern various intellectual objects uncomprehended by sensation; just so in the religious the sight is illumined by a light which uncovers hidden things and objects which the intellect fails to read. . . . The prophet is endowed with qualities to which

---

[26] August Schmolders, *Essai sur les écoles philosophiques chez les Arabes,* Paris, 1842. Cf Claud Field, *Wisdoms of the East,* London, 1909.

you possess nothing analogous and which consequently you cannot possibly understand. How could you know their true nature, since one knows only what one can comprehend? But the transport . . . is like an immediate perception, as if one touched the objects with one's hand."

This we have heard before and we shall hear it again, this assertion that there is a truth that the ungifted can neither receive nor understand, which can be submitted to no objective test but must be accepted as true because to those who experience it, though to them alone, it has all the attributes of objective reality—to them it *is* reality. It is not a doctrine that is new with al-Ghazzali. It is the foundation of all the teachings of Mohammed, St. Augustine, St. Paul, Jesus, Mani, the Jewish prophets, Zoroaster, of every religious teacher of this whole society. It is the foundation, perhaps, of all religions of every society. But for some centuries it was a teaching that had not commanded great prominence in Levantine affairs.

Always the forms of public worship had been gone through and always there had been religious individuals—as the existence of the Sufis shows—but men of great intellectual standing in Levantine society had had little to say on the subject. With al-Ghazzali there appeared for the first time the intellectualization of religious revival, the intellectual justification of the destruction of intellectual analysis as a method of obtaining usable knowledge.

Al-Ghazzali did not by any means confine himself to the distant retreats where by ecstasy he could gain certain knowledge of God. Despite his understanding that such knowledge is incommunicable, he nevertheless proceeded to communicate it to all Islam in a series of religious tracts cast in the form of scientific scholasticism—which was, of course, the then-prevailing mode. These tracts either had immense influence or—what is more likely and in historical reality is perhaps the same thing—they formulated as verbal propositions emotions that in the preceding thirty or forty years, had become widespread without anyone's having thought or said much about them. The climate of opinion must have become quite different from what it had been when al-Biruni and ibn-Sina were considered the intellectual glory of Islam.

The most famous of al-Ghazzali's tracts is the *Tahafut al-falasifa*, generally entitled in English, *The Destruction of the Philosophers*, but much more accurately *The Vanity of Philosophy*. In this al-Ghazzali attacks the Levantine Aristotelianism of his time on the basis that it was unable to furnish any sure evidence concerning the nature of God or the universe and that therefore, in effect, the internally certified truths of religion must stand unrefuted. Above all, he attacked the complex chain of causality that had been built up to account for the evident chain of event and consequence that appears to dominate the mundane world. He asserted in fundamental Levantine fashion that all causal knowledge of a scientific kind was impossible because there could be no system of causality. Under each separate event lay one and only one immediate and utterly sufficient cause—the will of God. The sequence of cause-and-effect which we think we see around us is, in reality, nothing but appearance—there is no necessity that ties effect to what appears to us as cause. The true and only cause of the effect is God.

On such doctrines, no mundane knowledge of any sort could flourish or even live long and these being the doctrines popular with the mobs of Baghdad and satisfactory to the Turks, on this note some three centuries of Levantine scientific inquiry came to an end. It was not a scientific effort that accords with our view of the way to go about it, primarily because it sought the answer to a different question from the one our scientific inquiry asks. But it was an attempt—perhaps the only one in human history—to discover whether there really is a rational explanation of what actually happens and why it happens when it happens. Perhaps these questions are incapable of rational answers. Perhaps only men of a fundamentally unscientific and unalterably religious society would even think of them and seek, for awhile, to find communicable, objectively testable answers.

One last, lonely thinker appeared in this gathering twilight of the mind of the Levant—ibn-Rushd, Averroës of the Latin West. Born at Cordova in 1126, grandson of the imam of the great mosque, he died at Marrakesh in Morrocco in 1198, almost an exile and his name a by-word for atheist throughout Islam. His writings were of great meaning for what Islam had been and had thought, but not of what it was to become. Out of the past, ibn-Rushd is a piece of Levantine history. Toward the future, Averroës is a part of the West, for only in the West were his writings kept and his thought, or what could be understood of it by the Latins, considered.

Ibn-Rushd wrote in the established tradition of Levantine scientific thought, both as to method and subject. His philosophical writings, principally a great commentary on Aristotle, and commentaries on al-Farabi now lost, followed the accepted pattern of the three preceding centuries. His philosophy, scientific and general alike, is in everything consequential to a Western mind indistinguishable from the philosophy of al-Farabi and ibn-Sina. His name is connected with the nominalists of the medieval West, but this is meaningless in Islam. Ibn-Rushd followed the surface language of Aristotle perhaps a little more carefully than his predecessors and doubted the authenticity of some of the more brazen Neoplatonic forgeries passing under Aristotle's name. Beyond this he could not be accused of originality. But coming as he did after al-Ghazzali, he wrote in a wholly different climate of opinion. He was thus forced to make precise issues left implicit in the earlier works. Attempting, then, to be rational he appeared, and perhaps he was, as irreligious as any Levantine can be. It was al-Ghazzali's position that upset ibn-Rushd for he saw at the end of that road of mystic self-certainty the destruction of all objectively verifiable knowledge. He argued, quite in vain, that the Koran gave no warrant to the claims or practices of the Sufis, indeed that its very text claimed its own religious completeness. He presented himself as a pious Moslem accepting the truth of the Koran in things religious and arguing Arabianized Aristotelianism as the truth of the world of fact and matter. But the inherent mysticism at the core of Levantine society had repossessed the thought of his time, and the authority even of the Koran was now insufficient to oppose the religious frenzy that was gripping the masses of Islam. The fact that a proposition was reasonable was in itself becoming proof that it was irreligious.

Only perhaps on the literal text of Biblical creation did he find it necessary to interpret the truths of religion to reconcile them with the facts of this world. Against the Biblical doctrine of recent creation, he offered a variant of an idea that had appeared and reappeared in Levantine circles ever since St. Augustine, namely, that time, too, was among the things created. Hence the Biblical creation is, in effect, the creation of time and as far as time is concerned, the universe has existed ever since there was time and hence is, for our purposes, eternal.

After ibn-Rushd, no Moslem again attempted to develop an orderly, rational philosophical system. Scientific thought became more and more narrow. Itineraries succeeded geographic and geodetic studies, herbals replaced attempts at general botany—and similarly in every department of knowledge. Within three centuries or less after ibn-Rushd's death, the intellectual level of the whole Levantine world had fallen to where it is today. And the point to be noted, which is often overlooked, is not simply that the Levantine level is pitiful in contrast to that of the contemporary West. It is pitiful in contrast to its own standing eight hundred to a thousand years ago.

The physical blow from which this society never recovered was the Mongol invasion. Far less numerous and potentially less powerful than civilized Islam, the Mongols began attacking the frontier cities along the Jaxartes River (the modern Syr Darya) in 1219. Both Khurasan and Transoxiana had long fallen under the political power of converted Turks, so it was as individual sultanates, not as a united empire under the caliph, that they attempted alternately to resist or to appease the armies of Genghis Khan. Back of the Khan were the resources and mechanical skills of the conquered provinces of northern China and armies trained by eleven years of war in central and eastern Asia. The Moslem defense was almost worthless. One after another the great commercial, civilized cities of western Asia were taken or surrendered, Samarkand, Bokhara, Tashkent, Kish, Merv, Nishapur, finally even Herat in the heart of Khurasan. These names are today either forgotten or the echo of a geographical romanticism. Some still exist as names, miserable towns in Russia and Afghanistan. But in the thirteenth century they were large cities, some of them probably with more than a million inhabitants. Their fate under the Mongols never varied. They were looted, the women raped, the men slaughtered save for special craftsmen sent back as slaves to Mongolia, the walls destroyed and the entire city burned. Of course, the open country fared the same way. Even the fruit trees were cut down. It is impossible to know how many people the Mongols killed in that summer of 1219, but it ran in the millions and it did not end in that summer.

After Genghis' death, his son and successor, Ogdai, pushed the Mongol conquests westward and southward. Mesopotamia and Armenia were overrun, Tiflis and Kars destroyed in 1236. For a few years there were then no further inroads against the Levant while the Mongols carried the war westward into Hungary and Poland. It was again resumed, however, in 1251 under Hulagu, brother of Kublai, who took Baghdad itself, February 15, 1258, and slaughtered more than a million of its inhabitants. In 1260, Aleppo and Damascus fell.

From this ruin Islam and all the Levant never recovered. In these lands had begun the Levantine civilization. There Mazdaism and Judaism, the two ancient religions of this society, had risen, flourished and been so largely absorbed into the Nestorian Christianity and Mohammedanism of which they themselves had been the moral and intellectual source. Here had lain the origin of Levantine architecture and Levantine science. Africa, Spain, Byzantium, Arabia itself, had been only political or cultural provinces of a civilization whose home and source now lay a ravaged and bloody ruin.

But in the world of ideals it was a great triumph. It was not the triumph sought by the promoters of the ideals. It certainly was not the goal dreamed of by the millions who believed they were moved by these ideals. But it was still a triumph. The theory of the Sufis on the worthlessness of terrestrial life was indeed vindicated—at least for Levantines and it was to them that the theory had been addressed. The egalitarian demands with which Abu Moslim had helped establish the Albasid caliphate, upon which the Ismailiya had ridden to power and wealth, were at last fulfilled—in the unarguable equality of all the conquered.

Chapter 5:

The Envy of Less Happier Lands

UNDERSTANDING THE SEPARATE and almost personal existence of these five civilizations in which most of mankind has lived its history, it becomes possible to turn at last to the origin of Western society. Once we comprehend the self-contained existence of these other societies, our own becomes an intelligible entity. It becomes also possible to understand why the philosophy of liberalism can grant to these five civilizations no significant place in our image of the past. Their pattern of youth and aging, their tragedies and triumphs, five thousand years of history eastward of Pompey's line, do not lead to us, do not progress to democracy, liberal religion and the Western mechanical sciences. They cannot, therefore, be part of meaningful history as liberalism must see it. To preserve the fiction of the progress of mankind, we must ignore the history of the great bulk of men. To admit that there is meaning for us in the histories of these distant and alien societies is to admit that historical life, like significant personal life, has the structure of tragedy, that the great societies, like great men, are driven by creative ideas which can never be completely fulfilled nor ever reach in the world of time and space the eternity that lies in the ultimate core of each idea. Creative life must always assert as a principle what all conscious living knows to be untrue, that somewhere there lies a land beyond the dominion of death. Each society has been in its own way the living argument of that principle. Beyond the ephemeral men who have composed them each has created something that does endure, that asserts and seeks its own eternity. But they have not been eternal nor have the three that still live escaped the fate of all the living, some day to become aged and weary.

To see the history of men in a perspective sufficiently removed from our own values and our own presuppositions to grasp its pattern of life, and

296

of death, discloses it as a breathtaking tragedy, but not as a moral homily on civic virtue and human progress. The great societies of men have been the most passionate, the most all-embracing, soul-consuming endeavors in which it is possible for men to engage. Sometimes for thousands of years a society has molded its men to the pattern of its ideas, led them and driven them into the great arts, the great politics, the great sciences that are the glory of men and mark us as something deeply different from all the other living creatures of the earth. It has not been the innumerable savage tribes but the few great societies that have accomplished those things that make us proud to be men. But if we refuse to look eastward beyond the Roman frontier, we can hardly sense this, nor sense either the greatness or the limits of our own society and of our own time.

In our historical tradition, Pompey's line has served to conceal the unadmitted unity of human history. For there is such a unity though it is not the proclaimed unity of humanitarianism, internationalism, and egalitarianism. It is not the unity of universal interfertility among all men, which may well extend to the higher apes. (Scientific curiosity on this point is interestingly silent.) Nor is it the ancient unity of men as savages. The development by all men of the basic elements of human life, language, social organization, the use of fire, tools and arms, these things lie in a past so remote that this unity has been long superseded by the disunity of the historical cultures. The one unity of mankind today lies in the identical pattern of historical life, the fact that all vital events which have happened to men for the past five thousand years have happened to them as members of one of the great societies. For more than fifty centuries, almost all men whose lives have been significant to other men have been members of one of these societies, molded by that society, creating in accord with its values, seeing the universe with its eyes, comprehending first and last things according to the age of that society at the time in which they lived. And the few men who have been exceptions to this have been only the barbarian enemies or conquerors of one of these societies, Cyrus, Attila, Alaric, Stalin and Genghis Khan.

But there has been another barrier to historical understanding, this one in time, not space: the Renaissance and the Reformation. Where Pompey's line conceals the real unity of human history, the Renaissance and Reformation—or more accurately our misunderstanding of these events—disintegrate the real unity of Western history. For though both were real events, though both immensely influenced the future life of the West, neither did what the partisans of each said that it did. But our received history accepts these false claims almost at face value. Neither the Reformation nor the Renaissance broke Western history into two almost unrelated sections nor did either, as each claimed to do, restore an actually broken continuity with the finished history of an older and alien society. Yet our understanding of our own past is so clouded by the turmoil of these events and by their modern accepted interpretation that the connection of our own life to the Middle Ages is largely unseen and the immense significance of the first five hundred years of Western life is almost unknown. Just as all history outside the line-of-progress scheme is the ignored domain of the specialist, so the Middle Ages are considered the field of the romantic archaist, the dilettante and the religious enthusiast. Nor, in the atmosphere of liberalism, is this unreasonable. If we grant the Middle Ages a serious place in our scheme of human advancement, we have no problem with the story of progress but it becomes impossible to keep mankind in the tale. Once the Middle Ages are accepted as the normal, organically connected youth of our society, it becomes obvious that our progress scheme is only the causally argued, mechanistic interpretation of the development within the West itself of ideas, passions and interests that have been inherent in Western society since it began.

What we do, in effect, is evaluate the Reformation and the Renaissance not on the basis of historical fact but in accordance with the standards of a political or ethical philosophy. They are interpreted as conscious creations of men deliberately seeking guidance in a distant past. They are seen, in short, as an example of archaism though that condemnatory word is never applied. Such a view is certainly in part correct, but the interpretation does not stop there. We endow these movements with a fictional personality and the mind is then able to apply this fictional concept as a causative agent in the later history of the West. Western history under this analysis becomes the chance consequence of the survival of Biblical and Classical literature and of the accident that the men of the Reformation and Renaissance happened to base their programs on these survivals, and by the agitation of these programs molded all the future history of the West.

The result of this process is that we begin serious Western history with the fifteenth century in our scale of emphasis if not openly in the texts of our history books. Only when the later history of the West has been rounded out as a consistent system stemming from Levantine Christianity and Classical antiquity, do we go back and supply as an ornamental supplement some odds and ends of information about the Middle Ages. This information is always false by omission and often wrong in positive statement, but it furnishes what our scheme of received history demands: an almost mythical backdrop for what we feel are the real beginnings of Western history: the Reformation and the Renaissance.

Yet these movements were not the beginning but the mid-point of Western history and to see that history as it was really lived, it is necessary to approach the Middle Ages not as an unimportant prelude to the great re-awakening of humanity in the fifteenth century, but as the beginning of everything that we Westerners now are. Western society as an organic unity began in the cruel violence and anarchy following the barbarian invasion of the western provinces of the already Byzantine Roman Empire. There the basic biological stock was formed from the invaders and the surviving fragments of the older population, a basic stock that has since remained almost a closed group. There the generative ideas of our society soon reached symbolic expressions and have remained ever since the source of the greatness of the West and the mark of Western men. The organic unity of men and ideas formed in those dim centuries has never since been broken.

Classical society did not die of a sudden nor did the political structure of the Roman Empire vanish from the western provinces in a few decades of war and public turmoil. The process by which the eastern parts of the Roman Empire became the Orthodox Christian nation of the Levantine society has been touched upon, at least, in its non-political aspects. The processes, cultural and political, by which *both* Classical society *and* the Levantine Roman Empire disappeared from the west has not. That these grim events were to have immense bearing upon the unborn West is evident.

From the legal and cultural lines that tie us Americans back to England more than to any other nation of the West, our picture of the centuries following the destruction of Roman political power in Spain, Gaul and Italy is falsified by an unconscious extension to these lands of the type of change that occurred in Britain. There the Roman garrison was withdrawn in a single summer and all trace and living memory of Roman life in the island wiped out in a few decades. The original Celtic-speaking population—how thoroughly Romanized we do not know—was slaughtered or driven to the western hills and the Breton peninsula. How many survived to live on under the conquerors is unknown. Probably some did, particularly towards the west, but they carried with them into the future England nothing but their blood. No scrap of their historical culture—Roman or Celtic—survived with them. The cities of Britain were not taken over for spoil or pleasure but destroyed. Although some English cities stand on the sites of Roman towns, probably none, except perhaps London, remained an inhabited community during the Saxon conquest.[1] Christianity and every trace of

---

[1] The problem of the fate of London is difficult. The Anglo-Saxon Chronicle says the British fled there after a defeat at Crayford in 457. Then for a period of one hundred and fifty years the Chronicle gives no further mention of the city, and when London is again heard of it is a heathen Saxon city. Yet the unique juridical position of London, even under the earliest Saxon kings whose legislation has come down to us, suggests that it may never have been completely destroyed or abandoned. Much of its Roman wall still stood in the early Middle Ages.

Roman speech and custom were wiped from the Island. Among all the immense accretions of foreign words to the English language perhaps not one [2] was added from contact between the Saxons and the Latin-speaking Britons of the fifth century. History records few conquests so savage and so thorough as the Anglo-Saxon occupation of Roman Britain.

Thus to the English tradition the tie to a Roman past is only bookish, a tie of documents, sacred and profane, long afterwards brought across the Channel, of images conjured from the fate of others. Even the indirect tie to Roman sources through the Norman conquest was at two drastic removes before it reached English soil: the Danish Duchy of Normandy [3] and that most significant of all the transient political creations of barbarian times, the Kingdom of the Franks.

But this literary connection with Rome, which the English share with the Germans and Scandinavians, was not the only one. There is another of which Italy, Spain and France are witnesses, the maintenance from Roman times of at least enough continuity for the Latin speech and the Latin Church both to survive. And if these withstood the ruin of barbarian times, how many other subtle but vital continuities existed under the shattered political surface?

These are at bottom the two traditions in which the West sees its historical connection with the Classical society. In the one all that is not wholly literary is wholly Christian. It is Gregory the Great punning in the slave market of Byzantine Rome. It is Augustine and his royal convert King Aethelbryht, and his Christian and Frankish Queen Bryhta, and the ten thousand men of Kent baptized in a month.[4] But the strands of this thread are little Roman and far more complex. In it there is also Aidan and his Irish monks out of Iona setting their monastery on the bleak sand spit of Holy Island to preach the word to the heathen of Northumbria—and leave us one of the earliest records of our ancient tongue: the Lindisfarne Gospels. And indeed, these two strands cannot be separated. The Church of England was Irish-founded and Roman-organized. Augustine was the apostle of Kent, but Aidan was the apostle of England.[5] For though the Roman Church organization absorbed the structureless Irish Church, this strange compound of hermits, missionaries and secret Pelagian-

---

[2] At most, scholars hazard two, port and kiln. There are, of course, place names of Roman origin in Britain.

[3] So we call these people when they seized lands in England and Ireland. For no good reason, fashion calls them Northmen or Vikings when they seized part of France. They were all the same people, the contacts between Norway and Denmark being extremely close.

[4] December 597

[5] Joseph Lightfoot, Bishop of Durham (1828-1889)

ism,[6] this church that had never known the Roman secular power and had never been a Levantine nation, was one of the most vital elements in maintaining Christianity in Gaul and establishing it in Britain and Germany. St. Gall and St. Columbanus were only the most famous of the Irish missionaries to the continent during the seventh and eighth centuries. Kilian is still remembered at Würzburg, Virgil at Salzburg, Cathald at far-off Taranto on the heel of Italy. And although the Englishman, Winfrith, St. Boniface, first Archbishop of Mainz, who died a martyr's death among the Frisians, is remembered in tradition as the apostle to the Germans, he did little but gather into the Roman organization the Christian Franks, Thuringians and Bavarians long converted by the Irish.

But equally deep in Western life is the other tradition, one that seems so much more direct and so much more Roman. In the lower valley of the Rhône it would be easy to believe, on the surface of things, that Classical society had changed but never died. The Roman aqueducts still stand. Automobiles use the Roman roads between cities that were there before Augustus received the Imperium. At Nîmes on summer nights, the moving pictures play in the Roman arena. In the hills above Avignon a simple memorial still expresses the sorrow of a proconsul of Gallia Narbonensis for the death of a cherished wife. On the farms, in the village cafés, in the control towers of the airfields, and in the cabs of the locomotives, it is Latin that the people talk. True, it is not a Latin that Cicero could have understood, but it is still Latin. Here in the ancient Provincia Romana—more truly Italy than a province, said Pliny—never since the days of the Gracchi has the Latin speech been uprooted. Never has one generation spoken a language different from that of their parents. So, too, across the Alps, despite the harsh hand of the Lombard—far different from the easygoing Burgundian—and beyond the Pyrenees, despite Goth, Arab and Moor, the evidence of Rome and the Latin speech still endure. Even in Caesar's Gaul beyond the Cevennes, where Rome is only archaeology, the language is still Latin.

> *Car nulle fleur ne fait pâlir tes violettes,*
> *Ville de Périclès! Et ce n'est pas en vain*
> *Que par la bouche d'or du plus doux des poètes*
> *Le dieu promit à Rome un empire sans fin.*[7]

---

[6] They became officially orthodox on this point in the fifth century, but its influence lingered for centuries. The Irish Church did not accept the Roman obedience until the twelfth century.

[7] For no flower can fade thy violets
Oh city of Pericles. Nor was it vain,
That by the golden mouth of the sweetest of poets,
The god promised Rome an empire without end.
—Frédéric Plessis (1851-1942)

But it was in vain. The Latin tradition is as literary as that of the north. Where it differs from the tradition of the north it is only archaeology and etymology. All of us live amidst the ruins of some past. All of us speak a language of unknowable antiquity. All of us have ancestors as far back as there were men—and beyond. It is not these things, which all men share with all others, that mark or could create the differences among the societies of men.

The two processes of extinction of Classical society and rise of the Levantine civilization were occurring simultaneously in the late Roman Empire, but they were not at all points the same process. This confuses our traditional picture of the decline of that empire, even though we recognize that the results in east and west were altogether different. In the east and in Africa, Classical society died and was replaced by the Levantine, or converted itself to the Levantine if you prefer. But in the northwest, Levantine civilization never took root and there all that happened was the extinction of the Classical. Under all its immense detail, this is in essence the difference between the fate of Gaul and Italy and the fate of Africa, Syria and Thrace.

The death of Classical society was prefigured from the end of the third century. The spread of Levantine culture in all aspects of art and thought is apparent. But there was also an unarguable political event. Classical men no longer felt it necessary to defend themselves, or the government of the Roman state no longer felt it politically wise or possible to ask the Romans to continue this task—which amounts to the same thing. Classical society did not want to die, but it left to others the brutal task of being ready to wage war in its behalf. Whether this was from idealism or cowardice or from mere political stupidity, it had no influence on the outcome. After the end of the third century the Roman army in the west never again contained any Romans. In the east, despite the great increase in the use of barbarian troops, it was always possible to raise armies in Syria and Anatolia, and as time went on the Byzantine army became composed almost entirely of Byzantine nationals. In the west, the inhabitants of of Gaul, Italy and Spain ceased to serve in the army. From the early fourth century their place was taken by barbarians, chiefly Germans, serving for Roman pay.

At first a sharp and deceptive difference was maintained between individual barbarians enlisted in the regular Roman army and barbarian tribes accepted willingly or fearfully as auxiliaries. The former had to be Roman citizens, were under Roman discipline, and in the beginning under Roman officers who used the Latin language. In contrast, the barbarian auxiliaries retained their own tribal organization and aided or opposed the

Roman state as suited their own whims or their own notion of their immediate advantage. But by the opening of the fifth century this distinction had become blurred.

With the increased settlement of Germanic tribes within the borders of the empire, more and more Germans qualified as Roman citizens with less and less wash of civilization of any kind. The regular legions rapidly came to resemble the barbarous auxiliaries. So far did the process go that in late Latin the word *barbarus* became a synonym for *miles* as the ordinary word for "soldier." Sidonius Apollinarus considered it one of the highest military assets of Syagrius, the last Roman commander in Gaul, that he could speak to the Roman troops in their own language. He had a fluent mastery of German. In Spain and Italy the situation was no different save that in these provinces instead of the Saxons, Alamanni and Franks of Gaul, the army was composed chiefly of Goths and Vandals.

The Roman officers' corps followed the same course. Thus, by Constantine's reign men of barbarian origin and even barbarian chieftains held the highest commands. A chief of the Alamanni, Eroc (Crocus), was perhaps the principal force in raising Constantine to the throne, and Frankish officers were always his favorites. Mellabaude, a Frank, was commander of the imperial guard in 378, and two other Franks were even consuls in 366 and 377. In the late fourth and fifth centuries the entire command in the west was barbarian, the Franks: Bauto, Arbogast and Richomer; the Goths: Gainas, Sarus, Fravitta and the most famous of all, Stilicho the Vandal.

That these men and their barbarous soldiers were the lords of the western provinces long before the legal extinction of the empire is evident in every trace that has survived from these times. Stilicho took to wife no less a lady than the niece of Theodosius the Great, and the latter's son, the Emperor Honorius, married Stilicho's daughter. The maternal grandfather of Theodosius II was the Frank, Bauto. Perhaps the most subtle and revealing evidence of where power really lay, of the true style of the times, is in the names the Romans began giving their children. During the fifth century, more and more children of unmixed Roman ancestry began to receive Germanic names.

Only the last trappings of power were beyond reach of these barbarians who called themselves Romans. They could not themselves become Emperors, just as their subordinates could not receive the dignity of the municipal senates. Nothing else seemed to concern the Romans, and so the emperors in the west after Arcadius were empty figureheads, the prisoners of one or another barbarian general.

Even long after what we officially consider the end of the empire in the west, the superficial aspects of late Roman times remained undisturbed. With the exception of areas where the barbarians drove out the older inhabitants—or indeed found them already gone and settled in deserted countrysides—Britain, northern and eastern Gaul, Raetia, Pannonia, Noricum and Illyricum, the myriad municipal governments which constituted in fact the political fabric of the Roman state continued their nominal government. The early emperors had been magistrates, not kings, presiding over the fiscal and military affairs of an empire which in legal form was a collection of cities tied to Rome by treaties. The Levantine monarchy of Diocletian and his Christian successors, despite its immense apparatus of state and the mass of its universal—and unenforced—legislation, did not entirely supersede these local governments. Under the barbarians, they continued to govern the private affairs of the Romans, while the barbarians governed themselves and all relations between Romans and barbarians, which was precisely what the barbarian Roman army had done for more than a century. True, in the disorders of the times the cities became less and less populous as they were sacked and looted and as commerce disappeared in anarchy, but this, too, was not a new or sudden development. In the countryside, many of the great landlords still kept their huge estates and still maintained the traditional social life of a Roman country gentleman. They still paid taxes and bribes to a barbarian commander, and it made little difference when he was no longer the nominal agent of a far-off emperor. In the shrinking cities, public amusements still played for the masses.

In a sense the German barbarians never conquered the western provinces. These were given to them. The barbarian wars of the late empire were between barbarians who, calling themselves the "Roman" army, had already become masters of the west, and the barbarians from beyond the old borders who desired to share, too, in the loot of an ancient society. The newcomers were divided and never in large numbers. The empire of the first and second centuries would have had little trouble fending them off.

Thus, east and west, the two processes ended in different results. In the east the supine lethargy of ancient Hellas was replaced by the energy of men from Syria, Africa, Anatolia, and even Armenia and Dalmatia. But these men in general were not uncivilized barbarians. They were—though they were not conscious of it—Levantines. They thought of themselves as Christians and occasionally as Mazdaists and Jews and Neoplatonists. But the principal point is that they were neither barbarians nor Hellenes—that is, true Greeks of Classical Hellas. They spoke Greek, but they did not come from Greece, and few things are so striking in the Byzantine Empire, early and late, as the complete unimportance of all the ancient sites of Classical culture, Attica, the Peloponnesus, Syracuse and the Ionian Islands. From the time of Hadrian to the loss of the western provinces, the new men from the Levant colored the intellectual and artistic life of the whole empire. But as the west fell from the imperial grip, it became evident that firm though this new civilization stood in the east, it had made little impression in the sparsely settled, thinly Romanized provinces of the west. It had affected Italy, but too little to rally that land and too briefly to bring it within the orbit of Levantine civilization.

Thus while in the east the Classical population permitted itself to be taken over by men of a new civilization, in the west the Classical population permitted itself to be taken over by men of no civilization at all, by semi-savages from the vast wilderness stretching between the Caspian and the Rhine. In neither case did the Classical society put up any struggle. In both cases the forms of a legal continuity were maintained—which seemed to be all that could excite the jaded masses of the Classical cities. In the east, the Classical society was absorbed into the Levantine, at first Christian and then in time more and more Mohammedan, as it stands today. In the west, the Classical society died in barbarism. Where Egypt had thrown out the Hyksos and China had civilized the Mongols and the Manchus, where even India had kept its inner life under Moslem conquest, the Classical society—its ancient source in Hellas firmly in the power of a young, vigorous civilization—could neither guard its western provinces from the barbarians, nor expel them nor make civilized Romans of them.

Each of the great divisions of the Latin-speaking Roman Empire, Africa, Italy, Illyricum, Spain and Gaul suffered a different fate in this destruction of the Classical west. Africa, the only Latin-speaking area where Levantine civilization ever seriously took root, passed about the middle of the fifth century under the brief dominion of the Vandals. Before the middle of the sixth it had been reconquered by Justinian and remained within the empire until the Moslems occupied it about a century later. Gradually both the Latin language and the Christian faith withered away to be absorbed in the triumphant Levantine Protestantism of the Arabic Empire.

In Illyricum and the adjoining areas along the upper Rhine and Danube, the Roman population was killed or driven out and replaced by heathen barbarians, the Germans, towards the west, Slavs and Avars towards the east.

In Spain, there rose during the sixth century a Christian Gothic Kingdom, Arian to be sure, but at any rate not heathen. The Roman provincial population was left almost undisturbed and the Goths, themselves never very numerous, lost their Arianism and gradually fused with the older population. It was, however, a community sunk in semi-barbarism and inertia. The conquering Goths became as Romanized and as torpid as their conquered subjects. The Gothic holdings in Gaul were soon lost to the Franks. Justinian reconquered the southeast with almost no opposition, and when the Mohammedans, with Christian aid, crossed the Straits of Gibraltar in 711, they needed little more than a military parade to reach the Pyrenees. The Latin Church and the Latin language survived among the lower strata of society—though cut off from effective contact with the Latin West—but for centuries Spain became a Levantine country and for a time one of the glories of the Dar-al-Islam. Spain as a Western land was a Spain which was conquered nearly five hundred years afterwards by a handful of men, chiefly of Gothic descent, who had fled to the northern mountains, immensely reinforced by men from beyond the Pyrenees who were almost as hostile to the ancient Mozarabic Christians as they were to the Jews and Mohammedans.

In Italy, Classical society, or what remained of it, was destroyed in the fierce struggle of Byzantine and barbarian. Although tradition remembers Alaric's Goths as the destroyers of Rome because Alaric is accounted the first barbarian to have captured the city itself, his capture differed little from the usual siege and sack which was the lot of many Roman cities in the struggle between rival generals for the imperial throne. Even the sack of Rome by the Vandals in 455, while far more thorough than Alaric's, did not destroy the city nor seriously interrupt its normal life. Under Theodoric, Italy presented much the same aspect as it had under Constantine more than two hundred years before. The "Roman" army was perhaps more openly barbaric, but on the other hand better disciplined. The sovereignty of the emperor at Constantinople was more shadowy, but in recompense Theodoric permitted no rivals or pretenders to wage civil war in Italy. The Romans still thought of themselves as Romans, and there was nothing very new in having a barbarian army under barbarian command stationed in their midst. The great landlords still farmed their immense tracts with *coloni*. That there were also powerful Goths who held land was not strange. The army had been rewarded with land for three centuries and had been manned by barbarians for as long. The Roman aristocracy was still an aristocracy. In Rome itself, the games were still held in the circus. The unemployment relief, or what had been begun six hundred years before as unemployment relief, still furnished free food and amusement, a life of penurious idleness and vicarious sadism, to the masses of the city. And the city, useless and politically unimportant as it was, was still immense. Under Theodoric, its population was still several hundred thousand and its physical plant almost as magnificent as it had ever been.

The destruction of Roman Italy came not from the barbarians but from the Levant. But where Spain and Africa were absorbed by the Moslems, Italy was sacked by the Byzantines.

In 536, Belisarius, fresh from his success over the Vandals in Africa, landed in Italy. Theodoric was dead and at first the Gothic troops offered little resistance. Rome was easily taken and Justinian began recalling his army. Unhappily for the Byzantines, the Goths rallied under a new and able leader, Totila and a long, ruinous war began. Totila began the siege of Rome in 537, captured Naples in 543 and finally took Rome in 546. In 551, Justinian sent over Narses with a new army, mostly Lombards, Huns and rebel Mazdaists. In 552, he retook Rome and in 554 defeated the last Gothic army. Totila was dead and the Gothic power destroyed, but Italy was an utter ruin after eighteen years of a war of extermination. Rome itself, three times besieged and captured, was a wreck. Much of it had been burned, the aqueducts had been destroyed and for many miles about it the countryside had been rendered uninhabitable. Its population had shrunk to a tenth of what it had been under Theodoric. The last consul had been named in 541; the last circus was given by Totila in 549. The last triumph was held by Narses in 552. The last mention of the Senate was in 579. The final end of the Classical city came when Justinian suspended the unemployment relief. With this ended, there was no further possibility of an urban population existing in this city which had neither commerce nor manufacture and had long ceased to be a political capital. It became a village housed in the vast and crumbling ruins of antiquity, a village ministering to the wants of its bishop, the custodian of an immense historical museum living on the trade of pious tourists who, as the centuries wore on, began flocking to the eternal city from the wilds of the newborn West.

Into this ruin flooded the Lombards, a half-heathen, half-Arian Germanic tribe, which alone among the barbarian invaders of Italy was to leave any trace, ethnic, linguistic or political on the future of the peninsula. The Byzantine holdings were reduced to Ravenna, the Adriatic shore that was to become Venice, Rome and the far south. Independent Lombard principalities were set up in the south and center, and in the north arose the Lombard Kingdom with its capital at Pavia. This was no longer a matter of barbarians pretending to be the Roman Army and posing to their Roman subjects as possessed of legal credentials from the dim imperial power at Constantinople. This was naked and alien conquest, and medieval Italy grew from Lombard Italy just as medieval Gaul grew from Frankish Gaul. True, the Lombard state succumbed to the Frankish and their subsequent political histories diverged widely, but both states were the creation of powerful, un-Roman invaders. Both states were the earliest political foundation on which was afterwards raised the new civilization of the West.

The only enduring political creation of barbarian times was the Kingdom of the Franks. From it there was to descend, directly and indirectly, the greatest part of the political structure of the future West. From it has come the name by which Westerners—even Americans—are still known in the Levant—Franks. In fact, the difference between French, Français and Frank is only a difference of language. There was never a time in which a group of people called French existed in distinction to a group called Franks. Even the brief, revolutionary title of Louis XVI and Louis Philippe, Roi des Français, would be rendered in Latin by the ancient title of Clovis, Rex Francorum. But it would be a mistake to see in this fifth century agglomeration of uncivilized tribes, this kingdom by courtesy and lack of a better word, anything remotely Western. It was not Western, but it left a heritage of political fact that has underlain the entire history of the West

The Kingdom of the Franks was less the creation of the Frankish tribes than of one of the several petty kings of the Salian Franks, Clovis, the grandson of a partly real, partly mythical chief—his mother conceived him from a sea monster—a certain Merovech[8] who fought beside the "Romans" against Attila's invasion of Gaul. Where the Gothic kings in Spain and the early Lombard kings in Italy were the descendants of chiefs who had led their tribesmen, as solid tribes, over the Roman border, the Franks of northern Gaul by the end of the fifth century had no unity and apparently no memory of a common government. Clovis did not lead a people against Rome. He gained lordship over tribes that were already solidly in place. His first strike for power was to defeat the last nominally Roman army in Gaul and incorporate its remnants—all Germans, of course—in his own. He then destroyed his rival Frankish kings scattered from modern Brabant to Maine and became the undisputed master of northern Gaul. Later he acquired supremacy over the Ripurian Franks of the Moselle and middle Rhine, conquered the Alamanni in modern Alsace and Baden and drove the Goths from their huge dominions between the Loire and the Pyrenees. Though he had less success against the Burgundians of the Saône and Rhône valleys, his successor annexed these, he had created in a few years the most powerful military force anywhere in the ruined west of the Roman Empire. But it was much more a personal than a tribal creation.

Besides his conquests, Clovis took another step which in his time was of great political advantage and was likewise to have long consequences in the future. He accepted Christianity, but unlike all the other Christian barbarian kings, he became a Catholic, not an Arian. He was baptized by St. Remy at Rheims, an event long remembered in the consecration of the kings of France. It had not the slightest effect on his treacherous,

---

[8] Latin, *Merovaeus*, Fr. *Mérovée*, whence the name of the Merovingian dynasty.

cruel and ambitious character, but in his own time it brought to his support the Roman bishops, who were then the real rulers of such towns as were left. It was a source of strength against the Arian Burgundians and Goths. It must also have made his rule seem more acceptable, or at least more legitimate, to his Gallo-Roman subjects.

Clovis' conquest of Gaul was accomplished largely with Frankish armies, and the Franks became a privileged group in his kingdom, but they do not seem to have dispossessed the Gallo-Romans. In most of the north and east, they and other Germanic tribes had already become the entire population and as far as the Loire there were fairly large, though perhaps isolated, Frankish settlements. Beyond the Loire, the Franks seem to have been primarily a political power. But the most important point was that though this dominion was called the Kingdom of the Franks, it was, in fact, not a state nor a kingdom nor a tribal conquest. It was the personal property of an individual. It was in reality the Kingdom of Clovis and all of it, Frank or Roman, was seen by its master and his successors in no other view than as their personal property.

They attempted to keep the remnants of the Roman tax system, primarily direct land and personal taxes, but only as a source of private enrichment. Their own Germanic speech never having been reduced to writing, they continued the use of Latin for the few records they kept. Their apparatus of state consisted only of single individuals placed as unrestricted autocrats over designated areas. Copying the Byzantines, they called these persons counts, but they bore no relation either to the count as government official of Byzantium or the count as feudal lord in the Western Middle Ages. The early Merovingian counts were appointed, removed and often executed at the king's pleasure, and their sole function was to extract as much wealth as possible from the fraction of the king's property placed in their temporary custody.

The system did not work for long. The Roman tax structure assumed the continuing existence of reliable records, something entirely beyond the capacity of the Merovingians, and in short order the king no longer knew who owed what. The sole revenue became whatever sum the king could exact from those unlucky enough to fall in his immediate power. Also, naturally, the counts stole for themselves, and the only dependable source of revenue soon became the fees that could be exacted from the dwindling flow of commerce wherever a place could be found through which it was forced to pass: harbors, bridges, ferries and mountain passes. Even these were soon appropriated for themselves by the king's agents assigned to collect them.

There is no indication that anyone, Frank or Gallo-Roman, felt an obligation of loyalty to anyone. Terror and bribery were the exclusive instruments of power, personal, political and ecclesiastical. Monogamy, except as a nominal form, was unheard of, and the only requirement of a bishop was that out of deference to an ancient convention he put aside his women when he assumed the episcopal office. This was not because a virtuous life was considered a worthy though unattainable goal. The bishop was like the holy man of innumerable savage tribes, a man set apart from his fellows and surrounded by taboos inapplicable to them. Later even this faded and all that remained was a bar against legal marriage.

Such a state of affairs obviously could not last. With command of neither loyalty nor a firm revenue, the king had to pay his bribes in land, not—as long afterwards—in the form of feudal tenure, but as outright possession. Naturally his counts tried to make themselves strong enough to keep their advantageous positions by their own power, and their sons tried to retain them. Since the kingdom was considered the personal property of the king, it was treated upon his death like any other private property and divided among his sons. The tribal Germanic custom of an elective kingship almost disappeared against this concept of inheritable private property.

Nevertheless, despite the frequent divisions, there was a growing feeling that the Kingdom of the Franks was some sort of a unit. The various parts always retained kings of the line of Clovis. As these kings died or were assassinated the fractioned pieces would always be put back together again. In time the realm tended to divide into three sub-kingdoms, Neustria, Austrasia and Burgundy, in the first two of which tradition has tried to see the origin of France and Germany. It is a vain attempt. Austrasia in the seventh century extended from the right bank of the Rhine across modern Belgium and Champagne into Aquitaine. It had no common bond of origin or language. It had been the arbitrary share of Clovis' eldest son and by the accident that for more than a century his successors had but one heir, it was not divided. This alone created its "nationality."

We do not know the origin of the magnates. Probably they were largely of Frankish descent, particularly in the north and east, but by the seventh century there had been much intermarriage and probably more interbreeding with the richer Gallo-Romans. In any event, they were not a nobility. Power and wealth were obtained by those who could get them and kept by those who were strong enough. Obviously a powerful father was an asset to a son, but in this society of every man for himself, men and families rose and fell rapidly. The only means of power were wealth and royal favor, both of which were precarious.

Even back in the time of Clovis, it is not known how much of a Roman landed aristocracy still remained after nearly a century of barbarian wars. But for a time there still continued to be subjects of the early Merovingian kings who insisted on their descent from the provincial senatorial order of

Roman Gaul. There may also have been a Frankish aristocracy of blood—the *aethelings* of Saxon England, the *adelenc* of Burgundy, but no document attests it in Frankish lands, and if it existed, it and the remnants of the senatorial order had vanished by late Merovingian times. Power was in the hands of those who could keep it by their own strength and cunning.

For two centuries the history of the Frankish kingdom—or more accurately kingdoms, for it was often divided—is known to us as little more than the chronicles of impolitic and often savage reigns, of endless civil wars for personal ambition, personal vengeance, of treachery and murder. Only the tradition of royal power, not its reality, survived, but the existence even of the tradition was something new. The Merovingians after a few reigns no longer ruled, but they did constitute a dynasty, even if it was a dynasty of assassinated and imprisoned kings. In immense contrast to the Roman Caesars, the blood of Merovech continued to occupy the throne.

The last Merovingian who exercised any real authority was Dagobert (629—639), and his authority was only a brief restoration. By his time, the magnates in the three divisions of the kingdom had gained most of the power and asserted the right to name the "mayor of the palace," originally the king's personal administrator, but increasingly a man able to convert his ministerial delegation into the personal possession of all the governmental power in the kingdom. The family that obtained the right to be mayors of the palace in Austrasia in the reign of Dagobert, that of Arnoul and Pepin, was to have an important future, but for more than a century after Dagobert nominal Merovingian kings were maintained on the throne while such real political power as remained in the Frankish state was exercised by the mayors of the palace in its three regions.

The establishment of the Frankish kingdom did not arrest the decay of civilized life in Gaul. The ruin of Classical society that became evident from the late third century continued under the Franks. The process is apparent in every aspect of life, and in such a far corner of the world as sixth century Gaul it is not confused by a concurrent rise of Levantine civilization. In Gaul nothing grew. Everything withered.

Under the early Merovingians, there were still "cities" in Gaul, that is, fortified Roman towns with populations perhaps between three thousand and six thousand, probably about one-fifth of what they had had in the second century. These were to become the *cités* of France, a town however small which, having once been a Roman *civitas,* was the seat of a bishop. In addition there were inhabited communities, generally smaller than the "cities," known as *vici.* The names of more than a thousand of these are known from early Merovingian times. By the end of this dynasty, all had disappeared while the number and the population of the "cities" continued to decline.

What little evidence exists concerning the economic activity of Merovingian Gaul confirms the disappearance of urban life. All the mechanical arts—never too robust among the Romans—withered to almost nothing. Architecture as an art ceased entirely after the sixth century, and as a technique almost stopped. To build in stone became beyond the capacity of the era and similarly with every craft, iron work, ceramics, except that of the silversmith which continued in active practice—but solely for religious articles. The great fair held regularly at Lendit near Paris traded in not a single fabricated article. Wine, honey and madder constituted the sum of commercial life by the year 700. The important Mediterranean carrying trade, which despite the barbarians still flourished in the fifth century, declined during the sixth and came to an end in the seventh as did the much more slender flow of commerce down the Danube to Constantinople and the Black Sea. It is customary to blame the Avar invasions of Central Europe for the second and the Moslem domination of the Mediterranean for the first, but the problem is not so simple. The collapse of commerce in Gaul had begun long before Mohammed was born and the Moslem power in the middle sea never interrupted Moslem-Christian maritime commerce in the east. Several centuries later the Western Christians found no difficulty in carrying on a profitable trade with the Moslems. The commerce of Gaul disappeared from the Mediterranean in the seventh century because there was no longer any commerce in Gaul itself.

The records of coinage tell the same story, plus the story of the disintegration of Merovingian royal power. The early kings merely continued minting Roman coins, both gold and silver, and not for many reigns did a Frankish king dare remove the Roman inscriptions and mint coins with his own effigy. But the royal monopoly did not last long. By the end of the sixth century, cathedrals, monasteries, prominent individuals, many of the *vici,* all were minting their own coinage, increasingly poorly struck and increasingly debased. By the opening of the eighth century gold ceased to be minted at all, (five hundred years later Louis IX minted the first gold coins of France). By the end of the eighth century even silver was rarely coined any more. Commerce gave place to a trickle of local barter.

The literature of Merovingian times was almost nil. In the fifth century there were still copyists of the Classical tradition—Ausonius in particular. In the sixth there was the chronicle of Gregory of Tours, written in a Latin of which the author, though descended from the senatorial class, was no longer the master. He knew enough to know that the Latin of his time was ungrammatical, but he did not know what that grammar ought to be. After him there was the author of an anonymous chronicle of Burgundy written in the same kind of Latin but worse. That was the end. Thereafter through Merovingian, and in truth even Carolingian times, Latin literature, even by the broadest definition, disappeared from the lands of the Franks. The language survived after a fashion, but it was used only for official purposes. Concerning Germanic literature, the evidence is less documented but equally clear. It had once existed, an immense series of barbaric epics, fragments of which—much modified by later times—survive from Germany, England and Iceland. The cognate material among the Franks had apparently become all but forgotten by the eighth century since Charlemagne had it recorded to prevent its complete disappearance. (These texts have not survived.) The memories from both sides of their ancestry were becoming dim beyond recall to the Franks of the eighth century.

Not only was the chain of language snapped. So was that of thought. The texts of Classical literature were not destroyed in the political fall of the empire. That literature still survived, probably in toto, to the middle of the sixth century. But by the end of the eighth there was less than the fragments we have today. Nor does it seem to have been lost through the accidents of war and public disorder. Most of it was destroyed to use the parchments upon which it was written for some more immediate purpose. To this value had the Classical past sunk to the men of the seventh century.

Even Christianity as a living faith did not survive except that out of deference to a sacred convention of our society we say that it did. The religion of Merovingian Gaul bore no resemblance either to the sayings of Jesus or the beliefs of the church that grew from Septuagint Jewry. Nor had it more than an organizational and textual connection with medieval Western Christianity. What existed in Merovingian Gaul was ignorant and universal superstition. Quite aside from the fact that there were almost no rural churches and that the *coloni,* as of old, worshiped wells and trees, the church of the episcopal towns had lost all touch with its source. Greek, of course, was an unknown language, and the most distant ecclesiastical horizon in Gaul reached only to the single patriarchate of which Gallic Christians knew, the see of Rome. They no longer knew that Rome was only one of five patriarchal sees. Beyond their own patriarchate, the only one within whose jurisdiction Latin was permitted as the sacred language, they knew nothing. They drew no real belief or standards of action out of the holy texts in their custody. These to them were no more than a magic rigmarole efficacious to appease mysterious powers. The intellectual level of the Merovingian church is attested by the fact that neither heresy nor theological discussion, neither devotional writings, nor mysticism, nor the desire to proselytize, ever developed within it. The church was indistinguishable from the base level of the laity. Only the monasteries offered a contrast, and that not by a higher level of thought or learning—but by complete withdrawal from the world about them. Only one of the great orders which later were to play such a tremendous part in the religious

and secular life of the West had yet been founded and that one, the Bene-
dictine, was still small and undistinguished. Indeed, its rule that monks
should live an active even though religious life, should farm and practice
handicrafts and spread improved knowledge of these techniques among the
laity, was strongly disapproved in the anchorite mood of the times. The
Merovingian church was the bishops, but these bishops were the creatures
of the debauched and incompetent kings who alone appointed them and
alone dictated to the increasingly infrequent Church Councils of Gaul.
The character of these kings, the baseness of their personal and political
lives, was fully reflected in most of the men they appointed as bishops. The
Roman Curia, itself in little better shape after the Byzantine invasions and
the Lombard conquest, had no shadow of power in Gaul.

It is true that by late Merovingian times, the church became rich—that
is, it held a larger proportion of the physical property of Gaul than at any
time before or since, but it was only a larger share in the universal poverty
and a testimonial to the depth of the general superstition. From the view of
either earlier or later times the only thing Christian about the Merovingian
Church was that it was the custodian of the sacred texts, texts which it
could scarcely read and from which it drew no real belief. The manuscript
as a magic talisman was more powerful than the content.

In truth, in this human debris of seventh-century Gaul nothing had
survived, either from the wilds of Germany or the civilizations of Rome or
of the Levant. What was alive under the last of the Merovingians was no
more than what is alive among all men, civilized or savage, the minimal
components of all human life: language, belief in supernatural powers, and
the mastery of some men over others. There was no memory or living
tradition of any other way of life. Rome and Germany had alike become
myths. Christianity was a name applied to the contemporary superstitions
of semi-savages. There were books, but few could read them, and these
could not understand them. What later times were to do in the name of
these books, sacred and profane, has no bearing on the life of the seventh
century Gaul. For the men of that time the books could as well not have
existed. The links with the past were severed. "Man" had returned, the
undifferentiated savage—or the newborn babe.

Into this drab ruin there reached in the opening decades of the eighth
century the long shadow of the Arabic Empire. It was not, as we sometimes imagine it, the clans of Arabia marching against Christian Gaul.
It was almost the whole Levant, suddenly brought into a political unity,
at last freed of every trace of the Classicism that had fractured the unity
of the Christian Levant. The Arabs were the political surface. The power of
their empire was the now mature civilization of the Levant.

From their occupation of Spain, the Moslem armies annexed southern Gaul without difficulty. In 732 they set out to destroy the apparently feeble remains of the Frankish kingdom. Perhaps if they had won their first battle, they might have duplicated what they had so easily accomplished in Spain. Contrasting the barbarous wreckage of Gaul with the complex, civilized world of the Arabic Empire, it is difficult to suppose that a decisive Moslem victory would not have made the fate of Gaul identical with the fate of Spain. Once the first levy of the Frankish troops had been destroyed, the feeble physical and moral resources of the corrupt and decadent kingdom hardly offered the chance of a rally. Most of the individual magnates of Gaul would have sought their own private welfare by submission to the Moslems as their counterparts in Gothic Spain had done, as in fact the Franks of the south had already done. A Moslem-held Gaul would have been another Spain, but with the immense difference that three hundred years later there would have been no France to attack the Moslem power from without and undermine it from within. There would have been only the weak Saxon Kingdoms of England, the stub of heathen Germany and distant Scandinavia beyond the power of the caliphs. Before it had even come into existence as a historical personality, the West faced destruction, faced being warped, not by books but by political and military facts, into a Levantine mold. Not until our own time has the life of the West ever hung in such a precarious balance as it did in that far away autumn of the year 732, when it did not yet exist.

But the first great battle was not won. There have been many battles that must have altered the history of the world, but in the history of the West, there was probably none of such immense consequence as that fought near Tours in October, 732. It was not a decisive military victory for the Franks. They merely held their own against the Moslems and the latter deemed it prudent to withdraw pending another attempt. They never had an opportunity to make it. A Berber revolt delayed them and detached part of their strength. A second invasion which reached Lyons, in 739, was unable to force the Franks to a decisive battle. Eleven years later the Abbasid revolution dethroned the Ommiads and ended the political unity of the Arabic dominions. Spain under an Ommiad prince, soon to proclaim himself an independent and rival caliph, was no longer the western province of a world empire.

The Byzantine conquest of northern Italy had been undone by the Lombards. The Arabic conquest of Gaul was blocked by the Franks. The soil of the future West had become beyond the military reach of the Levant, Christian or Moslem.

The man who organized the defense of Gaul was Charlemagne's grandfather, Charles surnamed Martel (the Hammer), illegitimate son of Pepin of Herstal, Mayor of the Palace of Austrasia. Charles Martel, as much as Charlemagne, was the founder of the latter's empire, and legend has with reason confounded the lives and actions of the two men. They mark a new turn in the history of the Frankish Kingdom. Indeed the roots go back to Pepin of Herstal who established the first firm Frankish power over all the German tribes, except the Saxons, and based his power less on bribing the distant magnates of all Gaul than on appealing to the vague loyalty and vigorous ambitions of his own Austrasians, high and low. Although Charles Martel continued a fictitious Merovingian king and left it to his son Pepin the Short to end the Merovingian dynasty and become in name as well as fact King of the Franks, Charles nevertheless established a new government in the Frankish dominions. Like his father's it was a government of his own associates from the Germanic parts of Austrasia. With it his grandson created the Carolingian Empire.

This short-lived dominion of the Carolingians, lasting little more than a century, is with good warrant felt to be the beginning of Western political history. From the earliest times, Charlemagne has been counted as Charles I and his son as Louis I in the lists both of the kings of France and of the medieval German emperors, the so-called Holy Roman Emperors. There is no doubt that the future political structure of the West developed to an extraordinary extent from this empire. The first tentative beginning was made at driving back the Moslems in Spain. The heathen Saxons were finally overcome and the Frankish dominions extended firmly to the Elbe. To contain the so-called Avars in what was to become modern Hungary, Carinthia and most of modern Austria were occupied. Scandinavia and Bohemia were brought into touch with the Frankish world. The Lombard Kingdom in central and northern Italy was annexed, beginning that long political association between Italy and Germany that was to last till the nineteenth century. Thus the Carolingian dominions were identical with the lands that have always been the core and source of Western society, Tuscany and Lombardy, France, the Low Countries and Germany west of the Elbe. Our society has extended its area beyond this original source, and since the sixteenth century, vastly beyond it, by settlement, by conversion and by conquest. But directly or indirectly all these settlements, conversions and conquests go back to the men and states of the ancient core.

The Carolingian Empire has often been called a renaissance. Charlemagne is credited with repairing the battered Latin of his time, of founding schools and encouraging study of the Classical Latin authors. By the end of the eighth century there could have been no confusion in anyone's mind of the distinction between Latin and the currently spoken language of the non-Germanic parts of the Carolingian domains. Whatever it was, and it differed between northern and southern Gaul, in Lombardy and still again in Tuscany, it no longer bore an intelligible relation either to what Latin had once been, or to the debased Latin of the church or that handed down since the times of Clovis as the language of record of the Merovingian court. It was this latter language that Charlemagne restored, recognizing, whether consciously or not, that it was no longer a spoken language and that there was no further need to be concerned about its relation to the spoken Romance tongues or of theirs to it. He also founded schools, one in each diocese, in which this corrected Latin—and little else —was taught, and he collected and prepared new copies of the surviving Classical literature. He established a new caligraphy in place of the debased and almost illegible letters of the Merovingian manuscripts. These were accomplishments of great importance for the future, but they hardly deserve the name of renaissance even if that name is applicable to any human event. The general intellectual level of the Frankish dominions remained what it had been, barbarous.

But if the Carolingian Empire was not a renaissance, it was in substance a revolution. It brought into power a new group of men. It not only replaced the decadent Merovingians on the Frankish throne, it drastically reduced the power of the church, whose abbots and bishops, like the Merovingian counts, had appropriated to themselves the royal power delegated to them. It likewise replaced the Merovingian magnates and even many of those in the Lombard lands.

It is true that lordship over land, and therewith over agricultural labor, went far back into imperial Roman times. It is true also that the triumphant barbarians did not disturb this system beyond appropriating for themselves many of the lordships. They set no tenants free and, indeed, introduced similar systems in the areas of solid Germanic settlement. In our passion, therefore, to see history as the history of institutions, there is a tendency to attach great significance to the continuance of tenant land tenure under the barbarians. But in reality this is of little significance. The point about agricultural land is not who works it, nor even who technically owns it, but who commands it. Who is its lord?

The Merovingians altered the lordship of the lands of Gaul though we do not know exactly to what extent, but the Carolingians altered it almost completely. Not that they suddenly transferred all the titles. They disturbed neither the tenants nor the still numerous holders in fee simple. But during their reigns there was a group of new men whose descendants were to become, and long remain, the political masters and the lords of most of the arable land of western Europe. The process was somewhat slow and by no means peaceful, but it stemmed from this origin.

In his struggle against his father's widow and his own legitimate nephews, Charles Martel built himself an army in the Germanic parts of Austrasia. Naturally, most of these men were of little social or economic consequence. For his wars against the Frisians, Saxons and Avars he drew more men from this source. It was this army, with a proportion of trained horsemen unusual for a Frankish army, that gave him dominance in Neustria and Burgundy and enabled him to check the Moslems. He faithfully rewarded these new men with possession of the vast lands of the church. He did not grant them title—ecclesiastical law forbad such alienation—but he gave them an indefinite right to the income of these lands, the benefice, which became later known as the fief. For the continuing administration of his dominions, he drew on the same men and again suitably provided for them with lands whose usufruct had formerly gone to others. Both his son and his grandson continued this policy, the latter making the grants legally hereditary, and by the death of Charlemagne there was hardly a corner of this huge empire that was not directly or indirectly under the command of one of these upstarts from Austrasia or even from beyond the Rhine.

But there was another component of this political embyro of the West, the church and the see of Rome. Between Justinian's reconquest of Italy and the rise of the Arabic Empire, the pope had been no more than another Byzantine patriarch. Whatever pretensions of supremacy, temporal or spiritual, may have been nursed in the intimacy of the curia these pretensions, if they existed, were strictly private. Even Gregory the Great, pope from 590 to 604, more than any one the literary founder of the tradition of the supremacy of the throne of St. Peter, was in fact little more than a Byzantine count in the temporal government of Italy and in spiritual matters outside his own archdiocese, only the author of hortatory epistles. "I am so storm-tossed in the seas of this world," he wrote in what is an accurate self-appraisal of the papacy and the Latin church at the turn of the seventh century, "that I cannot guide into port the ancient, half-rotten vessel to whose command the obscure designs of God have assigned me. . . . I tremble because I feel that once my vigilance is relaxed, the cesspool of vice will grow and against the raging storm the rotten planks will crack in shipwreck."

The position of the papacy grew steadily worse. By the time of Charles Martel the Lombard dominions were within forty miles of Rome and the Emperor Leo III had transferred ecclesiastical jurisdiction over Calabria, Sicily, Dalmatia and the Balkans from the see of Rome to that of Constantinople. Even as a Byzantine patriarchate, the papacy was sinking towards insignificance. In his extremity the pope turned even to the church robber of Gaul, but Charles was more interested in military assistance from the Lombards against the Moslems than in spiritual recompense from a grateful pope. But with Pepin the Short, the situation changed. Pepin wished to take the title of King of the Franks, and he feared to do so by the simple exercise of his own power. Meaningless as the Merovingian kingship had become, Pepin felt the need of a moral sanction to end it. The pope at last had something to give for what he wanted to get.

At Soissons in November, 751, Pepin went through the old Frankish ceremony of having himself elected by his magnates and then—something radically new—was annointed by Boniface, the pope's representative. For the first time there was a king in Europe "by the grace of God." Pepin never used the exact phrase, *Dei gratia, rex,* which with his successor became and still remains the titular formula of the kings of the West, but in an archaic form he styled himself the same way.[9] To that far-off date goes the origin of the doctrine of the divine right of kings. It was not, as later times came to misunderstand it, that royal absolutism was a divine institution. It was a personal matter. In order for a man to be legally king, he had to obtain his right to that office from God, a grant symbolized by consecration which only the church could perform. The image is from the Old Testament, Samuel, Saul and David, but as a political reality the idea had never operated in the Levant. No Byzantine emperor or caliph ever so received the divine attributes of his position. In the Levant there was no church as a poltical entity separate from the laity. Ex officio, the Commander of the Faithful held his trust by the grace of God.

What the pope desired in return was soon disclosed to Pepin. In October of 753 Stephen II set off over the Alps to confer with the new king at the abbey of St. Denis. There can be little doubt that he brought with him a recently composed document,[10] possibly even composed for the occasion, that was to have a long future in the West, so long that it is worth a brief consideration.

The document opens with the statement that it is the act of Flavius Constantinus, Emperor of the Romans, who in recognition of a miraculous recovery from leprosy and in gratitude for his conversion to the Christian faith by the personal efforts of Pope Sylvester, desires to assure to the pope, and to his successors as representatives of the Prince of the Apostles, a more ample power than that which he himself holds as emperor. He, therefore, first accords the pope and his successors primacy over the Patriarchs of Antioch, Jerusalem, Alexandria and Constantinople as well as over all the churches of the universe.

[9] For instance: *Juvante nos Domino, qui nos in solio regni instituit . . . Incipientia regni nostri . . . auxiliante Domino . . . Diplom Karol.* v. 1, No. 14, 25.

[10] Following G. H. Bohmer, in Herzog-Hauk *Realencykl.* (1902) and L. Halphen, *Charlemagne,* etc. (Paris 1947) there is some controversy on the point. See E. B. 11th ed. Article "Donation of Constantine."

For this purpose, continues the grantor, "to the blessed pontiff, our Holy Father Sylvester, the universal pope, to him and to his successors, we grant and yield . . . the City of Rome and all the provinces, all the localities, all the cities, both throughout Italy and in all the regions of the west, and by an irrevocable decision of our imperial authority, by virtue of this holy edict and this decree, we grant these in full possession to the Holy Roman Church, that she may enjoy them forever. Also we have judged it fitting to transfer our empire and the exercise of our authority into the eastern regions . . . because there where the dominion of the priests and the capital of the Christian religion have been installed by the Heavenly Emperor, it is not just that the earthly emperor should exercise his power."

In some respects the most extraordinary point about this extraordinary document is the evidence it furnishes of how utterly the Latin world had lost all touch with the past, even the past of the church. Possibly the forger was aware of the gross anachronisms in his composition but even if he was, he must have been certain that no one else, layman or cleric, could detect them. In the time of Constantine, Alexandria, Rome and Antioch were the only patriarchates.[11] The bishop of Constantinople was not such until 381 and Jerusalem was not so ranked until the Council of Chalcedon, more than a century after Constantine's death. These elementary facts must have been unknown in the Latin Church—for the papacy, if it still knew them, could not count on a conspiratorial cooperation from all the Gallic and Lombard bishops—or the forger would not have dared traverse them. So, too, all knowledge of the Christian emperors after Constantine must have been lost, or questions concerning the inapplicability of the Donation under such a pious emperor as Theodosius would have been raised. Along with knowledge, all abstract critical sense must have perished, for how explain the silence of writers like St. Ambrose and St. Augustine on such a vital ecclesiastical matter? But no one questioned the genuineness of this brazen fabrication.[12]

---

[11] Canon Six of The Council of Nicea in 325.

[12] It was first labeled a forgery in the eleventh century by Leo of Vercelli, Chancellor of the Emperor Otto III, but it was almost universally accepted as genuine by partisans of both pope and emperor until Laurentius Valla attacked it in 1440, beginning a controversy that lasted until the end of the eighteenth century.

Of it Dante said: (*Inferno* XIX, 115-17)

Ahi, Constantin, di quanta mal fu matre,
Non la tua conversion, mal quella dote
Che da te prese il primo ricco patre!

Oh Constantine, of how much harm the mother,
Not thy conversion, but that gift
Which the first rich pope took of thee.

The Spanish Inquisition expunged these verses from editions of Dante allowed to circulate in Spain.

Worse still, even in the Curia the chain of dogma seemed to have weakened. In his zeal to establish title to temporal power, the forger overlooked a vital point of Catholic dogma. Since when did the supremacy of the pope over all the bishops of Christendom stem from a grant by a temporal emperor? Was the succession of St. Peter and Matthew xvi, 18 no longer a sufficient title?

It is obvious also that the forger was not at all concerned with another indirect, but vital point concealed in his composition. The document sets out the papal position in the west with complete clarity, but what of his position in the east? In church matters he is supreme over not yet existing patriarchs, but what is his position with the terrestrial emperor? The very act of withdrawing imperial power from the west implies that it cannot be subordinated to the ecclesiastical and by the same considerations must be still supreme in the east. But this did not bother the forger. In his time all the patriarchates of the east were in the hands of the caliph and the basileus, and the one would have been as willing as the other to admit papal authority into his dominions. The forger had no interest in the east. Papal supremacy over its patriarchs was a pose solely for western eyes. His only concern was the Latin Church and the papal supremacy in· Latin lands. The Western Catholic Church as a political entity had begun.

The immense sovereign power to which the pope appeared to be morally entitled by this Donation seems not to have impressed Pepin as it was not to impress his temporal successors down to our own time. What he promised is unknown, but what he performed was substantially nothing. He intervened against the Lombard kings to the extent of giving the pope Ravenna, which the Lombards had just captured from the Byzantines, but he did not materially strengthen the pope's temporal position in Italy and he firmly refused to give the papacy any effective supervision over the Frankish Church. Under Charlemagne, the pope's position in reality became even worse, for though Charlemagne annexed the Lombard Kingdom, this merely substituted the powerful Franks for the weak Lombards as the pope's opponents in Italy. Far from gaining anything toward which the Donation looked, the only result accomplished by bringing the Franks into Italy was to make the papacy for more than a century an adjunct to the Frankish crown.

The event of Charlemagne's reign on which our progress-history most insistently dwells was his revival of the Roman imperial title, an insistence that tends—at times, seeks—to confuse the revival of the title with the revival or the intended revival of the empire itself. Few historical confusions are more absurd. An age in which such a forgery as the Donation of Constantine could be used in a practical political maneuver had so lost every link with even the Christian Empire that it would have been impossible to conceive of a revival. What they would have had to revive was unknown to them. They knew there had been a Roman Empire in the west, but this was, in reality, as far as their knowledge went. Also it was as far as their interest went. The Roman Empire was valueless to them. They would not have revived it even if they had known what to revive and had had the power to revive it. But the title of Emperor of the Romans had a contemporary value, not as reminiscent of a forgotten past, but as a useful political tool of the moment. At Constantinople the hated Greek emperor still called himself—when his Greek was translated —Emperor of the Romans, and the despised Greeks who refused to acknowledge the supremacy of the Latin and Frankish Church also called themselves Romans. The correspondence of the later Carolingian emperors, particularly Louis II, show that hostility to the Byzantines, not any archaistic dreams of the past, was the emotional force behind the revival of the title.

We moderns, with centuries of historical scholarship at our disposal, with centuries of a literary tradition asserting our tie to Rome, almost always see Charlemagne's empire as a vital link in this precious continuity. It comes as something of a shock to realize that he did not. We know the history of Rome, republic and empire, pagan and Christian. He did not. To him it was a few names and a maze of myths. On the other hand, we ignore as transitory phenomena of no future importance the political realities at the turn of the ninth century, the mighty empire of the caliph at Bagdad embracing all Africa, Egypt and Syria, possessing the preponderant naval power of the inner sea; the less powerful but still imposing Ommiad dominion in Spain; shrunken but great Byzantium, still a naval power, still the lord of Sicily and Sardinia, master of the Venetian coast and of Naples. But Charlemagne did not see these as we do, as unimportant temporary political creations that were not headed in the right historical direction. To him they were the world in which he lived, they were the great political powers with whom he had to deal, the civilized lands, the culture and technology of which far surpassed his own. As a model for his people he needed no dishonest literary reminiscence of the bygone and imaginary glories of Roman civilization. He had under his eyes the example of a civilization far above the semi-barbarism of the Frankish and Lombard lands.

But this we prefer not to understand though it is a commonplace phenomenon of world history—Romanoff Russia copying the mature West and posing, even like Charlemagne to the imperial title, as the heir of Byzantium; the Byzantines themselves in their time copying from the Mazdaists and posing as the heirs of the Caesars; Septuagint Jewry imitating the late Classical and inventing a past in the half-mythical Hebrew tribes. We know perfectly well the immense influence on other men of a powerful contemporary civilization, but we dislike to think of Charlemagne's empire in this role. To do so destroys the role we have assigned to it, the link to maintain our so passionately desired continuity from Rome. And since we do not want to see the actual power of the Levant even in this brief empire, we have to ignore what was significant about it and dwell upon those details that we can most easily distort. Of the latter the most obvious is the revival of the imperial title which we try to pretend indicated a desire to revive the empire. Another is Alcuin's reform of Latin, a mere technical necessity in a government that for more than three centuries had been using this language for its records. Another is the supposed fusion of Germanic and Roman institutions, in a land with no institutions save the Levantine episcopacy and a greatly modified Germanic kingship, a government that improvised everything else as the problems arose.

This excessive concern with trying to prove continuity hides the contemporary reality, the two disparate elements of Charlemagne's empire. That it was the political embryo of the West every historian has always admitted, but of this the men who created it certainly were not conscious. Its second and conscious strand is the one we do not like to admit, that it was a Latin caliphate. Charlemagne lived in a world whose great political powers, whose fonts of learning and civilization were the great Levantine states, the dominions of Leo the Isaurian at Constantinople, of Harun al Rachid at Baghdad, of the Spanish Ommiad, Abd er Rahman at Cordova. It was not Caesar or Trajan or even Constantine that Charlemagne copied. It was, as with most men, his great contemporaries. The Caesars were myths, the basileus and the caliph powerful living examples. He organized his dominions much as he thought they organized theirs. He introduced crafts and book learning from them—much of it of immense future value to the West. Like the Emperor Leo, he managed his church even on theological questions—to him and probably to him alone we owe the *filioque* clause in the creed. Like Harun al-Rashid, he thought he should be a patron of learning and in the grand manner affect it himself. And like every Levantine monarch he could devise no system of succession beyond the Levantine concept of the sacred family. His will alone is conclusive evidence that there was no notion of a revived Roman Empire. Drawn only six years after his acceptance of the imperial title, it has no trace of such a concept as the *Res publica*. Like his father and their Merovingian predecessors, he provided that the Frankish dominions were to be divided like private property among his three sons.

In important contrast to its interest in Charlemagne, traditional history has no interest at all in Merovingian times and very little in immediate post-Carolingian. It is not that these periods are not known or that nothing of interest or importance happened in them. The difficulty is that while the nature of Charlemagne's empire can be distorted to make a continuity from Rome sound superficially plausible, both the earlier and later cannot. The first did not revive the imperial title and the second threw it away without concern. They offer nothing that can be used to argue a continuum. They show in every detail that the West was a new entity with a definite beginning, not a selected part of the continuum of mankind, and that the most powerful influences touching its early life were not the literary remains of the Classical but the living political reality of the Levant.

Something of the falsity of the traditional picture can be realized by considering the time scale. From the so-called fall of Rome to the beginning of the medieval kingdoms, say to the Norman conquest of England and the accession of Hugh Capet to the throne of France, the period is treated as "transitional," and all attention is focused on the eighty-odd years of the Carolingian Empire. It is implied that very little else of any importance occurred during these times. The era is pictured as one in which the barbarian tribes were adjusting themselves to Christian and Roman culture before resuming the work of human progress. But consider the relative times. From the conversion of Clovis to the accession of Hugh Capet was the same length of time as from Hugh Capet to the discovery of America. Between the Saxon and Norman conquests of England, there was a greater span of centuries than that between the Norman conquest and the establishment of Virginia and New England, the annexation of New York and New Jersey. Out of so many centuries we select eighty years for serious treatment.

The reigns of the last Carolingians were as dismal as those of any of the Merovingians before them. Even under Louis the Pious, Charlemagne's sole surviving son who thus inherited the undivided property, the superficial aspects of a Latin caliphate vanished. The pretense of a centralized, learned court gave place to the reality of the territorial power of the illiterate local masters, not yet a feudal nobility but on the way to become one. There ceased to be any government officials. The counts asserted and maintained the right to keep the government of each county as hereditary property. The count became a vassal instead of an official. He came to owe fealty and no longer obedience to the sovereign. Benefices of all kinds, originally a means of current payment for services in a money-less economy, became equally hereditary. Not that the individuals holding counties and benefits did not change. In the rapid spread of local violence beginning in the reign of Louis the Pious, many a ruthless adventurer of obscure birth forced his way to the top in that anarchic society. Civil war, private murder, armed gangs roaming the country, Slav, Saracen and Norman raids all went unpunished and unrestrained. The genealogies of the noble and dynastic families of medieval Europe proclaim unarguably the social overturn during the reigns of the last Carolingians. Few even of the oldest and most famous can be traced back of the reigns of Charles III and Louis IV (d. 954). Even the lines of the Welfs and the Bourbons, descendants of the Capetians, vanish in the reign of Louis the Pious as does the lineage of the counts of Toulouse, long the uncrowned kings of southern France. The ancestry of the Dukes of Saxony, kings of East France and emperors in Germany and Italy from 919 to 1002 vanishes under Charlemagne's grandson, Louis the German. The dukes of Normandy, afterwards kings of England, descended from the savage Rolla, a Danish raider. It was a regime of new men from Charles Martel to the middle of the tenth century, and the great families that rose out of it, who must have known well their ancestors of only a few generations back, chose not to disclose the obscure and perhaps criminal origin of their founders. We know, by chance, that the great Norman house of Belesme, ancestors of the first earls of Shrewsbury, descended from an ordinary crossbowman in the reign of Louis IV.

On the political surface the disintegration was as evident as the revolutionary violence throughout society. Even in his lifetime, the sons of Louis the Pious began rebellions against him and civil wars against each other. The first division, creating an "East France" and a "West France," as they were contemporaneously known, and a long middle kingdom stretching from the mouths of the Rhine to Rome, did not last long. With the death of Lothair, whence the name Lorraine, the middle kingdom north of the Alps was divided between East and West France. In the meantime outside enemies had risen. In the south the Saracens, as they had come to be called, seized Sicily from the Byzantines and began occupying parts of southern Italy. Rome was besieged and the Rhône valley raided. In the north the raids of the Danes became more and more dangerous. Every estuary from the Elbe to the Garonne was open to them. Hamburg, Bordeaux, Nantes, Rouen, Paris, Amiens, Aachen itself were burned or looted. The heathen Slavs invaded from the east. Now and then the increasingly divided kingdoms would unite briefly against the Saracens or the Danes, but these unions accomplished little before personal rivalries and ambitions pulled them apart. Through it all from every church council, from every political bishop and from the kings who recited their pieces, went up the demand for "unity," "justice" and "peace." Indeed until our own time no period of Western history has found it so necessary as the late Carolingian to proclaim the unsullied purity of its poltical aspirations. It was hammered by foreign enemies against whom it rarely fought, its own politics the mere arena of a bloody struggle for power at every level of society, yet every act of treachery and personal ambition was proclaimed to be soley in the pursuit of these lofty ideals. Even its end was undignified. In 884 in all lands of the Carolingians, there was left but one adult, legitimate, male descendant of Charlemagne, so rapidly had their family degenerated—the emperor and king of East France, Charles III (the Fat). In 885, he became also king of West France, and for a brief moment the empire of Charlemagne was reconstituted. It was not for long. Stricken with a grave brain disorder, though not insane, he became increasingly unable to govern and abandoned by all his adherents, he died almost alone at Neidingen near the Black Forest, January 13, 888, the last occupant of the fallen throne of the West.

What was unified under Charlemagne was not a revived Roman Empire nor even, as events turned out, a Latin caliphate. Certainly to the men of those times the Levant was the living example of power and high civilization. They copied it, but they did not embrace its civilization. Unlike the other semi-barbarians scattered along the rim of the civilized world—the Abyssinians, the Slavs of Attica and Peloponnesus, the Vandals in Africa, the Khazars of the Black Sea, the Goths of Spain—the Latins did not become Levantines. It is futile to seek why. To all outward appearances the Latin Christians could easily have become a Levantine sect-nation as the Coptic Christians did, or the Khazar Jews. But they did not. Instead of adopting the developed civilization of others, they forewent much of any civilization at all and left to their descendants the founding of a new one. But of this they certainly had no thought.

What Charlemagne unified was the unborn West. In his reign the word "Europe" began to appear as the name for the home of "the Christian people" and "the Christian people" already explicitly excluded the Byzantines. Through this reign and through the dismal reigns that followed, the cry for unity of this "Christian people" is never ending, unity against the heathen Slavs and Danes, against the infidel Saracens, against the schismatic Greeks. Nor were the Greeks hated because they were schismatics. In truth they were made schismatics because they were hated. At root there is no other intelligible explanation of the zeal with which the West forced the *filioque* clause into the creed. The theological point involved is of the utmost obscurity. But to put into the creed an innovation which the Byzantines would not accept, that deprived these hated, civilized foreigners of the right to be considered truly Christians, of the right to proclaim the symbol that was long to be the mark of a Western man!

Tradition does not ascribe sufficient importance to this contoversy. As a matter of theology and church history it is even a little embarrassing to modern Christians. We do not quite see the importance of the theological question involved—whether the Holy Ghost proceeds from the Father alone or from the Father and the Son. We find it hard to see the necessity for forcing a change in the creed which had universally been the declaration of Christian faith for four hundred and fifty years, a change that even Charlemagne could not compel Pope Leo III to accept and so had to wait for his successor. That the Greeks would not adopt the innovation is only too understandable. But however obscure the theology of the *filioque* clause, there is no confusion in the clarity of its politics. It gave the Latins their own church. Whether there was a conscious motive to tear apart the fabric of the Christianities and tear it apart along the line that ever since has divided Levant and West, is perhaps a question beyond the capacity of human judgment. But that was the result.[13]

Though Christian disunity was thus pursued against the Greeks, within the Carolingian dominions Christian unity was sought passionately and established sufficiently well to endure for some seven hundred years. The disintegration of the empire was not permitted to cause the disintegration of the Latin Church, and against this unity the old separate laws began to break down long before the national laws of the successor states began to be differentiated. The multiplicity of law codes of the Carolingian Empire had been a barbarous version of the essential Levantine political structure that required every "nation" to keep its own law regardless of the nationality of the territorial sovereign. This had been carried down from the fifth century when there had been Frankish law for the Franks (indeed two of them), Burgundian law for the Burgundians, Roman[14] law for the Romans and so forth. These varying codes still survived in the ninth century though the different persons to which each was applicable no longer necessarily corresponded to their ancestry. Louis the Pious had begun to eliminate the extreme diversity among the different codes, but this was not sufficient for the partisans of unity. Agobard, Archbishop of Lyons, was one of these. "Whatever may be their racial diversity," he wrote to the emperor concerning the legal status of his subject, "whether different in sex, birth, and condition, nobles and serfs, all without exception pray with a common heart to the same God their father, 'Our Father which art in Heaven.' They call upon but one Father, desire but one kingdom, seek the fulfillment of but one will, all alike ask of Him the same daily bread and all alike the forgiveness of their sins. There is no longer gentile nor Jew, barbarian nor Scythian." St. Paul's phrase was not quite appropriate: "Aquitainian

---

13 "The rejection of the *filioque*, or of the dogma of the double procession of the Holy Ghost from the Father and Son, and the denial of the primacy of the Roman Pontiff constitute even today the principal errors of the Greek Church." *Catholic Encyclopedia* (1909), Art. *Filioque*.

14 i.e., Latin Byzantine.

nor Lombard, Burgundian nor Alaman, all are one in Christ. . . . Against this unity created by God should there be such a diversity of laws that in the same country, the same town, even in the same house, among five men . . . none is under the same law as another . . . ?" Agobard's solution was to put all under Frankish law. This did not happen immediately, but within a century it was accomplished. The first form of Western law made its appearance: the law of the territory is the law of all Christians living within it.

What the Carolingian Empire left in the way of countless popular legends from Spain and Italy to Norway, what Europe afterwards thought it had been and had meant, is not the same thing as what it historically was. It was not the full, clear flowering of Western society yet it marked the origin of the basic political frame of that civilization both in church and state. Charlemagne's own monument which he loved and built, the church of St. Mary at Aix-la-Chapelle, is its own epitome of the lands over which he ruled. It is only a copy of the early Byzantine church of San Vitale at Ravenna and its columns and capitals had to be dismantled from another church at Ravenna and hauled over the Alps to Germany. He could not find in all his dominions architects to design him a church or masons to cut him his stone.

After Charlemagne's death for more than a century in the darkness that lay over northwestern Europe, almost nothing occurred that gives any sign of the tremendous events that the few succeeding centuries were to produce. Almost nothing was written. Almost nothing was built. Of stone work, the immediate post-Carolingian period produced as little as the dark centuries before him. This little was of poor technical competence, massive half rubble, built with little or no style, decorated, when it was decorated at all, with direct copies of Byzantine designs.

And then with an extraordinary suddenness, without any event to signal the occurrence, literally without the least warning, a civilization, a compact way of life with a distinct historical personality, suddenly appeared in northwestern Europe.

Inexplicable as it may be, that is what happened. The line-of-progress history with its theories of influences, borrowings, slow development, here can do nothing but falsify the time scale. For five hundred years these lands had lain a social and cultural wilderness. There were many of the old basilicas left from the fourth and fifth centuries, built during the brief sway of Levantine Latin Christianity in Gaul, mosque-like with their innumerable lamps and columns, but this style did not survive and with the development of Romanesque architecture in the tenth century the few of these venerable buildings still standing were pulled down. In Carolingian times some buildings were built, of course, but the assemblage cannot be called a style of architecture and fewer were built than were destroyed. Some men wrote, crabbed annals or obscure, crude verse filled with awkward and childish imagery. There had been the Frankish dominions as the personal possession of their kings and the phantom kingdoms of the heptarchy of Britain. But with any meaning that these words could have in later centuries, it would be correct so say that for half a millennium in northwestern Europe there had been no architecture, no art, no letters, no intellecual life, no states; and then almost within the life span of a single man during the tenth century, there were all of them. Nor did they spread gradually from place to place. They appeared almost simultaneously from Lombardy and the Pyrenees to England and eastward into Germany.

It is probably not true that a man could compose alone from his own thoughts a book that would so impress his fellows that their way of life would be changed. Some books are said to have done so, but more probably they set down in precise form what was vaguely, from a thousand unknown sources, already in men's minds. Nevertheless although this is not probable, it is still imaginable. But it is not possible even to imagine one man creating a whole style of architecture. He might design a building, compose a new series of decorative motifs. The same man might even be imagined as capable of calculating all the needed engineering to handle the stresses, loads and thrusts that resulted from his design. But even if he would do all this, he still could have no building. What would he do for carpenters, masons, the stone cutters? Who are his quarry men? Who has the knowledge and equipment to calcine lime for his mortar? Who knows the right and wrong kind of stone to use and where it lies? Who has the wagons and tackle to move it? Who can build the sheers and blocks to lift it in place? Who has the forges, the knowledge of ore deposits and metallurgy to make the saws, drills, trawls, chisels, chains and bolts which he will need? Furthermore, who will pay for it? In an almost wholly agricultural society, who can afford the cost of diverting thousands of young men from the soil to train and then employ them in the innumerable crafts that are required for a great building?

It is with reflection upon these questions that the sudden appearance of what we call Romanesque architecture must be considered. In the closing years of the tenth century it appeared in Lombardy. A few decades later, it was in the Rhineland, a little later in Normandy, the Ile de France, England and finally Provence. There was no longer the crude taste and construction of the Carolingian builders. There was no more copying or pilfering of ancient stone. The design and the detail were the work of men who had envisaged for themselves the complete object they wished to create and who had devised the means to bring it into tangible existence. Not alone was there suddenly style in place of crudity and poor copy work. Instead of the trifling handful of buildings erected across five centuries, churches were suddenly erected everywhere. Throughout all western Europe there are hardly more than one hundred and twenty-five monuments, churches, baptistries, towers, which still stand or of which we can find any trace or record built between 500 and 1000. Yet in Normandy and the region about Paris alone we know of over six hundred and seventy-five edifices erected in the next two centuries and the number throughout western Europe is in the thousands.

Consider this immense enterprise spread throughout all northwestern Europe and northern Italy. Each area had its own sharp peculiarities of taste but all were unmistakably of this same style. Consider the financing of such a vast undertaking by a crude agricultural economy, not alone the great cathedrals, but the far more numerous parish churches and small abbeys. Consider the immense complexity of the development of all the subsidiary crafts required. It is evident that a vast community enterprise was in action, as a program unpreached and unplanned but irresistible and universal. Western civilization had begun.

Nor was it only our architecture that began in the tenth century; so did our music. Here again a break with the centuries of Levantine style marked the foundation of a new style involving what has been ever since the basic and unique principle of Western music. The eleventh century saw the introduction into the ancient Levantine plain chant of a second voice singing note by note a different melody. This was the foundation of polyphonic music. At first the interval was held rigidly at a fourth. Then a fifth was also permitted. The plain chant which had originally been above the second voice was placed below it as the holding voice (hence our tenor from tenere). Later more voices, each singing a different melody, and by Gothic times different words, produced the intricate web-like music of the high Gothic. We even owe the use of lines and clefs and the names of our notes to the Romanesque. Guido of Arezzo invented the former to record precise pitch in place of the vague indication of the Byzantine neuma which showed on the verbal text only whether the melody was rising or falling. As a mnemonic guide, Guido also took the appropriate symbols from a hymn to John the Baptist and used them for the names of the notes.[15]

The political structure of society changed with equal suddenness. The last trace of appointive officers of state disappeared. Hereditary territorial

---

[15] *Ut* queant laxis *re*sonare fibris
*Mi*ra gestorum *fa*muli tuorum
*Sol*ve polluti *la*bii reatum. Sancte Joannes.
Ut re mi fa so la are the notes *c d e f g a*; the name *ut* has been changed to *do* except in France.

feudalism became the universal political structure. There were no longer simply the rich and the poor, the serf and the slave. The millennial social structure of Europe made its appearance, barons, clergy and people. The remnants of the tribal past of the conquering barbarians vanished in an embryonic nationalism, leaving as a heritage the personal names of the modern West and a dim trace in the political institutions of the north, the tribal assemblies which are the far-off origin of the representative bodies that have existed in all the Western states since their origin.

Equally enduring was the state structure that arose in this period. On the map of Catholic Europe of the year 1000 is the skeleton of the state structure of Europe to this day. Scotland, Ireland, England, France, Germany, Bohemia, Poland, Leon, Castile, Navarre and Aragon were there as dynastic states. Only one state that existed in 1000 has disappeared— Burgundy. Scotland, and for awhile Ireland, merged with England. Leon, Castile and Aragon united to form Spain which absorbed the territory of Navarre, while France merged with its dynasty. Although Poland in the twelfth and thirteenth centuries, and again in the eighteenth and nineteenth, ceased to exist as a state, only Burgundy has vanished and it was, even then, no more than a legal fiction, having neither a dynasty of its own nor a popular consciousness of national individuality.

Surprisingly enough, even in the still heathen north and east, the political skeleton of our own time is evident. Norway had been officially and forcibly Christianized by Olaf I (995-1000), but the Kingdom of Sweden still worshipped the northern trinity whom we remember in the days of our week and for whose cause we abstain from eating horses, Oden, Thor and Frigg. In the southeast, Hungary had taken form under St. Stephen but was far from Christianized. Not only have all these states survived through a thousand years, but the only new ones that have ever been added were the four carved out of the dismemberment of the old German Empire and not reincorporated in the new, the Netherlands, Belgium, Austria and Switzerland. The one Western nation that appears as a name but not as a dynastic state on a map of the year 1000 is the only wholly intellectual creation of modern times, the triumph of cartography over history, Italy.

After the fluidity of the barbarian kingdoms, this crystallization, as it were, of the enduring institutions of society and of dynastic states that were to last so long is both an evidence that Western civilization had begun, and a commentary on one of the prime characteristics of our society, the immense durability of our institutions. That states without drastic changes in their borders should last for a thousand years does not seem extraordinary to us, but that is only because this is the way our states live. Except for the states of ancient China, it is quie untrue of the rest of the world. Whole civilizations have lasted that long and far longer, but not the territorial states which compose them. In this thousand years that the states of Europe have endured, political dominions within the Levantine world have risen and vanished. What has endured there has not been the territorial state but the sect-nation. The political structure of India has been one long flux in which no state endured for long. The empires of the Khans and of their successor, the Tartars, have risen, rolled up vast provinces and disappeared. Even China has endured more than one alien political master, and China is not comparable to the national states of the West, for China is not a nation but an entire civilization whose old naional states were long since rolled into a universal empire and as a universal empire, this society has endured since the days of the Hans.

The endurance of the states of the West is not a problem in modern political and social theory because no one even considers it a matter worthy of note. It is to us simply the way the politics of the world quite obviously should be organized. To us this is so clear that all our programs of world order presuppose the indefinite duration of the territorial political structure of the earth, once the proper boundaries are established—a generation ago by "self-determination," in today's fashion by the elimination of "colonialism." The world reformers do not see that they are proposing merely to enforce on men of other societies a political idea which has been rooted in Western society since it began but which has been an idea entirely strange and even unnatural to the men of other societies. In the Classical society, the only enduring political entity was the *polis,* whether it was independent or annexed to the power of another. In the Levantine, it was the sect-nation. In Egypt, it was the entire society. No political structure whatever could carry symbolic or ethical meaning to a society like the Hindu. Only in the West and in ancient China has the territorial state been an organization of human life consistent with the underlying ethics of the society.

We Westerners do not seem to consider it extraordinary that all human history gives us only one other example of a political organization of men comparable to our own. We have a dim awareness that there is an ethical base under our belief in the desirability of permanent territorial political units but we do not even wonder whether the ethics involved are not strictly the ethics of the West, inapplicable and even meaningless to the men of other societies. We could hardly do so, since we are not prepared to admit that ethics, too, is an aspect of the life of a historical society and that there have been as many ethical systems—however much each has had deeply in common with the others—as there have been historical societies.

The crystallization of the political structure of Europe occurred while the east and north were still heathen and while heathen customs and beliefs, some with a Christian sugar coating, were still widely prevalent in Germany, northern France and Britain. Unavoidably, therefore, there is raised the question of the connection between civilization and religion. Was it the conversion of the north and east that brought these areas within the borders of the West? How far is our society a Christian society? What connection exists between Christianity and Western civilization? These are not questions with which the liberal mood of our day is comfortable. Our modern non-sectarianism has been carried so far that most Western states are not only legally non-sectarian but for practical purposes non-Christian. To admit that our society had a Christian past necessarily gives a unique rank to Christianity. It may have no greater legal position then any other religion, but as the ancestral faith of the West, it acquires a greater social and cultural status, and strict egalitarianism is thereby violated. How can adherents of other faiths be considered truly equal to Christians if Christianity is recognized to have a special, even though only historical, connection with our civilization?

The proposition that there is such an identity, even historical, between a society and its religion raises objection from both the religious and the irreligious. For the latter, the proposition is objectionable because it asserts an importance in historical life of transcendental interests that are not today considered acceptable as part of the motive power of political action. Modern liberal thought does not, like leftist thought, outlaw religion, but it does require religion to be respectable, that is, to avoid the transcendental. Religious institutions can be allowed to provide a proper ritual for funerals and weddings—even with supernatural phraseology—but they must have no serious moral or intellectual purpose in society except the promotion of terrestrial egalitarian welfare. The same scale of values is applied to the past, and historical action that does not appear to accord with this scale is reproved as superstitious and discounted as being only a hypocritical disguise for the kind of practical motivation that would move a modern.

Therefore in strict liberal theory, Western society cannot be thought of as uniquely connected with Western Christianity. It is difficult enough to picture our civilization as essentially differentiated from all others without also tying in the unique faith of our ancestors. Yet it is manifest that the Latin Christianity of our medieval ancestors played a part in their lives that neither Judaism nor Mohammedanism did. Since this cannot well be denied, another escape must be found, and this is achieved either by minimizing the consequence of the religious beliefs of our ancestors or by stigmatizing as unsocial such of these consequences as are too obvious to ignore. Our ancestors thought of themselves before all else as Christians, and this has left in speech and custom certain habits and mannerisms that we are now taught to deplore. We cannot stage the *Merchant of Venice* because, even though it correctly reflects the view of sixteenth century England towards the Jews, it does not reflect the modern view, and our democratic age lacks the historical integrity to acknowledge as a fact of its own past a belief or an emotion that it no longer accepts. This sort of thing, on a huge but often subtle scale, operates through all our accepted picture of the history of the West. We feel obliged to reprove our ancestors for every departure from our own liberal principles. More serious than this, however, we feel that we must protect our principles by denying when we can, and ignoring when we cannot deny, that the illiberal, feudal, Catholic Christian society of the Middle Ages was the direct, lineal and exclusive origin of the civilization in which we now live.

Such is one aspect of the difficulty raised by the early history of the West, but there is another with which the religious are not too comfortable. How Christian was the Christianity of the Middle Ages? How much of the religion preached by Jesus was still contained in Latin Catholicism from the ninth to the fifteenth centuries? How much, even, of Greek Christianity as it developed to the Council of Chalcedon, was still part of the active faith of medieval Catholicism? It is these questions that are important to an understanding of the origin of our society, because though the connection between Christianity as a religion and Western civilization has always been obvious, it has been far from a simple relationship which anyone could understand at a glance. In contrast, the connection between Latin Christianity as a church and Western society is quite simple. There the relationship has been one of absolute identity. Western civilization and Catholicism were the same thing from the origin of our society until the breakup of the medieval church. Western civilization and Western Christianity, using the latter term to embrace all the successor churches established by the descendants of the medieval Catholics and stemming, whether their teachings admit or deny it, from medieval Catholicism, were again identical until far into the eighteenth century. Only with the rise of Western scepticism and the addition to Western society of men of a different historical ancestry—principally the Western Jews—did the obvious connection between our society and its religious expression become obscured. The problem, therefore, of the relationship between Western society and Christianity is in essence the problem of the relationship between Latin Christianity and Levantine Christianity. How far are they in fact the same religion? How far does an identity of holy scriptures establish as an identical religion two faiths which, in their understanding of ultimate reality, in their deep ethical principles, in their sense of God's purpose, are and have always been in every respect the diametrical opposite, one of the other? We have had little interest in Levantine Christianity. We have unconsciously falsified its history before Chalcedon and consciously ignored it thereafter. But the Levantine Church has never had any doubt that Catholicism and all its successor churches were a profound and intolerable perversion of the ancient faith. The Greek survivors of the papally-blessed capture of Constantinople in 1204 had no less deep in aversion to Latin Christianity than the Moslems of Jerusalem. Nor did the later centuries of Turkish lordship shake this old aversion. Even today in the shattered ruin of the Levant, the fragments of the ancient Levantine Christian churches at times make expedient religious alliances but still resist a real intimacy with their nominal coreligionists of the West.

The process by which Latin Christianity based a new religion on the texts and traditions of an older operated in many ways. Sometimes it shows openly in the altered meaning of ritual, sacrament or doctrine. Sometimes the shift in values has no conscious expression whatever and proclaims its existence in the unarguable language of symbolism. Sometimes, as in the role of the Virgin among the Latins, the change shows in the human means of comprehending the very existence of God. In no case is it ever formally admitted, beyond the admission implied in the accusation against the Greeks, that it was they, not the Latins, who had departed from the ancient faith. Manifestly, change could not be admitted, and to those to whom history is the record of formal documents, this vital fact in the life of the West must remain always a source of hidden and unadmitted confusion.

In the West, no real belief in eschatology ever existed. The end of the world was a form of words, not an actual event expected in a mundane though perhaps distant future. The hidden dualism of the doctrine of redemption became, too, the use of sacred language and a logical monstrosity whose illogic was studiously avoided, for no Western formulation could ever devise the image of any power from whom God had ransomed men. With this the meaning of the sacrament of baptism changed completely. This had been the central sacrament of the Levantine churches in that it symbolized the outpouring of the spirit, the pneuma of God by which the believer was made an inseparable part of the consensus of those who shared in the spirit. In the West, baptism became instead the symbol of the washing away of original sin, itself a doctrine honored in words and ignored in the living ethical system of the West. In the West, the central sacrament became the indissolvable pair, confession and communion, in which the Levantine doctrines of original sin and of grace as the operation of the unknowable will of God were blotted out by the Western doctrine of personal will and personal responsibility. Sin was not the generalized heritage of mankind—though this Levantine doctrine was, of course, not formally denied—but the conscious, purposeful act of an individual person. Absolution was not a small piece of the generalized redemption of mankind, but a specific grant to an individual who was knowledgefully contrite.

Time has partly obscured the clarity of these immense differences in religious beliefs—at least as characteristic of Western society as a whole

—because Protestantism with its keen sense of the surface of religious history has formally reversed all these changes and sought to establish in the West—to restore according to its own view—the ancient Levantine ranking of the sacraments, with the corresponding importance of the doctrines of original sin, and of grace as the agent of Levantine predestination. It has partly succeeded on the surface of religious events, but it has not altered the ethical structure of Western life save for a very few men for very brief periods. Instead it has largely deprived the Protestant churches of meaningful sacraments.

Indissolvably linked with the change in importance of the sacraments by Latin Christianity was a different ethical system that arose among the men of the West. For us modern Westerners, consideration of any ethical system, even our own, is made difficult because we no longer understand the nature of ethics. To some it is a silly notion invented to forbid our doing things we want to do. To others it is a pious whitewash for schemes of personal and imperial ambition ostensibly in the interests of world peace and the welfare of the masses. To still others, ethics is little more than the problem of maintaining chastity among young women. That an ethical system is the foundation of political and even of organic life, few of us would be prepared to admit. That men are driven by their largely unconscious, self-evident ideas of right and wrong and that these ideas, varying as they do from society to society, one and all concern survival, we would be even less prepared to admit. Such is our difficulty as moderns. As Westerners we have an additional difficulty in understanding the place of ethics in human history. The ethical life of the West has been confused as that of no other society has ever been. We have had our own ethical system by which with courage and unconcern we have unconsciously lived. We have also had scraps and fragments of the ethics of the Levant brought to us in the sacred writings that we profess as the foundation of our religious faith. These we have felt we should consciously learn and consciously follow. Usually it is only the latter that we think of as real ethics, so to our society—and to ours alone—ethics has appeared as a system designed not to further life but to encompass it with pitfalls and even contrive its ruin, something which could be dubiously approached but—though this we said in secret—fortunately never fulfilled. But this has been our misunderstanding of history, not the nature of ethical conduct.

The central duty under all ethical systems is to survive. What changes from society to society—and to a much lesser degree in each society from age to age—are the concepts of the entity that is to survive and of the world in which that survival is to take place. In India, being is to survive by stripping all the mortal qualities from the self; the deathless is to be attained by removing that which lives. In China, the family survives, link-ing its ancestors in the world of the spirit with its transient living members in the world of this earth. In Egypt, the *ka*, the mystic double of a man, was to survive among the spirits while in this world the cult and the Kingdom of Egypt as the symbols of purposeful endurance went on forever. In the Classical society, what could be made a myth survived in the timeless, shadowy world of the spirits, the hero, the great gesture that established the self-standing character of man against the blind, impersonal annihilation of fate. In the Levant, what was to survive was the consensus of the faithful, the mystic unity formed of all those who had received the spirit. But they were to survive only in the Kingdom of Heaven, for this world was a phantom which was soon to pass away.

The ethical system of all the Levantine religions stood upon this foundation. This world was a transitory illusion, not merely for each individual man as we sometimes picture it, but as an actual physical fact for all men and for all their descendants. The race of man like the earth itself was to be cut off. Nothing could endure in this world since this world itself was not to endure. All Levantine ethics, therefore, condemn all things of this world since all earthly things interfere with the approach of the soul to God. In this system no worldly interest is any more, or any less, sinful than another. Crimes exist in this society, violations of the good order of political and social life, but not sins in the Western sense. All men living actively in this world are in sin not because of some specific act which under temptation they have committed, but because living in this world cannot possibly be accomplished except by sinning. No one can act in accordance with chapters five and six of the Gospel of St. Matthew and exist long in a living, terrestrial society. No one can live contrary to Matthew five and six and receive the full spirit of God, which alone is the assurance of blessedness. The salvation of the worldly, if they are to attain it, is assured only by predestination, a predestination evidenced, but not strictly caused, by their membership in the body of the faithful, which, by definition, embraces the elect. But only the monk or the sufi by shedding all things of this world can bring himself closer to God, not thereby to assure himself more certainly of salvation, but by his nearer approach to God, by the greater outpouring of the spirit which his devotions open to him, to assure himself of greater bliss both in this world and in the next. It is true that the intense eschatological expectation of Jesus has given us in Matthew the Levantine code stripped of all compromise with earthly practicality, something we do not find in Talmudic Judaism, Mohammedanism and Mazdaism. Yet the essential meaning of the Matthean discourse, its ethical foundation in belief in the illusory and transient character of this world, is the ethical system of all the Levantine faiths.

The surface of this ethical system overlies our own. We have never accepted it, but we have never contradicted its validity. It is too firmly attested in our sacred scriptures for us to denounce it for what to us it is—meaningless, basically as meaningless as the Classical or the Hindu. We cannot accept its premises concerning what is to survive, where that survival is to take place nor the means by which that survival is to be accomplished. We cannot accept its basic dogma that sin has nothing to do with the knowledge and intention of the doer but inheres in the nature of man, not simply as a propensity but as a fact.

Levantine sin is the world itself. Active participation in its life is sin. This does not *cause* a man to risk his salvation. That could be caused only by the will of God, but such participation is dangerous evidence that the participant may not have been chosen by God to be among the elect. The sufi and the monk, the hermit and the dervish, do not by their own acts assure their election. The fact that God causes them to live the life of withdrawal from the world is a sign that he has chosen them. Levantine causality does not operate in Western ethics any more than it does in Western physics. In the West, sin has always meant a willed, personal act which causes its consequence. To abstain from sin is equally a willed act and equally causes, or would cause if it could be carried through a lifetime, its necessary consequence: salvation. Western ethics, therefore, even that part concerned with the salvation of the soul, has been an ethic of action. Good actions have beneficent consequences; bad actions have dangerous consequences. That is, the mechanics of our ethics has been quite different from the predestination of the Levant. Though we never admit it, we have all of us been Pelagians. We see a man's own will as the causative agent of his spiritual fate. Ethical conduct has meant a series of ethical acts during a man's stay in this world, not his withdrawal from it, while still clothed in its flesh.

In the ethical system of the West, what is to survive in this world is the personal will of the individual—which is to operate long after he is dead—and in the world to come his discrete, self-standing individual personality—what we call his soul. The personality of a man cannot survive in this world, but his purpose can. The purpose of one man or of many can bring about action, can create a function—which to us is a real, though conceptual, entity—which can act and endure even through many centuries, which in theory at least can be immortal. Willed, purposeful endurance both in this world and the next has always been the ethical purpose of Western men and on that base we have raised a group of enduring institutions, political, social and religious which act in the life of this world in accordance with the will of those who founded them and of those who generation after generation carry them forward. Our states, our learned institutions, our churches, our families, are enduring, purposeful entities, functions of this sort. Cognate institutions have existed in all societies but in none—save with the partial exception of China—have they displayed the purposeful endurance that they have in the West. In none has their ethical foundation been the same.

Concerning problems of what is to survive and how it is to survive in this terrestrial world, Western ethics have been almost untouched even by the surface coating of Levantine ethics, at least that has been the case until almost our own times. The political and family life of the West has been ethically based on the liens of loyalty. To be loyal has been right. To be disloyal has been wrong. Our earthly life has been a complex of such liens, obligations of obedience upward, obligations of care and responsibility downward. Like every ethical system it has not been free of conflict between the self-interest of individuals and the demands of some larger enterprise to which they belonged. But these conflicts, unlike conflicts of a different sort where Levantine ethics entered, have never posed an ethical *problem*. The ethical course was always clear even when it was not followed.

In the moral climate of today this relationship of a man to the vertical obligations which he assumes or inherits is extremely troublesome. We cannot deny the ethical character of the relationship, but since even the existence of such relationship presupposes a ranked rather than a leveled society, we feel driven to conclude that even though loyalty is a virtue, the existence of any personal relationship between men that requires personal loyalty is itself a relationship of inequality and therefore wrongful. Liberalism regards vertical relationship between men with serious misgivings. Few could deny their reactionary character. Leftism correctly sees in such bonds the essential cement of a differentiated, organic society and therefore the most important obstacle to the leveling and destruction of the West. And fashion is with both of them for we are today assured that the only ethical liens in a society should be horizonal between one man and all his equals, who are, of course, all other men. But since, in fact, horizontal relationships are innumerable, they cannot be personal and the loyalty demanded by egalitarian theory becomes a loyalty only to impersonal organizations and verbal concepts. But such impersonal loyalties have little ethical force. Verbal concepts have no life, and since there is nothing to survive, there is nothing to call forth the inherent ethical motives that lie in all men. Hence there is no counterweight to the promptings of narrow self-interest, and such conceptual and egalitarian enterprises are invariably the arena of naked and embittered struggles for personal advantage. The oligarchies of money and labor, the egalitarian state, whether parliamentary or dictatorial in form, are all obvious examples of this destruction of ethical conduct in the name of a "broader" or "higher" ethical concept.

But the moral fashions of today should not lead us into a historical error. Even now such vertical, personal obligations are not absent from our society, and in the past when they were carried with neither shame nor extreme self-consciousness, they were the ethics of Western society, the means by which what must survive in our society was enabled to survive. Our states and families, the noble and artisan classes, the learned professions, the crown and the peasant's holding, alike endured through the force of these ethical liens. What has happened in the West since these bonds have withered and the sense of these obligations has grown dim is not here in point. What is of consequence at the moment is simply to observe that until the rise of a different theory of public ethics, this was the ethical system that guided almost a thousand years of the terrestrial life of the West.

Such have been the ethical principles of Western men insofar as they were part of a political and órganic life that was, at least in purpose, immortal. But Western men like all other men have been individuals, and beyond their care for those things that can endure on this earth they, too, have sought a personal release from the dominion of death. Whether a real faith in personal immortality is still widespread in the West is by no means clear. Certainly it is more restricted and probably less vivid than in the past. But beyond question it was once a powerful motive in the lives of the Western peoples and ethical considerations directed to the survival of the soul were once important factors in the lives of everyone. And it is here, in defining acts injurious to the welfare of the soul, that we encounter the full impact of the Levantine ethical system and meet that unique phenomenon of Western life, the ethical problem. All societies are familiar with the conflict between self-interest and duty as the ethics of that society define duty, but only the West has had the ethical problem. The men of all societies have wished to do things they knew they should not do. Only Westerners have felt they should consider certain acts wicked when, in fact, they did not think them wicked. Only Westerners have felt that heavenly salvation conflicted with the *ethical* demands of terrestrial life. A man's duty to his family and his country, the whole network of obligations to men on whom he must depend and who must depend upon him, are ethical to us, but they count as matters of little consequence in the ethics of the Levant. Since we suppose that we have derived our ethical system from our religion, we feel that the conduct so explicitly recommended in the New Testament is ethical conduct, is perhaps the only ethical conduct. We feel that we should not only follow these maxims in our lives but in our hearts believe their violations to be as wicked as Levantine Christianity says they are. We try to put down our failure to follow such an unworldly course to our human weakness. We are always unwilling to admit that this is not the case, that we do not follow such a course because to us it would be a *wicked* course. It would violate *our* ethics. It would not be in the interest of the survival of those things for whose survival Western ethics exists. The flowering of earthly life in noble purpose, its indefinite continuance and growth, this to us is ethical action. We have differed among ourselves concerning what constituted a noble purpose in terrestrial life, but we have not differed that life should have such a purpose and that to carry it out was ethical action. No one ever taught this to us, but we have always known it. No one has ever been able to teach us that it was wicked. But it has been an ethical purpose in specific contradiction to that of Levantine Christianity.

From the beginning of our society this conflict has been evident in the personal lives of almost all thoughtful and sensitive men and women of the West. But in our public life prior to the French Revolution, the unworldly ethics of Levantine Christianity seem to have little influence. The terrestrial purpose of the West to grow and endure was carried out without too much paralysis of will from the recognition that this purpose was quite contrary to the ethics of the New Testament. To the irreligious days in which we live was left the absurdity of disbelieving in the Kingdom of Heaven, but under the slogans of liberalism seeking to impose by law and by war those relationships among men that God was to bring about beyond the grave.

In the past the great dynastic states and public institutions of all sorts, even the church militant as a terrestrial enterprise, generation after generation drew to their service the loyalty of the most significant men of the West. The ethical purpose of the state, in fact of public life in general, was accepted as self-evident. Our modern, democratic concept of the welfare state imputes no greater ethical purpose to the state than the medieval concept of its role, cast though it was in a noble and dynastic style. To be sure, where we picture the duty of the welfare state to be implicitly the leveling of society—everyone should be exactly as well-off as everyone else or the less well-off will still require more welfare—the Middle Ages envisioned it to be the increase of worldly welfare by all alike within the accepted frame of a legally differentiated society. The peasant was to have more to eat and the burger better clothes to wear, but at the same time the noble was to have a finer castle and the king a surer crown. The state was seen as the protector, not the reformer of society. There is thus an ethical difference. Indeed the two theories of the purpose of the state stand upon a different system of ethics, but in both the state is required to have an ethical purpose. To no Westerner can it be a mere machine for the private and transient advantage of those who hold its offices or control its operations. It exists for an enduring purpose, or it is not a state but only a gang of criminals masking its private adventures under the trappings of sovereignty. This idea is as old as the West, and though it is not unique with us, the type of state which it produced in the West is unique. The ethical function of the political state in the Levant was simply to act as a commander of the faithful, to shepherd the elect through their brief trials in this illusory world into the glory that awaited them. In this function so insignificant was what we would call politics that the Levantine state could exist with almost no political functions at all. Though we do not usually apply the term "state" to the internal government of the Levantine sect-nations when deprived of terrestrial power, as the Jews under the Sassanids and Mohammedans or the Orthodox Christians under the Turks, these were in fact examples of the Levantine state still carrying out its essential ethical function of using law and public policy in this world to care for the heavenly welfare of the faithful. Such should have been the states of the West had their existence been justified on the basis of Orthodox Christian ethics as it so obviously was not.

It was in connection with the survival of the soul not of the world that fragments of Levantine ethics were incorporated most firmly into the ethical system of the West, though even these fragments were selected in such a way that they did not destroy the ethical validity of purely Western values. Charity, chastity and forgiveness of personal wrongs were accepted as praiseworthy with the unspoken proviso that they should not be carried to an extreme that would wreck the functioning of civilized, earthly life. Charity that destroyed an ancient family holding, chastity that brought a dynasty to an end and invited civil war, forgiveness that refused to punish criminals; these were not virtues.

For the rest, the Levantine image of the Kingdom of Heaven was left much as the Westerners found it in the Bible and in the works of the eastern Fathers, though for the Levantine hierarchy within the Kingdom, the nearness to God to those who had more fully received the outpouring of his spirit, the Westerners substituted a general equality of all souls before the majesty of God. Other than this, the Levantine image of the supernatural life within the Kingdom was accepted unchanged. It was not then a matter of much consequence. Either to accept this image or reject it and fabricate a Western alternative could have had no influence on Western life. But the mechanics of reaching the Kingdom and the time and place of its arrival could, indeed, have affected Western life, and these were completely changed from their Levantine origin. The Kingdom of Heaven became a spiritual dominion whither the blessed went as they died, not a physically real, historical event which was to arrive on earth with the magical ending of time and history. Grace ceased to be favorable predestination and became a right granted all men to seek immortal happiness in God. Salvation, the immortal life of the soul, could be attained by the exercise of free will, and this freedom of the will, the *liber arbitrium,* was ranked as one of the greatest gifts of God to man.

We are taught, and we generally suppose, that our standards of personal conduct are derived from our Christian heritage. We maintain this illusion by refusing to recognize Levantine Christian ethics as the rounded, complete and altogether practical ethical system that it was. If we admitted it to be such, we would be forced to recognize its eschatological origin and to admit that it cannot be applied in anything resembling our concept of the world of earthly reality and continuing historical time. We prefer to interpret Levantine ethics as a lofty, "spiritual" goal which we should try to approach but which quite obviously we can never attain, which, if we wish to endure as a biological and political entity on the surface of this planet, we must be certain that we do not attain. To be sure nothing prevents our ascribing to a historical Christian origin the lofty and generous emotions which we—like the men of all civilzations—find in ourselves, any more than anything prevents our calling Christian the motives of treason, weakness and fear which, under the name of international idealism, are today the basis of our world political policy. But in neither case has the ascription anything to do with the ethics of Jesus.

Nowhere is this confusion of Western and Levantine ethics so pronounced as in the ethical purpose of the Western family, that is, in the sexual ethics of the West. It has been the burden of complaint of the irreligious for nearly two centuries that sexual unhappiness in the West was the consequence of a Christian morality. The devout have not agreed that this morality led to unhappiness, but they have been one with the impious in believing in its Christian origin. But both are largely wrong. Our family ethics have been like our public ethics, directed by the Western drive towards enduring purpose. The surface of Christian nomenclature has not changed that.

The sexual ethics of the Levant required not monogamy but abstinence, attainable only by the monk and the sufi, to be sure, but still the only truly ethical course. Anything short of that was unethical. An ordered sex relation might be endured as an unavoidable compromise with practical problems—so, for instance, St. Paul permits marriage as the lesser evil in contrast to the undiluted sexual standard of Matthew xix, 12. But while total abstinence was the only sex relation that was truly ethical in the Levant, sex was only one among many snares of this world, inherently no more sinful than any other. If a man could not be a sufi, he was already compromised by earthly interests, and his permissible sex behaviour could be anything compatible with public order and the Levantine type of family. Thus polygamy, divorce and concubinage were never considered improper. In the Levant, sex was never the agitated moral problem that it has always been in the West. We read into St. Paul and St. Augustine an insistence on sex that is not in the text because among all their concerns for the ethical life of their flocks, this is the only one that awakens an echo of reality to us. All the others strike us as the out-dated oddities of primitive Christianity, but where they warn against sex they are speaking of something meaningful to use.

There is a sexual ethic of the West, and its structure is the same as the ethics of our politics: purposeful endurance. The Western family is a private dynasty. It is patrilineal, monogamous and cannot be separated from its property. A family without property is as empty as a dynasty without a throne. Such become only names, not operating realities. Both lack the means of endurance. Without property, a man's biological strain can go on but the function, the enduring will, is ended. We should not here, as we often do, confuse wealth with property. Property may be worth little. It may not even be tangible since it can be a standing in a profession or a craft. It is nevertheless property since it is something a son takes with him when he follows his father's calling, something which can be of immense value to him which the sons of other men do not have.

On reflection, it is not surprising that the family structure of a civilization should resemble its state structure. The same purposes that operate to create the concept of what a family should be are the same purposes that mold the state. It is, therefore, natural that as the sense of the need for a dynasty dwindles in Western society, there should be increasing acceptance of divorce as a solution of erotic difficulties. Prior to about 1850, divorce in Western society was almost always for dynastic reasons. That is, divorce was resorted to when the purpose for which it was normally prohibited could only be served by permitting it, as in failure of heirs or the opportunity to merge crown or property. To liberal opinion these are admittedly the worst reasons for a divorce, but this shows how little liberal opinion understands the purpose of Western marriage.

In contrast to the bitter objection to divorce by medieval Catholicism, Orthodoxy, like the Jews and Mohammedans, always permitted it. Orthodoxy also recognized an approach to polygamy, which Mohammedanism, and Jewry until modern times, openly accepted, in the half-legal status of a concubine whose children had a right of succession in contrast to children born of mere casual contacts. A legal distinction between two kinds of illegitimate children is unknown in the West though there is an evident difference. Above all the Levantine family was not dynastic. The straight patrilineal descent universal in the West was absent. The head of the family was generally the oldest male of not-too-distant relationship, an uncle if there was no living grandfather. This structure shows plainly in the emperors of Byzantium, the Mohammedan caliphs and the later sultans, where sons succeeding their fathers to the throne were extremely rare. Even though we refer to various groups of these sovereigns as "dynasties," they were not dynasties in the Western sense but groups of men related by any degree of connection, provided that in them flowed the sacred blood that symbolized the pneuma of the dynasty.

The sexual ethic of the West is designed to promote the survival of the purposeful, propertied family. Hence it requires monogamy since polygamy would not establish cadet branches but fracture the property into distaff fragments. Hence, it cannot generally permit divorce which shatters the willed unit. Hence, its real code of conduct has always been the deplored double standard which adjusts the erotic shortcomings of monogamy without breaking the dynastic lines.

The educated modern world would recoil in verbal horror from accepting such a description of the ethical base of the Western family, though what ethical base is postulated in justification for the successive polygamy and polyandry of the accepted modern divorce-family would be hard to say. In what fashion it is ethically superior to a double standard, how it promotes the endurance of anything, is not apparent. But it does accord with the verbal formulae of liberalism. It is more egalitarian, and it is supposed to offer more freedom. It accords with the standards of both liberalism and feminism. Liberalism has destroyed our understanding of the ethical basis of property and feminism has destroyed our understanding of the difference of status and responsibilities of the two sexes. In fact, feminism is only liberalism applied to personal life instead of political. Just as liberalism started with the proposition that equality should be attained by making the masses like the gentry but ends in the leftist proposition that everyone should alike be sunk in the masses, so feminism began in the name of an elevation of moral tone by demanding that men act as scrupulously as women were supposed to do. But like its political parent it, too, finds idealistic goals unattainable, and in its modern form argues that it is right for women to behave not as men are supposed to behave but as men do behave.

But despite the verbal horror which convention would require us to express, no one is in any honest doubt about the real organization of the Western family for the past thousand years. It has been a sexual system based upon property considerations applying through successive generations. Men who were comfortable in erotic monogamy were faithful to

their wives. Men who were not, were unfaithful with equally good conscience. The latter was a situation that sometimes presented difficult practical problems but rarely disturbed the conscience. The practical difficulties
made it wiser to be faithful but not wicked to be unfaithful. The church
said it was a sin and feminism said it was "unfair," which in the context
is a synonym for "undemocratic," but the Western conscience raised no
barrier. It was not, for instance, in the class of incest or homosexuality.
An excess of infidelity, numerical or emotional, was, however, another
matter. That has always been considered unethical conduct, not because it
was a sex sin but because it diverted a man from his primary ethical
duty to promote the enduring welfare of his family. Generations of preaching and the occasional outbursts or revenge of angry wives have not
changed our real opinion in this matter. We are all willing to admit that
we ought to feel such conduct to be wicked but few of us have ever
been able to do so.

A somewhat similar situation has existed in regard to the chastity of
unmarried women. Again a formal rule has been supposed to apply to
all women, but, in fact, the dynastic family interests have provided the
ethical base. It was a matter not only of family but public importance
whether the unmarried daughter of the Count of Flanders became pregnant by a French prince, a German prince, on her father's groom. Her
chastity, therefore, involved a serious ethical point. The fate of a great
mercantile enterprise might hang on a similar problem. But in the immemorially transmitted peasant holdings, it made no difference by which
local boy a peasant's daughter became pregnant, so in these circles, as
among the propertyless then and today, marriage more often followed
pregnancy than preceded it.

There is no point, in regard to the ethical pattern of Western sex life,
in supposing that formal, moralistic exhortations represent ethical standards
and a thousand years of life lived with sober judgment and good conscience
represent sinful aberrations. It is not frozen phrases but acts done by men
and women and permitted—in fact, if not in word—by the surrounding
society that reveal the living ethics of a community.

But there is a curious point about Western sexual morality. Unlike
several other societies, particularly the Chinese and surprisingly enough
the Levantine, the sexual ethics of the West have always involved an irresolvable difficulty. It has not been solely an area of conflict between
Levantine and Western ethics, nor have the sexual inhibitions against
which the libertines protest been, as the impious say, the product of Christianity. Despite the element of Levantine ethics in the usual sermon against
sex, the deep element of sexual disharmony in the West has been inherently Western in origin. That sex alone among potential sources of sin

has produced the centuries of emotional difficulties of which our arts and literature are an immense testimony is not at its roots the result of Christion teaching.

> *The boast of heraldy*
> *The pomp of power*
> *And all the beauty that all wealth e're gave*

These, too, are deadly Levantine sins, as deadly as fornication, but they have never produced the long emotional tangle of sex in Western life. It is only in modern times that these latter goals of earthly interest have been put forward as sins, and then not as matters for the private conscience of individuals but as objects which it was the ethical duty of the state to remove in the interest of a more perfect, that is, less sinful world. But our difficulty with sex does not stem from such a transference of Levantine other-worldly ethics to the politics of this world. This difficulty goes back to the origin of our society.

The irreconcilable contradiction between causality and will, the contradiction that makes us imagine the past to have been cause-governed and the future to be under control of the will, exists in our attitude towards sex. Here the contradiction lies in our belief in the ethical validity of both willed action and endurance. In human generation it is impossible to reconcile them. The only means of human endurance are the direct antithesis of willed action. The ovum of a woman accepts indifferently anyone's seed. Her body industriously fabricates anyone's child. So obviously is this the contradiction of all we prefer to believe about the deep structure of life that if women rather than men composed the abstract ethical systems of the world and executed the artistic symbols that display such systems, some society believing as we believe—or like several believing almost the opposite of what we believe—would no doubt have used the image of the pregnant woman as the great symbol of will-less destiny that some have seen as the master of human life. But men, not women, compose such systems and execute such symbols. In the opening centuries of the Levantine civilization the church tells us how little it had come to expect of women in the way of abstract ethical thought, "wayward creatures of impulse, always curious to learn and never able to attain the knowledge of truth."[16] In the beginning of our own society, St. Anselm expressed a view of women that indicated that he, too, found women uninterested in abstract systems—and without such an interest there is no inner command to find symbols to represent the essential meaning of these systems.

[16] II Timothy 3:6

Femina nil horret, cuncta licere putat.
Audet quidquid eam jubet imperiosa libido
Et metus et ratio cedit et ipse pudor.
Haec leges sacras contemnit et omnia jura,
Turpe sit aut saevum, dum jubet illud amat.[17]

The artistic symbolism of all societies bears this out. Whatever it is, it is always from a masculine viewpoint. So it has been under the aspect of fecundaton, not gestation, that human generation has been displayed or denied as the great, revealing symbol of the relation of man to nature as each society has seen it. The symbol has never been the pregnant woman but the phallus.

We realize, of course, that the arts and religions of several other societies have employed an obviously phallic symbolism. We never recognize that in its own unusual way our society does so also. It is the exaggeration of Classical, Hindu and Babylonian phallicism that reveals to us that these societies required a symbolic expression of something they could not live with in comfort and self-composure, something that involved a contradiction in their image of first and last things. Our own exaggerated anti-phallicism reveals the same about us. The positive phallicism of these societies and the negative phallicism of our own show that, for all of us, human generation here raised problems that run deep into the ethical structure of the society. The carved pillars of Babylonia and India, the innumerable dramatic statues of Priapus which ornamented the public squares of Hellas, tell no more about these societies than a thousand years of Western art and letters tell about us. For these thousand years this secret which is a secret to nobody is never drawn, never painted, never mentioned. Not only is the secret personally familiar to almost all adults and most adolescents, but it is a commonplace to rural children. Yet in our arts, in everything that touches upon the willed direction by which we hold life should be governed, we assert that no such phenomenon exists.

It is silly to pretend that the phallus is absent from Western art because it is ugly or unattractive or unsuitable for artistic representation. These adjectives can never be *a priori* judgments of anything. Anything is suitable for artistic expression that is capable of fitting the unconscious symbolism underlying all artistic creation. Even as a matter of abstract aesthetic design anyone who briefly can take leave of his Western eyes and study Classical

---

[17] A woman recoils from nothing. She thinks she is free to do anything.
She dares whatever her imperious desire commands, and
neither fear nor consequence, nor even modesty, stands in her way.
She despises holy laws and very oath and let it be shameful or savage,
while she loves she is content.
—From *De contemptu mundi*, Migne, Patralogia Latina, Vol. 158, p. 693.

vases objectively can recognize that their phallicism produces no aesthetic disharmony. The negative phallicism of the West is not a matter of aesthetics but of ethics, and of the deepest, purest Western ethics at that. We cannot endure this intimate, powerful symbol of all that is immediate and improvident, all that ignores the conscious and purposeful ego, all that is a self-centered instrument bribed to a distant and impersonal purpose.

To the Classical society, to whom perpetuity was a horror and willed direction blasphemous, the phallus was, as it is to us, the principal symbol of the ephemeral, irresistible, blind fate which they asserted and we deny to be the master of the destiny of men. The same reason that led them to exaggerate its role out of all human proportions, to be unable to accept it as an ordinary human attribute along with innumerable others, leads us to do the same.

We have been unable to accept it either, but the contrast between the negative phallicism of the West and the positive phallicism of the Classical —a contrast that shows in all their arts and literature—seems less sharp than it really is because of the intervention of the Levantine society between us. We have never tolerated this symbol in our arts, but neither did the Levant. Nevertheless the Levant was never an example of negative phallicism like the West. It did not suppress the phallus because it could not endure it as a symbol. Except for the rigidly limited icons of the Orthodox church—and as everyone knows even they were the emotional issue of a fierce and ruinous civil war—it suppressed pictorial representation of every kind. But Levantine literature shows plainly that this society felt under no compulsion either to exaggerate or suppress the role of erotic acts and sensations in human life. All this world was evil, but if one did not withdraw from it, none of its aspects was any more evil than another. Since they accepted sex in this manner, much of their literature seems to us erotic. In a Classical sense it is not. One of the first and one of the last examples of Levantine storytelling are familiar in the West, *Daphnis and Chloë* and the *Thousand and One Nights*. Neither contains the least breath of the emotions that drove the Classical to offer divine honors to Priapus or the West to pretend that nothing exists of which he was the symbol.

We Westerners see the sensations and emotions that drive men and women into each other's arms as the mechanism by which endurance is effected. The sensations and emotions are not of themselves purposeful and certainly not willed. They seek only their own gratification, which is not enduring purpose as we understand it. Yet purposeless as they are, they are designed to effect a distant, sensorily unrelated purpose and they are furthermore the only means of effecting this purpose. The coupling of men and women—other circumstances permitting—is, therefore, natural and ethically right to us because it is the link in a chain of endurance. It retains this character even when conception is being consciously avoided because we recognize that the ethical connection is not between any specific act and its specific consequence, but between sexual love as a human desire and the conception of children as a general consequence. But just as we cannot single out one specific sex act as ethically right because it led to conception and hold the far more numerous couplings ethically wrong because they did not, so we cannot separate the sex act from its consequence and permit it to be considered by itself in art or literature. To do so buries the long-range ethical purpose under the overpowering present of sensation. The means cease to be means and become represented as ends. The purposeful endurance of the end is lost under the might of the will-less, purposeless moment. The sex act by itself, taken as it were out of context and pictured as an end in itself, becomes the symbol of everything that is unethical to the West: the momentary, the will-less, the indifference to consequence, the whole wild, curiously purposeless forefront of nature of which we know we are a part but over which we must assert our mastery.

It has been this aspect of sex, not teachings taken from Levantine Christianity, which has complicated the erotic life of the West. We believe in endurance, and, therefore, we have from the beginning endowed motherhood with symbolic significance. No one could count the statues, paintings and sketches of nursing mothers, usually, of course, representing the Virgin, with which Western art has been filled from its earliest days. But the means of attaining motherhood are the direct denial of will and conscious purpose so we can symbolize only the result, never the cause. The antithesis in Classical art is complete and exact. There are countless reproductions of Priapus, of goat-flanked satyrs with their human phalli, of ravished nymphs and naked goddesses. But in all that prolific array of the source of human generation there is not one representation of the enduring result. There is not one Classical representation of a nursing mother.[18]

Our arts, and their contrast to the Classical, never vary from this rule. We permit the representation of naked boys but not naked men—it is not physiology considered alone that disturbs us. Under the Classicist urgings of the Renaissance, we reluctantly admitted the naked woman to our permitted arts, but never the phallus.

It should not, therefore, be surprising that the attitude of the West toward homosexuality should be the opposite of the Classical. To the Classical society the sex act, or more properly the sex gesture, carried symbolic and even sacred significance, but its normal consequence while practically necessary was symbolically wrong, since it was an expression of perpetuity and a denial that man as he stood was a complete, self-contained

---

[18] There are, of course, Hellenistic, i.e. early Levantine, representations of the nursing Isis and of the Virgin.

and mythically enduring body. Seen from the aspect of birth, man became only a dependent link in an eternal chain and so the Classical world declined to look at him that way. To us only the consequence of the sex act has ethical symbolism, and the act itself, while ethically right as a means to its end, is symbolically wrong when considered by itself. Since homosexuality carried out the blind impulse at least partially and altogether avoided the normal result of the impulse, it did no violence to Classical ethics. For exactly the same reason it is ethically offensive to the West. We should not delude ourselves that our objection to homosexuality is because it is "unnatural" or "disgusting" or "horrible." These, too, are afterthoughts, and it is really no more unnatural than celibacy which we can tolerate and even approve when it is in the service of religion, where it serves the ethical purpose of survival in aiding the endurance of a higher life which to the believer has embraced the lesser—the church of God. Our objection to homosexuality is that it does not lead to the survival of anything whose survival is ethically required in the West, and it yields to will-less forces not as a necessary means to a long-range purpose, not as a natural response to a mechanism placed in men and women to drive them to accomplish that purpose, but as a perversion of that mechanism for fruitless self-indulgence.

These somewhat long considerations of ethics are prompted by two factors. The rise of Western society cannot be understood unless the relations of Latin and Levantine Christianity can be disentangled, and this cannot be accomplished without observing their different ethical systems. The second factor is the shallowness of much modern political thought which believes men are and always have been motivated only by the promptings of economic interest and egotistical thirst for power. Self-interest of all kinds has certainly never been absent from human life, and we should hope that it never will be, but to suppose that the powerful convictions of right and wrong do not also move men is to be ignorant both of history and contemporary life. To suppose, further, that these convictions are subconsciously derived from calculations of self-interest is to be equally ignorant of men. It is true in this day of moral confusion, of self-interest masquerading in verbiage derived from ancient ethical systems, that ethical motivation seems weak and crass self-interest almost irresistible. It is true that we are no longer clear concerning what must survive, but this does not make the ethical motive inherently less powerful.

With the ethical structure of Western society disentangled from the Levantine, the significance of the great change from Orthodox to Western Christianity becomes more clear. Every alteration of doctrine, ritual, sacrament, church organization and permissible personal conduct was in the direction of Western, purposeful, enduring wordly action and away from the consensus and earthly contempt of the Levant.

During recent centuries every Western state has been both creator and creature of its own language. As we have all become more democratic, we have become more conscious of our vernacular languages. In an age of mass education, the ability to speak a national vernacular, the one cultural acquisition that does not have to be learned by conscious effort, has become almost the only badge of nationality. In the same way, the literature that we associate with our various countries is the literature written in its language. Medieval writing, therefore, does not automatically fall into its proper national slot, because with only a few important exceptions all serious writing was in Latin. Where there exists an international corporation to which such writings can be mentally assigned—as is, of course, the case with theology—there is no difficulty in finding a mental home for this material in our image of history. Where we cannot do that, however, as we cannot with scientific or irreligious writings, there is no recognized place for such material and it becomes part of no particular history. Since received history is the history of chartered institutions like states and churches, of vested concepts like "liberty" or "sculpture" or, at the very end, of "mankind," there is no conventional classification for matters that belong to none of these but are attributes of a historical society. Thus Aquinas is part of the history of Catholicism and even Abelard lives in counterpoise to him. But the early scientific thinkers of the West are identified, to the extent that anyone has ever heard of them at all, only by the modern nation that today occupies the place of their birth. Thus Grosseteste and Bacon are identified as Englishmen, Fibonacci as an Italian, a type of classification that is obviously nonsense when applied to Aquinas or Abelard. In relation to the history of thought, all these men were simply Westerners, or as they would have called themselves indifferently, Catholics or Latins. But this is not the way our accepted history treats them. We tend, therefore, to have the curious anomaly that all the vernacular writings of the past are piously preserved in our image of history because they can be considered a part of the history of some modern state, and the theological writings are at least recorded as having existed because they belong to the international church. This means that almost all the rest, including all the serious but irreligious writing of the Middle Ages, is without a place in our picture of the intellectual abilities of our ancestors and the origin or our society. Popular romance and infantile piety grace the early vernaculars. Hymns and theological problems are enunciated in the Latin of the church —and in these two are embraced the accepted intellectual history of the Middle Ages. All else that exists in that immense mass of European Latin literature, politics, love poetry, science and the philosophy of science, ribaldry, a whole rounded literature of a young but vigorous people belongs to nothing whose existence we admit.

Buried in this forgotten field is the origin of Western physical mechanical sciences. What passes today in academic textbooks and among the educated public as the history of the origin of modern science is simply not so.

It may seem odd that the origin of Western science should be, as it has been, the subject of fable and slovenly fabrication. The sciences seem so clear and powerful that, by association almost, their accepted history could hardly be thought of as a field of mystery and tall tales. Actually, however, this is not odd. The history of the sciences is not a piece of science but of history and, as we have organized the subject, a specialty of history at that. Indeed, it has been a specialty that historical scholarship has neglected almost totally until recent years. French and German scholars began exploring this forgotten field toward the middle of the nineteenth century, but this pioneer work was necessarily a series of scholarly monographs that could not reach the general public—particularly not an English-reading public. This work has made available the facts about medieval thought, but this alone cannot bring these facts to the attention of the educated public and add them to our accepted image of history. It is only in recent years, thanks to Lynn Thorndike, C. H. Haskins and above all to George Sarton, that there exists in English even a preliminary and a bibliographic treatment of the field.

Thus in our received picture of the Middle Ages, no corner is left for the history of the origins of the Western sciences. To the conventional historian this is not felt to falsify the picture for he, like the layman, believes that the history of Western science does not go back into medieval times. If our science has any antiquity at all in his scheme, it is by jumping directly back from the Renaissance to Classical Greece.

The neglect of medieval science no doubt flows in part from the unfamiliarity of literary historians with the principles of Western science so that they would have difficulty understanding medieval scientific works, even if they took the trouble to dig them out of the forgotten archives. But it is also true that to find the early development of Western science in the Middle Ages is to reverse all the theories of the influence school and equally all those of the advocates of "mankind" as the engine of history. If mechanical scientific thought for nearly a thousand years has been the attribute of the ancestors of the present day Westerners, it is difficult to argue that it is an accidental development that could have happened to anybody under the appropriate influences of liberalism, democracy, coal, iron and the correct rainfall.

The fact of the matter is that the history of Western scientific thought exposes the hollowness of the liberal and Marxist theory of history. In a liberal age there has, therefore, been good reason to neglect it and along with it, to neglect the history of technology, even though it is from medieval technology that modern industry is directly and traceably derived. This and the succeeding two chapters are, therefore, an attempt to bring to light the early threads of Western secular thought, scientific and non-scientific alike since a sharp line cannot always be drawn in the early period; and indeed almost all medieval thought, even the religious, is a homogeneous body consistent with the civilization of the people who produced it. Medieval thought as a whole is Western thought and the chief reason to pay particular note to scientific thought is that our type of scientific thought has been unique with Western society since its origin. It has been one of the most striking examples of our historical personality. To note its presence among even our distant ancestors is part of the task of identifying our society.

To explore intelligently the history of Western science requires the realization that scientific thought must be a system of thought before it can become a system of facts. "Facts" do not exist in the world around us, and in order to make sense of the events that happen—and scientific "facts" are first of all events—there must be in men's minds a type of thought that can see events as raw material for factual analysis. It is easy for us today to forget that there are no "facts" in the scientific sense apparent in the world of physical reality. There is no such thing as gravity evident. Objects sometimes fall and sometimes fly upward. There is no such thing as heat. Some things are hotter than others. It is, therefore, in the type of thought applied to events about us that the history of Western science begins. It begins, therefore, with what has come down to us as philosophical speculation.

At the outset it is necessary to avoid the misconceptions that follow from treating the twelfth and thirteenth century speculations as merely one chapter in a universal history of philosophy. To consider these thinkers in series with Plato and Aristotle, or with the theologians and philosophers, Christian and Moslem, of the Levant, makes it impossible to understand what was taking place in medieval Europe. What these early Western thinkers were trying to do for their society was what the unknown Greek thinkers prior to Thales of Miletus (fl. 600 B.C.) and Pythagoras (fl. 530 B.C.), the earliest philosophers mentioned by Aristotle or known to us, must have worked out. Of these men we know nothing, not even of their existence, but Thales clearly had a foundation of astronomical and geometrical thought on which to base his own speculations and Pythagoras apparently drew on ancient Orphic speculations. We know a great deal more about the men in the Levantine world who, like the medieval school-men, were faced with the problem of the early exposition of the fundamental philosophy of their society. Among the Christians, they are the early writers from St. Paul and the author of the John Gospel to St. Augustine. Among the Neoplatonists, Plotinus and Porphy, among the Jews, the unknown oral composers of the Halaka, put later in writing as the Mishnah, and the authors of the various expositions in the Midrashim. These men were coping with the same kind of problem that faced the Western scholastics. Each attempted to formulate, primarily in religious terms, the underlying beliefs of a new society. It is with these schools of thought that Western scholasticism should be compared, not with the finished philosophers of a ripe civilization working against the detailed background of centuries of development of the thought of their society.

When the medieval schoolmen are compared with the early fathers of the Levantine civilization, even the most pious appears almost irreligious by comparison—if by religious is meant ecstasy and personal certainty of immediate divine revelation. The medieval schoolmen did not harbor doubts about the truths of the faith. They believed that the Christian faith had once been miraculously revealed, but they did not themselves expect to fall into divine ecstasy and have any part of it revealed anew. Even in these early days that we think of as the ages of faith, something of the cold, impersonal intellectual structure of Western thought is apparent.

The clash of science and religion is a standard pattern in all societies, but it occurs in the full development of a society after its science becomes thoroughly thought but and its religious myths have come to seem childish. So Aristotle stands in complete contrast to the Classical mythology, so in the Levant the Arabic sceptics who preceded Averroës were in conflict with pious followers of the Koran. But in these cases, the issue is whether a form of materialism or a form of mythology is the proper expression of the same faith. In the Western Middle Ages, the conflict was different. It was never a conflict between materialism and religion. Quite unconsciously, it was a conflict between the faith that men found in themselves and the faith they felt they ought to hold, between faith and "the Faith." For the medieval rationalists were men of profound faith. They lacked any compre-hensive body of evidence to show that the world of the senses was the real world and not the illusory phantom which the Levantines taught. They had no external reason to believe that one connected chain of causal neces-sity rather than the will of God immanent under each event governed the working of the physical universe. They never concretely formulated such a proposition, which is not surprising for even in our own day when this is the universally accepted premise of all the sciences, an exact philosophical formulation of this belief is still to be written.

In its origin, this belief existed rather as a germ than as a system. It was perhaps initially negative; Western thinkers could not believe in magic. Phenomena must have rational, that is Western rational, comprehensible and consistent explanations. This was a belief of faith, not evidence. But it clashed with the sacred books, which picture a universe run by the immediate action of the will of God. Such a world is unknowable and unpredictable by any method we Westerners would call scientific. The scientific limit in our meaning of the word "science" working under such a premise is a description of the appearance of the universe and to that, and to that alone, Levantine science was able to attain. To search for deep patterns, layer by layer of underlying causality, requires a belief that such a structure inheres in the physical universe, that no matter how far the chain of causality is followed, the borders of the material universe extend farther, that no chain of causality can ever encounter the will of God, for there it would end.

Medieval thought must, therefore, be considered in its setting. The problem is not to explore it for philosophical truths of current value but to examine it as a piece of history, one of those pieces that does lead to us.

Philosophical thought in the Middle Ages used concepts that we no longer employ. It sought immediate objectives that we have long ago tacitly abandoned. It lacked the classifications that we have found essential to the organization of knowledge. Physics, psychology, metaphysics, history, geography, zoology, mathematics, all alike appeared to require a common solution in every major problem that arose. To describe the aim of the medieval thinkers as the attainment of a synthesis, which is often done, is perhaps technically correct but conveys the wrong impression. Synthesis can at times be a polite name for unresolved confusion and such it was in the Middle Ages. The attempt at synthesis was forced upon medieval thinkers by their inability to separate the different types of problem with which they were concerned. Theology, psychology and mechanics, historical events and natural phenomena all had to be analyzed from the same set of axioms. There was also the problem of comprehension. Almost all our knowledge we gain by seeing. What mysterious relationship lies between the thing seen and our knowledge of what it is we see? A stone does not enter the eye but from something that does enter the eye we are able to know that it is a stone and to know that it is *there* outside us, not inside where the knowledge of it seems to be, that the stone is in some incomprehensible manner different from our only possible knoweldge of it. All we can certainly know is within our own nervous system. Yet the certainty convinces us that *it* itself is the phantom and that the external, which we know only by phantoms, is the certainty. Do not too condescendingly dismiss the early concern over this type of difficulty. Action at a distance is still a problem of physics. Psychology has not yet found the last secrets of consciousness. We are the beneficiaries of the discoveries that knowledge can be acquired with these problems unsolved and that different fields of inquiry can proceed from different premises.

The early medieval thinkers found themselves in a universe with certain fixed constants. Their environment, in the wide sense of the word, was, like ours, a historical past and a physical present. In the physical present, there was the community of Western Christendom, far more the "country" of these men than their feudal kingdoms. All used the same learned language. Everyone was under a multiplicity of feudal lords, but all belonged to the same church and quite aside from the temporal power of certain bishops in their secular capacity as feudal lords, the church, with jurisdiction over education and much of what is now the criminal law, was necessarily a unified political power. The political community to which they belonged was thus obvious to all of them: Latin Christendom. South of them was another community but, to them, one of infidels and schismatics. Eastward were the still barbarous Slavs. Whenever their philosophy touched upon men or history, they had, therefore, two units: "man" as a theological concept—the race of men whom Christ had potentially redeemed—and as a political reality the Latin Christians, they themselves, with whom alone this redemption had become actual. Their egotism, like that of every child and of every young civilization, was boundless.

Their historical environment, as they saw it was, therefore, "Christianity": the fact of the Western Catholic Church, the Bible, and the literature of the Levantine Fathers. Of the last, none had remotely the importance of St. Augustine. It is thus almost as silly to consider Western society and ignore Augustine as it is to ponder Western history and ignore the Christian church. The writings of Augustine are the synthesis of Levantine Christianity as the West received it. True, custom has established four Latin Fathers,[19] Augustine, Jerome, Ambrose and Gregory the Great, but only Augustine had a decisive influence on Western thought. Jerome was a scholar, not a theologian, Ambrose a poet and fantastic allegorist, Gregory an administrator whose theological interests, when they departed from being a mere copy of Augustine's, concerned the efficacy of relics and the power of demons and angels. The old Latin apologists, Tertullian, Minucius Felix, Lactantius and Arnobius, either avoided theology or were heretics. The later writers were worthies like St. Cyprian (d. 258) who wrote on local church problems and St. Hilary (d. 368) who composed obscure arguments against the Arians. Even the church at Rome used Greek until the middle of the third century. Thus Augustine was the only great Levantine thinker who wrote in Latin. His writings were part of a

---

[19] Technically *Doctores Esslesiae.*

living continuity of thought, most of which was expressed in the Greek and Syriac languages, and continued afterwards in Arabic. Other than Augustine there was no Latin Christian writer of intellectual consequence until the Westerners began discussing Western problems six hundred years after his death.

Custom likewise accepts the division of the Eastern and Western churches, but the distinction is established not on the basis of belief or of civilization but of language. The Eastern church is pictured simply as that of believers using the Greek language and the Western as the church of similar believers using Latin. It is an inadequate distinction. Only during the few centuries between the Severan emperors and the loss of the western provinces was a difference of language the only or the important difference between Christianity in Greek and Christianity in Latin. During this brief period, the Latin church was no more than a translation of the contemporary Greek and with the loss of the western provinces, Latin Byzantium disappeared and Latin Levantine Christianity disappeared with it—most of it ending in Mohammedanism. Some centuries later another and different group of Christians began using Latin, but this time it was a new church. They were different men and in other lands. The problems that concerned them had never occurred to the earlier Christians. Their deep and almost unconscious conception of what was real and what was illusory, instead of making them ripe for acceptance of the faith of Islam, made them its mortal enemies. Only the name of Christianity and the maintenance of surface formalities connected the independent Latin-using Western church of the eleventh century with the tiny Latin-speaking wing of the Greek church of the fifth. The two were no more one church than Charlemagne's empire was the same empire as Constantine's. The pretense of identity was much the same in both cases, though the one myth has endured somewhat longer than the other.

It is the hidden, unadmitted fact of this broken continuity that gives Augustine his importance in Western thought. The Levantine Greek Fathers have never weighed heavily in our lives. They have been little read even in translation and what was offensive in their doctrines has been charged to their Greek nationality, not to their Christian faith. But Augustine could not be so readily interpreted. As the only authentic Levantine Father intimately known, he was for centuries "historical" Christianity to the West. Long before the modern Protestants began seeking in the Gospels for this image of their own desires, the whole West had done so with Augustine. But in each case the texts have been disappointingly refractory.

All the great heresies that have wracked Western Christendom have, therefore, been either revolts against Augustine or, much more often, demands for firmer adherence to his theology. Age by age, men deeply imbued with Bible reading have found the church of their time or country unwilling to accept the meaning of the Bible as Augustine so powerfully and so passionately expounds it. The dualistic Cathari of the Middle Ages, the world-rejecting Lollards and Hussites, Wycliffe, Luther himself, the Jansenists, were all followers of Augustine. Calvin attempted to restore, almost verbatim, all he could understand of Augustine's doctrine of grace as God's method of accomplishing the predestination by which, in Calvin's view as in Augustine's, all human life was governed. In contrast to this long line of literalists, who so often have founded enduring heretical sects, rebels against Augustine's theology have been heresiarchs but never founders of sects. However firmly the churches of the West have proclaimed or believed that they expounded the true faith of the saints, all with the exception of the early Calvinist and Lutheran, have modified out of existence Augustine's central doctrine: predestination. Yet what Augustine taught, St. Paul taught. And certainly on this point, what Paul taught Jesus believed. There have thus been only a few conscious followers of Pelagius. Few have felt that their church, in the name of religion, should unequivocally take a position in contradiction to its religious documents. To the sincere but religious Westerner it has usually been sufficient that in day-to-day fact, the church already taught the contradiction. Those who have seen that it was a contradiction and have consciously preferred the contradiction to the ancient teaching, have more often ended in apostasy than in heresy. Like Pelagius against Augustine before Western Christianity began, only Arminius felt compelled to force the issue anew against the revived Augustinianism of Calvin.

But this day-to-day adjustment of Levantine documents to Western convictions has required a profound re-interpretation of the documents. The medieval church was never willing to say that Augustine erred and no modern sect is disposed to say so either. The Roman Catholic Church insists that Wycliffe, Luther, Calvin and the Jansenists all misunderstood Augustine—though all misunderstood him in the same sense. The modern Protestants, who on this point do not follow Calvin and Luther any more than the Roman Catholics, would seem to have a more difficult problem since it is easier to interpret Augustinianism out of Augustine than to remove it from the writings of Calvin and Luther. But Protestantism cares less for the theology of its founders than for their politics, and in the end modern Protestants occupy the same position on Augustine as the Roman Catholics. For both groups Augustine cannot have meant what he manifestly did mean. If we were to admit what Augustine meant, we would be driven to admit what St. Paul meant and from St. Paul it is but a step to Jesus himself. Since we have been reluctant to admit that we constitute a civilization of our own and that we have, therefore, necessarily placed our interpretation upon our sacred Levantine sources, we are forced to disguise from ourselves the actual meaning of these sources. What the life of Jesus and the teachings of Paul and Augustine meant in the civilization of the Levant has deep meaning to us. But that life *as if it had been lived among us men of the West,* and those teachings, *as if they had been addressed not to Levantines but to us,* have no valid meaning. The first has been profoundly entwined in our own deep religious beliefs. The second has been the surface of all our pious exhortations and a source of eight centuries of misery and anguish.

Augustine's theory of predestination is the central doctrine of his thought. It lies at the root of his theory of knowledge. Men, he believed, can neither learn nor be taught. When they hear or see something, they comprehend it or they do not comprehend it. They analyze it truly or falsely. But they do neither by the power of their own intelligence or the depth of their own experience. Only the light of the interior man, Christ himself, who resides within each, reveals to him the truth or falsity of the words and images that reach his mind. Thus neither the human teacher nor the pupil have decisive power in the acquisition of knowledge. All that the human teacher can do is present matters in such simple steps that the pupil is able to consult the inner Christ about each separately. What each man can apprehend is not in any way the result of anything his own, neither of his will, nor his experience, nor his intelligence, but only of the step-by-step revelations by the inner Christ who has thus built will and intelligence in some men and refused to build it in others. Knowledge of truth becomes not a question of objective fact but of the willingness of the inner Christ to reveal it,[20] and to Augustine the inner Christ is not, as it is with us, a phrase describing some human attribute acting in harmony with God's purpose. To Augustine the inner Christ was the presence of the Levantine substance of Christ physically within a man.

The outer life of man was as dependent on God as the inner, indeed the outer life was no more than the consequence of the inner. In his treatise, *On Grace and Free Will,* Augustine writes:

> ... *There is, however, always within us a free will—but it is not always good; for it is either free from righteousness when it serves sin—and then it is evil—or else it is free from sin when it serves righteousness—and then it is good. But the grace of God is always good; and by it it comes to pass that a man is of good will, though he was before of an evil one. By it also it comes to pass that the very good will, which has now begun to be, is enlarged, and made so*

*great that it is able to fulfil the divine commandments which it shall
wish, when it shall once firmly and perfectly wish. . . . the man who
wills but is not able knows that he does not yet fully will, and prays
that he may have so great a will that it may suffice for keeping the
commandments. And thus, indeed, he receives assistance to perform
what he is commanded. . . .*[21]

*. . . I think, too that I have so discussed the subject that it is not
so much I myself as the inspired Scripture which has spoken to you,
in the clearest testimonies of truth; and if this divine record be looked
into carefully, it shows us that not only men's good wills, which God
Himself converts from bad ones, and, when converted by Him, directs
to good actions and to eternal life, but also those which follow the
world are so entirely at the disposal of God, that He turns them
whithersoever He wills, and whensoever He wills—to bestow kind-
ness on some, and to heap punishment on others, as He Himself
judges right by a counsel most secret to Himself, indeed, but beyond
all doubt most righteous. . . .*[22]

*. . . God works in the hearts of men to incline their wills whither-
soever He wills, whether to good deeds according to His mercy, or
to evil after their own deserts; His own judgment being sometimes
manifest, sometimes secret, but always righteous. . . . Grace, however,
is not bestowed according to men's deserts; otherwise grace would
no longer be grace. For grace is so designated because it is given
gratuitously. Now if God is able, either through the agency of angels
(whether good ones or evil), or in any other way whatever, to operate
in the hearts even of the wicked, in return for their deserts—whose
wickedness was not made by Him, but was either derived originally
from Adam, or increased by their own will—what is there to wonder
at if, through the Holy Spirit, He works good in the hearts of the
elect, who has wrought it that their hearts become good instead of
evil?* [23]

There is no misunderstanding the consequence of Augustine's doctrine.
Everything that men do is the result of the will of God. His long and
more famous works, *The Confessions* and *The City of God*, are immense elaborations of this theme applied to his own life and the history
of men. The theological treatises merely bring the issue more sharply to
focus. As a result, in their argument against a doctrine of free will that
has been self-evident to us Westerners, they seem to us almost to impute

[21] *On Grace and Free Will*—Chapter XXXI
[22] *Ibid*, Chapter XLI
[23] *Ibid*, Chapter XLIII—A convenient edition of the writings of St. Augustine is
Basic Writings of Saint Augustine edited by Whitney J. Oates whose translation
is followed here.

an arbitrary evil to God. It is meaningless to us for Augustine to say that when God bends a man's will to evil he does so justly because of the unrighteousness of the man. Since man's will is at all times controlled only by God, a man's present evil will must have been made so by God himself at some point since birth. Even original sin is no answer. The elect whose wills have been inclined step-by-step to righteousness started with the same original sin as the damned.

But Augustine was not imputing evil to God. His denials on this point are not empty. Our difficulty lies in applying our concepts to his theories. To us an evil man is one who has an evil will. We cannot conceive of any way a man could be evil except by a series of willfully evil acts. To Augustine an evil will is what God develops in an evil man. He offers no more evident cause for a man being evil than we offer for a man being of evil will. But to us it seems that if there is any way in which a man could be evil other than by a series of willful acts, he must have been made evil through no choice of his own, though on the other hand we are sure that if he wills evil, he does so by his own choice. Against us Augustine says that a man is not responsible for willing evil, since his will is ultimately under the full control of God, but that he is responsible for being evil.

His polemics against the Manicheanism of his youth should not deceive us. In attacking the open dualistic mythology of the Manicheans, Augustine denied that the material universe could be evil. He went further and expounded from Plotinus the doctrine that evil has no real existence and is no more than the privation or misuse of the good. But this was a partisan argument and was far from representing in its entirety his understanding of the universe. Augustine was unwilling to concede the material universe to the Manichaean god of evil, but this was not to deny the existence of such a power. Above all, his philosophy stands on an inner not an outer view of man, on destiny as a drama of the soul, not of the world. In his long treatise, *On the Trinity,* he teaches that man was doomed to die because he was held in Satan's power, and Satan, not God, inflicted death upon him, having, however, a right to do so because of man's original sin. When Satan, without this warrant, put to death the sinless Christ, his further right to put men to death was extinguished. "The devil in that very death of the flesh, lost man whom he was possessing as by an absolute right. . . ."[24]

Whatever philosophical argument Augustine makes against the Manichaeans about evil being only the privation of the good, nevertheless in his understanding of the Atonement, evil is a power, and in his picture of the soul, evil is a reality, an emanation that takes possession of a man.

[24] *On the Trinity,* Bk. IV—Chapter XIII.

The elect are those from whom God drives out this resident evil. The damned are those so thoroughly possessed by this evil emanation that God will not enter their souls. This is not his statement but his thought. To us, this would make the possessed man morally guiltless. To the Levant, it does not. The elect of the Prince of This World are necessarily evil. If they had not been inherently evil, Satan would not have recognized them as his own. This is a kind of moral responsibility almost incomprehensible to us, but unless we attempt to understand it, however dimly, we can form no comprehension of Levantine ethics whether of Augustine or of Jesus. The Levantine universe is composed of the elect of the Kingdom of God and the elect of the Prince of Darkness, of the City of God and the Earthly City, and a man's task in this life is not to decide to which he will adhere but to discover to which he has been chosen. Faith and good works do not cause a man's election, they evidence it. The reason for a man's adherence to the faith and his continuance in good works is that a lapse in either would be a sign that he had deceived himself in supposing his heavenly election. The lapse would not be truly of his doing but of God's. It would not cause his damnation but reveal that he had not been elected.[25]

This concept of the ethical base of human life is so alien to the deepest beliefs of the West that from the origin of our society we have had to interpret it out of our Christianity. In our early days it was possible to grope along with Levantine concepts in physics and cosmology. Important though these are, they do not lie at the root of a man's being. But the base of a man's ethical system is an inalienable part of his personality. Without it he is a different man or not a man at all. Thus while it was possible to conform for some centuries to Levantine authority in such outward things as physics, it was never possible to conform in the deepest ethical thought. The crucial question, the one at the core of the entire difference between Levantine and Western ethics, was that of predestination. That God foreknew the fates of men was, of course, acceptable. That he predetermined them and that the will of the individual was, in the last analysis, not under his own control but only God's instrument in effecting what he had already predetermined, was intolerable.

It was a difficult transition. It required a direct contradiction of the teachings of the New Testament. What was perhaps even more difficult, it required an interpretive reversal of Augustine, more difficult because in the New Testament the ethical base is assumed more often than it is

---

[25] "Here is how the children of God and the children of the Devil are recognized. Anyone who does not practice righteousness does not belong to God ... let us put our love not into words or into talk but into deeds ... Thus it is that we may be sure we belong to the truth ..."
(I John 9, 18.)

stated, while in Augustine it is consciously elaborated, systematically and with great force and skill. Until modern times when the Bible itself at last became the object of critical, scholarly study and its historical sense thus became first clearly exposed, the great source of Christian discord in the West was always Augustine. It was relatively easy to misunderstand the intended sense of much scriptural language. It was extremely difficult to misunderstand Augustine. Yet the attempt had to be made. To substitute Western concepts for Levantine and still keep the Christian name in the West meant first misunderstanding Augustine.

Centuries of turning and twisting have left this problem precisely where the Middle Ages found it. Augustine is historical Christianity. He was the only Latin writer who systematized and reduced to intellectual exposition the theology of Levantine Christianity as he found it in the Bible and the Greek Fathers. He was the first great theologian of Levantine Christianity in the Latin language—and he was the last. In the development of Western secular and scientific thought his influence was immense. Modern convention requires us to separate the logical basis of our science from both the expressed and implied basis of historical Christianity. We make the assumption, if no more, of at least Levantine atheism, since God under Western science is not a worker of physical miracles contrary to the laws of nature. The Middle Ages were not yet able to do so and the early gropings of Western physical thought were begun under the towering moral and physical cosmology of Augustine.

Under the interpretation established by the Levantine Fathers and accepted in the early West, the Bible was a complete cosmology. The physical universe and man had a purpose and a history. Both had an inescapable destiny. The universe had been created for man, a rational creature endowed with freedom of the will, who willed to sin, thus bringing damnation and death upon himself and all his descendants. So far as this world was concerned, Adam's sin had an even more disastrous consequence. It corrupted man's nature. Adam in a state of innocence had free will. Once he had sinned, both he and his descendants lost this capacity. Christ's death, however, opened the way for Christians to be saved. To the Levantines, it redeemed from the powers of evil those whom God had predestined to be the elect. To the Westerners, it made it possible for Christians to seek salvation by the exercise of their own free will. The logical relationship between Christ's death and the Christian's salvation, that is, the precise meaning of the Atonement in the West, was impossible to establish; but this did not destroy the belief itself. The future history of the terrestrial universe was, therefore, simply the practical working out of this drama of salvation. To serve as the stage for this drama was why the universe still existed and why it would continue to endure. In theory, it had an end but that end was still far away.

Though the purpose of the universe was clearly established, its mechanism was not. God ruled even its every day operation, but in many things these day-to-day operations were conducted with an impressive regularity, so much so that some unchanging mechanism seemed to have been provided to carry out the will of God. This was obvious in astronomy, in the tides, in the rhythmical generation of men and animals, in repetitive experience encountered in all practical techniques. The purpose of the mechanism was clear, but how did it work? And since there was a common purpose in all things, must there not likewise be a common mechanism?

In this theocentric atmosphere where both nature and history existed for the divine drama of creation, fall and redemption, the only tools of analysis were Levantine and such disjointed elements of Classical thought as had been taken over and preserved by the Levant. They were thus sets of dual concepts, matter and form, substance and accident, genus and species (not in our restricted sense), subject and predicate, agent and patient, element and quality, which applied to our physical world of mass and energy have no meaning. Of the four Aristotelian[26] elements, fire, air, earth and water, none was the same thing as the physically obvious materials that bear these names. Each of them and therefore all objects within human experience—since all terrestrial matter was postulated to be compounded of these four elements—had its "natural" place in which it came to rest and towards which motion was "natural." All other motion was "violent" and required a mover. There was no continuing motion in the universe. Even the wheeling heavens required a source of constant motion. Even though they were postulated as composed of matter differing from the matter of earth and governed by different physical laws, yet the heavens, too, had a "natural" motion, circular. Even things moving "naturally" soon came to rest and would not again move except under the constraint of something else in motion. Since the Aristotelian cosmology embraced all types of change under the concept of motion, a constant source was required or the universe would come to a stand still. Somewhere there must be a continuous motion imparted by something which itself was not moved, for otherwise there would be an infinite regress. This ultimate source was God, who daily, even minute by minute, imparted the constant new motion without which the whole universe would soon perish, the stars and the sun cease to revolve, the winds cease to blow, the elements no

---

[26] The word "Aristotelian" is used to describe the philosophical system accepted under Aristotle's name both in the Levant and during the Western Middle Ages. Certain component details were derived from probably genuine writings of Aristotle and the immediate post-Aristotelian peripatetics, but Aristotelianism as a system of cosmology and philosophy was a form of Levantine neoplatonism.

longer transformed to give new sources of fire on the earth and water in the skies, the plants and animals doomed to immediate death as all things came to rest unmoved in their natural place.

The intellectual environment of the early medieval thinkers was thus an interlocked system of theology and physics, each reinforcing the other at every essential point. There were, to be sure, theological difficulties in trying unconsciously to interpret away the deeper Levantine concepts inherent in the Bible and the works of the Fathers. There were also specific contradictions between Aristotle and the Bible, and as the Aristotelian writings became more fully available during the twelfth and thirteenth centuries, these contradictions became the occasion for increasing difficulties. Aristotle, for example, taught that the soul was mortal and the universe eternal, that God exercised no immediate supervision over mundane affairs; but the Aristotelian cosmology as a whole coincided with the basic premises of the theology. Aquinas had no difficulty in using the Aristotelian laws of motion and causality to construct scientific proofs of the existence of God.

So at the outset there was no conflict between reason and faith. There were problems in seeking to resolve textual contradictions, but there was no group of men who consciously argued that the purpose of history and the mechanics of the physical universe were contrary to the teachings which all men, Westerners or Levantines, had theretofore drawn from the Bible.

We moderns use the word "science" to convey two meanings for which the Middle Ages used two different words: "reason," *ratio,* and "science," *scientia.* They like ourselves applied the word "science" to any interrelated body of knowledge, such as physics or geography. But where we use the same word to describe a method of knowledge or a set of mechanistic philosophical principles, in this meaning they used the word "reason," a practice continued into the eighteenth century. Hence, our word "science," in this sense, and the "reason" of the eighteenth century philosophers and the medieval schoolmen all meant the same thing: a set of conclusions logically derived from a group of facts and axioms from which all supernatural considerations had been removed, or at least had been removed so far as any thinker was conscious of them. The "facts" in each of the three cases differed enormously but the axioms very little. The latter were that knowledge of objective reality is possible even though limited and perhaps always inaccurate; that invariable temporal sequence is proof of causal connection, direct or indirect; that a causal connection is a necessity not a possibility nor a probability; that logical or mathematical reasoning, if correctly performed, is infallible and can only err from undetected errors in the premises, that is, in the assumed "facts."

We can have no quarrel with medieval reasoning as a method of seeking knowledge, but we would certainly object to the preliminary "facts" upon which that reasoning went to work. These "facts," like our own, were concepts, but an entirely different set from those to which we have given the name of facts. Naturally, most medieval thinkers, like most moderns, were unaware that their facts were concepts, but this ignorance involved them in more scientific difficulties than it does us. Our modern system of concepts bearing the name of facts, mass, energy, atom, the whole basic verbal structure of the sciences, has been refined by centuries of probing experience. The medieval set of physical "facts," substance and accident, matter and form, natural and violent motion, was taken over complete from the Levant, and it was not until the late thirteenth century that this system began to fall under serious critical scrutiny. But at all times the medieval thinkers had no doubt that reasoning was a valid system of knowledge quite independent of the truths of revealed religion.

Western speculative thought began in the eleventh century. The single apparent exception to this statement, or the single exception that some historians might argue, was John Scotus Erigena (Eriugena) brought from Ireland to the Continent by Charles the Bald about 840. Erigena was unquestionably a speculative thinker of systematic scope, but his strange isolation, two centuries before the great group of eleventh century thinkers—the continuity of whose thought has never been interrupted—was not an anomaly. So far as he was a systematic thinker, he was not Western. He was not at ease with the deep axioms of Levantine thought, but like many Irish of his time he knew Greek and was steeped in little else—Dionysius the Pseudo-Areopagite, Maximus the Confessor, St. Basil, Gregory and, of course, in Latin, St. Augustine. Erigena's world system, in his philosophical treatise *De divisione naturae,* is, therefore, a system of Neoplatonic emanations or ideas, flowing from God and at the point where they are most distant from Him, appearing to our eyes as phenomena in time and space. Even time and space are not realities, but only the outward realms of the universal circle of which God is the timeless and spaceless center. But since the appearances of phenomena both conceal and manifest ideas emanating from God, their destiny is to return to him and the dual role of Christ was, as man, to take upon himself all nature, animate and inanimate, and as the risen God take these with Him to heaven. Thus the return to God was begun by Christ and can be effected only through Him. Totally Levantine though the materials of this theology were, Erigena could not put it together into a logical Levantine system. He rejected every trace of open or hidden dualism and hence ran into impossible difficulties with the problem of sin. The power of matter, the existence of sex, all worldly interests and ambitions, Erigena saw as a consequence of original sin; but by refusing to postulate or even subconsciously accept a power of evil, he could not account for sin nor, like Augustine, insinuate it without explanation into a system that logically should be without it. As a result, Erigena really denied its existence. Sin he defined as a misdirection of the will resulting from a judgment that things were good when in fact they were not good. Hence, punishment became nothing but a concealed education because wickedness in the last analysis is not an evil will but an uninformed judgment. Thus hell has no physical existence. There can be no one to go there. All men, all nature, even the devil and the fallen angels, are in time to return to God who made them. Needless to say the Atonement had thus no purpose and the Eucharist, in a universe where matter was posulated to be only the appearance of ideas, could not be the physical body and blood of Christ.

This extraordinary system of Levantine physics, Christian nomenclature, and vague but profoundly Western ideas on the nature of the will and the impossibility of a dual causality in the universe, was founded, according to Erigena, on pure reason. Indeed reason played so large a part in his theories that he is often felt to have been the forerunner of rationalism. He denied all validity to authority unless reason could approve it, since authority depended for its validity upon reason, not reason upon authority. But since by the use of this reason he arrived not only at a completely pantheistic world but at one of neoplatonic emanations, his position in Western intellectual history is unavoidably confused. All the later rationalists used this method to work further and further away from such a universe.

Erigena was also not quite clear whether the Levantine emanations with which he dealt were substantial realities, as they were in the Levant, or only names as they later became to the Western nominalists. Erigena, like Pelagius, has faint, almost premature traces of Western thought. Both could be described as Levantine thinkers uncomfortable in trying to raise Western issues.

The first Western speculative thinker of systematic scope was St. Anselm, born of a Lombard family in Piedmont in 1033, prior and then abbot of the monastery at Bec in Normany and from 1093 until his death in 1109, Archbishop of Canterbury.

In a series of works[27] written over more than thirty years, Anselm attempted the composition of a rational, Christian theology. He saw the universe as he had learned it from his Levantine authorities, Augustine and Boethius' translation of the *Isagoge* of Porphyry, the last a commentary on Aristotle's logic. To Anselm the ultimate reality was God. The lesser

---

[27] Chiefly *Monologium, Proslogium, De Veritate* and *Cur Deus homo.*
First printed Nüremberg, 1491. *Opera Omnia*, Paris 1675.

realities were ideas. "Things" in a sense had no true existence but were merely visible impressions of the invisible ideas from which they derived their being. This was straight Neoplatonism, but Anselm was not quite content to leave it at that. He felt he had a duty to be an advocate of reason and that what faith revealed, reason could likewise prove. In defense of this position he argued that while the infidels could not be swayed by the authority of revelation, they might be won by the power of logic. He attempted, therefore, to derive his philosophy exclusively by rational methods. Starting with what he considered a rational proof of the existence of God he attempted to prove the truth of Christian revelation without resort to scriptural authority. It was an interesting attempt, and one of its lessons is the evidence of an eleventh century audience that in addition to an authoritative, demanded a rational, basis for the faith. The infidels were far away and Anselm's Christian reasoning was much more addressed to questioning Latins than to convinced Jews and Mohammedans.

This early Latin rationalism which troubled other churchmen than Anselm was not, as rationalism later became, even secretly hostile to religion. Western Christian theology had not yet formed as an unchallengeable system of truth. The situation of the Latins was in its way much like that of the Levantines nearly a thousand years earlier before the great councils had defined the correct theology for the Levant; that is, controversy was not heresy until the pope or a council ruled on the matter at issue. The texts of the decisions of the ancient Levantine councils had to stand, of course, but interpretations were possible and questions never raised in the Levant could be discussed. Nevertheless, in every attempt to raise questions and define dogma, while always avoiding an open clash with the decisions of the Fathers and the ancient councils, each new issue always threatened to carry the Latin Church a little further from its sacred documents. Thus shortly before Anselm's time, Berengar of Tours had argued against the dogma of transubstantiation, not on the ground that the physics of substance and accident was unsound, but on the Aristotelian basis that two different substances could not possess identical accidents. His view did not prevail, but the fact that he raised the issue brought about the first dogmatic decision on a matter that had been so evident and natural in a thousand years of Levantine Christianity that a doctrinal ruling had never been required.[28] Yet Berengar was not trying to assert Western concepts of physical reality against Levantine. He was arguing within the domain of Levantine physics itself. The clash of Western mechanical thought with Levantine never arose over the composition of matter, over molecules versus substance. It

---

[28] Apparently the word "transubstantiation" first came into use at this time, but here Protestantism made one of its few obvious historical mistakes in supposing the doctrine itself to have been medieval.

developed instead from Western concepts expressed in the laws of motion and was in full flower before the Western concepts of mass and energy were sufficiently developed to formulate a consistent hypothesis concerning the structure of matter. The Eucharist has always been a religious problem untouched by Western physics, since Western mechanical thought has no concept comparable to the Levantine concept of substance.[29]

But in his desire to present a reasonable Christianity to others, Anselm faced a serious rational problem of his own, again a problem which in a thousand years of Levantine Christianity had troubled no one. Anselm raised it in the very title of his treatise on the subject, *Cur Deus homo?* "Why did God become man?" What is the theological significance of Christ's death? If he died to redeem man from sin, from what *power* did he redeem him? In the dualism of the Levant, this had been no problem. From Satan, of course, had been the almost universal answer, though if Christ's death ransomed man from the devil it was a ransom paid to the devil, not only *from* God but *of* God as Gregory of Nazianzus pointed out. Few Levantine theologians were as disturbed by this conclusion as he. Ignatius avoided the more obvious offensive consequences of a ransom by the equally dualistic theory that Christ's divinity, concealed under his manhood, deceived Satan and, as Gregory of Nyssa phrased it, Satan, like a fish in seizing the bait of Christ's manhood, was caught on the concealed hook of his divinity. Yet however turned, the Levantine theory of the Atonement always involved Satan. It was always dualistic.

But from the very beginning of Western thought it could not be. Even Anselm, so soon and so devout an archbishop, could not accept the doctrine that Christ's death bought man free from the power of Satan. Such a view was automatic under the dualism of the Levant, but even in the infant West it was impossible. Satan could not be a coequal power whom God had to bribe or trick. God's power alone was sufficient to free man from any dominion Satan might hold over him. What, then, was gained by the death of God's Son? For it seemed clear to Anselm that the Son must have willed his own death since men could not have crucified an unwilling God. If redemption of man from a coequal power of evil was out of the question, what rational explanation could there be for God's sacrifice?

Anselm devised a curiously involved doctrine that Adam's disobedience, being an infinite insult to God, God's honor could only be restored by an infinite satisfaction, which could only be effected by the death of the God-man. Gone is all trace of Augustine's ransom in the sinless death paid

---

[29] The word "substance" in a material sense is today employed simply as a generic term for any unspecified material. Something of the Levantine and medieval meaning—where it was applied to matter—survives in our derived immaterial use of the word: "The substance of an argument . . ."

the devil in lieu of our sinful deaths still due him. Gone, too, and equally interestingly, was Augustine's insistence on the completely gratuitous nature of Christ's sacrifice in our belief. To Anselm it was a rational necessity flowing from the purpose of creation, to glorify God. So long as unforgivable sin exists, this glorification is not fully possible. Therefore, by necessity a means of forgiving sin must arise. As a theological theory, Anselm's has not had wide popularity—but then neither has any other in explanation of this difficult matter—but it is one more indication—and an important one—of the deep difference between Western and Levantine Christianities to find at the beginning of Western speculative thought an attempt to solve the theological mystery of the Atonement without resort to Levantine dualism.

There were two contemporary reactions against Anselm, each hostile not only to Anselm but partly to the other. The first was against his argument that reason paralleled faith and led to the same fundamental conclusions. If this were so, it was pointed out, we would have no need for the authority of scripture nor the teachings of the church. Christ would have come for nothing. Pagan reason unaided could have arrived at the truths requisite for salvation. No such conclusion can be accepted, and we must recognize in revelation truths that reason cannot attain. We must accept our faith on that authority.

The second objection was philosophical and came from those who afterwards denied the existence of Neoplatonist ideas as the reality behind things. There was no "justice." It was simply a name classifying separate just acts. There was nothing that existed corresponding to "man." There were only individual men. Nor could the issue be kept out of theology. Roscellinus applied the same doctrine to the Trinity, that is to the relationships subsisting within it that made it a formal unity, arguing that Father, Son and Holy Ghost were our names for different aspects of God, not three separate realities. This attempt to strike Neoplatonism from the core of the faith got nowhere, the authority of Nicea and Chalcedon were too evident and too ancient, but the philosophical conflict itself could not be suppressed. It went on far into the thirteenth century and ended not in a settlement but in the divergence of Western thought into two channels which ever since have been almost unrelated, physics and theology.

The age of Anselm saw the first and the last effort to develop a completely rational Christianity in the West. Thereafter, no one went any further along the rationalist road than Aquinas. The Trinity and the Atonement were accepted as mysteries beyond the reach of reason, known to us only by revelation. But it is important to notice that this was not what they had been in the Levant. Far from being thought of as revealed truth, they were held by the Levantines to be rational deductions formulated by human councils in answer to specific, intelligible questions. And under the physics of the Levant they were. But what was rational in the Levant could only be miraculous in the West and so these old efforts of Levantine reasoning —for obviously neither the Trinity nor the substance, persons or nature of Christ are attested in Scripture, nor is it explained from whom or by what mechanism Jesus' death is a ransom—have passed into Western Christianity to be believed as Tertullian felt belief should always be justified, *quia absurdum.*

It is unfortunate that the different rational structures of Levantine and Western Christianities and the different physics at the base of each of these structures are generally ignored. Nor has it been helpful that the physics, and the physical nomenclature, of an alien society should have been entangled in the theology of our own. It has left our theology with a self-contained vocabulary which, because it employs words with no other comparable application, has now become meaningless. No one any longer can convey thought by these words. They are only useful as signs of theological orthodoxy or heresy. But in the Levant this was not so. When the Fathers at Nicea, Ephesus and Chalcedon used the words that we translate as "substance," "person," "nature," "procession," (i.e. emanation) they used words currently applicable to the structure of material reality as Levantine men understood it, words that Levantine physicists were to use in purely scientific discussions for many centuries. Were a Western theologian to ask a Western physicist for a comparable definition, he could get no answer. These words have no meaning in our system of mass and energy and to defend our theology, we are driven to the false conclusion that nothing can be theologically sound unless it is physically unreal. We should know better. There is nothing in the creed of Chalcedon that a materialist sceptic like Averroës could not have accepted as sound physics even though, on religious grounds, he would have rejected it.

The acceptance of Levantine rationality as revealed truth in the West had an important consequence in the philosophical controversies of the Middle Ages. In the early days, as with Anselm, reason and revelation were seen as two independent means of arriving at the same truth. This was natural since what was called reason was still primarily Levantine reason, that is, logical deductions from Levantine concepts. It was the foundation of what was known as realism, a philosophical position directly opposite to what is called realism today. Medieval realism was Neoplatonism. It asserted that reality was not the multiplicity of tangible objects which our senses report, but the invisible, immaterial archetypes of such things. These archetypes were ideas in the Neoplatonic sense; that is, they existed as immaterial facts quite apart from the presence or absence of any such idea in any one's mind. In short, they were substances. Though the medieval realists thought of these ideas as existing in the mind of God, even this was not philosophically essential. The Levantine atheists had equally believed that such ideas were the ultimate reality.

The early medieval rationalist reasoned from this type of concept. They produced, therefore, no theological difficulties because Neoplatonism was the rational structure behind the Trinitarian and Christological decisions of the Levantine councils. Fundamentally, the same type of concepts lay behind the thought of St. Paul, and indeed was the subconscious understanding of reality held by the framers and most of the authors of the Bible.

But this era of intellectual peace did not last. Realism was challenged from a hostile philosophical position by men who came to be called nominalists; and the advocates of realism themselves felt unable to hold to an uncompromised Levantine position, which alone was logically tenable. Unconditioned realism had to deny the meaningful existence of individuals. If the only reality behind men was the idea "man," then whatever distinguished one man from another was, against ultimate reality, an illusion. Such a conclusion was inoffensive within a Levantine consensus, as St. Paul said, we are one body in Christ "every one members one of another." But to the Westerners it seemed to destroy the unconscious postulate at the root of all our thought, the separate existence of an individual, his self-managed will, his unconfusable identity—to the Middle Ages his own independent and immortal soul. Realism thus threatened to become pantheism.

Strict realism could find no way around this rock. Realism modified sufficiently to acknowledge the actual existence of individuals, animate or inanimate, broke down under its inability to formulate any intelligible explanation of how real arch types and real material things could co-exist. The second must either be illusory reflection of the first, as our inadequate minds and senses encounter these seemingly material expressions of the real, immaterial ideas; or else the ideas must only be names or mental concepts of the similarities that we observe in the multiplicity of real material things. The last was the interpretation of the nominalists, though in fact the issue was rarely forced to such extremes, both realists and nominalists having sound reasons for stopping short of the ultimate logical development of their respective positions. One ended in pantheism, the other in scepticism.

Thus what developed was a double contest, one within the other. Reason and revelation began as independent but converging methods of knowledge. But reason broke apart into two methods, realism striving to keep as much as it could of Levantine rationalism; and nominalism, officially devout but striking first at the Levantine rationalism of the creed and later at the validity of revelation itself. At the same time, modified realism became less and less competent to develop a rational justification of the entire body of revelation—which had been its original aim—and, in addition to the attacks it suffered from nominalism, became itself suspect to the pious. If the old realists like Anselm seem to be the spiritual ancestors of mere conservative churchmen, it is only because the churchmen never raised questions that disturbed the accepted dogmas, while the early realists answered all questions in perfect harmony with the dogmas. But in time, as rationalism became increasingly Western in its basic concepts, a rational realism ceased to be possible and the later realists fell back on a purely Levantine mechanism safe from the corrosive acid of Western thought, mysticism. All the later consistent realists were mystics, many of them heretics. In time, too, the devout began to insist that, regardless of how pious the motive, the truths of the faith must not be subjected to rational scrutiny, realist or nominalist. They must be accepted on the unquestioned authority of their divine revelation. The full development of these antagonisms was still far in the future, but the twelfth century saw their beginning. The twelfth century was the time not only of Anselm but of Abelard and St. Bernard.

Abelard was an unsystematic philosopher, so unsystematic, in fact, that it would be proper to deny him the name and call him simply a dialectician. His contemporaries admired him as a logician. That he was himself directly sceptical is doubtful, but his *Sic et non,* in which with neither commentary nor resolution he set in parallel the contrary opinions of eminent theologians on almost every important doctrinal point, at least hinted at scepticism and was in any case a scandal to the pious. But his chief affront to the churchmen was his unbounded confidence in the capacity of human reason. For Abelard, "human intelligence is all and leaves nothing to the faith," wrote St. Bernard.[30] Already the position of Anselm, that reason always would arrive at the conclusions attested by revelation, was becoming dubious; and unbounded confidence in reason an affront to the faith. There was also an immense difference between the contemplative reason of Anslem, matured in the repose of the monastery, expressed with decorous restraint, and the argumentative, logic-chopping reason of Abelard, developed in the acrimonious debates of the Parisian schools. Worse still, while Abelard may have had no inward doubts about the truth of the Christian faith, he felt no obligation to extend its mantle over a system of Levantine ethics. To Abelard sin was the act of a wicked will, not the presence in a man of the substance of evil. A sinful act was knowingly to do what the conscience recognized as wrongful. Acts were lawful or unlawful by their conformity to outward standards, but sin—right or wrong before God—was internal

[30] Migne, *Patrologia Latina,* vol. 182, p. 331.

and could never be truly known by any man but the doer.[31] Abelard protested his unquestioning faith in the Christian religion but under this ethical view, original sin was an impossibility and the doctrine of the Atonement absurd. When to this he added serious and frankly expressed doubts about the intellectual integrity of contemporary churchmen, what is surprising is that he suffered no worse a fate—at least from the church—than to have his writings condemned, a condemnation that did not prevent their illegal circulation.

Abelard's great opponent was St. Bernard, Abbot of Clairvaux. Bernard is sometimes called a mystic, but strictly he was merely anti-rationalist. His mysticism was little more than adherence to sacred tradition. There was nothing in him of the solitary ecstatic nor of the childlike, loving, innocent like St. Francis. He was an organizer, a great ecclesiastical politician, to whom abstract intellectual problems were non-existent. It was not important to him that theology should be understandable, whether through nominalism or realism. It was sufficient that it should not be debated. These things were better accepted as mysteries and men's efforts directed to the realities that seemed important to Bernard, those contributing to the advance of the faith as expressed in tangible form. His life thus centered in political institutions: his order—which he spread immensely; the kingdom of France—which for a time he all but ruled; the church—whose popes he dominated. His objection to Abelard was not that the latter's thought was erroneous—he was equally opposed to Abelard's realist opponents—but that it was *thought,* that it disturbed men's minds, confused their pursuit of salvation, and made the task of governing church and state more difficult.

Philosophy in the West has ever since worked within the rough boundaries of the three attitudes towards the Christian faith exemplified by Anselm, Bernard and Abelard. There have been those who believed a profound harmony must exist between Christianity and the conclusions of human reason. There have been those who sensed more often than they admitted the deep opposition between Western thought and historical Christianity, yet preferred to stand at all costs behind the faith. There have been those whose degree of acceptance of the outward form of Christianity has varied with the theological zeal or indifference of their age, but whose concepts of causation and of the nature of terrestrial reality, age by age, have carried Western thought further and further from the Levantine universe of its holy writings.

These three approaches to our life as a people and to our image of the physical universe—for both are subsumed in an ultimate philosophy—have come down to us in unbroken continuity through eight hundred years. Be-

[31] Cousin, *Ouvrages inédits d' Abélard,* II p. 637-8.

lief in the harmony between reason and the Christian faith, belief in the absolute power of human reason, belief in the primary importance of tradition—rational or irrational—and of the institutions that give life to these traditions, these have constituted the contradictory strands of the fabric of Western thought. At times one has seemed dominant over the others, but none has ever succeeded permanently in becoming the ultimate philosophy of the West.

The struggle among the partisans of these three attitudes has been the history of philosophy in our society. Indeed, the tension itself of this age-long conflict could almost be described as the living philosophy of the West; for Western philosophy never has attained—never can attain—a static repose within the antagonistic frames of Western causality and Levantine documentation. Western life has been lived since it began within these two frames and every man who has anchored himself firmly within either has cut from his life and his thought an inescapable part of the life and thought of his own people. Not the positions themselves but the struggle between them has been the essence of Western thought.

Philosophy could be defined as the deepest understanding of the total of existence. Each society has comprehended such a totality in its own fashion and so each has built its own philosophy. But to each, its own religious thought has also been a part of existence, and at the last limits of philosophy its religion has thus become inseparable from its secular thought. This has been true even in the West, but the surface of philosophy in the West has been warped as it has been in no other society. To us philosophy in the schoolmaster's sense and Christianity appear as two separate, often hostile, systems. Hardly anyone but Gilson has argued that a Christian philosophy is even possible. To most of us, if a system of thought were truly philosophical, it could not also be completely Christian. If it were Christian, it could not embrace the immense scope of Western secular thought without which nothing could properly be called a philosophy in the West. Western thought has thus always appeared to be divided between the merely pious—in which case it has not been thought at all—and the heretical, the agnostic and the atheistic, the progression in the case of the last three being largely a matter of the century of its occurrence.

But this division produces at best only textbook philosophy, that is, systems of thought attempting to stand within one or the other frame of historical reference—Christian or non-Christian. They have thus been either evasive or apologetic, in either case uncomfortably barren, in dealing with our ultimate concepts of "things and of God." It is the incompleteness of either position that suggests considering the tension between them as the living philosophy of the West. For Western thought has never been Levantine Christian thought to the exclusion of purely Western concepts.

We have not yet retreated back into the intellectual womb of our race. But neither has it been atheistic. We have not yet surrendered to this ultimate pessimism of purposeless despair. To the shallow—who must always in this matter be the bulk of men—great stretches of Western thought, medieval and modern, do seem agnostic and even atheistical because, to the shallow, religion and the accepted Christianity of their time have seemed synonymous. This was always unavoidable. Western thought from its origin has been mechanistic, and between this interpretation and the Levantine universe of the divine will immediately beneath each event, no harmony, no agreement, even no truce, was ever possible. But the Western mechanistic belief—that an unalterable chain of mechanical causation controls the entire operation of the physical universe —this belief concerns only our understanding of the methods, not of the purpose, of God. Yet since this faith of the West, for such it has been, denies the faith that lies at the root of historical Christianity, the tortured travail of Western thought has been inevitable—has, for all we know, been ordained from the beginning. And this struggle has been perhaps the great origin of the immense strength of Western thought. It has been able to shake the world, to alter the future of human life, not only of ourselves but of all men, because it has never been able to be at rest.

The history of Western thought cannot become intelligible unless the nature of this long struggle is understood. No one of these areas of thought has developed uncorrupted by the development of the others. No single side of the issue, authoritative Christian, rational Christian (as the ages have altered that concept), or anti-Christian, has ever embraced the full intellectual life of the West or ever could, of itself, be called the philosophy of the West. Thus to find medieval thought cast in seemingly more Christian modes than is the fashion of our own times, does not make it alien. It was dealing, in the style of its own time, with what has ever since been the underlying subject matter of Western thought, the two foci of our intellectual existence as a people: our own sense of physical reality and the sacred documents of the Levant.

Traditional history pictures the intellectual tension of the early Middle Ages as the struggle between realism and nominalism. But to us moderns the meaning of the contest is sometimes lost. True, it was no quarrel between materialism and religion, regardless of where the far distant heirs of the nominalists have since carried the controversy. The nominalists were devout men, but the logical consequence of a nominalist analysis of the world was the destruction of the philosophical foundation of the scriptures. Since nominalism considered the real to be the separate identities of every kind encountered in the universe, its foundation of fact became necessarily those things which to our senses actually do seem to exist. Since the obvious resemblances between things, one man has a number of obvious points of likeness with all other men, cannot be denied, and cannot be explained by the assumed existence of a real idea of "man" which somehow produces an endless series of material replicas of itself, the relation between things must be as real as the things themselves. That is, there must be actual material "somethings" behind real things, not real "ideas" but actual relations. To us today this is commonplace. Back of all sensible objects we see a web of sensible, material forces, but this is not the philosophy of scripture. The underlying Levantine concept is that the whole material universe is a thin veil of deception behind which are hidden the disconnected realities, the impalpable essences, the logos, the pneuma, the only true realities which have no direct or meaningful or discoverable connection with sensible things. This is the relationship St. Paul pictures when he says that the things that are seen are temporal but the things that are not seen are eternal. And when he says they are not seen, he does not mean they are not seen without electronic microscopes or recording instruments. He means they are not seen by the eye of the flesh.

By the end of the eleventh century, at the very outset of Western thought, one of the fundamental philosophical concepts of the West, in fact the most fundamental, thus forced its way into open controversy against the holy books. We believe in the existence of the world that our sense impressions describe to us. That it was a long task to refine, correct and coordinate these sense impressions does not diminish the significance of the twelfth century nominalists. Without belief in a real world of sense, there can be no sense impressions worth correcting and refining. There will be no data to coordinate.

What was involved in the controversy between the realists and nominalists was thus not religion versus science but the philosophy of one society against that of another. The nominalists thought of themselves as religious men, and on any test by which such a subjective state can be evidenced, they appear to have been. What they were attempting to do was to formulate within a group of religious propositions the foundations of one great branch of Western thought. It is a temptation to say the foundation of Western thought, but this would be incorrect. The heirs of realism live as well as the heirs of nominalism, but the philosophical line that has produced those intellectual developments that distinguish Western society from all other societies is of nominalist origin. Realism, transcendentalism, idealism, are all much of a kin and in this field of activity of the human intellect, Western society is undistinguished in comparison with the Levantine and the Hindu. Our great intellectual achievement is the formulation of Western mathematics and the Western physical sciences, and for these to develop at all required a society whose learned men believed in the reality of the data their physical senses reported and the reality of the calculated connections between these data.

It is not a question of the origin of the data of modern science. Before there could be any meaningful data, there had to be a philosophy, even an opinion, that such things as intelligible data could be gathered about the material universe. Few things more emphatically demonstrate the continuity of Western society than to find at the outset of our intellectual life the question basic to such a philosophy becoming of utmost importance to the keenest minds of the time. It is equally important to note that its resolution was in a direction that made the subsequent development of the physical sciences possible. This alone is of sufficiently grave historical importance. It should not be overlooked merely because in our own time the immense mechanical power of the sciences and the anti-historical fashion of modern thought focuses attention on the origin of data rather than on the origin of this type of thinking. For the second is the key to the first. The same data has been observable and much of it actually observed for millennia. But until about 1200, no one ever proposed a philosophical basis of belief that would permit the analysis of these data in the direction in which the West, and only the West, has analyzed them.

To be sure, the nominalist position was far too narrow for modern scientific concepts; for we see reality as functions not things, yet at least see these functions as those of real things. But from nominalism a way could be opened to intelligible data, while from realism no way led except back to the physics of St. Paul and St. Augustine.

But in the intellectual world of the twelfth and thirteenth centuries, the struggle of the nominalists against the realism of scripture and the Neoplatonists was complicated by the facts of history. There were also the Aristotelian writings, and so immense was the use of these that it was long the fashion to describe medieval thought as a struggle between Aristotle and Holy Scripture. In fact, the custom was to go further and ascribe all medieval thought about the physical world to Aristotle, or at least to his influence, either directly or through the Arabic commentators.

There is certainly no doubt that the writings ascribed to Aristotle were immensely used in the Middle Ages, nor is there any doubt that then and for long afterwards men who knew better but bowed to the climate of opinion, and learned and unlearned ignoramuses, shouted Aristotelian nonsense. This proves nothing about the actual development of Western thought. In all times, including our own, there is an intellectual style to which men conform, some more slavishly than others; but all conform. The problem is what is really happening under that general conformity.

Regardless of what the Aristotelian writings may have seemed to have meant to the intellectual rabble of the latter Middle Ages, to the great medieval thinkers, Aristotle was a hammer to beat Holy Scripture into a shape that could make it tolerable to rational Western minds. Even today argument from authority is more persuasive, at least on the basis of the number of people convinced, than argument from recondite facts or close reasoning. It may even have been more so in the Middle Ages. It was hardly convincing, or even wise, on the basis of a man's own concepts and reasoning to argue that the underlying picture of the universe in St. Augustine or St. Paul was weirdly nonsensical. The only sane approach was to maintain that such an understanding of the meaning of the saints was erroneous, that they really meant what Western rationalists wanted them to mean—which was, of course, not what they meant at all. In this process Aristotle was invaluable for he carried the authority of a venerated past.

The total of the Aristotelian picture of the universe was as un-Western as St. Augustine's but quite different from the latter's and in many specific details was adaptable to the Western position then at stake. Where we see a structure of mass and energy underlying all things and consider "things" to be merely names for the particular functions of mass and energy, Aristotle saw "things" as a molding of matter by form, each of which was potential, never actual, unless the matter was molded by the form and the form possessed of matter to mold. But Aristotle was not a Levantine. Even though much Levantine material was interpolated into the text, and even whole books like the *Liber de Causis,* passed under his name in the Middle Ages—and some probably still do—there is nevertheless a great core of Classical physics and causality that the editing of Proclus and the Levantine copyists left undisturbed. However strange to our concept of physical reality, Aristotle's concern about form and matter, accident and substance may be, he agrees with the West and disagrees with the Levant in two vital particulars: the material universe is the real universe; physical things have physical causes. His concept of the structure of the material universe is absurd to us, but he did not believe it to be an illusion that hid the unreachable reality of divine essences immanent in everything. His fourfold causality is not our monolithic materialistic causality, but it is at least a system of causality—not the assertion of an unanalyzable flow of the divine intelligence ordering all things by the unsearchable counsel of the divine will.

The great value of Aristotle is keyed by a little phrase of Aquinas in one of his arguments against the Levantine concept of the universal intellect in man where Aquinas insists on the complete personal integrity of each individual intellect, and the consequent separation of the act of understanding from the thing understood. "What is understood is in the intellect," he writes[32] "not in itself, but according to its likeness; for the stone is not in the soul, but its likeness is, as is said in *De Anima III*. Yet it is the stone which is understood, not the likeness of the stone, except by a reflection of intellect upon itself. Otherwise, the objects of science would not be things, but only intelligible species." The objects of the Western sciences have always been things, even though the objective of these sciences has been to dissolve these things into functions. The objects of the Levantine sciences, as al-Farabi succinctly shows, were not things but events.

For the rest, the Aristotelian concepts of form and matter, of natural and violent motion, of terrestrial and celestial elements, the inability to understand concepts that to us lead to ideas like energy and acceleration, these were not an asset to the growth of Western thought. But in the struggle against the Levantine physics of the medieval realists, the physics of Neoplatonism and of Holy Scripture, however much of this same spirit had been edited into the Aristotelian writings, the core of the Classical Aristotle was of immense value to the West. It is also important to recall that Aristotle was a logician and though logic is no more powerful than the verbal categories on which it is used, it furnished a powerful device against the method of belief by inward emotion which is as much a key principle of Levantine Christianity as belief by textual authority.

Another aspect of this same struggle against the philosophical concept of the universe implicit in the Holy Scripture was the rise of the Latin Averroists. Averroës was the last great Arabic commentator on Aristotle, and it was initially in the form of his commentaries and translations from Arabic that the West first obtained most of the Aristotelian writings. The Aristotle of Averroës was, of course, a Levantine philosopher justifying the Levantine universe of emanations. Man to Averroës is a creature who participates in the "active intellect," which is not an individual thing but the universal emanation from God which, as it were, stamps the individual out of the passive and transitory substance that composes him. But in the Arabic world, Averroës was a very late writer. Though his fundamental philosophy is that of the whole Levantine world, he was anti-religious in a Mohammedan fashion. (It is historically evident that there are as many ways to be anti-religious, in modern terminology agnostic or atheistic, as there are religions.) He pictured an eternal universe created by necessity, a necessity which he described as God's intellect. The universe forever moved from potential to actual, all real processes from stellar phenomena down to man being controlled immutably by successive emanations of the

[32] *Summa*, Q 76, Art. 2

divine intellect, the lowest of which was the "active intellect" of man, identical with human reason. It followed that human reason came from God and was, therefore, as infallible as faith. The last is evidently an irreligious formulation of Mohammed's dictum that the spirit of God was in his people and that they could, therefore, never agree in error.

Since Averroës was what might be called a Levantine materialist, his writings are in specific contradiction to much of the forefront of Scripture, specific creation and the last judgment, for example. Nevertheless, he was a Levantine, and his conception of the underlying nature of the physical universe was that of his society. He occupied, therefore, a curiously dual position to the Latin West. Philosophically, he was more akin to Holy Scripture than to the nominalists, but historically, like Aristotle, he wrote during the irreligious period of his own civilization. He was, therefore, an avowed partisan of reason as a counter power to faith.

It was as the champion of reason against revelation that the Latin Averroists used his writings during the late twelfth century. They were accused by their opponents of propounding as a formal proposition the notion of the two truths, *secundum rationem* and *secundum fidem,* and the accusation was substantially just. Since they felt that faith and reason could not be reconciled, they asserted, in effect, that these two could be contradictory and yet both be true. Although this idea has never been seriously pressed in Western thought since that day, and although it is a doctrine formally denied by almost everyone, religious and irreligious alike, nevertheless it has remained an unspoken method of intellectual procedure ever since.

Yet Western thought is much too passionately integrated into a single system to permit such a formal separation as the doctrine of the two truths would require. In Western thought, all that is known is either true or false. All that is not known is either probable or improbable. There is no possibility of accepting an intellectual dualism such as the Latin Averroists preached, and the only consequence of its formal acceptance would have been the rapid shattering of revealed religion under the lie that it was true by another way. Naturally, the Averroist movement withered rapidly under ecclesiastical pressure, but the essential difficulty remained. When the attempt to establish the desired synthesis between Western thought and Holy Scripture failed in the next century, the practice, though not the admission, of the two truths was resumed and has continued to our own time. All the practice really amounts to is postponing the open denial of religious propositions. It neither effects a synthesis nor honestly maintains the age-old tension.

This was the intellectual crisis of the twelfth century. It was not a debate about how many angels could stand on the point of a pin or such other rubbish as it has been the fashion since the eighteenth century to ascribe to medieval thought. The issues turned on matters of the gravest intellectual and historical importance. Is the physical universe actual or is it the illusory veil of a reality that cannot be reached in this life? Since reason leads to conclusions contrary to Holy Scripture, must reason perish in the West or shall the Western Catholic church cease to be Christian? Consequent on these questions were the foundation of Western science and the future political history of the West.

Of the thirteenth century alone out of the six centuries from 900 to 1500, a dim but recognizable image is accepted in our popular history. It is an image of the age of faith, of the purest expression of the world of monks and nuns, cathedrals, scholastic disputations, of religion as the dominant power in every walk of life. The century is pictured as the age of the great synthesis. It had evaluated life and society from the point of view of Christianity and established a marvelous but perishable unity.

Actually, it was a century like another. Events happened. The flow and growth of Western life went on. Gothic architecture attained its finest period. The idea of a possible political unity of the West in the so-called Holy Roman Empire ceased to be a reality, though it lingered long in the pages of propaganda and literature. Equally, the possibility of secular rule over the West by the papacy did not long survive papal triumph over the empire. Maritime expansion in the eastern Mediterranean overran the islands and peninsula of Greece. Expansion on land continued to push back the Slavs in the east and the Moslems in Spain. The struggle of crown and feudal nobility went on in every Western country, running sometimes with, sometimes against, the struggle of lay power against ecclesiastical, and of incorporated towns against the abutting feudal powers. The thirteenth differed from the other centuries of Western life as each has differed from all the others. It did not differ from the others to the extent that our accepted knowledge about it differs from our accepted ignorance about the others.

It is the one century out of the six before 1500 in which lived the two medieval thinkers whose names are still familiar to modern men, Roger Bacon and Thomas Aquinas, and the echoes these names recall, barren scholasticism and persecuted science, are almost the summary of our own vast misunderstanding. There was nothing barren about Aquinas' thought. Since the thought of his age was an essential link to our own, his work could not be without meaning to us even if there were no more than an ancestral connection. On the other hand, Bacon was neither a lonely intellectual giant born before his time nor a victim of ecclesiastical persecution for his advanced ideas. He was not persecuted and his ideas were not advanced. They were simply those of the men of his time interested in the phenomena of nature. In fact, his thinking was much more religious than that of Adelard of Bath a century earlier or of his genuinely scientific contemporaries discussed later in this chapter.

The thought of the thirteenth century was much more complex and of greater scope than the philosophical explorations of the twelfth. The Classical and Arabic texts had become fully available and had been pondered more carefully. Independent Western analysis was more self-assured. There appeared for the first time pioneers of genuinely scientific thought. The earlier traces of Western science had been only in the philosophical foundation, never in technical development. To be sure, all this early scientific thought was still in part theological. It was impossible in the thirteenth century to explore or reason about the physical world without considering God. The tacit divorce between actual and operable causality had not then been developed as an intellectual system—though in mechanics it was already in effect—and any reasoning about nature led necessarily to first causes, which as Aquinas rightly said, all men call God. We have avoided that answer only by ignoring the question, but need not hold too harshly against our ancestors their inexperience and youthful enthusiasm. They had just as much faith in the infallibility of scientific reasoning as we do, but there was an excitement and intimacy about their feeling towards God that we have long since left behind in the youth of our race.

There began also in that century diffusion of popular knowledge. There were more schools and more people sufficiently well-to-do to be able to attend them. The world of abstract learning was still a priest's world but an educated laity began slowly to appear. It was not a democratic laity and by our conventions it was not very well educated, but it was in its halting, early fashion the beginning of the "educated public" that has been with us ever since—at once the nurse and the unremitting enemy of thought.

No age, feudal or democratic, has been prone to dwell upon this antinomy. Education, and therewith the institutions that make it possible, are the prerequisite for the development and retention of learning. Almost by definition, therefore, the schooling given the educated would seem to represent the learning of each age. But we know that this has never been true. The unscholastic, often anti-scholastic, pioneering of every age must always be unknown to the educated of that time. Both its source and its tentative nature prevent presentation by the schools. As a result, any educated man, knowing nothing about it, knows it is false or unimportant. If it were not, he would have been told something about it. We are sometimes inclined to suppose that this is the inevitable consequence of the mass democratic education and the mass communication media of modern times coupled with the immense scope of modern knowledge. But these only make the matter glaringly conspicuous; for the same situation existed in the thirteenth century and can be seen in every age since. It appeared the moment an educated public appeared. From that date to the present it is necessary, in seeking to grasp the intellectual life of an age, to distinguish the dubious, tentative knowledge of the learned from the assured ignorance—not of the "masses", which is always assumed—but of the educated.

With the appearance of this educated public, there began a group of writings rather specifically prepared for it, encyclopedic summaries of general information, several of extraordinary bulk. None can be considered a milestone in the development of Western thought for none of the writers was a pioneer nor acquainted with the pioneering work of his times. These cyclopedias do show, however, that the general level of information available—and, from the large number of manuscripts, availed of—was fairly high and not particularly superstitious. Two of them were destined to remain the standard of popular educated information for three centuries.[34] Not that Western thought and learning stagnated during those three centuries. It grew immensely, but it grew in the esoteric world of the learned —and in the despised and ignored world of technology—not among the educated. Part of the phenomenon of the Renaissance was thus a revolution not in the knowledge of the learned but in the education of the educated. In the sixteenth century the educated began to be taught some of the facts discovered and some of the reasoning developed by the learned of the thirteenth and fourteenth.

The philosophical output of the thirteenth century was immense, much too immense to be given in a neatly condensed summary in these pages. Most of it could have little interest even as a historical monument, but scattered in the works of the outstanding thinkers of the time are the expressions of points of view that have come down through Western thought ever since. It seems wise, therefore, to mention, even superficially, the most important philosophical writers before discussing the eight or nine men with whom strict Western scientific thought began.

William of Auvergne, who was Bishop of Paris from 1228 to 1249, was one of the earliest writers to whom the bulk of Arabic translations had become available. His attempt to synthesize these works with Christian dogma was soon superseded by the full scholasticism of the end of the

---

[34] The *De Proprietatibus rerum* of Bartholemew the Englishman and the *Speculum maius* of Vincent of Bauvais. The first printed edition of the *De proprietatibus rerum* was in 1470; the last in 1609. The first of the *Speculum maius* was in 1473 and the last in 1624.

century, but his demand for a rational, causal system was possibly more insistent than among the later writers. He still had some of the naiveté of the twelfth century. Also his considerations on demons and magic were long influential and cast light on the degree of sacred and profane superstition entertained in the middle of the thirteenth century. William, despite his desire for a rational causality, of course, believed in demons. He could hardly do less since their existence is still an item of Christian belief.[35] He was, however, far from gullible about their powers and presence, feeling that their powers were probably limited to influencing men and could not affect the physical operations of nature. This is a view not far from that still held by many who hesitate to envisage divine or demonic interference with the physical laws of the material universe but, rather than deny the existence of such influence altogether, are willing to accept the mind or subconscious of man as a reasonable theater for its activity. Most natural operations that men did not understand, William felt, were the result of "natural magic." This he understood as a secret but not superstitious art, being, in his judgment, the "eleventh part of all natural sciences" which "the philosophers called necromancy," the art by which natural effects are brought about to the bafflement of the ignorant but within the understanding of the learned. Not every claim of the powers of this natural magic should be accepted at its face value, however, for if what the books on this subject say were true, the Chaldeans, Egyptians and Arabs, as masters of such a powerful art, would long since have conquered the world.

Despite his inevitable acceptance of astrology, his deep interest in Levantine magic and his position as a medieval bishop, his analysis of the world as he saw it is cast in the Western mode of causal analysis. "You should refuse to follow those," he writes, "who, in matters of this kind, take refuge in the all sufficient will of God, abandoning deeply involved questions and supposing that they have freed themselves when they have said that thus the Creator would have wished or that His will is the sole cause of such things. These go astray intolerably: first because they give a single answer for all questions; secondly because if they are asked concerning anything they assign the most remote cause. . . . while it was not the most remote, but the nearest cause that was in question."[36]

---

[35] Tanquery: *Brevior Synopsis Theologiae Dogmaticae*, 1923 p. 358.

[36] Similiter declinare debes a via eorum, qui in rebus huiusmodi ad imperiosissimam Dei volentem altissimi refugiunt, quaestiones indissolutas penitus relinquentes et liberatos se esse putantes, cum dixerint, quia sic voluerit creator, vel voluntas ipsius causa est solum rerum talium. Errant autem intolerabiliter: primo, quod omnium quaestionum huiusmodi solutionem unicam reddunt, secundo, quia interrogati propter quid, causam remotissimam assignant, cum . . . interrogationes, quae sunt propter quid causam remotissimam non quaerant: sed proximam.—*De Universo* ed. Venice 1591 pp. 944-5. Other printed editions of William's work were: Nüremberg 1496 (or 1497); Paris 1516; Baden 1674.

The matter of primary interest here is not so much a medieval bishop being unwilling to accept the will of God as an adequate explanation of phenomena. What is of principal importance about this passage is its comfortable acceptance of the idea of a scale of causality in which the near-by cause is the real, that is, the operable cause, and the remote is the grammatical or philosophical. It is well worth comparing this passage with Aristotle's fourfold causality where the efficient cause is not the nearest in a chain of successively embracing causes, but simply one cause quite independent of the other three. It is worth comparing also with the fatally locked Levantine causality of Boethius: ". . . Providence is an immovable and simple form of those things which are to be done, and fate is a movable connection and temporal order of those things which the divine simplicity hath disposed to be done." It is evident from which way of thinking about nature an operable, causal science could be developed.

Among thirteenth century men of extraordinary learning, none equalled the vast scholarship of Albert of Cologne, Count of Bollstadt, sometime Bishop of Regensburg, whom his contemporaries named, "The Great," Albertus Magnus.

Albert was the teacher and life-long defender of Thomas Aquinas—whom he outlived—and his repute has, therefore, suffered a little from exaggeration. It has been important to show that he was a great natural scientist who was almost the founder of Christian Aristotelianism, since to Thomism Christian Aristotelianism is felt to have been the origin of Western scientific thought. But Christian Aristotelianism was not the founder of Western science, though many Christian Aristotelians were also Western thinkers working at the foundation of that great mechanistic body of thought. Christian Aristotelianism was Christian, but Western science, as a body of thought—not inevitably as a group of thinkers—is necessarily unchristian. Western science is too mechanistic to be truly Christian. It assumes that nature never has and never will change the operation of mechanical laws to differentiate saint from sinner. Its causality is too conditioned and so far without purpose that it is necessarily atheistic within the limits that it seeks to study, namely the means through which natural phenomena occur. In the early days, it was "assumed" that God could, but did not, interfere in the natural world which, in substance, postulated an atheistic domain for purposes of study and comparison of cause. It was thus possible for Western Christians to investigate scientific questions, but it was not possible for the original impetus for this study to flow from any body of doctrine whose casual and physical principles were Levantine, however strenuous the attempts to Westernize that doctrine. It was here that Christian Aristotelianism was of value to the West, almost as valuable, though for different reasons, as the Thomists feel it to have been. Neither the scienific data of Aristotle nor his grammatical causality was of much value, and doubtless his errors outweighed his correct descriptions. But Aristotle's works were an attempt at an impersonal study of nature without assuming direct divine intervention. Championed by Christian Aristotelianism, these works threw the cover of a venerated past over the objective study of nature and protected the early growth of Western scientific thought from the wrath of the Western Sufis and the Levantine causality of the Holy Books. But when at last the religious radicals took over ecclesiastical control under the banner of the Holy Books in Reformation and Counter Reformation, Christian Aristotelianism ceased to have any function. It was inadmissible in Bible Christianity, Protestant or Roman Catholic, and having thus no longer a purpose in protecting scientific thought, it and all Christian forefront with it disappeared from Western science.

Albert was the first great Aristotelian of the West, though as an Aristotelian he has been unfavorably compared to his more famous pupil who is generally felt to have had the better philosophical grasp of Aristotle and a greater ability to synthesize this with Christian doctrine. This may well be, but for the purpose in hand it is irrelevant. It was Albert who invented the idea of Christian Aristotelianism and it was his pupil Aquinas who organized the idea into a coherent system that permitted the Western church to use it for three centuries as its philosophical interpretation of the world of nature.

In scientific thought Albert did not differ greatly from a number of medieval thinkers already mentioned. Inevitably, he accepted the belief that natural phenomena on earth are influenced by forces from the stars. He made the usual distinction between the two kinds of magic, one using natural forces known to the operator but unknown to his observer—that is, natural science under an older name—and the other an unnatural manipulation, perhaps of things but certainly of images, accomplished by demon aid. Naturally, he believed in demons though he records no personal encounter with them.

Through all his works run strains of doubt about reliance upon authority for statements of facts and of hesitation at accepting generalized concepts as substitutes for detailed knowledge of the phenomena of nature. Needless to say, his doubt of authority did not prevent his reporting many absurdities, and he lacked any method for systematic screening of reported "facts of experience" that would have permitted him to separate tall tales from actualities that only sounded improbable. Yet his pursuit of detailed natural facts was earnest and genuine, and this, rather than his abstract scientific thought, was his pioneering accomplishment; not that he gained the facts he sought but that he deemed it essential to seek them.

His chief scientific passion was what used to be called "natural history ":

zoology, botany and the vast ramification of their subsidiary sciences. Albert collected voluminous information about plants and animals from all over Europe, western Russia and the Arctic seas. As he grew older, his passion for detailed knowledge in this field grew upon him and grew in importance in his eyes. In his early days he apologized for it as better suited to rustics and unbecoming the pure knowledge of a philosopher. Later in life he vaunted detailed, specific, nature knowledge as "the best and perfect kind of science" ("optimum et perfectum genus . . . sciendi"). As Thorndike points out, Albert raised to the dignity of a science that passionate interest in the animate world that is so striking a mark of the men of the Middle Ages. The market for books on plants and animals seems to have been inexhaustible. Hawks, hounds and horses—that sacred trio of the nobility—peasant tales of wild and domestic animals, flowers, forest and meadows run through all their literature. Their cathedrals are almost a botanical museum so profusely and so accurately did they carve the flowers and trees of their countryside.

Albert's "natural history" is, of course, quite unsystematized. The concept of species and phyla was still centuries in the future. But he attempted to make concrete observation and report accurate data. In a few cases he conducted crude experiments—such as dissecting a cicada to study how it sings. He also wrote very sanely about alchemy, describing metals and salts and various pieces of chemical apparatus, quite without superstition or magical incantations. He states that the alchemists' synthetic metals resemble the natural, but are not the same thing. He records the discovery of a new metal, antimony, previously known only in its sulfide and oxide, and gives a recipe for gunpowder, as an explosive but not as a propellant.[37]

"For natural science," he wrote[38], "is not simply receiving what one is told, but the investigation of causes of natural phenomena." Albert did not get very far on this road but he was one of the first to describe it, however crudely. Neither Aristotle nor Averroës had ever conceived of science as the result of *investigation* of the causes of *phenomena*. Albert's writings were immense and very popular. He must have had a profound influence on many generations of Western thinkers.

Albert was also in all probability the author of an extremely popular little work, *de secretis mulierem—The Secrets of Women*—supposedly

[37] The last is in a work of doubtful authenticity, *De mirabilis mundi*, which is, however, a work of the same age and if not by Albert possibly by one of his pupils. It opens with the significant statement ". . . I learned that the work of the wise was to end what seemed, in the view of men, to be the miraculous nature of things . . ." Postquam sciuimus quod opus sapientis est facere cessare mirabilia rerum quae apparent in conspectu hominum . . .
Thorndike, Lynn, *History of Magic and Experimental Science* Cap. LXIII.
[38] Mineralium II ii, 1.

written for a priest to aid him in handling certain problems arising in the confessional. It suggests that even in matters of sex our medieval forefathers exercised an objectivity towards nature that was intolerable to the eighteenth and nineteenth centuries.[39]

The most famous intellectual figure of the thirteenth century was St. Thomas Aquinas. His memory is particularly cherished by the Roman Catholic Church, but no observer of Western history, no competent student of the development of Western science, ethics, sociology or juridical theory, can pass him by. Hence, his name is remembered and something of his philosophy is current in modern writings.

Aquinas was born in Campania in 1225, the son of Landulf, count of Aquino. This was Hohenstaufen territory, but Landulf supported the pope against Frederick II, which did not prevent the family bitterly opposing Thomas' ambition to join the Dominicans, an objective he finally accomplished in 1244. Thereafter he studied under Albert at Cologne and Paris, taught at Paris and in Italy, and died at Fossanuova near Rome, March 7, 1274, leaving behind him what is probably the greatest mass of philosophical writings ever produced by so young a man. By the common consent of the learned, including Protestants, he would probably be admitted to have been the greatest systematic theologian of the West. He was also one of the greatest systematic philosophers of the West, but this fact is obscured by the subsequent development of systematic philosophy. A tacit but nonetheless effective convention has grown up, particularly in the past two centuries, that while philosophy need not be anti-Christian, it must be indifferent to questions of faith, else it cannot be called philosophy. That Aquinas' philosophy was imbedded in a theological matrix was inevitable in the age in which he lived. To him and to all the men of his time, God and the historical Christian faith were as much a part of "nature" as any other natural fact in the universe about them. Reality to Aquinas was thus not alone the universe surrounding us in space—which is the "nature" of natural science and the "universe" of accepted philosophy. It was also what had been and was to be, though only insofar as past and future bore on the philosophical problem—for he was a Christian philosopher, not a historian. These departures from modern conventions must be kept in mind.

Needless to say, he lived under the physics of matter and form, substance and accidents. He believed in demons, sorcery and magic, which he considered the work of demons. Naturally, he accepted the influence of the stars upon all terrestrial events moved by natural causation—that is, upon

---

[39] The record of the profuse printing of Albert's works is too large to give here. See Sarton, *op. cit.* II 942. There were more than one hundred editions of his various works printed in nearly every continental country between 1472 and 1500.

everything except miracles, demon activity and the results of human free will. He believed in the true revelation of the Christian religion, the one perfect and unshaken form of which was that of the Western Catholic Church. He admitted that some things, the Trinity, for instance, could never be discovered by human reason and could only be known by revelation. But he was a rationalist. He denied that even revealed matters could be contrary to reason, and thus denied any possibility of conflict between faith and reason. Convention pictures him as primarily an interpreter of Aristotle, but he was also an interpreter of scripture and of the Church Fathers, seeking to make these conform to reason as, in a primitive Western way, he understood it. So he was a firm opponent of Levantine thought whenever he could disentangle it from scriptural backing.

Consider in connection with the foundation of Western scientific causality the following on the causal structure of the universe.[40] "They (Avicenna and his followers) add also that corporeal substance is the most removed from the first agent, and, therefore, they do not see how the active power can reach as far as corporeal substance. They maintain, therefore, that as God is purely active, so corporeal substance, being the lowest thing of all, is purely passive. For these reasons, then, Avicebron held in the *Fount of Life* that no body is active, but that the power of a spiritual substance pervading through bodies produces the actions which seem to be performed by bodies.

"Moreover certain Moslem theologians are said to have argued that even accidents are not the result of corporeal activity, because an accident does not pass from one subject to another. Hence they deem it impossible for heat to pass from a hot body into another body so as to heat it. What they say is that all such accidents are created by God.

"However, many absurdities arise from the foregoing positions. For if no inferior cause, above all a body, is active, and if God works alone in all things, then, since God is not changed through working in various things, no diversity will follow among the effects through the diversity of the things in which God works. Now, this is evidently false to the senses, for from the application of a hot body there follows, not cooling, but only heating, and from human seed only a man is generated. Therefore, the causing of inferior effects is not to be ascribed to the divine power in such a way as to withdraw the causality of inferior agents.

"Besides. If effects be produced not by the act of creatures (i.e. any created thing animate or inanimate) but only by the act of God, the power of a created cause cannot possibly be manifested by its effect, since the effect is no indication of the cause's power, except by reason of the action which proceeds from the power and terminates in the effect. Now the

[40] *Summa Contra Gentiles*. Cap. LXIX Pegis tr.

nature of a cause is not known from its effect except insofar as this is an indication of its power which results from its nature. Consequently, if creatures have no action for the production of effects, it will follow that the nature of a creature can never be known from its effect: so that all knowledge in the philosophy of nature would be denied us, for it is there that demonstrations from effects are chiefly employed."

Again taking issue implicitly with Augustine, Boethius and St. Paul and explicitly with Plato, Avicenna, and Avicebron, he writes: [41]

"But all these opinions seem to have a common origin. They all, in fact. sought for a cause of forms as though the form were of itself brought into being. But, as Aristotle proves, what is made, properly speaking, is the *composite*. Now, such are the forms of corruptible things that at one time they exist and at another time they do not exist, without being themselves generated or corrupted; but they become generated or corrupted by reason of the generation or corruption of the *composites*. For forms themselves do not have being, but composites have being through forms; for according to a thing's mode of being is the mode in which it is brought into being. Since, then, like is produced from like, we must not look for the cause of corporeal forms in any immaterial form, but in something that is composite, as this fire is generated by that fire. Corporeal forms, therefore, are caused, not as emanations from some immaterial form, but by the reduction of matter from potentiality to act by some composite agent."

These passages are not easy reading for a modern. The physics are hopelessly archaic, and argumentation by these ancient logical categories no longer seems convincing. But Aquinas' conclusions are as modern and as Western as anyone could wish: The universe of "corporeal substance," what we today would call the material universe, is not the unanalyzable flow of the divine will but the theater of action of "composite agents," that is of matter and material forces, the causal connections of which can be discovered by "demonstrations from effects." This last is of particular interest, since we are traditionally assured that Francis Bacon in the sixteenth century was the first Westerner to demand that the philosophy of nature be pursued by methods of induction, that is by demonstration of causes from their effects. Bacon was justly criticizing the academic scholasticism of his time, but he was not introducing a new scientific approach in Western thought. That it was the standard method of gaining knowledge of nature was as commonplace to Aquinas and many examples of its use in the Middle Ages will appear in this and the next chapter.[42]

[41] *Summa Theologica* (I Q, 65a4).

[42] Aquinas' complete works were so widely printed in the fifteenth century that cataloguing them here would be pointless. They were available everywhere in print in Western Europe before 1500.

Since the encyclical *Aeterni patris* of Leo XIII in 1879, Aquinas has been increasingly proclaimed as the exponder of the philosophical doctrine of the Roman Catholic Church. In the encyclical *Fausto appetente die* of 1921, Benedict XV asserted that the doctrines of Aquinas were the church's very own, "Thomae doctrinam Ecclesia suam propriam edixit esse," a position confirmed by Pius XI in *Studiorem ducem* in 1924. This makes the historical appraisal of Aquinas somewhat difficult. It suggests that in Thomism the Roman Catholic Church finds a synthesis between Western science and Christianity that Aquinas neither attained nor dreamed of— having obviously no notion of where the principles of mechanistic causality would lead. Many Protestants are thus further confirmed in their prejudice that the Middle Ages were the intellectual province of the present Roman Catholic Church and are less inclined than ever to disentangle the historical complex of which Aquinas was the eminent and for a time successful expositor.

It is not possible to make here an extended study of Aquinas, but it should be noted that he made will and responsibility the base of his ethical system avoiding Pelagianism by little more than formal wording. His political theory was the one which alone has ever had moral validity in the West, that the state exists for the welfare of its individual members—this, of course, did not make him democratic—and that rulers are the trustees of their country.

Aquinas was neither the father nor directly the protector of Western science. He was, however, the justifier of Western causality, precisely as he expressed it in the passages quoted above. It was this theologically based justification of an un-Levantine, and hence historically unchristian causality, coupled with the assertion of the real existence of the world of the senses, that permitted the intellectual youth of our society to postpone the conflict between Western thought and the historic Christian faith. But Aquinas did not accomplish the synthesis of these two vastly disparate means of understanding the universe, and no one else has accomplished it either, particularly not the semi-Christianity of modern times which asserts the right to reject in toto the causality, physics and historical meaning of the scriptures, yet to pick from this source such scraps as can be used for ethical or social precepts in the affairs of this world.

Aquinas' approach was to attempt the interpretation of Levantine Christianity into a Western mold to the extent that a Western cast of thought had consciously developed among the orthodoxies and venerations from the Levantine and Classical past. But he attempted the task long before the West had developed these data of history and natural science that seem so at variance with the causality and eschatology of the Levant. Hence what he felt he must interpret was not altogether what would trouble a modern

man. He went no further than defending the application of Western causality to the world of corporeal substance. He did not foresee that this
causality would someday assume the world of corporeal substance as the
be-all and end-all of life and bring into question even the existence of that
world of angels and demons in which he firmly believed.

To the modern Bible Christian, on the other hand, Aquinas is unacceptable precisely because of his modernism. Where the account of creation in
Genesis makes hard logical sledding, for instance, Aquinas was willing to
assume that Moses tailored his account to fit the ignorance of his hearers.
"Since Holy Scriptures can be explained in a multiplicity of senses, one
should adhere to a particular explanation only in such measure as to be
ready to abandon it if it is proved with certainty to be false."[43] This is
neither Calvin nor Loyola.

Aquinas was in effect the great medieval compromiser. He constructed
a system that made it intellectually possible to keep Western reason within
a society revering Holy Scripture and to keep Holy Scripture in a society
that aimed to employ Western methods of reason. His compromise was not
universal nor permanent. It required a degree of interpretation of scripture
that increasingly discomfited the Bible literalists. On the other hand, the
assertion of revelation as a source of knowledge unreachable by reason
left unsettled the vexing question of what in the Bible is revelation and
what is the human and, therefore, incomplete or erroneous understanding
of such revelation.

In Aquinas' own time, the trend of his thought antagonistic to historical
Christianity was evident enough. Most of the emotional religious men of
the thirteenth century, particularly the Franciscans, impassioned at the
time by a wave of Levantine millenarianism, bitterly opposed him. Two
years after his death, the University and Bishop of Paris condemned his
writings as contrary to the faith and full of what they called—and quite
miscalled—"Averroistic" errors. His old teacher, Albert, then a man of
eighty, came to Paris to defend him, but the condemnation went through
and the University of Oxford soon followed. In 1278, however, the Dominican Order, which then probably embraced the most learned men of
the church, officially adopted his doctrines, and by 1323, when he was
canonized by Pope John XXII—who was engaged in a bitter struggle with
the Franciscans—his doctrine became paramount throughout the whole
church, though not everywhere without dissent.

It is usual to credit Aquinas with having taken the lead in Christianizing
Aristotle. Few have considered his work as an attempt, perhaps tragic, to
Westernize Christianity, for it is an axiom of theology and of received
history that Christianity through all churches and sects from the teaching

[43] *Summa Theologica* (I Q, 68).

of Jesus to the present day is always one and the same religion. Yet in sober thought, most men will admit probably that even religions are in part at least the creatures of history. The problem to the Western Middle Ages was not what were the true and meaningful teachings of Christianity to the Levantine society, but what were these teachings to a Western society? Dogmatically, it was, as it still is, impossible to admit that these teachings could be different. There perhaps lay the tragedy. For the later inability to protect medieval Catholicism against revived Levantine literalism did not restore or establish "historical Christianity" in the West but drove one great section of creative Western thought out of Christianity altogether and out of real communion with any of the Western churches it has stayed to this day.

It is a curious subject for historical pondering, and one that has received little attention, that the society of the West alone among the great societies has lived in religious misery since it was old enough to have to think as well as to feel, that is, since the mid-thirteenth century. The tortures of conscience, the cruel zeal of all the different establishments, the inquisitions, the wars of religion, the stake and the noose, the flagellanti, the fires of Smithfield and the gallows of Salem, the weird, wild sects of seven hundred years, are one long and horrible testimony to the psychic disbalance of Western men in their vision of first and last things. No other society contains such a dreadful record of all the different manias clustering under the name of religion. Even the Levantine society itself, to our eyes the most religious of all societies, the only society where God, devil, angels and demons were immediately in everything and to whom the whole sensible universe was an illusion, even this society was never wracked with the bitter struggles that have been unending in the West. No great body of Levantine thought, religious or scientific, was ever a homeless alien utterly divorced from the official religion of its people.

It is, of course, a fair question whether the Western Catholic Church could ever have been Westernized sufficiently to keep within it Western scientific thought and still retain enough of the sacred tradition to be considered Christian. The long history of Bible fetishism suggests that it could not. But what might have been is not the point here. The matter of importance is simply to note the vital objective—undoubtedly not consciously thought out—of Christian Aristotelianism, the first and, to date, the last great attempt to keep a living unity between Western thought and the religious professions of Western men. It proved in time to be a failure and had only the curious consequence that having used Aristotle as a hammer to beat scripture towards a Western meaning, the implement became substituted for the purpose. For some centuries, scientific thought was at home in the Western church so long as it could wear an Aristotelian mask. True,

Aristotle with his corporeal universe and his disjointed mechanical causality is no more at home in the Bible than Newton or Darwin, as the Bible
Protestants were quick to see. But for some centuries, scripture had been
adequately interpreted to permit the alliance. Unfortunately, when the crisis
came, the compromise was hopelessly out of date. Next to the Bible on
the altar at the Council of Trent stood Aquinas' *Summa Theologica*, but
by then Western thought had far passed anything that could be interpreted
out of Aristotle alone, much less from an Aristotelian understanding of the
Bible.

The systematic, intellectual opposition to Aquinas—there was another
fierce emotional opposition—was led by John Duns Scot, a Franciscan
born about 1265 in the north of England or Ireland, who taught at the Universities of Oxford and Paris and died at Cologne in 1308. Where the
Latin Averroists had drawn support from Levantine naturalistic writings,
Duns Scot and his followers drew theirs from the writers of the Levantine
pietistic revival, Maimonides and above all ibn-Gabirol, Avicebron of the
Latins. The Moslem leaders of this movement, al-Ghazzali in particular,
were barely known in the West but the two Jewish writers were famous.

Following step by step the chain of ibn-Gabirol's thought, Duns Scot
was a realist, dissolving the world into an illusory forefront for mystic
"ideas" and "intelligences" (as Aquinas remarked, what the Levantines
called "intelligences" corresponded to what the Latins called "angels").
In this jungle of the direct action of God, human reason was a pitiful
weapon, and Duns Scot, therefore, denied Aquinas' postulate that reason
could arrive at the basic propositions announced by revealed religion. We
must, he asserted, accept the truths of faith solely on the authority of
revealed religion and not attempt to seek rational understanding of these
truths. Reason was applicable only to a limited field of minor natural
phenomena, and even here its hold was precarious. Revelation, the master
truth, itself uncontrollable by rational process, could always oust the feeble
conclusion of reason and any interpretation of revelation, however extreme, stood upon a firmer authority than the treacherous calculations of
reason. It was a system that purported to be intellectual but was so only
to the extent that it was not mystic. The mystic believes in the certainty
of revelation as he himself experiences it. Duns Scot demanded an act
of the intellect in consciously accepting the scriptures as revelation. He
should, therefore, not be confused either with the true mystics, nor—as is
sometimes done—with the Latin Averroists. He made no separation between reason and revelation, confirming each in its separate sphere. To
him, revelation and revelation alone—but a revelation already recorded
once and for all—was the only authority. The inward certainty of the
mystic was a snare. Reason could arrive at nothing prime and hold undis-

puted mastery of no domain. The commentary of centuries of Western thought upon this view of the universe is sufficiently expressed in the modern word "dunce," which is derived from the name of its great exponent, Duns Scot.

It is frequently argued that Duns Scot's separation between philosophy and theology benefited philosophy by freeing it from theological authority. This was the last thing Duns Scot sought and nothing in his teachings frees philosophy from theology. He desired to free theology from any control by rational philosophy and, thus freed, to leave it as the supreme arbiter of the human mind. There is no historical basis for supposing that his work had any other influence. Possibly the whole notion that Duns Scot in any way aided rational philosophy rests on the mistake repeated and repeated in historical and philosophical studies of the Middle Ages that the great nominalist, William of Occam, was a student and disciple of Duns Scot. He was not. Occam did not begin his studies at Oxford until 1312, four years after Scot's death and many years after Scot had left Oxford for Paris.[44]

But even before Aquinas was born, an opposition more profound and more enduring than that of Duns Scot had arisen against any attempt to compose a rational Christianity in the West. It was not a formal philosophy but an emotional attitude. By the last quarter of the thirteenth century it was a powerful force, particularly among the extremist Franciscans. As the centuries have passed, it has flourished and withered in Western life, but it has never been entirely absent. In our own time its modern version furnishes the moral self-justification of the most powerful movements on the surface of our politics.

In the thirteenth century this view of life was called Joachimism. It has since been called many names, millenarianism, utopianism, socialism, international communism,[45] for its outward program has always been in the style of its age. But under these shifts of fashion and intellectual formulae it has been one restless movement driven by the same powerful emotion. It has been built always on the same structural core: a passionate distaste for the kingdoms of this world and a mystical certainty that these wicked kingdoms will soon be replaced through the operations of powers that are not of this world. Whether these powers are given the name "God" or the

---

[44] The detailed record of the early printing of Scot's works is far too large to give here in full. A partial list: *Sentences*, Venice 1477, 1487, 1597, 1617; Nüremberg 1481; Paris 1513, 1518, 1600, 1661; Valencia 1603; Saragossa 1614; Antwerp 1620. There were over forty editions of other works variously printed between 1472 and 1624. See Sarton, *op cit.* II, 969.

[45] So far as the Westerners and Jews involved in Communism are concerned, it too is a millenarian movement. However, its Russian masters and other barbarous or civilized people now embraced within it are not millenarians but men of practical imperial ambition.

name "science" has been a difference of time, not of quality. The believers in each age have simply used the word current in their time for the mightiest power they could imagine.

Joachimism derived its name from Joachim of Floris (d. 1202), founder and abbot of the monastery of San Giovanni in Floris (Fiore) near his birthplace, Celico, in Calabria which—it must be recalled—had been Byzantine territory until 1057. The neat geographical unity of Italy deceives the mind into forgetting that southern Italy and Sicily were not originally Western lands. They were the first conquests of the West from the Levant in the early wars of eleventh and twelfth century imperialism. All the subsequent eastern conquests were lost, Crete, Cyprus, Athens, Constantinople, the countries of Antioch and Edessa, and the kingdom of Jerusalem, leaving southern Italy and Sicily the only Latin conquests still held in the southeast in 1500. From our habit of dating as much as possible about ourselves from the Renaissance, these lands have thus passed into our geographic image as though they were as integrally part of the West as the Rhineland or the Ile de France. At the time of Joachim's birth, less than a century after the Norman conquest—which merely dotted the territory with Norman castles and Norman lords—Calabria was still a Byzantine land. Even today the Byzantine ritual is followed in some of the churches of southern Italy.

Joachim's world views were in essence those of the Sufis and his monastic ideal was that of St. Basil. He divided the history of mankind into three ages, that of the Father—a period of blind obedience ending with Christ, that of the Son coming down slightly past his own time, and that of the Holy Ghost, which was soon to begin. He preached the redemption of the world, not as a transition of the dead to heaven but as a historical fact that was to transform the society of the living. It was to begin about 1260 and convert the earth into one vast Basilean monastery of solitary anchorites— a vision of the anti-clerical socialist state appropriate to his times and background. Accordingly, all the historical structure of the Western world into which the accidents of conquest had brought him to be born, church and state, property and learning, all these were transitory. The age of the Holy Ghost, so soon to start, would render them unnecessary. His version of what would happen to these crude realities of the mundane world was curiously like that of his irreligious intellectual descendant, Marx. Church and state, which Joachim, like Marx, taught had been historically necessary in the earlier periods, would not be violently abolished in the coming age of freedom—*plena spiritus libertas*—but would quietly wither away.

Lulled by the innocent gradualism thus asserted, and realizing quite properly that these views had a basis of sorts in scripture, the ecclesiastical authorities during Joachim's lifetime foresaw nothing of where the application of these principles would lead and his orthodoxy was never questioned prior to his death. By the middle of the thirteenth century, however, a collection of Joachim's Biblical commentaries—the natural Levantine form in which he expressed his doctrines—under the title *Liber Introductorius ad Evangelium aeternum* had become the master guide to a widespread political movement. The *Liber Introductorius* and its appended commentaries proffered men a method by which the unwritten Eternal Gospel could be read from an understanding of the true spiritual meaning of the Old and New Testaments. Thus could be gained a sure knowledge of the future of mankind here on earth. The necessary understanding could in turn be gained by all those who followed Joachim's spiritual disciplines and on whom the *intelligentia mystica*—the *ma 'rifat* of the Sufis—descended. The *Liber Introductorius* was banned by Pope Alexander IV in 1255 but it never disappeared from circulation.

The extremist wing of the Franciscans, the "spirituals," were profoundly infected by Joachimism and a whole body of ill-defined movements of varying degrees of heresy commonly embraced under the names of Fraticelli and Apostolici proclaimed one or another aspect of Abbot Joachim's teachings. All were anti-clerical, though some promptly established a hierarchy of their own, even to a pope and an emperor. All were egalitarian in doctrine, denouncing the sinful distinctions of worldly wealth as contrary to apostolic poverty which they felt to be the only manner of earthly life permissible to a true Christian. Furthermore, like their modern derivatives, though possessed of a science that proved the inevitable transformation of society by a power beyond human control, they nevertheless declined to rely on this power, but sought themselves to establish the millennium by direct operations in ecclesiastical and civil politics. Traces of these movements lasted in Italy into the fifteenth century, and in the north the Lollards of England and even the continental Anabaptists of the sixteenth century show many marks of Joachimism.

Nor was medieval Joachimism, any more than its modern forms, confined to the uneducated. It had its mass appeal as modern socialism does, but its power—its influence on history—lay not in the ephemeral quantity of its adherents but in the quality of a relatively few learned men whose thinking it touched. Even the upper circles of the Franciscans were affected by it and in time this was to play a profound part in the disintegration of the medieval church. Roger Bacon shows its influence and two such outstanding intellectual figures of the late thirteenth century as Ramon Lull and Arnald of Villanova were almost openly Joachimists. As two of the earliest "leftist" scientists, they deserve brief notice, though like some of their modern counterparts, they are more noted for their scientific repute than their scientific accomplishments.

Ramon Lull (c. 1235-1313) a Catalan—from Majorca—felt he had devised an infallible scientific method for converting the Mohammedans, an essential step to the accomplishment of the earthly millennium. He devoted most of a long life to propagation of this method and to preaching among the Saracens. It was in the latter cause that he met his death at the age of about eighty in a riot caused by his repeatedly and offensively preaching Christianity in the North African town of Bugia. His infallible method was simplicity itself—a logical machine with interrelated movable diagrams which mechanically brought the proper propositions into relationship with one another and thus produced the infallible answers. Most of his learned contemporaries—and his wife—thought he was crazy and his passion for a mechanized logical method completely blinded him to the fact that no calculating machine can ever give an answer independent of the data fed into it. Nevertheless, there was a certain grandeur in his passionate conception that the processes of reason could be freed from human error and the immense learning which he brought to his subjects. He himself became a fluent Arabist, composing some of his works in that language, and after a long struggle with the authorities he succeeded in establishing the study of Arabic, Hebrew and "Chaldean" (i.e., the eastern Aramaic of the Talmud) as approved subjects in the learned institutions of the West. The purpose was to aid in conversion, but the profit was to that vast and catholic learning which has been so long the unique tradition of the West.

In fairness to Lull and his embryonic thinking machine, it should be mentioned that his concept of the immense powers of symbolic logic earned the admiration of such a powerful thinker as Leibniz.[46]

Arnald of Villanova, a personal friend of Lull's, was primarily a physician and his writings on medicine were the standard blend of Galen and Avicenna, characteristic of his contemporary fellow physicians. He attempted, however, to base his scientific beliefs on observable evidence. Even though he accepted a host of superstitions himself, he postulated that all reliable knowledge has its sole source in the data of the senses. The intellect considering these data calculates abstract connections among them, and thus through the data of sense reaches knowledge of things that are not sensible, but hidden, difficult and subtle, a fact shown, he held, by the progress of both theology and medicine. As a Joachimist millenarian he was anticlerical, a bitter opponent of Aquinas and a firm believer from the Book of Daniel in the coming of Anti-Christ in the middle of the following century as the precursor of the Age of the Holy Ghost. Yet in the field of scientific knowledge he placed faith in neither authority nor revelation. Nor is this attitude unknown in our own times, although Daniel rarely serves

---

[46] The record of printings of Lull's works is complex and voluminous. His major works were in print by 1520. See Sartan, *op. cit.* II 900 pp.

as the source of revelation to the scientist turned seer. It need not, for the emotional content of Daniel has long since been transferred to later and ostensibly more mundane works.

The source of Joachimism in the thirteenth century is simple to identify. Its obvious evangelical trappings, its use of the name of God, parallel rather than mask the Levantine origin of its concepts on the nature of the historical world and of the forces operating in that world. With the adherents of the modern variants of millenarianism this simplicity is lacking. All are rationalist—though so was Arnald of Villanova—and many of them profess formal atheism. Since the irreligious of our time do not mean by the word "God" the same concept that the word conveyed to the men of the Middle Ages, this superficial difference in verbal usage permits the moderns to conceal from themselves the historical continuity of their own movement. They thus gain the intoxicating illusion of having freed themselves from the past, an illusion essential to this whole body of emotion.

But the continuity has not been broken. The meaning of words has changed. What the irreligious conjure in their minds when they use the word "God" is an anthropomorphic demon believed in by those they consider of slightly enfeebled intellect. The name to them is not that of a force—rational or irrational—but of a fantasy whose power is limited to the self-delusion of those who believe in it. Thus when they encounter the word "God" in the writings of the past, such is the image that rises to their minds. It never occurs to them to explore whether their image is an accurate representation of the concept held by others nor whether they themselves do not entertain under another name a concept that in all essentials corresponds to the concept for which the men of the past employed the word "God."

This easy word juggling hides from sight the continuity of utopianism—to call the whole movement by the name that even superficially is characteristic of every one of its manifestations, medieval and modern alike. But the continuity exists. Never have the successive believers doubted the tangible existence of the power that was to effect the transformation of the world. Never have they doubted that this power was as real as those they could see about them on the historical earth. Indeed the power upon which they counted to transform society was necessarily more powerful than the apparent forces of the world, for was not the world merely a creation of this power, God in the past, scientific causality in the present? How absurd, then, to offer arguments from the puny experience of life and history against an expectation based upon true knowledge concerning the power that had created the world itself? Thus in each age the believer has had what to him was unchallengeable authority, the one authority of his time that needed no troublesome reasoning on his own part, that could not be confused and compromised by the wearying intractability of mundane affairs. That in modern times the believers call this power "science" does not change its character. In all cases the power is to accomplish in the historical world transformations which the nature and forces of this world forbid. This is magic—the claim to knowledge of a power that causes the flow of events. To call it God does not make it holy. To call it science does not make it rational. To use one name or the other, to alter from age to age the surface aspects of the earthly paradise, even to denounce from age to age one's own utopian predecessors—none of these shatters the continuing identity.

It is evident that utopianism falls outside the three great intellectual positions that have constituted Western abstract thought. It has been neither traditional Christian, rational Christian nor pure sceptical rationalism. In fact, it has not been an intellectual position at all. It has never sought a logical consistency within any frame of intellectual or historical reference. It has not needed to because it has been an emotion concerning what ought to happen in the flow of political events, not an attempt to compose an understandable account of the mechanism by which the world endures.

From the Joachimists to the socialists, the utopian image has always been the image of the Levantine Heavenly Kingdom. In it there is to be neither risk nor want, neither small nor great, and indeed it is an image whose moral validity is accepted far beyond the circle of the utopians, though only they have ever expected to bring it about as a piece of practical politics in the kingdoms of this world. Thus utopianism, no less than rational and traditional Christian thought, shows the presence in Western life of the values and concepts of the Levant. But there has been an immense difference.

The image of the Heavenly Kingdom as it is set forth in our sacred writings is clear enough. But there is another thing that seems equally clear. This Kingdom is not to be achieved in a life like our own. Beyond the egalitarian standards that have fired the emotions of the utopians, there are changes exceeding the scope of natural life. There is to be neither marriage nor giving in marriage, neither birth nor death, no one can hunger or thirst or feel the chill of an icy wind. In short, since it cannot exist in this world, it must, we think, either lie beyond the grave or be offered us only as an ideal standard which must be modified to the requirements of earthly life. Such, at least, have been the interpretations of both rational and traditional Christianity in the West, and so long as one vital Levantine concept was ignored these interpretations could stand. But what was ignored in this interpretation of the scriptures was the logical key of the whole image: eschatology. Utopianism, consciously in the past, by almost forgotten tradition in modern times, has grasped that key. Utopianism has been the political struggle of the Western mind with eschatology.

This idea, so alien to our sense of reality, has never been capable of formal acceptance in the West. We have never been able to believe sincerely that the mechanical laws of the organic and inorganic universe would be magically changed. We have never believed, like the Levantines, that the will of God was the immediate and sufficient cause of each event. For us, therefore, to postulate a change in the physical universe has been to postulate a gigantic, unbelievable miracle. But for the Levantines the coming of the Kingdom required only a unique, not an unnatural event. Part of the task of Western theology has always been to interpret the Levantine concept out of our sacred documents.

But eschatology is too deeply imbedded in scripture for theological interpretation to disguise it always and from everybody. Someone is sure to sense that the Heavenly Kingdom in its full glory is literally promised here on earth, not simply reserved to the blessed after they die. True, the establishment of the Kingdom is to bring with it the overthrow of the Prince of This World and thus a total alteration of nature, but still it is promised here on earth, suddenly and to all the elect, the living as well as the dead.

Thus arises the immense logical difficulty in all utopias. Even the most ardent Western utopian cannot sincerely believe in a miraculous change in the physical universe. But the image of the Kingdom is too precious and too highly authenticated to be abandoned merely because the Levantine mechanism for its establishment is unsuitable. Since the goal itself is magical, there must be some magic route that avoids the stubbornly non-magical nature of the physical universe as we Westerners see it. Nor is the way long in being found and from Joachim to our own time it is always the same way. Magic is not to be applied, like the Levantines, to the world of nature. It is to be applied to the world of politics and history. Not nature but society is to be transformed.

It is not surprising that even atheistical socialism has a quality that seems in some way religious. The atheist socialist, no less than the Joachimist, has had faith, faith in infallible commentaries on his eternal evangel. By this faith he can apply the abstract doctrines of unworldly truth to foresee infallibly the tangled flow of future events. The socialist, too, partakes of the *ma 'rifat* that unites the almost mystic brotherhood of the comrades. Given the deep confusion in Western thought between religion and Levantine imagery, any encounter with Levantine causality and magic seems to the Western mind like an encounter with some aspect of religion. Indeed, whether socialism is considered religious or not depends on whether religion is defined, as we are often tempted to define it, as a Levantine view of the universe. But however this definition is turned, socialism is still

ethically crippled by the historical perversion at its base. It is untrue both
to its source and to its society. It accepts the image but not the reality
of the Levantine Kingdom of Heaven. It accepts the worldly values of the
Kingdoms of the West, the "good life" is to be a worldly life, but it denies
the structure of ethics and honor, of risk and responsibility on which the
greatness of the West has been raised. It is at home neither in Heaven nor
on earth. Its pose of virtue has in the end never been more than the mask
of hypocrisy worn by those who have used it for their personal ends.

It is true that every society when it had reached the age of the modern
West was wracked by the struggles of egalitarian politics. All experienced
the rise of adventurers, native and foreign, claiming power as spokesmen for
the masses. Their programs of mass welfare, in all societies, have been
essentially alike in that their basic appeal was not to ambition but to envy.
Instead of carrying out actions characteristic of their society, they destroyed
in each case much that was a personal attribute of that society. Thus Western society prior to the eighteenth century, despite its organic resemblance
to ancient Hellas or to the Levant prior to the fall of the Ommiad caliphs,
had built a set of political and social institutions, of ethics, of artistic and
intellectual styles marked by the most striking contrasts to the comparable
forms in the Classical world and in the Levant. But in our own time this
sharp differentiation has been reversed. Today Western politics and Western
arts more and more approach the politics and arts of post-Gracchian Rome
and of the Abbasid caliphate—perhaps of Hyksos Egypt. This has been
the role of egalitarianism in all these societies, to justify the revolt of "man,"
of the undifferentiated, the human animal, which all of us are whatever
else we may also be, against the dread responsibility of a highly personalized, unique society.

It is, therefore, absurd to suppose that in the West a political movement
so characteristic of all societies has been produced by the particular events
of Western history that have attached to socialism the emotional coloring
of eschatology in the form of utopianism. Nevertheless, utopianism with
its association of forgotten but none the less vivid religious imagery has
given Western socialism an appearance of political purity that confuses its
opponents and deranges the ethical judgment of its adherents and sympa-
thizers. The egalitarian movements of other societies seem to have lacked
this transferred religious coloration. Thus while none of these movements
ever cared too much whether its own political operations destroyed the
ability of its society to withstand the ambitions of barbarous or semi-
barbarous peoples, only Western socialism as a uptopian movement has
felt morally justified in consciously surrendering its society to the power
of the alien. And just as the elements of strength in our character, our
arts, our sciences, our deep political and personal ethics go back into the

youth of our society, so do our predispositions of weakness. We should not be surprised to find utopianism in the thirteenth century.

The first three hundred years of Western society, the eleventh, twelfth and thirteenth centuries, hold all the traits of historical personality that have since marked the West. They show the sudden establishment of a biological group not originally widely interrelated but embraced within a connubium that was to endure to this day and form the basic stock of Western civilized men. They show in embryo the geographical states that were to endure to our own time. They show the foundation of the type of Western family, Western dynasty, and the sexual dilemma that have been characteristic of the West ever since. They show the formulation of the Western ethic of action and of the supremacy of the will. They show the intellectual foundation in infinite causality and belief in the reality of the world of sense, of Western physical science. They show the trend of political centralization and imperial dominion that have long been so prominent an attribute of our society. They show the beginning of the great disparate lines of thought that have governed us ever since.

If these three centuries represented a smooth continuum with the times that preceded them, the identification of the historical personality of the West might be more arguable. If they flowed out of the Roman or Levantine society the way the Byzantine superficially appeared to emerge from Classical society, the picture would be less clear. But there is no resemblance between these different events. Here is a new group of peoples, some descended from inhabitants of the Roman Empire, some not. For five hundred years, a cultureless population devoid of arts, almost devoid of crafts, with no literature or intellectual life sinks deeper and deeper into barbarism. A few copies of the Levant, like Carolingian architecture or the writings of Erigena, are the cultural sum of half a millennium. And then suddenly there is in existence a youthful but complete society that builds what it wants to build and does so with immense strength and beauty, that casts the forms of millennial states, that establishes the intellectual principles of its own complex styles of thought.

Ever since eighteenth century liberalism became the standard for moral evaluation of the past, our received history has sought to destroy the living memory of these centuries. It has neglected their documents and ignored as best it could their monuments. It has libeled them with the fable of the ages of faith and the equally silly fable of the ages of superstition and barbarism. Its hatred of their political and social organizations has been so bitter that the intelligent viability of a feudal economy in the circumstances in which it was practiced has become almost impossible for modern men to understand, and the role of feudal government is scarcely even recognized—and this is an age whose own economy is fast going to ruin and whose governments have become the plaything of every anarchic power in society.

There is a reason for this hatred by liberalism of these centuries. Their mere existence as an organic past of the modern world destroys the foundation of liberal thought: its historyless concepts of egalitarianism and "mankind," its assertion that utilitarian programs of verbal intention are the generative power of history, at the last, its hope that there exists in this world some island of security in the river of fate. It does not like the centuries of our youth because they were centuries of danger and great adventure. It would, if it could, remove from modern life all "insecurity" which makes it the bitter enemy of such great political adventurers as William the Conqueror, or the Hohenstaufen emperors or the Hildebrandian popes. It is equally the enemy of the early thinkers, philosophic and scientific alike. Its fetish of science is superficial only. It seeks not power over the unknown but utility in the conventionally accepted. The conquest of space does not stir it. Its ideal would be to divert the great machinery of modern technology to provide the imaginary masses with more idleness and more amusements—which is the modern welfare state in practical fact.

But even two hundred years of liberalism have not wholly effaced from our lives the image of these centuries of our youth. To their memory still clings the perfume of their glory, the greatness of the enterprise which they began, of which we are the distant and embittered heirs, the mightiest, the most intellectual and the loneliest of the societies of men.

Chapter 6:

The Dragon's Teeth

AMONG ALL THE ENDEAVORS of this once mighty society of the West—for it remains with our own age to determine if it is still mighty—perhaps none has been so lonely and certainly none so intellectual as the creation of Western mathematics and the Western physical sciences. Like our arts, indeed like every enterprise of which we can be proud, our mathematics and sciences have been accepted by society in the aggregate, but their creation has been the work of an extraordinarily small number of men moved by interests and passions beyond the concern or comprehension of their contemporaries. The work of the men who erected the physical sciences has been the intellectual glory of the West, and most of us now living owe the fact that we came to be born to the application of these discoveries in agriculture, industry and medicine. So, too, do millions in China, India and the Levant though rarely, even in the West, is this aspect of the matter ever considered. But whether in the long run physical science will prove to have been part of the might or part of the weakness of the West, only the future can show. For it has been a perilous development. It has forced into an even greater specialization of its human components a society already differentiated far more than any other. It has increased almost beyond counting the number of men directly dependent for their lives upon the unceasing work of others. It has created its own vast, complex, technical tradition which must now be maintained unbroken from generation to generation, and that unending flow of able youth is less certain than we care to realize. When beyond this, the infantile politics of a democratic age attempts to operate in a world where Westerners and aliens alike are now armed with engines from seven hundred years of Western technology, it is a question whether we may not already have sown the dragon's teeth and only await the harvest. But for good or ill, this science has been ours, and we cannot well claim its glory without accepting the responsibility for having created it. All the aliens of our time are apt pupils in this one field of Western thought, but they have gone to school to the West.

We prefer to describe our sciences as "modern" rather than Western. While this soothes the mind with the unspoken implication of a natural growth, it does not remove the historical problem of why the development of this extraordinary modernity only occurred among the descendants of the Catholics of 1500, not among the half-barbarous Russians nor the civilized Chinese, Hindus and Levantines. Our general cultural histories, which are not histories of science but always mention the growth of the Western sciences as an example of progress, deal with this problem by reference to a vague causality. The spirit of free inquiry supposedly associated with the Renaissance and the Reformation, the beginning of democracy forecast in the growing power of the urban commoners against the rural gentry and nobility, these, it is indicated, allowed the sciences to grow. Why, at different times and in other civilizations, eras of free inquiry and the rise of urban mercantile interests did not equally produce our sciences is an embarrassment that is not discussed. Indeed it is a double embarrassment; for precisely these conditions accompanied the beginning of Classical science among the sixth century Ionians. Why then should that have developed into a science so different from ours? Equally, though less well known, the same conditions can be found in the Levant of the eighth century A.D., and again for more than three centuries, there was a great flowering of science, but still not of our sciences. There is almost enough evidence here to generalize a group of historical events into a phenomenon, to postulate a cause-and-effect relationship governing the connection between the particular age of a society, its social conditions, and the popular rise and spread of its sciences. But even this casts no light on why our sciences have been so different from those of other societies.

Even Sarton, who devoted a long life of rich scholarship to the history of the sciences, found no escape from the problem and indeed some difficulty in wrestling with it. "Down to the end of the fourteenth century," he writes[1], "Eastern and Western people were working together, (i.e. in the growth of science) trying to solve the same kind of problems; from the sixteenth century on, their paths have diverged, the fundamental if not the only cause of divergence being that the Western scientists understood the

---

[1] Sarton, George, *Introduction to the History of Science.* Vol. III, Pt. 1, p. 21.

experimental method and exploited it, whereas the Eastern ones failed to understand it." Unhappily here, as with all attempts to make causal history, appears pseudo-causality. Even granting the essential role of the experimental method—a concession open to grave argument—what caused this method to be used by the Westerners and not by the "Easterners," who incidentally were not a group, like the Westerners, but three independent groups flourishing in different times, the Chinese, the Hindus and the Levantines? What prevented others from using this wonderful device? Why should our ancestors, and only our ancestors, appear to have hit upon it? Even if no one else had ever thought of it before, why did not others immediately copy it from the sixteenth century West?

To be sure, the "working together" of East and West prior to the fourteenth century needs a more precise definition. It was hardly a cooperative endeavor broken by the arrogant withdrawal of the West into the experimental method. In all cases, within the different civilizations ineptly lumped under the word "Easterners" and between one or another of these and the West, the "working together" amounted to no more than the intellectual appropriation of such parts—and often misunderstood parts—of the sciences of some other society—almost always an earlier—that another civilization found useful within its own frame of thought. Thus the Levant appropriated parts of Classical mechanics but not Classical causality, Hindu mathematical notation, but not Hindu mathematics. The selective appropriation of the West—of more immediate interest to us but intrinsically no different—followed the same pattern. What then prevented the various "Easterners" of the sixteenth century from appropriating the experimental method from the West?

Deeper than this is the question whether the experimental method is, in fact, the fundamental explanation of the extraordinary operable power of the Western sciences—for that is the immense difference between our sciences and those of other societies. True, the experimental method has been present in Western scientific thought from the beginning and, therefore, appeared long before the sixteenth century, but why should Westerners and only Westerners have resorted to it? The answer would seem to be that only the Westerners asked the type of questions to which the experimental method is capable of giving an answer. The experimental method, after all, is not a universal method capable of producing every kind of desired knowledge. It has only a limited use. It happens to be a use of value to us, but this does not make it supreme for others, and there should be no reason to expect the scientists of any society to employ a method that could not give them the type of information they sought. The difficulty with the experimental method as the universal procedure of all science is that it can give answers only concerning phenomena. It is worthless in seeking the cause of an event. What experiment could be devised to discover the cause of something unique and unrecurring, "of what things would be found or not found at a certain moment of time?"[2] Only an interest in the cause of phenomena and a complete scientific disinterest in the cause of any particular happening could lead a science to adopt this technique. Should we, therefore, be surprised at its absence from Levantine science and its very minor role in the Classical where the cognates of our phenomena of change were static forms and where efficient causes were integrally part of every scientific explanation? Should we even be surprised to find it *in use* among the Levantines in their alchemy? For what the alchemists did seek was knowledge of phenomena, not events, but they sought something so out of key with the scientific thought of their society that they never devised anything but a few *ad hoc* recipes.[3] They could not use it to justify or disprove scientific theories, which has been its role in the West. The problem comes in the end always to the same point. The search is for the origin of a way of thinking, not of data or of methods, both of which have always been equally available, in their beginnings, to all men.

The origins of the Western mechanical sciences lie in the thirteenth century, even in part in the twelfth. Hardly had the philosophical presuppositions been formulated than the first tentative development of true causal science began.

It began quite naturally under the shadow of the highly developed descriptive sciences of the Levant, and its early tools of analysis were Euclid and Levantine mathematics. Its physical concepts were the "Aristotelian" laws of motion. It was already free of the Levantine causality of the immediate event, as William of Auvergne and Aquinas demonstrate, but though it had thus denied the scientific core of astrology, the repute of that science in the Levant was too great to permit open repudiation. For many centuries astrology was accepted but scientifically ignored, an attitude maintained as late as Kepler. The development of the Western sciences of the cause of phenomena was scarcely touched by this stubborn attempt at a science of events.

The view that the Middle Ages were dominated by superstitious ignorance is so usual in modern writings that it seems necessary to bring the times into better focus by noting something of the scientific information taken over ready-made from the Levant. This was much better, descriptively at least, than we usually suppose. Far from being the treasure of the suspected and persecuted few, it was the common property of both the learned and the educated.

2 Averroës. See page 262.
3 cf. al-Kindi's opinion page 278.

Consider the scientific writings of John of Halifax, usually referred to by the Latin form of his name, Sacrobosco. He was born in Yorkshire about 1200, studied at Oxford, and then lived in Paris until his death somewhere in the middle of the century. About 1230 he published a work on descriptive astronomy entitled *Sphaera Mundi*. There was nothing original in it, Sacrobosco depended entirely upon al-Farghani and al-Battani, but it was clear, well-organized and perhaps to the surprise of a modern, immensely popular. The work describes the correct form of the terrestrial globe, the mathematical consequences of using great and small circles as coordinates on its surface, the apparent motion of the stars, and the orbits—seen from a geocentric origin—of the planets (except, of course, Neptune and Uranus). The number of manuscripts of this work, the many vernaculars into which it was translated and the extraordinary number of printed editions are conclusive evidence of two things: first, that no one of any education in the Middle Ages could have supposed that the earth was flat: second, that the educated public of the Renaissance had still to acquire the basic intellectual heritage of the Middle Ages. Observe the evidence. Beyond the large number of manuscripts the work was widely commented on by both medieval writers and such prominent Renaissance figures as Regiomantanus, Lefevre and Melancthon. The Latin text was first printed at Ferrara in 1472, followed by more than twenty-five incunabula editions. Editions *for use in schools* were still printed as late as 1629 at Wittenberg and 1656 at Leiden.[4] Yet it was written in 1230.

Sacrobosco also wrote an elementary arithmetic, likewise from Arabic sources, equally sound, equally complete within its limits and almost equally popular. He used the so-called Arabic numerals throughout and covered the usual arithmetic operations through the extraction of cube roots.[5]

If the case of Sacrobosco can dispel the fable that the Middle Ages were a time of hopeless ignorance, the life and works of another Englishman may dispel the fable that they were times of slavish thought and tyrannical caste divisions.

Robert Grosseteste was a personality strikingly at variance with most of the popular modern images of the Middle Ages. He was born of very humble parents, at Stradbrook, in Suffolk, around 1175. In time he became the first chancellor of the University of Oxford and in 1235, Bishop of Lincoln.

[4] Translations: Italian: Venice 1537, 1543, 1550; Florence 1571, 1579; Siena 1604; French: Paris 1546, 1570, 1584; German: Nuremberg 1516, 1519; Strassburg, 1533; Spanish: Seville 1545; Madrid 1650. It was translated into Hebrew in 1399 and printed at Offenbach in 1720.
There were many printed Latin editions. The first Ferrara 1472.
[5] Printed at Strassburg in 1488 with many subsequent editions as late as Wittenberg 1550, 1568 and Antwerp 1559. Sacrobosco also wrote a Compotus (method of figuring the calendar) which was printed at Wittenberg in 1545 and 1550. Other editions at Antwerp 1547, Paris 1550, Venice 1564.

In the latter office as one of the principal leaders in the baronial opposition to Henry III, and in the embryonic nationalist opposition to Pope Innocent IV, he became one of the prominent political figures of his age. On the one hand he was a close personal friend of Adam Marsh, founder of the great Franciscan school at Oxford, on the other advisor to Simon de Montfort, Earl of Leicester—leader for the rebels against King Henry.

Beyond his political interests, Grosseteste was fascinated by scientific problems. There is no doubt that he conducted actual experiments of a scientific nature. Obviously, they bore little resemblance to a modern experiment, but in the beginning, when nothing in the field of physical knowledge had been observed under controlled conditions, any experiment directed at ascertaining a specific causal relation in nature was important and almost revolutionary. Roger Bacon, who was Grosseteste's pupil, praised him for having acquired the wisdom of Aristotle, not from reading Aristotle but through other disciplines and authorities (presumably Arabic) and through his own "experimentation." [6] "Experimentia" is much broader than modern "experiment," since Grosseteste used it to describe the worldwide astronomical observations that had led to knowledge that the earth was a sphere. But it also included something like our meaning because he used it to describe the change in the images of objects seen through lenses. This, he thought, was accomplished by the "visual ray" being broken up by the transparent object through which it passed. This showed us how "to make things very far off seem very close at hand" or how "to count sand, or grain, or grass, or any other minute objects." He was aware also that the determining factor was the shape of the lens: ". . . by a transparent figure interposed between the spectator and object seen, it is possible . . . that great things seem small and conversely, according to the shape given the interposed transparent object." The source of this is evidently al-Hazen, and it is repeated almost word for word by Bacon in his *Opus Maius*. Nor need we suppose that this accurate thirteenth century knowledge of the use of the lens was buried away in the forgotten manuscripts of a neglected genius and discovered anew in the Renaissance. It was not. By the end of the century, the use of lenses was so well known that the vernacular *Roman de la Rose* contains a generous account of the matter, and from the thirteenth century on spectacles became increasingly common. The confusion surrounding the supposed invention of the telescope in Holland in the seventeenth century is only natural, because it was not invented there or then. The systematic use of the telescope appears to date from Galileo, but the knowledge of how to make it had long been available.

[6] (. . . dominus Robertus . . . neglexit omnino libros Aristotelis et vias eorum per experimentiam propriam, et auctores alios et per alias scientas negotiatus est in sapientialibus Aristotelis—*Compenduum Studie Philosphiae*, Rolls Series I—469).

Some of the titles of Grosseteste's works show the scope of his scientific interests: On the errors of our calendar, on comets, on the origin of the stars, on the rainbow, on color, on the heat of the sun, on refraction and reflection of rays, on light. His treatise on the errors of the calendar was the basis of the reform of Pope Gregory five hundred years afterwards to give us the calendar we now use. In his treatise on light he describes experiments proving the uniform radiation of light in all directions and an attempt to discover its velocity, which he concluded was infinite. In this paper he also states that "some people" think the earth revolves around the sun but that true philosophy holds otherwise. He does not say who these people are and he seems to have dragged in the statement for no reason. This phrase was to have a longer history. Grosseteste was perhaps unintentionally a pioneer in another field which was to have a long future in the West: the research into the historical origin of Christianity. He translated from the Greek the seven epistles ascribed to Ignatius, Bishop of Antioch (died c. 110).[7]

Classical physical thought was never mathematical. The authors of their physical speculations—they could hardly be called theorists—were familiar with Euclidean geometry, the only scientific mathematics of the Classical world,[8] but used it as a source of plausible examples, not as a method of analysis of physical relations. The Levant made far greater use of mathematics and developed arithmetic, algebra and trigonometry as tools of analysis of the type of problem that interested their physicists. Much of their work, being concerned with the Levantine causality of events, has never interested us, though we have been quite willing to set to our purposes the Levantine mathematics themselves. We have even admired the scientific excellence of Levantine descriptive astronomy—complete with its numerical evaluation, so contrary to Classical practice—that was the technical base of their astrology.

[7] Thorndike, *op. cit.* Cap. LV treats rather fully of Grosseteste. Grosseteste's works were printed as follows:
Commentary on the system of the earth—*Compendium sphaerae*, Venice 1508, 1514, 1518, 1531.
On refraction and reflection—*Libellus de phisicis lineis angulis*, etc. Nüremberg 1503.
Commentary on Aristotle's *Posterior Analytics*, Venice 1494, 1497, 1499, 1504, 1537.
Super Libros Physicorum (of Aristotle) Venice 1506—Translated into Hebrew in 1537.
Commentary on Dionysius the (pseudo) Areopagite—Strassburg 1502.
Opuscula quaedam philosophica, Venice 1514.
Epistles of Ignatius, 1644.
An English translation of *On Light* has been published in modern times by St. John's College, Maryland.
[8] Arithmetic existed for practical purpose, of course, but hardly any Classical scientist except Archimedes ever employed it in scientific work.

Our own Western mathematics has differed in method and objective from those of either the Levant or the Classical, but we lose sight of this fact because of our convention that mathematics is a single, world-wide, millennial discipline created by "mankind." Of course, in this we ignore completely Chinese, Hindu and Mayan mathematics partly because we know much too little about them but largely because they cannot be fitted easily into a prelude to ours. Nevertheless, Western mathematics is a distinct body of mathematical thought, developed by Westerners, and bears no inward relation to Levantine or Classical mathematics. It bears a very pronounced outward relation to these predecessors, however, and the formal mathematics known to the great bulk of educated moderns is not Western mathematics at all but primarily those aspects of Levantine that have been found useful in everyday life where events dominate and scientific causality rarely enters.

Western mathematics thus has a datable history, and that history rather naturally begins with the appropriation of usable parts of the mathematics of the Classical and Levantine societies. There has never been any need to improve on Euclid for the exposition of Euclidean geometry—save to expose the contingent nature of his assumptions and detect those of which he himself was not conscious—but there was very early a need to pick out of the far vaster body of Levantine mathematical thought those operations that could be meaningful in the West. Magic squares, porisms and most of mobile geometry did not fall in this class, but the selection which we today call arithmetic, algebra and trigonometry did. The first two were made available in the course of the thirteenth century, the third early in the fourteenth.

Fibonacci, or Leonardo of Pisa, was born about 1170 and died about 1240. His father was the Pisan factor at Bugia on the north African coast, and Fibonacci there acquired a profound knowledge of Arabic mathematics. He was, however, much more than a simple translator. He not only mastered Arabic mathematics but he went slightly beyond it, twisting it in the direction that Western mathematics has followed ever since. In 1202, he published his *Liber Abaci*—which occupies 459 printed pages in its modern edition [9]—as complete and up-to-date an exposition of arithmetic as any written in our own day and far more complete than our usual high school text. It contains all the methods of calculating with whole numbers and with fractions, of extracting square and cube roots, proportional parts, arithmetic and geometric progression and compound interest.

It is considered a reproach to the learning of the later Middle Ages that after Fibonacci no one did more with arithmetic than draw on him. This is scarcely valid since to this day no one has done anything else in the field

[9] *Scritti di Leonardo Pisano,* B. Boncompagni (Ed.) 2 v. Rome, 1857-62.

of arithmetic unless one chooses rather arbitrarily to class some highly speculative modern work in the theory of numbers as arithmetic. The truth of the matter is that the West never had to develop arithmetic, the Levant had done it already and from Fibonacci's day to our own no more masterful summation has been needed. But Fibonacci went beyond arithmetic and, in time, beyond his Arab teachers. The *Liber Abaci* is also on algebra, handling equations of the first and second degree, determinate and indeterminate, with the use of letters as symbols. The proofs are rigid and usually geometrical.

In 1220 Fibonacci published his *Practica Geometricae* which assumes a thorough knowledge on the part of the reader of all currently existing books of Euclid and proposes to take the student beyond that point, though again primarily on the basis of Arabic work.

A few years later, in 1225, Fibonacci published his more original mathematical works, the *Flos* and the *Liber Quadratorum*. In the *Flos* problems of the solution of indeterminates received his attention. He realized the nature of positive and negative roots. He solved the equation $x^3 + 2x^2 + 10x = 20$ which those who believe in the intellectual backwardness of the thirteenth century may try to solve for themselves on the basis of the mathematics taught them by our advanced and scientific educational system. In the *Liber Quadratorum*, working from the principle that the sum of successive odd numbers gives the series of squares of the integers, he solved equations of the type $x^2 + y^2 = z^2$.

Fibonacci's works were not printed until the nineteenth century, but they remained in use in manuscript. It is interesting as a commentary on the roots of the Renaissance that in 1500 Luca Pacioli in his famous Renaissance masterpiece, the *Summa de Arithmetica*, followed Fibonacci throughout and, unlike some of his contemporaries, frankly admitted it, saying that anything in his work not specifically credited to a named authority was derived from Fibonacci. Pacioli was a close personal friend of Leonardo da Vinci, whom he assisted in calculations for casting the Sforza "Great Horse" at Milan.

Fibonacci has been remembered, perhaps because of Pacioli's scrupulous honesty, something not always prevalent among the revivers of learning in the fifteenth and sixteenth centuries. His fame is not particularly great, but at least our standard encyclopedias and histories of mathematics do mention him.

The introduction of trigonometry was the work of the two such dissimilar men as a blacksmith's son, Richard of Wallingford (1292-1335) who died abbot of St. Albans, and Levi ben Gerson (1288-1344), Jewish philosopher and mathematician of Provence. Both drew on the same Arabic sources and produced similar works. Judging by extant manuscripts, Richard's work was largely used in England and Gerson's, translated from Hebrew into Latin in 1342, was the chief source of trigonometric knowledge on the continent.[10] This largely closed the Western acquisition of the developed mathematics of other societies. The further development of mathematics in the West was the growth of a mathematical instrument capable of handling an entirely different type of thought. This will be touched on later.

The origin of Western mathematics is somewhat confused by the use we have made of parts of the mathematics of other societies and because the early, groping development of our own took place simultaneously with the acquisition of the finished work of others. No such confusion exists, however, in the development of Western mechanics, for here Western thought at the outset rejected completely the mechanics of other civilizations.

Jordanus Nemorarius is now largely forgotten. There is even some confusion concerning his historical personality. In all probability, the mathematician and physicist was the same person as the Nemorarius who in 1222 became the second general of the Dominicans and died in 1237. Duhem a generation ago thought they were different. Sarton in our day believed they were the same.

Jordanus was the first Westerner of whom we have record who studied problems of theoretical mechanics. Considering where knowledge of this subject has carried the modern world, the appearance of a work of correct though limited analytical power in this field during the thirteenth century is important evidence of the style and continuity of our thought. The subject itself had never been part of the corpus of the Levantine sciences; only Hero and Pappus had touched on a few problems studied long before by Archimedes and neither they nor their Arabic successors went any further. Essentially, mechanics in the thirteenth century stood where Aristotle and Archimedes had left it. Aristotle, it will be recalled, saw in the difference of *speed* of the two ends of a lever or unsymmetrical balance the explanation of the equilibrium of unequal weights at the two ends. Archimedes simply postulated the observed fact that in a balance, the weight times the length of the bar on one side balanced the same factors in the other. He made no attempt to explain why this should be so.

Jordanus in his *Elementa super demonstrationem ponderis* approached the problem by an analysis not of the static equilibrium like Archimedes, but like Aristotle of what happens to the weights and distances in a moving balance. Unlike Aristotle, however, he was not concerned with the self-contained changes in the system—the difference in speed at the ends of

---

[10] Regiomontanus, the Renaissance name of John Mueller (1436-1476) who is credited in the popular histories of mathematics with the Renaissance development of trigonometry simply rewrote Gerson's *De Sinibus* (*Sefer tekunah*), which **was not printed until modern times.**

longer and shorter arms—but with differences that appeared only against an absolute scale of reference. Undoubtedly he was not conscious of this new approach, which in itself is a point of historical interest on how unconscious are the characteristic modes of Western thought.

Jordanus formulated four principles concerning the relationship between weight and the force of a given weight:

"The movement of every weight is toward the center (of the world) and the force of that movement is the ability that it has to move downward and to resist contrary movement.

"In descending (a weight) is heavier (i.e. more forceful) the more direct is its motion towards the center.

"(A weight) is heavier (more forceful) according to its situation, to the extent that in this situation its descent is less oblique.

"A more oblique descent is that which, for the same descent, is less direct (towards the center).[11]

From these propositions, Jordanus derived the correct law of the lever in observing that a force sufficient to lift a given weight to a given height would lift half this weight twice the height. As Duhem points out this is the principle at the base of Descartes system of statics and Bernoulli's principle of virtual work.

Jordanus' treatise has come down to us associated with a group of mechanical studies of the same time, all of unknown authorship. One of these in particular entitled *De ratione ponderis* corrected some errors of Jordanus, began the quantitative as well as qualitative application of his principles and carried them further into the correct analysis of the action of inclined planes. Various erroneous solutions of this problem were still offered down to the time of Galileo, by da Vinci among others.[12]

What is particularly striking in this thirteenth century school of Western mechanics is the ability to distinguish the fundamental modern scientific concepts of mass, force and work even though their language lacks modern precise terminology. The difference between a weight (ponderosus) and the component of its motion directed downward (virtutem . . . ad inferiora)

---

[11] Omnis ponderosi motum esse ad medium, virtutemque ipsius potentiam ad inferiora tendendi et motui contrario resistendi.
Gravius esse in descendendo quando ejusdem motus ad medium rectior.
Secundum situm gravius, quanto in eodem situ minus obliquus est descensus.
Obliquiorem autem descensum in eadem quantitate minus capere de directo.
Quoted by René Dugas: *Histoire de la Mécanique*, p. 39,

[12] Jordanus also wrote on arithmetic, algebra and geometry, generalizing his operations by the use of letters instead of numbers much more than Fibonacci. His works were printed:
De ratione ponderis, edited by Tartaglia, Venice 1565.
Arithmetic, with a commentary by Lefèvre, Paris 1496, 1503, 1507, 1510, 1514.

is the distinction between mass and force. The realization that the same amount of force will raise different weights inversely to different heights is in itself the realization of the concept of work. True, these concepts, as concepts, are not defined, and certainly not quantitatively evaluated, but these early Western physicists were quite unconsciously thinking in these concepts, which then had neither name nor definition. No one could have derived them from Aristotle or Archimedes.

A little later in the century Giovanni Campano (Campanus) of Novara, Chaplain to Pope Urban IV and afterwards Canon at Paris, carried forward a study of Jordanus on the angle between a curve and a tangent. This led Campanus to a concept that he called "quantitates continuae," but which in modern terminology we would call infinitesimals. Here again, we find a wholly new type of analysis—infinitesimals as something numerically usable —introduced in connection with the concept of infinitesimally continuous motion. Nearly four centuries separate Campanus from the full development of the calculus, but its source lies in the thirteenth century. Campanus revised Adelard's translation of Euclid, adding notes of his own. He was also familiar with the work of Grosseteste and wrote on the sphere of the earth, the calendar and astronomical instruments.[13]

Long afterwards, Leibniz reproached Aristotle and all his followers for dealing only in what he called "dead force," such as the weight of an immobile object, and neglecting "live force" which "is born of an infinity of continued impressions of the dead force," as in an object which has already begun to fall. It is a difference expressed in modern terminology in the equation $F = m(\frac{dv}{dt})$ which becomes the "dead force" when the velocity is zero. The first realization that there is even such a thing as "live force" appears in the work of Jordanus. Furthermore, there is a living, unbroken chain of scientific thought from the work of Jordanus to the sixteenth and seventeenth century mathematicians and physicists and hence an uninterrupted, if now unconscious, tradition to modern times. It would be significant enough to find the roots of modern physical thought in the thirteenth century, but it is doubly significant that these early considerations were continuously available in the world of scientific thought until they became of historical interest only.

Against this rough survey of early Western scientific thought it becomes possible to make a more reasonable appraisal of the only medieval "scientist" whose name is generally known in modern times and whose imaginary history is treasured as an example of the fate of advanced thought in the

[13] His revision of the translation of Euclid was printed at Venice in 1482, Ulm, 1486, Vicenza 1491, re-edited by Paciola at Venice in 1509. His own mathematical treatise, the *Tetragonismus*, edited by Luca Guarico at Venice in 1503. His astronomical writing, *Sphera, Compotis*, etc., Venice 1518, 1531.

ages of theology and superstition: Roger Bacon. This is of some importance because Bacon and Aquinas are probably the only non-political figures of the thirteenth century whose names carry any ring of familiarity to the educated lay public of modern times and the different associations that their names recall reveal nothing of the Middle Ages but much of our misunderstanding of history. In the case of Aquinas, the modern image may be too narrow and seen without reference to the intellectual crisis of his time, but at least the image corresponds in part to the facts about the man. In the case of Bacon, however, the image is a caricature bearing no more resemblance to the man and his times than the popular sixteenth century picture, derived from popular legends of the fifteenth, that Bacon was a sorcerer. Bacon is today credited with being scientifically far in advance of his time for the curious reason that he was, in fact, scientifically somewhat behind it. This apparent paradox is also the reason for his earlier repute as a magician.

The explanation of such an odd turn of affairs is this. Bacon's writings, despite their excessive criticism of the shortcomings, philosophical and scientific, of all his contemporaries, either by name or by general reference, contain in themselves no scientific observations and no philosophical considerations that are not as well or better set forth in the works of other contemporaries. His discussion of magnetism is far inferior to that of Peter of Maricourt; his botany and zoology cannot compare to Albert's; his mechanics are derived from Jordanus and are less full than in the original. His discussion of the calendar is taken directly from that of his teacher, Grosseteste, and is not so thorough a piece of work. His studies on light are also from Grosseteste and add no new facts, though he does argue against Grosseteste that light does have a velocity. In philosophy he was a Neoplatonist and therefore a realist, and his concept of causality is accordingly a jumble. He preached the value of "experiment" as a source of knowledge, but so did Albert. He urged the study of Greek and Hebrew, but so did Lull. He harped on the value of mathematics but obviously did not have genuine mathematics in mind, for he objected to the years of study and complex proofs of the professional mathematicians. The only thing he thought important in mathematics was to teach simple arithmetic and a smattering of Euclid in a few months of study. This was hardly a novelty in the age of Fibonacci, and was certainly not an advance in mathematical thought.

Telescoped in this fashion, these statements sound derogatory to Bacon, which would be unfair for he was a definite though not important figure in the growth of Western thought. He was not, however, a man out of his times and his contemporaries and immediate successors made a roughly correct appraisal of his work. These were used through the fourteenth century to the extent that they added anything to the sum of Western thought, and then completely superseded—everything of value in them long taken over into the current body of living literature, they passed into intellectual oblivion. In comparison with the record of printings of other thirteenth century thinkers, there was no incunabula edition of any of Bacon's writings, and in the sixteenth century there were printed only three alchemical and one medical treatises under his name, two of the first certainly spurious. In the seventeenth century some more alchemy and only one treatise of some scientific significance, its ideas largely Grosseteste's, the *Specula mathematica,* were printed. In short, his writings were obsolete before the invention of printing. Out of deep ignorance of the thirteenth century, it might be possible for someone to assert that Bacon's writings were too advanced for that century. But only ignorance of the writings themselves could lead anyone to suppose that they were in advance of the sixteenth and seventeenth centuries. Unlike other medieval scientific works, they were simply not worth printing.

So far as the repute for sorcery is concerned, Bacon's own writings were sufficient base for that. They are full of wonderful things that he could do—some will be quoted below—which, of course, he could not do and had no idea how anyone else could do them. It is true that he asserts the ability to do these things by pure natural science, not magic—but that was the contemporary chatter of even the most brazen alchemist and in a time like the fifteenth century, the claim to do marvelous things by undisclosed means meant simply witchcraft and sorcery.

Bacon's principal scientific work, the *Opus Majus,* written for or at any rate sent by request to Pope Clement IV, was not printed until 1733—in other words not as part of a living scientific literature but as a historical curiosity. By that time the fifteenth and early sixteenth century printings of other medieval thinkers had long since passed out of general circulation. Their scientific ideas and data had been gathered up and individually forgotten in the ever-growing body of Western scientific thought, and the books themselves were no longer of current importance. In the naïve notions of history characteristic of eighteenth century enlightenment, these now forgotten medieval steppingstones of scientific growth simply did not exist. Bacon, being the only medieval scientific writer printed in the eighteenth century, was the only such writer the dismal theological centuries could have produced. Furthermore, the prejudices of the eighteenth century were skillfully appealed to by the editor of the 1733 edition. He suppressed the fifth book of the *Opus Majus* on theology and metaphysics—the purpose and climax of Bacon's efforts—terminating the work to the delight of the enlightened with Book IV, "experimental science." It was really as simple as that, and since the myths of eighteenth century enlightenment still dominate our popular image, such is still the usual image of Bacon. He is, therefore, the lonely pioneer of modern science. He must, therefore, have been persecuted and imprisoned for his advanced thinking by a superstitious and reactionary church. Even so eminent a medievalist as Henry Osborne Taylor in *The Medieval Mind* did not avoid falling into this eighteenth century trap, asserting that Bacon had been "obstructed by his Order" and "had evidently been forbidden to write or spread his ideas; he had been disciplined at times with a diet of bread and water." All this is "evident" solely because that is what we think should have happened to a man corresponding to our image of Bacon in times corresponding to our image of the thirteenth century. The facts are otherwise.

Bacon was born in England at Ilchester in Somerset, about 1214 of a well-to-do family, never identified, but by Bacon's testimony supporters of Henry III against de Montfort and exiled during the latter's period of control. He studied at Oxford under Grosseteste, went to Paris about 1236 and returned to Oxford as a regent master about 1251. Sometime between returning to Oxford and 1257 he became a Franciscan. In 1266, Clement IV, who before he became pope had known Bacon in Paris, requested Bacon to send him a major philosophical work which the pope believed Bacon had already written or was in the course of preparing. The response was the *Opus Majus*, followed by several brief compositions urging upon Clement the great advantage to Christian power and education of following Bacon's ideas. These were not at all new or revolutionary, but his exaggerated language and his sweeping and unfair criticism of his contemporaries were unusual in an age that conducted intellectual disputes—provided they did not touch the Faith—with considerable scruple and good manners. Nor is it Bacon's complaint that the times are backward—quite the contrary. His bitter criticism is against the modernity of his age, that it lacks the learning and sober discipline which adorned education and the sciences in the days of his great teacher, Grosseteste. His classification of the sciences important for the ends of Christendom are languages, mathematics (of which he himself had a most pitiful idea), optics, "experimental science" and moral philosophy, that is, theology and metaphysics—a classification distinctly reminiscent of al-Farabi's. Like al-Farabi, too, he considered metaphysics, "divine science," the goal of human thought and investigation. Even beyond this he felt that all truth of every kind is contained openly or metaphorically in the Bible and that anything not there contained is erroneous.

Between 1267 and 1292, nothing of Bacon's life is known, and legend pictures him as imprisoned by the Franciscans because of his advanced scientific views. The basis of the imprisonment story is a statement, written a century afterwards in the *Chronicle of the Twenty-four Generals*,[14]

[14] Little, A. G. (Editor) Oxford 1914 Essays, Bacon.

that Bacon was imprisoned for teaching "suspected novelties," that is, theological aberrations. This is possible but the date of the source—in a time when Bacon's repute as a sorcerer had begun—makes the matter highly questionable. In any event, he could not have been imprisoned for his scientific views which were those of every educated person, lay and clerical, of his times. But if he was imprisoned, he must still have been allowed to write; for in 1292, the year of his death, appeared his last work, the *Compendium studii theologiae.*

One of the most famous passages in Bacon, often cited as indication of his foresight and scientific interest, is the following from the *De secretia operibus naturae:*

> *Machines for navigation can be made without rowers so that the largest ships on rivers or seas will be moved by a single man in charge with greater velocity than if they were full of men. Also cars can be made so that without animals they will move with unbelievable rapidity; such we opine were the scythe-bearing chariots with which the men of old fought. Also flying machines can be constructed so that a man sits in the midst of the machine revolving some engine by which artificial wings are made to beat the air like a flying bird. Also a machine small in size for raising or lowering enormous weights, than which nothing is more useful in emergencies. For by a machine three fingers high and wide and of less size a man could free himself and his friends from all danger of prison and rise and descend. Also a machine can easily be made by which one man can draw a thousand to himself by violence against their wills, and attract other things in like manner. Also machines can be made for walking in the sea and rivers, even to the bottom without danger. For Alexander the Great employed such, that he might see the secrets of the deep, as Ethicus the astronomer tells. These machines were made in antiquity and they have certainly been made in our times, except possibly a flying machine which I have not seen nor do I know any one who has, but I know an expert who has thought out the way to make one. And such things can be made almost without limit, for instance, bridges across rivers without piers or other supports, and mechanism, and unheard of engines.[15]*

Bacon opens the passage with the statement that he will describe wonderful works of art and nature, show their causes and methods of operation and that no magic is involved.[16] He does, of course, nothing of the sort.

[15] Thorndike, Lynn, *History of Magic and Experimental Science* II, pp. 616-691 discusses Bacon's works and what is known of his life in considerable detail.

[16] Narrebo igitur nunc primo opera artis et naturae miranda, ut postea causas et modum eorum assignem; in quibus nihil magicum est . . . Brewer, J. S., *Bacon,* 533.

This is not scientific prediction of any kind, and the fact that certain of these things have been accomplished by means undreamed of by Bacon should not blind us to the spurious—indeed magical—nature of the others and of the passage as a whole. In line of intellectual ancestry Bacon here stands nearer to Nostradamus than to any scientific figure of the West.

Western mathematics is the mathematics of change. Euclid was concerned with the timeless, changeless relations holding between geometrical forms. Levantine mathematics studied instantaneous number relationships of all kinds. An algebraic equation discloses the relation between every specific value assigned to its unknown elements but cannot deal with magnitudes that grow or diminish. But to the West, the universe of nature is a changing universe. We are concerned with the relations that hold between changing magnitudes. Western mathematics, the mathematics of the analysis of varying magnitudes, began in the fourteenth century.

The great mathematical school of the Middle Ages was Merton College, Oxford, founded about 1263 by Walter de Merton, Bishop of Rochester. Unfortunately in the age of revived learning, the library and archives of the college were sold for waste paper and only a few manuscripts were saved by a contemporary mathematician, Thomas Allen (1542-1632). Even from these few chance survivals and from references in continental material the great mathematical importance of this school is evident.

One of the most eminent Merton mathematicians, or physicists, (it is at times difficult to distinguish the two in the Middle Ages) was William Heytsbury, fellow of Merton in 1340 and chancellor of the University in 1371. Five of his treatises have survived, three containing material of great interest in the history of Western mathematical and physical thought. In one, the *Sophistmata*, he elaborates on the idea touched on by Adelard of Bath that in the world of physical reality nothing is destructible. His development of the idea is still not quantitative but instead of Adelard's vagueness, there is at least qualitative precision: "If something is to be compressed, something else must be expanded. It is impossible for something to be heated unless something else is cooled." [17]

In his second paper, *De sensu composito et diviso*, Heytsbury shows a correct knowledge of the law of acceleration of falling bodies but we do not have his mathematical development of it. He simply states as a fact that in a second period of time a falling body falls three times as far as in a first period of the same duration. Yet his third treatise, the *Regulae solvendi sophismata*, shows that he must have been familiar with the mathematical analysis of this problem. In this treatise, he states that a body

---

[17] Necesse est aliquid condensari si aliquid rarefiat. Impossibile est aliquid calefieri nisi aliquid frigefiat.

whose increase in speed is "uniformly diform" (i.e. constant acceleration) will traverse in a given time the same space as it would traverse if it moved for the full time at the speed it had at the mid point of the time.[18]

Heytsbury had thus reached a clear comprehension of the difference between speed and acceleration. He had also reached a realization of the quantitative relation between speed and acceleration. The following passage shows that he was entirely conscious of it: "In a moving object which starts from rest, it is possible to imagine a 'latitude' of speed (velocity) which grows indefinitely; at the same time it is possible to imagine a 'latitude of intension and remission' (acceleration or deceleration) by which a moving object can accelerate or decelerate with a rapidity or slowness infinitely variable. This latter latitude is related to the latitude of movement (velocity) as the latitude of movement is related to the size of the distance traversed.[19] That is, not only can speed vary but the *rate* at which it varies can vary also; the two variations are directly related and both related to the space traversed. We write this much more simply by saying that if s is the distance traversed ds/dt is the speed and d^2s/dt^2 is the acceleration, but the idea is Heytsbury's. It is the fundamental idea of the differential calculus.[20]

Richard Swineshead, another mathematician trained at Merton, was born probably in Glastonbury, Somerset, early in the fourteenth century

---

[18] That is, $S = \dfrac{tV}{2}$, S being the distance and V the velocity reached at time t.

Two distances would then be related:

$$\frac{S_1}{S_2} = \frac{t_1 V_1}{t_2 V_2}$$

taking with Heytsbury $t_2 = 2t_1$

$$\frac{S_1}{S_2} = \frac{V_1}{2V_2}$$

taking $V = gt$ (uniformly diform intension)

$$\frac{S_1}{S_2} = \frac{gt_1}{2gt_2}$$

which again with $t_2 = 2t_1$

$$\frac{S_1}{S_2} = \frac{1}{4}$$

which Heytsbury announced.

In this modern notation it becomes at once obvious that the key equality is omitted, namely that resulting from the substitution of $V = gt$ into the equation $S = \frac{1}{2}tV$ to produce $S = \frac{1}{2}gt^2$. Such is one of the immense advantages of a sound mathematical notation which the medieval methematicians lacked. The equality is anything but self-evident in the verbal forms of the problem.

[19] Dugas *op. cit.* p. 65.

[20] Heytsbury's treatises were printed:

Regulae solvendi sophistmata—Pavia 1481. *De sensu composito et diviso*, Venice 1491, 1494, 1501 with a commentary Bologna 1504. His other treatises were printed Pavia 1483 and Venice 1517. A commentary on his works by the Italian, Gaetano da Thiene (1387-1465), was printed at Pavia and Venice 1483.

and became a Cistercian at Swineshead, Lincolnshire. The date of his death is unknown, in fact, all dates of his life are uncertain except that in 1348 as a student at Merton he took part in a riot of sufficient prominence to be recorded. Swineshead, whose name is frequently given as Suiseth, was the author of a theoretical treatise entitled *Calculationes,* which is mathematical in substance but has little to do with calculation. It is an exploratory treatise on the then frontier of Western mathematics, the problem of continuous change, what the fourteenth century mathematicians—for Swineshead was not a lonely figure—called intension and remission. This is what we today call the continuous change of a variable, but we have so long handled this problem by operations with mathematical symbols that its early, verbal enunciation becomes hard for us to follow.

Every child is aware that a falling stone hits the ground at a faster speed the higher it is thrown, that the longer a top spins, the slower it turns and the more it wobbles, that the steeper the hill the harder the climb. Millennia of human learning are not required to bring these relationships to view. How should we then explain that prior to the Western mathematicians of the fourteenth century, men of science never pondered the relationships shown in these simple things? Observe, too, in the strict domain of the learned that the Classical geometers were aware of the varying curvature of an ellipse, knew it changed at every point along the circumstance, yet to explore this obvious mathematical fact never occurred to them. The great Levantine mathematicians who developed trigonometry observed the changing relationship between an angle and its sine, but they interested themselves only in the instantaneous values, not in the variation.

Swineshead concerned himself with the mathematics of continuous change. The problem had never been thought out nor, of course, had anyone invented appropriate symbols or devised even the preliminary mathematical operations. Hence he was driven to the clumsy methods of language, which makes his work nearly incomprehensible today but did not at all diminish its value in the early centuries. He seems, incidentally, to have been the first mathematician to realize the mathematical nature of maxima and minima (which he could not solve), of infinity, and vaguely, of the consequence of infinite series. Studying the series $1/2$, $2/4$, $3/8$, . . . $n/2n$, he correctly reasoned that the sum of this series if carried to infinity will simply equal 2 though he was unable to formulate a rigorous proof. Like Heytsbury, he was aware of the correct relation between the acceleration of a falling body and the distance traversed.

Nor was Swineshead's work neglected. It was widely used in manuscript and was printed as early as 1477.[21] The Renaissance mathematicians,

---

[21] At Padua, reprinted at Pavia, 1498, and Venice, 1520.

Politus, Alvarus Thomas and Pomponazzi, published discussion of the *Calculationes,* and Carden felt that Swineshead was one of the twelve greatest thinkers of all times.[22] Even Leibniz thought highly of Swineshead, felt that he had introduced mathematics into scholastic philosophy, and thought that there should be a new edition of the *Calculationes*—in the full seventeenth century. In fact, Swineshead remained an important figure in the intellectual history of the West as late as the middle of the eighteenth century,[23] but with the final triumph of the Renaissance myth he has been dropped into oblivion. The Renaissance humanists, Mirandolo and Vives in particular, having a sound awareness that he was the powerful representative of something at deep variance with the Classical and Levantine traditions, (their devotion to the latter was unknown to themselves) detested him. The ages of liberalism have followed that lead. Yet even Swineshead's technical language, which was that of his contemporaries—fluxus and fluens for the rate of change and the variable changing—are the terms and concepts Sir Isaac Newton used in his formulation of the differential calculus.[24]

Mathematics was not alone in moving towards Western methods of analysis. Philosophy, still completely scholastic in form, accompanied it, and in that age was more ready than the schoolroom philosophy of later days to include scientific thought within its compass. The philosophical pioneer of the early fourteenth century was William of Occam, born at Ockham[25] in Surrey late in the thirteenth century. He studied at the Franciscan College at Oxford and taught theology there until 1324. Despite the constant repetition of the mistake by even careful modern writers, he did not study under Duns Scot and his views were very far from those of Scot. In 1324, Occam was ordered to Avignon because of opinions on church organization expressed in his commentary on the *Sentences* of Peter Lombard. He was not condemned, but in 1328 having become the most

---

[22] His list was: Archytas of Tarentum, Aristotle, Euclid, Archimedes, Appolonius of Perga, Vitruvius, Galen, al-Khwarizmi, al-Kindi, Jabir ibn Aflah, Duns Scot and Swineshead.

[23] He is so treated in Jacob Brucker's *Historia critica philosophiae,* 1742, 1744 (III 849-53).

[24] Modern scholarly opinion on Swineshead tends to be noncomittal ... Sarton (*op. cit.* III, 1, 737) says that he "tackled awkwardly many of the fundamental questions of mechanics and physics, introducing new abstractions, which were not very fertile yet stimulated thought." Thorndike (*op. cit.* III—371) considers the large body of late medieval writings, of which the *Calculationes* is a conspicuous example, somewhat more fruitful in that "in reality it was laying the foundation for the later development of the mathematical method in physical science; that it was striving to express in words and arguments what was later put much more forcibly and conveniently into symbols and equations ..."

[25] Which should be the form of his name, but custom has established the other spelling.

outspoken leader of the spiritual Franciscans, he was imprisoned by Pope John XXII. Later in the year, together with several other friars and Michele da Casena, General of the Franciscans, he escaped from Avignon and joined the excommunicated Emperor Louis of Bavaria at Pisa. He spent the rest of his life in Italy and Germany under the emperor's protection and died, probably at Munich, in 1349.

At the time, pope and emperor were engaged in one of the ever-recurring quarrels about the extent of the secular and ecclesiastical powers. Occam was not originally interested in this aspect of contemporary politics, though he later wrote voluminously in favor of the emperor's cause. His quarrel with John XXII stemmed from his views on the necessity for evangelical poverty. This issue had become almost an open split between the Avignon Curia and the Order of St. Francis and was aggravated by the powerful Joachimist faction in the latter. Joachimism was not Occam's position, but he was a firm believer in the desirability of ecclesiastical poverty.

Occam's attacks on the pope were to earn him the enthusiasm of the early Protestants, but his influence in Western thought lay in his philosophy and logic, and even in his rather groping scientific thought, rather than in his ecclesiastical opinions. He destroyed realism as a tenable philosophical position and divorced logical thought from religious thought. Logic, he held, was an operation conducted with verbal counters. Words were not "things" and when used for concepts and universals they were not even the symbol for things but only the symbols for non-existent abstractions. Nothing exists but separate, distinct, independent things. We do not, he felt, logically deduce generalizations from these discrete things—much less find such generalizations in exterior nature—but by an intuitive process we see a likeness among certain classes of things and this likeness becomes a species in our minds and acquires a name, a term. It is with these last that logic works.[26] We cannot, therefore, prove the existence of universals and any notion of a logical demonstration of such matters as the existence of God, in the fashion of Aquinas, is nonsensical. It is impossible, he argued to know by evidence that God exists. Such belief is, therefore, irrational, though to Occam nonetheless valid as a matter of faith.

Occam is rightly felt to have brought medieval scholasticism to an end, in the sense that after him traditional scholasticism became nothing but a complex paraphernalia of minute verbal distinctions, of logic chopping with verbal counters standing for concepts that contained no meaning. Western thought of any worth was no longer carried forward in this now antiquated vehicle and after a century or so, the vehicle itself ceased to be used even by second-rate minds. But Occam did not succeed in driving out of Western thought the habit of verbal spinning with intuitive concepts

[26] The relation to Hobbes is obvious.

as barren of meaning as those of the late scholastics. The continuing history of philosophy reveals more than one famous name whose works are immense commentaries on notions as empty of physical nature as the universals of the medieval realists. Kant and Hegel, for instance, despite their acute observations on details of human reasoning, could have profited from more careful pondering on the insight of the great fourteenth century nominalist.

The key to Occam's thought was his refusal to confuse tangible evidence of the senses with concepts that were only derived, not observed—and derived by what he considered a process of uncertain validity. To him a concept was neither something we observe in outer objective reality nor a truth intuitively perceived within ourselves. It stood upon sense data and was entirely derived from these by our own mental operations. It followed that the public meaning of a concept, that is, of any word so used, was like the meaning of an algebraic symbol, a convention agreed on in advance. The conversion of "truth"—for so all schools of thought then and since prefer to define their concepts—into conventional postulates led him to formulate a rule of thought that is still the cardinal principle of scientific hypotheses and still goes under the name of Occam's razor—the rule of minimum assumptions. We are not warranted in using more assumptions, asserting more numerous "truths," to explain what can be explained by fewer.[27]

On this principle he began the analysis that was to end in the total collapse of Levantine physics and Biblical cosmology. He denied the validity of the Aristotelian concept of "natural" and "violent" motion, a doctrine sacred to Bacon, Albert and Aquinas, indeed, apparently, to all previous thinkers. Where, he asked, was the Aristotelian "mover" of a thrown stone after it left the hand of the thrower? He cited evidence to show that it could be neither still with the thrower nor in the air about the stone. The Aristotelian concept of motion must, therefore, be a mere mental invention, an unwarranted assumption to get around a special difficulty. He admitted, however, that he himself had no idea why a stone continued to move after it was thrown. This was typical with Occam. He knew that there was something very much the matter with the respectable thought of his time, and he knew in a general way what the matter was, but he had no creative ideas of his own. His greatness was that of a critic.[28] But he had a pupil.

[27] *Frustra fit per plura quod potest fieri per pauciora.*

[28] Occam's philosophical and logical works remained in constant demand. His principal work on philosophy, *Super quattor libros Sententiarum*, was printed in part at Strassburg in 1483 and in full at Lyons in 1495. Lesser philosophical works were variously printed at Strassburg in 1491, 1506; Bologna 1494; Paris 1487, 1488; Venice 1506; Rome 1637.

His principal work on logic, *Suma totius logicae*, was printed at Paris 1488;

Occam, product of Oxford, not of Merton though he must have known the men of that college, and until his flight to the empire, professor at Paris, bridged the two great centers of scientific learning of his time. As Oxford had become the great mathematical center of the Middle Ages, Paris had become the center of physics. One of Occam's pupils, a man who should be remembered—though he is not—as the first of that long and distinguished line of genius, the great physicists of the West, was Jean Buridan, born at Bethune in Artois probably in the closing years of the thirteenth century, rector of the University in 1328, canon of Arras in 1342. He died at Paris sometime after 1358. Buridan was a philosopher as well as a physicist, and he is dimly remembered in the history of philosophy for "Buridan's ass," the donkey who starved to death between two identical piles of hay because by deterministic principles there was as much reason to go to one as to the other and hence the donkey could get to neither.[29] There are slight variants of the story and none has ever been found in Buridan's writings, nor is the philosophical problem itself of much consequence to be the chief thing for which so powerful a thinker should be remembered. Buridan's great work was on the problem of motion. Following his teacher, Occam, he denied that there are any motions whatsoever in nature that correspond to the Aristotelian teachings concerning "violent" and "natural" motion. But he went far beyond Occam and disclosed the nature of motion—at least if the Western idea of motion is what motion "really" is.

We have from Buridan a study on this problem which is worth detailed attention. It is perhaps the earliest scientific paper of the West that can still be understood without having to substitute modern terminology and modern mathematical concepts for the cumbersome and difficult verbal symbols of the Middle Ages.

Aristotle, it will be recalled, taught that an object in "violent" motion was always moved by something, his "motor." A stone fell without "cause" since that was its "natural" motion, but when it was thrown it was moved by a "motor" and this "motor" necessarily moved with it during its flight and, like the source of all "violent" motion, rapidly lost its force. Hence

---

Bologna 1498; Venice 1508, 1522, 1591; Oxford 1676. It was translated into Hebrew late in the fifteenth century. A smaller logical work, *Expositio aurea, etc.* was printed at Bologna in 1496. Most of his political treatises against the Pope were also widely printed: variously, Louvaine 1481; Lyons 1494, 1495, 1496; Paris 1476; Venice 1513; Frankfort 1614.

[29] The story of Buridan's ass probably arose from the fact that he was an opponent of the extreme volitionists. He argued that free will is only the freedom to choose between alternates offered by the intellect in its estimate of desires and the consequence of different courses of action. The most the naked will can do, he taught, is postpone a decision and let the intellect work up more persuasive arguments for one course in preference to another.

all "violent" motion soon came to a standstill. The "motor" of an object thrown through the air was said to be the air itself, which had been set in motion by the thrower, and the nearer air constantly moving the more distant, the continuum of the air pushed the object along until the force died away.

Buridan's paper opens with an examination of concrete, rather than logical, objections to Aristotle's theory. How does the air get behind a top to keep it spinning? A grindstone goes on revolving long after the blacksmith stops turning it and does not move from its stand to allow air to occupy its former position. Furthermore, if it is closely covered with a tarpaulin to exclude moving air, it turns just as long. A spear sharpened at both ends can be thrown as far as one with a blunt rear, though in the first case there is no surface for the following air to push. The moving air should carry a feather much more easily than a stone, but no one can throw a feather as far as he can throw a stone. A ship along a dock or in a canal continues to move long after men stop hauling on her cable and the seamen on her deck, far from feeling the air pushing the ship, can feel the ship moving through the air. It is interesting to see how carefully Buridan had been observing the world of mundane actuality.

From these criticisms, which are akin to those of Occam but more concrete, Buridan proceeded to develop a causal thesis of his own: "During the time that the mover moves the moving object (i.e. while the thrower swings his arm with the stone still in his hand), he impresses upon it a certain *impetus,* a certain force capable of moving the object in the same direction in which the mover moved it, whether it is upward, downward, sidewise or in a circle (i.e. as a wheel, or a stone on a string). The faster the mover moves the object, the more powerful is the force that he impresses on it. It is this *impetus* that moves the stone after the thrower has himself ceased to move it. But because of the resistance of the air and also (with objects thrown upwards) because of the weight which causes the stone to move contrary to the direction of the force of the *impetus,* this *impetus* is continuously weakened so that the movement of the stone is continuously slowed. This *impetus* ends by being overcome and destroyed at the point where gravity becomes more powerful than the *impetus* and from there on the stone moves towards its natural place [an Aristotelian phrase for falling].

. . . "The more a body contains matter, the more of this *impetus* it can receive and the greater is the intensity with which it can receive it. A feather receives an *impetus* so slight that it is immediately destroyed by the resistance of the air. Similarly if someone throws with the same speed a light piece of wood and a heavy piece of iron, the two pieces having the same volume and the same shape, the piece of iron will go further because the *impetus* impressed on it is more intense. It is for this reason that it is more difficult to stop a large grindstone turning rapidly than a smaller wheel . . ."

The *impetus,* Buridan says further, "seems to be the reason why the natural fall of objects constantly accelerates. At the beginning of this fall gravity alone, in effect, moves the object. Thus it falls more slowly. But soon this gravity impresses a certain *impetus* on the falling object, an *impetus* which moves the object at the same time as gravity. The movement then becomes more rapid, but the more rapid the movement becomes, the more intense becomes the *impetus.* It can be seen therefore that the movement will go on continually accelerating." Buridan does not use the word "inertia" any more than Jordanus used the modern terminology of mass and force, but Buridan had the idea of inertia. What he is talking about is itself inertia, the *function* of mass to resist every change in its velocity, plus or minus.

As if this accurate description of the dynamics of motion for which Descartes afterwards developed the mathematical analysis were not a sufficient milestone in Western thought, Buridan carried the idea into the field of cosmology: "One cannot find in the Bible that there exist intelligences charged to communicate their proper motions to the celestial orbes. It is, therefore, permissible to show that there is no necessity for supposing the existence of such intelligences. It could be said, in substance, that God, when he created the world moved as he pleased each of the celestial orbes. He impressed upon each of them an *impetus* which has moved them since then. Thus God has not had to move these orbes any more, unless in the sense of a general influence similar to that by which he gives his approval to all things that happen. . . . This *impetus* which God impressed upon the heavenly bodies has not subsequently been weakened or destroyed because there has not been with these bodies any requirement toward other movements nor has there been any resistance, which could corrupt or diminish this *impetus.*"[30]

On what was science and what was not in the Middle Ages, it is worth comparing these passages with that of Bacon quoted earlier.

This bold conception of Buridan's was the foundation of the overthrow of Levantine cosmology. Here, not later, Western scientific thought was freed from the physics of its religious texts. Popularly, it has been entirely eclipsed by the later mathematical exposition of the same ideas by Kepler and Newton, but the formulation of the concept itself had to precede its mathematical analysis and proof. We today are comfortably accustomed to the idea that the same physical universe embraces both the earth and the stars. No other society ever thought so.

Buridan went even further. Like Grosseteste, but with riper thought on

[30] This follows Duhem's translation quoted by Dugas, *op. cit.* p. 47.

the subject, he considered whether the earth has a daily rotation: "utrum terra semper quiescat in medio mundi" and assembled the arguments in favor of a diurnal motion—without, however, committing himself on the subject. Like Occam, whose thought influenced him at so many points, he was concerned with sufficiency of hypotheses. But he went much further than Occam in a modern direction by being willing to accept a hypothesis when events occurred as though the hypothesis were true. This is, of course, the modern scientific position. Hypotheses are to make facts intelligible. The facts do not prove the hypotheses. These are tentatively accepted so long as they introduce intelligible order into the chaos of facts and are not disproved or shown to be improbable. With Buridan it was an Occamist position, which seeks the definition of usable assumptions, not conceptual "truths."

Buridan's influence on Western scientific thought was permanent and decisive. Many of his students became teachers in different European universities and his works continued to be used into the sixteenth century. Albert of Saxony and Nicholas of Cusa, sources of scientific thought for Copernicus, Kepler and da Vinci, and the great Nicole Oresme, were profoundly affected by his work.[31]

It must be noted that although Buridan so developed the concept of *impetus* that its establishment in Western thought stems from him, he did not invent it. Like every profound idea it appeared and seemed acceptable in a particular milieu at a certain time. Francis of Marchia, a Franciscan lecturing on the *Sentences* at Paris in 1320, as a long aside in a work considering whether supernatural power resides in the sacraments, mentions the idea and also extends its application to the heavenly bodies. He did not call it *impetus* but *virtus motiva* and thought that maybe some sort of Aristotelian motor might also be involved through the medium. There is

---

[31] Printed editions of Buridan's works, unfortunately an incomplete list, were:
   Summulae logicae—Lyons 1487, 1499; Venice 1499; Paris 1504; Oxford 1637; London 1740.
   Sophismata—Paris several editions after 1496.
   Consequentiae—Paris 1493, 1495.
   Questiones super VIII libros physicorum—Paris 1509.
   In metaphysicen questiones—Paris c. 1480.
   Questiones in libros de sensu et senato, etc.—Paris 1516, 1518.
   Questiones de anima—Paris 1516.
   Questiones super VIII libros politicorum—Paris 1500, 1513; Oxford 1640.
   Questiones super X libros Ethicorum ad Nichomachum—Paris 1489, 1513, 1518; Oxford 1637.
   His commentary on the *De caelo et mundo* in which he discussed the diurnal motion of the earth was not printed until modern times (Cambridge, Mass. 1942), but his friend Albert of Saxony practically reproduced it in his commentary, and the latter was printed Pavia 1481; Venice 1492, 1497, 1520; Paris 1516, 1518.

even a faint trace of the same concept in a few Levantine authors. Al-Bitruji, a Spanish Moslem astronomer of the twelfth century whose works were translated into Latin by Michael Scot during the thirteenth century, used such a concept—though an *impetus* that died away by its own nature—in his strange anti-Ptolemaic theory of concentric celestial spheres each turning slower than the next outer sphere, and as an example of the postulated driving force he cited the continuing motion of a thrown stone. No one paid more attention to this theory than to denounce it. Somewhat the same idea had occurred long before to the sixth-century Alexandrian Byzantine, Simplicius, and to another Alexandrian, Philoponus.[32] Before that Plutarch theorized that the moon stayed aloft because its speed circling the earth offset its tendency to fall.[33] As an idea it was known to both Albert and Aquinas and the latter specifically refuted it on the ground that the presence of such an impressed force would alter the substantial form of a projectile.[34]

In this, as in almost any fundamental physical idea, the notion itself is simple, and has almost always occurred to someone, somewhere, in the immense learning of one or another of the great societies. But if it is meaningless in the deep philosophy of that society, nothing develops from it.

Nicole Oresme was born near Caen in Normandy in the second decade of the fourteenth century, entered the college of Navarre at Paris in 1348, became principal of it in 1356, canon of Rouen and Paris (benefices since he continued to teach at Paris), dean of Rouen, and from 1377 until his death in 1382 he was bishop of Lisieux back in his native Normandy. He was also the personal advisor to Charles V of France, and Buridan was his intimate friend. The influence of each of these men can be seen in the thought of the other.

Oresme is almost as difficult to discuss as Aquinas but for different reasons. No modern institution, no accepted school of social or political philosophy proclaims his importance so that in assaying his part in the development of Western thought, the assayer, if he concludes that Oresme was a man of immense consequence, is forced to a personal judgment unsupported by anyone's convention. Duhem describes him as "one of the principal founders of modern science,"[35] but Duhem was an enthusiast and sought, whenever he could, to find medieval Frenchmen as the source of Western scientific thought. "One of the greatest men of science of the

---

[32] Sixth or seventh century, there seems to have been two men of such names (Isis 18, 447) much confused.

[33] *De facie in orbe lunae* quoted by Pierre Duhem, *Systeme du monde* I, 363.

[34] Commentary on the *de Caelo,* Bk. III, Lecture VII.

[35] *Catholic Encyclopedia*, Vol. XI, p. 296, a concise summary of Duhem's view elsewhere voluminously expressed.

fourteenth century. One of the greatest mathematicians, mechanicians and economists of the Middle Ages; one of the founders of the French scientific language and of French prose in general." Such is Sarton's summary of Oresme,[36] but Sarton, despite his immense scholarship, was a disciple of the "mankind" school and more than a little severe on the medieval Westerners for their lack of clarity and their doing little more than "adumbrating" the modern scientific theories. It is a severity that he does not always extend to the finished work of the Levantines, despite its slight value to us. Avicenna he describes as "The most famous scientist of Islam and one of the most famous of all races, places and times;" an enthusiasm perhaps even more intense than Duhem's but in behalf of a different vision of the past.

Oresme was a philosopher as well as a mathematician and physicist, something which of itself would make his importance in Western thought difficult for us to gauge. The later specialization of these disciplines—Leibniz was perhaps the last who mastered them all—inclines us to classify these early thinkers as unspecialized amateurs, and in modern scholarship no role is so despised as that.

In philosophy Oresme was a follower of Occam, but a stricter rationalist, and carried Occam's reliance on sensory evidence considerably further—a point of some importance in his scientific thought. Despite his ecclesiastical position, he was not a Biblical literalist and among a number of doubts that had risen in his mind was one on the existence of demons. "If the Faith did not declare that they do exist," he wrote, "I would say that they could not be proved to exist from any evidence, because everything (supposed to show the existence of demons) can be explained naturally."[37] Most of the supposed activity of demons, he thought, was the result of delusions or more often of statements by people who had never seen the thing they were talking about but were merely passing on what they had heard. He noted the fondness of men for believing the impossible and miraculous while they were unwilling to believe the possible.[38] Beyond this, the number of physical qualities which the senses must report, position, magnitude, mass, density, shape, motion and so forth, of itself gave room for serious error and misunderstanding. He had a low opinion of the accuracy of most reports of what men thought they had heard or seen and felt that human credulity had been and would continue to be one of the great dangers to

---

[36] *op. cit.* Vol. III, Pt. II, p. 1486.

[37] Nisi autem poneret eos esse dicerem quod ex nullo effectu posset probari esse quia naturaliter omnes possunt salvari.—Quodlibet—23, quoted Thorndike *op. cit.* III—466.

[38] Propter quid homines sepe credunt impossibilia et mirabilia et extranea et tamen possibilia et vera nolunt credere. Quoted by Thorndike op. cit. III-452.

learning and religion.[39] He himself completely disbelieved the mounting mass of confessions concerning diabolical intercourse which the growing witchcraft frenzy was bringing forth. "Many from violent torture confess what they never did," he wrote. Others, he thought, were so stupefied by fear of torture that they did not know what they were saying. Still others may indeed have entered what they thought were diabolical alliances, but, in fact, nothing happened from any such performance.

In somewhat the same vein of rationalism, Oresme was strongly opposed to astrology, writing what is probably the earliest rational attack on it— there had, of course, been religious attacks based on the doctrine of human free will and the impossibility of the will of God being bound by the power of the stars. Oresme did not reject these arguments, but he added two of a scientific sort, first that correlations between celestial motions and earthly events were too few to serve as a valid base; the positions of the stars had not even been collated with reported weather data. Secondly, he observed that where celestial forces could be tangibly identified they turned out to be heat and light; and wherever terrestrial effects could be traced to such causes, they alone seemed largely to account for the effects without leaving much room for the astrological disposition of the stars.

Oresme likewise composed a penetrating study of money, the *De origine natura jure et mutationibus monetarum*. It is evident from this full treatise on the subject that the feudal economy of payment in kind was completely wrecked and Western society already deep in a money economy. Oresme was aware of the basic principle of the market, that money always goes where it can obtain what its possessor thinks will be the highest value. He was aware of the consequences of depreciated money and felt that the sovereign had no right to change the value. He differed from Aristotle's view that money is only a measure of the value of other things and believed that money was a piece of merchandise having a value of its own. That was certainly true of the metallic money of the Middle Ages before the bank-credit money of modern times proved Aristotle correct concerning conditions, such as his own, in a mature money economy.

Oresme's mathematical works dealt with the same general subjects as Heytsbury's and Swinesheads', but they carried these ideas somewhat further. The problem of how to handle a variable was the great concern of all of them. Oresme's method was the use of graphs to show the changing value of the variable by the changed position of the curve. He constructed these graphs as we do today by the use of ordinate and abscissa, which he and his contemporaries called intension in latitude and extension

---

[39] videtur mihi quod facilite credere est et fuit causa destructionis philosophie naturalis, et etiam in fide facit et faciet magna pericula ... Thorndike *op. cit.* III—455.

in longitude, that is, a "quality"—approximately what we would today call a "function"—was represented horizontally by an extension in longitude and any variation of this quality, intension or remission in latitude, by verticals of varying heights. Joining the tops of the verticals would thus form a line representing the change. A uniform intension would produce a horizontal straight line, a uniformly diform intension a slanted straight line, a diformly diform intension, a curve.[40] But though Oresme realized that there was a relation between the position of a point on such a curve and a numerical value, and was aware that the slope of the curve depended on the degree and type of intension, the full expression of this relationship in an exact mathematical equation was beyond him—as it was beyond his successors for some centuries. He did, however, grasp the mathematical nature of maxima and minima, realizing that the least amount of change in the latitude (ordinate) for a given change in the longitude (abscissa) corresponded to the points of maximum and minimum. The complete mathematical formulation of these facts had to await the development of the differential calculus in the seventeenth century, what we express today by the relation $dy/dx = 0$. He was also aware that if the extension of a line of varying intension represented motion with varying velocity, then the distance travelled was represented by the area under the curve. This was the exact method used by Galileo in his exposition of the law of falling bodies and is today the general interpretation of the meaning of integration.

Oresme then considered the problem of representing a quality graphically when the number of variables was increased. He realized that a quality with two variables corresponded to a surface formed by the sum of the infinite number of perpendiculars whose tops formed the curve of the quality. In partly modern terminology, if a diform intension was such that its curve corresponded to the equation $y = x$, the total change in the quality would be the area between this line and the abscissa of origin to any value of x, and that this would equal x multiplied by the value of y at the midpoint, or $\int y = \frac{1}{2}x^2$. He then carried this analogy to the representation of qualities with three and four variables, which he called "qualités superficielle" and "qualités corporelle."

"The 'qualité superficielle'," he wrote, "is represented by a body and no fourth dimension exists. One cannot even be imagined. Nevertheless it is necessary to conceive the 'qualité corporelle' as having a double 'corporéité.' It has one true one, by the effect of the extension of the subject, extension that takes place in all dimensions, but it has also another, which can only be imagined. It comes from the intensity of the quality, a quality

---

[40] Those familiar with modern calculus or analytical geometry will have no difficulty recognizing what Oresme was inventing.

which is repeated an infinite number of times by the many surfaces that can be drawn in the body of the subject." [41]

Despite its fourteenth century source, the meaning of this can perhaps be grasped only from some familiarity with modern technical practice. A phase rule diagram of a three-component system with defined pressure and variable temperature is an example of Oresme's "qualité superficielle." Each of the three pure components is represented as the apex of an equilateral triangle and variation of temperature as the third dimension converting the triangle into a prism. On each plane of constant temperature, curves will mark the conditions of equilibrium of various solutions and solid phases for all proportions of the three components. If now this complete system is imagined as a "qualité corporelle" and the pressure made an additional variable, the original three-dimensional freedom remains, but each of the infinite number of planes of constant temperature can now be imagined as giving rise to an infinite number of parallel planes of different pressure with the differing equilibria, all contained not only within the prism but within the constant temperature plane itself. It is a geometric conception not reached again for many centuries after Oresme.

Oresme pioneered in another branch of Western mathematics, exponents. Like his "qualité corporelle," exponents required him to ponder the meaning of powers, or dimensions, beyond the three of sensory space. Denying the physical possibility of a fourth dimension but realizing, as he had with the "qualité corporelle," that its mathematical expression could still have valid meaning, he dropped all connection between exponents and sensory space and conducted purely mathematical operations with these exponents. From this he arrived at the first known realization of the possibility of fractional exponents and devised correct rules for operating with them. Nowhere in the mathematical records of all other civilizations is there evidence that the possibility of fractional exponents had ever occurred to anyone. Neither modern engineering nor physics would be possible without this development of Western mathematics.

Oresme's physics was that of Buridan. He accepted the idea of *impetus* and extended it to action and reaction, citing, as an example, a hammer bouncing from an anvil. He concluded that gravity was an inherent property of matter, that therefore there need not be postulated any Aristotelian fixed center of the universe toward which the heavy and away from which the light elements naturally moved. Hence to define absolute motion, he felt it would be necessary to postulate an immovable infinite space beyond the stars. Like his contemporary mathematicians at Merton, he arrived at the correct interpretation of the average speed of a uniformly accelerated

---

[41] From the *Tractatus de figuratione potentiarum et mensuarum difformitatum*, quoted by Dugas, *op. cit*, p. 59.

body, but no more than they was he able to develop the full qualitative form of the law. To express their thought in modern terminology, all of them realized that uniformly diform intension produced $V = gt$. They also knew that $S = \frac{1}{2}tV$. No one apparently pierced to the core of the problem and grasped the fact that $S = \frac{1}{2}gt^2$ was the fundamental quantitative expression for what they were seeking. Nor was Oresme able to free himself from the Aristotelian error of believing that differences in weight affected the acceleration of falling bodies.

In regard to planetary motions he wrote a French treatise *Traité du Ciel et du Monde,* in which he set forth a detailed argument for believing that the earth had a diurnal rotation which, he said, "some people" thought it actually had. It will be recalled that this was precisely how Grosseteste had written on the problem a century before, and though no writings on the problem except those of Buridan have come down to us, nevertheless as early as 1277, Etienne Tempier, Bishop of Paris, had declared that consideration of the possibility of a diurnal motion of the earth was not contrary to faith. That the subject had reached a degree of prominence requiring a ruling by the Bishop of Paris indicates that it must have been more widely considered and perhaps accepted than our surviving documents alone would indicate. No documentary consideration survives from the particular years of Tempier's ruling, yet he certainly did not rule on a matter that no one raised.

Oresme's arguments for a diurnal motion of the earth were much the same as Buridan's. He pointed out to begin with that so far as casual observation was concerned it was meaningless. A man in the sky able to see the details of the earth, supposing the sky were moving, would suppose that he was watching the earth turning beneath him, just as we suppose we see the sky turning above us. Against Aristotle's argument that the earth cannot be turning eastward because, if it were, something thrown in the air would fall to the westward, Oresme relied on Buridan's principle of *impetus.* All things on the surface of the earth have the same eastward *impetus* and never lose it. Against the difficulty that the Bible states specifically that the sky, not the earth, moves, Oresme urged that in these passages the Bible speaks "a la manière de commun parler humain," as he felt it did in a number of places. Finally, an immobile earth would require an inconceivable speed on the part of the incredibly distant stars in order for them to make their daily passage above the earth. Of an astronomical argument, he cited one of the best. If it is admitted that the earth moves from west to east, this accords with the other eastward planetary motions "The moon in one month, the sun in one year, Mars in about two years and the others the same way."

Of course, Oresme was a man of his time. To his scientific arguments for the diurnal motion of the earth he added several religious considerations. Thus theology teaches that the heavens are noble and the earth vile, while rest is more noble than motion since we pray God to give rest to the dead, whom we hope are blessed. Therefore, it is more appropriate that the vile element earth should be in motion and the noble heavens beyond the planets be at rest. Furthermore, God wisely arranges things so that his miracles produce a minimal disturbance of nature. Therefore, when God appeared to stop the sun for Joshua, it is more reasonable to suppose that he stopped the local motion of the small earth than a vast motion of the immense heavens.

Oresme was a pioneer in still another field. He was the first Western scholar to use a vernacular for learned purposes. He did so reluctantly under pressure from the king, for he complained of the difficult and tedious process of composing in French, when he always thought in Latin and thus always had to translate mentally as he wrote. This first use of French for learned purposes required Oresme to compose a learned vocabulary, and his neologisms have remained ever since the basic scholarly vocabulary of French. As well as composing in French, he translated some of his own writings and three of Aristotle's, the *Ethics, Politics* and *Economics*.[42]

Oresme's religious considerations are merely a pointed example of something that is true about all medieval scientific thought. None of it is modern. Thus when we confuse Western scientific thought with its particular modern expression, when we concentrate upon its aspect of modernity and ignore its "Westernness," the medieval thinkers become a problem because they certainly lack all trace of modernity. They were not specialists. They did not even postulate atheism, let alone believe it. Since they were not working as we do on a foundation of centuries of development of each field, their definitions and their nomenclature were as vague and disorderly

[42] Two of Oresme's three principal mathematical treatises were printed:
　　Tractatus de latitudinibus formarum, Padua 1482, 1486; Venice 1505; Vienna 1515.
　　Tractatus proportionum, Paris ? c. 1500, c. 1510; Venice 1505.
　　His *Algorisimus proportionum*, which contains his discussion of fractional exponents was not printed until the nineteenth century. Though restricted in circulation it remained known to mathematicians for there survive of it five manuscripts, one from the fourteenth century, three from the fifteenth century and one from the sixteenth century.
　　His French translations of Aristotle were printed at Paris in 1488 and 1489. Oresme delivered a stern sermon on the abuses of the church before Pope Urban V at Avignon on Christmas Eve 1363. It became a great favorite in the Reformation, being first printed at Basel in 1556 and many times reprinted. Oresme's own French version of the *De origine ... monetarum* entitled *Traictie de la première invention des monnoies* was printed at Bruges about 1477. The Latin text was printed at Paris early in the fifteenth century and reprinted at Lyons in 1605 and 1677. His *Traicté de l'espère*, Paris 1508.

as those of children. In contrast, "modernity" is evident on every page of Aristotle's physical treatises, of Euclid, of Archimedes, even, for those who bother to look, of Avicenna and Averroës. All were scientifically speaking atheists. All worked in developed disciplines, rigidly defined, in subject matter and nomenclature, by centuries of scientific work within their own societies. There is thus no lack of modernity in their writings. What is missing is any trace of Western thought. If we seek the source of "modernity," the thought of these men might seem to be the place to find it, but if the problem is the origin of the "Westernness" of Western thought, they are of little help. Further if we suppose, as historical evidence seems to give us the right to do, that modernity, like old age, is not a contagious disease but an attribute of an organism or of any living association having an organic quality, then it is pointless to seek exterior causes for this aspect of our present sciences. The modernity of Archimedes and the modernity of modern mathematics have no causal connection.

If we bear in mind this distinction between modernity and Westernness, the thought of the groups of mathematicians and physicists from Grosseteste to Oresme—and there were many more, the men discussed here being only the most distinguished examples—acquire a meaning that is not apparent if we seek only for modernity. If we add to this strictly scientific thought, the philosophical considerations on the nature of objective reality, on causality, and on the validity of sensory evidence, that is, the philosophers from Abelard to Occam, all the root ideas of even our most modern scientific thought appear. Among the philosophers we find concern for the causality of phenomena, for experimental evidence, for mechanistic consistency in nature. Among the mathematicians we find the pursuit of an entirely new concept, the mathematics of change, and the attempt to free mathematics from all sensory limitations. Among the physicists we find the revolt against form, substance and accident as usable concepts for analyzing nature and while the analysis of matter was not even thought of, the analysis of physical processes was begun in a uniquely Western direction with the problem of motion.

In the history of Western thought the early Western thinkers cannot be dismissed merely because they were not modern and failed to produce a finished body of science, nor because our conventional history avoids stating the fact, discussed below, that the continuity of their thought has been unbroken to our own times. The value of medieval writings does not lie in any scientific use they could have today. They have none. The importance of these works is only their place as the origin, not the completion, of Western physical and mathematical thought.

This kind of importance, curiously neglected in Western pure science except for the supposed influence of Classical thinkers, is yet always realized in regard to specific mechanical inventions. No one thinks that James Watt did nothing of importance by inventing the condenser and thus making the steam engine (which he did not invent) sufficiently efficient to become of commercial importance. The fact that his machine would be worthless today does not detract from its importance when it was invented. Nor would the *name* Watt gave to a condenser have made any difference. Its operation is sufficient for us to have recognized it regardless of the name. But to recognize this pattern of development in the field of pure science is more difficult, for there immediate tangible fulfillment is lacking and vague archaic language has to be thought into modern symbolic terminology. Yet the situation is the same.

No one could pretend that medieval mechanical and mathematical thought was a clear body of scientific doctrine or that it was free from almost childish errors. Nor does it have any apparent bearing upon these fields of scientific thought that embrace the problems of the moment and are to some extent the fashion of current popularizers: relativity, wave and quantum mechanics. But medieval scientific thought was none the less genuine Western scientific thought. It dealt with the problems, and was cast in the concepts, of physical reality as Western science has always understood reality. In later times these same problems and concepts formed the structure of Western mathematics and physics as these were developed from Newton to Lagrange. And this body of physical data and abstract reasoning *is* Western science. Our modern work makes this material not erroneous but a special case in non-Newtonian mechanics. Historically the situation is just the reverse. Modern mechanics is a special case of Newtonian mechanics from which it is derived both logically and historically.

The basic concept of Western science is the distinction of matter and energy, whether that distinction is asserted to be an ultimate reality as by Newtonian mechanics or denied as by some of the moderns. In both cases the problem is to disentangle the operations of energy regardless of what the real nature of the inert remainder may be. It is only a debate whether the remainder is "matter," whatever that may be, or a form of energy whose potential barrier is above some pre-defined threshhold. To the West all matter on analysis breaks down into energy and a remainder. In studying the gravity of a falling body, a piece of iron is wholly "matter" and the energy involved is the motion of the fall. From the view of thermodynamics and electromagnetism the iron is no longer "matter," but the scene of complex energy relationships between bits of "matter" which are now called molecules. In subatomic physics the molecules become in turn arrangements of energy, and the "matter" becomes at most the electrons, neutrons and protons which, no doubt, will someday themselves be similarly dissolved.

In substance in Western scientific thought matter, at each particular "cut" of reality, is the object that acts or is acted upon. Energy is the action, and potential energy the possibility of action. It makes no difference whether that action is ordinary motion through space or molecular re-arrangements, or the absorption of photons or the distortion of a magnetic field. "Matter" in each case is only the part of the phenomenon that is not action at the level considered.

No other society ever believed in or observed this division in the structure of nature. That things act and are acted upon al-Farabi believed. But that action itself as a concept could be abstracted from the things that act, could be rationally analyzed as the basic causality of all phenomena, was an idea which his society never entertained. To Aristotle even physical motion meant only the object moved. Motion was a state of things, an "accident," part of their description like their shape or their color, never an extrinsic reality, never, in his language for our concept, a substance of which the thing moved was the accident. It was precisely this basic concept of the reality of energy that prompted the work of the medieval physicists. That is what is disclosed in Jordanus' separation of weight as such from the effective weight along the perpendicular component, in Buridan's concept of the *impetus* in a moving body.

Viewing motion not as the thing moved, but as the motion itself, necessarily raised a new set of mathematical relationships that neither Classical nor Levantine mathematics had ever had to consider. Euclidian geometry is capable of analyzing the static "dead" forces in equilibrium in a balanced lever but not the "live" forces of a lever in motion. Levantine algebra and trigonometry were capable of analyzing an indefinite number of successive states but not the transition between these states. Accordingly, it is not surprising to find the early mathematicians like Swineshead and Oresme working on the problem of continuous variation, their diform extension in latitude, for this is the mathematics of motion. And here perhaps more than in mechanics our lack of perspective destroys our understanding. The mechanics of the Classical and the Levant are so absurd by our concepts that medieval physical thought is at least respectable pioneering. On the other hand, Classical and Levantine mathematics were admirable tools of static analysis, and were finished tools, before our society began. They are basically no better today than they were in 1200—the Western addition of logarithms has immensely speeded calculation and we have solved algebraic problems which the Levantines never could, but these improvements have not changed the analytical power of these ancient mathematics. But the development of the mathematics of continuous change, the differential calculus and its derivatives, was entirely the work of Westerners and they undertook its beginnings almost at the same time that they were learning what they desired from the finished mathematics of Hellas and the Arabs. Their own creative efforts seem—and were—crude and awkward in comparison with the speed and skill with which they learned the finished import.

We are thus faced with a minor historical puzzle. How does it come that the work of the thirteenth and fourteenth century mathematicians and physicists has not been recognized as the source of Western scientific thought? Why should convention date the beginning of our sciences at the Renaissance, with the names of Copernicus, Kepler, da Vinci, Galileo and Descartes, names back of which is draped as mere stage setting, vague remarks about the "hints" that might have been extracted from the ancients? Why has an obvious chain of developing thought, a chain with tangible links in books and manuscripts, been ignored—or even denied—and a completely tenuous, unnatural and inherently improbable chain, devoid of all physical links, been invented in its stead?

There are probably several answers. There is first a complex problem in the intellectual history of the fifteenth and sixteenth centuries, for there is evidence of a definite retrogression of Western scientific thought from the late fourteenth century until far into the sixteenth century, a retrogression that makes late sixteenth century material seem more extraordinary than it was because it is usually observed only against its immediate antecedents. This difficult matter is discussed more fully in the next chapter, but one important historical fact should be noted here: all the men discussed in this chapter were born and educated before the Black Death. There is secondly the fact that historians, and after Leibniz, philosophers, have with the rarest exceptions lacked intimate knowledge of Western mathematical and scientific thought. They would have hesitated, had they encountered such material in a fourteenth century thinker, to form a personal judgment on its value in the development of a body of thought in which they themselves were so ill-grounded. On the other hand, among men of science a taste for serious historical research has been extremely rare. As a result, the field of the history of science has been the specialty largely of those interested in the scientific thought of their own time and therefore quite willing to accept without serious examination accounts of the origin of our sciences which they found already in print. The latter process goes step by step back to the Renaissance writers, and there it necessarily stops because these writers did in general announce a source for their thought: Classical antiquity. Why, therefore, seek further?

What has been overlooked is that this Classical background proclaimed by many Renaissance writers, though not by all, was only a fad of the times. It was not serious history and could not have been so intended even by the writers themselves. They were not writing history but science, and they presented their thought in a way that appealed to the taste of their readers. Just as no modern physicist would fly in the face of his audience by dwelling on the esoteric, undemocratic, inherently Western quality of our sciences; just as no nineteenth century physicist would have dared admit that he arrived at the key to a difficult problem in a dream, albeit a perfectly normal operation of thought; just as few physicists in any age have been willing to admit that they guessed the right answer and only afterwards composed the equations from which they appeared to derive it—so no Renaissance physicists would have ruined the acceptance of his thought by admitting that it grew from works composed in a Latin quite unlike the Latin of Erasmus, works written by men who thought Aristotle an overrated windbag, men who attended mass under their lofty Gothic vaults and felt no need either for a new religion or an architecture decked out with the domes and colonnades of early Byzantium, which the Renaissance in its innocence thought were Classical.

The scientific writers of the Renaissance did what their confrères have always done. They arrived at their conclusions and theories within the living body of thought of their time and then presented them in the manner expected by their public. In those times this manner required a Classical, or supposedly Classical, background. So once having arrived at their conclusion, the Renaissance physicists riffled through Classical authors to find some reference that could be twisted to serve as a vague antecedent. In no case is this difficult to demonstrate. The documented sources used by Copernicus and Kepler will be mentioned. Agricola's *De re metalica* is an almost comical example of an invented Classical background. Like many another Renaissance figure, George Bauer, a mining engineer and metallurgist, put himself at the outset in the style of his times by translating his name into Latin. He then composed an exhaustive and valuable account of mining (other than coal) and metallurgical practices as they stood in the opening of the sixteenth century, complete with detailed drawings adequate to reproduce the machines in question—that is, the equivalent of modern blueprints. His machines include hoists, pumps, fans, blowers, cupola and blast furnaces, stamping machines, a variety of technical apparatus driven by water or animal power undreamed of by Levantine or Classical engineers. They were the product of some three hundred years of early Western technology, but Agricola salts and peppers his account with irrelevant references to the Greek and Roman authors wherever he can find the vaguest reference to anything to do with metals. He does not precisely say so, but the reader is left free to assume, if he likes, that all these power-driven machines and complex metallurgical processes were inspired by reading Homer, Horace, Virgil, Pliny, Livy, Plutarch, Diogenes Laertes, etc., whose irrelevant quotations sprinkle Agricola's paper.

There is also the fact that from the middle of the sixteenth century, mathematicians did more than pose as continuers of the Classical tradition. They felt bound to try to stay within it and while they could do little with Euclid and Aristotle, Archimedes offered them a mathematical model of far higher order. Archimedes was not concerned with the mathematics of change. There is no evidence that even he any more than other Classical mathematicians ever conceived that there could be such a mathematics. His interest was to find the numerical value of areas and volumes. To accomplish this he devised a technique, which we miscall that of exhaustion, which has been superficially—and erroneously—labeled as the precursor of modern integration. It was a technique of great mathematical brilliance but it was not the Western calculus nor the foundation for it. Nevertheless for almost a century after 1550 Western mathematicians tried generally to stay within it or, more often, to develop the growing concepts of the calculus—concepts of change and increase towards a limit—within the Archimedian method of addition of static geometric areas and volumes. This formalization of much mathematical work during this period in terms of Archimedean principles has been deceptive. It has led many historians of mathematics to picture the "influence" of Archimedes on the growth of the calculus without realizing that this growth took place *against* the basic principles of Archimedes and in spite of them.[43]

If we were to find only one or two of the root ideas of Western science among the medieval thinkers, or if we were to find these ideas expressed by isolated, ignored or persecuted men, the case would be different. But we find all these ideas expressed over a period of more than a century in various parts of the Catholic West. Nor were they the ideas of lonely men. They were the ideas of bishops and friends of kings. They were taught in the greatest institutions of learning, at Oxford and Paris. They were the ideas carried from these institutions to every corner of the West and taught in turn in the new universities founded during that century in Germany and northern Italy.

Further, these ideas; phenomenal causality, *impetus*, the identity of terrestrial and celestial mechanics, change as a mathematically expressable relation, mathematics divorced from sense concepts, constituted an interrelated whole. They formed a unique conception of nature that had never appeared among the thinkers of any earlier society. Not even one of the individual ideas taken alone had ever been the doctrine of any previous society. Isolated versions of some had been mentioned by chance individuals in other societies, but none had ever been developed. Some of the most important had never been thought of by anybody.

Nor are we driven to mere conjecture about the continuity of fourteenth

---

[43] This subject is excellently reviewed by Carl B. Boyer. *The Concepts of The Calculus*, New York, 1949.

century physical thought into the sixteenth and seventeenth centuries. The record of printing of medieval works is fairly conclusive, for these would not have been printed without a demand in the learned world. This, of itself, indicates a general continuity of thought, but there is more specific evidence. We know that Kepler studied the writings of Nicholas of Cusa, he said so himself and praised Cusa as "divinus mihi Cusanus." Cusa (1401-1464) student at Heidelberg and Padua, afterwards Cardinal and Bishop of Brixen, reproduced item by item Buridan's arguments and examples of *impetus*, terrestrial and celestial. We know that da Vinci studied Cusa, Jordanus and Albert of Saxony (1316-1390) and that Albert, before he became first chancellor of the University of Vienna, had studied at Paris in the days of Buridan and Oresme, and like Cusa published their view not only on *impetus* but on the diurnal motion of the earth. His works were profusely printed from 1481 to 1580 in France and Italy. We know that Buridan's doctrines were still taught at the College of Montaigu at Paris far into the sixteenth century and that his books were printed there. We know from the physical and mathematical writings of Soto, St. Vincent, and above all from the official "father" of calculus, Cavalieri, that these men had studied the medieval mathematicians and physicists. We know the same thing from the testimony of Pacioli, Tartaglia and Cardan. We know that this body of material was studied by Galileo—he cited both Swineshead and Heytsbury by name and used arguments and diagrams identical with those of Oresme—and that Descartes had available to him Oresme's *Tractatus de latitudinibus formarum*. We know the testimony of so great a mind as Leibniz on the value of the *Calculationes*. We know that Newton used the concepts and terminology of Swineshead.

With these facts there is no argument. There is only avoidance of the subject. The printing record of Classical mathematicians is cited, but the far more profuse printing record of medieval mathematicians passes almost unmentioned.[44] In regard to the diurnal motion of the earth, it is always carefully remarked [45] that Oresme's *Traité* was never printed, which is felt to show that it could not have been known to Copernicus. This is unproved and, indeed, not too probable, since manuscripts continued to circulate and even be recopied long after the introduction of printing. But even if the *Traité* was unknown to Copernicus, because unprinted, did the lack of this single book cut him off from the whole body of medieval scientific thought, most of which was in print? Yet we insist that Copernicus could have had no contact with this material and must have obtained his heliocentric ideas from fanciful "Pythagorean" notions which the Italian humanists were supposedly teaching while Copernicus was in Italy around

[44] For instance, Struik, *Concise History of Mathematics*, N. Y. 1951
[45] by Sarton, Dugas and Thorndike alike.

1500. And indeed traces of this Classical material are evident in Copernicus —in his errors, his insistence that the paths of the planets must be circular because this was a more noble form of motion and therefore, according to Plato, the only possible one for a celestial body.

There is no doubt that in antiquity Aristarcus sketched a heliocentric system, that Heraclides of Pontus sketched a partial one, having Venus and Mercury revolve around the Sun. Nor were these facts lost track of to be discovered in any revival of Classical learning. The famous description of Aristarcus' system is in Archimedes' *Sand Reckoner* and hence probably unknown both in the Levant and the Middle Ages (it was not among the works of Archimedes translated by William of Moerbeke), but Cicero refers to a heliocentric system, ascribing it to a certain Hicetas of Syracuse. Diogenes Laertes, in his *Life of Philolaus*, says "Philolaus was the first to claim that the earth moved in a circle, others say that it was Hicetas of Syracuse." The pseudo-Plutarch *De placitis philosophorum* (Lib, iii Ch. ix) says that Heraclides and Ecphantus attributed a daily rotation to the earth, and so does Eusebius in his *Preparatio Evangelica* (Lib. XV Cap. LVIII). Proclus in his commentary on the *Timeus* says (ed. Diehl, Leipiz 1906, Vol III p. 138) "Heraclides of Pontus professed the opinion that the earth moved with a circular motion; Plato on the contrary believed it to be immobile." Simplicius in his commentary on Aristotle's *De caelo*: "Heraclides of Pontus and Aristarcus believed it possible to save appearances (i.e. to account for the apparent motion of the stars and planets) by making the earth turn from west to east about the poles of the equator, and that in such a manner that it makes almost one turn a day. They add the word "almost" because of the movement of the sun which is one degree a day." Seneca in the *Natural Questions* (Lib VII, Cap. II) says: "It could be explored whether the universe revolves about an immobile earth or whether the earth turns within a stationary universe . . . whether the rising and setting of the stars come from the movement of the heavens, whether we ourselves set and rise. . ." Plutarch in *De facie in orbe lunae* says "Aristarcus offered the hypothesis that the heavens remain immobile and that the earth traverses the ecliptic at the same time that it is turning on its own axis." Ptolemy himself refers to the theory of a moving earth.

There was never a time in the West when Cicero was not read and probably the same thing is true of Seneca. In any event, the record of first printings shows how well-known most of these texts must have been in the fifteenth century West: Seneca, Naples 1475; Plutarch, Aldine 1507; Diogenes Laertes (Latin translation), Venice 1475. Nor is there any lack of witnesses to the continuing awareness among the learned of theories based upon a moving earth, Grosseteste in the twelfth century, Etienne Tempier in the thirteenth century, Oresme and Buridan in the fourteenth,

Nicholas of Cusa in the fifteenth (incidentally a list worthy of meditation, four bishops, one of them a cardinal, and a university professor). There is no basis, therefore, for supposing that this idea was unknown to the learned of the medieval West and required a sudden rediscovery. It was known and long and carefully considered; and the reason it was not hastily adopted is evident in the writings of those who considered it. Until a physics of the sky could account causally for the motion of the planets, astronomy was concerned only with "saving the appearances," that is, prediction of the observable future positions of the planets and stars, and for that task the Ptolemaic system was far superior to any heliocentric system prior to Kepler.

But Copernicus wrote not for the learned but for the educated. And like Agricola he decked his work out in the best current style by making opening references to Classical authors as justification for his idea. *The De revolutionibus orbium coelestium* is neither a physicist's study of celestial motions, like Kepler's *Astronomia nova*, quite properly subtitled a "Physics of the Sky"; nor an astronomer's manual for calculating the position of the planets. No one could use it for anything but public agitation, and precisely so it was used by Galileo, to the great damage of learning and the church to found a memorable and false tradition of ecclesiastical opposition, as false as the tradition that Copernicus derived his heliocentric notions as a result of Renaissance revival of the learning of antiquity.

Instead of a rediscovery of a Classical oddity, there was an unbroken tradition of Western thought constantly growing firmer and becoming better buttressed by deduction from observed facts, for three hundred years from Grosseteste to Copernicus. Nor did it end there, for without Kepler's work that of Copernicus would have been almost as tentative as Oresme's and we are able to document some of Kepler's medieval sources. Beneath it all there is in any case one indisputable scientific fact. Without the mechanics of Jordanus and Buridan a heliocentric system would be a mere description, as unscientific, as unrevolutionary, in Western thought as pointless, as the Ptolemaic. It is not the apparent motion of the heavens but their physical nature that has been the revolutionary discovery of the West. The core of that discovery is our concept of the nature of motion. The idea of impetus was the beginning of an understanding of motion as self-existing apart from the thing moved, and this separation is the base of our concept of energy as something distinct from the manifestations of things energized. All our physical sciences stand upon this foundation and without it they could never have been created. Its first application to cosmology was the concept of the diurnal rotation of the earth and the maintenance of both terrestrial and planetary motions by the sole continuing effect of the *impetus*, identical in the heavens and on earth. This, not the description of relative celestial motions was what struck at the heart of Levantine cosmology, though the new picture of the skies, derived from it and more comprehensible to the educated, created the popular sensation. It was not the heliocentric description but the idea of *impetus* that destroyed the need for an external mover, for any intelligences, angels or *primum mobile* to maintain the continuing existence and order of the universe. The image of a world over which God need no longer keep a daily watch, of a world that ran by machinery, was the creation of this medieval concept of motion.

All the complex machines of power and wealth which we have so casually spewed over the earth have been the incidental derivative of this conviction. And this has been our achievement, no one's else. It is no matter that today, or indeed for many decades in the past, individuals from other societies have been able to become competent operators and even pioneers in one or another branch of Western physical thought. Particularly today, with a vast developed corpus of technology and abstract scientific reasoning, with the necessary tools of mathematical analysis prepared, anybody on earth who wishes can learn to practice what our ancestors have made and provided. But regardless of what use or what peril this dangerous body of thought may become to men of other societies or to our own distant offspring, it remains inescapably Western, as Western as Vedic thought was Indian, as the eschatology of Jesus and the ecstasy of Plotinus and St. Paul were Levantine.

Chapter 7:

Within a Darkened Forest

Nel mezzo del cammin di nostra vita
mi ritrovai per una selva oscura,
chè la diritta via era smarrita.
Ah quanto a dir qual era è cosa dura
esta selva selvaggia e aspra e forte
che nel pensier rinnova la paura!

IT IS THE EVE OF GOOD FRIDAY, April 7, 1300, when in his allegory Dante at the mid-point of his life thus finds himself in a darkened forest where his way is lost and where the wildness and tangle of the woods is such that even to tell of it renews his terror. It could as well serve as an allegory of our society during the two hundred years that opened with Dante's lifetime. These centuries separate the breakdown of Gothic architecture from the rise of the Renaissance. They are the same centuries that separate the end of what is so often called the age of faith from the beginning of the Protestant revolt.

To the superficial optimism of the opening years of the present century, no period in the life of the West is more unpalatable than this era of wars and social uprisings, of the first beginnings of the power of commerce and money, of a strange collapse of religious prestige, of the decadence of Gothic architecture, of the Black Death of 1348 destroying perhaps half the population of Europe. All the romance, real or imaginary, of the Middle Ages is absent from this grim age. No tales of Robin Hood or Richard Coeur de Lion can be spun about the political struggles of the

Hundred Years' War. Out of the ruins of medieval church and empire the vernacular nations, embryonic since the tenth century, began emerging as the brutal engines of political reality. All that remains in our accepted image of these times are the evil associations of the Middle Ages; violence, superstition, backwardness and profound ignorance. Yet to us modern men of the West, no period is more meaningful, for here emerge the unmistakable traces of modern times. The childlike innocence of the twelfth and the juvenile sophistication of the thirteenth change to a dreary and often sordid practicality. Neither the doctrine of the two truths nor the attempted synthesis of Aquinas could any longer hold Western thought within even an artificial frame of unity. Scepticism and Bible mysticism were no longer, as in the earlier days, merely tendencies pulling the same officially united body of thought in opposite directions. Thought and religion hereafter generate two separate and opposed bodies of belief. No community includes either the words or the personalities of two such men as Oresme and St. Thomas à Kempis. They could as well belong to two different civilizations.

This Catholic Europe of 1300 had become a complex affair. It was dotted with towns and universities. Commercially, it was already knit together by roads and canals. Its seaborne commerce had, even then, produced the manufacturing cities of Flanders and the carrying-trade, maritime republics of northern Italy and Germany. It was a complexity standing on about three hundred years of intensive technological development, uniquely Western both in the speed of this development and in the manner with which technical problems were handled.

At the end of Carolingian times the physical heritage of the West was practically nothing. The Roman roads were in ruins, there were few stone buildings, no industry, a bare trickle of commerce in a few staples. There were scarcely any towns or ships, and meager subsistence agriculture with pitifully few domesticated plants was almost the sole economic occupation. Draft animals were few and small.

Details of the early growth of a more advanced technology have not come down to us. We see only results attained at sporadic points in later times, yet enough to gather the sweep of events. From the earliest days, one search that dominated all others was for sources of power. In the beginning, wind, water and animals were the only sources available and all were in full exploitation by the twelfth century. None strictly speaking was a Western invention though the iron shoeing of horses, the development of harness for heavy draft work and the deliberate breeding of strong work animals were certainly Western improvements on existing techniques. But something more specifically Western appeared in the twelfth century, the power-driven trip hammer and valved bellows in iron forging and the use of glass windows. So, too, began the first paved roads.[1] Technologically it is not much of a crop, particularly under the unspoken assumption that these things had existed since prehistoric times and had been the general development of "mankind." Considered against the conditions of a community without them, their consequence on the wealth and welfare of a civilization are more impressive. Considered not as the vague creation of "mankind" but as the specific development of the twelfth century West, however often and partially developed independently by other societies, they tell much about the type of civilization that was beginning in Catholic Europe.

With the thirteenth century, the technical developments became broader and more rapid and by the fourteenth they attained the outlines of mass industrialization—limited in location and restricted by lack of power, but nonetheless already faintly modern. The earliest industry seems to have been weaving. The spinning wheel came into use in the thirteenth century. Today we would scarcely consider this an industrial item (though the modern textile industry simply uses power to drive what is essentially the same device), but in comparison with hand spinning it was. It so greatly increased thread production that industrial weaving became possible. It produced also what appears to be the first record of an unending complaint in the West: technological unemployment. In order to protect employment among hand spinners, the weavers' guild of Speyer in 1298 forbade cloth manufacturers to use wheel-spun thread in the warp, limiting the use of the new invention to the woof.

By the end of the thirteenth century, paper had been invented (or reinvented for the Chinese had long known it)[2] and paper mills came into

---

[1] Or revival of paved roads, if you prefer, though strictly speaking the Romans did not pave roads. They built underground stone walls whose tops were roughly level with the ground surface. Twelfth century technology is reviewed by Des Noettes, *Le Mercure de France*, May 1932.

[2] This problem occurs constantly in any serious history of technology in the West. How much of it began as an idea derived from contemporary Chinese practice? Possibly a great deal, because Chinese technology was considerably more developed than that of the early medieval West and after the middle of the 13th century there was a fair amount of knowledge available about China. This aspect of Western history was ignored by the line-of-progress historians because by definition the Chinese, ancient or modern, are not in that line. Today it seems likely that the unity-of-mankind school will overdo the matter in the other extreme by arguing from Chinese priority, which is undoubted, to Chinese causal influence as the hidden author of Western mechanics. But this equally misses the point. There were no Chinese blueprints nor Chinese engineers available to teach the West. At most there was knowledge that somehow or other the Chinese were able to make such-and-such a product or had designed such-and-such a machine. The medieval Western engineers were willing to try any good idea,

existence. The fate of this new industry was tied to the weaving industry since the early paper was exclusively made of cloth fiber and the producers depended for raw material on linen cloth being sufficiently abundant and sufficiently cheap to encourage the discarding of all sorts of old cloth as rags. The general increase of the wealth of the West was sufficient for this and with the blossoming of the paper industry came printing, first in the mid-fourteenth century with what is technically known as xylography —each page a solid wooden block—and then, as everyone knows, printing with movable type early in the fifteenth. Gutenberg was the promoter of the idea, and very successful at it, but he did not invent it. It was invented probably a generation earlier and certainly in a xylographic printing plant. Xylography was not extensively used for texts by the early printers, but a great deal of illustrated material and short texts were printed this way for about a century before Gutenberg. (The modern invention of the various forms of stereotyping has, of course, revived the principle so that today the great bulk of printing is once more on plates, though not, of course, on wood plates.)

The technical flower of the thirteenth century was its church architecture. This had its origins back in the late tenth century and had become a great art and a masterly though incomplete technology by the twelfth. Its artistic climax, however, was in the thirteenth and the technical development continued for two hundred years longer.

Gothic architecture enjoys great popular fame, rising and falling to be sure, with the degree of romanticism prevalent at any particular time, but one of its most important aspects—to the problems here under review— is the restricted domain of the experts: the engineering in these buildings. From this point of view, these are the most remarkable structures theretofore built by any society. They advertise to the world that their builders are the first men who ever cared enough about stress analysis to undertake its study and apply its principles. These buildings are immense glass inset lanterns, their vaults carried on structural ribs, their walls abolished, the weight and wind stress carried by an exactly fitted skeleton of piers and buttresses. Our steel-skeletoned, flat vault, reinforced concrete floored, curtain-walled buildings of today are no more thorough expressions of stress engineering than these works confined by necessity to stone.

The influence school of art history has had a difficult time with these

wherever it came from, plus some partially original ideas of their own. Their contemporaries in the Levant, or in India, or Bali or the Negro kingdoms of east Africa, were not, though all of them had available as much or more knowledge about China. The subject of technological contacts between the West and China is thoroughly explored in *Science and Civilization in China*, Joseph Needham, Cambridge, 1954 (and later). See particularly Vol. I, p. 241.

Gothic buildings. Their total aesthetic quality as a complete artistic entity is without precedent, so this, the central historical problem, the aesthetic purpose of the whole enterprise, is rarely discussed. Next, the decoration is radically different from any earlier style, either Classical or Levantine. Since this exists in manifest detail, it cannot be ignored. Hence it is set down as an interesting but unimportant bit of local originality, developed from Classical ideas on how to treat a capital or corbel table.

But since the buildings are buildings, they must use structural members, and since the number of structural members is limited, brilliant search can be made for influences in this field. Since intersected barrel vaults were used by the Romans and there are even rare cases where they built rib vaults, this is obviously the origin of the Gothic vault. The Syrian churches of pre-Moslem times often used solid external buttresses in place of the massive masonry or lateral walls of the Romans, so this perhaps is the origin of the flying buttress. The Moslems used the pointed arch, which popular opinion often assumes to be the distinguishing mark of Gothic architecture, so this feature was clearly imported from the Arabs.

Briefly, this is rubbish. The early Western builders, the Romanesque of Lombardy is the earliest example of their work, were familiar with the Roman groined vaults. They built some themselves. If they were familiar with the Roman use of ribs, it would be extraordinary but unimportant for they did not use the Roman rib system. They developed the rib in a unique structural way by carrying their vaults on two diagonal crossing ribs and four side ribs, two transverse and two wall ribs in technical terms. From this vault, the northern builders developed the finished Gothic vault by discovering the exact points where the stresses of the vault reached the piers, the direction of thrust at these points, and a method of carrying these thrusts outward and downward. The first use of the pointed arch was probably a geometrical consequence of desiring to retain the great structural strength of semicircular diagonal ribs while still keeping the soffit of the main vault level. (In a similar problem the Romans used weak elliptical groins.) A semicircular transverse rib with semicircular diagonals would have covered the nave with a series of dome-like vaults, not with the level sweep that is so striking in Gothic buildings, made possible by the use of pointed transverse ribs.

Nothing has survived to tell us how the engineering problems were worked out. The failure of some buildings, Beauvais is particularly famous for this, and the awkward structural compromises in others, show that the methods for finding engineering solutions were crude and not always accurate. But though we do not know the method—and have ourselves so long become accustomed to the complex mathematics of modern engineering that we cannot even imagine how an engineering problem could be solved otherwise—the fact remains that no mere happy accident but engineering thought lay at the base of this architecture.

As radical as Gothic architecture, but in a less permanent medium, was Gothic shipbuilding and though the medium was ephemeral, the art was to alter the political face of the earth. The Gothic shipbuilders produced the ocean-going vessel that in succeeding centuries gave Europe access to the entire globe and from that access, for awhile, its mastery.

No contemporary technical discussion of Gothic shipbuilding has survived, and unlike the great cathedrals, the vessels themselves have long since gone; but from the scant pictures, the seals of maritime cities and chance contemporary references, the major steps of the development can be followed. In the opening years of the thirteenth century, the standard ship was small, partially decked, with one mast and either a steering oar or an outboard rudder, sometimes a pair of such rudders. By the end of the century, the size had increased, the decking was full and the rudder was inboard in its present place. During the fourteenth century, most vessels probably still carried a single mast amidships, but more and more a second and often a third mast were added. Flush planking universally replaced the earlier clincker-built hull.

There has survived a detailed description of a vessel, the *Rocheforte*, rented by Louis IX from the Venetians for his Crusade. She was over one-hundred feet long, forty-foot beam, with two full decks and partially decked under her bow and stern castles. She carried two masts, the foremast seventy-five feet high and the mainmast sixty-nine feet, an oddity of rig that did not survive. She carried several different-sized sails for each mast, but apparently only one was worn at a time. Nor was her size unusual. The king returned from the Holy Land on a vessel with eight-hundred men aboard and contemporary ordinances of the city of Marseilles record numerous vessels carrying a thousand or more people.

These were also the centuries of cannons and clocks, two unarguable Western inventions—though cannon may be a reinvention, again paralleling our so kindred society of China. That they were a Gothic, not a modern, invention is useful to remember since so often in the modern West both are felt to be the symbols of tyranny, physical and spiritual. But cannon and clocks are only specifically Western and efficient means to the same ends pursued by every society, creation and survival.

Back of these, indeed back of the architecture, the shipbuilding, the development of farm tools and of the light industries, lies the less obvious technical foundations of all of them, competent metallurgical practices and embryonic foundries and machine shops of some sort. The details are lost but again the major line of development is known.

Machine shops there must have been to produce the accurate parts for the clocks and the mine pumps that began to be used during the fourteenth century. Only foundries could produce cannon. In metallurgy the traditional sponge iron process began to be supplemented by the blast furnace. The former process never obtained a temperature high enough to melt the low-carbon iron it produced. Accordingly, such iron could not be cast but only worked by heat and constant hammering. The blast furnace, in contrast, produced a high-carbon iron with a melting point low enough for the furnace to attain, and hence iron castings became possible. The earliest such furnace recorded was one working at Namur in 1340. A later one was built at Liège in 1400. At the same time the skillful handling of bronze is shown by the remarkably large cannon cast during the fourteenth century and the number of memorial plaques and effigies that were made in those years. Although charcoal was used for smelting by the fourteenth century metallurgists, coal was beginning to be used for heat. Liège became a center not only of metal working but of coal mining, and the records of coal exports from Newcastle to London and France go back to the reign of Edward II (1307-1327).

There was another technical development of a sort, though we rarely think of it as such, the establishment of the universities. Bologna, Paris, Montpellier and Oxford go back to the end of the twelfth century; Cambridge, Padua, Toulouse, Salamanca and a number of others to the thirteenth; Grenoble, Lerida, Coimbra, Pavia, Ferrara, Cologne, Heidelberg, Vienna, Prague, Cracow and many more go back to the fourteenth.

We usually forget that neither tools nor universities are the inventions of mankind. Other societies have developed some of the tools that ours rediscovered, but none from its earliest days painstakingly and thoughtfully applied itself to devising means to accomplish an almost endless series of practical results. As for universities, which are in a way the tools of the mind, other societies have had institutions for training the young in law and religion and have had occasional but ephemeral academies as the homes of philosophical or even mathematical disciplines, but no other society conceived and created millennial institutions for the preservation and advancement of all learning. That the four most ancient universities and many almost as old still endure in unbroken, living continuity with their medieval foundation is far more extraordinary than it seems to us to whom the vast endurance of the institutions of our society is a matter of course. It is extraordinary, too, that by direct branching from these ancient institutions, most of the universities of the Western world have been derived, even those of America, for Cambridge was founded out of Oxford, and from Cambridge was founded Harvard, from Harvard, Yale and from Yale, Princeton It is a strange disease of modern men to hate the past, to seek to cut all the threads that connect us to it, and yet to treasure so much that it has given us.

By 1300, the political community of the West had moved far from the feudal anarchy of the tenth and eleventh centuries. The empire had risen in its great struggle with the papacy, been defeated during the thirteenth century and collapsed into a mere name for a collection of independent principalities and mercantile city republics. The Kingdoms of France and of England were becoming centralized monarchies filled with ever growing cities. In Scandinavia, the crown was gradually destroying the territorial power of the nobility and erecting a political government. Beyond the Pyrenees, Portugal and the still separate Kingdoms of Castile and Aragon had all but driven out the Moslems.

By the end of the eleventh century, the earlier semi-private attacks on the Mohammedans in Spain and Sicily were replaced by a vast, organized effort of the whole community, the Crusades, to destroy the power of the Moslems and the Byzantines. To destroy the Greeks was never officially the purpose of any Crusade, even of the Fourth which sacked Constantinople and founded the Latin Empire, but in Western practice and unofficial sentiment the feeling toward the Byzantines differed little from the feeling towards Moslems or Jews. All through the twelfth century, the successive crusading armies found themselves in ever deeper hostility toward the Byzantines, and the Normans in Sicily made no pretense but waged open war against Constantinople. At home in Western Europe, and not surprisingly, the fever of these wars officially for the faith turned bitterly against the enclaves of Levantine society, the Jews, physically resident in Western lands, but socially and culturally part of the great civilized, urban world of Spain and the Levant. Jewish segregation, originally by the choice of the Jews themselves, had existed since the Jews had entered western Europe, but anti-Jewish legislation and popular violence against Jews appears to have begun during the excitement of the Crusades. But it should also be noticed that while the intellectual and ruling classes of the West had no love for the Jews and were often anxious to expel them, they did their best to prevent personal outrages and violence. The terrible slaughters that accompanied the crusading fever in Germany were the work of mobs in the control of a man whose name alone would betray his social status, Walter the Penniless. That this savage and debased hostility was a democratic passion not shared by the upper classes and the learned seems indicated by another fact. In this century of the fiercest hostility against the Levantines, the utmost effort was made to translate from Greek and Arabic—and to a far lesser extent from Hebrew because there was far less in Hebrew—every scrap of useful knowledge that these alien peoples appeared to possess.

A psychological unity of the Latin-speaking Catholics had come into existence—at least as a unity against all other men. Even in legal theory, this political unity was accepted, since the Western image represented all Catholics as ultimately temporal subjects of the emperor and spiritual subjects of the pope. Of course, no such government existed, any more than its modern counterpart of a united West, but this image was the ideal of feudal theory till the fall of the Hohenstaufen dynasty and the narrowing of the empire to Germany.

With a conscious unity, if not a common political government, there began an attempt to picture the history of this unity. The Crusades produced many narratives of the wars and of events in the Levant, but they also produced the first attempt at a history of the West as a society—still seen under the Frankish name—and the first gropings towards a philosophy of history. Otto, Bishop of Freising, grandson of the Emperor Henry IV, brother of Conrad III and uncle of Frederick Barbarossa, thus rather well-placed for contemporary information, wrote a *History of the Two Cities*, the heavenly and the earthly,[3] which contains the following passage:

> *Thus worldly power passed from Babylon to the Medes, then to the Persians, afterwards to the Greeks, finally to the Romans and under the Roman name has passed to the Franks. ... But lastly the Franks, skilled though they were in arms, were to have their kingdom desolated as foretold by the Gospels. Though they had vastly extended the boundaries of their realm, and brought under their dominion Rome, the capital of the world, though they had made themselves dreaded by all peoples and seemed invulnerable—and their kingdom, shifted from east to west might have been thought to have attained peace and stability—yet it was rent within itself not only city against city but by the power of brother against brother. ... Thus from all the ruined kingdoms of this world we may assign an end to this five times repeated event. For even the kingdom of the Franks, the last worthy to hold Rome, is seen to be shrunk, and we who write the record of these manifest changes are, by this change of power as by a sufficient reason, turned to the changelessness of the Heavenly Kingdom.*[4]

[3] *Chronica sive historia de duabus civitatibus*—printed at Strassburg 1515.

[4] Ita nimirum potestas temporalis a Babylone devoluta ad Medos, inde ad Persas, post ad Graecos, ad ultimum ad Romanos et sub Romano nomine ad Francos translata est. ... Denique armis experientissimi Franci, cum regni terminos

In the same years Hugh of St. Victor foresaw the end of the world in the final culmination of civilization along the shores of the Atlantic. Our own received history and the accepted moral objectives of our world policy—allowing that we must transport the Kingdom of Heaven to earth —appear but massive and pedantic glosses on Hugh and Bishop Otto.

Finally, it should be noted that even by 1100 this community of northwestern Europe had become a power. Its internal organization, its agriculture and its technical crafts had become sufficiently expert to serve as the base of political and even a start at external imperial power. Even then western Europe was not a backward community eking out a drab existence on inefficient, subsistence agriculture. There was sufficient wealth and technical skill for this community to be able to raise, equip and maintain armies and fleets. The importance of the latter is too often overlooked. Such vast and successful endeavors, with the maze of crafts and skills involved, the immense managerial problems of assembling and financing men and materials needed to build and navigate seagoing fleets, such are not the operations of dull-witted peasants, brutal lords and mystics entranced by the divine vision. Furthermore the political consequences of Western naval power have reached the whole world, yet we forget that the West became a sea power in the twelfth not in the sixteenth century. We do not have the record of any famous naval action in that period. We have instead a slow, relentless destruction of Byzantine and Mohammedan naval power in the Mediterranean.

At the opening of the eleventh century, the Moslems held the coast of Spain from a few miles south of Barcelona, the Balearic Islands, Corsica, Sardinia, Sicily and Malta. The Byzantines held the heel and toe of Italy, the peninsula of Greece proper, the Aegean Islands, Crete and Cyprus. These powers possessed what seemed appropriate naval power for these widespread maritime dominions. At the outbreak of the Crusades a century later, Pisa had captured Sardinia and Corsica, and the Norman adventurers had taken Sicily from the Saracens and southern Italy from the Byzantines. A little more than a century after this, Byzantium had been destroyed forever as a power, and the Mohammedans driven from

---

plurimum dilatassent mundique caput Roman in suam dicionem transfudissent, cum iam omnibus gentibus horribiles facti essent et inexpugnabiles viderentur, in se ipsos non solum civiliter sed et intestine fratribus auctoribus divisi, regnum, quod ab oriente ad occidentem tamquam fugiens statum et requiem invenisse putabatur, desolandum fore iuxta evangelium praesagiebant. ... Igitur omnibus regnis mundi imminutis, cum et Francorum, qui ultimi Romam habere meruerunt, minoratum apparet regnum, nos qui ad ostandendas mutationes rerum res gestas scribimus hac regni mutatione tamquam sufficienti argumento ad regni caelestis immutabilitatem missi huic quinto operi finem imponamus. (*Chronica—Scriptores Rerum Germanicarum,* V-36).

the sea. Aragon had seized the Balearics and shortly afterwards came into possession (from the Venetians) of Athens and most of the Morea (ancient Peloponnesus). The Spanish coast was held beyond Cartagena. Venice had seized the Dalmation coast, Crete, the Negroponte and the lower Aegean Islands. Genoa held Chios and the upper islands, the Crimean coast, the north shore of the Sea of Azov, and Tana, near the modern Rostov, at the mouth of the Don. Rhodes was held by the Knights of Rhodes, Malta by the Knights of Malta. Cyprus was the dominion of the exiled Latin kings of Jerusalem. Although the Crusades founded no enduring power on the mainland, they did establish Western naval supremacy in both the eastern and western Mediterranean. The loss of the east followed the rise of the Ottoman Sultanate in the fifteenth century. Athens, in 1458 and the Crimea in 1475, the last possessions, fell after more than two centuries of Western rule. To ignore, as we usually do, the medieval rise of Western imperial power in the Mediterranean and Black Seas completely distorts the sixteenth century oceanic expansion. It contributes again to the illusion of a sudden discontinuity in our society. Four hundred years before Columbus, the West had learned to master winds and tides and armed enemies at sea.

With this medieval maritime development it should not be surprising to find the origin of true maps in the twelfth and thirteenth centuries. They appeared, the *portolani*, seaman's charts, which bear no resemblance to the monastic map, designed not for use but for the edification of the pious and fastened in our popular image as the map of the Middle Ages. The *portolani* were built by triangulating on compass bearings and hence produced a Mercator projection, the only projection on which all compass bearings are straight lines. It is not known whether the correct mathematical theory was consciously employed, though the level of contemporary spherical trigonometry was quite up to it. The fact remains that these were excellent practical charts by which accurate navigation was possible. No *portolani* of the thirteenth century survive but they did exist. On Louis IX's Crusade against Tunis, for instance, the King was shown the ship's position on a chart while out of sight of land, and even back in the late eleventh century, Adam of Bremen mentions them. Lull in the *Arbor Scientiae*, written about 1296, says men find their way over the sea by the use of chart and compass. Navigators also had the astrolabe by which they could find the altitude of the sun or stars and hence know their latitude very closely. They had no accurate method of finding longitude, but this remained true well into the eighteenth century.

These medieval charts were of immense consequence. They were the first method ever devised that made it possible to keep track of a ship's position when out of sight of land and without such certain and continuous knowledge, oceanic navigation would be the occupation of madmen. Whether the ancient Chinese ever devised a similar method we do not know, but neither the Classical nor Levantine societies thought of anything approaching them. They are the inescapable prerequisite for oceanic navigation and, without them, the exploration of the sixteenth and seventeenth centuries could never have taken place. It is true that they might have been devised then, but the fact is that they were a creation of at least the thirteenth if not the twelfth century.

All the alien contacts of the West were not hostile. Peaceful knowledge of the other societies of the earth was likewise gained by personal travel. On April 16, 1245, Fra Giovanni del Pian di Carpine set out from Lyons with a letter from Pope Innocent IV to the Great Khan. About a year later, Fra Giovanni having crossed most of Europe and Asia delivered his message at Qaraqorum, the Mongol capital south of Lake Baikal, obtained a reply and was back at Lyons before the end of 1247. The Khan's answer is still preserved in the archives of the Vatican.[5] Fra Giovanni wrote an accurate account of his trip entitled *Historia Mongolorum* etc., which was promptly abridged by Vincent of Beauvais in his *Speculum historiale*. At about the same time, Innocent sent a Dominican, Ascelivi, to deal with the Mongols in Persia. His report, too, reached Vincent of Beauvais and was incorporated in his *Speculum*.

A few years later, Louis IX sent his own mission, headed by William of Rubruquis, a Flemish Franciscan, to the Mongol court. William left Constantinople by sea in May, 1253, landed in the Crimea, crossed central Asia and reached Qaraqorum in April, 1254. He was the first European to describe the Caspian as landlocked, to note the correct courses of the Don and Volga, the existence of Korea and of the two kingdoms of Cathay. He reported the existence of the Nestorian Christians of China. Although he did not enter China proper, his description of it was excellent. He recorded the narrow eyes and generally short stature of the people, their method of medical diagnosis by use of the pulse, their employment of paper money and character writing in lieu of letters. His work was known to Roger Bacon but seemingly not to Vincent of Beauvais.[6]

By the end of the thirteenth century, the Mongols had moved their capital from the arid steppes about Qaraqorum into the wealth of con-

[5] Printed in *Revue de l'Orient Chrétien*—Vol. 3, p. 1923.

[6] An Italian translation was printed in 1537 and both it and the *Historia Mongolorum* were printed in *Hakluyt*, London, 1598.

quered Cathay at Khanbaliq (modern Peking). Thither, in 1289, Pope Nicholas IV sent Giovanni de Montecorvino with letters to Kublai Khan. Giovanni, an Italian Franciscan, who had already been at the court of the Il Khan in Persia, crossed Persia to Ormuz on the Gulf and then proceeded by sea along the Malabar and Coromandel coasts of India to Madras. Here he was joined by a Dominican, Nicholas of Pistoia, and the two attempted to found a mission. After Nicholas' death in 1291, Giovanni went on by sea to Cathay, arriving at Khanbaliq in 1292 where he remained in considerable favor with Kublai Khan until his death there, probably in 1328. Giovanni had little success converting the Nestorian Christians but made some headway with the heathen Mongols. He translated the New Testament and the Psalms into Mongolian, built at Khanbaliq not far from the Khan's palace the first Catholic church in China and in 1307 was named by Pope Clement V the first Archbishop of Khanbaliq. Giovanni's letter from India no longer exists, but there is a contemporary Italian translation. It contains an account of the climate and peoples of India and the Hindu-Moslem division of that country. His letters from China were more concerned with ecclesiastical problems but gave considerable information about the country. Oddly, one of the Archbishop's worst difficulties was an irreligious Italian surgeon who turned up in Khanbaliq on his own private adventures in 1301 and told the Chinese scurrilous stories about the Franciscans and the Roman Curia.

It seems almost needless to mention the famous journey and the long residence in China of the Polo family except to place it as the most famous, yet still only one, of the series of Western travels to India and China in the thirteenth and fourteenth centuries. The two elder brothers, Niccolo and Maffeo, had met Kublai Khan in western China in 1266 and after returning to Venice in 1269 took Niccolo's fifteen-year-old son Marco with them and went back to China overland across central Asia. They arrived at Khanbaliq in 1275 and remained there in the Khan's service for seventeen years. With the Khan's permission, they then returned to Europe, going by sea to Ormuz, staying for some time in Java and Sumatra on the way.

After his return to Venice, Marco was captured by the Genoese at the Battle of Curzola in 1298 and while a prisoner of war dictated to a fellow prisoner, Rustichello, the famous account of his travels. Rustichello wrote it in French, but it was soon translated into Latin, Italian, German and Spanish. It was the fashion in the eighteenth and nineteenth centuries to deny as much as possible of the accuracy of Marco's account, presumably on the ground that medieval Europe had no right to be so much better informed about the Far East than the prevailing popular opinion on the subject. There was no doubt also a desire to maintain intact the silly opinion which rose in the late Renaissance and has since endured that the heathen were barbaric or vile or both, the moral position, for instance, of the popular Protestant hymn *From Greenland's Icy Mountains.*

These twin views not only dismissed a serious study of Marco until recent times but served to conceal the immense and excellent addition to geographic knowledge made available to—and promptly used by—Westerners from the reports of Polo and others mentioned above. Thus, Polo's information was used by Peter of Abano early in the fourteenth century, by John of Ypres some years later. Polo's geographical reports are fully used in the Catalan map of 1375, and Prince Henry the Navigator studied them with great care. It is a commentary on Columbus that he had not too much use for Polo and relied implicitly on the fantastic rubbish of Sir John de Mandeville, whose imbecilities, islands of women, cities of gold, he reported finding in Cuba and Hispaniola.

Something of the same sort shows, too, in the popular confusion from the Renaissance into almost modern times over the medieval geographical discoveries. It was long the fashion to consider Cathay, Mangi and Zipangu, Khanbaliq and Zayton (the principal port used by Western and Levantine travelers, Ch'üanchow in Fukien) as almost mythical places for no better reason than the common fate of names to be changed either by the natives or by a new foreign approach. Yet, Cathay (Kitai) is still the Russian name for China. Khanbaliq became Peking and then in our own time briefly Peiping. and again Peking, yet the Polos still lived there for many years and Giovanni de Montecorvino was still its first Catholic Archbishop.

Marco Polo's account was immensely popular and, studied with the reports of other travelers, gave an educated Westerner of the early fourteenth century an essentially sound idea of India, Central Asia and China. This knowledge was never lost.[7]

The alien contacts of the West during the fourteenth century receive little attention in our accepted history. The Crusades were over and oceanic expansion had not yet begun. Likewise the age of direct Arabic intellectual influence was finished for there were practically no translations from Arabic after the middle of the thirteenth century. Nor had the later wave of Levantine military expansion begun. In time naval control of the Mediterranean and possession of the Danube basin were to be fiercely fought over but there was no dramatic event of the fourteenth century to remind conventional history that Western society still existed in a world of other societies. In the thirteenth century, the flimsy screen of half-barbarian Slavs that alone

---

[7] The earliest printing of Polo's account was in German, Nüremberg 1477, reprinted at Augsburg in 1481. There were two different Latin texts printed respectively at Zwolle, probably in 1483, and at Antwerp in 1485 (the edition used by Columbus). Other texts and editions are: Italian, Venice 1496, Brescia 1500; Portugese, Lisbon 1502; Spanish, Seville 1503; French, Paris 1556; English, London 1579.

separated the West from the universal empire of the Mongols had been easily pierced. The principal Slav fortress towns, Ryazan, Vladimir and Kiev had been sacked in 1237 and in 1241 Hungary was overrun and the Mongol armies had reached the Adriatic. Only the death of the Khan Ogotai—Genghis' son—in far-off Qaraqorum led the Mongol commanders to call off their proposed invasion of the West. In the fourteenth century, however, the whole military situation of the east had changed. The Mongol Empire was divided and its greatest part had become thoroughly Chinese. Finally in 1368 a native Chinese dynasty, the Ming, overthrew the heirs of Genghis and began a Chinese invasion of Mongolia. Although Mongol power still pressed on the Levantine world from the Black Sea to India, Europe had become beyond their reach.

Nor was the military power of the fractured principalities of Islam any threat to the West. The Latins had been driven from the mainland of Asia Minor, but in turn had taken most of Spain and held all the important islands of the Mediterranean. Almost the last, Rhodes, had been captured from the Greeks in 1309 by the Knights of St. John. An uneasy balance of power lasted through almost all the fourteenth and fifteenth centuries, ending in the late fifteenth with the rise of the Turkish power in the eastern Mediterranean and the Spanish in the western.

Of course, the fourteenth century was not without talk of new crusades. The crusade was still proclaimed as the self-evident and only moral goal of political action. The fact that it was military nonsense and psychologically out of date did not quiet the clamor, since neither of these reasons led anyone to propagandize against the notion. One crusade was actually staged in 1365, that of Peter I of Cyprus, which accomplished nothing but the sack of Alexandria and left the King's chancellor, de Mezieres, to wander for nearly forty years through the courts of Europe trying to preach this bankrupt ideal. The truth of the matter was that the possession of the tomb of Christ had ceased to be of any importance to the West. Only some of the literati and a few professionals like de Mezieres still cared or still hoped to wring profit from the venture.

Though relations between the West and the great civilized Levantine world did not reach the level of dramatic history in the fourteenth century, this aging, cultured society still flourished from Spain to India. We have of this society as it stood in the fourteenth century an extraordinarily full picture in the written travels of ibn-Batuta which, unlike most later Arabic writings, is available in both French and English translations.[8]

Ibn-Batuta was born at Tangiers in 1304. When he was twenty-one, he left for the Meccan pilgrimage and traveled for most of the rest of his life.

8 *Voyage d'Ibn Batoutah*, Defremery and Sanguinetti, Paris 1859.
Ibn-Batuta—H. A. R. Gibbs, London 1929-1939.

On his way to Mecca, he took side trips up the Nile to Edfu and across Syria to Damascus. After he had been at Mecca, he began his travels in earnest, visiting Baghdad and Mosul, the Persian Gulf, Yemen, Anatolia, the Crimea, Southern Russia, Astrakhan, Constantinople, then back to Samarkand, Bukhara and the Indus valley. He then spent seven years in India visiting Delhi, the Malabar coast, the Maldive Islands, then to Bengal where he took ship to China. Here he visited Canton and Peking and returned via Sumatra and Calicut to the Persian Gulf. He then turned westward, traveled through Sardinia, visited his home at Tangiers briefly, and crossed into Spain where he visited Andalusia and Granada. Later still he crossed western Africa to Timbuktu. Sir Henry Yule (1820-89) estimated that he traveled in all about seventy-five thousand miles. Throughout all these vast wanderings he found himself always at home among people of his own civilization, either in politically Moslem lands or among groups of Moslems forming little islands of Levantine civilization in alien lands, just as Western travelers until recently would have found themselves at home in a little island of Westerners whether at Peking, Calcutta, or Cairo. Furthermore, throughout the vast dominion of the Dar al Islam, ibn-Batuta found men who knew others half across the earth. In Alexandria he met a man who asked him to visit one friend in India, another in the Indus valley and a third in China. In China, he met Moslem physicians and merchants from west Africa, in Granada some from Persia. Everywhere he found a great mercantile civilization with men actively in touch with other men in all parts of the world. Commerce and religious observances were the concern of everyone and very nearly their exclusive concern. In comparison with the shut-in provincialism and the emotional and intellectual agitation of the contemporary West, the cosmopolitan, fashionable, intellectually superficial world of the Dar al Islam—everybody knew everything worth knowing—was distinctly modern.

Another Moslem writer, a generation younger than ibn-Batuta, casts a different light on the aging Levantine society and the young West. 'Abd al-Rahman ibn-Khaldun, the last Moslem philosopher of history—so late in his own society that he was forgotten by the Levant until modern Arab nationalist propaganda learned of him from the West and began a synthetic cult of veneration.

Ibn-Khaldun was born at Tunis in 1332 of a family originally from southern Arabia which, settling in Spain in the ninth century had come over to Africa after the rise of Christian power in the thirteenth. He spent most of his life in Tunis, Morocco and Granada and acted as ambassador for the last state to the Court of Peter I of Castile. In 1374, he retired to Oran and began working on his *History of the Arabs*, the *Kitab al 'ibar*. In 1401 he went to Damascus, where he met the new Mongol conqueror, Timur. In 1406, he died at Cairo.

The problem that concerned ibn-Khaldun was the problem that had troubled al-Kindi and al-Mas'udi four hundred years before—the problem, indeed, that is the concern of this book six hundred years afterwards—the rise and decay of the societies of men.

Ibn-Khaldun necessarily felt that the will of God lay immediately beneath all events. He was likewise a very pious Moslem and believed that the welfare of states like the welfare of individuals is ultimately determined by their submission to God's will—which, of course, is implied by the very meaning of the word Islam, the company of those who submit. Yet he was impressed by the pattern of decay that he sensed in his society. Unlike al-Kindi, he sought no astrological explanation for the decline of the empire of the Arabs. It was not that he disbelieved in astrology on scientific grounds, but he and his age had become too pious to accept a rigidly mechanistic and irreligious theory as a substitute for the will of God. So he composed what is much more valuable to us, a long detailed consideration of all the objective facts of Moslem society: "History is information about human social organization, which itself is identical with civilization. It deals with such conditions affecting the nature of civilization as, for instance, savagery and sociability, group feelings, and the different ways by which one group of human beings achieves superiority over another. It deals with royal authority and the dynasties that result and with the various ranks that exist within them. It deals with the different kinds of gainful occupations and ways of making a living, with the sciences and crafts that human beings pursue as part of their activities and efforts, and with all the other institutions that originate in civilization through its very nature."[9]

Semi-savage peoples, such as the nomads of the desert, possess the power to create civilizations, but once these civilizations flower in cities and settled agricultural countrysides, the very nature of urban, civilized life begins to corrupt the society. Physical degeneracy, moral corruption, political folly, military weakness flower from the very conditions that are the prerequisite for the rise of the arts and sciences and of humane institutions:

"The goal of civilization is sedentary culture and luxury. When civilization reaches that goal, it turns toward corruption and starts being senile, as happens in the natural life of living beings. Indeed, we may say that the qualities of character resulting from sedentary culture and luxury are identical with corruption. Man is man only in as much as he is able to

[9] Ibn Khaldun, *The Muqaddimah*, (i.e. *The Introduction* to his *Kitab al 'ibar*) translated by Franz Rosenthal. New York 1958. Vol. I, p. 71.

procure for himself useful things and to repel harmful things, and in as much as his character is suited to making efforts in this effect. The sedentary person cannot take care of his needs personally . . . He has no courage as a result of luxury and his upbringing under the impact of education and instruction. He has become dependent upon a protective force to defend him. He then usually becomes corrupt with regard to his religion, also . . . When the strength of a man and then his character and religion are corrupted, his humanity is corrupted and be becomes, in effect, transformed."[10] Hence, he felt that civilizations must inevitably succeed each other, and as he pondered the lost sciences of the Babylonians and Assyrians and the static intellectual life of his own society, he remarked that even then logic, philosophy, physics and mathematics were flourishing among the Latin Christians.

This digression from the youthful, provincial life of the West into the great aging society of the Levant is prompted by an event of the fourteenth century that brings home the fact that though history is the history of the societies of men, nevertheless man is also an animal and all men, regardless of their society, are a particular species of mammal inhabiting the earth together. Historically, "mankind" is a fiction. Biologically, "man" is a fact. Consider across the societies of the fourteenth century the spread of the Black Death. There is no record in the written annals of men or in the conjectured restoration of pre-history that any such vast destruction of human life ever occurred before or since.

The first recorded outbreak in the series that was to sweep the civilizations of the world began at Muttra on the Sumna River between Delhi and Agra in 1332. By a calamitous coincidence this was the year of a great pilgrimage which occurred every twelve years. The returning pilgrims spread the disease in all directions. By 1351 it had reached the eastern borders of India. Westward its progress was faster. It reached Constantinople in 1347, and by the fall of that year was in Sicily, Naples and Genoa. Early in 1348, it appeared in Venice, Damascus, Jerusalem and Cairo, and by fall was prevalent throughout the western Mediterranean lands, Latin and Moslem alike. In 1349 it reached its peak in England and Germany, and by 1352 it had spread from the Baltic coast deep into Russia. It probably also had entered southern Russia from the Black Sea commerce some ten years earlier.

Ibn-Khaldun, whose father died of it at Tunis in 749 A.H. thus comments on it: "In the middle of the eighth century (A.H.), civilization both in the east and the west was visited by a destructive plague which devastated nations and caused populations to vanish. It swallowed up many of the good things of civilization and wiped them out. It overtook dynasties at

[10] *ibid.* Vol. II, p. 296.

the time of their senility, when they had reached the limit of their duration. It lessened their power and curtailed their influence. It weakened their authority. Their situation approached the point of annihilation and dissolution. Civilization decreased with the decrease of mankind. Cities and buildings were laid waste, roads and way signs were obliterated, settlements and mansions became empty, dynasties and tribes grew weak. The entire inhabited world changed. . . . It was as if the voice of existence in the world had called out for oblivion and restriction, and the world had responded to its call. God inherits the earth and whomever is upon it. When there is a general change in conditions, it is as if the entire creation had changed and the whole world been altered, as if it were a new and repeated creation, a world brought into existence anew. Therefore there is need at this time that someone should systematically set down the situation of the world among all religions and races, as well as the customs and sectarian beliefs that have changed for their adherents, doing for this age what al-Mas'udi did for his."[11]

It is impossible to know what proportion of the population of the civilized societies of the earth died in the climactic years of the Black Death. The estimates of scholars run at about one quarter, though admittedly the mortality was much higher in certain places, but even for the West where our records are better it is difficult to make a sound estimate, and for India, China, and the Levant conditions are even more difficult. What few actual statistics exist do, however, show that the mortality in the West in the years 1348 and 1349 was enormous. Out of sixty-nine metropolitans of the Western church, twenty-five died. Out of 575 bishops, 207 died. If the disease had been wholly of the bubonic form, contagious only through vermin, the assumption might be made that the populace must have suffered a greater proportion of deaths than the bishops and archbishops, even allowing for a certain difference in average age. Records indicate, however, that the directly contagious pulmonary form was equally prevalent, so any variation of the percentage mortality is uncertain. But merely to extend the known mortality of the higher clergy over the population as a whole, is to show a catastrophe that justifies the general tenor of unbelievable horror and disaster that runs through all the contemporary accounts.

Ibn-Khaldun saw in the plague the seeds of destruction of Levantine society, and it is true that the Levant declined more and more rapidly during later centuries despite the great military revival of Turkish power in the fifteenth and sixteenth centuries and the powerful dominions of the Great Mogul in India in the seventeenth. Yet the decline had long preceded the Black Death and even the miseries of his society that ibn-Khaldun pictures went far back of 1348 and, as he said himself, he was picturing the

---

[11] *ibid.* Vol. I, p. 64.

influence of the plague on those who "had reached the limit of their duration." Above all, the West, which suffered certainly as great a mortality, entered no decline despite some evident scars that have lasted to this day. The plague undoubtedly damaged the continuity of learning. Untrained men had to be made teachers and priests and the rapid decline of Latin throughout Europe, and of French in England, may well have been one of the results. This must in turn have intensified the demand for vernacular scriptures, as much for the benefit of ignorant priests as for pious laymen. It seems probable also that the terror of the plague, coupled with ignorant priests and vernacular scriptures, vastly increased the wave of superstition that had already pretty well replaced Gothic faith that a rational interpretation of both life and religion was possible. Not only did the witchcraft craze increase, a hysterical frenzy arose against the Jews who were accused of causing or spreading the plague. This was no program arranged from on high. Clement VI in vain tried to rally the shattered clergy of Europe to stop it, pointing out that Jews died as plentifully as Catholics and that the disease raged in areas where there had been no Jews for centuries. It was a mass frenzy and nothing stopped it. In contrast, while the plague raged in Damascus, Jews, Moslems and eastern Christians prayed together for deliverance.

It might seem that the horror of the Black Death serves only to remind us that even the West is composed of men, and like all other men, creatures of this planet. It seems hardly worthwhile to mention such a fact in a day when internationalism enjoys the moral prestige which it does in our own. The point is different. The point is to observe those aspects of life in which civilizations do not divide men. In some respects, we are all of us part of the species man. But in the field of history, biology is only the base, not the pattern. It can strike across the pattern of history, possibly alter it somewhat as the Black Death perhaps did, but it is not of itself the pattern. We men of all of the great societies never cease to be men, subject to the fate of men. But each of us is also subject to another and different fate: the fate of his society.

One special, unique aspect of the relation of the West with other civilizations remains to be noted. Through all the intellectual and technical development that has been barely sketched here, through all the turmoil of politics, one alien group lived physically in the midst of the Western peoples but almost aloof from their life, almost untouched by the strains and intellectual problems that beset the West: the Western Jews. Now and then, as has been noted in connection with the various Western writers, some Western work was translated into Hebrew, but except for medical works it was noticeably rare. The intellectual life of the Western Jews in these centuries was still much like the life of their fellow Jews in barbarous Scythia or in the civilized Dar al Islam. In the West, they had ceased to use Arabic, partly replacing it for learned works with Hebrew—theretofore apparently confined to religious uses—and for common speech employing the vernacular of their locality.

Their position was more odd than we usually picture it. The custom of cultural islands in the midst of other peoples was universal in the Levantine world—so the Jews, Nestorians and Orthodox Christians lived among the Moslems as they had lived among the Mazdaists before them. It is still common for civilized people among savages. Until the recent downfall of the Western empires in further Asia, it was likewise common there. Briefly in China under the Mongols this was also the custom for all the non-Chinese groups. But none of these cases quite reproduces the situation of the Jews in the medieval West. They were not there by the grace of distant but available military power like the one-time Western status in Asia. After about 1000 they were not there as civilized men among semi-savages—though that would have been true earlier and it was undoubtedly in this way that they long thought of themselves. Even in later times, they probably regarded their relation to the Catholic society about them as only an unpleasant form of the relationship of the Jews in the Islamic world toward the Moslem territorial sovereigns.

But the Westerners could not think of them in the same way. Western states and nations are territorial, not confessional like the Levantine, and it is notable that the West permitted no other people to form groups in its midst. No one ever dreamed of permitting islands of Moslems or Nestorians or Manicheans to dot the West. But the Jews as the sacred people of the Old Testament were felt to be entitled to this exception. It seems evident that it was an unpopular exception permitted by the consciences of prelates and the calculations of princes, not by the emotions of the masses. It is assumed in our time that democracy and religious toleration go hand in hand and that anti-semitism is a product of hierarchical instigation, lay or clerical. The Middle Ages do not offer much support to these beliefs. The forced conversions and expulsions in southern France and Spain in the fifteenth and sixteenth centuries were matters of state and ecclesiastical policy dictated by political consideration along this frontier against Islam, and fear of the large body of conquered Jews and Moslems who came under Christian power as the Spanish conquests were pushed southward. But the widespread dislike of the Jewish communities throughout all Western Europe, the willingness to believe ominous and nonsensical slanders about them, to countenance and encourage both petty and dreadful outrages against them, these stood unhappily on a firm mass footing. Without the support, even though unenthusiastic and often ineffective, of the church and the religious tradition of the higher laity it seems almost certain that the Jews of all the Western lands would have been forced back into the political world of Islam and the westernized Jews of modern times would never have come into existence. For had there been no Jews remaining within Western society during and since the Middle Ages, the Jews of today would appear to Western eyes as the Moslems, the Parsees or the Armenian Christians do. Without their long residence physically within the West and their adoption of many of its customs and modes of thought, a process that long preceded its more sudden and dramatic appearance after the French Revolution, all modern Jews would indeed resemble those examples of unaltered Levantine civilization, the Jews of Iraq and the Yemen. The Western Jews are a product not only of the Levantine society from which their nation derived its whole original civilization, but of entirely alien influences long absorbed from the West. Even so in reverse, Western society is a product of its own basic modes of thought and action, yet deeply modified by the Holy Books of the Levant which it has always venerated and over which it has pondered so long and so vainly.

To return, then, to the intellectual life of the West during the fourteenth and fifteenth centuries.

The most ominous, though perhaps the most subtle thread in the intellectual life of that age was the breakdown of religion. Under the disparity between the way Western thought compelled men to think and what the Holy Books said they should think, the psychic balance of a whole population began to be disturbed. It became increasingly impossible to derive joy out of religion. How could one derive joy out of a doctrine in whose unstated postulates one could not fully believe? But it could not be wholly disbelieved either. Its antiquity was too powerful a proof of its truth, and there was as yet no firm base of objective irreligious knowledge. All that remained then was terror, of the unknown, of death, of the certified demons, all made the more torturing by the doubts that most minds must have fiercely denied even to themselves. And so instead of the lofty Gothic architecture, the religious life of the fourteenth and above all the fifteenth century seems almost to be lived before the solemn-robed judges of the Holy Inquisition and in the incredible, almost universal belief in witchcraft. Does not the Book of Samuel prove the existence of witches, and Exodus require their destruction? Do not suppose that this was an ecclesiastical plot from above or a politically engineered matter like the Albigensian Crusade or the destruction of the Templars. This was a psychic breakdown among the mass of the people. Untold thousands denounced themselves as heretics or witches, confessed, pleaded for punishment. There exist ecclesiastical directives to the inquisitors ordering them to disregard such confessions as much as they could, but nothing checked the hysteria.

At the same time less broken souls began a spiritual withdrawal from all rational attempts to cope with the world of earthly reality. Such were the German and Low Country mystics, Meister Eckhart and Thomas à Kempis, such in part Wycliffe and the Lollards. All had in common the belief, however indirectly stated, that since reason and religion were in hopeless conflict, the only defense against a broken mind and a wrecked life was firm, unquestioning self-immolation in scripture. The continuance of this position into early Protestantism and Counter Reformation mysticism is manifest.

But there were others who had the mental ability to put the truths of religion to one side, not disbelieved but simply not applied very vigorously to earthly affairs, and there were still others, perhaps the great majority, who must hardly have thought about these problems at all and proceeded with the activities of a busy and energetic life. For there is a bustle of the modern world in the tremendous technological developments of the fourteenth century—even to those two grim pillars of modern industrial society —coal and iron, for here appears on the stage of history, coal mines and blast furnaces.

The great period of Gothic architecture came to a close somewhere about 1275, leaving its masterpieces in France unfinished as they stand unfinished to this day. It is important to note that not one of the great cathedrals of northern France, the home and source of the Gothic style, was ever finished. The reasons usually offered are varied and none in itself is convincing: the Hundred Years' War, the Avignon Papacy, the ruin of the Templars and the increased secular taxation of the church. But like any other major historical event, it is impossible to assign a cause that will stand under analysis. To the extent, for instance, that secular taxes on the church reduced its building revenues, we are faced with the much graver causal problem of why society late in the thirteenth century permitted the secular authorities fiscal powers that would have bordered on sacrilege a century before. We can take the whole situation, however, as clear evidence that great as the power of religion still was over the minds of Western men some aspects of that power was fading. With the decline of twelfth century mysticism something of the childlike innocence of religious thought came to an end. With the end of high Gothic, something of the aesthetic power of religion ended also. Once again, centuries afterwards, in the brief, flickering reawakening of deep religious emotion in Reformation and Counter Reformation, religion once more earned the service of a great art, music—but this was all. Except for this, the church has ever since purchased decoration as it needed it, to be in style and show good taste, not received it because aesthetic and religious expression were self-evidently synonymous.

St. Peter's for all its splendor—and St. Paul's to a lesser extent—is still a church decking itself out with ecclesiastical magnificence, not simply the ordinary self-evident way to build as are the Gothic churches great and little of the medieval North. It was not that these Gothic churches were the spontaneous outpourings of mass religious emotions—that silly aesthetic democracy of Viollet-le-Duc's has been well exploded—they, like St. Peter's were the deliberate creation of a restricted, rich and powerful church. But the religious values of the medieval Catholic Church prior to the fourteenth century included aesthetic values that were in harmony with the values of the most able and thoughtful men of the time. It would be difficult to affirm that this remained so true in later ages.

Contemporaneous with the decline of French Gothic appeared the first traces of the witchcraft hysteria and of Bible mysticism. It may seem inappropriate to associate these two manifestations of Western intellectual life. The one we deplore and the other, though we moderns rarely practice it, is certified as worthy of our admiration. Furthermore in selecting what we consider good and what we think bad in our heritage, there would be no hesitation in the choice we would make between a belief in mysticism and a belief in witchcraft. But our preference would not sever the tie between the two beliefs. They arose at about the same time early in the fourteenth century. After a gradual increase they reached their zenith together during the sixteenth and each slowly faded late in the seventeenth. Their emotional and logical sources were the same, the conviction that the world of the spirit was more powerful than the world of the flesh and that spiritual powers could, and sometimes did, interfere in the operation of the natural. In this matter modern sentimentality inclines toward a ridiculous position. We may believe or we may pay only lip service to the belief in spirits, but if they exist, for us they are always good spirits. We may be dubious whether angels operate in the physical world, but we are certain that demons do not. Our ancestors were both more logical and more respectful of the plain sense of their religious documents.

The history of witchcraft in the West is the story of the curious merger of lycanthropy and demonology. The first, belief that the souls of men can take up temporary abode in the bodies of animals, is as old as man and as universal. Of its existence among the ancient heathen Germans, and the Celts of Roman Gaul and Italy we have little direct evidence but it is reasonable to suppose that so universal a belief was part of their folk heritage. In contrast the learned doctors of the church during the early Middle Ages believed in demons, the fallen angels of the apocryphal books of the Bible, but denied the reality of lycanthropy and hence the existence of the *striga*, the night-riding, bloodsucking hag capable of assuming animal or other human shapes whose power covered the whole range of popular superstitions, from generating storms and making herds and flocks infertile to spreading plagues and causing love-madness or impotence. There is no doubt, however, that despite the doctrines of the church, belief in the *striga*, the German *hex*, was almost universal among the masses, and though originally the creature itself was considered a monster, not a human, by post-Carolingian times it had fused with the lycanthropic conceptions and become the magical manifestations of a *human woman*. In general, the official position of the church itself until well into the fourteenth century was that the *striga* was imaginary and that those who confessed to being such—as many increasingly began to do, not only under torture but of their own will—were suffering from delusions. Neither the church nor any civil law, however, denied the reality of *malificium*, the effecting by magic —whether spells or potions—of the death, injury, uncontrollable sexual desire or impotence (two very common charges in marital disputes) of another person. It seems certain, also, that *malificium* was no imaginary crime. We may dismiss the supposed magic and still see the consequence of drugs, poisons, hypnotism and suggestion. Both civil and ecclesiastical law also recognized the existence of *subcubae* and *incubi*, demon partners in sexual intercourse, and accepted as possible evidence of demon activity, manic possessions, sortilege and similar aspects of necromancy. Thus the true witch of about 1500, as the image came to be accepted by the masses and the educated alike, was the result of attributing to an imaginary folk creature, the lycanthropic *striga*, certain powers that had concrete, discoverable manifestations, others believed to be real but demonic, and then identifying this new concept of the *striga* with any unfortunate woman who chanced to be suspected. The introduction of Christian doctrine to give the reputed existence of this creature ecclesiastical and popular moral sanction was the identification of the names *striga* and *malifica*. (Ex. xxii, 18, Deut. xviii, 10 where the Vulgate uses the latter name and instructs that they be put to death.)[12] Beyond this it was decided that all the powers of a witch were derived by a pact with demons or with the Devil himself. Furthermore, since a pact had been entered into with the Devil, baptism must have been foresworn and so heresy was involved.

It is a commentary on the inaccuracy of our usual historical image that many suppose the belief in witches to have been medieval, to have been, indeed, one of the blights of that dark past which the enlightenment of the Renaissance removed from our lives. The facts are precisely the reverse. The belief in witchcraft, at least by the controlling elements of society, and the pursuit and execution of persons accused of being witches was entirely a phenomenon of the Renaissance. It was, in fact, connected with

---

[12] A. V. translates *maleficium* in these passages as "witch," R. V. as "sorceress" and "sorcerer" and D. V. as "wizard."

many of the mass psychological strands that can be detected in other Renaissance events. In the Middle Ages there were many trials of both men and women accused of *maleficium*, which we can inaccurately translate as "witchcraft," but most of them were trials for what was undoubtedly poisoning or were the use of charges of *maleficium* to get rid of a personal enemy. In short, there was always an intelligible reason—whether virtuous or not—for prosecuting the particular person charged with *maleficium*. There was no belief, as there was during the Renaissance, that abroad in the land were thousands of witches, unknown and apparently harmless, who had to be systematically searched for and executed.

The more pleasant aspect of the increasing belief in the unnatural was the spread of Bible mysticism. One of the most famous, though not quite the earliest, of the preachers of popular mysticism was Meister Eckhart, born in Thuringia about 1260, graduate in theology at the University of Paris in 1302, Provincial of Saxony and later Prior of Strassburg and Cologne where he probably died in 1327. Eckhart was a mystic, a gifted poet and the founder of a long and important school of mystical writers. He regarded God as the only reality and aside from God all was illusion. His breach with scholasticism was complete, though not officially argued as it was by the later Protestants. He made no doctrinal break with the church. But religious truth to him was not to be derived by the scholastic method of logical or purportedly logical derivation from both scripture and the objective world of the senses. His thought is the thought of Plotinus, although almost certainly not by direct knowledge of the great Neoplatonist Father. It was something he must have found implicit in Augustine and the New Testament. (Only his sermons survive and the development of his thought cannot now be traced.) Religious truth was gained not by rational analysis of the Biblical text but by personal mystic insight, something possessed by the authors of the New Testament and still the only method by which a modern man could understand the true meaning of the Bible and comprehend the purpose of the world. His disciple, Johann Tauler, born at Strassburg about 1300, established at Basel a group of mystics known as the Friends of God, and another friend, Heinrich von Berg, known as Suso, beatified in 1831, wrote and preached widely.[13]

The most famous and politically most important of these fourteenth century German mystical writings was the *Theologia Deutsch*, a compilation of Eckhart's and Tauler's views made about the middle of the century by an unknown follower. It was first printed by Luther at Wittenberg in 1516, before any thought of a break with Rome. By the middle of the

[13] The works of all three men, Tauler's and Suso's wholly in German, were extensively printed in incunabula and early sixteenth century editions.

sixteenth century, it had been translated into Latin, French, Flemish and English. Luther said of it that only the Bible and St. Augustine had given him more.

In the Netherlands, Eckhart's teaching influenced Jan van Ruysbroeck (1293-1381), who wrote an extensive series of mystical treatises in Flemish which in turn profoundly molded the thought of Geert Groote (1340-1384). Groote was more a revivalist than a contemplative mystic, and his doctrines, by keeping the language of Eckhart's mystical Neoplatonism but insisting on a more practical view of everyday life, came much nearer the practice of later Protestantism. He preached a simple, personal life filled with study of the truths of scripture and charitable service to one's fellow men. Naturally, he advocated the use of the Bible in the vernaculars.

Groote founded an order, The Brothers of the Common Life, of both lay and clerical members for purposes of devotional meetings and education. Towards the end of his life, worried by ecclesiastical opposition, he decided that a formalized monastic order was safer and took the clerical part of his movement as a separate group into the Augustinian canons. By the middle of the fifteenth century, the schools of The Brothers and the monasteries of the Augustinians following Groote's "moderna devotio" had established schools and monasteries in the Low Countries, northern France and western Germany. Something of the meaning of this movement can be sensed from the fact that Luther was an Augustinian, and added a personal expression of indebtedness to Groote, and that both Erasmus and Pope Adrian VI, who tried to meet Luther on clerical abuses—though not doctrinal points—were students at the schools of The Brothers of the Common Life.

In literature, the most famous product of Groote's movement was the *Imitation of Christ* written somewhere between 1380 and 1424 by Thomas à Kempis,[14] an Augustinian canon regular. There is scarcely a page that is not a tissue of Biblical echoes. It is the most famous and most poetic expression of the Bible mysticism common to this whole movement. Despite its threads to Protestantism, it has remained a treasure likewise to the Roman Catholic mystics, and where the *Theologia Deutsch* was published by Luther, the *Imitation* has earned the praise of such saints of the Roman church as Borromeo, Loyola and Francis de Sales.

"Our opinions and our senses often fail us and see but a little way. What profits a great sophistry about hidden obscure matters when our ignorance of such things cannot be held against us on the Day of Judgment? What do we care for genera and species, we to whom the eternal word is spoken, we who are freed of the tangle of many opinions?" The inner voice of

[14] It was first printed Augsburg 1471. There were at least twenty-five incunabula editions.

Christ says: "I teach without the din of words, without the confusion of opinion, without the arrogance of honors, without the struggle of arguments. I am he who teaches to loathe and despise the things of this earth, to seek heaven, to hope for the eternal. There is more profit in giving up everything than in studying deep secrets." [15]

As can be concluded from these quotations, the schools of the Brotherhood were not pioneers in philosophical and scientific thought. They were designed as primary schools for simple people who had no intention of becoming learned, and confined themselves largely to the humanities of the trivium—grammar and Classical literature—which raised no confusion of opinion and probed no deep secrets.

But the seeds of Protestantism were not all mystical. Not every objection to ecclesiastical wealth or papal power flowed from devotion to the text of the Bible and distaste for the incurable earthliness of worldly life. Those who felt they could appropriate the wealth of the church for themselves were equally fervent advocates of evangelical poverty. Those who felt hierarchical authority inherently sinful were joined by those who objected to hierarchical authority only so long as it was in other hands than their own. Naturally, then as now, these were never anyone's proclaimed motives. The reasons of the mystics sounded better and, properly applied in practical politics, could accomplish the same results. Such fourteenth century rebels were not numerous and none founded a great mass movement of religious revolt, but they existed, primarily filling the role of specialized instruments for particular sovereigns. In time their lives came to be looked back on as furnishing valuable precedents for the later popular revolts, and some element of what they stood for always remained in Protestantism. After all, however mystical the origin and intention of a movement may be, open revolt against ecclesiastical authority is not solely a mystical operation. There is in it necessarily an element of adventure, of contempt for at least some theretofore holy things. It draws not only the mystic but the partial sceptic, the unworldly super-believer but the potential unbeliever also.

Of the latter class, the fourteenth century opened with a noteworthy example, William de Nogaret. Incredibly distant though he may have been from the pious mysticism of Eckhart and Groote, never claimed by Prot-

---

[15] Nostra opinio et noster sensus saepe nos fallit et modicum videt. Quid prodest magna cavillatio de occultis et obscuris rebus, de quibus nec aguemur in iudicio quia ignoravimus? ... Et quid curae nobis de generibus et speciebus? Cui aeternum verbum loquitur, a multis opinionibus expeditur I-3. ... Ego doceo sine strepitu verborum, sine confusione opinionem, sine fastu honorem, sine impugnatione argumentorem. Ego sum qui doceo terrena despicere, praesentia fastidere, coelestia quaerere, aeterna sapere. Plus profecit in reliquendo omnia quam in studendo subtilia. III-43.

estantism as its hero, indeed utterly disavowed, nevertheless he belongs by the facts of history with his mystical contemporaries. The master arranger of Anagni, the indirect assassin of Boniface VIII, the man who destroyed the sacerdotal aura of the medieval papacy and brought on the political popes of Avignon, cannot escape his laurels as one of the great if unintentional founders of Protestantism. On the long white wall that carries the monument to the Reformation at Geneva no statue or inscription comemorates this one-eyed hatchet man of King Philip IV of France, but history is no more bound by the myths of Calvin than by any other. De Nogaret was the first political Protestant.

He was modern in another respect also. He was the first professional lay politician, certainly the first of significant importance. De Nogaret was born near Toulouse some time before 1270 and was professor of civil law at Montpellier when Philip IV, who had came to the throne at the age of seventeen in 1285, called him to Paris in 1296 as a member of a small group of professional administrators whom the king drew around him. None was noble and none was a cleric. Clerical officials of common birth had been commonplace for centuries in every monarchy of the West, but this group that Philip brought together in the closing years of the thirteenth century was a departure from the past; they were commoners but not clerics. The new policy of the king and his common ministers was equally revolutionary. Like all great political enterprises, it had a consistent principle of tangible, large-scale purpose guiding all the particular shifts and expedients of policy. The purpose was the destruction of the feudal political order of France and the establishment of a central government powerful enough to govern. The practical working core of this new conception of government was a staff of professional bureaucrats, not noblemen on leave from their fiefs nor priests beholden, even if only in their consciences, to another sovereignty than the king's. To destroy the feudal political structure required not only the exercise of direct royal power in the great fiefs, such as independent Champagne and Flanders and English Guinne, but equally its use to end the feudal position of the church. It also involved a fiscal revolution since it forced the crown to finance a permanent professional state in place of the ancient personal household of the king traditionally paid for by the feudal revenues of his own personal lands.

From the outset of Philip's enterprise it was obvious that it was managed by lawyers. The favorite device became the judicial proceeding, as hollow and fraudulent as might be necessary, and backed and made effective solely by military power, but always under the mask of formal legalism. The Count of Flanders was deposed by such a trial, but the subsequent revolt of the Flemish cities—by then the center of a tremendous textile industry and dependent on England for wool—destroyed Philip's hope in the northeast.

Here, indeed, one revolution came to clash with another, for Philip's design of founding the centralized national state came in conflict in Flanders with the ambitions not only of the feudal count but of the rising urban bourgeoisie, and while Philip's ambitions were modern his weapons were archaic —his army was still the feudal levy. It was the trained infantry of the Flemish towns that routed the French knights at Courtrai in 1302.

Against Edward I's possessions in the south, the method of legal proceedings was never carried to its full limits precisely because Philip was never able to build anything better than a feudal army. Despite his attempts to construct a navy and to organize a continental alliance, his military power never allowed a full-scale attempt to oust the English, and the adherence of Flanders to the English side was always a fatal gap in his continental system. Eastward juridical-military adventures, bribery and marriage were more successful, and Philip succeeded in annexing Lyons and Champagne to France and in laying a legal foundation for the future acquisition of Burgundy.

The financial operations of this new state administration were those standard for all political adventures, inflation and taxation. Lacking the full development of a Western fiscal system, having neither a printing press nor a Federal Reserve System, the only mechanism available for the necessary increase in the money supply was debasement of the coinage, and this was carried to such an extent that the king earned the title of the royal counterfeiter. Against taxation, a new thing in an age of feudal dues, the king's lay subjects had no recourse but grumbling imprecations, but taxation of the church brought an independent political power into the struggle, the Roman Curia. Taxation of ecclesiastics was not new, but theretofore it had been the monopoly of the Curia itself. The old controversy over the investitures, which destroyed the medieval German Empire, had been a struggle for the right to obtain the allegiance of the ecclesiastical princes. A victorious empire would have dismembered the political structure of the church. Philip struck the church in a more immediate and tangible way than through the problematical future of human loyalties. He struck at the secular foundation of the throne of St. Peter itself, the revenues of the Curia.

Boniface VIII felt himself secure on the throne of Gregory VII. He was the heir and exemplar of the Hildebrandian Papacy which had humbled a long line of powerful emperors and destroyed the German state. He attempted to treat this rebellious king and his upstart ministers by the same means that Gregory had used to humble Henry III and Innocent had perfected in the destruction of the Hauenstaufens.

The struggle had begun at the very outset of Philip's reign, for Boniface in the bull *Clericis laicos of* 1296 had forbidden Philip to tax the clergy without papal consent. The king's strong position in the early years of his reign forced Boniface to retreat on this point, but the French disaster at Courtrai created an opportunity for the pope to re-establish his position. In 1302 he promulgated the bull *Unam Sanctam*—of which modern Roman Catholics hold only the last sentence to have been uttered *ex cathedra*— the most sweeping statement of papal secular power ever made. The consistent application of its principles would have reduced all secular office to little but tenancy at the papal pleasure. It was accompanied by assurances that further defiance would lead to the king's excommunication and back of that lay the near certainty that the pope would offer the crown of France to someone else. The last was not an idle threat, for the papacy had already transferred the crown of Sicily from the Hauenstaufen to the house of Anjou and was even then claiming the same right to dispose of the crown of Hungary. Also Boniface was rather a good lawyer himself, having arranged the legal formalities incident to the abdication of his predecessor, Celestine V, and begun the trial—in absentia—of Edward I for interfering in Scotland which Boniface, though not the Scots, considered a papal fief.

With his army destroyed at Courtrai, *Unam Sanctam* in force, and excommunication and papal deposition a near certainty, Philip's position was grave. De Nogaret, by now vice chancellor, persuaded him of his remedy. De Nogaret proposed that he himself go secretly with a few men to Italy, there gather a few more from among the Colloni, bitter enemies of the Gaetani, the pope's family, (a bitterness recently intensified by the pope's promotion of Gaetani interests all over Italy) and by an action so impossible that no protection could exist against it, turn the whole tide of events. De Nogaret's scheme was to kidnap the pope into French territory, try him for heresy, convict and depose him. It was not necessary to make any provision for acquittal. Individual popes had more than once been the victim of the internal politics of the great ecclesiastical families of Rome, but this had affected only an individual pope, not the institution of the papacy which had remained Roman and independent. This time de Nogaret aimed by seizing the pope to capture the papacy.

In March of 1303, de Nogaret received the king's commission to set out. On September 10, with a band of only sixteen hundred men, he seized the town of Anagni where the pope was staying and made him prisoner. Some chroniclers say that the pope was shamefully abused. The weight of modern historical opinion is that he was only threatened and that de Nogaret saved his life from the murderous designs of Sciarra Colonna. The details hardly matter. De Nogaret had accomplished the politically impossible. The sacred person of the pope could be sacred no longer against the powers of a national state. The might of his spiritual power when extended into secular affairs could never again by itself protect him from a secular counter power. Since September 10, 1303, the independent secular power of the pope has ceased to exist. Thereafter the popes have been dependent for the exercise of such power on finding some state to exercise its power on their behalf. Since no state has ever been willing to do this without some corresponding advantage to itself, the secular power of the papacy after 1303 became more and more enmeshed in nationalistic struggles to the great damage of its international moral power. Finally after some centuries of captivity, first to French and afterwards to Spanish imperial interests, the fact, and to a large extent even the idea, of papal secular power dwindled away till it ceased to be a political reality in the West.

The first stage, however, was capture of that power by the French king and this was de Nogaret's task. He almost failed, for after three days Anagni was recaptured and the pope set free. He returned to Rome, but his prestige was hopelessly destroyed and the family politics of Rome, released by the French action, broke into violence. The Orsini, another family hostile to the Gaetani, imprisoned the pope in the Vatican and on October 11 he died—possibly of mistreatment, certainly of anguish and humiliation.

The new pope, Benedict XI, elected October 22, 1303, was a timid and conciliatory man as far as he felt he could be. He appeased the Colloni since they represented only a Roman factional quarrel, but to the political demands of the French he would give nothing. In June, 1304, he excommunicated de Nogaret who had returned to France, been suitably rewarded by Philip and was back again in Rome. Exactly one month after this excommunication Benedict died, reportedly poisoned. Whether this was the fact, and if so whether de Nogaret arranged it, is unknown, but the pope's death and probably the suspicion that de Nogaret had effected it gave de Nogaret what he wanted. The terrible French were too much for the cardinals to resist. After eleven months of deadlock and negotiation, they elected a man who was neither a cardinal nor an Italian: a Frenchman, Bertrand de Got, archbishop of Bordeaux, a nice technicality since this was English territory.

Whether the new pope, Clement V, had made any previous agreement with Philip, or merely yielded to French power is problematical. But he did yield. He created ten French cardinals. He modified *Clericis laicos* and *Unam Sanctam* till they no longer meant anything. He reluctantly gave in to Philip's desire to destroy the Templars and seize their property—a foretaste of the destruction of the other monastic orders some two hundred years later. He established the papal residence at Avignon, technically in imperial territory, but directly across the Rhone from a powerful French castle. In only one thing was he stubborn—the absolution of William de Nogaret. That was too great a scandal even for Clement V.

The French response was typical of the new politics of the times. The matter was of considerable importance to the king's prestige since de Nogaret had been the royal agent and had been publicly honored for his work in Italy. Accordingly, with magnificent legal indirection that is suggestive of some of the great trials, national and international of modern times, not the pope, but Guichard, bishop of Troyes, who had once supported Boniface VIII, was imprisoned and brought to trial on the charge of bewitching Jeanne of Navarre, queen of France, and later accomplishing her death by diabolical means. The trial was deliberately kept dangling from 1308 till de Nogaret's death in 1313 with vast amounts of seamy and probably false testimony as a reminder to Clement of what a trial of other ecclesiastics, or a posthumous trial of Boniface VIII, could be made to produce. Finally in April, 1311, Clement capitulated, absolving de Nogaret under severe penances that the lawyer never bothered to perform.

It is a curious speculation whether a man who had no fear of the ghostly powers of Boniface could have believed in the witchcraft charges he pressed so extensively against Bishop Guichard or the perjured testimony of heresy he produced against the Templars. Probably he believed in neither. But these great and famous trials were known from one end of Europe to the other, and what to de Nogaret was probably only an indifferent means to a practical end became certified to millions as realities and mind-devouring terrors.

This episode was thoroughly Western. It had in it also an air of modernity. The establishment of central royal power against the independence of the church and of the feudal nobility was a democratic process. That the opinion of the rural peasantry was not involved did not make it undemocratic. They did not count, as political opinion, even in the French Revolution. Democracy in operation is concerned not with everyone's opinion—that is merely its technical modern form—but only with the organized opinion of those whose opinions can be made politically effective. In the time of Philip IV, the masses whose favoring opinions were sought were the commoners of the growing mercantile and manufacturing towns and the intellectual world of the universities. It was not idle chatter when William of Occam promised to defend the emperor with his pen. Literate opinion had become a political factor. There was, therefore, that characteristic so common to all democratic processes, the casting of an issue in terms of emotional viewpoints presumed to be held by the masses, that is, by that part of the masses whose opinions mattered. The Templars were pursued *as* heretics but not *because* they were heretics. The object was to destroy their organization and seize their wealth, but since this was not a purpose suitable for public discussion, the same end was attained by ostensible pursuit of a different and publicly-approved objective. In the case of Bishop

Guichard, the method was similar: to threaten the pope without the public realizing that he was being threatened.

The political struggle with the papacy in the early fourteenth century was not entirely confined to the devices of practical policy. An important part of it involved the development of Western political thought. Two men are the outstanding examples, Marsiglio of Padua and John of Jandun, and even some parts of the writings and life of William of Occam place him in the same group. All three were ex-communicated. All three were protected by the emperor, Lewis of Bavaria.

Marsiglio dei Mainardini was born at Padua between 1275 and 1280. He studied medicine at Padua, became rector of the University of Paris in 1312 where he met John of Jandun, and became his lifelong friend. In 1316, Marsiglio was appointed canon at Padua and John of Jandun canon at Senlis, both by Pope John XXII. For how great a period either was absent from Paris is unknown, but during these years Marsiglio wrote with considerable assistance from John his famous *Defensor Pacis*, The Defender of the Peace. Immediately on the publication of this work both men felt it wise to leave Paris secretly and took refuge together in Nuremberg. They were denounced by a bull of 1326 and excommunicated in 1327. John died in 1328, Marsiglio probably in 1342.

The *Defensor Pacis* is an unqualified argument for secular and even partially democratic power against ecclesiastical. It is not democratic in our sense of the word, for this now includes an unspoken but intended egalitarianism. Marsigilo thought rather in terms of a graded community of which every rank was a part.

His philosophical basis resembled Hobbes'. Society has a purpose, its own good, and its greatest good is peace. This, he felt, is the social equivalent of physical health to the individual. The struggle between secular and ecclesiastical authority destroys peace, from which it follows that the church should have no secular power and therefore no property and no courts to proceed against heresy. The only law that should have force, that is, the only *law,* should be civil law. This, in turn, must be drawn by professional lawyers since it is a technical matter, but subject to popular approval by the whole community and then be enforced by the prince, the prince being placed in office by the vote of the people or their representatives and being accountable to them for the just discharge of his duties. Brief consideration of these principles reveals at once that they are those of the three-functioned state of the eighteenth century philosophers incorporated in the Constitution of the United States. In fact, they are realistically a little more accurate than our orthodox version of how the separation of state powers should work. Though our constitution limits only interpretation of law to the professional lawyers, and even that not by its letter, political practice has in effect followed Marsiglio, not Montesquieu. Our laws are not only interpreted but enacted by lawyers.

On purely ecclesiastical matters, Marsiglio objected to papal power. He wished not only to subordinate the church to the state, but to deny it a unified organization. In his view, the pope was simply the bishop of Rome, ranking the other bishops in dignity but not in authority. The only ultimate and general authority in the church should be a general council, summoned as needed by the emperor, on which laymen as well as clerics should sit. Bishops should be appointed only by secular authority and popes elected by the councils. It would be a mistake, however, to suppose that Marsiglio was irreligious. He was too deeply influenced by the spiritual Franciscans for that. He was simply anti-clerical. A heretic himself, his imagined secular power would have pursued heresy as vigorously as ever the Roman Curia—a complete identity with the later views of the Calvinists.

Much of Marsiglio's theory of the proper purpose and function of the state had been developed by earlier Western thinkers even before Aquinas. His views of the powers of the pope and the need for ecclesiastical poverty had been expressed by many Franciscans, and even, hardly a decade before, by no less a person than Hervé Nédélec, general of the Dominicans.[16] But the combination was new, and the added and extensive catalogue of church corruption and abuses gave it spice. What was perhaps most novel was the unequivocal demand for the complete separation of church and state and the relegation of the former to being either a voluntary organization or a mere extension of state power. So seriously was this work taken in its time that John XXII declared that the Emperor Lewis had forfeited the imperial throne for the single crime of sheltering such a heresiarch as Marsiglio. The pope, however, lacked the means to make the forfeiture effective.

The *Defensor Pacis* was a great literary success, for numerous fourteenth century manuscripts still survive. It was soon translated into French[17] and into Italian in 1363. It apparently passed out of wide circulation in the fifteenth century, for there are no incunabula editions. The Reformation brought it back.[18]

---

[16] His *De potestate papae* was printed in 1506.

[17] Oresme was often accused of having made this translation. He denied it under oath.

[18] It was first printed in Latin at Basel in 1522, Frankfort 1592 (for Henry IV), 1612, 1613, 1614, 1622, 1623, 1692, Heidelberg 1599. An English translation was printed at London in 1535 at the expense of Thomas Cromwell and an abridged German at Neuburg in 1545. Neither the French or Italian translations appear to have been printed. Marsiglio was also the author of another

In England the Bible mysticism of Groote and the secular political ideas of Marsiglio were partially fused and even a good deal of Joachimite millenarianism appeared in the more popular expressions of the late fourteenth century religious and secular discontent. It was the age not only of Wycliffe and the Lollards but of Wat Tyler's rebellion.

John Wycliffe has been seen in something of a heroic light by many Protestants. He is pictured as the great precursor rising in the time of an obscurantist, papally-dominated church to announce the deep principles of the Reformation: national churches, the doctrinal supremacy of scripture alone and the denial of transubstantiation. That his writings were of some consequence in the Protestant revolt a century and a half after his death is undoubted. But he himself differs in one important particular from the leading Reformers of the sixteenth century. It is not always easy to be sure whether Wycliffe's politics grew from his religious convictions or whether his theology was developed and modified by the calculations of political expediency.

Wycliffe was born in Yorkshire about 1324 and attended Balliol College, Oxford. His early life is obscure, but by 1374 when he was named one of the royal envoys to negotiate with the Curia he had become a popular preacher at London and a noted participant in the philosophical disputations of Oxford. There is no evidence that prior to 1374 he had ever entertained doubts on doctrinal matters of any kind. It was at this point that the senility of Edward III coinciding with the mortal illness of the Prince of Wales set the stage for the political ambitions of John of Gaunt. Gaunt's program was to confiscate the wealth of the church for the benefit of the faction whose support would make him the master of England through the anticipated minority of the future boy king, Richard II. Wycliffe became the clerical apologist for this first seeding of the red rose of Lancaster.

The doctrinal position that Wycliffe developed in support of the ambitions of the house of Lancaster was that of *dominium*. On a foundation of standard scholastic realism derived from Duns Scot, he established that all things having true existence are emanations of God, earthly reflections, so to speak, of their heavenly prototypes. Since God exercises lordship, lordship itself is a divine institution and men may properly exercise it in terrestrial affairs. On the other hand, property, something indefeas-

---

treatise which for awhile bedevilled European historical thought, the *De Translatione imperii romani*, arguing that the medieval empire was a true continuation of the Roman. After all, he was in a different but no greater error than Gibbon. This was widely printed: Frankfort 1614, 1621, 1668; Basel 1555, 1566; Heidelberg 1599; London 1690. His *De Jurisdictione imperatoris in causa matrimoniali* was printed in 1598.

ibly the possession of a human being, reflects nothing that exists with God and the claim to hold it is, therefore, a sin. Furthermore, since lordship, *dominium,* emanates from God, those who possess it over other men or over physical wealth are, as it were, tenants of a fief held of God and maintain their tenure not by any right of ownership but by the continuing performance of the obligation attached to the divine fief. This obligation is manifestly righteous service to God. Thus the church may not lawfully own wealth, but it may hold *dominium* over wealth so long as it performs righteous service. Since unrighteousness voids the tenure, the vacant fief may in such cases be lawfully transferred to another tenant. The key question, which translated this dry piece of Scotist scholasticism into a revolutionary political engine, concerned the power that may lawfully decide whether the church has forfeited its *dominium* by unrighteousness. To this question Wycliffe answered unequivocally: the state.[19]

With the beginning of the Great Schism, Wycliffe's thoughts turned to the propriety of such an institution as the papacy. Applying his doctrine of *dominium* he decided that by accepting the Donation of Constantine, Silvester I had acquired not a *dominium* from God, but sinful property from man and that, therefore, he and all his successors had cut themselves off from the true Christian faith. But since earthly problems required earthly answers, and since Wycliffe had voided the authority of the throne of St. Peter, an alternative and equally final moral authority must be found capable of enforcing on earth righteousness in accordance with the laws of Heaven. This authority Wycliffe found in the king. The king, not the pope, was God's vicar. He held *dominium* over both the spiritual and temporal welfare of the subjects placed by God in his charge. The narrow technical exercise of priestly powers was assigned to priests, but the obligation to see that the priests righteously performed this function lay upon the king. Accordingly, even the spiritual jurisdiction of a bishop derived from the king.[20]

Logic drove Wycliffe one step further. The one flaw in his doctrine of royal supremacy was the sacerdotal powers of the priest. The priest and the priest alone could perform the miracle of changing the bread and wine of the eucharist into the body and blood of Christ, and only by partaking of the eucharist could a man be saved. The power to perform this miracle and hence the ultimate power to damn men or offer them a means to salvation could not be derived from any royal grant or authority. If the doctrine of transubstantiation were true, the king had an earthly superior, the priest, and a superior in a matter of graver importance than any other, the life or death of the soul. To complete his doctrine Wycliffe was driven

---

[19] *De domino divina.*
[20] *De officio regis.*

the final step. He denied transubstantiation, not, like Berengar, because it seemed impossible under Aristotelian concepts of substance and accident, not, as a modern sceptic might do, because the physics of mass and energy cannot deal with such concepts, but because it struck down the ultimate moral authority that he wished to confer upon the king.

This time, however, he had gone beyond the interests of his patron. The Duke of Lancaster had no objection to clerical anguish over debates about church property, but profound, unarguable heresy was another matter. He peremptorily ordered Wycliffe to cease preaching on such matters and the latter withdrew to his county parish and lived there in silence for the few remaining years of his life. He died in 1384. Thirty years afterwards the Council of Constance decided in retrospect that he had been a heretic and ordered his body disinterred and burned.

Wycliffe's work was not confined to abstruse Latin scholasticism in behalf of the political ambitions of the mighty. The influence of his ideas in the peasant revolt of 1381 is evident, though no direct connection by Wycliffe with this fierce civil war has ever been validly established. Nevertheless, his ideas spread in vernacular translations. He himself organized "poor priests" to preach throughout England in competition with the endowed clergy—in effect the foundation of the Lollards—and he assisted the spread of the vernacular Bible, a translation of which is popularly though erroneously ascribed to him.

The Lollards, however, carried out Wycliffe's logic more ruthlessly than he had been willing to do. He had considered the problems of property and lordship as they concerned the church. The Lollards applied the same reasoning to secular property and political lordship. There, too, property as such must be sinful. There, too, lordship must be a fief held of God and equally must be voided by unrighteous conduct on the part of the tenant. Thus, all titles of land and nobility, the crown itself, must be Godly fiefs which become vacant if their possessors act unrighteously. To the question concerning what power is competent to decide whether these fiefs were vacant, the Lollards replied: the people, that is, they themselves as the informed and righteous spokesmen for the people.

But the embryonic Protestantism of Wycliffe's movement went no further in the fourteenth century, and even in England the threads of later Protestantism back to Wycliffe were not openly continued on English soil but brought back into England from the Continent. The political combinations that had found Wycliffe useful developed in a manner that made Lollardy dangerous. In 1399, Gaunt's son, Henry of Bolingbroke overthrew Richard II and became himself Henry IV. Revolutionary doctrines, scholastic or popular, were no longer of advantage to a man who had gained the crown. Nor were they of continuing advantage to any powerful group within his dominions. Unlike the situation in Germany under Charles V more than a century afterwards, there were no political factors that made toleration of the new heresy advantageous or even expedient to anyone. The peers of England stood in no such relationship to the kings of the House of Lancaster as the princes of the empire stood to Charles. To them as to the king, the Lollards meant only peasant revolts, not territorial independence. The parliament of Henry IV himself passed the statute *de haeretico comburando* and the Lollards as a selfconscious group were destroyed. Secretly much of it must have lasted, for there still survive numerous manuscripts of Wycliffe's sermons and more than one hundred and sixty, an enormous number for such scarce items as medieval manuscripts, of the so-called Wycliffe Bible. The mystic side of this movement survived even in high places. Henry IV's great niece, Margaret Beaufort, Countess of Richmond, mother of Henry VII, began the first English translation of the *Imitation of Christ*.

After the death of Richard II's Queen, Anne of Bohemia, in 1394, her train went back to Prague taking with them several Lollard converts and a large number of Wycliffe's work. These began to circulate in Bohemia early in the fifteenth century and what John Huss taught, he had learned from Wycliffe. In the philosophical history of the West, the work of Luther and Calvin is one almost entirely of outward, political operation. In the world of thought, Protestantism began when the attempt of scholasticism to unite Western thought and Holy Scripture came to an obviously unsuccessful end early in the fourteenth century.

Such was the complex, vibrant, passionate society in which were to develop those involved and curiously interrelated historical phenomena that we blanket under the names Renaissance and Reformation. Thus it is here that these perhaps overlong considerations of distant history come to an end, for if their purpose of identifying the personality of the West is not yet accomplished, the task is beyond the power of the author and pursuit of this identity through the events of later times would be futile. The notes on the French Revolution, which will be found in the succeeding section are not history as the term has been used heretofore. They are not biographical items in the life of a great historical personality, though of course, the events discussed happened in the life of that personality, but considerations of present political problems carried back to their immediate roots. They do not seek, as historical writing should seek, to create the image of a living entity. They can be called history in a restricted sense only because they deal with certain events in the past. But they are in fact only discussions of narrow, even if important, matters in current political controversy. Furthermore, there is no need, in attempting to project an image of Western history for modern men, to extend that image closer to our own day than the end of the Middle Ages. Thereafter the image of fact and the image of tradition seem in fair accord, and once the misconceptions concerning earlier times and alien societies are observed, little more is needed. Nor has a reader anyone but himself to blame if he is not familiar with the major lines of the history of Europe and the Americas from the fifteenth century to the First World War and with the relations of the West to the other peoples of the earth during this period. It is a period exhaustively treated in our received history. No writer could consider himself sufficiently wise or sufficiently informed to improve upon the immense historical coverage long since given these centuries.

There remains, however, one historical matter. It is not germane to the identity of the West seen in contrast to other societies, but it is of consequence in an understanding of our own inward history. Viewed in our received image of history as the beginning of what we now are, the Renaissance and the Reformation carry quite other meanings than they do when they appear in the course of the life of a society already five centuries old, already rich with the traditions, values, worldly and intellectual interests that we still prize. Looked at not backwards from modern times but, as it were, forward from the Middle Ages, they appear not as a beginning but almost as an interruption. How truly were they such and how much of a mere coincidence was it that both movements arose together after five hundred years of Western life? Was there any deep connection between them and was either something more than proponents or detractors have declared them to be?

It is more difficult to pierce the intellectual barrier of our understanding of the Renaissance than it is to overcome the limitation of suspending history at Pompey's line. The latter is a definable geographical item. It did exist. It had a specific place on the face of the earth, and it is possible to know what cities and what men were on one side or the other. We know when it came into existence and when it disappeared. But what was the Renaissance? What can be said to precede something that has neither assignable beginning, identifiable apex nor discoverable end? What influence can be ascribed to something that is neither a movement, nor a program, nor a particular length of years? The very vagueness of what each writer means when he uses the word Renaissance confounds concrete analysis. Sometimes the word means a supposed rediscovery of Classical art and literature, sometimes only a revived taste for Classical material long known in the West. Sometimes, as in music, philosophy and the sciences, in commerce and in politics, it means phenomena of the fifteenth and sixteenth centuries that have no conceivable connection with anything Classical whatsoever.

The word thus has more an emotional than a factual meaning, and it is often applied not to convey information but to assert a philosophy of history. Its function then is to deny or belittle the continuity of Western life and by asserting, however vaguely and guardedly, a "revival" of some undefinable Classical influence, to offer amid the welter of negative proof from all the millennia of human history, one pitiful and unsure example of a continuity of history across the boundaries of a historical society.

In its etymology and in the first usage of the term it obviously meant such a rebirth. So Michelet and Burckhardt used it in their mid-nineteenth century writings popularizing the term, and even its first historical use, by Vasari (1511-1574), was in this sense. But as historical study has exposed the impossibility of a rebirth—the lack of any element of genuine Classical civilization being even known, let alone revived, in those centuries —the term has taken on other meanings. Sometimes it becomes a mere handy name for a period of Western history, as the term Middle Ages is today no more than a proper name for a stretch of time, almost like the names of our months, in the *magnum annum* of the centuries. But on other occasions and even by the same writer, the word is used as though it described a movement or even a conscious program.

It used to be the custom to indicate in a vague way that the capture of Constantinople by the Turks in 1453 must have been a causative factor in the Renaissance because Byzantines fleeing from the Turkish conquest— which they did not do—carried with them Classical Greek texts theretofore unknown in the West. Oddly the schoolbooks, where this sort of tabloid imbecility is most prevalent, never remark on the sixty years in the thirteenth century when the Latins held the city for themselves and could have taken any Greek manuscript they pleased, nor on the fact that 1453 merely marks the fall of the city of Constantinople, almost all the territory of the Byzantine Empire having come under Turkish government nearly a century before. The magic of 1453, however, has withered—even in schoolbooks— as modern scholarship has been unable to find any important Classical work that reached the West in accordance with this superficial theory. Nevertheless, though the fact is not explicitly stated, the inference is allowed to remain that the Renaissance saw a great new access of Classical texts. Obviously, the very base of the conventional picture of the Renaissance requires this belief. If men had been reading and considering these texts for some centuries before 1450, then the sudden chatter about them means something different from the excitement of a sudden discovery. The second might be argued as a revival of something long lost and hence a kind of Renaissance. The first would be only an intellectual fashion. Such it was.

It was not new *texts* but new *editions* of Classical works that appeared with the Renaissance.

The mere attempt to date the Renaissance indicates part of the difficulty in defining it. Convention dates it from the mid-fifteenth century. Burckhardt, finding it desirable to include Petrarch, Boccaccio and Giotto as men of the Renaissance, felt obliged to include the fourteenth century. Vasari himself thought the rebirth had begun in the thirteenth. On the other hand, the usual history of science begins with da Vinci in the sixteenth and the same type of thought applied to music bring us to Monteverdi in the opening decades of the seventeenth century.

Walter Pater and J. A. Symonds dodged the difficulty about dates by describing everything they knew and liked about the thirteenth century as Renaissance phenomena, precursory and preparative, but under no circumstances to be credited to benighted medievalism. They disclose, in fact, the real meaning of the word to the Renaissance enthusiasts: every phenomenon of several centuries of Western history of which the author approves. In this sense the word represents not a historical fact, but a subjective invention of nineteenth century romanticism—elaborated in large part from the historical concepts of eighteenth century liberalism—to embrace those philosophical and aesthetic programs that the romantics understood and valued. This use requires, therefore, a calamitous unawareness of the integrity of Western history and, as a necessary base, a deliberate refusal to observe the known facts of Classical society. When Symonds [21] said that he meant by Renaissance "the recovery of freedom for the human spirit after a long period of bondage to oppressive ecclesiastical and political orthodoxy—a return to the liberal and practical conceptions of the world which the nations of antiquity had enjoyed," his emotions are revealed in every word. But quite aside from what he obviously did not know about the Middle Ages, it would be interesting if he had told where in Classical antiquity he discovered "liberal and practical conceptions of the world"? In mass slavery, in licit and open homosexuality, in rowboats as seagoing vessels, in technological poverty and scientific shallowness, in the endless petty bloodshed of the Greek city states, in the mixture of short-sighted apathy, personal tyranny and civil war that is the history of most of the life of the Roman Empire? These were the facts of the matter, and they are far closer to the reality of that society than a careful selection of Classical poets and dramatists, Aristotle's theory of aesthetics, a few carefully chosen ruins and pieces of broken statuary. It is from these last, not from the sense of a once living society that we conjure the image of an antiquity that never existed and with this invention from texts and fragments, proceed to apply it as a causal agent in the history of the West.

[21] E. B. 11th Ed. v. 23 p. 84.

There is a further important point in our general picture of the Renaissance that is realized but whose significance is lost because of our erroneous picture of the general history of the Mediterranean lands. It is always recognized that there is a firm connection between Italy and whatever phenomenon is considered to be part of the Renaissance. What is here overlooked is that in no part of Italy was there any continuing tradition going back to Classical times, while in contrast a great deal of the peninsula had been for centuries under the unbroken living influence of Levantine Byzantium, under whose political dominion much of it had remained until the twelfth century. Outside of Lombardy most of Italy had no early Gothic period at all, and its arts at that time were in the style of Byzantium. The Italian "revival" of the fourteenth century, which was the direct origin of the fifteenth century work, was primarily a turn from Byzantine styles to those of northern Europe. A good part of the reality about the *Italian* Renaissance was the introduction into central Italy of the concepts, not of Classical, but of Western life. This is unarguably the case with Italian fourteenth century painting and music. It was equally true of sixteenth century Italian scientific thought.

Even a brief consideration of the technical foundation of the arts shows the impossibility of a Classical causation operating in the Renaissance. In painting the great problem of the age was the mastery of handling spatial depth. This could hardly be gained from study of Classical art, which resorted to any device it could invent to deny depth of space and showed all its figures, human or inanimate, as outlines, never as solids. It is even ridiculous to suppose that the great Western art of music, already rich with medieval counterpoint and the beginning of systematic harmony, needed or could get guidance from Classical music—which was in fact unknown at the time and whose singsong monophony would have sounded insulting to men whose art already stood on more than three hundred years of developed polyphony.

But to correct the absurdities of the enthusiasts does not entirely clarify the problems of the Renaissance. There was no revival of antiquity, but Raphael did paint in a different style from van Eyck. Bernini and Bramante did build quite differently from their Gothic predecessors. A man has only to walk across the transept of St. Denis to see for himself that a sudden and extraordinary change of outward style had touched the very top level of Western society. Against the grave Gothic dignity of the effigies of the medieval kings and queens of France, the tombs of Louis XII (d. 1515) and Henry II (d. 1559) with their marble arches, their bas-relief medallions and "Classical" statuary, may seem a delight or a garish shock depending on the taste of the observer, but no one could feel that all were in the same artistic tradition. And what is true in miniature at St. Denis is true of palaces and monumental architecture across all northern Europe and Italy. True, this is not Roman or Greek architecture. Its proponents called it Classical, and we still repeat this obvious falsehood, but they took care to build nothing resembling the still standing Greek temples of Sicily and southern Italy, of whose existence and Classical authenticity they could hardly have been ignorant. Renaissance architecture, despite the use of occasional Classical components, no more resembled Classical architecture than Raphael's paintings resemble those on the walls of Pompeii, but where Raphael, different as he was from Giotto, was aware, as were all the painters of the Renaissance, that they were the "moderns" of a great tradition going back to Giotto and beyond him to the forgotten painters of the medieval north, there is nothing about St. Peter's that even suggests the tradition of Chartres and Amiens.

Furthermore, monumental architecture never returned to the Gothic tradition and the poor quality of what has been produced by occasional archaism, by the periodic "revivals" of Gothic style in ecclesiastical and academic structures, testifies how completely this tradition has been lost and how impossible it has been to recapture it. To be sure, it is difficult to see how a style could "progress" artistically from Amiens or the unfinished stub of St. Ouen, though the later English Gothic, despised as it is by the coterie of the romantic enthusiasts, is nevertheless a work of magnificent beauty, and the brick Gothic of north Germany and Denmark, and the even stranger Gothic of Langue d'oc and northern Spain, testify to the extraordinary elasticity of this style while its tradition remained living. It might, therefore, be rash to assume that the Gothic was abandoned because it had reached aesthetic perfection and the only alternative to abandonment was to go on changelessly copying it. Since most of its greatest monuments were never finished, perhaps many factors more complex than aesthetics alone were present in its extinction. Furthermore, in domestic architecture, in clothing and furniture there was no sharp break with the styles of the Middle Ages. Domestic Gothic blends imperceptibly into Renaissance (Tudor) and Baroque (Georgian and Colonial).

Though none of the events whose aggregate we call the Renaissance were a revival of Classical thought or Classical style, the spirit of these events was manifestly at odds with part at least of the memory of the Middle Ages. That much is clear about all of them and the aspect of revolt against the Middle Ages, not the supposed authority in an imaginary Classical past, is what is significant about them. It is essential, also, to realize that the revolt was not against our present-day, conventional image of the Middle Ages. No such imaginary horror had ever existed. The Renaissance was not the assertion of beauty against ugliness because the Middle Ages had produced some of the most exquisite beauty of our society. It was not the rise of free thought against obscurantism, because the thought of the Renaissance was not at all free and that of the Middle Ages not particularly obscurantist. It was not the assertion of rationalism against superstition because the Middle Ages were less superstitious than the Renaissance, as the increase in the belief in witchcraft and the boldness of much medieval thought show. It was not an increase in knowledge because there is no evidence of any such increase. What, then, was the turmoil of the Renaissance all about? Perhaps one thing of which a trifling example has already been given illustrates the most meaningful factor common to all the developments that we associate with the Renaissance. It was not new Classical texts that appeared in the Renaissance, but new editions. The Renaissance marked not the acquisition of new learning but a great increase in the number of the educated, and perhaps—it is hard to be qualitatively precise in such a complex matter—something of a decline in the learning of the learned. The attempt to exploit alien artistic motifs, to seek justification for both art and thought in the falsification of distant history, are not signs of strength and growth. They betray an inner insecurity, a desire to escape the relentless, disturbing dynamism of Western society which has never been content to leave well enough alone but must always probe for deeper secrets.

Seen in this relation to the life of the West, the Renaissance must be pondered in connection with its twin, the Reformation. The difficulty in definition which complicates discussion of the Renaissance is not involved in considering the Reformation, but in compensation there is another and worse difficulty. Almost all modern Westerners by personal allegiance or by family tradition are either Roman Catholics or Protestants. It is almost impossible for us to evaluate the Reformation and Counter Reformation— for one is meaningless without considering the other—except in the light of values derived from our open or unconscious allegiance to some side of this long controversy. We approve or disapprove of these events by their consequences on some sect or church, not by their consequences on the West as the common society of us all. There is another difficulty. Since Roman Catholics assert that the medieval Catholic and the modern Roman Church are identical, not merely in legal continuity, and since, extraordinarily enough, most Protestants are willing to agree that such is the case, the Protestant revolt comes to be thought of by all sects almost as though it had been a revolt against the Roman Catholic Church of the present day. The changes that four hundred years have worked in the Roman Catholic Church—its own national particularism and its own theological developments—are duly recorded but are not permitted to alter the fundamental conviction of identity between Roman Catholicism and the medieval church. It is almost as though the liberal Protestant justifies Luther in anticipation of the pontificates of Pius IX and Leo XIII, the Roman Catholic applauds

Borromeo because of the worldliness of many aspects of twentieth century Protestantism. It is part of the illusion of seeing the Reformation and the Renaissance as the beginning rather than the mid-point of our history. If, instead, we view Protestantism not as a revolt from the modern Roman Catholic Church but from the united Catholic Church of the West, and Roman Catholicism, not as the continuum of that united church of the West, but as a specialized, geographically narrowed, reaction to this revolt, the image that results is less to our tastes but far truer to the facts.

This is doubly necessary because there is a natural tendency, since the north became Protestant, to view the later intellectual accomplishments of Englishmen and Germans as the accomplishment of Protestants rather than of Englishmen and Germans. This is made easier by the political decadence of Spain after the destruction of her attempt at European hegemony, and her gradual decline in the seventeenth and eighteenth centuries. The bracketing England-Protestant, Spain-Catholic and the drawing of desired conclusions from this agreement of outward fact, is only another example of the ascription of causality to the endless complexes of history. But what we cannot determine, and the only fact that would permit a judgment on the question, is what the north would have become had it remained loyal to the medieval church, had neither Protestantism nor Roman Catholicism come into existence.

The medieval Catholic Church, being by its own definition the Church Militant, not the Church Triumphant, was a human institution which, despite its divine guidance, was necessarily subject to the evils and shortcomings of all human institutions. It was a vast political government intermeshed with the secular powers of the newly-risen national states. It was immensely wealthy yet immensely costly to operate. It was eternal, yet its eternity could be maintained only by maintaining its transitory earthly interests. That it was corrupt and that its relation to the new centralized kingdoms needed readjustment, everybody admitted. That it had to be destroyed as the only alternative to maintaining the corruptions and the archaic political relations is not so certain.

Under the various issues of theology and ecclesiastical discipline which arose in the Reformation, two underlying historical assumptions came in time to be accepted by all Protestants. The first was that the medieval church had been led far away from the true Christianity taught by Jesus. It was not simply that the church had developed the human abuses incident to power and wealth. These could be seen and corrected. What was difficult to remedy was not worldly corruption but spiritual error, the inability to see or the refusal to admit that the medieval church, even at its best, did not teach or practice the Christianity of Jesus. The second assumption was that Protestantism was the restoration of this true, historical Christianity, long lost by the Western church.

To be sure, these assumptions were not particularly new in the religious life of the West. The fourteenth century mystics implied as much and the Franciscan spirituals all but said it. Among heretical movements like the Joachimists and the Lollards this position was openly proclaimed. The Cathari had gone even further by striking down the authenticity of both canon and ritual in contrast to their own undoubtedly ancient (though partially Manichean, certainly not Catholic) texts and practices. Yet in the sixteenth century this view of the history of Christianity in the West produced not isolated mystics, nor a fervent wing of the church uncomfortable under orthodoxy but still orthodox, nor scattered heresies that commanded too little political power to survive. Instead it produced a profound, and to all evidence, permanent division in Western Christianity. The abuses and corruptions of the church were old. The demands of the reformers were not new. What was new was the political situation of sixteenth century Europe and while to postulate this as the cause of Protestantism would be absurd, no comprehension of that great revolt is adequate without reference to its politics.

Running like a thread of consistency through all the complex developments of the Reformation, there is one political fact that emerges from a geographical study of where it triumphed and where it failed. In the end there appeared a distinction between Protestant and Roman Catholic lands that was not racial, nor linguistic, but entirely political. The Reformation did not triumph in those nations where the kings had already destroyed the political power of the feudal nobility and in fact, though not in form, deprived the church within their dominions of independent political power.[22]

In Castile, long a military frontier against Islam, the royal control over the church was probably more absolute than anywhere in Europe and with the formation of a united Spain, the same royal absolutism was extended against the liberties, lay and ecclesiastical, of Aragon. Even the Holy Inquisition did not operate in Spain, its place being taken by the Spanish Inquisition, under royal, not papal, control.

In France, under the Pragmatic Sanction of Bourges in 1438, the objectives of Philip the Fair were finally obtained: effective political control of the church within France itself. The cancellation of the Pragmatic Sanction by the Concordat of 1515 satisfied the papacy by its renunciation of conciliar principles—its admission that the supreme authority in the Church was

---

[22] Poland alone constitutes an exception. There the legalized anarchy of the constitution made the Polish government all but a fiction, Protestantism spread for awhile particularly in Lithuania, but largely succumbed in the three-cornered struggle with Roman Catholicism and Russian Orthodoxy with which Poland alone among the Western states had any serious contact

the pope, not a council—but within France itself fastened royal control ever more firmly over the episcopate. Thus in France, where Protestantism did not triumph, it offered nothing to a state already centralized and already dominant over the church within its borders. There Protestantism became the cause of those who did have something to gain from it, the uprooted feudal nobility in chronic revolt against the last weak Valois kings. When the able Henry of Navarre abandoned Protestantism, he likewise abandoned his leadership of the revolting nobility by suddenly becoming, in the face of the most improbable odds, the legitimate King of France.

The hereditary Burgundian lands within France had been annexed to the French crown by Louis XI on the death of Charles the Rash in 1477. The Burgundian lands within the empire were briefly united with the Hapsburg dominions by Charles V and then separated by his grant of the Hapsburg lands to his brother Ferdinand as emperor, and the Burgundian to his son Philip as King of Spain. In the southern part of this dominion, Franche Comte, Lorraine and Luxembourg, the hereditary authority of the Burgundian princes had been well established. In the northern, the counties of Brabant, Flanders and Holland, and the Duchy of Gelderland, the numerous mercantile cities enjoyed practical independence. By the end of the sixteenth century, Calvinism became the cause of these urban communities and equally the cause of this fractured piece of German nationalism against the hated Spaniards.[23] In the Hapsburg lands to which in 1526 were added Bohemia, Silesia and Hungary where the emperor ruled by hereditary right, not imperial election, the authority of the crown had been firmly established. Political control over the church within these territories and the reform of the more aggravating financial abuses of the church were thus easily effected by the agreement of Regensburg negotiated by Campeggio on behalf of Clement VII in 1524.

In contrast, throughout the rest of the empire, the imperial government was little more than a high-sounding name. The local principalities, counties, free cities, imperial episcopal sees provided in each locality the only effective rule. The power of both the emperor and Imperial Diet were in legal theory supreme over all the local governments, but there was no machinery of state to enforce either edicts of the Diet or commands of the emperor. Beyond this, the great principalities had themselves centralized their own political power within their own dominions at the expense of

---

[23] The United Netherlands, the modern Kingdom of the Netherlands (Holland) was part of the German Empire until 1648, when it achieved independence from both the empire and the Spanish crown, hence the ambiguous meaning of the English word Dutch, as in Pennsylvania Dutch, i.e. German. The remainder of the Spanish Netherlands passed from the Spanish to the Austrian Hapsburgs in 1714, was annexed to France in 1801, abortively united with Holland from 1815 to 1831 and since then has been the Kingdom of Belgium.

the smaller territorial nobility. They were, therefore, in the dual position of centralized dynasties toward their own local nobility, but firm adherents of feudal anarchy in their relations with the emperor, and since the imperial office always remained elective, the successive emperors tended to be very gentle toward princes upon whose franchise they depended for the continuance of their dynasty on the imperial throne. Some of these principalities were states of considerable consequence. Others were little more than the castles of robber barons, but all alike presented the geographical crazy quilt of feudal land tenure, a geographical monstrosity which existed throughout the West insofar as title to land was concerned, but only in Germany still fractured the exercise of sovereignty. During the particular years of Luther's early preaching, there was the further political factor that the emperor happened to be Charles V, embroiled in a world of other interests in Spain and Italy. His hostile relations with the pope made it impossible for him to force the church to remedy the valid grievances of the still inchoate religious rebellion in Germany, and his need of the German nobles for war against the Turks and the French made it impossible for him to suppress the dissidents by force.

In Scandinavia, the civil wars incident to the dissolution of the Union of Colmar and the feeble position of a still largely elective kingship furnished the background for the rapid spread of Lutheranism. Nowhere were the politics of the Reformation so naked, or the religious issues so superficial, as in Sweden where Gustave Vasa was in revolt against the crown of Denmark and at war with the Archbishop of Upsala, the head of the Danish faction in Sweden.

In Scotland, where the royal government had never been much more than a name, the long minority of James V was a period of almost complete anarchy. Bribery, murder and the endless intrigues of the French and English parties was the atmosphere in which the kirk advanced. As in France, Protestantism became the cause of the burgesses and the nobles against the theory of a royal government that could govern. But in Scotland it became also the cause of the English party and it was the English party that won.

In England the outcome of the religious revolt was unique, precisely as the political situation in England was unique. There the territorial independence of the nobility had been ended, but not their political power. As a group, the nobles of England, through Parliament, held political power which the nobility of France and Spain had not been able to transfer to the Estates General and the Cortes as their territorial independence was destroyed by the Crown. What would clearly have been to the taste of Henry VIII would have been a position over the English Church similar to that enjoyed by the King of France over the French. He could not obtain it because the political weight that England could bring to bear on the papacy could not equal that of either France or Spain. Henry could not put troops into Italy as Francis I could, nor like Charles V seize Rome itself. It is a trifle naïve to see, as some historians have done, considerations of mere sensuality on the part of Henry and of high Christian morality rather than Spanish politics in Clement VII's tortuous negotiation and final refusal of the divorce that Henry deemed essential to the preservation of his dynasty. The papacy was simply not a free agent in matters of high European politics and had not been so since the pontificate of Boniface VIII. Inevitably with political separation from Rome, differences of doctrine and ritual were not long in being added as they served various practical purposes. Henry confined his reforms to seizing monastic properties and declaring himself, in effect, pope in England, but the state-controlled Church of England which he created was made Protestant by his successors, Edward VI and Elizabeth I. With them Protestantism—though a Protestantism tinged with "Romish" trappings intolerable to the seventeenth century Calvinists and the nineteenth century Methodists—became identified with nationalism and has largely remained so to this day. How far any real points of conscience dictated the reform theology and ritual of the Church of England is perhaps beyond historical assay, since the question turns on the inner spiritual life of such complex personalities, and of politicians in such difficult practical positions, as Cranmer, Thomas Cromwell, the Protector Somerset and Queen Elizabeth herself. There is little doubt that papal power was unpopular in England. The political struggle between crown and papacy had gone on since the days of Henry II, and the English churchmen themselves had more than once objected to granting English benefices to foreigners. The type of political difference that arose between Henry VIII and the pope was not new, and the king's settlement of it, while drastic and unprecedented, seemed more a political than a religious matter and raised no serious opposition from the English clergy or laity. But the doctrines of Calvin and Luther were another matter. When Somerset, the Lord Protector and uncle to the boy Edward VI, began bringing reformers into England, translating the liturgy from Latin into English, establishing increasingly Protestant doctrines as the standard of the English Church, opposition began to rise. In the religious see-saw of the successive short reigns of Edward VI and Mary, the matter did not come to a head, but when Elizabeth restored the Edwardian changes, the ancient ties were at last severed. Of the twenty bishops of England, only one accepted Elizabeth's legislation and of the lower clergy about half. What popular sentiment may have been, there is no way to tell.

There is one other aspect of the politics of the Reformation. It could not have triumphed in Scandinavia, the Netherlands, Scotland and England unless it had first triumphed in Germany. It is part of the history of the West, but it is particularly part of the history of Germany.

Luther's *Address to the Christian Nobility of the German Nation*, written in 1520, breathes hardly a word of deviation from the doctrinal system of the medieval church. The enemy is not the false theology of the church, but the grasping fiscal and disciplinary jurisdiction of the Roman Curia. He shows how much better the German princes could manage the church, how idle and thievish monks could be eliminated and how German money need no longer pour over the Alps into Italy. The *Address* was an immense success with the German nobility, particularly in the north. It was Luther's political master stroke and gave his movement what no previous heresy had ever had in the West: political power. Thereafter, whether they liked or disliked where Luther took his theology, the North German princes remained his partisans. Campeggio's agreement of Regensburg, which came to be generally accepted in southern Germany, was unacceptable in the north.

It was centuries since the snows of Canossa or the bloody dust of Benevento. In 1520 perhaps hardly a German thought of these old monuments to the ruin of the German state, but they played their part in the surge of support that Luther's *Address* brought forth. It was an assertion of German nationalism in the face of historical facts. It sought to reverse history and restore not only a Christianity but a Germany that had never existed. For it was pure, irrational emotion. All Germans wanted a Germany but they wanted no German government. They were sick and terrified of the ruinous anarchy that Germany of 1520 had become, its impoverished petty nobility, the slowly strangled commerce of its commercial cities losing the ocean trade to the organized efforts of the maritime kingdoms and perishing at home under the multiple taxation and indeed robbery of the anarchic jurisdictions, the sullen, hostile peasantry so soon to rise in the slaughter of the Peasant War of 1524. For all this, each man desired a remedy, but only a remedy that would destroy the anarchic advantages of others, not his own, and this was as true of the great princes in the Diet as of such a mere robber baron as Sickingen, insolently independent behind the walls of the Ehrenburg, not ten miles from Worms itself. For the Diet would not let the emperor rule, nor would the individual princes in the Diet let the Diet, as an organ of state, rule them in their private domains. They used their membership not to legislate to their own advantage as the ruling group in Germany but to veto whatever would have limited the sovereignty of each within his own petty dominion.

Into this Luther tossed his firebrand: no one but Rome need sacrifice his advantages. Demolish the ancient church and all will be solved, the German nation reconstituted, its wealth restored from the estates of the church, its future evils removed by purging the old religion of papistical superstitions. The sixteenth century was not an age in which demagoguery had yet attained the refinements of democratic procedure, but Luther's appeal, whatever else it may also have been, was, in sober truth, pure demagoguery. It proposed remedies that bore no factual relation to the ills they were offered to cure. It played upon the emotions of frustrated patriotism, but far from erecting a governing state, weakened the already phantom state even further. In the name of the Christian gospels, it set resonating the chords of greed in every scoundrel throughout the broken kingdom of Germany. We ourselves in our own time have seen this great nation, torn by the anarchy so frequent in its tragic history, rise with the most natural of human emotions and then, in the hands of demagogue or madman, pull down upon itself and upon the whole society of the West vast and enduring catastrophes. We were not the first to have seen this. Even Luther himself, secure and isolated in the Wartburg during the lonely summer of 1521, more than once suffered wracking agonies of conscience at the mounting havoc he had let loose over Germany. But not even he could have foreseen that it would be one hundred and twenty-seven years before the reign of blood and ruin in Germany came to a halt, and not then until it had wiped out a third of her people.

From that summer of self-torture in the seclusion of the Wartburg, Luther has left us many notes and jottings that allow us some insight into the agonized confusion of his soul. In one he records, "I am unable to pray without at the same time cursing. If I am prompted to say 'Hallowed be thy name!' I must add: 'cursed, damned, outraged be the name of papists.' If I am prompted to say 'Thy Kingdom come, ' I must perforce add: 'cursed, damned, destroyed must be the papacy.' Indeed I pray thus orally every day and in my heart without intermission." [24]

When a man professing a religion that bids us forgive our enemies cannot recite its central prayer without injecting into the sacred text such imprecations, he is obviously struggling with issues beyond his own conscious awareness. He is possessed of hatreds that he is unable to bring to rational focus. It was not the worldly indolence and spiritual incapacity of the Medici popes that set off such horror in Luther's heart. It was not the greed of the Curia nor the pompous and immoral lives of so many of the clergy. Against these things he had, or would have had if he had limited his attack to these, many allies throughout Europe. The very preaching of the sale of indulgences which had begun his break with Rome had been forbidden in Spain by Cardinal Ximenes. But Luther's true antagonism was not toward the papacy or the corruption of the church. His destruction of the hierarchy and the sacraments, his flattening of the liturgy and hatred of church art,

---

[24] *Samtliche Werke*, XXV, p. 108 Erlangen, 1826-57.

his inability to reason with anyone—foe or partisan—about anything—reason, the "pert prostitute," which toward the end of his life he came to fear and hate more than all else—these things reveal what his tortured soul could not abide, the West itself, symbolized to him in the medieval church.

That nothing resembling this church exists today, that it could not be reconstituted and would not be tolerable if it were, has no bearing on the historical significance of the motives and passions that led to its destruction. At that time it was the visible symbol of the unity of the West and the choice to destroy it rather than reform it, for such in the end was the choice of the Reformers, was a choice against the West. It was not, as it superficially seemed, a revolt against tortuous theology or excessive ecclesiastical organization. It was not a demand to establish a more rational or restore a purer Christianity. It was a flight from the complexities, the responsibilities, anxieties and deep compromises inherent in the intellectual greatness of the West. To divide the church was to shatter something of the West. For that venerable church of our ancestors had been one of their great creations and had served them well. Though they built it, it had taught them and nurtured them. It had raised them from savagery to a lofty and noble civilization. It was both a symbol and an instrument of that achievement. The record of the profound learning that had arisen under it, the enduring beauty of the art that had been given to its service, these things proclaim its position in the hearts of our forefathers with an eloquence that no objection of theological niceties, no wails of virtue outraged by the human errors of power and corruption, can ever drown.

In the long view of the West, how can we consider as anything but a retrogression an age that placed on the throne of Gregory VII, Leo X and Clement VII; in Anselm's old see, Thomas Cranmer; that for spiritual insight substituted Luther and Loyola for Aquinas and Bonaventura; that for ecclesiastical organization preferred Calvin and Borromeo to St. Bernard; that as the intellectual lights of the church produced Melancthon and Bellarmine in the place of Grosseteste and Oresme?

It has often been pointed out that the Reformation was merely one facet of the long process of dismantling the universal church of the Middle Ages. But particularly, it was the method of dismantling the medieval church adopted in those nations that had not developed strong central governments or firmly established dynasties. This, at least, is what the politics of the Reformation accomplished. What other triumph it achieved is less easy to be sure of. What other tangible goals the reformers themselves sought is equally difficult to specify. The writings of Luther and Calvin, of Zwingli, Hooper and Bucer are available to all men to read, but to envisage a translation of their words into practical, Western institutions presents many problems. The reformers did not preach those things which today we so commonly credit to them. They did not preach freedom of conscience or religious toleration. Their teaching of the supremacy of scripture was conditioned as rigorously as the Roman Church conditioned its own similar views of scripture. For both, the Bible is the supreme authority *as the church interprets it.* The reformers arrived at some new interpretations because they founded a new church, but each was convinced that his own interpretation was correct and allowed of no other. Thus, once the challenge to the old church was successfully laid down, dissident groups in turn challenged the new and the Reformation broke into many pieces. But this was not the original intention of the reformers. Each wanted a church as universal as the medieval. The nature of their political backing rendered this a dream from the outset, but a multiplicity of churches was not their goal. Neither, it would seem, was the almost immediate control of the Reformed Church by the secular power part of the original hope of the reformers. Such control was inevitable in England and Scandinavia where the state itself had introduced the doctrinal and ecclesiastical changes. But even in Germany, the Reformation did not move from principality to principality entirely on a wave of popular conviction. Even there the decisive action was the decision of each local prince to establish the Reformed Church within his dominions. With no effective internal disciplinary power of its own, with no governing hierarchy, the new church had to choose between dissolution into religious anarchy or dependence on the existing secular powers. Calvin alone escaped this peril. He organized a disciplined church with an operable, though unofficial, hierarchy; but even Calvinism, where it decisively triumphed—in the United Netherlands and in Scotland—did not dispense with reliance upon the secular power. Calvinism, instead of becoming the creature of the state, captured it.

In the perspective of history it is the politics more than the theology of the Reformation that looms in importance. Neither Roman Catholic nor Protestant could admit this as doctrinally correct, yet to modern men of the West, how grave were the strictly religious questions on which this great revolt justified itself? Transubstantiation, masses for the dead, the intercession of the saints, if those seemed superstitious to the early reformers, do they today seem any more superstitious than the infallibility of scripture, the predestination of the elect, the reality of witchcraft, the Virgin birth and many another which the reformers never denied nor questioned? That is, can we today detect in the views of the reformers a consistent, intelligible theology which made logical sense of their choice of ancient practices and doctrines for acceptance or rejection? Denial of Roman supremacy is another matter, in fact, though not in form, a political question, but in theology what was gained at the cost of the religious unity of the West?

Luther in his *Babylonish Captivity of the Church* and *Freedom of the Christian,* published in 1521, sought to justify the demolition of the entire theological and ecclesiastical structure of the Middle Ages. He denied the historical authenticity of the papacy. He rejected Latin as the liturgical language, yet went back to Augustine to reassert predestination. He denied the efficacy of the sacraments as means to salvation, indeed, denied even the validity of most of them, and argued that salvation is not something attainable by man's efforts, is not a goal towards which man can progress, but is a static condition which God grants to his elect, to those who *believe* utterly in God and have no confidence in themselves. Manifestly, this preference for the uncomplicated processes of belief over the difficulties of handling evidence and reason, a preference as keenly felt but differently organized by both Thomas à Kempis and Loyola, goes back to the fourteenth century mystics and gave Luther an emotional, popular support without which the practical politics of the German princes would probably have been futile. But the subject matters that he thereby brought into controversy in the upper intellectual life of the West were as profitless as their argumentation has been bitter.

Naturally neither Protestants nor Roman Catholics evaluate the foundation of the Reformed Churches in quite this manner. Both Roman Catholics and Protestants are convinced of the doctrinal importance of the issues raised in the Reformation. Beyond doctrine, Protestants feel that they personally exercise a liberty of judgment and conscience denied to Roman Catholics. Although they also attach importance to the doctrinal differences, almost to a man they no longer understand them and are indeed very far themselves from the doctrinal position of their founders. The rigid predestinarianism of both Calvin and Luther has today almost no adherents. The real presence and the manner of its substantiation could hardly be intelligently debated today by any theologian, Protestant or Roman Catholic. The frozen words of ancient arguments can readily be repeated, but to assign any comprehensible meaning to these words is no longer possible.

For unhappily one of the fruits of the Protestant revolt was to open questions whose argumentation could not but be sterile within the frame of Western thought. To attack the delicately interrelated structure of dogma and ritual of the medieval church was a hazardous undertaking. This structure contained a set of doctrines, self-consistent and each as valid as another within the frame of Levantine causality and Levantine physics. It also contained a series of compromises and interpretations that made the structure viable in Western life. Logically, therefore, the medieval church could be attacked from the point of view of Western scepticism, that its Levantine core was invalid and hence its Western compromises unnecessary. This would have meant destroying the faith as well as the church. Equally, a logical attack could lie from the point of view of Byzantine orthodoxy, but though this would have destroyed the papacy, it would not have destroyed the hierarchy, the sacerdotal priest nor the monastic orders. Naturally, the reformers based their attack on neither ground. They justified acceptance or rejection of parts of the medieval church on historicity, on what they thought the church had been in the apostolic age. They supposed they could discover the true nature of that church from study of the Bible and such of the works of the Fathers as they were able to comprehend, which meant, in fact, almost entirely St. Augustine. This led them to abandon all the Western compromises of the medieval church because for these they could find no Biblical or Patristic warrant, but it also led them into an illogical and actually unhistorical rearrangement of the Levantine remainder, because the problem of understanding Levantine Christianity was far beyond their capacity as historians or indeed their will as pious men but unavoidably Westerners. As historians, they could not grasp the significance of the fact that the New Testament came to them composed in Greek, not Hebrew or Aramaic, nor understand by what perfectly proper historical warrant the distrusted Vulgate stood upon the long extinct Septuagint, not the Torah and Writings of the sixteenth century Jews. Having no notion of the Levantine concept of eschatology, they did not know how to interpret references to the Heavenly Kingdom, so their extremist wings were constantly tending to Joachimism. Being unfamiliar with Levantine physics they misconstrued the silence of the Fathers on transubstantiation to mean its denial, not its self-evidence. Not understanding Western causality and scientific thought any better than they understood Levantine—for they were not by any means the most learned men of their age—they could not foresee that they must accept Levantine physics as religious mysteries or end by denying any rationality to the Christian faith. To open discussion of Levantine doctrines from the standards of Western thought could not leave some "nonsuperstitious" part but could end only in the total demolition of all of them.

It is true that almost no modern man of the West would desire to live under the power of the medieval church, but that is not what was at stake in the Reformation. Though we feel it perfectly proper for a man to be necessarily subject to some state, we no longer feel that any of the attributes of sovereignty should be possessed by a church. We no longer believe that men can or should be compelled to believe. In a vague way we assign to the Reformation the release of the West from this ecclesiastical sovereignty of which we no longer approve. But this is a dubious assignment.

Certainly, the rise of religious tolerance and indifference—intimately related though we dislike to admit the connection—followed the Reformation
but followed it by almost two hundred years and was certainly not something the reformers themselves desired. Their churches were as sovereign
as the Pope's and in some countries more so. Whether the Reformation
was the unintended cause of religious toleration would seem, like any historical causality, unprovable. In the light of the history of other societies
it would seem even improbable. All societies in their respective ages of
money and democracy were as indifferent religiously as ours is today.

What we have left as the enduring remains of the Reformation is, in fact,
only its politics, only the organizational breakup of the Western church.
The rest, the great doctrinal reforms, the freedom of conscience, the separation of church and state, the whole host of advantages which Protestant
tradition has ascribed to the Reformation, today either no longer mean
anything or are not inherently derivatives of the Reformation at all.

Misunderstanding of the rise and spread of Protestantism and confusion
between the declared intentions of its founders and the consequences of
their work are among the great difficulties that beset an attempt to comprehend the historical personality of the West. The underlying unity of all
Western thought appears to have no existence when this breach about first
and last things cuts our society socially and historically in two. There is
a further difficulty. The myth of the Renaissance stands on the fact of the
Reformation. However much the schools of liberalism and aesthetics skirt
a frank statement about the source of their assertions of a break in the
continuity of our society, the manifest evidence for such an official break
in religious affairs is what allows them to feel safe in asserting discontinuity
in the field of art and secular thought. For the founders of Protestantism
declared that in fifteen hundred years the traditions of Christianity had
become so corrupt that the religious beliefs and practices of their time were
a fabric of error. They declared their own purpose to be a return to the
original Christianity taught by Jesus, and they and their protagonists to
this day declared that this was what they accomplished. Despite the soften-
ing to accord with the tastes of an age of material wealth and spiritual
poverty, in their position on ultimate and essential matters, all Protestants
agree with the position of their fundamentalist faction that Protestantism *is*
the faith delivered to the saints. There are thus two propositions concealed
in one. First, that one and the same religion, one and the same system of
ethics, causality and metaphysics, could be transferred across the centuries
from one civilization to another utterly different from it; and second, that
even though that continuity was gravely injured by the corruptions of
medieval Catholicism, it was possible to restore it by conscious effort based

on reading a book. Neither proposition is so. Protestantism did not restore the faith delivered to the saints, even though it was correct in its suspicions the medieval Catholicism was not that faith. It could not have done so, and had it known or truly desired to know the historical actuality of the faith that was delivered to the saints, it would not have sought to restore it. The idea that Protestantism recovered, even in any part, the teachings of Jesus or Paul requires for its acceptance a false image of what Jesus and Paul believed and taught. Accordingly from age to age Protestantism, to live up to its claim to be historical Christianity reincarnated, has had to create age by age a different image of the past, a different "historical" Jesus. Thus we have had the Redeemer God Jesus of early Protestantism, the predestinarian Jesus of the Calvinists—the one image touched by a faint wash of historical accuracy—the later ethical Jesus, a sort of magnetic Sunday School teacher, finally the socialist Jesus of our own day. These images in all their full development in Protestant literature are a wonderful commentary on the spiritual needs of the people who invented them, but they bear no resemblance to the historical Jesus or the ideas of the early Levantine Church.

But the actual historical Levantine Christianity of Jesus—belief that the end of the world was at hand when the Messiah would alter all mundane reality—this was not the "historical Christianity" that Eckhart, Groote and Wycliffe, and after them Luther and Calvin, tried to restore. The end of the earth in historical time was never a real belief of the West, and, therefore, none of the basic ethical teachings of Jesus could be restored. Utter indifference to the welfare of state and family, abandonment of all practical responsibility for the affairs of this world in lofty human kindliness and ecstatic contemplation of the approach of God's Kingdom on earth, these are the prerequisites of the morality of Jesus. They have always been unacceptable premises as the base of a moral life in the West. We are taught to venerate the specific ethical propositions of Jesus, but we are not taught their metaphysical foundation and would not accept it if we were. One of the results is our acute embarrassment in handling religion as a part of history.

If we were not a society that has always thought in strongly historical terms, this would create little difficulty. But one of the great warrants for the truth of Christianity to the West has been its antiquity. We feel we must believe, if we believe in a Christianity at all, that our present faith is indeed that delivered to the saints. The difficulty is that the West never could accept the principles of the Christianity of Jesus and of the early Levantine church. Only one approved road has, therefore, been open, that of misunderstanding ancient Christianity, asserting that the Christianity of the moment is what ancient Christianity actually was. From the nature of their conception of the church and of their own origin, this has been a sharper requirement to Protestants than to Roman Catholics. But for both, it has interposed difficulties in arriving at an objective historical understanding of the several Christianities. And for both, it has confused understanding of the Reformation. That revolt could never have hoped to restore what it never could have believed in—eschatology, the doctrine of the imminent end of the world.

Protestantism and the Counter Reformation were thus in part an inward break with the continuity of the West. Where the medieval Catholics had attempted to fuse their image of the world and their idea of God, to understand each in the light cast by the other, Protestantism proclaimed that all needful things were already known, that the idea of God was complete—once and for all revealed fully in the scriptures. For the unhappiness of men who found, in the growing light from the historical world, the necessary interpretation of the Bible more and more difficult, the answer of Protestantism was not to seek deeper for religious understanding but to shut out the light of the world so far as the religious image was concerned, to let no element of the vast, fascinating, mysterious, cause-governed universe as Western men see it, influence the inward religious image. Should we be surprised then that Protestant religiousness has been textually Biblical and the scientific thought of Protestant lands atheistic? Certainly Roman Catholicism was not wholly free of this same reaction but suffered it far less acutely.

All this is less obvious if we date Protestantism from its completion in the Protestant revolt of the sixteenth century, instead of the Protestant withdrawal in the fourteenth. But the former is outward political history only, confused with the superficial wrangle of clerical abuses, the accidents of German history, and made and unmade by the irrelevant political adventures of the Houses of Hapsburg, Valois, Bourbon, Tudor and Stuart.

Yet even this outward history is significant. Protestantism is nationalistic. All the Protestant Churches are historically national churches, and the partial variation from this principle today is the result of a dismembered Germany and the one-time British colonies in North America. Yet this too is characteristic of the age of its origin, for nationalism as a conscious, political idea first appears in European life in the fourteenth century. The rise of the vernacular speech, the rise of the vernacular state, and the rise of the vernacular church all quite naturally came together.

Since men became aware of them as historical phenomena, the words "Renaissance" and "Reformation" have always been a couplet, always in some unclear way bracketed together. Historians have dwelt at length on their complete difference, yet always treat them together. Here instinct has been sounder than accepted historical doctrine. They must be treated together because they are at bottom the same thing: a revolt from the Middle Ages, and in both is the same mark of popularization and the decline of the quality of Western thought and politics. Both shared another trait. Each movement sought authority for its revolt in the tradition of the early Levant, but neither knew that this was their authority. They had no conception of the existence of such a society. The Reformation declared its authority to be the Bible and made no further inquiry concerning the civilization that had produced the Bible. Protestantism did not rise to restore a long suppressed Western theology which the official church had repressed. To the contrary, it revolted against the Western theology that had been painfully built up in the conflict between Western thought and the necessity of staying within some sort of bounds laid down by the holy books.

The humanists of the Renaissance declared that they were reviving Classical learning and Classical art without observing that what remained of Classical learning had been effectively known in the West for five hundred years, and what they called Classical art was early Byzantine. When Renaissance artists unconsciously used some detail of Classical art, they did so as the Byzantines had done long before by taking some separate Classical detail of structure, a column or an arch, and using it in a completely unclassical way. No one rebuilt a Classical building or recarved a Classical statue. No one polished a bronze or painted marble. The only art the Renaissance really affected was architecture, and in the world of thought its sole accomplishment was to hasten or possibly insure the destruction of Latin as the international language of the West. It has long been the fashion to proclaim the artistic and intellectual life of the West since 1500 as in the main derived from the intellectual stimulation and reawakened curiosity ascribed to the Renaissance, but this presupposes an intellectual and artistic wilderness in which the clamor of the humanists suddenly set men off on new and wonderful enterprises. The record of medieval learning, barely sketched as it has been in these chapters, disposes of the notion of a cultural wilderness before 1500. The mere record of printings of these works disposes of any notion that the climate of thought after 1500 was a departure from the great tradition of the Middle Ages.

When Luther came to the conclusion that the papacy was barely four hundred years old, he decided that it was un-Christian. When he encountered the Roman law, he decided that no one had ever put together such wisdom on worldly matters. When Bramante set to work to design St. Peter's, he announced that it was his ambition to set the dome of the Pantheon on the Basilica of Constantine. He thought they were Classical buildings as Luther thought the *Corpus Juris* was Classical law. In each case, the apostle of the Renaissance and the apostle of the Reformation was mistaken. Neither was admiring Classical civilization, and neither really knew anything about that long vanished society. Both needed authority for their retreat from the West and both found it where such authority so usually appears in Western civilization: the records and monuments of the Levant.

Bramante and Luther were in the same confusion that had vexed Western thought before their time and still vexes it. The life of Western society has been more complex than our tradition portrays. The fact that Classical society had perished some centuries before our official "fall of Rome" and had been succeeded by a radically different civilization introduces into our intellectual and political heritage much of Levantine society under the name of "Roman" and much that cannot be called Roman under that of "Hellenistic" Greek. So generally is this the case that the more carefully the Levantine and the Classical heritages are examined, the more certain it appears that the true Classical heritage was extraordinarily slight, extremely narrow in its application, and invariably the result of conscious effort by a few particular men.

The truth of the matter is that we Westerners have always loathed the Classical society and to keep our official veneration intact we have had to shield ourselves from too accurate and too direct knowledge of it. We dare not translate its great writings honestly. Vital elements of its arts we have to suppress as pornography and the balance we can only admire if they are shattered and discolored fragments. Even in a democratic age its politics seem to us incredibly brutal and childish. Its saturnalia and the ghastly shows in its arenas we cannot conceive as actually happening to human beings. Who cares to remember that "love" to the great Plato meant homosexuality and to Ovid fornication, that the blasphemy which Alcibiades committed the night he sailed for Syracuse was to knock off the phalli from the statues of Priapus in the streets of Athens, phalli on which young girls hung votive garlands on feast days? Who likes to remember that crucifixion was not a horrible and unusual punishment particularly reserved for Jesus but a normal sentence of Roman criminal law? No, of the Classical civilization we have kept the languages and venerated the name. All else has been falsified out of recognition and even the language, while it was used, not mummified, was so altered that it became a Western, not a Classical, tongue.

In contrast the Levantine civilization has permeated our lives at a thousand unconscious points. We are not Levantines and very far from being such, but the Levantine has been the only alien society that has appreciably altered the life of the West. We have always been nominal Christians, and our ancestors lived in political and intellectual intimacy with this society in the days of its greatness. With no group of men has the West been so deeply involved as with the Levant. Always we have seen it close to and under many of the innumerable facets that any society presents. We touch in our Bible, in Constantine and Justinian, in Mohammed, in the Jews, in medieval texts, in the Crusades, in the Orthodox Church, in St. Augustine, at the battle of Lepanto and the siege of Vienna. All our life as a society we have lived in intimate contact with this great alien, and when any aspect of its life or thought could be given the Christian or Roman name, its authority has been almost incontestable. It has reached our lives in so many ways and over so many centuries that it is difficult for us to withdraw from it far enough for these immensely looming, seemingly disparate, details to take, in the perspective of distance, their place in the great unity of which they are a part. And failing to realize the existence of this society, we have confused much of it with our own and thereby lost not the sense of the existence of the West—for that is too obvious—but of our own origin and our own destiny, the reality of our past and the possibilities of our future. The confusion of Luther and Bramante neither began nor ended with them.

It was moral indignation over the sale of indulgences as a means of financing Bramante's great Levantine dome over St. Peter's that led Luther to post the ninety-five theses on the door of the Castle Church at Wittenberg, October 31, 1517. Even in the coincidence of external trivia the two great revolts were intertwined.

There is a relation that has often been noted connecting the Reformation and Renaissance with the appearance in Western society of an urban, moneyed class. These new movements are thus pictured as signs of enlightenment, liberation and progress undertaken by new men from the lower ranks, a new class determined to break free from the fetters of a feudal and hierarchic society. As such, these revolts are considered worthy of praise as the first steps in the march of our civilization towards democracy. Since in modern thought progress and the rise of democracy are believed identical, the Renaissance and Reformation would be considered steps in the advancement of mankind even if we were not also taught that their specific accomplishments were likewise progressive in detail. But there is another side to consider.

In the case of the politics of the Reformation, tying religious emotion and ecclesiastical organization into the structure of the national territorial states ended in destroying the concept of the West as the unit of our common civilization. The full flower of that disaster was not to be apparent until our own day, but from this far-off source stems part at least of the fearful political disunion of the West, a disunion that beclouds the borders of our society, that makes us unsure who is within and who without, or even whether such a society exists at all, that at times makes a deadly enemy a nation's favorite and petted ally. Nor were the disasters of the Reformation limited to politics. Its religious consequences were not wholly to the benefit of the West. Admittedly, Protestants cannot be expected to view as unfortunate the religious revolution to which they owe their separate identity. Less obviously, the same is true of Roman Catholics. Naturally, Roman Catholics cannot approve the division of the church, but in their turn they would scarcely deplore the doctrinal re-emphasis brought on by the Reformation and Counter Reformation. Thus if each must think as partisan of his own church, neither Protestant nor Roman Catholic can sit as an uncommitted Westerner in judgment on this great crisis. Neither is free to ponder whether it was to the long advantage of the West to introduce doctrinal differences on purely Levantine concepts, or whether it deepened the religious life of the West to make the badge of loyalty to their respective churches formulae without meaning in a Western understanding of the universe. Neither can admit that it was a disaster to the West to insist upon belief in the literal truth of the Christian documents—in the manner each has understood that literal truth—as the public emblem of religiousness in the West. Though perhaps only the Protestants intended to do so, the consequence of the Reformation on both Protestants and Roman Catholics was to shatter, apparently forever, the attempt to build a Western Christianity. Perhaps there was no way to do it that was both reverant to its Levantine origin and still meaningful within the understanding of nature and history that has always marked the West. Perhaps the task could never have been accomplished, but after 1520 it was never again tried and after that date religiousness and Levantine literalism have been accepted as unchallenged identities in the West. The attitude of Oresme and at times of Aquinas—the will to interpret the Bible—as written "a la manière de commun parler humain," has since 1520, been branded an irreligious attitude. From this has flowed the long and logically absurd clash between "religion" and "science" which has in fact been only a clash between Western and Levantine physics, the former posing as atheism and the latter as religious truth. From this has also flowed what is far more serious, the clash between history and religion, which brings every religious Westerner, if he is also thoughtful and possessed of a sense of history, into irreconcilable conflict with the Levantine understanding of the documentation of the Christian faith. Reimarus, Bauer, Weiss, Loisy, Dollinger are only the most prominent Protestants and Roman Catholics to have come to grief with their churches over this historical impasse. Far more important are the unknown thousands whose ill-comprehended but insolvable differences with the Christian texts have deprived them of a true communion in the faith of their fathers.

The conventions of our religious tradition forbid our seeing in clear focus the misfortunes that flowed from the Reformation. The conventions of liberalism fill the same office for the Renaissance. To see wherein the artistic and intellectual life of the fifteenth and sixteenth centuries was in part a decline, not an advance, requires more than the facts that justify the statement. It requires recognition of the fact that to level society—and popularization is the first step towards leveling—is not to advance it.

To discuss the aesthetic changes associated with the Renaissance would be futile for in this field there are no objective standards. Every man is free to proclaim whatever tendency he pleases as evidence of the progress of the arts. Perhaps as near to objectivity as it is possible to come in this highly subjective matter is simply to recall again that the alleged Classicism introduced by the Renaissance was fraudulent. In architecture the new taste was early Byzantine. There was no Classical influence whatever operating on Renaissance painting and music. In literature there was no more Classicism than there had been ever since the days of John of Salisbury. The apparent difference was simply that in the Renaissance, Classicism appeared for the first time in the vernacular writings, not because this was a new trend but because the vernaculars were replacing Latin as the literary language. Despite Michelangelo, the Renaissance was never able to establish a Western art of sculpture. Westerners have, of course, made statues but to classify their products as an art comparable with Western music, painting or literature is simply silly.

But there are aspects of the Renaissance that can be subjected to qualitative evaluation. In the sciences there are large areas where facts, not opinions, are decisive and here the influence of the Renaissance in impoverishing Western thought shows itself. The two methods of impoverishment were those standard in all phenomena of the Reformation and Renaissance: popularization and recourse to authority, usually Levantine, but in the case of mathematics, Classical.

The great mathematical task of the sixteenth and seventeenth centuries was the formulation of the calculus. It did not, of course, flower full-blown in the heads of Newton and Leibniz. It is a curious fact also that all through the fifteenth century there was no mathematical pioneering, and the subject still stood where Oresme and Swineshead had left it. The ideas of the fourteenth century mathematicians were kept alive but scarcely carried any further. Only Nicholas of Cusa made the concepts of the infinite and the infinitesimal a little more precise. He recognized the circle as an infinite-sided polygon, each side being, of course, infinitesimal, and regarded zero and infinity as the lower and upper limits of the series of natural numbers. He also described a straight line as an infinite circle.[25] Aside from

---

[25] Kepler, *Opera Omnia,* II 595 says: Et Cusanus infinitum circulum dixit esse lineam rectam.

Cusa, and the principal interests of his life were theological not mathematical, there was no fifteenth century work of importance. It is not easy to account for this stagnation. On the one hand, there was during that period the growing popularity of humanism, which always lacked the intellectual competence to handle mathematics. On the other hand there was the more tangible fact of the grave damage to the higher academic tradition following the terrible mortality of the Black Death. Perhaps humanism itself, the response of the partially learned, was also a consequence of this rupture in the chain of learned men. However that may be, when mathematical pioneering was resumed in the sixteenth century, the full authority of the Renaissance was in force and the examples of Classical learning were the models from which men hesitated openly to depart.

The works of Archimedes were known in the Middle Ages—about a dozen manuscripts from the twelfth to the fifteenth century have survived,[26] but the medieval mathematicians showed no disposition to follow his methods. In 1543 Tartaglia published parts of his works, in a medieval translation by William of Moerbeke. In 1544 the complete Greek text was published at Basel and in 1588 Commandino published a translation at Venice. From then until far into the nineteenth century, the irrelevant shadow of the great Syracusan lay across the development of Western mathematical thought.

The situation is curious and of extraordinary interest, because historians and mathematicians alike, far from seeing any disadvantage resulting from the imposition of Archimedean concepts, ascribe to this very intrusion the foundation of the calculus. The matter is of some importance because the belief that the influence of Archimedes led to the foundation of the calculus is probably the only case in which the learned still accept any part of the popular Renaissance myth that a revival of Classical learning was a beneficent stimulus to the growth of Western thought. But even here, for all of Archimedes' genius, the myth is still only a myth. The calculus does not owe its origin to the Renaissance devotion to the texts of Archimedes. Three things account for this misunderstanding. First, unlike most ancient authorities used by the Renaissance, Archimedes was not a mere compiler but a mathematician of extraordinary genius. No one could study his works without profit regardless of the utterly different mathematical concepts of his society and of ours. Secondly, the mathematicians of the sixteenth and early seventeenth centuries proclaimed the genius of Archimedes and sometimes cited him as the source of their inspiration even when they departed completely from his methods and used those of their medieval predecessors. Thirdly, there has been a great reluctance to observe that

---

[26] See Thorndike and Kibre: *Catalogue of Incipits of Medieval Scientific Writings in Latin*, Cambridge 1937.

the development of the calculus from the late seventeenth to the mid-nineteenth century gradually stripped from it every element of an Archimedean surface and left exposed as its generative principles the concepts of infinity and change totally absent from all Classical mathematics but first enunciated by Swineshead and Oresme.

The core of the difficulty can be understood by examining the long wrangle on the nature of the differential as Leibniz formulated it. What meaning can dy/dx have when dx is zero? Yet if it is not zero the differential equation is false. So long as the Archimedean tradition lasted, dx was not zero, it was felt to be infinitesimal, yet not devoid of all magnitude and the calculus was, therefore, not an exact mathematical discipline but a convenient approximation devoid of truth and hence of philosophical consequence.

Archimedes had designed a method of ascertaining areas of plane figures (and an equivalent method for solids) by breaking them up mentally, and sometimes physically, into a very large number of very small triangles or rectangles and then summing all these smaller figures. Similarly, it will be recalled, Oresme had concluded that when a curve of diform intension represented velocity of motion, the area under the curve—that is, the theoretical sum of all the verticals (which might be thought of as an infinite number of infinitely tiny rectangles)—represented the distance traversed. The two methods seem much alike, but there are two unbridgeable differences between them. Archimedes' purpose was not to deal with change so that while his work bears a superficial resemblance to the integral calculus, it has no bearing on the differential calculus which was its logical and historical foundation. In the second place, Oresme, like Swineshead and Cusa, was sublimely indifferent to the problem of how the addition of even an infinite number of infinitesimal magnitudes could have a finite sum. If the infinitesimal units are thought of as possessing any magnitude at all, however small, an infinite aggregate of them ought to have an infinite sum. If they have no magnitude at all, the problem would appear to be zero times infinity, which should still have zero as an answer. Archimedes involved himself in no such difficulty because he never permitted the concept of infinity to enter his work. He dealt with very small and very large numbers, often indeterminate, but never with the infinitesimal or the infinite. Yet only the willingness to conceive of these and use them as the conceptual limits of a series lies at the base of the calculus. The fourteenth century mathematicians were intuitively correct in their willingness to use these concepts, even though under the mathematics of their times, largely Levantine and Classical as it was, they were not logically justified in doing so. Only long afterwards were these concepts rigorously defined and their use logically justified. In the meantime, however, the Renaissance and early seventeenth century mathematicians almost surreptitiously used them under an Archimedean mask, but what they brought to flower was neither the method nor mathematical purpose of Archimedes but those of Swineshead, Heytsbury and Oresme.

Consider the problem in connection with the equation of accelerated motion, $S = \frac{1}{2}gt^2$, which differentiates to $V = gt$, where V is the instantaneous velocity at time t. But what is an instantaneous velocity? How can there be a time of zero duration? Furthermore, since velocity is distance traveled divided by time of travel, it would seem to be non-existent if the time in question were of zero duration. Observe, however, that $V = gt$ has been derived from $V = gt + dt$. Now, obviously, as dt is given a series of decreasing values, $gt + dt$ likewise decreases towards the limiting final value of gt itself when dt is zero. In the limit, therefore, the instantaneous velocity V is represented simply by gt. So far as our physical senses are concerned, a time of zero duration remains just as meaningless as ever, but we are able to arrive at a usable and logically valid number at the end of an infinite series of other numbers. Western mathematics has, therefore, been willing to disregard whether a result is capable of sensory or even conceptual realization, provided it is logically justified. Not so the Classical. There are no Classical concepts in mathematics, anymore than in any other field of thought, that cannot be grasped by the hands and seen by the eyes.

Cusa's definition of a circle as an infinite-sided polygon is exactly mathematical thought of this nature. Consider a polygon circumscribed about a circle, its sides constantly being increased in number and, therefore, reduced in size. Obviously, as each side is allowed to grow smaller the number of sides increases, but the perimeters of the successive polygons get smaller, approaching at the limit, where the sides are of zero length and of infinite number, the circumference of the circle. Again sensory realization is impossible, but the logic is unimpaired. Swineshead similarly examined the infinite series $\frac{1}{2} + \frac{2}{4} + \frac{3}{8} + \ldots n/2^n$ and calculated that though it had an infinite number of terms, they added to the finite value 2. The fact that no last term could even be imagined did not bother him. Yet this was the solution of Zeno's paradox of Achilles and the tortoise, which Classical mathematics had never been able to solve.[27]

In contrast, Archimedes in his *Quadrature of the Parabola* proceeded in

---

[27] Roughly, Achilles runs twice as fast as the tortoise, but the tortoise has a mile head start. When Achilles has run the mile, the tortoise has gone half a mile, when Achilles has run the half mile, the tortoise has gone a quarter. Every time Achilles reaches where the tortoise was, the tortoise is half the distance ahead. How can he overtake him? This is the series $1 + \frac{1}{2} + \frac{1}{4} + \frac{1}{8} + \frac{1}{16} \ldots + \frac{1}{2^{n-1}}$

an interestingly different way. He observed that the area of a parabolic section could be indefinitely approached by drawing a triangle with its base coinciding with the section and its apex at the vertex. This in turn would produce two smaller parabolic sections on each side of the triangle in which two smaller triangles could be inscribed in the same way, and so on indefinitely. This gave him a series of 1, 2, 4, 8 . . . n triangles of total respectives area 1, ¼, $\frac{1}{16}$ . . . $1/4^{n-1}$ so that the area of the parabolic section was approached by the successive polygons formed by adding the triangles $1 + \frac{1}{4} + \frac{1}{16} \ldots + 1/4^{n-1}$. He observed that regardless of where this series is stopped, if ⅓ of the last term is added to it, the sum is always the same, namely ⁴⁄₃. From this he concluded, and then proved by a double *reductio ad absurdum*, that the area of a parabolic section was equal to ⁴⁄₃ of the area of the inscribed triangle. But what Archimedes did not do, in this or in any other problem, was observe that the perimeters of the successive polygons approached the parabola as a limit. Had he done so he would have had an infinite series with no definite or imaginable last term. The difference is not simply a matter of greater or less mathematical subtlety. It is a profound difference in the comprehension of reality and lies at the root of the vast difference between the sciences of the two civilizations. To us the logical though unimaginable is none the less real. To the Classical only what could be sensed could exist. It is the difference between the comprehension of change, and the acceptance of static endurance. Furthermore, it is a difference not founded on any observation, good or bad, of the data of nature. If anything, the Classical concept is far closer to what can be observed than is ours. The difference is solely in a way of thinking. No observation of nature could ever give rise to such mathematical concepts as those of the West.

It is because Archimedes' understanding of the meaning and relations of numbers was so at variance with that of the West, and because the purpose of his methods never even approached the purpose of the Western mathematicians, who were not seeking to find static volumes and areas but to develop a mathematics capable of measuring change, that it is historically false to insist that the Renaissance mathematicians developed the foundation of the calculus from their study of Archimedes.

On the contrary, since Archimedes as a Classical man could not conceive of infinity as a reality, much less of an infinite succession of numbers varying towards either a finite sum or a limiting value, the attempt of the Renaissance mathematicians to be guided by Archimedean principles while developing an utterly un-Classical mode of mathematical thought, introduced vacillation and confusion into their work. They feared to strike down the Archimedean limitation which held mathematics to comprehensible magnitudes. They hesitated openly to follow the medieval mathematicians in using concepts beyond sensory representation, infinity and the relationship of variables at a limit. But, in time, despite the authority of the Classical, they did just that. In the calculus as it stands today not one trace remains of the methods or concepts of Archimedes, except perhaps the inept notation for the differential, dy/dx, which inevitably suggests a ratio between quantities and this it never is. The West owes nothing else to Archimedes, Classical genius though he was.

Even the Renaissance mathematicians, despite their bowing to the climate of opinion, tacitly admit this. Torricelli and Wallis, for instance, both betray how little they really depended upon Archimedes. Both expressed the belief that he had not derived his conclusion by the methods set out in his works, but must have had a secret analytical method, such as they and their contemporaries were even then employing. They were in part correct, but not precisely in the way they supposed. Archimedes did have a method not disclosed in his works, and when it was discovered and published in 1906, it appeared to confirm this belief. But, in fact, it does not. For Archimedes' private method—it was not secret but used only for approximation and thus never included in his finished calculations—no more than his formal method employs an infinite series. It recognized a surface as composed of elements which are not infinite in number, but for Archimedes' purpose need not even be partially numbered, as in the example of the area of the parabolic section. Even had this method been known in the Renaissance, it still would not justify ascribing to Archimedes a part in the development of the calculus.

In mathematics and in the arts, criticism of the supposed value of Classical influence during the Renaissance suffers from an insurmountable handicap. It is forced to compare what did happen with what might have happened. It is forced to point out the alien nature of the Classical and Levantine elements so passionately asserted in this period, and then trace the much slower and almost always unadmitted process of sloughing them off, a process which has never been entirely completed. But because the medieval base which remains after the Classical and Levantine materials were removed was fundamental to our thought, though by modern standards obviously undeveloped at the onset of the Renaissance, criticism can only argue that from this base the arts and sciences would have flourished as they did, or better than they did, without the temporary addition of alien fashions. Since even the styles of the present day require us to deny such a proposition, and since it is entirely beyond proof, its acceptance or rejection must rest for each man on his own concepts of the historically probable, his own sense of the potential elasticity of the past, his grasp of the creative power of a great society.

But there happen to be two quite unrelated fields of human endeavor, one minor and the other of considerable human importance, in which the damage of the Classical or supposedly Classical fashions of the Renaissance is factually demonstrable. These fields are geography and medicine.

It will be recalled that the portolani from the thirteenth century onward began to make available in the West fairly accurate maps of the coasts of Europe, North Africa, the Near East and the Mediterranean islands. By the late fourteenth century these maps even included such distant islands in the Atlantic as the Azores, Canaries and Cape Verdes. For Asia, there were available the excellent accounts of the fourteenth century travelers which furnished no detailed maps, of course, but at least established the rough position, north and east, of the major land masses.

In 1409, Giacomo d'Angelo translated into Latin directly from the Greek Ptolemy's geography, supposing that he was restoring a lost treasure of Classical antiquity. The translation circulated fairly widely in manuscript and then with printing and the full Renaissance, it became the unchallenged geographical authority, going through seven editions before 1500.[28] Precise Western knowledge was promptly abandoned by the educated and there rapidly appeared in general circulation the absurd maps which our schoolbooks still reprint, not as examples of Renaissance ignorance but as a charge against the stupid Middle Ages which never used them. The Mediterranean is once again misshapen, the coasts of Africa hopelessly distorted, the Atlantic islands lost, the peninsula of India disappears and China becomes a huge appendage running southeastward from the mouth of the Ganges toward an imaginary Antarctic. Such was the accepted geography of the educated in the time of Columbus.

This geographic retrogression was apparently of no importance in the life of the West. Mastery of the sea had already been assured by the medieval development of the ocean-going ship and the tide of exploration soon removed Ptolemy from the shelves. But it does furnish an example, whose lesson can be extended to fields where such documentation does not exist, of the inability of the educated men of the Renaissance to think for themselves when faced with the fashionable authority of the supposedly Classical.

Medicine has not heretofore been touched upon in these pages because it is not a causal science and most of its history is not germane to the development of the thought and philosophy of a society. Even today the inability to establish a complete causality in medicine leaves great stretches of the discipline devoid of scientific foundation as the West understands a science, and thus requires the services of the skilled empiricist. Prior to the modern knowledge of biochemistry and physics, this was even more

[28] Including Vicenze 1475, Florence 1478, Ulm 1482, 1486 (E.B. 11th Ed. 17-643), Bologna 1482, Greek text, Bâle, 1533.

sharply the case. Throughout Western history well into the nineteenth century, the inexact or erroneous notions of physics and chemistry prevented the development of even a partial scientific foundation for medicine. The best that could be expected, therefore, of medieval medicine was a growth in the knowledge of structural anatomy and the gradual increase in precision of diagnosis—which required general agreement upon classification of symptoms, and a slow accumulation of notes on successful empirical treatments. With the thirteenth century, Western medical writings began to show a start in these directions despite the general adherence to Galenic concepts and an almost universal acceptance of the role of astrology in health and sickness. In the thirteenth century began also the series of *concilla*, records of actual clinical cases, that in the course of time built up an immense factual record without which the classification of diseases and symptoms would have been impossible.

But the thirteenth century did a little better than this. It also produced two physicians who recorded two empirical discoveries accepted by their contemporaries and now known to be correct, though we erronously suppose that they were discoveries of the eighteenth and nineteenth centuries. These men were Theodoric Borgognoni and Gilbert the Englishman (Anglicus). Theodoric, who was a Dominican as well as a physician and died in 1298 as Bishop of Cervia near Ravenna, wrote several treatises on the medical uses of arsenicals, alums and salts, all of which are lost—which is of no consequence. But he also wrote a treatise on surgery in which he disclosed a method developed by his father, likewise a physician, of preventing the festering of wounds by washing them with wine. We have, therefore, to consider the decline in empirical surgical knowledge between Theodoric and Lister, for the necessity of letting wounds become infected was an article of medical faith from the fifteenth to the nineteenth centuries.

Gilbert the Englishman, Chancellor of the University of Montpellier, in 1250 wrote, along with a number of miscellaneous medical treatises, a *Compendium medicinae*, which, true to its title, summarized available medical and surgical knowledge. It contained the first recorded awareness of the contagious nature of smallpox and of the impotence of drug treatment for cancer, for which Gilbert advised surgery. This was sensible but not particularly important. But Gilbert likewise advised travelers to drink only distilled water and for sea voyagers to eat fruit. Again we have apparently a partial decline in medical knowledge reaching into the eighteenth century, for only then was the necessity of these practices realized.

Borgognoni's discoveries were not lost because of the benighted stupidity of his age. Henry de Mondeville, who was born somewhere around 1270, studied medicine at Montpellier and Paris and then under Theodoric in Italy. He returned to France to become chief surgeon of the French armies during the reigns of Philip the Fair and Louis X. On the basis of his wide experience with the living laboratory of the French armies he wrote a surgical treatise. He had tried Borgognoni's ideas on treating wounds with the object of preventing infection and found that they worked. Not only must wounds, including operative incisions, not be probed, they must be washed only with wine. Dressings, thread and needles must be as clean as possible. In regard to Galen, he acknowledged his greatness, as even medieval convention demanded, but added the phrase of John of Salisbury, that even though we are pigmies and stand on the shoulders of the giants of the past, yet we still stand on their shoulders and can see further than they.

So medicine stood in the West when Niccolo da Reggio made the first Latin translation of Galen direct from the Greek, supposing, as d'Angelo supposed about Ptolemy, that he was making available a Classical treasure that need no longer be taken indirectly from the Arabic texts. Its effect was not immediate nor direct, but it proved to be disastrous. Late in the century, Guy de Chauliac, physician to Popes Clement VI, Innocent IV and Urban V, decided to write a surgical treatise. His only warrant for doing so—for he was a person of no intellectual capacity—was the one he stated himself, that having available Niccolo's translation of Galen, he was the first medical writer to enjoy the immense advantage of direct knowledge of the works of the Classical—as all supposed—master. Accordingly, all the new anatomical discoveries of the Italians were rejected and all the errors of Galen reintroduced. Worse still, since Galen thought suppuration of wounds necessary, the proved aseptic methods of Borgognoni and Mondeville were completely rejected. In fact, Guy's *Chirugia Magna* was little but a compilation from Galen with now and then an item from ibn-Sina. The style of the times soon took over from there. Guy was the voice of Galen and, therefore, just what the Renaissance wanted. Where Mondeville's real foundation for the work of Pasteur and Lister was never translated and never printed until as a historical curiosity in the nineteenth century, Guy's revival of supposedly Classical learning enjoyed extraordinary popularity. By the sixteenth century, it had been translated into French, Provençal, Catalan, Spanish, Italian, English, Dutch, Irish and Hebrew and before 1600 had been printed in innumerable editions all over Europe.[29]

[29] The Latin text: Venice 1498, 1499, 1500, 1519, 1546; Lyons 1537, 1559, 1572, 1585 and later.
Italian: Venice 1480, 1493, 1505, 1513, 1521 and later.
Dutch: Antwerp 1500, Leiden 1507, Amsterdam 1646.
Catalan: Barcelona 1492.
Spanish: Seville 1493, 1498.
English: (part only) London 1542, 1579.
(For French editions see Ed. Nicaise, *La Grande Chirugie*—Paris 1890).

Yet not even a mechanical reason drove the Renaissance into the deadly embrace of Galen. Though Mondeville's work was not printed, Borgognoni's was almost as widely translated as Guy's—Spanish, Italian, French, English, German and Hebrew before the height of the Renaissance—and even printed, though only in Italy.[30] This knowledge was not lost by accident. Under the whip of an intellectual fashion and in the face of concrete evidence, it was deliberately disregarded in professional and educated circles and then gradually forgotten. Yet it survived, almost like an old wives' superstition, in the self-medication of the common people.

To see the Renaissance and Reformation as two manifestations of the same retreat from the exacting moral and intellectual responsibilities of Western civilization is to run afoul of the dearest conventions of modern times. We revere these movements (with the sole exception of the view of Roman Catholics on the division of the church) as the source of those things of which we approve in the modern world. Furthermore an age, such as our own, which defines responsibility as reaction and irresponsibility as moral progress, could scarcely accept the notion that any other age should be subject to criticism for acting somewhat under these same definitions. Yet even so, we can only preserve our illusions by maintaining intact a distorted image of the Renaissance and Reformation. We refuse to admit the manifest connection between the witchcraft frenzy and the religious excitement and Bible fetishism of the Reformation. We refuse to see the intellectual shallowness of humanism and protect our treasured picture of the adolescent verbiage of so much Renaissance literature by ignoring the serious literature of the Middle Ages. We offer scientific incense to Copernicus, da Vinci, Kepler and Galileo, but ignore medieval scientific thought which had trained and inspired them and of which they were only some of the links to us. It would be absurd to say that there were not great accomplishments in the fifteenth and sixteenth centuries. These centuries were an age in the life of the West, and like all the rest of that life since the tenth century, had their great part in this immense enterprise. But the greatness lay not in the superficial clamor and garish show of the Renaissance, nor in the religious fever of the Reformation, not in the things of which the men of that age boasted, but in the things that they were and tried themselves to ignore. For in spite of their proclaimed purpose, they did continue and did develop the civilization of the West, not that of Hellas nor of Christian Byzantium. But it is not incumbent upon us to admire the men of that time for their follies, nor to forget that though the continuity of the West

---

[30] Latin text, Venice 1498, 1499, 1500, 1513, 1519, 1546. Similarly Gilbert's *Compendium* was printed at Geneva in 1508 and at Lyons in 1510, but all the fleets of the West continued to be rotted with scurvy and black water fever till far into the eighteenth century.

survived this turmoil, in the meantime one hundred and fifty years of humanism and superstition had flowed over Europe and the foundation of anarchy as the principle of Western international politics had been thoroughly laid.

What seems to have happened was indeed what the enthusiasts of democratic principles have pictured. There was a new urban, moneyed class. It had considerable power and some prestige, and with the invention of typography it probably furnished one of the chief markets for books. It went to school, but to the kind of school founded by Grotte's Brotherhood of the Common Life. It will be noted, in examining the Western thinkers discussed earlier, that almost all of them were clerics. Much of their lives, certainly the early years, were devoted to study—study no doubt of a large amount of rubbish but of sound thought and intricate reasoning as well. Not only were these men such students, but their audiences at university lectures and the readers of their manuscripts were such students also. Here and there some popularizers have been noted, and more existed, but in general, medieval writings were intended for a highly professional group. It was a group that had clerical duties, but the ecclesiastical life also offered time and opportunity to most of the original and speculative thinkers of the time. A similar situation has existed since the seventeenth century with the academic world of the great universities furnishing the basic group in which speculative thought has developed.

It is true that neither the church nor the universities have produced some of the most original and powerful thinkers of the West, but in their respective times they did furnish the body of competent, trained opinion without which the continuity of thought would have been lost and the great thinkers would have had neither background to understand nor an audience by whom they could have been understood.

With the new moneyed men of the fifteenth and sixteenth centuries, the situation was quite different. Like so many liberal moderns—for they were in fact the liberals of their time—they considered themselves educated with all the education that anyone needed, though their studies rarely exceed the trivium. They could read and write their vernaculars. Some could read Latin. They could do sums and read a multiplication table. They knew that Euclid had invented geometry, Galen medicine, and that natural science stemmed from Aristotle. This was the audience for the humanists of the Renaissance. Naturally, it was a popular doctrine that true wisdom and culture lay in writings that could be thoroughly understood on the basis of this education. Naturally, Swineshead's uniform and diform extension in latitude and Oresme's fractional exponents seemed like rubbish. "In quantum mechanics physical quantities or observables are not represented by ordinary variables, but by symbols which have no numerical value but determine the possible values of the observables in a definite way. . . . These symbols can be added and multiplied with the proviso that multiplication is non-commutative: AB is in general different from BA." Does this not sound like rubbish even on the basis of a modern non-technical education? (It is from one of Max Born's Oxford lectures on chance.) We would not say so only because the powerful tradition of modern science leads us to accept what we cannot understand if it bears the sacred imprimatur of science. That tradition was lacking in the Renaissance and the more democratic doctrine of humanism was obviously more comfortable.

Somewhat the same thing was true in the field of religious thought. The intricate reasoning of the twelfth and thirteenth century theologians required abstruse study. The understanding of the Bible derived by a graduate of the trivium was at once much easier and much more popular. Like humanism it was, therefore, equated with truth.

On one thing alone did the three great protagonists of Renaissance, Reformation and Counter Reformation agree. Erasmus, Calvin and Loyola, all three detested and all three bitterly condemned the College of Montagu at Paris where Jean Dullaert was teaching Buridan's doctrine of *impetus* and printing his books.

There is a current phrase that in all its ramifications can be applied to one subtle trait of both Renaissance and Reformation and thereby clarify to us moderns an aspect of these movements that we recognize but whose full significance we rarely ponder. In the life of the West these movements marked the first age of the common man. True, he was not yet in complete control of politics, not yet herded into depersonalized masses under the whip of irresistible publicity, not yet far removed from the traditions of honor and loyalty; but yet common, untrained and arrogant in ignorance, instinctively resisting the hard discipline of the West. We should not fool ourselves into supposing that the core and source of strength of Western civilization can ever win the conscious applause of the great bulk of Westerners. Unconsciously they live by and treasure the standards of their civilization, but the intellectual acknowledgment of these standards runs counter to so many demands of self-esteem and self-justification, of childish hopes and pathetic dreams that most men can never verbally make this acknowledgment even secretly to themselves.

For the historical personality of our society is not kindly toward the common man. Whatever lies within the easy grasp of everybody has never counted for much in the life of the West. Whatever has been easier to believe than to discover has never been what created the unique greatness of our society. Not the comforting satisfaction of inward belief, but the potential humiliation of outward fact has been the last standard of truth in the West. Ours has, therefore, been an esoteric, not a popular society, requiring for competence in every field of its life a degree of devotion and specialization that few, even from the West, have been able to give and probably none completely to enjoy. It has also been a society whose inward convictions have been at hopeless variance with the outward professions that the events of history have forced it to make. Thus it has destroyed the peace of mind of every able man of the West for a thousand years and required us to live under an inner tension, indeed with an inner sadness, so close does the West bring the structure of tragedy into its life. That men should at times revolt from this hard responsibility scarcely strikes us as unnatural. Indeed such revolts, for all their dangers, perform one invaluable function. They protect us from stagnation, from smug self-complacency which threatens all life that becomes too sheltered, too secure in the appearance of unchallengeable mastery. That we who live in an age of such revolt should admire our predecessors in retreat is equally natural. But we should not delude ourselves that our conduct and our admiration are in behalf of those modes of thought and goals of action by which the West stands, pattern and envy to the world.

Chapter 8:

The Politics of Hope and Disaster

THE PREAMBLE OF THE DECLARATION OF INDEPENDENCE was neither a hurried step nor a hasty draft. As far back as the previous December, Congress had declared the colonies independent of the power of Parliament so that the Declaration, weightily considered and as it did, applying only to the symbol of the crown, was not a practical but a moral document. It affirmed a view of history and appealed to the conscience as well as the nascent national pride of the Americans. The appeal to the conscience was a justification of the social revolution—not yet democratic—that accompanied the incipient nationalism of the struggle against Great Britain. For among the strongest partisans of the American cause were new possessors of estates seized from Tories or from suspected Tories, or from mere possessors of estates who, it was thought, might have become Tories.

"We hold these truths to be self evident: that all men are created equal and that they are endowed by their Creator with certain inalienable rights among which are life, liberty and the pursuit of happiness."

To an American, these words are so familiar that they are usually known by heart. But they are known as a block, not as words in sequence composing grammatically ordered thought. They seem to us to have a meaning, but the meaning is contained in the passage as a whole, not in the ordered summation of separate, intelligible parts. We take the entire sentence as a meaningful symbol. We do not read it as though it were a message from a stranger, the sense of which we had to ascertain for the first time. Yet it can be so read and when it is, there emerges a historical significance far greater than the justification of vague, optimistic egalitarianism for which this passage has so long been famous.

We are first told that some "truths" are to be enunciated, not facts—these follow later in the list of grievances against the British Crown. The preamble deals only with "truths." What is a truth? It is not the same as a fact nor is it admitted to be a hypothesis. It means something different from the adjectival use of the word, where the sense is simply correct in contrast to incorrect.[1] Thus to speak of "truths" is not the same as to speak of the abstraction "truth." Truth is a concept, but "truths" are propositions, specific, verbally formulated beliefs that are asserted to be true. They are what the language of an older day would have called articles of faith.

These truths, we are told, are self-evident, and here we again encounter an act of faith. The only things that are self-evident are those incapable of proof, those accepted by the mind not from outward evidence but from inward certitude. It is a process known to the religious as revelation and except that the deistic Jefferson lacked an accepted revelatory mechanism, such is precisely what "self-evident" means in this passage—revealed, perhaps, through the inspired writings of the eighteenth century philosophers.

The articles of faith that are revealed are two: that all men are created equal and that all are endowed with certain rights. Oddly, men are not said to be born equal, though the only way by which men appear in the world of politics and history is to be born into it from the womb of a woman. Here, however, they are created.

Probably the Declaration avoids saying that men are born equal because they manifestly are not. But if Jefferson did not deem it prudent or truthful to use the word "born," what sense did he desire to convey by the word "created?" Jefferson was not so slovenly a linguist that he supposed, as some moderns would read the passage, that one word was the indifferent synonym of the other. Yet, in the world of politics men are born. It is only in the universe of theology that man is created. But if the equality of all men is a divine creation applicable within the kingdoms of this world, it has been singularly ill-applied, and in that sense the mere political equality that Jefferson elsewhere taught would here credit only lawyers' pettifogging to the Creator of the Universe. Somehow no accurate sense seems applicable to the phrase.

With the rights with which the Creator endowed his creatures the sense is equally hard to define. That we are endowed with life seems almost redundant—we obviously have life while we live—but under no circumstances is our right to it inalienable. That it will soon be taken from us is the very exemplar of all things unarguably certain. What sense can Jefferson have intended in talking about an inalienable right to life? He could hardly

---

[1] In older English this was nakedly evident. Piers Plowman, for instance, uses the expression "false truths" for erroneous or deceitful opinions, and Locke, on whom Jefferson leaned so heavily, felt even the adjective could properly be applied only to verbal or mental statements, not to objective reality.

have meant merely that men assert the right not to have their lives arbitrarily taken from them by other men. That was hardly a novel proposition at any time in any society—civilized or primitive.

The rights of liberty and the pursuit of happiness seem to present less difficulty if we understand by inalienable not something that *cannot* be alienated, but something that ought not to be. But the seeming clarity is illusory. What difference is there between "liberty" and the "pursuit of happiness?" Presumably if a man enjoyed the first, he would use it for the second; if he were engaged in the second, it must be by reason of possessing the first. Further, what can the phrases mean in the humdrum world of ordinary life? They cannot mean "do whatever you like," for that is anarchy. If they mean "do whatever does not bother the powerful," that "right" has always existed and still exists, everywhere. Yet if they meant freedom to do what the new government allows but the old government forbade, that is the same thing.

The odd inability to find a precise sense in the preamble of the Declaration is not because it contains lofty philosophical ideals or outlines a goal towards which we should strive but of which we have naturally fallen somewhat short. That is not the difficulty. Even a lofty philosophy, if it bears any relation to reality, has somewhere a concrete meaning however abstruse the expression. The preamble is not abstruse. It is quite simple, but it is apparently meaningless.

But there is a meaning. If the verbal images are translated from the deistic jargon of the eighteenth century back into the theological concepts of the Middle Ages, if they are thought of as applicable not to an "ideal" condition in this world but to a "real" condition in the world to come, then all confusion and peculiar definitions vanish and the preamble becomes clear and intelligible.

"We hold these articles of faith to be the revealed truth: all souls are created equal and they are endowed by God with certain inalienable rights among which are immortality, free will and access to grace."

If these religious propositions are again translated, this time into the Medieval Latin in which they were developed, the connection is even more striking. In English, we do not customarily describe immortality as the "life of the soul," but such was the standard Latin phrase, *vita animae*. With "liberty" there is even the etymology of the word itself. "Free will" is *liber arbitrium* and in Medieval Latin one sense of *gratia* is almost a perfect translation of the word "happiness" as used in this passage, the goodness and joy of life.

Certainly Jefferson and his committee, John Adams, Franklin, Roger Sherman and Robert Livingston, did not knowingly draw the principles of their political morality from medieval theological formulations. No more were they aware that their political theories on the source of state power and on the legitimate objectives of state policy were the theories of Aquinas and Marsiglio of Padua. On the contrary, as has been often noted, they were floating on the stream of eighteenth century liberal thought, and neither they nor their contemporaries had any historically accurate notion of the sources of that stream. In the usual fashion of the eighteenth century they liked to ascribe Greek or Roman origins to the ideas of which they approved, and it would have been a profound shock for the liberal Jefferson had he discovered behind his great preamble not the togaed ghost of Tiberius Gracchus but the black-robed schoolmen of the Gothic Ages.

But the ignorance of the eighteenth century about the sources of its thought does not alter the historical fact of what those sources had been. No more than the sixteenth does the eighteenth century mark a break in the continuity of Western society. These eighteenth century liberal philosophers were dealing with hopes and opinions reaching them out of their own past, even though it was a past of which they were almost willfully unconscious. When they applied medieval considerations concerning the soul and the Kingdom of Heaven to the body and life of this world, it was not with any religious intention nor any awareness that they were seeking to apply ghostly standards to earthly matters. They were in search of moral justification for certain worldly ambitions, of their own, and of the groups in society with which they identified, if not themselves, at least their interests. They found this justification unconsciously in their forgotten heritage of religious thought which they applied to the only real object they could envisage: the kingdoms of this world. And that is essentially why their political thought seems so lofty and so utterly incapable of fulfillment.

Custom does not permit us to call these eighteenth century liberals what in historical perspective they really were: leftists. Nor is the objection based on a mere anachronism. It is unarguably offensive to link the treasured names of the past with the current crop of Soviet agents, partisans and apologists. But in this aspect of the question the Soviet Empire is not involved. Leftism is a genuine Western movement, in full development long before the present lords of the Kremlin captured the tottering apparatus of the Russian state. There are Levantine influences in it, largely from the Bible, but there are no traces of Russian. Even today when all effective action by the movement is firmly controlled in the interests of Soviet policy, it is still entirely a product of Western life. It is not the Russian angle that inhibits applying the name leftism to eighteenth century liberalism. It is the offense to convention.

Yet eighteenth century liberalism was in fact the direct intellectual and moral ancestor of modern leftism, and there is grave political importance in understanding the connection tying even the most modern liberalism and leftism to the derailed religious imagery of the eighteenth century philosophers. The connection is the greatest single element of intellectual strength in Western leftism. These religious images of the good life in the hereafter are the most highly authenticated set of principles in Western life. They have been woven into the fabric of our thought and literature for a thousand years. They are not always so completely and compactly translated to worldly affairs as they are in the Declaration, but idealistic, reform and revolutionary publicity has proclaimed all or part of these principles, sometimes in religious, sometimes in deistic or even atheistic, form ever since political operators began using mass public opinion as one of the levers of political action.

It is immaterial that the political movement operating under the moral authority of eighteenth century liberalism long since won control of all the states of the West. It is immaterial that this movement established in the seats of the mighty a new group of men and new methods of attaining power and wealth. Naturally these men then became "conservative." They had no desire for other individuals to apply against them the mechanics of mass appeal by which they had ousted their predecessors. But this has nothing to do with the continuity of the principles. Leftism considered as part of the history of thought is a body of doctrine, but in the affairs of life and politics it is a mechanism for organizing masses so that those who control the organization can destroy the current possessors of power and wealth and grasp these for themselves. Naturally the heirs of successful revolutionists of the past, violent or political, became the target of the present. It is a drama in which the leading roles are constantly being played by new understudies, but we should not lose track of the sweep of the play through excessive attention to the personalities in the cast. Nor should there be confusion because the technical means of power and wealth change from age to age, sometimes even within decades. Power is power whether it is obtained by heredity, possessions of money, elective office, control of a political organization or of a labor union. Wealth is wealth, whether under the wheel of time it is conferred by title or mere effective possession, whether it flows from land, factories, speculation or taxes, whether coveted objects are paid for with gold or bank credit, taken by simple seizure or acquired officially in the name of the state. These details of the ever-changing forms of wealth and power have no inner importance. Distinctions in regard to them are of consequence only for outward political purposes, to convince the naïve and the childish, to confuse the simple. The essential unity of leftism has come down to us through two centuries, the moral validation of earthly ambitions by unconscious appeal to the religious convictions of our past.

Despite the offense involved in calling eighteenth century liberalism by the accurate though anachronistic name of leftism, it is essential to do so in order to keep apparent the source of modern leftist thought. The modern form has become immensely more sophisticated and complex than its predecessor. It has different mechanisms both for reaching public opinion and bringing about political action. It has a different group of men in the masses on which it operates, men with somewhat different historical images and other emotional catch words than the masses of the eighteenth century. It has involved itself perhaps inextricably with the world-conquering ambitions of an alien empire. Also almost two hundred years have gone by and we are now far away from the last living nobility as a political power in the West. All these changes contribute to the bad manners and grotesque naïveté characteristic of modern leftism—its great skills are in gaining petty immediate advantage and on the stage of world politics, it would be comically inept if world politics were not so deadly and the source of such vast disasters. These things distinguish modern leftism from its eighteenth century predecessor, but its fundamental set of moral principles are the same. Its principles are the morality of the hereafter, and it professes that these principles can and must be applied to the affairs of the living.

In a profoundly irreligious time like ours, the pious will deny with indignation that this transference of religious values is inherently fraudulent. To recognize the imposture is to recognize that the function of religion is not to bring about the good life here on earth and this the pious of our day cannot do. What else can religion be for but to reform this world, since by modern practice and belief, if not by public admission, the hereafter counts for little? There is *only* this world and it must, therefore, be here that the good life is to be attained, even though a good life as defined by the holy canons. The last betrays the origin of the image. For the versions of the good life as envisaged by both the pious reformer and the atheist leftist, while they differ in minor details, are alike in that this imagined life resembles nothing that has ever been lived but of old was forseen beyond the grave. In later times, it has been proclaimed but never approached and its principles are at variance with everything that we know or can estimate about the behavior of men on this earth. Its perfect form, which is supposed to be the ultimate goal, is complete equality, complete sinlessness—the categories of sin differ but each advocate has his own list of sins that are to cease—complete lack of personal responsibility in the beneficent embrace of the state, whose divine attributes are proclaimed even in the words used to describe it. And like the Kingdom of Heaven, when once established, this good life is to endure unchanged forever. No evil manipulator can arise within its happy ranks, no outward wickedness can assail it. The reign of Satan will be at an end.

This perverted religious image has been the moral driving force of the great social movement that since the eighteenth century has made the political history of the West. Whether we call it liberalism or leftism is hardly more than a matter of fashion, or perhaps of whether for each of us the process seems to have culminated in our own success or is still regarded as the vehicle of our unfulfilled ambitions. The movement is not thereby made diverse and the men who have ridden it to power have each in turn ousted their predecessors and the masses to which it appeals have generation by generation become larger and their level of political intelligence lower. Not only has the population of the West increased greatly but the proportion of urban and technically literate people has increased even more. But it is all one movement. The fact that the leftists and industrialists of today have almost destroyed the power of the bankers of yesterday, and both have destroyed the merchants and landholders of 1800, does not break the movement into contradictory parts. Every revolution is a process— among other things—of destroying the early revolutionists, and the process is the same whether it is on the century scale of great movements, or the annual scale that governs the personalities during the phases of open violence. That the Mountain destroyed the Girondists, that Robespierre guillotined Danton and then was himself guillotined by the surviving members of the Convention does not make several contradictory movements of the French Revolution.

Actually the time scale of contemporary leftism is not abnormal compared to other great political and intellectual movements in the West. The development of Protestantism from Ruysbroeck and Groote to Luther occurred over two centuries, and the conversion of the feudal political structure of the West to the centralized dynastic states of the sixteenth century occupied about the same years. The great period of the dynastic states, the struggle for oceanic empire and the firm establishment of Great Britain, was a process of about the same length, occupying roughly the years from the destruction of the dream of a Hapsburg continental empire late in the sixteenth century to the French Revolution. It is only because we are intimately involved in the politics of leftism that we see details, above all details of the internal struggles for personal power, enlarged out of all proportion.

For two centuries this movement has been the religion of the irreligious. There is no need to discount the political effectiveness of the familiar mechanics of mass politics, the appeal to special group interests, the power of a well-organized minority in an evenly divided electorate, the use of money and intimidations of all kinds. These are all effective pieces of political machinery and without them, the political history of the West would be quite different from what it has been. But these are only possible against the background of certain moral presuppositions about society, and it is these latter that the secular leftist movement has furnished.

Of course, these two centuries of liberalism have not accomplished the moral goals of the movement. They have neither leveled society nor abolished crime nor established peace. Many great things have been done in these two centuries and many formal propositions of leftism written into law and enforced in custom, but not the great moral principles. It was, to be sure, fashionable to explain this failure by the assurance that we are on the way and that distinct progress toward all goals could be observed in comparison with our society in 1750. Today, we can see that even outwardly this can only be true of the egalitarian goal of leftism and that even here it applies chiefly in formal legal status, and in matters of manners and methods of personal address between individuals. So far as the substance of power is concerned, the gulf that separates Walter Reuther from an obscure mechanic, John L. Lewis from an unknown miner, or the President from a simple voter, is at least as great as any that existed in the eighteenth century.

It should not be surprising that liberalism has failed to reach its declared goals. Indeed, it is a little simple to expect or even hope that it some day will. All that we know of human life assures us that this movement can be used to do many things, but this it cannot do. It is not that these goals can be shown causally to be unattainable. In a proper way of speaking, they do not exist. They are only concepts and images of the hereafter and they, therefore, can have no existence on this earth. They are almost like those empty verbal propositions that can be so readily composed: "The circular edge of the square is a true triangle." Each part has some meaning somewhere in the world of thought, but the grammatically assembled whole has no meaning. What it is talking about in perfect grammar simply does not exist.

Almost the only internal politics of the modern West is leftist, the leftism of the oligarchy of money against the leftism of the oligarchy of labor, the leftism of the internal struggles within the different oligarchies. And because this is so it seems almost absurd to question the moral foundation of the whole movement. After all, there is nothing else that has political reality in our time. Since the only domestic politics of the West is today leftist politics, the struggle of the ambitious leftists of today against the successful leftists of yesterday, what good can be accomplished by suggesting that men examine the moral foundation of the whole movement?

Furthermore, to examine the wide divergence between political events and declared political purposes during the past two hundred years and to seek to question rather sharply the validity in wordly life of the declared purposes, suggests doubt about the wisdom of the events themselves. Nothing so foolish is involved. Judging by our own earlier history and by the history of other societies, something like the major political events of the past two hundred years was inevitable so long as the West remained a living society. That the new oligarchies would rise to political rulership was inescapable so long as these oligarchies came into existence at all. Yet the details of their rise to power need not have been precisely what they were, and a sense of the wise and unwise managing of these details is what can be of political value today. Yet these cannot be understood unless the moral basis of the movement is understood. Otherwise pseudo-moral and emotional viewpoints are introduced and the political successes of the past are hopelessly confused with the disasters of the present, since both proclaimed the same moral objective.

Furthermore, in the long history of the West the individuals who have risen and fallen in these two hundred years of leftist politics matter little more than the personal fates of kings and ministers, bishops, and burgesses in the centuries of feudal and dynastic politics. That the Reuthers and the Rockefellers have ousted the Morgans and the Vanderbilts is no more a disaster to the West than that the former ousted the Livingstons, the Carrolls and the Randolphs or that these in turn had ousted the peers of Stuart and Georgian England. This is the nature of a living society. Sometimes it seems that one method of changing the rulership of society is preferable to another, that for instance the English custom of absorbing the new men into the old forms gave—at least for a time—a stronger and more gracious society than the French method of violently abolishing the old forms, or the American of abolishing the forms legally and attempting to practice them privately—what we call "society." But these differences are perhaps matters of taste, for none of the great states of the West has been able to come through these two centuries with even a second-rate group of rulers in control of its politics. All are in the hands of political imbeciles and have been so for more than a generation. All have a public opinion saturated with the moral principles of leftism.

This movement has been more than the religion of the irreligious. True to the style of the age in which it flowered, it has borne the mark of popularity. It has been the political philosophy of the common man, the moral foundation of the concepts of progress and political optimism that have set the style and outward purpose of the public life of these two centuries. Under its mandate there have occurred those great accomplishments of political progress with which we are familiar to the point of boredom. There is point neither in retelling these manifest changes in Western public and private life nor in seeking totally to discredit them because of their fallacious base or because unadmitted seeds of disaster were sown during the harvest of democratic progress. Like all Western history, these two centuries of liberalism present the irresolvable tensions, the inseparable benefits and dangers that have made the complex greatness of the West. Nor have there been absent elements of irony, profitless as it is to note the ironic; for here what purports to be an utterly materialistic interpretation of human life is disclosed to be based on the forgotten transcendentalism of our ancestors and a school of thought that urges us to despise history foresees unrolling into the long future only an image of life once conjured in the past. But there is profit, as these two hundred years draw to an end, as the shadows of potential disaster stretch longer and darker over the society of the West, in seeing whether and how often this political philosophy of the comman man has achieved neither the goal that it proclaims nor the tangible advantage sought by its momentary promoters, but merely the ruinous consequences of sheer incompetence. For the political operations conducted in the name of this philosophy of democracy, almost generation by generation have brought new men to the seats of power and it is a proper subject for examination whether the moral justifications by which they persuaded others of the virtue of their rise did not blind these men themselves to the needless follies that both the logic and the emotions of their political philosophy led them to commit. Perhaps the most perilous of all political dangers is that men who must lie in order to govern may come in time to believe their own lies, and in the great political crises of these two hundred years—crises that have marked the rise and the decline of the age of liberalism, the French and American Revolutions and the two World Wars—this has been their most characteristic political trait.

The three great wars of the first sixty years of the eighteenth century came to a close with the French Empire shattered and the method of dynastic politics no longer the paramount instrument of Western politics.

The British Empire became the principal military power in the West, disguised though this was by standing on a maritime foundation, and mercantile politics the prevailing method. Enrichment by commerce became the accepted mode of personal advancement and this commerce stood in its final foundation upon the colonial trade. In England, the governing families, largely of the Stuart and Georgian peerage, partly shared in this trade themselves and partly accepted into their restricted group the most effective of the new mercantile families. In France, however, the nobility, though it still possessed vast legal privileges, had long ceased to govern. Instead, it maintained an aloof and social superiority toward both the *nouveaux riches* of commerce and the *noblesse de robe*, the higher officials of the governing bureaucracy. In British America, as in England, commerce became the chief means of becoming rich and powerful though being a newly settled country, land as a source of great wealth was still available to new men. In the other Western states, there was as yet little mercantile wealth, and the landed gentry and nobility remained the monopolists of political power. In Spanish lands, there was also the hierarchy of the Spanish church as an immensely powerful political factor, and in northern Italy there were the old merchant families of bygone times, still locally of consequence, but of little weight in the politics of Europe.

The rise of the new men in England was accompanied by the sudden appearance of the literature of enlightenment and political liberalism. This began rather soberly in England and was taken up extravagantly in France. What it really meant, when the sense is distilled out of the confused transference of medieval religious concepts, was that success was more than coronets and great wealth than Norman blood. True to its ghostly origin, it was cast in universal terms, but both reader and writer saw only themselves as the concrete equivalent of the universal "man" whose rights were so clearly discerned. All of it boils down to one practical idea: the rich are as good as the peerage.

In England, where the rich were, in fact, becoming as good as the peerage, some sense of political responsibility and restraint survived in this literature of moral justification. In France where the idle nobles rebuffed the new men, and where neither possessed any mechanism of political power, this literature flowered with neither responsibility nor restraint. Since there seemed not the remotest chance that either reader or writer would ever have to take the risk of carrying out any of these wonderful ideals in actual governmental practice, no sobering second thought bothered anyone. Thus there grew up what we would today call an "informed public opinion," a talkative, literary group which knew exactly what ought to be done about everything but no member of which could be responsible for doing it. Yet irresponsible as this clamor was, it was not without effect on the governing bureaucracy and directly and indirectly on the person of the king. It can be discerned in the folly of the War of the Austrian Succession, where this same informed public knew that Austria was the hereditary enemy. A few intelligent people foresaw that the ultimate danger to France lay in a powerful Germany built up around Prussia and in a British maritime empire. But all the intellectuals knew better. They hated reactionary Austria. From reasons of political theory they admired liberal, mercantile England and efficient, anti-Catholic Prussia. Under the pressure of these views expressed in the innumerable pamphlets of the time—the eighteenth century version of a press campaign—the idiot alliances of that war were concluded, the French navy allowed to deteriorate, and Prussia immensely strengthened at the expense of Austria.

True to her interests rather than to her liberal principles, England eventually sided with Austria, and in the end France invested eight years of war only to acquire a great increase of her unwieldy internal debt. The episode was perhaps the first example of the operation of democratic foreign policy in any Western state. Like so many of these, the unforeseen consquence was not long in arriving; the crushing defeat of France in the Seven Years' War at the hands of Prussia and England, the loss of India, Canada, the Mississippi Valley, the last of the French islands in the West Indies except Haiti, the destruction of the French merchant marine and the ruin of the navy. So far as the interests of France were concerned, her support of the revolting British colonies in 1777 was simply an unsuccessful attempt to reverse the disasters of the Seven Years' War. Napoleon's oceanic policies were the same. Yet some fifty years afterwards when the French intellectuals at last held responsible political power as the Girondists of the early years of the Convention, the wisest policy they could devise was to start a war against tyranny personified in the throne of Austria. Perhaps there was even a trace of this moss-grown popular image in the policies of the Third Republic leading up to the first World War, for no political considerations could have led France to seek or permit the destruction of Austria-Hungary. Financial advantage to banking and industrial interests may have been served, and undoubtedly the verbiage of international ideals, self-determination and the ending of monarchies—but the tangible welfare of France was not benefited by turning the Danube basin into the anarchy of paper theory-states to which Nazi Germany and then the Soviet Empire fell heir.

The government of the Kingdom of France during the last fifty years of its life is dealt with rather awkwardly by our accepted history. The battle cry of the French Revolution was that it overthrew tyranny, and since we consider that Revolution a necessary step in the rise of democracy, we feel bound to acknowledge at least this much of its own evaluation of itself. The difficulty is that examples of tyranny in the reigns of Louis XV and Louis XVI are hard to find. There were great social gulfs between the nobility and the peasants and urban craftsmen, and there were what the historians call "inequities" in the tax structure. But since the equity of any given tax structure depends on the personal view of each taxpayer and non-taxpayer, without any possibility of objective establishment, and since even modern democratic practice has not succeeded in forcing egalitarianism, neither of these objections seems an example of unbearable tyranny. In fact, by the Jeffersonian analysis that the best governments are those that govern least, it would be necessary to conclude that the reigns of Louis XV and XVI furnished the finest governments ever known in the West. Paralysis, not tyranny, was the prime quality of both reigns, particularly that of Louis XVI. Over and over necessary administrative measures were vetoed by the Parliament of Paris or their enforcement effectively suspended by one of the provincial Parlements. Incompetents with a claque among the innumerable political pamphleteers could not be removed from office. Taxes could not be collected nor decrees enforced. The greatest paralysis of all was fiscal. The exemption from direct taxation enjoyed by the nobility—once a valid distinction when they furnished to the crown military and civil service at their own cost—could not be ended nor could the richer commoners be stopped from acquiring patents of nobility simply to escape the income tax. The French nobility had become that useless and dangerous social appendage, an aristocracy.[2]

The Estates General had not developed into the equivalent of the British Parliament. France had never become a republic of the nobles and country squires posing as a titular monarchy. In France the government was the royal bureaucracy restricted by ancient customs and provincial privileges, deriving all the authority that it had from the person of the monarch, to be sure, but by no means possessed of unlimited power. In essence, the restrictions on royal power that existed in England existed likewise in France. They had come down in both from feudal times when the king's powers were those of feudal custom and only the consent of his feudal tenants could give him more. But where in England Parliament, as the organ of the feudal tenants, used its possession of these reserved powers to become itself the font of authority, in France these reserved powers were held by nobody. The king was absolute in the fields where custom permitted him to govern. In other fields there was neither government nor organ of state that could assign these powers to the king or exercise them itself. There were only the Parlements which could not govern nor grant power, but could always veto its extension.

France was rich but, denied an adequate revenue, the government was bankrupt. Its expenses were far from disproportionate to the wealth of France yet it was literally powerless to increase the taxes—hardly an attribute of tyranny. Even the onset of the Revolution was the act of this government that could not govern. To call the defunct Estates General

---

[2] It has always been implicitly evident that though often confused, the words "nobility" and "aristocracy" are not synonyms. "Aristocracy," brought into the language like its equally dishonest cognate "democracy" by conscious theorizing and deliberate adaptation from Greek, is absurd by its etymology. Under no circumstances do "the best" rule, nor is a nobility ever "the best." When it exists, it is simply the hereditary group holding the political power in a community. Quite properly language revolts at calling a group "noble" after it loses the essential function that made it a nobility. For this reason the word "aristocracy" is useful if its meaning, not its etymology, is attended to. The same remark, of course, applies to "democracy" as the name not of rule by the people, which never exists, but of rule by the managers of the people, whether they wear crowns, or hold formally elective office, or rule from no official position at all.

without a mechanism of election, without the least notion of what its powers were or what actions it was to take, was not a belated restoration of ancient, usurped rights but an act of political suicide. But the eighteenth century liberals ignored these facts. Such facts were historical not reasonable. To the liberals it was sufficient to declare the ancient Estates General to be what it was not and never could be, what in fact no elective body of any kind could ever be—the government. In their superficial misunderstanding of history they did not recognize that the British Parliament was not the government of England but the conference committee of the great families that ruled England. The government of England was the apparatus of state, and control of this apparatus, not its destruction, was the objective of parliamentary politics. All this was overlooked in the liberal enthusiasm of Paris in 1789, though fortunately not completely in Philadelphia three years before. On the assemblage of the Estates General, the old royal bureaucracy ceased to be the government and the Estates became it, without the least idea of how to govern, nor what to govern for, nor possessed of any technical machinery for issuing commands or enforcing them. The partial anarchy of the king's government was succeeded by complete anarchy. And then followed what always follows anarchy, the organization of means of self-seeking power, in this case the "sections," the organized mobs of Paris recruited from the growing mass of destitute and ruined men, a mass that did not exist in 1789 but resulted from the laxity of the government, the commercial disasters of anarchy, the flight of the emigrées and the worthlessness of the currency. "Une immense populace accountumée depuis une année à des succés et à des crimes," so Mirabeau himself described Paris in the late fall of 1790. Things were not much different throughout all France.

The picture of an aroused populace spontaneously rising for its rights still finds a place in our image of that Revolution, though the picture itself is known to be false. All the famous "popular" riots of the Revolution, the storming of the Bastille (July 14, 1789), the forced residence of the king at Paris (October 6, 1789), the overthrow of the king and the Girondist-dominated Legislative Assembly (August 10, 1792), all were the work of mobs specifically organized for the purpose. All were possible because each of the governments in office at the time feared to take the easy steps to prevent them: troops under the command of the government itself, not of the Jacobin-dominated municipality of Paris, timely arrests of the men who organized these mobs. Always each government went to the guillotine as the next group to the left seized power, until in final desperation the last survivors of the Convention, fearful of their own lives at the hands of Robespierre, attacked the problem of dealing with the "people" at its source: they seized the organizers of the sections, the men who could bring the mobs into the streets, Santerre and Hanriot. That day Robespierre fell, 9 Thermidor An II (July 27, 1794).

But all these were incidental operations in the struggle for personal political power which for more than five years had spread bloodshed and destruction throughout France. They had nothing to do with the deep political objective of the Revolution which was simply the attainment of power by men of money. It has been the fashion of leftists since Marx to picture the sweep of the Revolution up to Thermidor as a bid for power by the "workers" and the Thermidorian reaction as a bourgeoisie counter-revolution. This was not so, for in that time no politically powerful group stood to the left of the men of money. The organized oligarchy of labor did not then exist and the "extremism" of Danton, Marat and Robespierre was the extremism of demagoguery appealing not to existing powerful interests in society but to a temporary, dissolute and partly hired mob. The revolution of money could not be overthrown so long as there remained a France, neither by Napoleon nor all the powers of Europe because it represented the achievement of political power by that group which had come to dominate the personal lives of Frenchmen. But the overthrow of the personal managers of mere mobs was a simple matter once the mechanism of mob pressure was understood and once a government acquired sufficient nerve to take the necessary simple steps. But it could have been accomplished as easily in 1789 as in 1794 without the destruction of the historical forms of society, without the terror, without the long wars that the Girondists began and even Napoleon could not win.

Nowhere does the dreadful political inexperience of the new men show more sadly than in the naïve theoreticians who composed the new Legislative Assembly of 1791, a group which then and in the later Convention has passed into tradition under the name of Girondists. Almost to a man, they were members of the well-to-do, moneyed class. As a class, they had already attained power and as individuals it was theirs to exercise. They had already converted the ancient kingdom into a constitutional monarchy. They had already ended the archaic privileges of the aristocracy. Title to the soil of France had already been very largely vested in those who used it. But these liberals had been born and reared on eighteenth century rhetoric, and they believed that words and concepts were the masters of political reality. Like Louis XVI himself they could not grasp the nature of power, that however disguised its exercise, it stands in the last analysis on the use of force. Against the organized, domestic violence of the ambitious they deployed the weapons of oratory and political maneuvers. Against the military force of foreign states they hurled the Declaration of the Rights of Man. They disliked the French monarchy, even in limited constitutional form, because it was historical, not rational, and because the king opposed them on two points, their strong anti-clericalism and their flippant indifference to the dangers of foreign war. Again from a lack of understanding of the nature of political power, the Girondists could not comprehend the function of the monarch in the state, and in pursuit of their concepts and their verbal animosities they sought to destroy the king without the least awareness—until they reached the guillotine—that once the monarchy was gone, nothing stood between the Girondists themselves and the insatiable ambition of the men on their left, men who used rhetoric as they did, who as willingly profited from mob violence as they did, but who knew what the Girondists ignored, that mobs are not ruled by appetite and oratory, but by organization.

In the meantime the Girondists chose as their means of destroying the king's position a foreign war. They thought it would be popular since they talked—and probably thought—in terms of "tyrants" and "liberated peoples" and apparently supposed that these words corresponded with political facts. Lacking any real knowledge of politics, they knew that what was said about affairs was what was so about them. Just as in 1740, all the educated knew that Austria was the enemy of France, and a "tyranny" to boot; that Frederick the Great's Prussia and merchantile England were "liberal" states favorable to the rise of moneyed men like the Girondists. Everyone could see that a war against Austria—which the king bitterly opposed—would solve all their problems.

Louis XVI had never asserted a right to oppose the great constitutional changes in 1789. He had not even used his legitimate power to check the growing anarchy. His attitude towards the new men was one of indolent disdain and weak inconsistency, not firm political opposition. But he saw foreign policy as a French not a constitutional question and as one in which he had a right and a constitutional duty to have an opinion. And under the Constitution of 1791, he was correct. But neither his last-minute wisdom nor the legality of his position prevented war nor saved his life and throne. His belated awakening to political facts in a world of rhetoric, his concern for the welfare of the French state in a world of armed states, was represented in the prevailing demagoguery as the foreign influence of his queen, Marie Antoinette, aunt of the emperor. The campaign of the Girondists to discredit the king succeeded thoroughly. They declared the war they desired in April, 1792, and the mob of August, 1792, in accordance with Girondist expectations and Girondist slogans destroyed the monarchy. But it was a Jacobin-controlled mob and brought to power men who promptly destroyed the Girondists, while the war they had so cheerfully started as a piece of domestic political tactics was waged throughout Europe and on the oceans for twenty-two years and reduced France to a never-acknowledged, at times an unwilling, but in essential questions of foreign affairs, an actual vassal of England.

From the point of view of a modern, living in a society where money is an admitted political power, yet who sees about him the possessors of such power cooperating in enterprises designed, though never proclaimed, to render money itself politically powerless, one of the most fascinating figures in the French Revolution was the king himself. Our conventional accounts of that Revolution rarely go beyond dismissing him as incompetent—which he was. They do not ponder the type and source of incompetence that harried this last descendant of a line of kings whose political management had been sometimes poor, sometimes brilliant, but on the balance of eight hundred years always successful and had thereby created the French state and the France we know. So much turned on the character and decision of this one man, so much of the modern West has been marked by the events and the memories of the French Revolution, that we cannot wisely ignore the character and training of this king who, though not the author of that Revolution, was certainly responsible for its catastrophes.

Louis XVI was a liberal. True, the political platitudes of 1774 differed in phraseology from those of our day but this identifies him only as an old-fashioned liberal as it equally identifies Roland and Danton. There is also the vague feeling, handed down from the Jacobin fiction, that merely by being king he must *ex officio* have been a tyrant and, therefore, not possibly a liberal. But these points are irrelevant. All that needs clarification in order to see the liberalism of Louis XVI is an aspect of liberalism itself. Like almost every doctrine, liberalism has both an active and a passive form. It is a useful instrument for those who manage it, but it is also the master of those who believe it. Not all liberals seek to use its methods of manipulating public opinion to gain power for themselves or for the group with which they identify their interests. Most of them are among those whose opinions are thus manipulated. All liberals, to be sure, are convinced that they have arrived at this viewpoint by the independent application of their own critical judgment to the objective facts of life and history. They suppose that they have attained this viewpoint—which they like to fancy as esoteric, not the most commonplace conventionality of the educated—by their own mental efforts and that it represents not only truth and public virtue but the protection and advancement of their own earthly welfare. But this is evidently not so, either concerning the consequences of liberal politics or the considerations, practical and psychological, that lead men to become liberals. Like adherents to other conventional doctrines, most men who adhere to liberalism do so because they have been taught to do so, by their parents, or by their teachers, or by the social and intellectual environment in which they flourish. Louis XVI became a liberal under the influence of all three and by the time he was faced with the responsibility of government, he was too firmly molded to change.

Francois de Salignac de la Mothe Fénelon, (1651—1715) Archibshop of Cambrai, does not today enjoy the fame of Rousseau and Voltaire as one of the founders of modern political thought. Certainly he was a more pious Roman Catholic than the other founders of liberalism, and the France that emerged from the Revolution was not the France he set forth as an ideal. But the revolutionary philosophers of 1791, when they placed his statue beside that of Jean Jacques Rousseau on the façade of the Pantheon at Paris judged better than the moderns. Not the completeness of Fénelon's liberalism but where it took effect and the enduring influence it exerted were what made it important. Fénelon was the tutor and life long advisor to the Duke of Burgundy, grandson of Louis XIV and father of Louis XV. Though Burgundy himself never reigned, and though Louis XV showed little influence from Fénelon's thought, the Duke of Burgundy had nevertheless firmly implanted this form of pious liberalism in the royal family. Louis XVI's father, estranged son of Louis XV and again a dauphin who never reached the throne, was brought up in this tradition, and despite the scepticism of his father, openly used Fénelon's *Télémaque* as a manual for the education of the future Louis XVI. After his death, the boy, trained to bitter hostility towards the vices and worldly empiricism of his grandfather, grew up in the guard of his five maiden aunts, pious ladies as saturated with genteel optimism and political innocence as anyone in France.

What Fénelon taught was the early eighteenth century equivalent of modern liberal internationalism. Political virtues were given a more Christian cast than is today the fashion, but otherwise there was little difference. Man as Fénelon saw him was not an evil, corrupt, ambitious and ruthless animal. He was by nature good, kindly, pious and civic-minded. All that was needed to bring out these virtues were suitable institutions, institutions of education, government and international concord, all of which were to operate by the rational benevolence of all concerned. As a result, he saw no need for a state capable of governing, either monarchic or of any other sort. Perhaps the idea of such a state never occurred to him, since it could be required only to deal with men of contrary and hence, by definition, evil will, and in Fénelon's pious rationalism no such thing could exist under the beneficent institutions that he envisaged. His ideal for the French state was a hierarchy of harmonious councils, local and provincial, heading up to the Estates General, councils that would convey to the pious, ever-rational monarch the cooperative will of the people—

but also assess and collect the taxes. That the ambitious or contrary-minded could ever destroy this national harmony, or foreign states ever disturb its concord, did not enter his calculations. He never realized that his multiple layers of debating societies, empowered not to govern but solely to cripple the finances and administration of the state, could end only in anarchy and revolution. He did not live long enough to see almost exactly what he planned come to pass at the assemblage of the Estates General in April, 1789.

Beneath Fénelon's political imaginings lay the conviction, which better became an archbishop than it does a modern agnostic, but even today underlies every form of liberalism, that all men are equal before God and the good life of universal egalitarian meekness is required by Christian principles. Since this is so, it is wrong to have a society in which some men, even good men, prevail over others equally good. In the politics of celestial rationalism, good prevails over evil; it has no conflict with other good. Fénelon, true to the core of liberal thought, thus could not grasp the essential nature of the state: that it must be a mechanism for carrying out the concerted will of some, even against the concerted will of others equally virtuous. To Fénelon force was at no point the root of all politics, the indispensable attribute of every sovereignty.

Even had Louis XVI not been deliberately educated in such beliefs, he would have required extraordinary strength of character and rare political sagacity to have escaped them. They expressed the verbal consensus of all that was brilliant and fashionable in the upper circles of French society. Re-enforcing them was that imprecise but undoubted sense of guilt, which troubled the French aristocracy as it troubles the modern rich, which, in fact, gnaws at the political judgment of all men who enjoy advantages but are not required personally to exercise power and responsibility to retain them. In this atmosphere and against this intellectual background, the youthful training in the ideals and political theories of Fénelon remained the governing force in the character of this bewildered king. He never forgot that once when a boy, his father brought him the parish record whereon was recorded his baptism and showed, preceding his own name, that of a simple artisan. "Learn from that," said the Dauphin, "that all men are equal by natural right and in the eyes of God who created them." It was a lesson that the last authentic king of France was never able to forget. In his own eyes he represented only another human being, not a unique man whom the accidents of birth had charged with responsibility for the historic French state. On the last fatal night of the French monarchy, August 10, 1792, when Santerre's mob was debating whether to storm the Tuilleries, the king would not have it defended. Who was he to kill fellow Frenchmen? Even after he abandoned the palace and the loyal troops that guarded it—he had refrained from sending for many more that ringed Paris—and sought refuge from an armed mob among the debaters of the Assembly; even then when his troops, attacked and by habit counter-attacking, found the whole "aroused people" suddenly disappearing and the Jacobin citadel, the Hotel de Ville itself, practically in their hands, even then the king ordered them to desist. He wanted no one killed for his sake. And so in the morning the king was the prisoner of the unresisted mob, but so was the Assembly and so was the Convention that soon followed it. For almost two years the masters of this mob were the masters of France, which they could not govern but did their best to sack. When the king refused to defend himself, he did more than refuse to defend the French monarchy. He also refused to defend the continuing existence of the French state, and from the consequence of that disaster France and the whole West have never recovered. To the end, the king could see himself only as a private person. In the secret recesses of his own mind, all men *were* created equal and to be King of France meant only to hold an empty title.

In 1815, the series of wars for the imperium of the West had been waged with only brief interruptions for seventy-five years. Violent revolutionary situations of one sort or another had been going on for forty. At last peace and formal reaction came together. But the reaction was formal only, as none knew better than the arch-reactionary Metternich, who felt that Europe was doomed and that all he could do was try to hold its society together as long as possible. But among the victors of these great wars—which in the sweep of Western history should perhaps be accounted the first World War—Prussia, England and the United States, Metternich's pessimism was premature. The ruling groups in each felt themselves possessed of a great future, England as mistress of commerce and of the seas, Prussia as the hard core of a new Germany, the United States as the lord of a vast, rich and undeveloped continent. And so each pursued its own road to the ultimate and fateful crossing a hundred years later.

But along the eastern borders of Western civilization, these forty years of revolution had brought a change more profound for the life of Western society than even the principles of the Rights of Man, though in time the two were to be fused. Russia as a power factor in the politics of the West had at last come into existence.

Ever since the days of Ivan III (1462—1505), a Russia had been in existence in the form of the dominions of the Grand Dukes, afterwards Tsars, of Muscovy, once tributaries of the Tartar Khans. A far earlier Russia, that of the Viking princes of Novgorod and Kiev, become in time completely Slav, had troubled the Lithuanians and the Poles, the Teutonic knights along the Baltic coast and now and then the Swedes. But no Russia, neither that of Vladimir of Kiev nor that of Ivan III and his successors, had ever been a factor in the civilization or the politics of the West, nor could it be said to have had a civilization of its own. Its intellectual life was non-existent. The complexity of its economy consisted of a few emporia where its own primitive raw materials were exchanged for the fabricated products of the three great civilizations which touched the edges of this vast semi-wilderness: China, the Levant and the West. Its religion in the form of the Russian Orthodox Church had been derived from Byzantium during the centuries of worldly glory of that Levantine power, and was little more than the fetishes of medicine men whose magic rites were performed under the formulae of Greek Orthodoxy. In time, however, these rites were to become powerful enough to make acceptance of the Russian Church the sufficient and exclusive determinant of Russian nationality.

This Ivan, who was only less "The Terrible," than his grandson Ivan IV, was for Russia what Clovis was for the West. He created the Russian people as Clovis created the Frankish—recalling what the name still means outside the West. Back of both there had been tribes and tribal names and the confusion of fractured politics. After them there existed, and continued to exist, an enduring relation between a biological group and its political organization. Even in the time scale of subsequent developments there is a certain analogy. From Ivan III to Peter the Great a long era of disorder and civil strife corresponds to the Merovingian times in Gaul. From Peter the Great to Stalin there extend something over two centuries of Russian consolidation, expansion, immitation, yet withal increase in Russian self-consciousness, comparable in some ways to the two centuries from Charles Martel to Otto the Great, though to be sure, the first Russian analogue of Charlemagne (or of Charles Martel) appears to be Stalin himself, who bears some resemblances to the Carolingians but none to the Saxon. Yet considering the different personalities of the two societies, if Russia is the beginning of such a society, and above all the very different environments of the infancy of each, the differences are less notable than the resemblances.

Ivan III and Clovis not only created their respective peoples; each founded the great symbol of the future society built by this people. Where Clovis by his conversion made the Latin Church for centuries the rallying point and symbol of the West, Ivan III by his dramatic marriage to Sophie Palaeologus, landless and penniless heiress of the last Byzantine dynasty, established the long-enduring symbol of Russia, the transformation of Moscow from a mere city to the sacred, historic emblem of imperial power. It has been a symbol which even today hidden in Communist phraseology still remains the ethos of action wherever the Russian banners fly, Moscow the holy city of the world, the third Rome, true and only heir of the Caesars and the *basileis*, guardian of the past, promise of the future.

Like every primitive and barbarian people, the inhabitants of the Russia of those times, essentially the upper valleys of the Dnieper and the Volga, imported from their civilized neighbors such of the crafts of the different civilizations as they could absorb and use. They were too remote from China—their contacts were at secondhand through the Mongols—to acquire much from that distant and indirect source, so that prior to the late fifteenth century they copied the Levant, above all the Christian Levant of Byzantium. The motifs of their primitive arts, the form of their religion, their letters, all came from Constantinople. But with the fifteenth century the decline of the Levant and the rising civilization of the West gave a new pattern for their masters to hate and to copy. Ivan III was the first of the many masters of Russia who sought in the West for weapons to use against the West. Under him Pietro-Antonio Solario of Milan tore down the wooden palisades and built the great crenelated stone walls of Moscow and the huge gate of the Kremlin opening on Red Square. Under Ivan, Paoli Debrossis equipped the Russian troops for the first time with firearms, even artillery, and Fioravanti degli Alberti of Bologna built in the center of the Kremlin the famous edifice that was once the Cathedral of the Assumption. Peter the Great was neither the first nor the last practitioner of a custom already two hundred years old when he came to the throne. From Solario and Debrossis to Pontecorvo the motives have changed but never the process.

Back of the symbol of Moscow, the holy city, lies a view of world history significantly different from ours, and one that may be an unconscious element in the appeal which the Soviet Empire holds to so many irreligious Jews. Traditionally we see ourselves representing "mankind" in the main line of human progress from Rome and Christianity. Traditionally we regard the whole Levant, Christian, Jewish, Mazdaist and Moslem, as fruitless deviation from this true line of progress. Under the symbols of Ivan III, the Russians see "mankind" proceeding through the Levant to Russia, and regard the West, not the Levant, as the erroneous deviation. To us, Russia joins the march of "mankind" to the extent that it Westernizes itself. To the Russians, the West must be copied for its mechanical power but hated for its moral and intellectual principles. To the Russians the West can rejoin the true line of progress only by becoming Russianized. Although this is contrary to the historical theories of Marx and might not even be verbally accepted by the Russian masses (the deep motives of no society probably ever are), it has not been too difficult to express in Communist terminology and move forward in practical Soviet politics. Today "world revolution," whether so intended or not, means simply destruction of the power of the West as the first and essential step to its Russification.

The territorial ambitions of Ivan III against the West did not extend beyond the Lithuanians and the Poles, as those of Peter never extended beyond the Swedes and the Germans of the Baltic. Whatever the dreams of the Tsars of Muscovy, whatever their hatred of their Slavic neighbors who refused to accept the Russian Orthodox faith, they lacked the power to pierce this shield of Slavic Catholics and reach the heart of the West. Never had they been able to extend their dominions beyond the Duna and the Dnieper except for the tiny bridgehead of Kiev siezed by Boris Godunov late in the sixteenth century. But then suddenly in the disbalance of European politics that followed the appearance of revolutionary France, the frontiers of the Russian Empire were moved from Riga, Smolensk and Kiev to Thorn and the eastern tributaries of the Oder. In a little over twenty years of war and revolution among the Western states, from the second partition of Poland in 1793 to the Congress of Vienna in 1815, Russian power moved five hundred miles into eastern Europe. It was the first barbarian lordship over Western peoples since our society began, and except for the Turkish possession of Hungary from 1541 to 1699, it was the first alien lordship of any kind.

To be sure, in the guise of Petrine Tsarism, with its formally Europeanized bureaucracy, the Russian Empire of 1815 did not seem so alien as it was. The powers of Europe considered it a strange, semi-barbarous state but they did not class the tsar with the sultan or the emperor of China. Deceived by the name Christian, by the thin surface film of westernized Russians and Westerners in the Russian service, they accepted Russia as an oddity but not an alien. Had their sense of history not foundered in eighteenth century rationalism they might have grasped more clearly the profound difference that separated Russia from themselves, but even so there would have been little they could have done about it. Their own politics had opened the borders of the West. Nor at first did there seem any reason to be disturbed. After its sudden gigantic acquisition of territory, and after the re-establishment of order in the West, the Russian Empire withdrew largely from strictly European matters into its own strange affairs, its waves of weird religious frenzies, its pogroms, its anarchists and assassinated tsars, its Slavophile conspiracies and its vast, dreary literature of frustration. Checked by diplomatic action and once by war from expansion southwestward into the Balkans, the empire contented itself—for the time—with pushing its dominion eastward and southeastward, crossing the Caucasus Mountains, annexing Turkistan (1864-73) the eastern shore of the Caspian (1873-81) and the valley of the Daria from the Aral Sea to the borders of Afghanistan (1884-5). In the Far East, the territory between the Amur and the Sea of Okhotak was taken from China in 1858 and Sakhalin and the coast area between the mouth of the Amur and the Korean border was gradually annexed between 1858 and 1895. Vladivostok itself was founded in 1860. In 1900 Manchuria was occupied, but defeat by the Japanese in 1905 postponed possession for forty years. This defeat likewise checked Russian expansion in the Far East and thereby diverted the restless ambitions of that empire back to the long quiescent Balkans and to the summer of 1913.

INDEX